Legal Writing
and Other Lawyering Skills

ASPEN COURSEBOOK SERIES

Legal Writing
and Other Lawyering Skills

Sixth Edition

Nancy L. Schultz
Professor, Dale E. Fowler School of Law at Chapman University

Louis J. Sirico, Jr.
Professor of Law and Director, Legal Writing Program
Villanova Law School

Wolters Kluwer
Law & Business

Copyright © 2014 CCH Incorporated.

Published by Wolters Kluwer Law & Business in New York.

Wolters Kluwer Law & Business serves customers worldwide with CCH, Aspen Publishers, and Kluwer Law International products. (www.wolterskluwerlb.com)

No part of this publication may be reproduced or transmitted in any form or by any means, electronic or mechanical, including photocopy, recording, or utilized by any information storage or retrieval system, without written permission from the publisher. For information about permissions or to request permissions online, visit us at www.wolterskluwerlb.com, or a written request may be faxed to our permissions department at 212-771-0803.

To contact Customer Service, e-mail customer.service@wolterskluwer.com, call 1-800-234-1660, fax 1-800-901-9075, or mail correspondence to:

Wolters Kluwer Law & Business
Attn: Order Department
PO Box 990
Frederick, MD 21705

Printed in the United States of America.

1 2 3 4 5 6 7 8 9 0

ISBN 978-1-4548-3102-0

Library of Congress Cataloging-in-Publication Data

Schultz, Nancy L., author.
    Legal writing and other lawyering skills / Nancy L. Schultz, Professor, Chapman University School of Law, Louis J. Sirico, Jr. Professor of Law and Director, Legal Writing Program, Villanova Law School.—Sixth edition.
        p. cm.
    Includes bibliographical references and index.
    ISBN 978-1-4548-3102-0 (alk. paper)
    1. Legal composition. 2. Oral pleading–United States. I. Sirico, Louis J., Jr., 1945- author. II. Title.
    KF250.S38 2014
    808.06′634—dc23

                                                                                            2014001205

About Wolters Kluwer Law & Business

Wolters Kluwer Law & Business is a leading global provider of intelligent information and digital solutions for legal and business professionals in key specialty areas, and respected educational resources for professors and law students. Wolters Kluwer Law & Business connects legal and business professionals as well as those in the education market with timely, specialized authoritative content and information-enabled solutions to support success through productivity, accuracy and mobility.

Serving customers worldwide, Wolters Kluwer Law & Business products include those under the Aspen Publishers, CCH, Kluwer Law International, Loislaw, ftwilliam.com and MediRegs family of products.

CCH products have been a trusted resource since 1913, and are highly regarded resources for legal, securities, antitrust and trade regulation, government contracting, banking, pension, payroll, employment and labor, and healthcare reimbursement and compliance professionals.

Aspen Publishers products provide essential information to attorneys, business professionals and law students. Written by preeminent authorities, the product line offers analytical and practical information in a range of specialty practice areas from securities law and intellectual property to mergers and acquisitions and pension/benefits. Aspen's trusted legal education resources provide professors and students with high-quality, up-to-date and effective resources for successful instruction and study in all areas of the law.

Kluwer Law International products provide the global business community with reliable international legal information in English. Legal practitioners, corporate counsel and business executives around the world rely on Kluwer Law journals, looseleafs, books, and electronic products for comprehensive information in many areas of international legal practice.

Loislaw is a comprehensive online legal research product providing legal content to law firm practitioners of various specializations. Loislaw provides attorneys with the ability to quickly and efficiently find the necessary legal information they need, when and where they need it, by facilitating access to primary law as well as state-specific law, records, forms and treatises.

ftwilliam.com offers employee benefits professionals the highest quality plan documents (retirement, welfare and non-qualified) and government forms (5500/PBGC, 1099 and IRS) software at highly competitive prices.

MediRegs products provide integrated health care compliance content and software solutions for professionals in healthcare, higher education and life sciences, including professionals in accounting, law and consulting.

Wolters Kluwer Law & Business, a division of Wolters Kluwer, is headquartered in New York. Wolters Kluwer is a market-leading global information services company focused on professionals.

Contents   *ix*

Preface   *xxiii*

Chapter 1.   Overview   1
Chapter 2.   Managing Your Time   7
Chapter 3.   Learning About the Legal System   13
Chapter 4.   Research Strategy   25
Chapter 5.   How to Brief a Case   35
Chapter 6.   Introduction to Legal Analysis   47
Chapter 7.   Purpose, Context, and Structure   71
Chapter 8.   Make Your Main Themes Stand Out   81
Chapter 9.   Help the Reader to Understand You   93
Chapter 10. Meeting the Client   111
Chapter 11. Introduction to the Memo   121
Chapter 12. The Memo: Heading, Issue, and Conclusion   127
Chapter 13. Practice with Drafting Memos: Headings, Issues, and Conclusions   135
Chapter 14. The Memo: Facts and Discussion   141
Chapter 15. Practice with Memos: Facts and Discussion   153
Chapter 16. Writing the Client Opinion Letter   163
Chapter 17. Practice with Client Letters   171
Chapter 18. Advising the Client   181
Chapter 19. Negotiating   189
Chapter 20. Mediation   203
Chapter 21. Settlement Agreements   211
Chapter 22. Communicating Electronically   223
Chapter 23. Drafting Pleadings   231
Chapter 24. Practice with Pleadings   239
Chapter 25. Writing Persuasively   249
Chapter 26. Writing Pretrial Motions and Trial Briefs   257

Chapter 27. Appellate Process and Standard of Review   265

Chapter 28. Introduction to Writing Appellate Briefs   269

Chapter 29. The Appellate Brief: The Introductory Parts   273

Chapter 30. The Appellate Brief: Statement of Facts; Summary of Argument   281

Chapter 31. Practice in Writing the Statement of Facts and Summary
of Argument   287

Chapter 32. The Appellate Brief: Argument and Conclusion   295

Chapter 33. Basic Principles of Oral Communication   309

Chapter 34. The Appellate Argument   321

Appendices

I.   Memoranda   329

II.   Client Letters   351

III.   Settlement Agreements   369

IV.   Pleadings   385

V.   Briefs and Oral Arguments   405

VI.   Grammar and Punctuation   445

Index   455

CONTENTS

Preface   *xxiii*

Chapter 1
Overview

§ 1.01. Introduction   1
§ 1.02. The Legal System and Legal Analysis   1
§ 1.03. Types of Legal Writing   2
    1. The Case Brief   2
    2. The Memorandum   2
    3. The Client Opinion Letter   2
    4. Settlement Agreements   3
    5. Communicating by Email   3
    6. Pleadings   3
    7. Motions   3
    8. Briefs   3
§ 1.04. Writing Style   4
§ 1.05. Citation Form   5
§ 1.06. Communications Skills   5
    1. Client Interviewing and Counseling   5
    2. Negotiation and Mediation   6
    3. Oral Argument   6

Chapter 2
Managing Your Time

§ 2.01. Managing Your Time in Law School   7
§ 2.02. Managing Your Workload by Planning Ahead   7
§ 2.03. Managing Your Writing Assignments   8
    1. Different People Have Different Writing Methods   8
    2. Dealing with Writer's Block   8
        a. Stop Researching and Start Writing   9
        b. Write a "Zero Draft"   9
        c. Write the Easy Parts First   9
        d. Use the Buddy System   9
        e. Talk with Your Professor   9

§ 2.04. Getting Your Document Written: Five Pointers   9
         1. Plan Your Writing Process   10
         2. Plan for Multiple Drafts   10
         3. Be Realistic in Planning Your Deadlines   10
         4. Build in Some Time for Complications   11
         5. Leave Time for the Details   11

Chapter 3
Learning About the Legal System

§ 3.01. The Legal System and Legal Writing   13
§ 3.02. Sources of Law and Their Hierarchy   13
§ 3.03. The Court System   14
         1. The State Courts   14
         2. The Federal Courts   15
§ 3.04. The Common Law   16
         1. Mandatory Authority   16
         2. Persuasive Authority   17
         3. The Weight of Authority   18
§ 3.05. Statutes and Their Interpretation   18
         1. The Supremacy of the Legislature and the Legislative Process   18
         2. The Relationship Between Statutory Law and Common Law   20
         3. The Roles of the Court and the Legislature—An Illustration   22

Chapter 4
Research Strategy

§ 4.01. Introduction   25
§ 4.02. Where Do You Start?   25
         1. Statutes   26
         2. Treatises   26
         3. Restatements   26
         4. Legal Encyclopedias   27
§ 4.03. Other Resources   28
         1. Digests   28
         2. A.L.R. and Legal Periodicals   28
§ 4.04. Computer Research   29
         1. Traditional Legal Research Sources   29
         2. Not Purely Legal Resources   30
         3. Books versus Computers—How Do You Decide?   30
§ 4.05. Updating Your Research   31
§ 4.06. When Do You Stop?   31
         1. Look for the Most On-Point Cases First   32
         2. Stop When You Come Full Circle   32
         3. Do Not Follow Every Lead   32

§4.07.   How Do You Keep Track?   33
§4.08.   Research Checklist   33

Chapter 5
How to Brief a Case

§5.01.   What Is a Brief?   35
         1. Briefing Is Taking Notes   35
         2. The Purposes of Briefing   35
§5.02.   How to Brief   36
         1. The Format   36
         2. Parts of the Brief   36
            a. An Exercise   36
            b. Name of the Case   39
            c. Citation   39
            d. Facts of the Case   39
            e. Procedure   39
            f. Issue   40
            g. Holding   41
            h. Analysis   41
            i. More Sample Briefs   41
         3. Problem   42
§5.03.   Beyond Briefing   45
         Exercise   46

Chapter 6
Introduction to Legal Analysis

§6.01.   Introduction   47
§6.02.   Arguing Deductively   48
         1. Limitations   49
         2. Maximizing the Use of Deductive Reasoning   49
         3. Application   49
§6.03.   Applying the Law to the Facts   50
         1. The Basic Approach   51
         2. An Example of Legal Analysis   51
§6.04.   Case Analysis   55
         Exercise   62
         Exercise   64
§6.05.   Statutory Analysis   64
         Exercise   69
         Exercise   70
§6.06.   Legal Analysis Checklist   70

Chapter 7
Purpose, Context, and Structure

§7.01.   Introduction   71
§7.02.   Purpose   71
§7.03.   Context   72
§7.04.   Structure   72
    1. Outlining   72
       Exercise   74
    2. Deciding on a Structural Strategy   74
    3. Roadmaps, Topic Sentences, and Transitions   76
       Exercise   77
    4. Organizing Within Arguments   77
    5. Placement of Policy and Equity Arguments   78
§7.05.   Context and Structure Checklist   78

Chapter 8
Make Your Main Themes Stand Out

§8.01.   Introduction   81
§8.02.   Make the Outline of Your Argument or Discussion
    Stand Out   82
§8.03.   Put Your Conclusion First   83
§8.04.   Write Effective Paragraphs   85
    1. Use Topic Sentences   85
    2. Write Cohesive Paragraphs   87
       a. Write Focused Discussion Sections   87
       b. Avoid Extraneous Sentences   88
    3. When Necessary, Use Transitions and Repeat Words   89
       Exercise   90

Chapter 9
Help the Reader to Understand You

§9.01.   Introduction   93
§9.02.   General Advice   94
    1. Get to the Point   94
    2. Use Concrete Language   94
    3. Use the Active Voice   95
    4. Avoid Legalese   97
    5. Define Technical Terms   98
    6. Write in the Appropriate Tone   99
       Exercises   100
§9.03.   Structure   101
    1. Write Short Sentences   101
    2. Put the Parts of Your Sentence in a Logical Order   102

3. Avoid Intrusive Phrases and Clauses   103
4. Use Full Sentences   104
5. Use Parallel Structure   104
§ 9.04. Content   106
1. Use Positives Rather Than Negatives   106
2. Avoid Ambiguous Words and Phrases   106
3. Avoid Colloquialism   107
4. Do Not Personalize   108
5. Avoid Excessive Variation   108
Exercises   108

Chapter 10
Meeting the Client

§ 10.01. Introduction   111
§ 10.02. Purpose of the Initial Interview   111
§ 10.03. Planning the Initial Interview   112
§ 10.04. Greeting the Client   112
§ 10.05. Preparatory Explanation   113
§ 10.06. Getting the Client's Perspective   113
1. Getting Started   114
2. Keeping Track   114
3. Getting the Details   114
4. Goals and Priorities   115
§ 10.07. Preliminary Assessment of the Client's Problem 116
§ 10.08. Developing Options   116
§ 10.09. Fees   116
§ 10.10. Closing the Interview   117
Exercise   118
§ 10.11. Client Interview Checklist   118

Chapter 11
Introduction to the Memo

§ 11.01. What Is a Memo?   121
§ 11.02. The Purposes of a Memo   121
§ 11.03. The Parts of a Memo   122
1. The Heading   123
2. The Issue   123
3. The Conclusion   123
4. The Facts   123
5. The Discussion   123
§ 11.04. The Hallmarks of a Well-Written Memo   124
1. Thorough Research   124
2. Good Judgment   124

3. Objective Analysis 124
4. Clear Writing Style 124
   a. Good Organization 125
   b. Write for the Reader 125
   c. Precision and Clarity 125
5. Creativity 125
6. Correct Citation Format 126

Chapter 12
The Memo: Heading, Issue, and Conclusion

§ 12.01. The Heading 127
§ 12.02. The Issue 128
§ 12.03. The Conclusion 131

Chapter 13
Practice with Drafting Memos: Headings, Issues, and Conclusions

§ 13.01. Exercise I 135
§ 13.02. Exercise II 137
§ 13.03. Exercise III 138
§ 13.04. Exercise IV 138

Chapter 14
The Memo: Facts and Discussion

§ 14.01. Facts 141
§ 14.02. Discussion 144
§ 14.03. Make Your Reasoning Readily Apparent 147
   1. Avoid the "Digest" Approach 147
   2. Avoid the "Historical Development of the Law" Approach 148
   3. Avoid the Use of Too Many Quotations from Legal
      Authorities 149
   4. Avoid the "Abstract Writing" Approach 150
   5. Avoid the "Law Discussion Only" Approach 150
   6. A Good Example 151
      Exercise 152

Chapter 15
Practice with Memos: Facts and Discussion

§ 15.01. Introduction 153
§ 15.02. Drafting the Facts Section 153
§ 15.03. Editing the Facts and Discussion Sections of a Memo 157
§ 15.04. Drafting the Discussion 161

Chapter 16
Writing the Client Opinion Letter

§ 16.01. Introduction   163
§ 16.02. Write in an Appropriate Style   163
    1. Focus on Your Audience   163
    2. Be Concrete   163
    3. Avoid Sounding Colloquial   165
    4. Avoid Jargon and Stilted Language   165
    5. Use Correct Spelling and Grammar   166
§ 16.03. Answer the Question   166
    1. Include Important Facts Provided by the Client 166
    2. Be Accurate   166
    3. Explain Your Answer   167
    4. Do Not Promise What You Cannot Deliver   168
    5. Address Your Client's Concerns   168
§ 16.04. Tell the Client Where You Are Going   169
    Exercise   169

Chapter 17
Practice with Client Letters

§ 17.01. Introduction   171
§ 17.02. Editing a Letter   177
§ 17.03. Drafting a Letter   180

Chapter 18
Advising the Client

§ 18.01. Purpose of the Consultation   181
§ 18.02. The Scenario   181
§ 18.03. Planning the Consultation   182
§ 18.04. Beginning the Consultation   183
§ 18.05. Reaffirming the Client's Goals and Priorities   184
§ 18.06. Developing Options   184
    1. Likely Consequences   184
    2. Advantages and Disadvantages   185
§ 18.07. Choosing a Course of Action   185
§ 18.08. Getting Settlement Authority   187
    Exercise   187
§ 18.09. Consultation Checklist   187

Chapter 19
Negotiating

§ 19.01. Introduction   189
§ 19.02. Purposes of Negotiation   190

§19.03. Theories of Negotiation   190
    1. Adversarial Models   190
        a. Game Theory   190
        b. Economic   191
        c. Social-Psychological Bargaining   192
    2. Problem-Solving Negotiation   192
§19.04. Styles of Negotiation   193
§19.05. Planning for Negotiation   194
    1. Evaluating the Case   194
    2. Planning to Exchange Information   194
    3. Establishing an Opening, Target, and Bottom Line   195
    4. Analyzing Needs and Interests   196
    5. Planning for Personalities   197
§19.06. Beginning the Negotiation   197
§19.07. Information Exchange   197
§19.08. Trading   198
§19.09. Closing the Negotiation   199
§19.10. Negotiation Ethics   199
§19.11. Negotiation Checklist   200
    Exercise   200

Chapter 20
Mediation

§20.01. Introduction   203
§20.02. What Is Mediation?   203
§20.03. What Do Mediators Do?   204
§20.04. Confidentiality   204
§20.05. The Stages of a Mediation   204
    1. Preparation   204
    2. Mediator Introduction   205
    3. Party Opening Statements   205
    4. Agenda Development   205
    5. Caucuses/Conferences   206
    6. Brainstorming/Negotiating   206
    7. Resolution   206
§20.06. Writing for Mediation   207
    1. The Agreement to Mediate   207
    2. Mediation Briefs   208
    Exercise   209

Chapter 21
Settlement Agreements

§21.01. Introduction   211
§21.02. What Do Settlement Agreements Look Like?   211

1. Descriptive Title   211
2. Caption   212
3. Transition/Language of Agreement   213
4. Recitals/Background   213
5. Definitions   214
6. Operative Language   214
7. Contingencies   216
8. Declarations   217
9. Closing   218
§ 21.03. Who Does the Drafting?   219
§ 21.04. Releases   220
    Exercise   221

Chapter 22
Communicating Electronically

§ 22.01. The Trend : Communicating with Email   223
§ 22.02. Know Your Audience   223
§ 22.03. Format Your Email Appropriately   224
§ 22.04. Send a Message That Is Not Too Simple or Too Complex   224
§ 22.05. Email with Caution   225
    1. Anticipate the Unexpected Reader   225
    2. Maintain a Professional Tone   225
§ 22.06. Email Advice   226
    1. Begin Your Email with a Summary of the Query   226
    2. Be Aware of Differences in Email Systems   226
    3. Watch Out for the "Reply All" Button   226
    4. Proofread   226
    5. Be Cautious with Humor and Avoid Sarcasm   226
    6. Avoid Emotions   227
§ 22.07. Sample Emails   227
    Exercise   229

Chapter 23
Drafting Pleadings

§ 23.01. Introduction   231
§ 23.02. The Purpose and Language of Pleadings   231
§ 23.03. Following Rules   232
§ 23.04. Captions   232
    Exercise   233
§ 23.05. The Complaint   233
§ 23.06. The Answer   235
§ 23.07. Verifications   237

Chapter 24
Practice with Pleadings

§ 24.01. Introduction   239
§ 24.02. Plaintiff's Facts   239
§ 24.03. Drafting the Fact Allegations   240
§ 24.04. Drafting the Legal Claim   240
§ 24.05. Critiquing a Complaint   241
§ 24.06. Drafting the Answer   244
§ 24.07. Critiquing an Answer   . 245

Chapter 25
Writing Persuasively

§ 25.01. Introduction   249
§ 25.02. Make Your Argument Clear and Credible   250
        1. Make Your Argument as Simple as Possible   250
        2. Write in a Persuasive but Credible Style   250
§ 25.03. Write a Well-Organized Argument   251
        1. Structure Your Argument   251
        2. Put Your Best Arguments First and Develop Them More Fully   251
§ 25.04. Adopt a Persuasive Writing Style   252
        1. Be Concrete   252
        2. When You Want to Emphasize a Word or Idea, Place
           It at the End of the Sentence   253
        3. When Appropriate, Use the Same Subject for a Series of Sentences   253
§ 25.05. State Your Facts Persuasively   254
§ 25.06. Make Equity and Policy Arguments   255
§ 25.07. Use Precedent Persuasively   255
        1. Argue that Adverse Precedent Is Consistent with Your Argument   256
        2. Interpret Precedent Narrowly or Broadly, as Appropriate   256

Chapter 26
Writing Pretrial Motions and Trial Briefs

§ 26.01. Purposes of Motions   257
§ 26.02. Form of Motions   257
§ 26.03. Motions to Dismiss   257
        Exercise   258
§ 26.04. Motions to Compel Discovery   258
§ 26.05. Motions for Summary Judgment   259
        Exercise   260
§ 26.06. Ethical Considerations in Motion Practice   260
§ 26.07. Checklist for Motions   261
§ 26.08. Trial Briefs   261
§ 26.09. Examples   263

Chapter 27
Appellate Process and Standard of Review

§ 27.01. Introduction	265
§ 27.02. How Cases Come Up on Appeal	265
§ 27.03. The Record on Appeal	265
§ 27.04. The Standard of Review	266
1. Clearly Erroneous	266
2. Abuse of Discretion	267
3. De Novo Review	267
4. The Importance to the Practitioner	268
§ 27.05. Available Forms of Relief	268

Chapter 28
Introduction to Writing Appellate Briefs

§ 28.01. What Is a Brief?	269
§ 28.02. Procedural Rules for Appellate Briefs	270
§ 28.03. The Parts of a Brief	271
1. The Title Page	271
2. Table of Contents	271
3. Table of Authorities	271
4. Jurisdictional Statement	271
5. Questions Presented	271
6. Constitutional and Statutory Provisions	271
7. Statement of Facts	271
8. Summary of Argument	272
9. Argument	272
§ 28.04. The Hallmarks of a Well-Written Brief	272

Chapter 29
The Appellate Brief: The Introductory Parts

§ 29.01. Using the Record	273
§ 29.02. The Title Page	274
§ 29.03. Table of Contents	274
§ 29.04. Table of Authorities	274
§ 29.05. Jurisdictional Statement	275
§ 29.06. Questions Presented	275
§ 29.07. Text of Constitutional, Statutory, and Regulatory Provisions	278
Exercises	278

Chapter 30
The Appellate Brief: Statement of Facts; Summary of Argument

§ 30.01. Statement of Facts	281
1. Tell What Happened	282
2. Tell the Truth, but Put Your Best Foot Forward	283

3. Hold the Court's Attention   285
    Exercise   285
§ 30.02. Summary of Argument   285

Chapter 31
Practice in Writing the Statement of Facts and Summary
of Argument

§ 31.01. Exercise I   287
§ 31.02. Exercise II   288
§ 31.03. Exercise III   288
§ 31.04. Exercise IV   288

Chapter 32
The Appellate Brief: Argument and Conclusion

§ 32.01. The Argument   295
  1. Structuring the Argument   295
    a. Use Headings   295
    b. How to Write the Headings   296
    c. Using Headings as an Advocate   297
    d. How Many Headings?   298
    e. Final Considerations   298
  2. Preparing the Substance of the Argument   298
    a. General Considerations   299
      i. Understanding the Appellate Process   299
      ii. Familiarity with the Record   299
      iii. Research: Do It Right but Know When to Stop   299
      iv. Compliance with the Rules of Court   299
      v. Simplicity in Substance and Style   300
    b. Formulating the Arguments   300
    c. The Organization and Substance of the Arguments   300
    d. What to Avoid   302
    e. Using Precedent   303
      i. Hierarchy of Precedent   303
      ii. Handling Adverse Precedent   303
      iii. Rebuttal of Opposing Arguments   304
      iv. Parentheticals, String Cites, Signals, Quotations,
        and Footnotes   304
    f. Writing Persuasively   305
      i. Control Tone   305
      ii. The Final Touches   305
§ 32.02. The Conclusion   306
§ 32.03. A Checklist   306

Chapter 33
Basic Principles of Oral Communication

§ 33.01. Introduction   309
§ 33.02. Consider the Audience   309
         1. Do Your Homework   309
         2. Adapt to Your Audience   310
§ 33.03. Consider the Setting   310
         1. Study the Physical Surroundings in Advance   311
         2. Understand the Occasion   311
§ 33.04. Structure for Maximum Effect   311
         1. Structural Strategy   312
         2. Methods of Proof   312
         3. Organizational Patterns   313
              a. Chronological   313
              b. Cause to Effect   313
              c. Problem to Solution   313
              d. Pro Versus Con   313
              e. Topical   314
         4. Introductions, Conclusions, and Transitions   314
§ 33.05. Write for Sound Appeal   314
         1. Useful Tools   315
              a. Humor   315
              b. Novelty   315
              c. Conflict   315
              d. Suspense   315
              e. Emphasis   316
              f. Theme   317
              g. Language   317
                   i. Rhetorical Questions   317
                   ii. Repetition   317
                   iii. Imagery   318
         2. Not So Useful Tools   318
§ 33.06. Apply the Fundamentals of Good Public Speaking   319
         1. Maintain Eye Contact   319
         2. Be Heard   319
         3. Do Not Read   319
         4. Use Emphasis   319
         5. Use the Pause   319
         6. Use Appropriate Gestures   319
         7. Watch Your Posture   320

Chapter 34
The Appellate Argument

§ 34.01. Introduction   321
§ 34.02. The Setting of the Oral Argument   322
§ 34.03. Preparing the Oral Argument   322
    1. Know the Record   322
    2. Study the Authorities   323
    3. Know the Arguments   323
    4. Outline Your Arguments   323
    5. Prepare Argument Aids   323
    6. Rehearse the Argument   324
    7. Advise the Court and Your Opponent of New Information   324
§ 34.04. The Structure of the Oral Argument   325
    1. Basic Argument Structure   325
        a. The Introduction   325
        b. The Roadmap and Key Facts of the Case   325
        c. The Argument   326
        d. The Conclusion   326
    2. Rebuttal   326
§ 34.05. Questions From the Judges   327
§ 34.06. Oral Argument Checklist   328

Appendices

  I.   Memoranda   329
  II.   Client Letters   351
  III.   Settlement Agreements   369
  IV.   Pleadings   385
  V.   Briefs and Oral Arguments   405
  VI.   Grammar and Punctuation   445

Index   455

PREFACE

We have used the materials in this book to teach legal writing and analysis to students at Villanova Law School, George Washington University Law School, and Chapman University School of Law. We wish to thank them for all they have taught us about teaching the subject. Most of the sample documents in this book are the products of our students and former students. The names of the authors of documents reproduced in the appendices appear with their documents.

We would also like to thank our research assistants for their invaluable contributions to this latest edition. Nancy Schultz thanks Jared Berman and Billy Zakis for their very capable assistance. Lou Sirico thanks Tehrim Umar for the same.

Legal Writing
and Other Lawyering Skills

CHAPTER 1

Overview

§ 1.01. INTRODUCTION

To be a successful lawyer, you must write and speak effectively. In your profession, you will spend much of your time crafting legal documents and speaking with clients, courts, and other lawyers. In this book, we help you learn some of the skills you will need to be a lawyer. You will learn how to draft case briefs, memoranda, opinion letters, pleadings, motions, briefs, and settlement agreements. You also will learn about client counseling, negotiations, mediation, and how to make oral arguments in court. You will master an approach that emphasizes precision, good organization, and plain English. By learning to communicate clearly, you will increase your effectiveness as a lawyer.

Law school is an exciting, but demanding experience. It places far more demands on your time than your undergraduate education probably did. Coping with these demands requires you to lead an organized life. In Chapter 2, we offer suggestions on how to organize your time and how to tackle writing assignments that will be new to you. If you prioritize your obligations and set aside time to meet them, you still will have time to relax and socialize.

Our educational philosophy is to teach you how to write and argue in a traditionally accepted style. As you gain experience, you will develop a style that reflects your personality and particular strengths. At this stage, however, you should learn the standard method as a foundation for later growth.

This chapter gives you an overview of the book. It briefly discusses the legal system and legal analysis and then describes the major types of legal writing. It also explains our approach to writing style, discusses citation form, and introduces the lawyering skills you need to learn.

§ 1.02. THE LEGAL SYSTEM AND LEGAL ANALYSIS

Before you can make legal arguments or draft legal documents, you need to learn about the American legal system and about accepted methods of legal analysis. You need to learn more than television and the movies have taught you. You also need to unlearn some of what they have taught you.

Television and the movies offer a simplified view of the law. Though they frequently portray trials, they rarely show lawyers engaging in legal research and drafting documents. The media spend little time on pretrial proceedings and on courts that hear appeals from trial decisions. The media almost never tell us that this country has many court systems: every state has its own courts, and the federal government has not only the United States Supreme Court, but also trial courts, appeals courts, and various specialized courts.

The media also fail to offer even a glimpse of how lawyers construct legal arguments. Though television and the movies frequently present arguments based on common sense, they do not show how these arguments must be stylized to become legal arguments that judges will find persuasive.

Legal analysis is not particularly difficult or different from other methods of reasoning. Nonetheless, you must expend considerable effort to become good at it. In this book, we teach you about the legal system and legal reasoning. Over the next several years, these subjects will occupy much of your time. Becoming proficient in the methods outlined in this introduction will aid you in your other courses.

§ 1.03. TYPES OF LEGAL WRITING

1. The Case Brief

A case brief is a summary of a court opinion. As a student, you undoubtedly are writing case briefs in most of your courses. Writing the brief helps you prepare for class. During class, the brief serves as an accessible set of notes on the case. Chapter 4 offers help in reading and briefing cases.

The word "brief" has another meaning. It also refers to the written argument that a lawyer presents to a court deciding a case. See Section 1.03[8].

2. The Memorandum

By "memorandum" or "memo" we mean the interoffice memorandum. It discusses the law concerning a client's legal problem and predicts how a court or other body would decide the issue presented. The memo, then, is essential in determining how to proceed. The writer of the memo first must research the law thoroughly and then explain how it supports his or her conclusion. In legal practice, memos may take many forms, as we discuss later in the book.

The word "memorandum" sometimes is used to describe the written argument that a lawyer presents to a court or an administrative agency. The lawyer may write this type of memo to support or oppose a pretrial motion, to summarize the argument in a trial or administrative hearing, or to support the client's argument before an appellate court. In the latter case, most courts would call the document a brief. In all cases, the document is similar to a brief in that its goal is to persuade rather than to summarize the law. See Section 1.03[8].

3. The Client Opinion Letter

The client opinion letter advises the client how the law applies to a particular problem and suggests a course of action. The lawyer should explain any legal concepts in lay language.

4. Settlement Agreements

This is another important form of legal writing. When disputes are settled by negotiation or mediation, the agreement must be formalized in a way that clearly and accurately reflects the agreement the parties have reached. The agreement should anticipate possible future areas of dispute and provide a mechanism that will prevent future litigation between the parties.

5. Communicating by Email

The legal profession is not immune to the electronic revolution. Today, lawyers communicate by email and other types of electronic media. In the recent past, new lawyers usually forwarded their research and other assignments in printed memoranda that would require at least several pages. Now, they frequently send out their work by email and expect their supervisors to read it on an iPhone.

Email demands that the lawyer be concise but still accurate. Although all legal writing calls for conciseness and accuracy, electronic communication takes those requirements to a new level.

6. Pleadings

Pleadings are the written papers that a lawyer serves on the opposing side and files with the court to begin litigation. In a noncriminal case, for example, the plaintiff's lawyer files a complaint asserting that the client has suffered a legal wrong and that the defendant is liable. The defendant's lawyer files an answer and may file a counterclaim asserting claims against the plaintiff. Other pleadings may also be filed.

Complaints are the first opportunity the lawyer has to state the case in writing. They must be drafted clearly and precisely, and establish sufficient facts to support the alleged cause of action or the court may refuse to hear the case and dismiss the complaint.

7. Motions

Before, during, or after trial, a lawyer may file a motion asking the court to deal with a particular issue. For example, the defendant's lawyer might move to dismiss the plaintiff's claim and argue that even if all the plaintiff's assertions are true, the defendant still would not be liable. Motions are persuasive documents and should follow the principles of advocacy writing. There are very few universal rules that govern the format of motions, so you will need to learn the procedures that are followed in your jurisdiction and in the law office where you work.

8. Briefs

By "brief," we primarily mean the appellate brief. It is the written document that the lawyer submits to the court when the client's case is on appeal. It includes a factual explanation of the case and an argument based on detailed legal analysis of relevant cases and other authorities as well as fairness and social policy concerns. Some courts call the brief a memorandum. See Section 1.03[2]. "Brief" may also refer to the written argument that the attorney presents at the pretrial or trial level, or even prior to a mediation.

Different courts have different rules for the format of the brief. In this book, you will learn a standard form that you can easily adjust to meet the requirements of a particular court. We also provide specific examples of different kinds of briefs.

§ 1.04. WRITING STYLE

This book is about writing and speaking like a lawyer. A lawyer should write and speak clearly, concisely, and forcefully. So should other professionals. Our profession faces a particular problem: it has inherited a tradition of poor writing. Many of the court opinions in your casebooks offer sad examples of this tradition. If the judges had written the opinions clearly, you would understand the decisions better and spend less time reading and briefing them.

Lawyers frequently justify lapses in comprehensibility by emphasizing the need to convey highly technical information and complex ideas. We reject such excuses. As a lawyer, you can write and speak clearly. Lawyers and scholars concerned with this matter agree. Current books and articles make clear that short sentences and plain English are the trend. Rambling sentences and legalese are out. You may recognize this philosophy if you have read *The Elements of Style* by Strunk and White[1] and *On Writing Well* by William Zinsser.[2]

Some first-year students are shocked when they receive their writing assignments back from the writing instructor. They find their papers covered with red-penned criticisms. Often the real shock comes to students who always believed they were excellent writers. In undergraduate school, they received praise and good grades and gained confidence in their ability. For them, legal writing seems to be a totally new form of writing.

Throughout this book, we use the written work of our students to provide good and bad examples of legal writing. The bad examples were written by intelligent, capable students. Most of the students came to law school confident about their writing abilities. They discovered they had more lessons to learn if they were to be good legal writers. They mastered those lessons and improved their legal writing style.

Your pre-law writing experience may not be a valid predictor of your initial performance in legal writing. Legal writing can be equally difficult for students of all backgrounds.

You may have been an English major who wrote brilliant essays or poetry for years. You may experience strong feelings of hurt and discouragement if you receive a paper that the writing instructor has torn apart. The instructor then gently tries to lessen the pain by explaining that you now are learning a new and very different method of writing. It is best for you to accept this fact now, before you hand in your first assignment.

On the other hand, you may have been an accounting or science major in undergraduate school with little writing experience and with many fears about legal writing. You may be delighted to discover that you can write very well in the legal setting.

---

1. William Strunk & E.B. White, *The Elements of Style* (4th ed., Allyn & Bacon 2000).

2. William Zinsser, *On Writing Well* (30th ann. ed., Harper 2006). A number of books urge lawyers to write in plain English. They include Irwin Alterman, *Plain and Accurate Style in Court Papers* (ALI-ABA 2002); Gertrude Block, *Effective Legal Writing* (5th ed., Foundation Press 1999); Louis J. Sirico, Jr. & Nancy L. Schultz, *Persuasive Writing for Lawyers and the Legal Profession* (3d ed., LexisNexis 2011); Richard Wydick, *Plain English for Lawyers* (5th ed., Carolina Academic Press 2005).

We do not claim that the writing style we teach is superior to all other writing styles. Many great works of literature conform to other styles. Much good journalism lacks the precision that we demand. We make only one claim: the writing style that we teach is the best style for legal writing.

Many lawyers cling to the old ways. Some of your future employers may be among them, and you may have to compromise if you cannot persuade them to give you a free hand. But the tide is turning. Your efforts at communicating clearly will pay off. Judges, clients, and other lawyers will be more likely to understand you. They will also find you more persuasive. Lawyers who refuse to abandon verbosity and jargon may find themselves viewed as dinosaurs in a modern world.

§ 1.05.   CITATION FORM

As a lawyer, you will rely heavily on constitutions, statutes, prior cases, and other authorities. To cite authority means to refer to specific statutes, cases, and the like when you prepare an analysis of a legal point or make a legal argument. You may cite authority to provide important information, to support your argument, or to acknowledge adverse authority that you must distinguish or contest.

When you cite authority in a written document, you must include enough information so that the reader can make an initial decision about the authority's importance. For example, the reader may find it important to know how old a case is, whether the court is a local one, and whether the court is prestigious. You also must include enough information to enable the reader to find the authority in the library or online. For a case, a successful library search requires knowing the case's name, the set of books in which it appears, the volume, and the page number. A successful online search requires knowing the case name, jurisdiction, and date.

Two competing manuals set out rules on what information you must include in a citation and what format you should use. They are the *ALWD Citation Manual* (created by the Association of Legal Writing Directors and Darby Dickerson) and *The Bluebook: A Uniform System of Citation* (published by a small group of law reviews). Fortunately, for most citations that you will use in a first-year law course, the citation rules of both manuals are virtually the same. However, the *ALWD Citation Manual* is much more student oriented and much easier to understand than the *Bluebook*. The *ALWD Citation Manual* is the manual we follow for citations used in this book.

§ 1.06.   COMMUNICATIONS SKILLS

1. Client Interviewing and Counseling

Lawyers have occasion to generate written documents only if they have clients to represent. You must be able to convince a potential client that you are the right person to handle the important and delicate matter that he or she proposes to hand over to your keeping. You will be able to do this if you plan your interviews to maximize the likelihood that you will get all necessary information and be able to accurately assess the client's problem and develop appropriate options for resolving it. You will have satisfied clients and lots of work if you can help clients to resolve their legal dilemmas in ways that meet their needs and take their goals and priorities into account. To be able to do this consistently requires skill and practice. We will introduce you to some of the fundamental skills and concepts that underlie this vital work. We will also explain how research and writing relate to client representation.

2. Negotiation and Mediation

The vast majority of legal problems are resolved outside of court. Negotiation is a critical lawyering skill. In this book, we introduce you to some issues of fundamental importance to effective negotiation—preparation, information exchange, keeping track of concessions, and the tone and style of the negotiation. We discuss both adversarial and problem-solving "win/win" strategies for negotiating. You will discover that negotiating is a very human process, with few rules and lots of psychology. You will also discover that good legal research and writing skills make you a more effective negotiator and lawyer.

Mediation takes place when negotiations fail and the parties need assistance in communicating to resolve a dispute. In this book, we introduce you to the fundamentals of mediation—what a mediator does and how lawyers function in a mediation. There are several forms of writing that relate to mediation: agreements to mediate, premediation briefs, and settlement agreements. We teach you about all of them.

3. Oral Argument

Lawyers make oral arguments before legislatures and administrative bodies and in courts. In this book, you will learn specifically how to make an oral argument when a court is hearing your client's case on appeal. In an appellate court, you submit your written argument in a brief, and you also may get the opportunity to address the court in oral argument.

Appellate argument differs in style from college debate and other speaking occasions. A formal etiquette governs what you say and how you say it. By using this book, you will learn when to sit, when to stand, how to begin your argument, and the like. You also will learn how to structure your argument, what to emphasize, and how to answer questions. In addition, you will learn how to be persuasive.

Learning effective legal writing and oral advocacy is a demanding and exciting task. We wish you well.

CHAPTER 2

Managing Your Time

§ 2.01. MANAGING YOUR TIME IN LAW SCHOOL

For many students, dealing with the demands of law school is a challenge. In undergraduate studies, you probably had sufficient time to complete the required work. At that level, students sometimes postpone their studies until a few days before the final exam or write a paper the night before it is due. Law school, however, is different. You must complete your homework before each day's class. And writing assignments require more than a single, hasty draft.

The demands of law school require students to manage their time very carefully. In this chapter we first offer guidance on managing your time and then turn to completing your writing assignments efficiently, including some tips on dealing with writer's block. It's worth noting, however, that no one method of time management works for everyone. Therefore we offer general guidelines that you can adapt to your own personality and needs.

§ 2.02. MANAGING YOUR WORKLOAD BY PLANNING AHEAD

The best advice on managing your time is to plan ahead. Without advance planning, you run the risk of dealing with your law school workload by handling the current urgent assignment. In no time at all, you will fall behind in meeting your obligations and begin to wonder how you will ever stay afloat. On the other hand, if you plan ahead, your law school assignments will become a manageable, daily flow of work.

Start by making a timeline for at least the next six weeks, or, preferably, for the rest of the semester. Mark the deadlines for your long-term projects—for example, major legal writing assignments, other important assignments, mid-term exams, and final exams. If you do not know those dates, ask. You may know of other big, personal dates—for example, an undergraduate homecoming, a wedding, or a family reunion. Mark those dates on your timeline as well. To the extent that you can, break down your major projects into small, intermediate tasks and set deadlines for completing them. For example, set deadlines for outlining segments of your courses, for completing the research on a writing assignment, and for meeting with your career advisory staff.

Now that you have scheduled plans for long-term projects, turn your attention to your day-to-day tasks. Those tasks include preparing for each class, reviewing your notes after each class, and completing short, written assignments. Use your timeline to plan your week. For example, decide when you will study for each class, when you will work on research for your next big writing project, and when you will craft your resume. Don't forget to schedule time for relaxation, exercise, meals, and parties.

Each evening, briefly review your day to make sure you are roughly on schedule. When you conduct your review, you will sometimes discover that you are behind your schedule or possibly even ahead of it. In either case, you now have the chance to revise your schedule for the coming days to make sure that you can complete all your tasks.

Of course, although this plan sounds quite logical and manageable, reality may intrude and complicate your schedule. You may come down with the flu, break up with the love of your life, or realize that a given project will require far more time than you expected. You should not respond by tossing out your timeline. Instead, adjust it. If you allocate more time to one project, you may have to make the difficult decision of reducing your commitment to another. You may decide to skip a party or your favorite television show, or even devote only adequate time to preparing for tomorrow's classes. In any event, make sure that you have clearly identified the high-priority tasks in your life and are allocating to them the time that they deserve.

§ 2.03. MANAGING YOUR WRITING ASSIGNMENTS

1. Different People Have Different Writing Methods

Often, Legal Writing professors emphasize only one method of completing a writing assignment: complete the research, make an outline, fill in the outline with text based on your legal research, edit your draft, and keep revising your drafts until you are satisfied. For some students, this linear method works perfectly. However, for other students, it does not work at all.

How we plan our writing and then execute it depends on our particular personalities and cognitive styles. In order to draft a document, some writers need to work through, say, seven drafts. Other writers spend a good deal of time thinking about a draft before committing their thoughts to paper; for them, the first draft may need only limited revision. Some writers prefer to construct a detailed outline and then insert text. Others freely write or follow their own organizational system and then proceed to organize their writing in a linear outline format.

The point: In order to write successfully and efficiently, you need to know what method works best for you. Your only obligation is to finish with a well-organized document that conforms to an outline format and that largely follows the lessons that this book offers.

2. Dealing with Writer's Block

Sooner or later, probably every writer comes to a full stop; you cannot seem to turn your thoughts into words. The causes vary. You are afraid that your product will be inferior. You cannot find a way to organize your thoughts. You tell yourself that you cannot write until you do more research. Still, the deadline approaches, and you need to get moving.

To get the words flowing, no one method works every time. You need to try different methods and see which works for you in a given situation. Here are a few that you might try.

a. Stop Researching and Start Writing

Sometimes, we continue researching because we know that once we stop, we will have to start writing. Researching, then, becomes an excuse for not writing. Remind yourself that after you begin to write, you always can return to your research. When you have spent enough time researching, start writing. As you write, you may discover that you have very little productive research yet to perform.

b. Write a "Zero Draft"

Often, the way to break through the blockage is simply to start writing—writing anything. You are not writing a first draft. You are writing a "zero draft." Forget about the outline. Forget about starting by writing the introduction to the document and then systematically continuing to the end. Just write what comes to mind. You may find that much of what you write you can use without much revision. More importantly, the simple act of writing may free you to continue with your project.

c. Write the Easy Parts First

This technique is sometimes called the "Swiss cheese method." Imagine a mouse confronting a slice of cheese. The mouse nibbles a hole in the slice and then nibbles another hole. Eventually, the slice looks like Swiss cheese. In the end, the mouse consumes the entire slice.

Imagine your project as a slice of cheese. The difficult parts of the project are keeping you from writing. You are not sure how to write about them. Instead, you identify the easiest parts of the project and start by tackling them. You are like the mouse nibbling holes in the cheese. When you finish nibbling away the manageable parts, you may find that the difficult parts are few and are not as much of a challenge as you feared.

d. Use the Buddy System

Find a friend who has the same or a similar writing project as you. Without engaging in any forbidden collaboration, talk about your projects and agree on some deadlines—for example, when you will complete the first round of research, when you will write the first few pages, when you will conform your authorities to the prescribed citation manual. By using this system, you and your buddy give one another support and motivate yourselves to meet deadlines.

e. Talk with Your Professor

Your professor probably has dealt with many students who are fearful of writing. With that experience, he or she can help you through your difficulty. Lawyers become legal writing professors because they like to help students develop into confident, successful lawyers. They want to help you.

§ 2.04. GETTING YOUR DOCUMENT WRITTEN: FIVE POINTERS

If you plan the writing process, break it into stages that are expressly scheduled, and leave yourself time to get the details right and to handle problems, you will find that writing is less stressful and more productive than it might otherwise be. It may seem that in making suggestions for managing the writing process, we have added steps that will all take time. This is true—these steps will all take time—but if carefully followed, they also will prevent stress, save time that might otherwise be spent on needless editing and revision, and leave you with a finished written product of which you can be proud.

1. Plan Your Writing Process

The most important aspect of planning the writing process is having a plan. That sounds simple, but like many simple statements, it is true. As we emphasized at the beginning of this chapter, planning is essential. For some writers, starting with a "zero draft" is a helpful way to get started. However, sitting down at the computer the night before an assignment is due and just writing will likely result in a stream-of-consciousness product. In the end, it will require more editing and revision than you have time for, and the finished product will not resemble a carefully planned and structured document. So do not think that you can save time by skipping the planning and preparatory steps. Structuring your approach to writing will ultimately save time and will almost certainly result in a better final product.

2. Plan for Multiple Drafts

In law school, you need to schedule at least a first draft and a final draft. If you have time, you may want to think about an additional, intermediate draft. Each draft should be a full, written version of the document; it is not a good draft if you leave gaping holes in the discussion with a note that you will get to it later. You need to see your writing in front of you in order to figure out if it works. Do the arguments make sense? Are they clear? Are there gaps in the logic? Are they adequately supported by authority? If you write more than one full draft, you will have the chance to correct both analytical and stylistic problems with your writing.

As a near-final step, consider printing your document. It may look different in hard copy than it does on the computer screen. If so, you may want to revise the format.

3. Be Realistic in Planning Your Deadlines

You will have a deadline for almost any legal document you write, whether it is a paper for class, a memo for a supervisor, or a brief for court. So you should start your writing process by being honest with yourself about how much time each step of the process will take—research, outline, first draft, final draft. You should assume that each step will take a significant amount of time, and you need to schedule these steps around whatever else is going on in your professional and personal lives. So be realistic. How much time do you have between the day you get the assignment and the day it is due? How much time do you have each day and week to devote to the assignment?

You should give yourself a minimum of 24, and preferably 48, hours before your deadline to leave the document untouched before a final review for minor errors. You will miss errors if you keep working on the document right up until the deadline. By reviewing your document after some time away from it, you will be able to compare what you meant to say with what you actually said, and make any necessary changes. And you will be better able to catch typographical and grammatical errors, as well as citation errors.

Thus, you should complete your final draft two to three days before the deadline. You should complete your rough draft a week before that. And you should complete your outline a week before your first draft. You should give yourself a significant amount of time to prepare an outline after you have completed your research; a good outline will make writing the first draft significantly easier and more efficient.

Obviously, you need to adjust your internal deadlines according to how much time you actually have to prepare the assignment. Our guidelines are intended to give you a relative idea of how much time you need to leave for each phase.

4. Build in Some Time for Complications

As a group, legal writing professors are becoming less tolerant of late papers. If you fail to meet a deadline, you may receive a reduced grade or a failing grade. Because some personal problem may arise along the journey to the deadline, be sure to build into your schedule a bit of extra time in case you need it.

It has been said that machines have "critical-need detectors." This means that when you need them most—the printer, the copier, or the computer—they are most likely to suffer malfunctions. If you wait until the last possible moment to produce your finished product, you will not have time to deal with technical difficulties. We have all heard the stories of computer crashes in the middle of the night that result in missed deadlines, or copiers that jam when we are trying to produce documents for court. If you are stressed out because you have left your work too close to the deadline, consider the possibility that that very stress may cause technical problems because you are in a hurry and are not handling the equipment as you should.

Even if you have done nothing to contribute to the problem, leaving yourself extra time will allow you to find that other printer or copier. In addition, back up your work while you are writing. This precautionary step may save you from that disastrous computer crash. There are many options for preserving your work—on a flash drive, in "the cloud," and so on. Use them!

5. Leave Time for the Details

Perhaps the single most common mistake made by inexperienced writers is not leaving enough time to get the details right. Legal documents tend to have several parts, whether multiple required sections such as are found in briefs or simple cover sheets and technical requirements for filings. You need to get in the habit of caring about the details, including grammar, spelling, punctuation, and citation form. You cannot place your sole reliance on software that checks spelling or auto-corrects errors. Those programs cannot recognize every error. For example, they will not catch the word that is a real word but is misused in a sentence.

The only sure way to catch the minor mistakes is to carefully proofread your document with a fresh pair of eyes. To give yourself the best chance of actually catching your mistakes, remember to put the document aside for at least 24 hours before you proofread it. Details matter. Get into the habit of making sure your writing is technically correct and professional looking. This practice will give your writing the polished appearance that will impress your professors, supervisors, clients, and judges.

CHAPTER 3

Learning About the Legal System

§ 3.01. THE LEGAL SYSTEM AND LEGAL WRITING

Much of the legal writing you will do in your career will involve analyzing legal problems. To analyze a legal problem, you must understand the sources of our law and their relationships to each other. You must also understand the workings of our legal system. This chapter provides a broad introduction to our court system, the common law, and statutory law and interpretation. Once you understand these aspects of the legal process, you will be able to evaluate a legal problem properly and prepare an accurate and well-reasoned legal analysis.

§ 3.02. SOURCES OF LAW AND THEIR HIERARCHY

There are three primary categories of law: constitutions, statutes, and common law. The Constitution of the United States and the 50 state constitutions set out the structure and powers of government, protect individual liberties, and define the reach of statutory authority. Statutes are passed by legislatures and govern a host of areas ranging from crime to social security benefit levels. The common law is the law judges make when they rule on cases. When a case is decided, it becomes a precedent for future similar legal conflicts in the same jurisdiction.[1]

An applicable constitutional provision, statute, or common law rule always governs the outcome of a legal problem. The existing case law will assist you in interpreting the statute or constitutional provision in the context of your particular case. When there is no relevant constitutional provision or statute, as there often is not, the common law is the sole source of authority for evaluating and resolving your case.

---

1. The word "jurisdiction" means different things in different contexts. Here we use it to refer to the geographic area or court system in which a case is decided. It can also mean the power of a court to hear a case, as in "personal jurisdiction" (jurisdiction/power over a party) or "subject matter jurisdiction" (jurisdiction/power over the issue presented to the court).

§ 3.03. THE COURT SYSTEM

Two court systems operate simultaneously in the United States: the state court system and the federal court system. In both the state and federal court systems there are two types of courts: trial courts and appellate courts. The following is an overview of each system.

1. The State Courts

Each of the 50 states has a court system. Although the structure of that system differs from state to state, it is always hierarchical. There are trial courts, often an intermediate appellate court, and a court of last resort—the tribunal at the top tier of the court system. In addition, there may be numerous other courts that perform specialized roles, such as small claims courts, juvenile courts, and housing courts.

A trial court is presided over by one judge, and may or may not include a jury. The function of a trial court is to determine the facts by evaluating the evidence in a case and to arrive at a decision by applying the law to the facts. Trial courts at the state level may be divided into courts of limited jurisdiction and courts of general jurisdiction. Pursuant to the provisions of the state constitution and state laws, courts of limited jurisdiction rule on certain specific matters such as violations of criminal law. Courts of general jurisdiction are empowered to hear a broader range of civil and criminal matters and often also review appeals from courts of limited jurisdiction.

From the decision of a trial court, the losing party may appeal to the next level, the appellate court. The appeal is heard by a panel of three to five judges, of whom a majority must agree on a particular result. That result forms the basis of the court's opinion deciding the case. The appellate court evaluates the lower court's decision and determines whether it committed any legal error that would warrant reversing or modifying the decision or ordering a new trial. The decision of the appellate court may be appealed to the state's highest court, which often has discretion to choose the cases it will hear. The decisions of the courts of last resort are final, and there is no further appeal of state law issues.

This diagram of the California courts illustrates a typical state court system, though you will find that states name their courts differently—for example, New York calls its court of last resort the Court of Appeals rather than the Supreme Court.

CALIFORNIA COURT SYSTEM

```
┌─────────────────────────┐
│     SUPREME COURT        │
└─────────────────────────┘

┌─────────────────────────┐
│      COURT OF            │
│      APPEAL              │
│   (6 courts of appeal)   │
└─────────────────────────┘

┌─────────────────────────┐
│    SUPERIOR COURT        │
│   (58 trial courts,      │
│     which handle         │
│  all criminal cases, all │
│  civil cases, appeals of │
│   small claims cases &   │
│    civil cases worth     │
│   $25,000 or less,       │
│      appeals of          │
│  misdemeanor- cases)     │
└─────────────────────────┘
```

Source: Superior Court of California County of Santa Clara, Self Service Center, Overview of the State Court System, http://www.scscourt.org/general_info/community/courtsystem.shtml

2. The Federal Courts

The Constitution and certain federal statutes establish the federal courts and empower them to hear certain kinds of cases. Federal courts hear all cases that arise under federal law, such as those involving the United States Constitution or federal statutes, disputes between two states, or cases in which the United States is a party.

Like the state systems, the federal court system is divided into trial courts, appellate courts, and a court of last resort. The trial courts are called district courts. Each state has at least one district court, and that court's jurisdiction is limited to the territory of its district. In a district court case, a judge sits with or without a jury, depending on the nature of the case and the wishes of the parties.

The intermediate appellate courts in the federal system are called the United States courts of appeals. The courts of appeals hear appeals from the district courts located in the same circuit. A circuit is a designated geographical area usually encompassing several states. The United States is divided geographically into thirteen circuits. Eleven of these circuit courts are identified by number, for example, the United States Court of Appeals for the Third Circuit. There is also the United States Court of Appeals for the District of Columbia and the United States Court of Appeals for the Federal Circuit, which hears appeals in patent cases, certain international trade cases, and some cases involving damage claims against the United States. Usually, three judges sit on a panel to decide a particular case, and at least two must agree for a decision to be reached.

The Supreme Court of the United States, consisting of the Chief Justice and eight Associate Justices, is the highest court in the federal system. The Court hears a limited number of cases from the courts of appeals and, on certain issues, from the district courts and the highest state courts. The Court must accept review of certain types of cases, but these are rare. Typically the Court selects which cases it will hear by issuing a writ of certiorari. Cases heard by the Supreme Court generally involve new or unresolved questions of federal law affecting people throughout the country and interpretations of federal statutes or the United States Constitution.

This diagram illustrates the federal court hierarchy:

FEDERAL COURT SYSTEM

SUPREME COURT OF THE UNITED STATES	

COURT OF APPEALS FOR THE FEDERAL CIRCUIT	**UNITED STATES COURTS OF APPEALS (for all 11 circuits & D.C.)**

U.S. COURT OF FEDERAL CLAIMS	**U.S. COURT OF INTERNATIONAL TRADE**	**U.S. DISTRICT COURTS 94 judicial districts U.S. Bankruptcy Court**

MILITARY COURTS (trial & appellate) COURT OF VETERANS APPEALS U.S. TAX COURT ADMINISTRATIVE AGENCIES

§ 3.04. THE COMMON LAW

The phrase "common law" refers to legal principles created and developed by the courts independent of legislative enactments. It is the body of law judges create when they decide cases. The doctrine of stare decisis mandates that a court follow these common law precedents. Under our system of precedent, however, courts must follow only those precedents that are mandatory or have binding authority. Case law that is not binding is often referred to as persuasive authority.

1. Mandatory Authority

Mandatory authority is authority that you must rely on because it binds the court in your jurisdiction. It is unethical to omit from a legal argument mandatory authority that is adverse to your client's interests.

When you are presented with a legal problem, you research the statutory and case law of the controlling jurisdiction to resolve that problem. If there is an applicable statute, the court is bound to follow that statute as previously interpreted by the courts. If there is no statute, you will look for case law that is binding on the court where the case is pending.

A precedent becomes binding on a court if (1) the case was decided by that court or a higher court in the same jurisdiction, and (2) the material facts of the pending case and the decided case, as well as the legal reasoning applicable to the two cases, are indistinguishable. For example, a state trial court is bound by the decisions of that state's intermediate appellate courts and its highest court. A federal district court is bound by the decisions of the court of appeals of the circuit in which the district court is situated and the decisions of the Supreme Court. District courts are not bound by the decisions of other district courts or by those of the courts of appeals of other circuits. The courts of appeals are bound by their own decisions and those of the Supreme Court. They are not bound by the decisions of other courts of appeals.

Suppose you are arguing a case in a jurisdiction and your research discloses a case from a higher court in the same jurisdiction with identical material facts and applicable reasoning. The material facts are the facts the court actually relies upon in reaching the decision. The court you are before is bound by the holding of the previous case; the earlier case is "on point" with your case. The holding is the court's decision on the issue before it. All other discussion of tangential issues is called dicta and is not binding. You will rarely, if ever, have a case that is directly "on point" with your case—most cases will be distinguishable on some material basis.

2. Persuasive Authority

Sometimes your research will show that your jurisdiction has neither a statute nor legal precedent to govern your case. You must then rely on persuasive authority to help analyze the issue. Persuasive authority is non-mandatory legal authority. It is authority that may persuade a court to decide a certain way but does not require a particular decision. Persuasive authority includes:

- Primary authority that does not control your case because the rules are not directly applicable or the relevant facts are distinguishable. For example, assume that in a particular case a court finds that the defendant was liable for assault for brandishing a real gun at plaintiff. This holding may not apply to a subsequent case in which a defendant brandishes what is obviously a toy gun at a plaintiff.
- Secondary authority, such as treatises, hornbooks, or law review articles, which present only authors' viewpoints about law but are not themselves the law.
- Dicta in court opinions, which are discussions that are explanatory, but not necessary, to the decisions. For example, the court in the gun assault case may suggest that brandishing a knife also can constitute an assault. An actual case involving brandishing of a knife, however, may not involve an assault unless all the circumstances create that offense. The victim, for example, may have felt no real threat from the defendant's brandishing the knife, and therefore no assault occurred. The court deciding the knife case will not be constrained by the suggestion in the earlier case that brandishing a knife may be an assault.
- Precedents from other states that have decided your issue are persuasive authority. In the federal system, precedents from other district courts and other courts of appeals are persuasive authority.

3. The Weight of Authority

When you draft your legal papers for the court, you must decide which cases to include in your discussion to present the most compelling argument. Certain cases will be more persuasive than others. How persuasive a case is, that is, what weight it carries, depends on a number of factors, including:

(a) The level of the court. The decision of a higher court is more authoritative than that of a lower court.

(b) Factual similarity. When the cases you cite have facts similar to your case, their value as precedent increases.

(c) The year of the decision. A more recent opinion is more useful than one that is dated.

(d) The judge. Look for an opinion written by the judge presiding over your case or by a judge with a good reputation.

(e) Majority decisions. Language from a majority decision carries more weight than that from a concurring or dissenting opinion.

(f) The state in which the court deciding the case sits.

(i) Geographic proximity. A case from a state that is relatively close geographically is often more helpful than one from a state that is far away.

(ii) Certain states, like New Jersey, are often at the forefront of emerging case law.

(g) The number of other courts that have cited the case approvingly; that is, a developing trend in the law.

§ 3.05. STATUTES AND THEIR INTERPRETATION

1. The Supremacy of the Legislature and the Legislative Process

Under our system of government, the United States Congress and the state legislatures are the supreme lawmakers, subject only to the limitations of the federal and state constitutions. Therefore, statutes provide the binding rules of decision that courts must follow. Statutes prevail over common law if there is a conflict between the two. Here is a brief discussion of how statutes come into being.

A member of Congress introduces a bill in either the House or the Senate.[2] It is then referred to the appropriate committee, which conducts hearings and issues a report. There is discussion of the bill on the floor, and a vote is taken. If it passes, it goes to the other chamber, where it goes through a similar process. If different versions of the bill are passed by the House and Senate, the bill may be sent to a conference committee for resolution of the differences. Finally, it goes to the President for signature or veto. If the President vetoes the bill, Congress may try to "override" the veto with a two-thirds majority vote, meaning they can pass it anyway if they get enough votes. Otherwise, the President's veto means the bill will not become law.

In finished form, state and federal statutes usually have certain parts: a preamble, which may include a statement of policy or purpose; a definition section, which attempts to define

---

2. For our purposes, we simply note that the processes in the federal and state systems are similar.

the significant words used in the statute; the substantive provisions; and any procedural provisions. Consider the following Maryland statute:

MD. CRIM. CODE ANN. § 10-701. "Flag" defined
In this subtitle, "Flag" includes any size flag, standard, color, ensign, or shield made of any substance or represented or produced on any substance, that purports to be a flag, standard, color, ensign, or shield of the United States or of this state.

MD. CRIM. CODE ANN. § 10-702. Scope of subtitle
This subtitle does not apply to:

(1) an act allowed by the statutes of the United States or of this State, or by the regulations of the armed forces of the United States; or

(2) a document or product, stationary, ornament, picture, apparel, or jewelry that depicts flag without a design or words on the flag that is not connected with an advertisement.

MD. CRIM. CODE ANN. § 10-703. Marked flag and merchandise
Scope of section

(a) This section applies to a flag of the United States or of this State, or a flag that is authorized by law of the United States or of this State.

Prohibited—Advertising marking

(b) For exhibition or display, a person may not place or cause to be placed a word, figure, mark, picture, design or advertisement of any nature on a flag.

Prohibited—Public display of marked flag

(c) A person may not publicly exhibit a flag with a word, figure, mark, picture, design, or advertisement printed, painted, or produced on or attached to the flag.

Prohibited—Merchandise marked with flag

(d) A person may not publicly display for sale, manufacture, or otherwise, or sell, give, or possess for sale or for use as a gift or for any other purpose, an article of merchandise or receptacle on which a flag is produced or attached to advertise, decorate, or mark the merchandise.

Penalty

(e) A person who violates this section is guilty of a misdemeanor and on conviction is subject to a fine not exceeding $500.

MD. CRIM. CODE ANN. § 10-704. Mutilation
Prohibited

(a) A person may not intentionally mutilate, deface, destroy, burn, trample, or use a flag:

(1) in a manner intended to incite or produce an imminent breach of the peace; and

(2) under circumstances likely to incite or produce an imminent breach of the peace.

Penalty

(b) A person who violates this section is guilty of a misdemeanor and on conviction is subject to imprisonment not exceeding 1 year or a fine not exceeding $1,000 or both.

MD. CRIM. CODE ANN. § 10-705. Construction of subtitle

This subtitle shall be construed to carry out its general purpose and to make uniform the laws of the states that enact it.

MD. CRIM. CODE ANN. § 10-706. Short title

This subtitle may be cited as the Maryland Uniform Flag Law.

As you see, while the Maryland statute has no preamble, it does have a definition section and substantive and procedural sections, including penalty and construction provisions.

2. The Relationship Between Statutory Law and Common Law

After the applicable constitutional provisions, enacted statutes are the highest authority in a jurisdiction. The courts are bound by them. A legislature may enact a statute that overrules or modifies existing common law. It may enact a common law rule into a statute. Courts, however, rule on whether statutes are constitutional.

When deciding a case governed by a statute, the court must decide how to apply and enforce that statute. Courts rely on certain aids in interpreting the meaning of a statute. You will rely on those same aids in urging the court to adopt a particular construction.

Most statutes are deliberately drafted in broad language because they are written to establish a principle rather than to solve a specific problem. The general language serves as the basis for common law development of the statute by the courts. It is the court's application of a statute to particular cases that gives meaning to the statute's language and provides guidance for future cases.

To interpret broad and ambiguous statutory language, courts look to the following for guidance:

- The actual language of the statute, (i.e., the words chosen by the legislature).
- The context within the statute. What is the subject or purpose of other headings or sections in the same statute? What language do complimentary statutes contain? Is there a statutory statement of legislative purpose? Legislatures sometimes attempt to avoid ambiguity problems by including statements of legislative purpose as a preamble to the statute itself.
- The legislative history of the statute. A statute's legislative history provides information to the court about the legislature's intent in adopting the statute. It consists of the "official comments," the floor debate, the committee reports, and the committee hearings. Unfortunately, on a state level, the legislative history is often nearly nonexistent, and on every level it may be very difficult to obtain.
- Administrative interpretations by the agency charged with administering the statute. They occasionally provide a more specific indication of the statute's meaning. For example, the Food and Drug Administration issues regulations and interpretations of statutes governing the food and drug industries; the Federal Communications Commission issues regulations and interpretations governing cable and television, among other communications services, and the Department of Transportation issues

regulations and interpretations governing all the various forms of transportation, such as trains.

- The interpretation of other courts. A court will consider how courts at a higher level, the same level, or even a lower level have applied the statute.
- The broader context of the statute. What kinds of events were taking place that caused the legislation to be created? What goals were to be furthered by enacting the statute? If a statute overrules common law or tries to fill in a gap in the common law, understanding the problems that led to the enactment can help define the scope of the statute.
- The common law. When a statute codifies existing common law, the body of cases that developed the common law rule provides highly useful guidance.
- A comparison with similar statutes of other jurisdictions.
- Scholarly interpretations, if available.

Courts sometimes also look to canons of statutory construction. These are maxims intended to provide guidance. However, courts are free to disregard them. Here are the most commonly used canons:

1. The "plain meaning rule." In construing a statute, the court shall not deviate from its literal meaning except as required by internal context or the need to avoid absurd results.
2. The rule of "negative implication." When the legislature has covered a certain subject in a statute, it must have intended to exclude everything not mentioned.
3. The principle of construing penal statutes narrowly.
4. The principle of construing statutes in derogation of the common law narrowly.

Although some canons of interpretation have themselves been adopted by statute,[3] as a rule they reflect common sense and do not provide technical help in construing a statute. As between the available aids to interpretation, courts will more likely be persuaded by intrinsic factors such as the statute's language and "plain meaning" than by extrinsic factors such as legislative history.

---

3. A Pennsylvania statute states:

RULE OF STRICT AND LIBERAL CONSTRUCTION

Statutes in derogation of common law—

(a) The rule that statutes in derogation of the common law are to be strictly construed, shall have no application to the statutes of this Commonwealth enacted finally after September 1, 1937.

Provisions subject to strict construction—

(b) All provisions of a statute of the classes hereafter enumerated shall be strictly construed:

    (1) Penal provisions.

    (2) Retroactive provisions.

    (3) Provisions imposing taxes.

    (4) Provisions conferring the power of eminent domain.

    (5) Provisions exempting persons and property from taxation.

    (6) Provisions exempting property from the power of eminent domain.

    (7) Provisions decreasing the jurisdiction of a court of record.

    (8) Provisions enacted finally prior to September 1, 1937 which are in derogation of the common law.

Provisions subject to liberal construction—

(c) All other provisions of a statute shall be liberally construed to effect their objects and to promote justice.

1 Pa. Cons. Stat. Ann. § 1928.

3. The Roles of the Court and the Legislature—An Illustration

The question of whether flag burning is permissible has been addressed by the legislature and courts in turn. It provides an excellent illustration of the interaction between the two in the context of statutory interpretation.

The Texas Penal Code stated:

Desecration of Venerated Object.

(a) A person commits an offense if he intentionally or knowingly desecrates:
(1) a public monument;
(2) a place of worship or burial;
(3) a state or national flag.

(b) For purposes of this section, "desecrate" means deface, damage or otherwise physically mistreat in a way that the actor knows will seriously offend one or more persons likely to observe or discover his action.

Tex. Penal Code Ann. § 42.09 (West 1989).[4]

While the Republican National Convention was taking place in Dallas in 1984, Gregory Lee Johnson participated in a political demonstration that included the public burning of an American flag. He was convicted of desecrating a flag in violation of Texas law. This conviction was affirmed by a Texas district court of appeals, but was subsequently reversed by the Texas Court of Criminal Appeals. The United States Supreme Court granted certiorari.

Texas claimed its interest in preventing breaches of the peace justified Johnson's conviction under the statute. In fact, however, there was no breach of the peace. The Supreme Court heard the case on appeal and observed that Texas was essentially making the argument that an "audience that takes serious offense at particular expression is necessarily likely to disturb the peace and that the expression may be prohibited on this basis." *Texas v. Johnson*, 491 U.S. 397, 408 (1989). The Court also found that the asserted state interest in "preserving the flag as a symbol of nationhood and national unity" could not survive the scrutiny imposed on state actions that attempt to regulate speech content protected by the First Amendment. *Id.* at 420.

The federal flag burning statute in effect at the time of the *Texas v. Johnson* ruling stated:

Desecration of the flag of the United States; penalties

(a) Whoever knowingly casts contempt upon any flag of the United States by publicly mutilating, defacing, defiling, burning, or trampling upon it shall be fined not more than $1,000 or imprisoned for not more than one year, or both.

(b) The term "flag of the United States" as used in this section, shall include any flag, standard, colors, ensign, or any picture or representation of either, or of any part or parts of either, and of any substance or represented on any substance, of any size evidently purporting to be either of said flag, standard, colors, or ensign of the United States of America, or a picture or a representation of either, upon which shall be shown the colors, the stars and the stripes, in any number of either thereof, or of any part or parts of either, by which the average person

---

4. This statutory section now relates to cruelty to animals.

seeing the same without deliberation may believe the same to represent the flag, standards, colors, or ensign of the United States of America.

(c) Nothing in this section shall be construed as indicating an intent on the part of Congress to deprive any State, territory, possession, or the Commonwealth of Puerto Rico of jurisdiction over any offense over which it would have jurisdiction in the absence of this section.

18 U.S.C. § 700 (1989).

Congress responded to the *Texas v. Johnson* case by removing the "casts contempt" language from subsection (a) of the statute, reasoning that now the flag burning prohibition was not content-based. The revised statute read, in relevant part:

AN ACT

To amend section 700 of title 18, United States Code, to protect the physical integrity of the flag.

Be it enacted by the Senate and House of Representatives of the United States of America in Congress assembled,

This Act may be cited as the "Flag Protection Act of 1989".

SEC. 2. CRIMINAL PENALTIES WITH RESPECT TO THE PHYSICAL INTEGRITY OF THE UNITED STATES FLAG.

(a) In General—Subsection (a) of section 700 of title 18, United States Code, is amended to read as follows:

(a)(1) Whoever knowingly mutilates, defaces, physically defiles, burns, maintains on the floor or ground, or tramples upon any flag of the United States shall be fined under this title or imprisoned for not more than one year, or both.

(2) This subsection does not prohibit any conduct consisting of the disposal of a flag when it has become worn or soiled.

(b) Definition.—Section 700(b) of title 18, United States Code, is amended to read as follows:

(b)(1) As used in this section, the term 'flag of the United States' means any flag of the United States, or any part thereof, made of any substance, of any size, in a form that is commonly displayed.

18 U.S.C. § 700 (Supp. II 1990).

Shortly after the passage of the revised Flag Protection Act, Shawn Eichman and two friends set several United States flags on fire on the steps of the United States Capitol during a political demonstration. Their protest was, in part, intended to demonstrate their objection to the newly enacted statute. In *United States v. Eichman*, 496 U.S. 310 (1990), the Supreme Court found that the revised language failed to make the statute constitutional.

Although the Flag Protection Act contained no explicit content-based limitation on prohibited conduct, it was nevertheless clear that the Government's asserted interest was related to the suppression of free expression and concerned with the content of such expression. The Government's interest in protecting the physical integrity of a privately owned flag rests upon a perceived need to preserve the flag's status as a symbol of our Nation and certain national ideals. But the mere disfigurement of a particular manifestation of the symbol, without more, does not diminish or otherwise affect the symbol itself in any way. For example, the secret destruction of a flag in one's own basement would not threaten the flag's recognized meaning. Rather, the Government's desire to preserve the flag as a symbol of certain national ideals is implicated only when a person's treatment of the flag communicates a message to others that is inconsistent with those ideals.

Moreover, the precise language of the Act's prohibitions confirmed Congress's interest in the communicative impact of flag destruction. The Act criminalized the conduct of anyone who knowingly mutilated, defaced, physically defiled, burned, maintained on the floor or ground, or trampled upon any flag. Each of the specified terms—with the possible exception of "burns"—unmistakably connotes disrespectful treatment of the flag and suggests a focus on those acts likely to damage the flag's symbolic value. And the explicit exemption for disposal of worn or soiled flags protected certain acts traditionally associated with patriotic respect for the flag.

Although Congress cast the Flag Protection Act in somewhat broader terms than the Texas statute at issue in *Johnson*, the Act still suffered from the same fundamental flaw: it suppressed expression out of concern for its likely communicative impact. *United States v. Eichman*, 496 U.S. 310, 312-326 (1990).

It is clear that Congress wanted to enact a law that prohibited flag burning. However, it seems equally clear that regardless of the form of such a statute, it most likely would not survive a constitutional challenge. Reread the Maryland flag burning statute at the beginning of this section. Is it possible that the Maryland legislature has drafted a statute that would survive constitutional scrutiny? The statutory language suggests that the statute will be enforced only when the circumstances surrounding the flag burning are likely to create a breach of the peace.

As you see, enacted statutes have no meaning or effect until they are interpreted by the courts and applied in context. Statutory analysis is an important function of our court system.

CHAPTER 4

Research Strategy

§ 4.01. INTRODUCTION

For purposes of this discussion, we assume that you have already learned or are learning how to use specific materials in the library. The goal of this chapter is to teach you how to integrate your knowledge of the materials in the library with what we are teaching you about legal writing and analysis.

In other words, once you have your writing assignment in hand, how do you approach the research process? Where do you start? How many places do you look? How do you balance book and computer research? When do you stop? How do you keep track of your research so that you don't end up covering the same ground repeatedly? We will take up each question in turn, using the Paul Trune problem presented in Chapter 6. The issue in the case is whether Mr. Trune can bring a civil action for false imprisonment. Before continuing, go to Section 6.04 and read the facts of the case.

As we go through this discussion, do not be concerned if you see angles that are not discussed. Our approach shows you how one person might effectively research this particular problem. If you see other approaches, try them; you may find that they work for you, or you may find they were not included because they were unproductive.

§ 4.02. WHERE DO YOU START?

As you begin the research process, identify the key legal terminology that will help you access the appropriate research sources. If you are unfamiliar with the area of law presented by the research problem, begin your research with a secondary resource that discusses the broad legal principles and rules that govern the area. Examples of such sources include hornbooks, treatises, and legal encyclopedias. If you do have some knowledge of the field, you can go directly to sources of primary authority such as digests and annotated statutes.[1] We will discuss the use of each of these resources in Mr. Trune's case.

---

1. If you are researching a question that might be the subject of a law review article, that would be an excellent place to start. Law review articles will give you a head start on primary source research, as well as an idea of arguments that can be made on your topic. You can find law review articles by using a published index to periodicals or by doing an online search.

1. Statutes

Many law students reflexively think of statutes when beginning research tasks. If you are re⌐earching a problem in an area that is likely to have been addressed by a legislature, that is not a bad instinct to have. When you are unfamiliar with the law in your jurisdiction, begin by determining whether there is a relevant statute. Is there a false imprisonment statute in Wisconsin? Section 940.30 of the Wisconsin Statutes, governing false imprisonment, provides that "[w]hoever intentionally confines or restrains another without the person's consent and with knowledge that he or she has no lawful authority to do so is guilty of a Class H felony."

Before you start searching the annotations under § 940.30 for helpful cases, read the statute carefully. The question you have been asked is whether Paul Trune can bring a *civil* action for false imprisonment. You are researching false imprisonment as a tort, not a crime. Thus, the statute's characterization of false imprisonment as a felony should tip you off that the statute does not apply to your client's situation, and you should ignore it.

2. Treatises

If you are researching an area such as tort law that tends to be governed almost exclusively by common law decisions, how do you begin? The answer depends in large part on how familiar you are with the subject matter of your research project. If you know the elements of false imprisonment and are familiar with the key terminology, you can probably begin with the relevant digests. However, if you do not, you will first need some background information about the topic. For that, you should consult a secondary source such as a treatise.

In a treatise, you can read generally about the applicable legal principles as well as begin to identify specific cases. Dobbs, *The Law of Torts* (West 2000) is one of the primary treatises in the area of tort law. If you look on pages 67-75, you will find an explanation of the tort of false imprisonment. You will also see some Wisconsin cases in the footnotes: *Drabek v. Sabley*, 31 Wis. 2d 184, 142 N.W.2d 798 (1966) (p. 69, n. 16; p. 71, n. 18; p. 73, n. 4); *Herbst v. Wuennenberg*, 83 Wis. 2d 768, 266 N.W.2d 391 (1978) (p. 70, n. 12; p. 71, nn. 17 and 19); and *Dupler v. Seubert*, 69 Wis. 2d 373, 230 N.W.2d 626 (1975) (p. 71, nn. 16 and 17). *Herbst* and *Dupler* are discussed at length in Chapter 6.

3. Restatements

Another good source of general rules, at least in areas of the law for which they exist, are the Restatements. Restatements are common law treatises on legal subjects, such as Torts, Contracts, and Property, created to collect and present current rules and cases. Although the Restatements are not the law, unless the courts in your jurisdiction have adopted the relevant provisions, they are often persuasive. In any event, the Restatements provide a good discussion of basic principles, with examples of how those principles can be applied. The Appendix volumes contain relevant cases, so you can determine whether the courts in your jurisdiction have cited the Restatement. If a Restatement provision applies to your case, do not overlook this resource as you search for applicable law.

First, consult the general index at the end of the pertinent Restatement (i.e., Torts, Contracts, etc.). The general index will direct you to the appropriate volume, which will include a more detailed index. False imprisonment is covered in §§ 35-45 of the Restatement (Second) of Torts. The applicable language of many of these sections is quoted in the decisions discussed in Chapter 6, so we have not reproduced it here.

If you look in the Appendix volumes, which are organized chronologically, you will find annotations of cases from various states. The Restatement is cited extensively in both *Herbst* and *Dupler*, so you should not be surprised to find the *Herbst* case in the appropriate Appendix volume. If you check earlier volumes of the Appendix, you will also find *Dupler*. If you check later volumes, you will find other Wisconsin cases. Remember that you must check several volumes to be sure you have discovered all of the relevant authority.

4. Legal Encyclopedias

Finally, legal encyclopedias are another good source of general rules and a good starting point for finding primary authority. If you have found a good treatise, you may not need to check an encyclopedia as well. Looking in an encyclopedia may also be unnecessary if there is an applicable Restatement, at least if the Restatement has been adopted in your jurisdiction. If, however, you have not located any other resources that can help you learn the basic rules and terminology of your field of inquiry, encyclopedias should do the job. Until you become comfortable with legal research and the resources available to you, you may want to check more than one source anyway, to be sure you genuinely understand the legal issues involved and to see if the different sources contain different types of useful information.

If your state publishes its own legal encyclopedia, start there. In this discussion, we will take on the slightly more difficult task of trying to find Wisconsin precedent in the general encyclopedias, *Corpus Juris Secundum* and *American Jurisprudence*; the research procedures, however, are the same. If you look in volume 32 of *American Jurisprudence 2d*, at the start of the chapter on false imprisonment, you will find an outline that breaks the topic of false imprisonment into analytical elements. As you scan the outline, Part B, "Elements," should look like a good place to start. More specifically, section 2, dealing with the basic elements of confinement, should look particularly interesting. The subsections will give you a general discussion of what constitutes sufficient restraint.

The next step is to look for cases in your jurisdiction that demonstrate how the courts have applied those concepts. When you look under sections 10-20, however, you will find that only footnote 65 cites a Wisconsin case: *Weiler v. Herzfeld-Phillipson Co.*, 189 Wis. 554, 208 N.W. 599 (1926) (holding that there is no false imprisonment where a supervisor interrogates an employee suspected of dishonesty in the supervisor's office for a lengthy period; the court pointed out that the employee was being compensated for the time and was under the direction of the employer so long as she remained an employee). An examination of the pocket part discloses no additional Wisconsin cases. The case you have found will get you started on the question of what constitutes false imprisonment in Wisconsin, but given its age, you should try to find something a little more recent.

An examination of volume 35 of *Corpus Juris Secundum* will yield a similar outline. Part B, "Manner and Character of Restraint," again dealing with the basic requirements of restraint, should look like a good place to start. In the main volume, you will find one Wisconsin case: *Herbst v. Wuennienberg* (§ 15, n. 6, and § 17, n. 11). (*Herbst* is discussed in Chapter 6.)

§ 4.03. OTHER RESOURCES

1. Digests

Now that you have a greater familiarity with the elements of false imprisonment and have identified a few cases to read, you can move on to the digests. While digests will not give you general descriptions of the law, they will probably provide you with more cases. Again, you should use a state digest if your state has its own, but you can also look in West's regional digests. In the *North Western Digest 2d*, you will find an outline for false imprisonment. Assuming that your primary goal is to determine what the cases have to say about the sufficiency of restraint as an element of false imprisonment, you should find notes 5 and 6 relevant. Here are the Wisconsin cases contained in the annotations under those key numbers:

Johnson v. Ray, 99 Wis. 2d 777, 299 N.W.2d 849 (1981)
Drabek v. Sabley, 31 Wis. 2d 184, 142 N.W.2d 798 (1966)
Schaidler v. Mercy Medical Center of Oshkosh, Inc., 209 Wis. 2d 457, 563 N.W.2d 554 (1997)
Peters v. Menard, Inc., 224 Wis. 2d 174, 589 N.W.2d 395 (1999)
Miller v. Wal-Mart Stores, Inc., 219 Wis. 2d 250, 580 N.W.2d 233 (1998)
Herbst v. Wuennenberg, 83 Wis. 2d 768, 266 N.W.2d 391 (1978)
Hainz v. Shopko Stores, Inc., 121 Wis. 2d 168, 359 N.W.2d 397 (1984)

At least two of these Wisconsin cases are familiar, but several new ones appear also. The advantage of the digests over the treatises and encyclopedias is that the digests provide brief general descriptions of the cases, which you can use to decide whether you want to read any particular case in full. In making this decision, always remember that such a short description of the case cannot possibly alert you to every aspect of the decision that might be useful, and that these "squibs" are occasionally inaccurate.

Even so, you can often use the annotations to eliminate cases that have no relevance to the situation you are researching. For example, if you look at the descriptions of *Johnson*, *Schaidler*, *Miller*, or *Hainz*, you should conclude that you are not likely to find anything helpful in those cases because the facts are so different as to make them difficult to compare. Given that you have other cases that outline the general requirements to make a claim of false imprisonment, you do not need these cases for any general language they might contain.

An examination of the pocket part to the digest will reveal no new Wisconsin cases, so you should start to feel fairly confident that you have now identified the most relevant and up-to-date precedent on your issue. Also note that you are starting to see some of the same cases repeatedly, which is a good sign—it means that you are finding the limits of the legal universe in which you are operating.

2. A.L.R. and Legal Periodicals

If you wish to be especially thorough and find out what others have written on your topic, you might want to consult sources such as the *American Law Reports* (A.L.R.), the *Current Law Index*, or one of the indexes to legal periodicals. For a topic as straightforward as this one, involving an intentional tort that has been reasonably well defined by the courts, such additional research will probably not be necessary. If you were doing this research in a firm, at a client's expense, you would almost certainly not go to such lengths.

While you are in law school, however, and are still learning the law with the luxury of enough time to fully investigate all potentially helpful options, you might want to at least take a quick look at these kinds of supportive resources. If you happen to come across an annotation or law review article specifically on your topic, you might even *save* time on your research.

If you did look at the A.L.R. index, you would find brief descriptions of a number of annotations on specific aspects of false imprisonment. And, if you searched the *Current Law Index* for false imprisonment, you would again find brief descriptions of articles on specific aspects of the topic. The *Current Law Index* is organized chronologically, so you might have to check several volumes for relevant articles. The vast majority of articles and annotations listed in these sources deal with criminal false arrest and imprisonment; the few that have any civil or tort implications do not appear to be relevant. You can use your judgment as to whether you would read any of these annotations or articles, but again, if you were doing this research at a client's expense, you should consider whether the expenditure of the time required would be cost-effective.

§ 4.04.   COMPUTER RESEARCH

1. Traditional Legal Research Sources

Most law schools provide free access to LexisNexis and Westlaw.[2] LexisNexis and Westlaw can be used most efficiently when you have enough of an understanding of the legal terminology that you can frame a search that will retrieve only relevant cases. For example, if you search a database of Wisconsin state cases using "false imprisonment," you will retrieve 10,585 cases on LexisAdvance and 941 cases on WestlawNext.[3]

When a client is paying for your time on the computer, you simply cannot read through hundreds or thousands of cases. Even if a client is not paying, it makes no sense to go screen by screen through all those cases when a glance through an encyclopedia, a treatise, or a digest will let you know much faster whether you need to read the cases in their entirety. In all likelihood, the vast majority of the cases do not deal substantively with false imprisonment, or they may involve criminal charges or aspects of the tort that are not at issue in your case.

Do not use the specific facts of your case to narrow your search. It is highly unlikely that you will find other cases involving fact patterns just like yours, and your real concern is to find cases dealing with the same issues that your case raises. For example, you could narrow your search by adding "farmer" to your search request, but that will not reduce the number of cases you find, nor will it add to the number of useful cases. You should know by now that it does not really matter that the defendant is a farmer, and such a search will only waste your time.

As you narrow your search, focus on terminology that will call up cases dealing with the elements of the tort with which you are concerned. Your primary concern in Mr. Trune's case is whether there was sufficient restraint. Thus, you might try a terms and connectors search along the lines of "false imprisonment and restrain! w/20 suffic!", which will yield

---

2. Your school may also have subscriptions to other legal research services, such as Loislaw, which can be accessed at http://www.loislaw.com.

3. As of September 2013.

65 cases on WestlawNext and 15 on LexisAdvance. If you perform the search, you will note that at least some of these cases look very familiar. You can also try a natural language search to see what you find.

WestlawNext is also very efficient in finding an updated, digital copy of a legal digest or legal encyclopedia. For example, let's look at "false imprisonment" one more time. Log onto WestlawNext and go to the front page. From there, click on the tab "Tools," located under the broader tab "Browse[.]" Next hit the first link titled "West Key Number System[.]" A list of 450 legal topics should pop up. You can manually search for "false imprisonment" or you can use the search key (on a PC, use control+F; on Mac, use command+F) and search for "false imprisonment[.]" This should take you to number 168—false imprisonment; go ahead and click on the link. The top two links on the next page under "Civil Liability" will bring you to a table of contents like page, similar to the digest. The bottom two links under "Criminal Responsibility" will list relevant cases, which you can refine based on the jurisdiction you want to search.

Many other websites offer access to legal sources; some are free, others are not. Try searching yourself to see what you find, or consult your legal writing instructor or law librarian to see what other sources they recommend. LexisAdvance and WestlawNext are very expensive to use in practice, so you should not assume that you will be able to do all of your research using those services once you are out of law school.

2. Not Purely Legal Resources

You no doubt already have experience researching online using Google or other search engines. For that reason, we do not discuss here all the sources available; we merely suggest one or two sources that may be helpful.

Google Scholar is a free research engine that produces surprisingly good legal research results, at least for some users. If you input a search, Google Scholar will come up with cases on the topic, plus citations to the cases in articles. It does not have an updating feature, so you cannot tell whether the case is still good law, and the cases come up without headnotes or other features available on LexisAdvance and WestlawNext that can lead you to other relevant sources. Law librarians and legal writing instructors who have tried searches on Google Scholar report both pleasant surprise about the speed and accuracy of the results, and concern about the lack of some familiar and helpful features. If you search for Wisconsin civil cases on false imprisonment you will come up with 249 cases—more than you want to scroll through.

You are probably already familiar with Wikipedia, especially since it appears in so many search results. Wikipedia can be very helpful for finding general information on a topic, or as a launching pad for research in a particular area. We do not recommend it for formal legal research, however, because any Wikipedia user can add information on the site. As a result, you cannot guarantee the accuracy or reliability of the information you find there.

As when using other research tools, it is always a good idea to check your research by trying multiple sources. The information that comes up repeatedly is likely to be the most helpful and reliable.

3. Books versus Computers—How Do You Decide?

Many practicing attorneys report frustration and disappointment at what they see as inadequate research training and skills on the part of recent law graduates. Many law students assume that everything worth finding can be found on the Internet. However, the Internet is not always the answer—it may be inefficient, excessively costly, and unable to give you what you need. One senior attorney points out that Internet research has two major shortcomings—it cannot work with either concepts or analogies, both of which are critical to legal analysis.[4] Sometimes books in the library lead to faster and more accurate results. You may even find key cases in the books that would not have turned up in a computer search. Sometimes this is the result of what we call the "inspiration factor." As you are scanning an outline in an encyclopedia, digest, or annotated code, you may see a heading that will lead you to important cases, but it may not use the words you would have thought to use for a computer search.

All in all, the safest approach often is to try both book and computer research. You should start with books, to gain familiarity with the relevant concepts, and use visual scanning to see connections and terminology that may not have occurred to you just sitting at your computer. Turn to the computer when you have narrowed your research sufficiently to choose the best search terms, or when you are ready to look for specific cases and statutes.[5]

§ 4.05. UPDATING YOUR RESEARCH

Always update your research, not only to make sure the cases you plan to build your argument on are good law, but also to see whether there are any subsequent cases that might be even more helpful. Updating services such as Shepard's from LexisNexis or KeyCite from Westlaw can be just as useful as case finders as they are citators. Updating online is much more efficient than using the Shepard's volumes in the law library, but you should use whatever updating tools you are taught in your legal writing class. The important thing is to make sure that you are relying on the most recent authoritative sources, and are not going to embarrass yourself by citing a case that has been overruled or is otherwise no longer good law.

§ 4.06. WHEN DO YOU STOP?

Perhaps the most frustrating element of legal research for those who are learning it is knowing when to stop. In their zeal to leave no stone unturned, fledgling lawyers tend to explore every conceivable alternative, to look in every resource book the library has to offer, and to read every case that even mentions the type of cause of action at issue in the case they are researching. Telling you that you will develop instincts that will help you avoid wasting time in the library or online (which you will) may offer some long-term comfort, but it will not get you through those frustrating early efforts. Thus, we offer a few guidelines that should help streamline your first research efforts.

---

4. Scott Stolley, *The Corruption of Legal Research*, For Def. 39 (Apr. 2004).

5. A recent study by LexisNexis suggests that young lawyers are spending most of their research time online and are not using legal classification systems. Lastres, "Rebooting Legal Research in a Digital Age," located at http://www.lexisnexis.com/documents/pdf/20130806061418_large.pdf. Whether they are approaching research in the most efficient manner possible is, of course, the question, but the study makes interesting points about how legal research is evolving.

1. Look for the Most On-Point Cases First

Students sometimes try to identify the entire universe of available case law before beginning to read the decisions and then read all the decisions in no particular order. You will save yourself time and effort, and conclude your research sooner, if you identify the most useful cases right from the start and then read them before you go on. Identify these cases by looking for factual similarities or statements of holdings that sound like they could easily apply to your case.

Shepardizing these close cases, and reading cases cited in the decisions that support propositions important to you, should allow you to narrow the scope of your subsequent research. Using these cases as a jumping-off point will eliminate the need to read cases that do no more than outline general principles without offering useful applications to your situation.

2. Stop When You Come Full Circle

One of the surest signs that you should stop looking for new cases is repeatedly coming across citations to the same cases in different sources. Thus, if you find the same cases in the digest and the encyclopedia, even when you are researching different key words, you can be confident that you have identified the most relevant case law. Focus any additional research on leads provided by those key cases.

3. Do Not Follow Every Lead

One of the most common problems encountered by students is the frustration that comes from realizing that you have wasted valuable time reading cases that have only the most tangential relevance to your situation. Often, this is the result of deciding to read a case of possible but questionable relevance, then discovering a citation to an even more tenuously related decision, following up on that one too, and perhaps going on to follow the chain even further afield. While you do not want to miss any genuinely useful authority, you must constantly remind yourself what your case is really about.

To avoid these trips down blind alleys, draft a one-page outline of your tentative analysis and keep it with you at all times. By regularly referring to the outline, you will keep focused on the real issue in your case. If you are not ready to draft an outline, find another way to stay focused, for example, keeping with you any written information that you have about your assignment.[6] Creative analysis of problems is to be encouraged, but if you are finding it difficult to connect the product of your research to your main issue, imagine how difficult it will be for your reader!

Even when you stay focused, sometimes you will not find cases on point, but only cases tenuously related to the topic of your research. In this predicament, your only recourse is to read many cases in search of the few that contain some useful language or fact patterns. All you can do is try to analogize these cases to yours, either factually or by looking at the underlying legal or policy issues.

---

6. If you do end up reading irrelevant cases, avoid the temptation to find a way to work them into your written product anyway, just to show your instructor (or your supervisor) how much work you did. You will only frustrate the reader by overwhelming him or her with useless information, and you may make him or her wonder whether you really understood the issue at all.

Finally, if you believe that you are spending an inordinate amount of time researching, consider whether you might be procrastinating. Students are often afraid to begin writing. Let's face it: it's no easy task to put your ideas and research findings into some logical order, and then craft them into sentences, paragraphs, and pages. Spending time on research can be justified, but once you pass the point where it is really productive, move on. Writing can actually be fun if you give it a chance!

§ 4.07.   HOW DO YOU KEEP TRACK?

To avoid wasting time later, spend time early on creating a research path. When you consult a digest or encyclopedia and find a relevant case, copy down the case's full name and citation. This way, you will not spend valuable time tracking down missing parts of citations or pulling cases off the shelves only to discover that you have already read and rejected them.

When you read the case, make a note next to the citation that indicates whether it was helpful or not, and whether you plan to return to it or cite it in your written analysis. Most of us find that making copies of useful cases is a good way to keep track of them, and to make sure we have all the necessary information for citation purposes. The problems tend to arise in losing track of the cases we decide not to use, and it is worth a few extra minutes of your time to make a complete record of your research process.

Whenever your notes get disorganized, it is worth stopping to make a clean list of useful cases and rejected cases. This way, you will not have to wonder whether you have already read a case.

§ 4.08.   RESEARCH CHECKLIST

The following checklist will remind you of basic sources and approaches as you research a project. You will not need to follow each step for every assignment, but the checklist should enable you to consciously reject a step or resource rather than forgetting its existence.

I. Process
- Start with secondary sources such as treatises and encyclopedias if you need to learn the fundamental rules that govern your area of the law.
- Look for an applicable statute if you think there might be one, but be sure the statute actually applies before reading any annotated cases.
- Go to the digests when you know the key words that will help you identify relevant cases.
- Use computer sources as appropriate, depending on cost, efficiency, and your understanding of the subject matter.
- Update your research, and check the validity of the sources on which you intend to rely.
- Read on-point cases first, Shepardize them, and read cited decisions on important points. Don't follow tenuous leads.
- Stop when you see the same cases repeatedly.
- Keep a research path.

II. Sources
- Statutes
- Treatises and hornbooks
- Restatements
- Encyclopedias
- Digests
- Computer-assisted legal research (if it is cost-effective and you know the key words)
- Shepard's, KeyCite, AutoCite (use as a case finder, not just to check whether a case is good law)
- A.L.R.
- Periodicals
- Other sources, such as looseleaf services, that might apply to different types of problems

CHAPTER 5

How to Brief a Case

§ 5.01. WHAT IS A BRIEF?

1. Briefing Is Taking Notes

In your first year of law school, your professors will expect you to brief the cases that they assign. The word "brief" has two meanings in law. A brief is a written argument that an attorney submits to a court deciding a case. A brief also is a summary of a court opinion. In your initial law school classes and in this chapter, your concern is with this second type of brief.

Because briefing is new to you and because law school is also new, you may think that briefing is very different from anything you have done before. If you examine the task closely, however, you will discover that it is a very familiar one.

Briefing a case is taking notes on the case. By this time, you are a veteran at taking notes on what you read. You probably started taking notes in high school or college. Briefing a case seems different because it is a highly structured method of taking notes. It requires you to identify various parts of a case and summarize them.

2. The Purposes of Briefing

Briefing has two purposes. First, it helps you to focus on the important aspects of the case. A court opinion may ramble on page after page. Your brief, however, will be no longer than one or two pages. Briefing forces you to get to the heart of the case to grapple with the essentials.

Second, briefing helps you prepare for class and serves as a source of reference during class. You cannot brief a case properly unless you understand it. Briefing ensures that you understand the case before you discuss it in class. During class, you will find yourself referring to your brief. The discussion in a law school class goes far beyond what the brief contains. Your professor uses a court opinion only as a springboard to a sophisticated treatment of legal doctrine and legal process. Without the sort of understanding of basic aspects of a case that briefing demands, you will not get off the springboard and will fail to gain what the class has to offer.

Your case briefs are your personal notes. Your professors are not going to grade them. They probably never will read them unless you ask for assistance. Few students refer to their briefs when preparing for exams. View your briefs as your private study tools for class preparation.

Because you will not be handing in your briefs to your professors and will not use them at semester's end, you may be tempted not to brief cases. Briefing can be time consuming, and your time is limited. We strongly encourage you to stay with briefing at least for the first few months of law school.

At the initial stage of your legal education, you should brief all assigned cases. As your grasp of the law grows, you will switch to writing short summaries or even writing notes in the margins of your casebooks. For now, however, brief your cases diligently. Briefing will help you understand what is going on in class, not always an easy task.

§ 5.02. HOW TO BRIEF

1. The Format

The typical brief includes the name of the case, its citation, the important facts in the case, the case's procedural status, the issue in the case, the court's holding, and the court's reasoning.

Different professors may ask you to brief cases in different ways. We offer you a typical format for a case brief. If a professor asks for a slightly different format, be sure to oblige him or her. You will find that despite deviations in format, all professors want you to abstract essentially the same information.

2. Parts of the Brief

a. An Exercise

Here is an exercise to help you learn about briefing cases. After reading the trial court's opinion in *Conti v. ASPCA* (which you may read again in your property course), go back and take notes on it. You need not follow any particular format. Just take notes as if you were taking notes on a college reading assignment. Following the case is a brief of the case. Please do not read it until after you have completed taking notes.

As you read the opinion, note its format, the typical format for this sort of opinion. It begins with the name of the case, with the plaintiff's name coming first. It then lists citations, which tell you what library books contain the opinion. Next is the name of the judge who wrote the opinion. Finally comes the text of the opinion. It contains the facts of the case, the court's reasoning, and the court's decision.

Conti v. ASPCA
77 Misc. 2d 61, 353 N.Y.S.2d 288 (Civ. Ct. 1974)

Martin Rodell, Judge.

Chester is a parrot. He is fourteen inches tall, with a green coat, yellow head and an orange streak on his wings. Red splashes cover his left shoulder. Chester is a show parrot, used by the defendant ASPCA in various educational exhibitions presented to groups of children.

On June 28, 1973, during an exhibition in Kings Point, New York, Chester flew the coop and found refuge in the tallest tree he could find. For several hours the defendant sought to retrieve Chester. Ladders proved to be too short. Offers of food were steadfastly ignored. With the approach of darkness, search efforts were discontinued. A return to the area on the next morning revealed that Chester was gone.

On July 5th, 1973 the plaintiff, who resides in Belle Harbor, Queens County, had occasion to see a green-hued parrot with a yellow head and red splashes seated in his backyard. His offer of food was eagerly accepted by the bird. This was repeated on three occasions each day for a period of two weeks. This display of human kindness was rewarded by the parrot's finally entering the plaintiff's home, where he was placed in a cage.

The next day, the plaintiff phoned the defendant ASPCA and requested advice as to the care of the parrot he had found. Thereupon the defendant sent two representatives to the plaintiff's home. Upon examination, they claimed that it was the missing parrot, Chester, and removed it from the plaintiff's home.

Upon refusal of the defendant ASPCA to return the bird, the plaintiff now brings this action in replevin.

The issues presented to the Court are twofold: One, is the parrot in question truly Chester, the missing bird? Two, if it is in fact Chester, who is entitled to its ownership?

The plaintiff presented witnesses who testified that a parrot similar to the one in question was in the neighborhood prior to July 5, 1973. He further contended that a parrot could not fly the distance between Kings Point and Belle Harbor in so short a period of time, and therefore the bird in question was not in fact Chester.

The representatives of the ASPCA were categorical in their testimony that the parrot was indeed Chester, that he was unique because of his size, color and habits. They claimed that Chester said "hello" and could dangle by his legs. During the entire trial the Court had the parrot under close scrutiny, but at no time did it exhibit any of these characteristics. The Court called upon the parrot to indicate by name or other mannerisms an affinity to either of the claimed owners. Alas, the parrot stood mute.

Upon all the credible evidence the Court does find as a fact that the parrot in question is indeed Chester and is the same parrot which escaped from the possession of the ASPCA on June 28, 1973.

The Court must now deal with the plaintiff's position that the ownership of the defendant was a qualified one and upon the parrot's escape, ownership passed to the first individual who captured it and placed it under his control.

The law is well settled that the true owner of lost property is entitled to the return thereof as against any person finding same. (*In re Wright's Estate*, 15 Misc. 2d 225, 177 N.Y.S.2d 410) (36A C.J.S. Finding Lost Goods § 3).

This general rule is not applicable when the property lost is an animal. In such cases the Court must inquire as to whether the animal was domesticated or ferae naturae (wild).

Where an animal is wild, the owner can only acquire a qualified right of property which is wholly lost when it escapes from its captor with no intention of returning.

Thus in *Mullett v. Bradley*, 24 Misc. 695, 53 N.Y.S. 781, an untrained and undomesticated sea lion escaped after being shipped from the West to the East Coast. The sea lion escaped and was again captured in a fish pond off the New Jersey Coast. The original owner sued the finder for its return. The court held that the sea lion was a wild animal (ferae naturae), and when it returned to its wild state, the original owner's property rights were extinguished.

In *Amory v. Flyn*, 10 Johns. (N.Y.) 102, plaintiff sought to recover geese of the wild variety which had strayed from the owner. In granting judgment to the plaintiff, the court pointed out that the geese had been tamed by the plaintiff and therefore were unable to regain their natural liberty.

This important distinction was also demonstrated in *Manning v. Mitcherson*, 69 Ga. 447, 450-451, 52 A.L.R. 1063, where the plaintiff sought the return of a pet canary. In holding for the plaintiff the court stated, "To say that if one has a canary bird, mocking bird, parrot, or any other bird so kept, and it should accidentally escape from its cage to the street, or to a neighboring house, that the first person who caught it would be its owner is wholly at variance with all our views of right and justice."

The Court finds that Chester was a domesticated animal, subject to training and discipline. Thus the rule of ferae naturae does not prevail and the defendant as true owner is entitled to regain possession.

The Court wishes to commend the plaintiff for his acts of kindness and compassion to the parrot during the period that it was lost and was gratified to receive the defendant's assurance that the first parrot available would be offered to the plaintiff for adoption.

Judgment for defendant dismissing the complaint without costs.

Now that you have completed reading the case and taking notes on it, compare your notes with a typical brief of the case.

Conti (pl.) v. ASPCA (def.)
77 Misc. 2d 61, 353 N.Y.S.2d 288 (Civ. Ct. 1974)

FACTS: ASPCA owned Chester, a show parrot. On June 28, he escaped to a tree and def. could not retrieve him. The next day, he disappeared. On July 5, pl. found Chester and enticed him to his home. ASPCA learned about this and took Chester back. Pl. brought replevin action. (There was a question whether the parrot really was Chester, but the court decided he was, based on the evidence.)

PROCEDURE: Action for replevin. Court dismissed the complaint, in def.'s favor. (Note: This is a trial court decision.)

ISSUE: Whether, when a domesticated animal escapes, ownership passes to the person who next captures it.

HELD: The parrot here is a domesticated animal (no discussion). When a domesticated animal escapes, ownership remains with original owner.

ANALYSIS: The owner of a wild animal (*ferae naturae*) loses ownership when it escapes with no intention of returning. This rule does not apply to domesticated animals (animals that have been trained and disciplined). They are treated as lost property, and ownership remains with the original owner. The court fails to state a rationale explicitly, but cites the *Manning* case: a contrary holding would contradict "all our views of right and justice." The court relies on three cases:

  Mullett: A sea lion is treated as ferae naturae. Upon escape, the new captor gains ownership.

  Amory: Court treats wild geese as tamed and therefore unable to gain their natural liberty.

Manning: Escaped pet canary is treated as a domesticated animal and as belonging to the original owner.

––––––––

Your notes probably contain most of the information that the sample brief contains. The organization, however, may be quite different. You can see how the briefing format forces you to focus on essential information and state it concisely in a logical order. Now let us use the *Conti* case and the sample brief to examine the parts of a brief.

b. Name of the Case

Copy the name of the case. When you determine which party is the plaintiff and which is the defendant and, on appeal, which is the appellant or petitioner and which is the appellee or respondent, write down this information as well. Some opinions are written in a way that makes these vital facts difficult to discover. In *Conti*, the plaintiff's name comes first, but in some cases it comes second. If you fail to write down which litigant is which, you may forget this information at a crucial moment in class.

c. Citation

The citation contains the information that you need to find the case in the library. If you do not know how to use a cite to find a case, you will learn very shortly. Most casebooks offer abridged versions of cases. Your curiosity sometimes will lead you to search for the complete case in the library. If you have the cite in your brief, you will not have to return to your casebook to find it when you head for the library.

d. Facts of the Case

Write down the facts that you think were important to the court in deciding the case as well as any additional facts that are important to you. Court opinions often contain pages of facts. You would be wasting time and paper if you were to copy them. You want only the essential facts. If you read the entire case before you begin to brief it, you will have a much better sense of which facts are the essential ones. If you fail to read the case first, you run the risk of getting mired in a complex set of facts and writing pages of useless information.

The *Conti* case has relatively few essential facts. These facts are that Chester, a domesticated parrot, flew away from its owner, the ASPCA, and ultimately landed in the home of Conti, who now claims ownership. Chester's height and coloring are not significant. These characteristics would be significant if the opinion focused on whether Conti's parrot really was Chester. Therefore you need not write down Chester's description. The details of Chester's escape and ultimate welcome at the Conti household also are not essential. We know we can disregard this information because we have read the rest of the case.

e. Procedure

Answer three questions:

(1) *Who is suing whom for what?* In *Conti*, the answer is clear.

(2) *What is the legal claim?* Here, the plaintiff is suing in replevin. In some other case, a plaintiff might sue for breach of contract, false imprisonment, negligence, relief granted by a statute, or on one of many other grounds. If you come across a word like "replevin" and do not know its meaning, look it up in a dictionary. "Replevin" tells us that Conti was

asking the court to order the ASPCA to return the bird to him. If you did not know the meaning of replevin, you might have thought that Conti might have been satisfied to receive the dollar value of the bird.

(3) *How did the lower court rule in the case?* It heard the arguments, considered the evidence, and rendered the decision. The trial court wrote the *Conti* opinion. Therefore we have no decision by an even lower court. Suppose Conti was dissatisfied with the court's decision and appealed to a higher court, which decided the case and issued a written opinion. If we were briefing that opinion, we would note in our brief that the court below had dismissed Conti's complaint.

f. Issue

The issue is the legal question that the court must decide in order to reach its conclusion. In *Conti*, the issue is whether the owner of a domesticated animal loses ownership when it escapes and someone else captures it. Sometimes a court opinion will state the issue explicitly. Sometimes it will state the issue only implicitly and leave you the task of articulating it explicitly.

The *Conti* court states the issue in a very shorthanded way: "[I]f it is in fact Chester, who is entitled to its ownership?" We are ignoring the court's first issue—whether the parrot is Chester—because the court finds the issue uncontroversial and quickly decides it without analysis. You must flesh out the issue in order to state it in more general terms. The issue deals not just with a parrot named Chester, but with any domesticated animal that escapes and undergoes capture under similar circumstances. Ultimately the court must decide the case on the basis of a general rule applicable to similarly situated individuals and animals.

How narrowly or broadly you phrase the issue is, in part, a matter of taste. In the sample brief, we phrase the issue broadly:

> Whether, when a domesticated animal escapes, ownership passes to the person who next captures it.

Another lawyer might phrase it more narrowly—that is, more tailored to the facts of the specific case:

> Whether, when a domesticated parrot escapes, ownership passes to the person who next captures it.

Still another lawyer might phrase it even more narrowly:

> Whether the finder of Chester, an escaped parrot, owns it when the parrot was a domesticated animal that the ASPCA trained and disciplined and used in educational exhibitions.

In our experience, beginning law students frame issues too narrowly or too broadly. When they frame an issue too narrowly, they focus too much on the facts of the case and fail to understand that it applies to a broad range of cases. When they frame an issue too broadly, they fail to appreciate how important the specific facts of a case are to the court deciding it.

Learning to frame an issue is an art that takes time to learn. Your professors will give you guidance in mastering the art. They also will let you know how narrowly or broadly they want you to frame issues in their respective courses.

g. Holding

The holding is the court's decision and thus its resolution of the issue in the case. It usually requires rephrasing the issue from a question to a declarative sentence. In *Conti*, the holding is:

> When a domesticated animal escapes, ownership remains with the original owner.

As with framing issues, different professors will have individual preferences on how broadly or narrowly they want you to state the holding.

h. Analysis

Explain the court's reasoning in reaching its decision. Again, reading the case before you brief it will save you an enormous amount of time. Understanding the court's reasoning is not always easy. Sometimes the reasoning will be unclear or contain gaps in its logic or require the reader to discern what the court is saying only implicitly. These defects and similar ones often will be the subject of class discussion.

A court frequently explains that its decision furthers important social policy. In your brief, identify these policy considerations. In *Conti*, the court quotes an earlier decision to the effect that a contrary holding would contradict "all our views of right and justice." If the *Conti* court had written a more expansive opinion, it might have stated that its holding protected the right of property ownership because it forbids an individual to casually seize and keep the property of another.

Court decisions often include dicta. Dicta are discussions of law that are not necessary to the court's decision in the case before it. The singular of "dicta" is "dictum." The discussion of the *Conti* court about the rule to follow when an undomesticated animal escapes is dictum. The court's discussion of that situation is not essential to deciding the case of a domesticated parrot that escapes. It is a wise practice to note dicta in your brief.

Be sure to read any footnotes. Most cases appearing in law school casebooks are edited versions. The editor has omitted most footnotes. If the editor has retained a footnote, he or she believes that it is important to the student's understanding of the case. A footnote sometimes contains the key to the case.

Do not ignore dissenting and concurring opinions. Again, if an editor retains a dissent or concurrence, he or she has done so for a reason. Do not be surprised if your professor asks you if you agree with the majority or the dissent. If you fail to brief the dissent, you probably will be unable to answer the question.

i. More Sample Briefs

Here are two additional briefs of the *Conti* case. Each differs slightly from the sample brief we have studied. Our purpose is to show you that there is not just one way to brief a case. Just as different people take notes in different ways, different people brief cases in different ways. In each, however, the essential information is the same.

First Sample Brief

Conti v. ASPCA
77 Misc. 2d 61, 353 N.Y.S.2d 288 (Civ. Ct. 1974)

FACTS: on June 28, 1973, the ASPCA's parrot, Chester, flew away. On July 5, Conti (Pl.) found a bird the court determined was Chester in his backyard. Conti caged the parrot and called the ASPCA for information on parrot care. The ASPCA (Def.) suspecting the parrot was Chester went and took the parrot from Conti. Def. refused to return the parrot to Pl.

PROCEDURE: Trial court decision on a replevin action. Replevin is an action where a person seeks to recover possession of particular goods.

ISSUE: Who has rightful possession of an escaped parrot originally owned by one party and recaptured by another?

HELD: Ownership of a domesticated animal does not terminate upon escape, but remains with the original owner.

ANALYSIS: The true owner of lost property is entitled to its return. Ownership of a wild animal (ferae naturae) ends when it escapes and returns to its natural liberty. A domesticated animal (one that has been trained and disciplined) is treated as lost property and is subject to return upon recapture.

In determining whether the parrot was domesticated or wild, the court considered three cases and three guidelines. *Mullet* found an untrained sea lion to be ferae naturae. *Amory* held geese that had been trained were domesticated. *Manning* determined extinguishing ownership of a pet canary was "wholly at variance with all our views of right and justice." Chester had been trained, disciplined and was like a canary. Ownership continued to be held by the ASPCA because Chester was domesticated.

Second Sample Brief

Conti v. ASPCA
77 Misc. 2d 61, 353 N.Y.S.2d 288 (Civ. Ct. 1974)

FACTS: Defendant ASPCA conducted a demonstration with a parrot named Chester during which the bird escaped. A week later, a parrot with markings and colorings similar to Chester's appeared in plaintiff's yard and remained with the plaintiff for two weeks before being caged. The ASPCA removed the bird after plaintiff called for advice about its care. ASPCA claimed the bird was Chester and belonged to the organization.

PROCEDURE: Action for replevin—plaintiff wants the bird back.

ISSUE: Court identified two issues: 1. Whether the bird is actually Chester; and 2. Who gets him?

HELD: ASPCA gets the bird because: 1. The court found that the bird was Chester; and 2. As a domesticated animal, Chester does have a true owner, whose rights are not lost when the bird escapes.

ANALYSIS: The key issue in determining ownership was whether the rule of ferae naturae applied. This rule states that an owner acquires only qualified rights in a wild animal that are extinguished if the animal escapes. The court found that Chester was subject to training and discipline and therefore was not wild.

3. Problem

Here is another case that many of you will read during your first year in law school. Please brief it. Following the opinion are three sample briefs of the case. Compare your brief to them. Please do not read these briefs until you have written your own. If you ignore this instruction, you will learn far less.

As you read the opinion, note that it is an appellate opinion. The trial court decided in favor of the defendant, and the plaintiff has appealed to the appropriate appeals court, here, the Massachusetts Supreme Judicial Court.

Note also the format of the opinion. It begins with the name of the case. Here, the first name is McAvoy, the name of the plaintiff, who is now the appellant. Though some courts put the name of the appellant first, others do not necessarily do so. In each case, you need to check. Next is the citation you need to find the case in the library. Then come the facts of the case and, then, the name of the justice who wrote the opinion. Most of the time, the name of the judge appears before the statement of the facts. In virtually all appellate cases, several judges decide the case, and one judge writes the opinion. Here, Justice Dewey had that task. After the opinion discusses the case, it gives the court's ruling. In this case, the court overruled the plaintiff's exceptions and upheld the decision of the trial court. Exceptions are the grounds on which the plaintiff sought the appeal.

McAvoy v. Medina
93 Mass. (11 Allen) 548 (1866)

[Tort action to recover sum of money found by plaintiff in defendant's shop.]

At the trial in the superior court, before Morton, J., it appeared that the defendant was a barber, and the plaintiff, being a customer in the defendant's shop, saw and took up a pocket-book which was lying upon a table there, and said, "See what I have found." The defendant came to the table and asked where he found it. The plaintiff laid it back in the same place and said, "I found it right there." The defendant then took it and counted the money, and the plaintiff told him to keep it, and if the owner should come to give it to him; and otherwise to advertise it; which the defendant promised to do. Subsequently the plaintiff made three demands for the money, and the defendant never claimed to hold the same till the last demand. It was agreed that the pocket-book was placed upon the table by a transient customer of the defendant and accidentally left there, and was first seen and taken up by the plaintiff, and that the owner had not been found.

The judge ruled that the plaintiff could not maintain his action, and a verdict was accordingly returned for the defendant; and the plaintiff alleged exceptions, (Citations omitted.)

Dewey, J. It seems to be the settled law that the finder of lost property has a valid claim to the same against all the world except the true owner, and generally that the place in which it is found creates no exception to this rule. 2 Parsons on Con. 97. *Bridges v. Hawkesworth*, 7 Eng. Law & 7. Eq. R. 424.

But this property is not, under the circumstances, to be treated as lost property in the sense in which a finder has a valid claim to hold the same until called for by the true owner. This property was voluntarily placed upon a table in the defendant's shop by a customer of his who accidentally left the same there and has never called for it. The plaintiff also came there as a customer, and first saw the same and took it up from the table. The plaintiff did not by this acquire the right to take the property from the shop, but it was rather the duty of the defendant, when the fact became thus known to him, to use reasonable care for the safe keeping of the same until the owner should call for it. In the case of *Bridges v. Hawkesworth* the property, although found in a shop, was found on the floor of the same, and had not been placed there voluntarily by the owner, and the court held that the finder was entitled to the possession of the same, except as to the owner. But the present case more resembles that of *Lawrence v. The State*, 1 Humph. (Tenn.) 228, and is indeed very similar in its facts. The court there makes a distinction between the case of property thus placed by the owner and neglected to be removed, and property lost. It was there held that "to place a pocket-book upon a table and to forget to take it away is not to lose it, in the sense in which the authorities referred to speak of lost property."

We accept this as the better rule, and especially as one better adapted to secure the rights of the true owner.

In view of the facts of this case, the plaintiff acquired no original right to the property, and the defendant's subsequent acts in receiving and holding the property in the manner he did; does not create any. Exceptions overruled.

First Sample Brief

McAvoy v. Medina
93 Mass. (11 Allen) 548 (1866)

FACTS: Pl. customer found a pocket-book lying on a table in def.'s barbershop. Def. agreed to hold it in case the owner returned. The owner never showed up and apparently was a transient customer. Def. refused to give pocket-book to pl.

PROCEDURE: Pl. brought tort action to recover money in the pocket-book. T.C.: Pl. could not maintain the action; verdict for def. Pl. appeals. Ct. here affirms (exceptions overruled).

ISSUE: Does the finder have a valid claim to property that the owner voluntarily placed in a given location and forgot to retrieve (i.e. property that the owner mislaid)?

HELD: No.

ANALYSIS: The finder of lost property has a valid claim to it as against all but the true owner. But property that is voluntarily placed somewhere, like the table in the barbershop, and accidentally left behind is not lost property. The finder has no right to it. The owner of the location has the duty to take reasonable care of the property until the owner calls for it. This rule is better adapted to secure the rights of the true owner.

Second Sample Brief

McAvoy v. Medina
93 Mass. (11 Allen) 548 (1866)

FACTS: McAvoy (P) was a customer in Medina's (D's) barbershop. P found a pocket-book containing money on a table in the shop. P & D agreed (at least at the time of trial) that it was placed on the table and accidentally left by a transient customer. P left the pocket-book with D who promised to advertise it. No one claimed it, and D refused to give P the money found in it.

PROCEDURE: P appeals from the trial court, which found he could not maintain a tort action for the value of the money.

ISSUE: Whether the finder of property determined to be accidentally left has the same property right as the finder of lost property.

HOLDING: The finder of mislaid or forgotten property acquires no right to the property found against the shop owner where the article was left.

ANALYSIS: Property voluntarily placed and accidentally left in a shop does not give the finder a valid claim against all but the true owner. A shop owner has the responsibility to use due care for the property until the true owner returns. Creating a property interest in the shop owner supports its return to its proper owner.

The court uses *Bridges* and *Lawrence* to show that finding the property in the shop is not the determinative factor. The distinction is between deciding if it is lost (*Bridges*—found on the floor), in which case the finder gets it, and finding if it is mislaid or forgotten (*Lawrence*—found on a table).

Third Sample Brief

McAvoy v. Medina
93 Mass. (11 Allen) 548 (1866)

FACTS: Plaintiff McAvoy saw a purse on a table in def.'s barbershop and asked def. to give it to the owner or to advertise it. When the owner did not show up to claim the purse, pl. demanded it.

PROCEDURE: Action in tort to recover money. Pl. appeals from lower court verdict for def.

ISSUE: If the purse is not treated as lost, but as accidentally left behind, would the finder be entitled to keep it if the true owner does not show up?

HELD: Pl.'s appeal was denied (exceptions overruled). The court held that the purse would not be treated as lost under the circumstances and thus pl. acquired no right to the property.

ANALYSIS: The court relied on *Lawrence v. State* in which the court distinguished between property "placed by the owner and neglected to be removed" and property lost. The court felt that treating the mislaid property differently and giving it to the owner of the location created a rule that was "better adapted to secure the rights of the true owner."

§ 5.03. BEYOND BRIEFING

Briefing is just the beginning of preparing for class. Once you brief a case, you need to think about the opinion critically. You will spend most of your time in class evaluating the opinion rather than merely restating what the court said. By the time class is over, you may decide that you disagree with the court. After a class on the *Conti* case, you still may agree with the outcome, but you may question at least some of the court's reasoning. In a class on the *McAvoy* case, you may learn that the trend among courts is to reject its holding. Here are three questions to help you think about the cases you have briefed.

(1) *Do you agree with the court's holding and reasoning?* Does the logic flow? Does the court rely on assumptions—explicit or implicit—with which you disagree? Do you agree with the social policies that the court purports to further?

(2) *Would you use the court's holding to decide a case with similar, but not identical, facts?* In *Conti*, suppose Chester was an untamed wolf instead of a tamed parrot? Suppose he was

a tiger that escaped from the zoo? Would the court still find for the ASPCA, even though the animal was undomesticated? Would you?

(3) *Why did my professor and the casebook's editor select this case?* What larger lessons are they trying to teach? Why are *Conti* and *McAvoy* usually near the beginning of property casebooks, as opposed to the middle or end? If you think about each case as part of a series of cases that you are studying, do you see a big picture in addition to a series of narrow rules?

Exercise

Pick a case that you have briefed for one of your classes. Ask your professor to read it and suggest ways to improve it. You will discover that most professors will be very willing to spend the time with you.

CHAPTER 6

Introduction to Legal Analysis

§ 6.01. INTRODUCTION

Largely because of the adversary system, American legal analysis has at its core the common law doctrine of stare decisis, which means "to stand with things decided." In other words, earlier cases are precedents whose holdings determine the outcome of later cases. Constitutions, statutes, and other sources of law are frequently the bases of court decisions. Courts must determine the meaning of these law sources as they apply to specific situations. Thus, analysis of case precedent forms the core of legal analysis, and legal analysis is primarily applying court-made law to the facts of the current case. In every case, lawyers on opposite sides will be using the same facts and law, but hoping to persuade the court to reach diametrically opposed conclusions.

There are three steps for developing a legal argument:

1. Determine all legal authority, or general rules, applicable to your case.
2. Apply this legal authority to the facts of your particular case.
3. Draw a conclusion based on the legal authority that you have applied to your case.

For example:

Step One General Rule:	A lawyer may not knowingly make a false statement of material fact or law to a tribunal.
Step Two Particular Case:	Sandra North is a lawyer, and she knows that an important case she wanted to rely on in her brief has just been overruled.
Step Three Conclusion:	Sandra North must not rely on the overruled case in her brief because that would be a false statement of material law.

The next two sections discuss legal authority and how to use deductive reasoning to apply authority to your case.

§ 6.02. ARGUING DEDUCTIVELY

Legal analyis frequently relies on deductive reasoning. When you argue deductively, you take three steps:

1. apply a general rule (of law), which usually derives from a particular statute or case but also may derive from a variety of different sources,
2. to a particular case, and
3. draw a conclusion.

For example:

General Rule:	All teachers are cruel and heartless.
Particular Case:	John Doe is a teacher.
Conclusion:	John Doe is cruel and heartless.

In a legal argument, the general rule is the relevant legal authority; the particular case is the facts of your case; and the conclusion is the result reached by applying the legal authority to the facts.

For example:

The general rule is a court decision stating that all golfers have a legal duty to avoid injuring other golfers, and a golfer fulfills this duty by yelling "fore" when hitting a golf ball. In this particular case John Doe is a golfer. Therefore, the conclusion is that John Doe has a duty to avoid injuring other golfers, and he can fulfill this duty by yelling "fore" when he hits a golf ball.

When broken into its components, the deductive reasoning applied here looks like this:

General Rule:	All golfers have a legal duty to avoid injuring other golfers and can fulfill this duty by yelling "fore" when hitting golf balls.
Particular Case:	John Doe is a golfer.
Conclusion:	John Doe has a legal duty to avoid injuring other golfers and can fulfill this duty by yelling "fore" when hitting golf balls.

In your legal writing or other law school classes, you will probably learn about IRAC (Issue, Rule, Application/Analysis, Conclusion), or some other version of the acronym (CRAC, CIRAC, etc.). You will also hear this acronym when you start preparing for your bar exam, and you may hear it from practicing attorneys. It is the formulation of deductive reasoning that has been most commonly used in law schools for many years.

Almost all approaches to legal analysis use some form of what we teach you here— identify your issue and rule, apply the rule to your case, and state your conclusion. Most teachers and supervisors in law offices will also tell you to state your conclusion up front, which leads to CRAC or CIRAC. Whatever it is called in your classroom or office, the basic premise remains the same—use a structure that contains the essential elements of legal analysis and that presents those elements clearly for your reader to follow.

1. Limitations

Deductive reasoning is only a framework or a starting point for formulating a legal argument. It does not always dictate the outcome of a case with great precision and may only give you a "ballpark" prediction of what the outcome of your case should be. Remember that the party on the other side of the case also will apply deductive reasoning, using the same facts and law, to arrive at a very different conclusion about the case. Deductive reasoning is only as valid as your interpretation of the general rule and your application of that rule to the particular case.

For example, with regard to the case above, suppose you found the general rule in a California case, but New York law governs your case and does not follow the California rule. If New York law is settled, it controls; that is, if New York law specifically holds that yelling "fore" is not required, the California case has no precedential value. If it is unsettled, then the California rule is, at best, persuasive authority. Thus, if New York courts have said only that golfers must take "reasonable steps" to avoid injuring other golfers, you might want to argue that the California rule is more specific and should be adopted.

With regard to the same case, suppose John Doe the golfer is a child. Or suppose he was incapable of yelling "fore," either because he could not speak or he speaks a foreign language. These differences in the facts might make your authority nonmandatory and maybe not even persuasive.

If the general rule is very broad or very narrow, or if your understanding of how the rule applies to the particular case is in some way not totally accurate, your conclusion may not be persuasive to a court. Reasoning deductively is not always as easy as it appears, but it is still a useful framework for legal logic.

2. Maximizing the Use of Deductive Reasoning

To use deductive reasoning for legal argument, you must:

1. Be sure that your general statement, or rule of law, is correct by analyzing all relevant law and predicting accurately the rule you think the court will apply to your case.
2. Be sure that your statement of the facts in the particular case is accurate and does not ignore anything that might alter application of the general rule.
3. Be sure that your application of the rule to your facts is thorough and fair, taking into account all relevant analogies and distinctions.
4. Be sure that your final conclusion follows logically from the rule and facts.

If there are several issues in your case, you should apply deductive reasoning to each issue separately, again taking great care as to your interpretation of what the law is and its application to your own situation. One issue may contain many sub-issues, each of which requires a separate application of deductive reasoning.

3. Application

When writing your argument with deductive analysis, we recommend that you always state your conclusion first because readers of legal writing do not want to be left waiting in suspense for the conclusion. After you state the conclusion, identify the key issue and the applicable rule, and present the relevant legal authority. Next apply the legal authority to the facts of your case. Finally, restate the conclusion you have drawn from your analysis.

Here is a brief example of this form of analysis:

Conclusion:	The defendant here had a duty to shout "fore" to the plaintiff.
Issue:	The key issue is when a golfer has a duty to yell "fore" when hitting a golf ball in the direction of another golfer on an adjacent fairway.
Major Premise: (Relevant legal authority or rule)	In *Allen v. Pinewood Country Club, Inc.*, 292 So. 2d 786, 789 (La. App. 1974), the court held that golfers have a duty to yell "fore" if they hit a golf ball and another golfer on a different fairway is standing in the ball's line of flight. The court found that all golfers have a duty of reasonable care and must avoid injuring other golfers. *Id.* To fulfill this duty, a golfer must give timely and adequate warning to other golfers in the golf ball's line of flight. *Id.* Therefore, a golfer has a duty to yell "fore" when hitting a golf ball that veers toward another fairway and a golfer on the other fairway is standing in the ball's line of flight. *Id.*
Particular Case: (Applying the relevant legal authority to the facts)	Under *Allen*, the defendant in the present case had a duty to yell "fore" to the plaintiff. The defendant hit a golf ball from the fairway of the sixth hole. The ball hooked toward the fairway of the fifth hole. The plaintiff was standing on the fairway of the fifth hole and was in the direct line of flight of the golf ball hit by the defendant. Therefore, the facts of the present case fall squarely within the holding in *Allen*.
Conclusion:	Since the defendant hit a golf ball that hooked toward the plaintiff who was on an adjacent fairway and was in the direct line of flight of the golf ball, the defendant had a duty to shout "fore" to the plaintiff.

The conclusion at the end is not just a simple paraphrase of the conclusion at the beginning. It should be developed more fully and should include the relevant, concrete facts of the case.

§ 6.03. APPLYING THE LAW TO THE FACTS

As you may have surmised from the preceding discussion, a legal argument is meaningless unless you apply the relevant legal authority directly to the facts of your case. The most important aspect of legal argument is taking the general rule of law and applying it to the particular situation. Applying the law to the facts makes your argument concrete and tells the court how you think it should resolve your case. The rest of this chapter shows you in detail how to do this. After a brief overview of the process, you will see a legal analysis of an issue arising out of a case similar to the *McAvoy v. Medina* case presented in Chapter 5. We will then proceed step-by-step through two examples of legal analysis, one relying solely on cases and one adding statutory construction to the mix. As we go along, you will be asked to write out the analysis that follows from the discussion.

1. The Basic Approach

The single most important thing to remember about legal analysis is that completeness is everything. The goal is not to arrive at an answer as quickly as possible, but to lay out, in what often seems like excruciating detail, how you got from the question to the answer. In most cases, if a thought goes through your head that helps you arrive at a conclusion, it should appear on the paper. Readers of legal analysis, generally busy practitioners and judges, do not want to work at analyzing the problem while they read. They want to pick up the document you have submitted, read through it quickly, and understand instantly how you reached every conclusion you present.

How does this process work? Assume you have been asked to predict the outcome of a particular client's situation. You have identified the relevant case law and are preparing to write out an analysis that explains how the case law applies to your client's situation. Until you become comfortable with this analytical process and develop your own personal style, you should go through the following steps *in writing.* First, brief the cases you will be analyzing. Summarize the facts, holding, and rationale of each decision. Find and identify the rule of law applied by the court in each case. Add the procedural history, if it is relevant to the discussion.

Once you have the building blocks, try to formulate a general principle or principles that explain the decisions reached by the courts. Are they applying the same rules? If the courts seem to be arriving at the same end by different routes, compare and evaluate the various approaches. If the courts arrive at different results, try to figure out what distinguishes the cases. Are the facts different? Are the courts trying to implement different policies?

When you have figured out why the courts reached the decisions they did, look for analogies between the decided cases and the case you have been asked to analyze. Compare the facts. Identify the policy or policies behind the decisions, and try to decide what outcome that policy would mandate in your case. By policy, we mean the societal interest or goal that is served by the decision. Look at the equities—did the courts seek out the "fair" result, and what would that be in your case? How do these policy and equity arguments relate to the legal rules announced or applied by the courts?

After you have gone through these steps, it is time to begin writing out your analysis. When you do, *integrate* your analysis of your case with your discussion of the decided cases. Integration means you do not present all of the relevant law and then discuss its application to your case. An effective legal analysis will make comparisons between the decided cases and the case being discussed wherever appropriate, whether those comparisons are of facts, applicable policies, or equities. You want to synthesize the existing law and your client's situation by demonstrating how they fit together, and by explaining how what has happened in the past will or should inform the decisions of those faced with the current situation.

2. An Example of Legal Analysis

This section will present a sample legal analysis of a question regarding whether a piece of property was "lost" or "mislaid," and thus who can claim ownership of it. First, reread the *McAvoy v. Medina* case from Chapter 5. Assume that the only other relevant authority is the following case:

Durfee v. Jones
11 R.I. 588 (1877)

July 21, 1877. DURFEE, C.J. The facts in this case are briefly these: In April, 1874, the plaintiff bought an old safe and soon afterwards instructed his agent to sell it again. The agent offered to sell it to the defendant for ten dollars, but the defendant refused to buy it. The agent then left it with the defendant, who was a blacksmith, at his shop for sale for ten dollars, authorizing him to keep his books in it until it was sold or reclaimed. The safe was old-fashioned, of sheet iron, about three feet square, having a few pigeon-holes and a place for books, and in back of the place for books a large crack in the lining. The defendant shortly after the safe was left, upon examining it, found secreted between the sheet-iron exterior and the wooden lining a roll of bills amounting to $165, of the denomination of the national bank bills which have been current for the last ten or twelve years. Neither the plaintiff nor the defendant knew the money was there before it was found. The owner of the money is still unknown. The defendant informed the plaintiff's agent that he had found it, and offered it to him for the plaintiff; but the agent declined it, stating that it did not belong to either himself or the plaintiff, and advised the defendant to deposit it where it would be drawing interest until the rightful owner appeared. The plaintiff was then out of the city. Upon his return, being informed of the finding, he immediately called on the defendant and asked for the money, but the defendant refused to give it to him. He then, after taking advice, demanded the return of the safe and its contents, precisely as they existed when placed in the defendant's hands. The defendant promptly gave up the safe, but retained the money. The plaintiff brings this action to recover it or its equivalent.

The plaintiff does not claim that he acquired, by purchasing the safe, any right to the money in the safe as against the owner; for he bought the safe alone, not the safe and its contents. See *Merry v. Green*, 7 M. & W. 623. But he claims that as between himself and the defendant his is the better right. The defendant, however, has the possession, and therefore it is for the plaintiff, in order to succeed in his action, to prove his better right.

The plaintiff claims that he is entitled to have the money by the right of prior possession. But the plaintiff never had any possession of the money, except, unwittingly, by having possession of the safe which contained it. Such possession, if possession it can be called, does not of itself confer a right. The case at bar is in this view like *Bridges v. Hawkesworth*, 15 Jur. 1079; 21 L.J.Q.B. 75 A.D. 1851; 7 Eng. L. & Eq. 424. In that case, the plaintiff, while in the defendant's shop on business, picked up from the floor a parcel containing bank notes. He gave them to the defendant for the owner if he could be found. The owner could not be found, and it was held that the plaintiff as finder was entitled to them, as against the defendant as owner of the shop in which they were found. "The notes," said the court, "never were in the custody of the defendant nor within the protection of his house, before they were found, as they would have been if they had been intentionally deposited there." The same in effect may be said of the notes in the case at bar; for though they were originally deposited in the safe by design, they were not so deposited in the safe, after it became the plaintiff's safe, so as to be in the protection of the safe as *his* safe, or so as to affect him with any responsibility for them. The case at bar is also in this respect like *Tatum v. Sharpless*, 6 Phila. 18. There it was held, that a conductor who had found money which had been lost in a railroad car was entitled to it as against the railroad company.

The plaintiff also claims that the money was not lost but designedly left where it was found, and that therefore as owner of the safe he is entitled to its custody. He refers to cases in which it has been held, that money or other property voluntarily laid down and forgotten is not in legal contemplation lost, and that of such money or property the owner of the shop or place where it is left is the proper custodian rather than the person who happens to discover it first. *State v. McCann*, 19 Mo. 249; *Lawrence v. The State*, 1 Humph. 228; *McAvoy v. Medina*, 11 Allen, 549. It may be questioned whether this distinction has not been pushed to an extreme. See *Kincaid v. Eaton*, 98 Mass. 139. But, however that may be, we think the money here, though designedly left in the safe, was probably not designedly put in the crevice or interspace where it was found, but that, being left in the safe, it probably slipped or was accidentally shoved into the place where it was found without the knowledge of the owner, and so was lost, in the stricter sense of the word. The money was not simply deposited and forgotten, but deposited and lost by reason of a defect or insecurity in the place of deposit.

The plaintiff claims that the finding was a wrongful act on the part of the defendant, and that therefore he is entitled to recover the money or to have it replaced. We do not so regard it. The safe was left with the defendant for sale. As seller he would properly examine it under an implied permission to do so, to qualify him the better to act as seller. Also under the permission to use it for his books, he would have the right to inspect it to see if it was a fit depository. And finally, as a possible purchaser he might examine it, for though he had once declined to examine it. And the defendant, having found in the safe something which did not belong there, might, we think, properly remove it. He certainly would not be expected either to sell the safe to another, or to buy it himself without first removing it. It is not pretended that he used any violence or did any harm to the safe. And it is evident that the idea that any trespass or tort had been committed did not even occur to the plaintiff's agent when he was first informed of the finding.

The general rule undoubtedly is, that the finder of lost property is entitled to it as against all the world except the real owner, and that ordinarily the place where it is found does not make any difference. We cannot find anything in the circumstances of the case at bar to take it out of this rule. We give the defendant judgment for costs.

Here are the facts of the case to be analyzed.

FACT PATTERN: LOST OR MISLAID?

While collecting books for reshelving, P., an employee at a law library, discovered a black valise lying on its side on the floor between two bookshelves. He picked up the valise and brought it to the circulation desk, where he searched the contents for some identification of the owner.

A few days later, D., a student at the law school, came to the circulation desk to find a black valise she had lost. P. showed D. the found valise. D. said that it looked like her case but wished to check the contents to be sure. P. agreed and opened the valise for D.

While examining the contents, D. discovered a secret compartment that contained a diamond engagement ring. D. pocketed the ring, leaving her name with P. in case the original owner should turn up, and left the library. P. followed, requesting that D. return the ring to the valise. D. refused. P. now sues for return of the ring.

D. claims that the ring was lost, so D., as finder, is entitled to it unless the real owner claims it. P. claims that the ring was intentionally left in the secret compartment and, as a result, was not "lost" in a legal sense. P. insists that he is a custodian of the mislaid property and is entitled to keep the ring unless the real owner claims it.

ANALYSIS

The principal issues to be addressed in this case are whether either the ring or the valise fits the legal definition of "lost," and thus whether D. could legally have "found" the ring. Although the valise was "lost," and the ring was not, D. does not have a legal claim to custody of either one.

The rule that "the finder of lost property is entitled to it as against all the world except the real owner," *Durfee v. Jones*, 11 R.I. 588 (1877), applies to the valise. P. found the valise lying on its side, in a manner and in a place suggesting it was not left there intentionally. Consequently, P. acquired a legal interest in the valise analogous to the interest acquired by the plaintiff in the *Durfee* case when he purchased a safe containing money that had slipped into a crevice inside the safe. Durfee did not find the money while the safe was in his possession. The defendant legally acquired custody of the safe from Durfee, found the money, removed it and then returned the safe. Durfee sought the return of the money as well, but the court held that the money had not been intentionally placed into the crevice and was thus "lost." Therefore the defendant had title to the money, subject only to the title of the true owner. The only difference between the interests of Durfee and P. is that Durfee was entitled to the safe against all others whereas P. is only entitled to the valise if the original owner does not turn up.

Conversely, if the original owner places property in a particular location, intending to retrieve it, the finder is not entitled to the property but is expected to "use reasonable care for the safe keeping of [the property] until the owner should call for it." *McAvoy v. Medina*, 93 Mass. (11 Allen) 548 (1866). In that case the owner of a shop was held to have the obligation to keep a pocketbook left on a table by a customer. The plaintiff "found" the pocketbook and later attempted to obtain custody of the money inside it from the defendant shopkeeper, but the court rejected the plaintiff's claim.

These cases lead to the conclusion that an individual who acquires possession of a piece of personal property assumes only a custodial interest over any property intentionally hidden inside it. In the present case, D. cannot argue that the position of the ring within the valise was the product of some accident, as was the location of the money in *Durfee*. The ring had been deliberately placed in a secret compartment in order that it be protected. Since P., as finder, was entitled to the valise, D. could not lay claim to anything intentionally hidden within it, even if P. did not know of its existence.

Even if D. could legally "find" the ring, P. gave D. leave to look inside the valise solely to determine the identity of its owner. D. did not have to search for secret compartments to see if it was her case. The court in *Durfee* indicates that a finder must have at least implied permission to examine the property. In the present case, P. opened the case so that D. could check to see if it belonged to her. P. did not give D. permission to conduct an exhaustive search of the lining, and there was nothing inherent in the determination of whether it was D.'s valise that would have implied permission to do so.

Thus, P. may claim the valise against all but the true owner, but has only a custodial interest in the ring. D. has no claim whatsoever to either the valise or the ring.

§ 6.04. CASE ANALYSIS

Now that you have seen what the final product looks like, we will break the process into its component parts so you can learn how to produce a good legal analysis when you are assigned to do so. Assume that you are an associate in a law firm and a partner has presented you with the following situation:

A few days ago, a business client of ours came to us with a personal problem. Paul Trune, an auditor for the Internal Revenue Service, was making a pilgrimage to Baraboo, Wisconsin, to visit the birthplace of the Ringling Bros. & Barnum & Bailey Circus. Unfortunately, while on the way to Baraboo, Paul became quite lost and ended up driving down some unknown Wisconsin back road with an overheating radiator. Paul was forced to pull off the road next to a stretch of woods. He grabbed an empty bottle that he kept in the car for such emergencies and began walking in search of water. After a mile or so, the woods gave way to a clearing in which there was a well. Paul looked around for a farmhouse or any other building, but he didn't see any. Seeing no fences or signs either, Paul walked up to the well to take some water.

Just as Paul was raising the bucket from the bottom of the well, he heard a voice ring out behind him. Paul turned to see a farmer gesticulating wildly and yelling at him about "trespassing." As the farmer got closer, Paul saw he had a dead, bloody rabbit in his left hand and a rifle slung around his back. The farmer then bellowed at Paul that he "knew how to take care of trespassers," and ordered him to start walking in the direction of a small hill. Seeing that the farmer had a gun and the ability to use it, and given the man's irate state, Paul decided that it was best not to say anything and just obey.

Once at the crest of the hill, Paul saw a small farmhouse and barn below. The farmer marched Paul into the barn and told him to wait until he called the sheriff. The farmer closed the door to the barn, but didn't lock it. Paul feared for his safety so he stayed put. After about two hours in the barn, with no sign of the farmer or a sheriff, Paul peeked outside. Not seeing the farmer anywhere in sight, he took off.

Paul now wishes to know if he has a cause of action against the farmer for the intentional tort of false imprisonment.

Next, assume that there are only two cases in Wisconsin that address the tort of false imprisonment. Here they are, in relevant part:

Dupler v. Seubert
69 Wis. 2d 373, 230 N.W.2d 626 (1975)

OPINION: WILKIE, C.J. This is a false imprisonment action. On April 23, 1971, plaintiff-appellant Ethel M. Dupler was fired from her job with the defendant-respondent Wisconsin Telephone Company. She was informed of her discharge during an hour-and-a-half session with her two superiors, defendants-respondents Keith Peterson and Helen Seubert, who Dupler claims, falsely imprisoned her during a portion of this time period. A jury found that Peterson and Seubert did falsely imprison Dupler and fixed damages at $7,500.

The trial court gave Dupler the option of accepting a lower amount—$500—or a new trial on the issue of damages. The option was not exercised, judgment for $500 was entered, and Mrs. Dupler appeals. We reverse and remand for a new trial on the issue of damages, but give plaintiff-appellant an option to accept $1,000 damages in lieu of a new trial.

Dupler had worked for the Telephone Company as a customer service representative since 1960. At approximately 4:30 on April 23rd, Seubert asked Dupler to come to Peterson's office. When all three were inside, sitting down, with the door closed, Seubert told Dupler the Telephone Company would no longer employ her and that she could choose either to resign or be fired. Dupler testified that she refused to resign and that in the conversation that followed, Peterson discussed several alternatives short of dismissal, all of which had been considered but rejected.

At approximately 5 o'clock, Dupler testified, she began to feel sick to her stomach and said "You have already fired me. Why don't you just let me go." She made a motion to get up but Peterson told her to sit down in "a very loud harsh voice." Then, Dupler testified, she began to feel violently ill and stated "I got to go. I can't take this any more. I'm sick to my stomach. I know I'm going to throw up." She got up and started for the door but Seubert also arose and stood in front of the door. After Dupler repeated that she was sick, Seubert allowed her to exit, but followed her to the men's washroom, where Dupler did throw up. Following this, at approximately 5:25, Seubert asked Dupler to return to Peterson's office where she had left her purse to discuss the situation further. Dupler testified that she went back to the office and reached for her purse; Seubert again closed the door and Peterson said [in] a loud voice, "Sit down. I'm still your boss. I'm not through with you." At approximately 5:40 Dupler told Peterson her husband was waiting for her outside in a car and Peterson told her to go outside and ask her husband to come inside. Dupler then went outside and explained the situation to her husband who said, "You get back in there and get your coat and if you aren't right out I'll call the police." Dupler returned to Peterson's office and was again told in a loud tone of voice to sit down. She said Seubert and Peterson were trying to convince her to resign rather than be fired and again reviewed the alternatives that had been considered. Dupler then said: "What's the sense of all this. Why keep torturing me. Let me go. Let me go." She stated that Peterson replied, "No, we still aren't finished. We have a lot of things to discuss, your retirement pay, your vacation, other things." Finally, at approximately 6:00 Peterson told Dupler they could talk further on the phone or at her house, and Dupler left. When asked why she had stayed in Peterson's office for such a long time, Dupler replied:

> Well, for one thing, Helen, Mrs. Seubert, had blocked the door, and tempers had been raised with all the shouting and screaming, I was just plain scared to make an effort. There were two against one.

Peterson and Seubert did not dispute that Dupler had been fired on April 23rd, or that the conference lasted from 4:30 to 6 p.m., or that Dupler became very upset and sick to her stomach and had to leave to throw up. Peterson admitted that Dupler had asked to leave and that he requested that she stay and continue talking so she could indicate whether she wished to resign or be fired. Seubert said Dupler did not so indicate until "within three minutes of her leaving." Both denied that any loud or threatening language had been used, or that Dupler was detained against her will. Peterson said neither he nor Seubert even raised their voices. He said the session was so lengthy because Dupler continued to plead for another chance, and to request reasons for the dismissal.

The jury found that both Peterson and Seubert falsely imprisoned Dupler and fixed her damages at $7,500. At the same time, the jury found that Dupler's co-plaintiff husband was not entitled to any damages. It found that Peterson and Seubert had not acted maliciously and thus did not award any punitive damages. . . .

The issue raised by a motion for review filed by defendants-respondents is: Is the jury's verdict, finding that Dupler was falsely imprisoned, supported by the evidence?

The essence of false imprisonment is the intentional, unlawful, and unconsented restraint by one person of the physical liberty of another. In *Maniaci v. Marquette University*, the court adopted the definition of false imprisonment contained in sec. 35 of the Restatement of Torts 2d, which provides in part:

False Imprisonment

(1) An actor is subject to liability to another for false imprisonment if
   (a) he acts intending to confine the other or a third person within boundaries fixed by the actor, and
   (b) his act directly or indirectly results in such a confinement of the other, and
   (c) the other is conscious of the confinement or is harmed by it.

Secs. 39 and 40 provide that the confinement may be caused by physical force or the threat of physical force, and the comment to sec. 40 indicates the threat may either be express, or inferred from the person's conduct. As Prosser comments:

Character of Defendant's Act

The restraint may be by means of physical barriers, or by threats of force which intimidate the plaintiff into compliance with orders. It is sufficient that he submits to an apprehension of force reasonably to be understood from the conduct of the defendant, although no force is used or even expressly threatened. . . . This gives rise, in borderline cases, to questions of fact, turning upon the details of the testimony, as to what was reasonably to be understood and implied from the defendant's conduct, tone of voice and the like, which seldom can be reflected accurately in an appellate record, and normally are for the jury.

This is precisely such a case and we conclude that the record contains sufficient evidence from which the jury could have concluded that Mrs. Dupler was intentionally confined, against her will, by an implied threat of actual physical restraint. She testified that defendant Peterson ordered her in a loud voice to remain seated several times, after she expressed the desire to leave. She reported being "berated, screamed and hollered at," and said the reason she did not just walk out of the room was that "Mrs. Seubert had blocked the door, and tempers had been raised with all the shouting and screaming, I was just plain scared to make an effort. There were two against one." The jury obviously believed Mrs. Dupler's rather than the defendants' account of what transpired, as it had the right to do, and we conclude her testimony was sufficient to support the jury's verdict.

Herbst v. Wuennenberg
83 Wis. 2d 768, 266 N.W.2d 391 (1978)

OPINION: Abrahamson, J. Carol Wuennenberg appeals from a judgment entered by the trial court on a jury's special verdict finding that she falsely imprisoned Jason A. Herbst,

Ronald B. Nadel, and Robert A. Ritholz ("plaintiffs"). Because there is no credible evidence to sustain a finding of false imprisonment, we reverse the judgment and order the cause remanded so that plaintiffs' complaint can be dismissed and judgment entered in favor of Wuennenberg.

I

In April 1975, plaintiffs initiated a civil action charging Wuennenberg with false imprisonment, malicious prosecution, and abuse of process. Plaintiffs' cause of action for false imprisonment arose from an incident which took place on September 19, 1974 in the vestibule of a three-unit apartment building owned and lived in by Wuennenberg and located within the district which Wuennenberg represented as alderperson in the city of Madison. Plaintiffs' causes of action for malicious prosecution and abuse of process arose from trespass actions brought against the plaintiffs by the city of Madison after Wuennenberg had registered a complaint about the September 19, 1974 incident.

On September 19, 1974, the plaintiffs were comparing the voter registration list for the City of Madison with names on the mailboxes in multi-unit residential dwellings in Wuennenberg's aldermanic district. Plaintiffs' ultimate purpose was to "purge the voter lists" by challenging the registrations of people whose names were not on mailboxes at the addresses from which they were registered to vote.

The plaintiffs and Wuennenberg gave somewhat differing accounts of the incident which gave rise to the action for false imprisonment, but the dispositive facts are not in dispute.

According to Ritholz, whose version of the incident was corroborated by Herbst and Nadel, when the plaintiffs reached Wuennenberg's house at approximately 4:30 p.m. they entered unannounced through the outer door into a vestibule area which lies between the inner and outer doors to Wuennenberg's building. The plaintiffs stood in the vestibule near the mailboxes, which were on a wall in the vestibule approximately two feet inside the front door to the building. Neither he nor the other plaintiffs touched the mailboxes, stated Ritholz; he simply read the names listed for Wuennenberg's address from a computer printout of the registered voters in Wuennenberg's district, and the others checked to see if those names appeared on the mailboxes.

When they were half way through checking, testified Ritholz, Wuennenberg entered the vestibule from an inner door and asked plaintiffs what they were doing. Ritholz replied that they were working for the Republican party, purging voter lists. According to Ritholz, Wuennenberg became very agitated and told the plaintiffs that she did not want them in her district. "At first she told us to leave," testified Ritholz, "and we agreed to leave, but she very quickly changed her mind and wanted to know who we were. Since we already agreed to leave, we didn't think this was necessary."

After the plaintiffs had refused to identify themselves to her, Wuennenberg asked them whether they would be willing to identify themselves to the police. Ritholz replied that they would be willing to do so. Nonetheless, testified Ritholz, he would have preferred to leave, and several times he offered to leave. Both Nadel and Herbst, who agreed that Ritholz was acting as spokesman for the group, testified to Ritholz's statement to Wuennenberg that the plaintiffs were willing to identify themselves to the police.

Subsequently, Wuennenberg's husband came to the vestibule to see what was going on, and Wuennenberg asked him to call the police. About this time Wuennenberg moved from the inner door to a position in front of the outer door. According to Nadel, Wuennenberg blocked the outer door by "standing there with her arms on the pillars to the door to block our exit." The plaintiffs agreed that Wuennenberg had not threatened or intimidated them and that they neither asked her permission to leave nor made any attempt to get her to move away from the doorway. When asked why he had not attempted to leave the vestibule, each of the plaintiffs answered, in effect, that he assumed he would have had to push Wuennenberg out of the way in order to do so.

The plaintiffs waited in the vestibule, stated Ritholz, until the police came some five minutes later. They gave their names and explained their errand to a police officer who told them that they were not doing anything wrong and that they could continue checking the mailboxes in the district.

Wuennenberg testified that she and her husband were in their living room watching television and reading the paper when she heard the plaintiffs enter her vestibule. She came to the inner door, noted Herbst with his hands on the mailboxes, and asked the plaintiffs if she could be of any assistance to them. Ritholz answered "No." She next asked if they were looking for someone in the building. Ritholz again answered "No." . . . Ritholz . . . stated that the plaintiffs were election officials, volunteering their services. At this point, stated Wuennenberg, she told the plaintiffs that it did not seem proper for citizen volunteers to be interfering with mailboxes and that she considered the plaintiffs to be trespassing on her property. Ritholz, speaking in "an authoritative tone," replied that the vestibule to Wuennenberg's building was "just like a public street" and that he had a right to be there.

After Ritholz told Wuennenberg that the plaintiffs would not identify themselves to her, but that they would identify themselves to the police, Wuennenberg's husband came out to see what was happening. She explained and then told him, "It looks like you'll have to call the police." Her husband looked at the plaintiffs, and they "nodded their approval to this."

After her husband left to call the police, testified Wuennenberg, she positioned herself in front of the outer doorway because she could watch for the arrival of the police from that vantage and because "I didn't want someone trying to run away at that point." She stated she did not brace her arms against the door frame. She would not have made any effort to stop the plaintiffs had they attempted to leave, stated Wuennenberg, because, "I'm not physically capable of stopping anybody."

Plaintiffs' causes of action for false imprisonment, abuse of process, and malicious prosecution were tried before a jury. At the close of the evidence, the trial court granted Wuennenberg's motion for a directed verdict on the causes of action for malicious prosecution and abuse of process but denied Wuennenberg's motion for a directed verdict on the cause of action for false imprisonment.

The jury returned a special verdict finding that Wuennenberg had falsely imprisoned the plaintiffs and awarded Herbst, Nadel and Ritholz a total of $1,500 in actual damages. The jury found that Wuennenberg's acts had not been malicious and thus declined to award punitive damages.

II

We reiterate the rule which this court must follow in reviewing the record to determine if the jury verdict is supported by the evidence: A jury verdict will not be upset if there is any credible evidence which under any reasonable view fairly admits of an inference supporting the findings. The evidence is to be viewed in the light most favorable to the verdict. A jury cannot base its findings on conjecture and speculation. We hold that the evidence adduced in the case before us does not support a finding that the plaintiffs were falsely imprisoned, and accordingly we reverse the judgment of the trial court.

The action for the tort of false imprisonment protects the personal interest in freedom from restraint of movement. The essence of false imprisonment is the intentional, unlawful, and unconsented restraint by one person of the physical liberty of another. *Dupler v. Seubert*, 69 Wis. 2d 373, 381, 230 N.W.2d 626 (1975). There is no cause of action unless the confinement is contrary to the will of the "prisoner." It is a contradiction to say that the captor imprisoned the "prisoner" with the "prisoner's" consent. Harper & James, The Law of Torts sec. 3.7, p. 227 (1956).

In *Maniaci v. Marquette University*, 50 Wis. 2d 287, 295, 184 N.W.2d 168 (1971) and in *Dupler v. Seubert, supra*, 69 Wis. 2d at 381, we adopted the definition of false imprisonment given by the Restatement of Torts, Second, sec. 35:

> (1) An actor is subject to liability to another for false imprisonment if
> (a) he acts intending to confine the other or a third person within boundaries fixed by the actor, and
> (b) his act directly or indirectly results in such a confinement of the other, and
> (c) the other is conscious of the confinement or is harmed by it.

After review of the record we conclude that the evidence is not sufficient to support the conclusion that Wuennenberg's acts "directly or indirectly [resulted] in . . . a confinement of the [plaintiffs]," a required element of the cause of action.

The Restatement lists the ways in which an actor may bring about a "confinement": "by actual or apparent physical barriers"[Sec. 38, Comment *a*]; "by overpowering physical force, or by submission to physical force"[Sec. 39]; "by submission to a threat to apply physical force to the other's person immediately upon the other's going or attempting to go beyond the area in which the actor intends to confine him"[Sec. 40]; "by submission to duress other than threats of physical force, where such duress is sufficient to make the consent given ineffective to bar the action" (as by a threat to inflict harm upon a member of the other's immediate family, or his property) [Sec. 40A]; "by taking a person into custody under an asserted legal authority"[Sec. 41].

The plaintiffs do not contend that confinement was brought about by an actual or apparent physical barrier, or by overpowering physical force, or by submission to duress, or by taking a person into custody under an asserted legal authority. The parties agree that the central issue is whether there was confinement by threat of physical force and thus argue only as to the applicability of section 40 of the Restatement, which we cited and applied in *Dupler v. Seubert*, 69 Wis. 2d at 382. Section 40 provides:

> § 40. Confinement by Threats of Physical Force
> The confinement may be by submission to a threat to apply physical force to the other's person immediately upon the other's going or attempting to go beyond the area in which the actor intends to confine him.

The comments to section 40 provide that a person has not been confined by "threats of physical force" unless by words or other acts the actor "threatens to apply" and "has the apparent intention and ability to apply" force to his person.[1] It is not a sufficient basis for an action for false imprisonment that the "prisoner" remained within the limits set by the actor. Remaining within such limits is not a submission to the threat unless the "prisoner" believed that the actor had the ability to carry his threat into effect.[2]

Dean Prosser comments on the elements of false imprisonment as follows:

Character of Defendant's Act

The restraint may be by means of physical barriers, or by threats of force which intimidate the plaintiff into compliance with orders. It is sufficient that he submits to an apprehension of force reasonably to be understood from the conduct of the defendant, although no force is used or even expressly threatened. The plaintiff is not required to incur the risk of personal violence by resisting until it actually is used. It is essential, however, that the restraint be against the plaintiffs will; and if he agrees of his own free choice to surrender his freedom of motion, as by remaining in a room or accompanying the defendant voluntarily, to clear himself of suspicion or to accommodate the desires of another, rather than yielding to the constraint of a threat, then there is no imprisonment. This gives rise, in borderline cases, to questions of fact, turning upon the details of the testimony, as to what was reasonably to be understood and implied from the defendant's conduct, tone of voice and the like, which seldom can be reflected accurately in an appellate record, and normally are for the jury.

As plaintiffs state in their brief, the question before this court is whether there is any credible evidence which supports a conclusion that the plaintiffs did not consent to the

---

1. Restatement of Torts, Second, Section 40, Comments:

   a. Under the rule stated in sec. 35, the actor's threat may be by words as well as by other acts. It is not necessary that he do any act actually or apparently effectual in carrying a threat into immediate execution. It is enough that he threatens to apply and has the apparent intention and ability to apply force to the other's person immediately upon the other's attempting to escape from the area within which it is the actor's intention to confine him.

   b. The submission must be made to a threat to apply the physical force immediately upon the other's going or attempting to go beyond the area within which the threat is intended to confine him. Submission to the threat to apply physical force at a time appreciably later than that at which the other attempts to go beyond the given area is not confinement.

   c. Submission to threats. The other must submit to the threat by remaining within the limits fixed by the actor in order to avoid or avert force threatened to the other. The other's remaining within such limits is not a submission to the threat unless the other believes that the actor has the ability to carry his threat into effect unless prevented by the other's self-defensive action or otherwise, and that it is, therefore, necessary to remain within these limits in order to escape or avert the violence threatened.

   d. It is not necessary that the force threatened be such that a reasonable man would submit to confinement rather than sustain the harm threatened; it is sufficient that the actor threatens physical force with the intention of confining the other and that the other submits to the threat.

2. Other commentators have agreed that submission must be to an apprehension of force and that a voluntary submission to a request does not constitute an imprisonment. For example, Harper and James have stated that:

   . . . In ordinary practice, words are sufficient to constitute an imprisonment, if they impose a restraint upon the person and the party is accordingly restrained; for he is not obligated to incur the risk of personal violence and insult by resisting until actual violence is used. . . . *If the plaintiff voluntarily submits there is no confinement, as where one accused of crime voluntarily accompanies his accusers for the purpose of proving his innocence.* And where no force is used, submission must be by reason of an apprehension of force or other unlawful means, *mere moral persuasion not being sufficient.* 1 Harper & James, *Torts* sec. 3.8 (1956).

confinement and that they remained in the vestibule only because Wuennenberg indicated by standing in the doorway that she had "the apparent intention and ability to apply" force to their persons should they attempt to leave. We have reviewed the record, and we find that it does not support this conclusion. Ritholz testified that Wuennenberg had not verbally threatened the plaintiffs, and since none of the plaintiffs asked Wuennenberg to step aside, it could be no more than speculation to conclude that Wuennenberg would not only have refused this request but also would have physically resisted had the plaintiffs attempted to leave. At best, the evidence supports an inference that plaintiffs remained in the vestibule because they assumed they would have to push Wuennenberg out of the way in order to leave. This assumption is not sufficient to support a claim for false imprisonment.

We do not intend to suggest that false imprisonment will not lie unless a "prisoner" attempts to assault his captor or unless he fails to make such attempt only because he fears harm. The plaintiffs in the case at bar were not required to obtain their freedom by taking steps dangerous to themselves or offensive to their reasonable sense of decency or personal dignity. See Restatement of Torts, Second, sec. 36. At a minimum, however, plaintiffs should have attempted to ascertain whether there was any basis to their assumption that their freedom of movement had been curtailed. False imprisonment may not be predicated upon a person's unfounded belief that he was restrained. *White v. Levy Brothers*, 306 S.W.2d 829, 830 (Ky. 1957). *Cf. Riggs National Bank v. Price*, 359 A.2d 25 (D.C. App. 1976).

. . . Plaintiffs were not "berated, screamed, and hollered at"; they outnumbered Wuennenberg three-to-one; and they gave no testimony to the effect that they were frightened of Wuennenberg or that they feared she would harm them.

Viewed in the light most favorable to plaintiffs, the evidence shows that the plaintiffs were willing to identify themselves to the police, but that they would have preferred to leave Wuennenberg's premises. It is not a sufficient basis for an action for false imprisonment that the plaintiffs remained on the premises although they would have preferred not to do so. Because plaintiffs did not submit to an apprehension of force, they were not imprisoned.

Judgment reversed, and cause remanded with directions to the trial court to enter judgment in favor of Wuennenberg dismissing plaintiffs' complaint.

You are now faced with something of a dilemma. You have only two cases, and they reach opposite conclusions. You must decide which case is more like Mr. Trune's situation, and why. If you feel strongly that Mr. Trune's case is more like either *Herbst* or *Dupler*, try to figure out why. Identify the key facts, and the rule that makes those facts relevant.

Alternatively, you may have noted similarities (and differences) to both cases, and may be thinking that Mr. Trune's case could go either way. If so, welcome to the reality of law practice! In our adversary system, there will always be lawyers on both sides of a case, using the same facts and law to argue for opposite results. Your job is to make your argument more persuasive than the other side's.

Exercise

1. Identify the issue(s) in *Herbst* and *Dupler*.
2. State the rule each court applies.

3. Write down the relevant facts from each case.
4. Write down the holdings of both cases.
5. Write out the rationales for both decisions.
6. Identify the policy or policies served by the decisions.
7. Decide whether the results are fair, in a purely equitable sense. Why or why not?
8. Identify the similarities and differences between *Herbst* and *Dupler* and Mr. Trune's case.

Now you must make a prediction. Will Mr. Trune be able to make out a case of false imprisonment? Why or why not? One of the most difficult ideas to get used to is that it almost does not matter which way you answer these questions. There is no right or wrong answer, only strong or weak analysis. Even so, you should still try to reach a conclusion about the most likely result. It is almost never enough merely to describe the applicable precedents; your reader will want you to predict the most likely result when those precedents are compared to the case under consideration.

Once you choose a position, you should be prepared to explain it. Identify factual analogies, previous applications of legal rules, and policy and equity considerations that make your predicted result seem likely. You should start with a statement of the applicable legal rule as presented by the courts, explain how that rule has been applied in the past and why, and then explain how it applies to your case.

The structure of your analysis will depend on the type of question you are discussing. In our case, dealing with the tort of false imprisonment, the courts tend to break the tort down into specific elements that must be satisfied. See *Dupler* and *Herbst* excerpts. Where the decisions give you this kind of structure, use it. The format of your analysis should generally track the format of the analysis presented by the courts. It is always easier for a reader to process a message if it is structured in a familiar manner.

If you structure your analysis by elements, instead of case by case, you will probably find that you discuss each case more than once. You can avoid redundancy by presenting the facts and any other relevant aspects of the case in detail the first time you cite the case, and then referring to the case subsequently using a shorthand form, offering detail only on the portion(s) of the case on which you are relying at that point in the discussion.

You should discuss the application of each element to your case at the same time you discuss the application of that element to previously decided cases. Do not wait until you have discussed all the elements to go back and try to explain all at once how the elements apply to your case. If you save all of your application for the end, you force the reader to remember too much at once. It is much easier to deal with one element at a time, and to thoroughly understand the application of that one element, both to the decided cases and to the case being discussed.

In a truly good legal analysis, you will not stop at supporting the result you think is most likely. You will also identify, explain, and respond to the arguments likely to be made by the other side. You do not want to make better or more persuasive opposing arguments than are likely to be made by opposing counsel, but you must deal with any arguments you *know* must be made on behalf of the other party. A good lawyer understands that there are two sides to almost every argument and acknowledges the legitimacy of the other side, while at the same time explaining why the preferred result is more likely. Consider: Are the factual differences between the adverse authority and your case more significant than the factual similarities? Are the policy goals behind the rule better served by a decision along the lines you advocate? Is fairness better served by the result you have predicted? These are the questions you must answer if your legal analysis is to be considered complete and persuasive.

Exercise

Write out a full analysis of Mr. Trune's case in essay form. Can he make out a case for false imprisonment? Why or why not? What is the applicable rule? What do the decided cases hold? What are the reasons for those decisions? What policies are served by the decisions? How are the facts of those cases similar or dissimilar to Mr. Trune's case? How do those factual similarities or dissimilarities affect the rationales for the decisions and the policy goals being served? Why is the result you predict equitable? What are the arguments on the other side? Why are they less persuasive than the arguments in support of the result you advocate? (Remember, you should reach a conclusion regarding the most likely result in Mr. Trune's case.) If you answer all of these questions, you will be well on your way to writing good legal analysis.

§ 6.05. STATUTORY ANALYSIS

Here is another example, this time adding the variable of a statute that must be interpreted and applied to the client's situation. These are your facts:

I was visited today by the son of an old client who found himself in a bit of trouble over the weekend. Apparently there was a gathering of Vietnam veterans at the Vietnam Veterans' Memorial on the Mall [in Washington, D.C.] on Saturday. This young man, R. Abel Rowser, chose this occasion to protest what he sees as continuous U.S. aggression against weaker powers around the world. Wearing a sign on his back that said "Vietnam, Iraq, Afghanistan—NO MORE!!!," he climbed to the top of the wall, pulled out an American flag, poured kerosene on it, and ignited it.

Mr. Rowser says that he truly believed that most Vietnam veterans would agree with him that U.S. military involvement in places such as Iraq and Afghanistan is a mistake. He believes that the Vietnam experience should have taught us to keep our noses out of other people's business. He used the flag burning to get their attention and then fully expected to lead a rally and perhaps even a march on the White House in support of his position. We may, perhaps, question his grip on reality, but I honestly believe that his description of his intent is sincere.

Mr. Rowser's recollection of what happened after he burned the flag is a bit fuzzy, perhaps because he was running for his life at the time, but he recalls a great deal of yelling and shouting. Several of the gathered veterans apparently started running in his direction in a manner that led him to believe he may have made an error in judgment, and he took off. He escaped, so there were no face-to-face confrontations with any of the veterans.

Mr. Rowser is also not entirely clear about what was happening when he arrived, but he thinks it may have been some sort of religious service. There was a man standing at the front of the crowd wearing a clerical collar, and the group was singing something.

Please read the D.C. disorderly conduct statute and the applicable cases and let me know whether you think the statute applies to Mr. Rowser's conduct under these circumstances.

This is the relevant statute:

§ 22-1121. Disorderly conduct.[1]

(a) In any place open to the general public, and in the communal areas of multi-unit housing, it is unlawful for a person to:

(1) Intentionally or recklessly act in such a manner as to cause another person to be in reasonable fear that a person or property in a person's immediate possession is likely to be harmed or taken;

(2) Incite or provoke violence where there is a likelihood that such violence will ensue; or

(3) Direct abusive or offensive language or gestures at another person (other than a law enforcement officer while acting in his or her official capacity) in a manner likely to provoke immediate physical retaliation or violence by that person or another person.

(b) It is unlawful for a person to engage in loud, threatening, or abusive language, or disruptive conduct, with the intent and effect of impeding or disrupting the orderly conduct of a lawful public gathering, or of a congregation of people engaged in any religious service or in worship, a funeral, or similar proceeding.

(c) It is unlawful for a person to engage in loud, threatening, or abusive language, or disruptive conduct, which unreasonably impedes, disrupts, or disturbs the lawful use of a public conveyance by one or more other persons.

(d) It is unlawful for a person to make an unreasonably loud noise between 10:00 p.m. and 7:00 a.m. that is likely to annoy or disturb one or more other persons in their residences.

(e) It is unlawful for a person to urinate or defecate in public, other than in a urinal or toilet.

(f) It is unlawful for a person to stealthily look into a window or other opening of a dwelling, as defined in § 6-101.07, under circumstances in which an occupant would have a reasonable expectation of privacy. It is not necessary that the dwelling be occupied at the time the person looks into the window or other opening.

(g) It is unlawful, under circumstances whereby a breach of the peace may be occasioned, to interfere with any person in any public place by jostling against the person, unnecessarily crowding the person, or placing a hand in the proximity of the person's handbag, pocketbook, or wallet.

(h) A person who violates any provision of this section shall be guilty of a misdemeanor and, upon conviction, shall be fined not more than $500, imprisoned not more than 90 days, or both.

Whoever, with intent to provoke a breach of the peace, or under circumstances such that a breach of the peace may be occasioned thereby: (1) Acts in such a manner as to annoy, disturb, interfere with, obstruct, or be offensive to others; (2) congregates with others on a public street and refuses to move on when ordered by the police; (3) shouts or makes a noise either outside or inside a building during the nighttime to the annoyance or disturbance of any considerable number of persons; (4) interferes with any person in any place by jostling against such person or unnecessarily crowding him or by placing a hand in the proximity of such person's pocketbook, or handbook, or handbag; or (5) causes a disturbance in any streetcar, railroad car, omnibus, or other public conveyance, by running through it, climbing through windows or upon the seats or otherwise annoying passengers or employees, shall be fined not more than $250 or imprisoned not more than 90 days, or both.

---

1. This statute is currently codified at D.C. Code § 22-1321.

Assume that the only relevant cases are these two (edited here to include only those parts of the discussion useful for our purposes).

Rodgers v. United States and District of Columbia
290 A.2d 395 (D.C. 1972)

OPINION: HOOD, Chief Judge: In a concurrent trial before a judge and jury, the judge found appellant guilty of disorderly conduct, and the jury found him guilty of destruction of property but acquitted him of assault. Appellant makes a feeble attack on the destruction of property conviction, but we find no merit in it. His attack on the disorderly conviction requires more consideration.

Appellant was arrested following a series of incidents which occurred in and around the Crampton Auditorium on the Howard University campus. On that night a blues concert was being held in the auditorium outside of which a large crowd had gathered.

Appellant, who had no ticket, made numerous attempts to gain entry to the concert. He first presented an invalid press pass which was not accepted. He then repeatedly attempted to enter the auditorium by carrying instruments for band members. This ploy also failed. Appellant then attempted to enter through the basement accompanied by a large group of people. He finally kicked the glass out of a portion of one of the doors in the main entrance. In the course of attempting to gain entry appellant sought the assistance of the crowd outside by shouting obscenities at the campus policemen inside the auditorium and by threatening to kick down one of the doors if the crowd would follow. These activities continued for approximately 2 hours until three members of the University Special Police Force approached appellant, placed him under arrest after a scuffle and turned him over to the Metropolitan Police Department.

Appellant attacks his disorderly conduct conviction on four grounds. He first claims the information was insufficient. The information, filed under D.C. Code 1967, § 22-1121, the pertinent part of which is set out below, charged that appellant did:

> . . . under circumstances such that a breach of the peace might be occasioned thereby act in a manner as to annoy, disturb, interfere with, obstruct and be offensive to others by *loud bois-terous [conduct] and fighting* in violation of Section 22-1121(1) of the District of Columbia Code.

It is appellant's contention that the information is insufficient in that it fails to charge that he engaged in any activity with an intent to provoke a breach of the peace or under circumstances which threaten a breach of the peace. We disagree. This court has held that an intent to provoke a breach of the peace is not an essential element in the proof of disorderly conduct. *Sams v. District of Columbia*, D.C. App., 244 A.2d 479 (1968); *Rockwell v. District of Columbia*, D.C. Mun. App., 172 A.2d 549 (1961). It has likewise been held that proof of an actual breach of the peace is not required under § 22-1121. *Stovall v. District of Columbia*, D.C. App., 202 A.2d 390 (1964); *Scott v. District of Columbia*, D.C. Mun. App., 184 A.2d 849 (1942). It is sufficient that the alleged conduct be under circumstances such that a breach of the peace might be occasioned thereby.

Appellant further contends that the evidence presented at trial was not sufficient to support his conviction. It is argued that the conviction should be reversed because appellant's "conviction is unsupported by any evidence to show . . . that anyone other than the police were annoyed or disturbed." We disagree. Appellant was not convicted merely for conduct which was annoying or disturbing to the policemen present, but rather, he was convicted for disorderly conduct carried out under circumstances whereby a breach of the peace might have been occasioned.

The Supreme Court in *Cantwell v. Connecticut*, 310 U.S. 296 (1940), concluded that not only violent acts but acts and words likely to produce violence on the part of others were included within the purview of breach of the peace. Here we have evidence of a course of action including both acts and words which can be said to be likely to produce violence among some or all of a crowd estimated at between 300 and 400 persons. Appellant's conduct over the 2-hour period with which we are concerned included several instances falling within the purview of § 22-1121 which may be deemed disorderly conduct. In examining his conduct as to interfering with others, it is readily apparent that appellant's conduct interfered with the orderly progression of events related to attendance at a concert where such attendance was limited to those persons holding valid tickets, a requirement which appellant did not meet at any time during the course of the evening. The record plainly reveals numerous attempts by appellant to gain entry into the auditorium. Each attempt invoked counterefforts by the special police whose task it was to maintain order during the concert. These actions on the part of the appellant were obstructive to persons holding valid tickets.

By their very nature appellant's actions would tend to slow down and even halt orderly ingress to the auditorium. The holders of valid tickets, seeking orderly admission, have a right to peaceful enjoyment of the concert without unwarranted disturbances by trespassers. It is these same ticket holders to whom appellant's actions would be patently offensive, as well as annoying and disturbing. *Heard v. Rizzo*, 281 F. Supp. 720, 741 (E.D. Pa. 1968), *aff'd*, 392 U.S. 646 (1968).

Rockwell v. District of Columbia
172 A.2d 549 (D.C. 1961)

Hood, Associate Judge. Appellant, the leader of the American Nazi Party, was arrested for disorderly conduct on July 3, 1960, after rioting and fighting broke out at a rally he and his followers were holding in the park area at Ninth Street and Constitution Avenue, N.W. While awaiting trial on that charge he was again arrested for disorderly conduct on July 24, 1960, this time at Judiciary Square during the course of another outdoor gathering which he was attempting to address.

The two informations were consolidated for trial without a jury, and appellant was found guilty on both charges. He appeals the two convictions claiming that his freedom of speech, as guaranteed by the First Amendment, was obstructed by the arrests for disorderly conduct; that he was unable to obtain service of process on key defense witnesses; and that a certain letter he offered in evidence was wrongfully excluded by the trial court.

At trial the evidence revealed the following circumstances leading to the arrests. On July 3, 1960, appellant and his followers held a rally at Ninth Street and Constitution Avenue, N.W. At about 2:00 p.m. appellant began to speak from a platform within a roped-off area. Standing inside the enclosure were appellant's followers, some of whom wore red swastika armbands. Numbering 100 to 300 people, the audience outside the enclosure included many opponents of appellant's theories and party. Fourteen members of the U.S. Park Police were also in the audience, though only eight of them were in uniform. The spectators greeted appellant's opening words with hissing, booing and derisive chanting, the noise at times growing so loud that appellant could not be heard. This turmoil continued for about an hour and a half until suddenly an unknown number of spectators breached the enclosure and attacked appellant and his followers. As the fighting began the police moved in and arrested appellant, all of his followers and apparently some of the spectators who had participated in the attack.

During the trial there was a great deal of prosecution testimony concerning appellant's reaction to the crowd noises interrupting his speech. Witnesses testified that at different times they heard appellant shouting [various negative and offensive comments regarding Jews]. . . .

One Government witness also stated that at one point appellant started shouting, "Jews, Jews, sick—dirty Jews, filthy Jews . . . ," and shortly thereafter the spectators broke through the ropes and attacked appellant and his followers. Another prosecution witness testified that in the course of his speech appellant referred "to the Jewish race as traitors; or labeled the race as traitorous to our country."

Conceding he impatiently shouted, "Dirty Jews. Rotten Jews. Miserable Jews. Shut up, Jews. Go on and yell, Jews," appellant denied he made the other statements attributed to him. He stated he had been forewarned of possible disorder by Government officials and had done all in his power to prevent trouble, short of refusing to exercise his constitutional right of free speech. Even during the course of his speech he sent several of his men to warn the police that the crowd was getting dangerously unruly. According to appellant, the police replied to his warning by informing his men that the way to restore order was for appellant to stop talking.

On the second occasion that appellant was arrested he was conducting another rally in Judiciary Square. This time appellant—his followers in two ranks directly behind him— began to address an audience of about fifty people. As soon as appellant began his speech the spectators started to heckle him. Appellant responded by calling them "Jews" and "cowards," thereby increasing the intensity of the badgering from the audience. According to one prosecution witness, appellant "sort of lost his temper, and he turned around, and he says, 'Go get 'em, boys.' " At the command appellant's followers with their arms folded in front of them moved into the audience. One spectator was struck under the chin, and as a result appellant and his men were arrested for disorderly conduct.

Denying that anyone in the audience had been assaulted, appellant explained his actions on July 24 by referring to the near riot on July 3. Conscious that more trouble was to be expected if he spoke again, he had trained his men to move out into the audience at the first sign of possible disorder. Apparently these men were to surround hecklers and shout back at them, all the time under strict orders to keep their arms folded in front to avoid any suggestion of an invitation to combat. As to the command he gave on July 24, appellant testified he merely said, "First and second squads move out," which was the signal for his men to go into the audience in the manner described above. . . .

The conviction that grew out of the July 24 charge of disorderly conduct does not even raise a constitutional question. It is clear from the record that appellant ordered his followers into a hostile audience to stop the heckling that was interrupting his speech. Under the circumstances we cannot conceive of a better way to cause disorder than that adopted by appellant. Whether appellant intended that result is not controlling. An assault on one of the spectators did occur as a direct result of appellant's command to his followers to move into the audience and the trial court could without error convict appellant of disorderly conduct. . . .

. . . Appellant, however, was charged and convicted under a statute which reads in part as follows: "Whoever, with intent to provoke a breach of the peace, or under circumstances such that a breach of the peace may be occasioned thereby. . . . " Code 1951, § 22-1121, Supp. VIII. It is clear that the language quoted is to be read disjunctively, and that one lacking an intent to be disorderly may nevertheless be guilty of the charge if his conduct is "under circumstances such that a breach of the peace may be occasioned thereby. . . . " The only question the trial court had to decide was did appellant's statements constitute disorderly conduct under the circumstances of July 3. As we have indicated, we believe there was sufficient evidence for the trial court to answer as it did.

Affirmed.

While both *Rockwell* and Mr. Rowser's case have fairly obvious free speech implications, confine your analysis to the question of whether Mr. Rowser's actions amount to disorderly conduct. Any time you are analyzing a legal question involving a statute, you should begin with an analysis of the language of the statute itself. The relevant language of the D.C. disorderly conduct statute seems to be the following:

> Whoever, with intent to provoke a breach of the peace, or under circumstances such that a breach of the peace may be occasioned thereby: (1) Acts in such a manner as to annoy, disturb, interfere with, obstruct, or be offensive to others. . . .

Look at the statute and be sure you understand why we have chosen this language.

Did Mr. Rowser intend to provoke a breach of the peace? Does that matter? Why or why not? What do the cases say on this point?

Did Mr. Rowser act under circumstances likely to occasion a breach of the peace? How do you know? Can you answer this question without reference to the decided cases?

Exercise

1. Identify the issue(s) in the *Rodgers* and *Rockwell* cases.
2. Identify the statutory language applied by the court in each case.
3. Identify the relevant facts of each case.
4. State the holdings of those cases.
5. Describe the rationales of those cases.
6. Identify the policy or policies served by the decisions.
7. Decide whether the results are equitable. Why or why not?
8. Identify the similarities and differences among the *Rodgers* case, the *Rockwell* case and Mr. Rowser's situation. Consider facts, issues, policies, and equitable issues.

Now go through the same process you went through with Mr. Trune's case. What is the most likely outcome? Why? Have you identified the arguments on both sides? (Be careful here—since both of the decided cases find disorderly conduct, many people have a tendency to find it automatically in Mr. Rowser's case as well.) How will you structure your discussion? Since there are no elements here, you may find it useful to deal briefly with the intent question first, then analyze the decided cases in detail in the context of whether they took place under circumstances likely to cause a breach of the peace, comparing Mr. Rowser's situation to each case as you go along.

If another approach seems more logical to you, try it—you will find that your written product is better and more persuasive if you structure it in a way that makes sense to you. Many students make the mistake of trying to copy examples or to write the way someone else writes. Use your own instincts, while observing the guidelines discussed here and following any instructions offered in your legal writing class.

Exercise

Write out, in essay form, your analysis of Mr. Rowser's case. Predict whether he will be convicted of disorderly conduct and justify your prediction, using both the language of the statute and the decided cases. Focus on important facts, and use policy and equity arguments where appropriate. Don't forget to discuss and analyze the arguments on the other side, explaining why you find them less persuasive.

§ 6.06. LEGAL ANALYSIS CHECKLIST

Until you have performed enough legal analyses that the process becomes second nature to you, you might want to refer to this checklist to be sure you have not left out any important steps that your reader will be expecting to see in your written product. There is no magic format that will work in every context or for every style, so you will have to experiment until you find the right structure for you, the case you are addressing, and the particular audience for the document. Nevertheless, any good legal analysis must contain the following information, presented in some logical order.

— Make your prediction. Your written analysis should begin with a statement of your ultimate conclusion.
— Identify the rule that governs your case and cite to its source, whether statutory or common law.
— Identify the structure of your argument, using elements of a tort, statutory requirements, or any other method that will help the reader understand how your ideas relate to each other.
— Identify the key facts of your case.
— Discuss the facts, holdings, and rationales of all important relevant cases.
— Compare the facts of those cases with the facts of your case and explain why the courts' rationales apply or do not apply. Do not forget to argue the equities of the case or the policies behind the courts' decisions, if such arguments are helpful to your position.
— Identify any persuasive adverse authority or arguments likely to be presented by the other side. Explain why your predicted result is the better outcome. Be careful here; remember not to make arguments that are better than opposing counsel is likely to make.
— Summarize the key points in your argument. Persuade the reader of the overall strength of your position by reminding him or her of the highlights of what you have presented.

CHAPTER 7

Purpose, Context, and Structure

§ 7.01. INTRODUCTION

In their eagerness to get on with the writing process, many writers forget to think about the "big picture" aspects of what they are writing about. If you consciously address the elements of purpose, context, and structure *before* you start constructing sentences and paragraphs, your finished product will be much more polished and comprehensible. This chapter will discuss each in turn and offer strategies for incorporating this kind of thinking into your writing process.

§ 7.02. PURPOSE

It seems fairly obvious to say that you should understand why you are writing a document before you begin putting words on paper. Surprisingly, many writers are so anxious to get their ideas into concrete form that they do not stop to think about what the document must accomplish and what the intended reader needs from the document. Here are two key questions to ask yourself before you begin writing (or, for that matter, before you begin researching):

- For whom am I writing this?
  - Client (consider education, level of sophistication about legal matters, anxiety level, stage of case, nature and length of relationship between you and client)
  - Supervising attorney (consider what you know about expectations based on your and others' previous experiences)
  - Judge (consider what you know about judge, level of court, stage of proceeding)
- What am I trying to accomplish?
  - Answer a specific question (keep that question in mind at all times and be sure you actually answer it)
  - Advise reader generally on the state of the law in a particular area (consider why reader needs information and tailor presentation to what you know about that need)
  - Persuade reader to adopt a particular course of action (Do you want your client to do something? Do you want the trial court to grant or deny a motion? Do you want the appellate court to affirm or reverse the trial court? Do you want opposing counsel to respond to a settlement offer?)

Your answers to these two questions should go a long way toward dictating the structure and tone of the final document. For example, a letter to a client who wants to know if she has a malpractice claim will have very little in common with a motion for summary judgment to the trial judge on that same claim. If you keep the intended audience and goal in mind at all times, you should be able to avoid the trap of going on at great length about issues the reader does not care about, or simply has no need to think about. Likewise, you will be sure that you actually do address the issue or issues that are of primary importance to the reader.

§ 7.03. CONTEXT

Context is closely related to purpose, but it encompasses a few additional elements. In addition to remembering for whom you are writing and what you need to accomplish, you need to consider the forum in which you are writing. Is this a memo in a law office? A brief to a court (trial or appellate)? A letter to a client? Each type of document involves different expectations regarding format, tone, amount and type of information, and writing style. A brief to a court will be presented in a very formal tone and must conform to fixed and specific rules regarding format, while the tone and format of a letter to a client are more flexible. An office memorandum should be presented in a tone and format that are consistent with the expectations of the particular office in which it is written.

We will discuss several different types of documents in this book, but if you need to draft a document not covered in this book, you should find similar documents intended for the same or a similar audience, and learn whatever you can about the contextual expectations. Read the samples, ask questions (preferably of the intended reader, if possible), and look at any written guidelines, such as court rules, that may govern the final product.

§ 7.04. STRUCTURE

The structure of a document is much like the foundation and framework of a building. Both need to be carefully constructed, and, if done well, both will strengthen and define the finished product. All of the many aspects of the structure of a written piece require conscious thought and strategic planning. We will discuss structural issues such as outlining and the placement of arguments, and signaling tools such as road map paragraphs, thesis sentences, and transitions. We will also briefly touch on the placement of authorities and different types of argument within an argument or discussion. Because we do discuss the specifics of particular types of documents in later chapters, the approach here will be to present more general rules that should guide your preparation every time you write.

1. Outlining

For most people, the really important thing to know about an outline is that you should do one.[1] There is no formula for outlining that will work for everyone. What is crucial is

---

1. We say "for most people" because there are those who can construct a perfectly coherent, logical discussion every time they sit down to write. If you are one of those rare people, the extra step of creating an outline may not be a terribly useful or efficient way to spend time. For most of us, however, whether we are writing memos, briefs,

that you sit down before you begin to write and plan the flow of your discussion. Here are some considerations you should take into account in that planning process:

- What are the key points to be analyzed?
- How many points do you need to make?
- What is the most logical order in which to make those points?
- How do the different parts of your discussion relate to each other?
- Which are your strongest and weakest points?
- How does the legal authority you intend to rely on fit into your arguments? Are there different cases or statutes on each point, or do you need to use the same authority to support several arguments?

Once you have done enough research to get a preliminary idea of the types of arguments you need to make, you should make a sketchy outline. There is no need to write out full sentences in the outline at this point; you will most likely be identifying only the major points to be made. You should keep this preliminary outline with you as you continue your research and analysis. It will help to keep you focused as you sort through the available authority.

You may find that the initial outline is incomplete or that it does not present the parts of the discussion in the most logical order. You should be flexible enough to recognize this and to adjust your outline in any way and as many times as seems appropriate. Even in the midst of writing, you may need to rethink your outline and restructure your presentation.

When you have collected all the authority you intend to rely upon, go back to your outline and "plug in" the authorities. Decide which cases or statutes are most helpful on particular points, and add them to the outline in the appropriate places. Then organize the authorities into the proper order.

As you finalize the outline, you may want to flesh out your major points. You can do this by writing them out in full sentences and by adding subpoints. Some writers need to, and should, construct very detailed outlines, while others can write just as efficiently with less thorough guidance. Regardless of your approach, do not forget to identify the purpose, audience, and context of your document before constructing your final outline. *Now* you are ready to begin writing.

Keep your outline in front of you at all times during the writing process. This will keep you from trying to make all of your points at once or in the order they occur to you as you are writing, which may or may not be the order that makes the most sense. Also, referring to the outline when you are struggling to develop a point may help you understand how that point relates to the rest of the document, which may sometimes be enough to get the writing process back on track.

If the outlining approach discussed here does not work for you, there are alternatives. You can create a very general heading-only outline, write up the discussion, and then rearrange sections of the discussion as necessary. You can write the sections in a different order than set forth in the outline if one or two points are giving you particular trouble.

---

or law school exams, making the effort to outline the structure of our argument before we flesh it out in full paragraph form is the only way to ensure that the final product is a sensible, focused communication to the intended reader. This is true even though outlining is a more natural process for some than for others. There may be writers for whom it is a sufficiently foreign way of thinking as to be almost counterproductive, but in the context of legal writing it is usually a necessary, if difficult, endeavor, because it is the only way to ensure that our ideas will be communicated in a way that is useful to our busy readers.

Starting with the easier section or sections will at least get the writing process started, and you may then discover that the difficult sections become more manageable. You also can write without an outline to get the ideas down on paper and then superimpose an outline on the discussion after you have written it, to be certain your final structure makes sense.

Let's go back to the lost ring case discussed in Chapter 6 and outline the analysis in Section 6.03. Remember that there are many ways to outline any discussion, but here is one approach.

I. Was the valise lost?
    A. *Durfee*—definition and rule for lost property
    B. *McAvoy*—definition and rule for mislaid property
II. Was the ring lost?

[Note that you will only apply the rules here since you have already defined them in Section I, and it would be unnecessary in such a short document to repeat your discussion of the cases]

III. Who gets the ring?

    Durfee—finder must have permission to examine property

This is obviously a very simple discussion, and the outline is likewise simple. You can apply the same process and principles to a much more complex discussion, and it will give you a clearer picture of where the document is going and what it will accomplish when you are finished.

Exercise

Select a memorandum from Appendix I in the back of the book and outline the discussion.

2. Deciding on a Structural Strategy

One of the decisions about structure you need to make as you begin writing is the order in which you will present the arguments. Sometimes there will be an inherently logical approach to ordering the arguments; for example, if you are discussing a tort or statute that sets forth specific elements that must be, or always are, discussed in a particular order, you should order your discussion accordingly.

The false imprisonment problem discussed in Chapter 6 presents just such a situation. Both cases rely on the Restatement (Second) of Torts, which presents the elements in a specific order: (1) intent to confine, (2) actual confinement, and (3) consciousness of confinement. In this situation, it is easier and more likely to meet the expectations of your reader to follow this structure. However, do not feel that you must devote equal time to each element. If there is a genuine issue as to whether one or two elements are present in your case, while the other element or elements are clearly satisfied, you can allude only briefly to the elements not at issue and devote the bulk of your analysis to the elements in dispute. If you are writing an advocacy document, most experts will advise you to start with your strongest argument. This is good strategic advice, as long as it does not create a conflict with the type of inherent order discussed above, and so long as it does not cause you to make the argument in an order that does not make logical sense.

Some people will also advise you to end your discussion on a strong note, so that you leave a favorable impression with the reader. Again, if you can do so logically, this is sound advice. If you have not already guessed, this strategic approach to ordering your arguments will leave your weaker points in the middle of the discussion, where they are most likely to be forgotten.

For a concrete example of strategic structuring of an argument, look at the following outlines of an argument from two appellate briefs on opposite sides of the same issue. The issue addressed by both briefs is whether a decedent's estate can bring a tort action against the hospital that employed the decedent. The decedent was murdered while working at the hospital on the late shift. The hospital sought to bar the claim by arguing that the only available remedy lay in the applicable workers' compensation statute. The crux of the argument was whether a statutory exception to the exclusivity of the workers' compensation remedy applied.

In the hospital's brief, the statutory argument is outlined as follows in the table of contents:

I. WORKERS' COMPENSATION SHOULD BE THE EXCLUSIVE REMEDY FOR INJURIES SUSTAINED BY AN EMPLOYEE IN THE COURSE OF HER EMPLOYMENT FROM AN ATTACK BY A THIRD PERSON WHEN NO RELATIONSHIP BETWEEN THE THIRD PERSON AND EMPLOYEE EXISTED PRIOR TO THE ATTACK.
   A. *Workers' Compensation Is Intended to Be the Sole Remedy for Injuries Sustained in the Course of One's Employment.*
   B. *The Attack upon Charla Louis Was Not for Reasons Personal Within the Meaning of the Workers' Compensation Act and Is Only Compensable Through Workers' Compensation.*

Here is the outline of the statutory argument from the Estate's perspective:

I. THE ESTATE OF A HOSPITAL EMPLOYEE WHO WAS ATTACKED AND MURDERED WHILE WORKING, BY AN ASSAILANT WITH PERSONAL MOTIVATION TO COMMIT SEXUAL ASSAULT, IS NOT LIMITED BY THE REMEDIES OF THE WORKERS' COMPENSATION ACT.
   A. *An Exception Provided by the Act Disallows Compensation for All Personally Motivated Assaults by Third Parties.*
   B. *The Fact that the Victim Was Present on the Premises of the Employer as Required by Her Job Does Not Limit Recovery to that Provided by the Act When the Third Party Attack Is Personally Motivated.*
      1. Preexisting personal animosity is not dispositive or even highly indicative of the assailant's motivation since his motivation at the time of attack is at issue.
      2. The nature of sexual assault indicates personal motivation in the form of anticipated sexual gratification; rape is not usually motivated by work-related activity.
   C. *An Employee Who Is Not Required by Her Job to Have Personal Contact with the Public Does Not Assume the Risk of Personal Assault so as to Bring Sexual Assault by a Third Party Under the Provisions of the Act.*

The exception is most helpful to the Estate, and you will notice that it appears prominently in the outline of the estate's argument—as the first subpoint of the argument. While the Hospital's argument deals with the issues raised by the exception, it is not even mentioned explicitly in the outline, thus diminishing its apparent importance. The first point in the Hospital's argument is the exclusive nature of the workers' compensation remedy.

In addition to thinking strategically about the order in which you present your arguments, you should consider how much space you will devote to each argument. A reader is likely to assume that an argument that occupies a substantial amount of room is important. Why would a writer spend a lot of time and effort developing a point that is of only passing significance? No writer would, unless that writer got so caught up in developing a tangential or tenuous analogy that the writer lost sight of the need to do a cost-benefit analysis during the writing process. Ask yourself whether the amount of time and space you spend on an argument is proportional to the persuasive impact the argument will have in the context of your overall presentation. If not, consider whether the argument can be edited substantially, or perhaps cut altogether.

3. Roadmaps, Topic Sentences, and Transitions

It is not enough to have a structure for your document. You must let the reader know what that structure is. If the reader knows up front where the document is going and gets messages along the way that help to orient him or her, the document will be easier to read and the analysis will seem more logical and possibly even more persuasive.

The simplest way to orient the reader early on is to provide a "roadmap" paragraph. This introductory paragraph highlights the most significant parts of your analysis and states your ultimate conclusion. At the risk of abusing our analogy, by identifying the destination and the major landmarks at the beginning of the journey, you make the trip easier and more comfortable for the traveler.

A roadmap paragraph can be very explicit, as is this paragraph:

The Estate's action is premised on a negligence theory of liability. However, as the court emphasized in *Murphy v. Penn Fruit Co.*, 274 Pa. Super. 427, 418 A.2d 480 (1980), negligence is not established by the mere happening of an attack on the decedent. *Id.* at 432, 418 A.2d at 483. The Estate must plead and prove each element of the tort to establish liability. The necessary elements to maintain a negligence action are a duty or obligation recognized by the law, requiring the actor to conform to the standard required; a failure to conform to the standard required; a causal connection between the conduct and the resulting injury; and actual loss or damage resulting to the interests of another. *Morena v. South Hills Health System*, 501 Pa. 634, 642, 462 A.2d 680, 684 (1983), quoting Prosser, *Law of Torts*, § 30 at 143 (4th ed. 1971). Each of these elements will be examined in turn as they apply to the facts of this case.

You can also take a slightly less detailed approach, as the writer of this memo does:

Ms. Holmes was falsely imprisoned by Dean James. Dean James had probable cause to question Ms. Holmes about the materials found in her locker, but he acted unreasonably in confining Ms. Holmes and causing her to miss her exam. Dean James's conduct was without legal justification, and the confinement was therefore unlawful.

Both examples inform the reader of the writer's ultimate conclusion, and provide information about how the argument will progress. That is all a roadmap paragraph needs to do.

Topic sentences and transitions are the landmarks that let readers know where in the discussion they are at any given point. The first sentence of any paragraph should give the reader a clue as to what the rest of the paragraph will be about. As a general rule, a single paragraph should not develop more than one idea, and the purpose of that first, or topic, sentence is to identify that idea. We discuss paragraph construction in greater detail in Chapter 8.

As you shift between the major points you identified in the roadmap paragraph, make a conscious effort to put distinct transitions between them. Sometimes the transitions will be as simple as an introductory sentence that identifies the element you are about to discuss, as you will see if you look at the first memo about false imprisonment in Appendix I.

Exercise

Choose one of the remaining memos in Appendix I, and identify all thesis sentences and transitions. Are there any paragraphs that do not begin with topic sentences signaling what the paragraph is about? If so, does this cause confusion or frustration as you try to pull the central idea from each paragraph? If not, it may be that the topic has been implicitly signaled in some other way. Do the transitions act as landmarks that relate back to the roadmap? Does this help you, as a reader, understand the progression of the discussion and where you are in the analysis at any particular point?

4. Organizing Within Arguments

Thus far, we have explored ways of structuring your document at the "macro" level— outlining the progression of the discussion, choosing the order in which to present your points, and making your organizational scheme apparent to the reader. In this section, we will discuss organization at a more "micro" level. How do you decide where to present authorities within an argument or part of a discussion, and how much space do you devote to each? How do you integrate law, policy, and equity arguments? The answer is that you apply the same principles we discussed earlier, that is, you start with the stronger authorities and arguments, and devote proportionally more space to them as well.

How do you know which authorities are strongest? We discussed the different types and weight of authority in Chapter 3. Here is a summary that should help:

1. On-point decisions by higher courts in your jurisdiction are binding and should be featured conspicuously. If such decisions go against you, first look for a relevant way to distinguish them, pointing out differences between the facts or policies at issue in those cases and your case. If they cannot be distinguished, you need to deal with them in other ways, perhaps by arguing that they were wrongly decided or that times have changed sufficiently that a new rule is called for. Unless such adverse decisions are truly dispositive of your case, you can still place them strategically in the middle of your argument, using the more prominent beginning and ending positions for authority that is more helpful to you.

2. Decisions by lower courts in your jurisdiction are very persuasive and should also be given appropriate space and position. The same rules about distinguishing or otherwise dealing with adverse authority apply.

3. Recent decisions are generally more persuasive than older decisions, all other things being equal (i.e., if the facts in the older decision are significantly more analogous to your case, you might want to spend more time on the older decision).

4. Federal decisions interpreting state law are persuasive and should be given some attention if they fill in gaps in the state decisions or articulate the rationale for the state

decisions particularly clearly. Unless you have no better authority, you do not want to use disproportionate amounts of space on such decisions.

5. Decisions from other jurisdictions and secondary authorities are only as persuasive as you make them. This almost inevitably means that you will have to devote considerable space to making analogies or articulating policy justifications for adopting rules from such sources. If you have no other authority, perhaps because the question you are addressing is a novel one in your jurisdiction, it may be worth your effort to do so. You may be able to discover and argue a developing trend in the law that supports adoption of the rule you advocate. If, however, you have other authority that the reader is likely to find more useful, you should think twice about using valuable space and reader energy on such subordinate points. Remember that the reader is likely to equate the time needed to develop and understand an argument with the importance of that argument, so make your decisions accordingly.

5. Placement of Policy and Equity Arguments

Keep your strategic sense working on the question of integrating law, policy, and equity arguments as well. As you learned in Chapter 6, policy arguments are based on societal goals that would be served by the result you seek, and equity arguments are based on notions of general fairness as applied to the particular facts of your case. Remember that courts of law are essentially conservative institutions, bound to a large extent by precedent and notions of stare decisis. This means that you should feature your legal arguments in the prominent positions and devote more time to them. Policy and equity arguments are supportive and will seem more persuasive if they are closely tied to your legal arguments. Therefore, on any given point, you should start with your legal arguments and authorities, and then follow immediately with related and reinforcing policy and equity arguments.

If you do not have on-point authority to support your position, you may be able to find authority to support pure policy arguments. Think about other areas of the law that have important similarities to yours and that serve the same policy goals. Look for cases in those areas that have similar facts and the result you want. Policy arguments should generally be given more prominence than purely equitable, fact-based arguments. While equitable arguments are useful, and judges generally like to feel that they are being fair in rendering their decisions, you do not want to devote a lot of time to such arguments or lead off with them, unless you have nothing else.

§ 7.05. CONTEXT AND STRUCTURE CHECKLIST

— Identify and articulate the goal of your document.
— Identify your audience and any expectations you know or suspect that audience has for your document.
— Outline the major points you need to make in the document to accomplish your goal.
— Fill in details such as legal authorities and revise the outline as necessary as you go along.
— Make sure you start and end with a strong point, to the extent logic permits.
— Organize your legal authorities according to the appropriate hierarchy, giving more space to more persuasive authorities.

— Organize your legal, policy, and equity arguments so that the more persuasive arguments receive greater prominence in terms of both position and space.
— Write your roadmap paragraph and check your document for transitions and thesis sentences that will let the reader know where in the analysis you are and where the analysis is going.

CHAPTER 8

Make Your Main Themes Stand Out

§ 8.01. INTRODUCTION

Sometimes we read a court opinion, a memo, or an appellate brief and do not understand its message until we reach the end. After we finish reading the document, we think about the conclusion and try to synthesize all the information and analysis that we have read. As we synthesize, we may find ourselves returning to earlier paragraphs in the document and puzzling over them. If we think about this process of digesting information, we probably will conclude that it is inefficient and creates the risk that the reader will misunderstand the message that the writer seeks to convey. When it comes to writing, we may conclude, there must be a better way.

There is a better way. From the very beginning of the document, let the reader know what your message is. Instead of waiting until the end to pull the rabbit out of the hat, make your main themes stand out throughout the document. Let the reader know where you are going.

To accomplish this task, apply three principles: make the outline of your argument or discussion stand out; put your conclusions first; and write well-organized paragraphs.

First, as suggested in Chapter 7, make an outline of your writing. An outline will clarify your organization for you, and your reader will benefit because of it. Because your first draft is never your best work, you should revise your outline and your writing several times.

Second, in any legal document, put your conclusions at the beginning of your writing. At the outset, the reader wants to know your conclusions about the law as applied to the facts of your case. Although you may well decide to recapitulate your conclusion at the end, the end is not the place to state your conclusion for the first time.

Third, write well-organized paragraphs. Within your document, paragraphs are major units of discourse. If the reader easily grasps the idea of each paragraph, follows the discussion of that idea, and can make a smooth transition to the idea in the next paragraph, he or she will understand your message.

§ 8.02. MAKE THE OUTLINE OF YOUR ARGUMENT OR DISCUSSION STAND OUT

As we discussed in Chapter 7, to make the outline of your argument or discussion[1] stand out, you should begin with an outline. Many students are not accustomed to making outlines of their writing in advance. They write first and outline later. For most people, this approach just does not work. Make an outline.

Your initial outline is a simple listing of the major points in your discussion or argument. As your research and analysis progress, you can develop a more comprehensive outline using full sentences. You also may decide to reorganize your outline.

Here is part of a sample sentence outline in an appellate brief concerning a case that takes place in Pennsylvania. The plaintiff in the case is attempting to take ownership of a property from the owner who has a deed to that property. Under Pennsylvania law a trespasser can gain ownership of property by possessing it for twenty-one years and performing certain acts of ownership. The doctrine is called "adverse possession."

Sample Sentence Outline:

I. SMITH HAS ACQUIRED SUFFICIENT INTEREST IN THE DISPUTED TRACT OF LAND TO ENTITLE HIM TO OWN THE LAND BY ADVERSE POSSESSION.
    A. Smith's Possession of the Disputed Tract of Land Has Been Actual, Continuous, Visible, Notorious, Exclusive, Distinct, and Hostile for the Statutory Period of Twenty-One Years as Required to Satisfy the Elements of Adverse Possession.
        1. Because Smith intends to hold this land for himself and has manifested his intention by many acts of possession, his decision to discontinue one act, grazing sheep, during the requisite period does not break the continuity of his possession.

Here is another example. In this case, two workers had a verbal dispute that was work related. Six months later, they engaged in a personal fight during working hours. One of the workers was injured and now seeks recovery under the Pennsylvania Workers' Compensation Act. An outline for part of a memorandum on the case might look like this:

Sample Sentence Outline:

I. BECAUSE THE FIGHT WAS PURELY PERSONAL, THE INJURED WORKER CANNOT RECOVER UNDER THE ACT.
    A. As interpreted by case law, the Act excludes injuries arising when the attacker acts for purely personal reasons.
    B. As interpreted by case law, the Act is remedial and should be liberally construed in favor of the injured worker.

---

1. The word "argument" here means arguing your client's case in a brief that goes to the court. You will learn more about writing effective briefs in Chapters 28-32. The word "discussion" here means an objective discussion of the law, without argument, in legal memoranda and client letters. You will learn more about writing effective memoranda and client letters in Chapters 11-17.

    C. Nonetheless, all similar cases permitting recovery were over work-related issues with no mention of personal matters.

    D. In light of the case law, the earlier dispute is too remote to permit describing the fight as work related. Therefore the injured worker probably will lose.

To complete this outline, you would fill it out by including throughout some information about the cases that you plan to discuss.

To make the outline of the argument stand out, you should follow it in your writing. With the outline in hand, you should find that you will write more easily. If you run into difficulties, you may decide that your outline is faulty and that you need to revise it.

After you turn your outline into a draft, do not let the first draft be your final writing. First-year students face many time pressures and often want to save time by not revising their writing. Many students who receive lower grades in legal writing than they expected readily admit, "Well, I didn't revise my writing. I wrote only one draft."

The usual reason the student gives is lack of time. Lawyers face just as many time pressures. Bear in mind that you will be working for clients when you become a lawyer, and your best writing is never the first draft. Your rule of thumb should be to go through at least three drafts, if not more. Make the time to go through as many revisions as necessary to make your final product the best it can be.

Once you have written a first draft, go back over it and make sure it follows your outline perfectly. If you find that the outline is forcing you to organize your discussion in an awkward way, revise your outline.

Structure your discussion so that your organization is clear to the first-time reader. In this book you will learn and relearn many rules that will help you achieve this goal. As you go through your revisions, make sure you apply each rule.

§ 8.03.   PUT YOUR CONCLUSION FIRST

A conclusion is usually at the end of a writing. To make your theme stand out, however, put it at the beginning. Depending on what you are writing, you may find it desirable to also recapitulate it at the end.

The basic rule of expository writing is:

Tell your readers what you are going to say.
Say it.
Tell them what you just said.

Tell your reader your conclusion at the outset. Then discuss the rationale for your conclusion. Then remind the reader of the conclusion you have justified in your discussion.

The reader wants to know, right up front, what the law is as applied to the given situation and does not want to be "held in suspense" until the end of the memorandum, brief, or letter. You are not writing a mystery novel!

Do not make the reader wait until the end to see where you are going. If you think your writing will become repetitive, you are right. Some repetition is necessary to make your point.

The following is an edited excerpt from a student's legal memorandum. In this sample, the student stated the conclusion at the beginning of the discussion and provided an emphatic recapitulation at the end.

In this case, a court should hold the minor operator of a rider mower to an adult standard of care because the fourteen-year-old's operation of the mower was a dangerous activity that adults normally perform. Courts generally require a minor to exercise the same standard of care that would be exercised under similar circumstances by a reasonably careful minor of the same age, intelligence, and experience. Nonetheless, they make an exception in the case of motor vehicles.

In two cases involving the operation of motor vehicles by minors, the Supreme Court of Arkansas decided to hold minor operators to an adult standard of care. In one decision the court required an adult standard of care from a fifteen-year-old boy who was riding a motorcycle on a public street. *Harrelson v. Whitehead*, 365 S.W.2d 868 (Ark. 1963). In a second decision the court held that a fourteen-year-old boy operating a farm tractor in a cotton field should adhere to the same standard of care as a reasonably careful adult. *Jackson v. McCuiston*, 448 S.W.2d 33 (Ark. 1969). In *Jackson*, the court recognized that applying an adult standard of care to a minor who operates a motor vehicle is "an exception to our general rule that a minor owes that degree of care which a reasonably careful minor of his age and intelligence would exercise under similar circumstances." . . .

The court should impose an adult standard of care on a minor operator of a rider mower. This activity requires an adult standard of care for the safety of the operator as well as for the safety of anyone else in the vicinity. The exception to the general rule is justified because rider mowers are inherently dangerous, and adults normally operate them. A minor who undertakes the operation of a dangerous adult activity in the business world of adults cannot avoid the standard of care of a reasonably careful adult.

Some lawyers would call the first paragraph of this excerpt a "thesis paragraph," because it states the conclusion and indicates how the writer reaches it. More specifically, in stating the conclusion, it presents the issue in concrete terms by using the facts of the case and justifies the conclusion by identifying the applicable rule, statute, or case precedent and briefly explaining how it applies.

Putting the conclusion first creates a roadmap in the reader's mind. Because the reader knows where the writer is going, the reader finds the discussion more meaningful from the outset. As readers, we find nothing more frustrating than plodding through a legal memorandum or brief that does not give us this roadmap. Without it, we find ourselves silently asking, "Now where is this writer taking me?"

Even though the student stated the conclusion at both the beginning and end of the discussion, the discussion is not too repetitive. The writer tells you what the conclusion is, explains the rationale for the conclusion, and then restates the conclusion at the end as justified by the discussion. You do not have to guess at the outset where the writer is taking you—there is no mystery here.

Note that the writer's conclusion at the end does not simply repeat the conclusion at the beginning. Instead, it makes clear the justification for the court decisions. Often the conclusion at the end will be more concrete or more emphatic than the conclusion at the beginning. Frequently, it will contain new information or a new insight.

Sometimes you will decide not to place a conclusion at the end because you find it superfluous. In such instances, the conclusion is so dominant throughout the discussion that you see no need to repeat it. Still, do not let your ending trail off. End with some emphasis, perhaps by using a pithy sentence, a compelling example that justifies your conclusion, or a suggestion on what to do next.

Compare the following edited excerpt from another memorandum on the same subject with the one above:

Courts have tended for the past twenty years to create exceptions to the general rule governing minors' responsibility for their negligent actions. In this society with rapid technological change, courts have faced the necessity of changing many rules to keep up with the use of sophisticated equipment in the form of farm machinery, automobiles, and the like. Public policy has compelled these changes in the interest of safety in a changing world.

Although minors have had to adhere to a minor's standard of care, exceptions have evolved. Today's minors operate very sophisticated equipment, and public policy requires a higher standard of care from them. Minors do have accidents as a result of their handling sophisticated equipment, and safety requires that they be responsible to a greater extent than they were in the past.

The writer gives you no idea at the outset what the memorandum will conclude. After reading two paragraphs, you have no idea what this memorandum will say about the case involved. The main theme does not stand out. In comparison, the first sample memorandum excerpt requires only a quick glance for the reader to know what the writer's conclusion is.

At the outset, always let the reader know what your conclusion is. Then explain that conclusion within the context of the discussion. Finally, if desirable, present a recapitulation at the end.

§ 8.04. WRITE EFFECTIVE PARAGRAPHS

In making your main theme stand out, you must pay attention to how you present and develop ideas. You present and develop them within your primary units of discourse: sentences and paragraphs. In this section, we discuss writing effective paragraphs. You will learn how to present the idea in a paragraph, how to develop that idea, how to give the paragraph unity and direction, and how to connect sentences and paragraphs so that your analysis flows smoothly.

1. Use Topic Sentences

Every paragraph should present one major idea. In most paragraphs, you will first present that idea in one sentence or in a group of sentences called topic sentences. (Most of the time, you will use one topic sentence.) These sentences provide the topic for the discussion that goes on in the rest of the paragraph.

Here is an example of a paragraph with a topic sentence in its most typical location, the very beginning. The writer is arguing against a court decision that upholds a statute as constitutional.

The majority defines the right at stake too narrowly and treats the developmentally challenged as second class citizens with second-class rights. No legislature would even consider drafting a provision like § 4693(c) and applying it to legally competent adults. Just as with the legally competent, individuals like D.T. must enjoy their fundamental liberty and privacy rights if they are to develop to their maximum economic, intellectual, and social levels.

In this paragraph, the topic sentence clearly states the point. The rest of the paragraph develops the point by explaining why the writer disagrees with the majority.

Here is the same paragraph with the sentences arranged in a different order:

> No legislature would even consider drafting a provision like § 4693(c) and applying it to legally competent adults. The majority defines the right at stake too narrowly and treats the developmentally challenged as second-class citizens with second-class rights. Just as with the legally competent, individuals like D.T. must enjoy their fundamental liberty and privacy rights if they are to develop to their maximum economic, intellectual, and social levels.

This paragraph is unsatisfactory because the topic sentence is in the wrong place. A paragraph works well when the topic sentence states the idea and the remaining sentences develop that idea. Here, the paragraph begins with the development, then states the topic, and then continues the development. In its original form, the paragraph succeeds because it begins with the conclusion and then develops it.

Instead of being at the beginning of the paragraph, the topic sentence can be at the end. In this instance, the paragraph builds to a conclusion. Here is an example:

> Just as with the legally competent, individuals like D.T. must enjoy their fundamental liberty and privacy rights if they are to develop to their maximum economic, intellectual, and social levels. Their development, however, is frustrated by § 4693(c). No legislature would even consider drafting a similar provision and applying it to legally competent adults. By upholding this statute, the majority defines the right at stake too narrowly and treats the developmentally challenged as second-class citizens with second-class rights.

You often will write this type of a paragraph as an introductory or concluding paragraph to a document or to a large section of a document. In these locations, readers frequently prefer a paragraph that builds to a conclusion. However, in other locations, be cautious about putting the topic sentence at the end. As you know, readers normally like conclusions to come first and therefore like topic sentences at the beginning.

Consider this paragraph:

> The State and the independent counsel for D.T. filed identical motions requesting the Probate Court to dismiss the parents' petition. They argued that § 4693(c) bars the relief requested and that it is constitutional. The court granted the motions and dismissed the petition. On appeal, the Superior Court issued a brief per curiam opinion affirming the Probate Court's opinion.

This paragraph lacks an explicit topic sentence. Nonetheless, we know the theme of the paragraph: the procedural history of the case. As the paragraph illustrates, sometimes a paragraph has no topic sentence.

You can omit a topic sentence when the general idea of the paragraph is clear to the reader. In a sense, the idea is present by implication. Narrative paragraphs are the most typical example.

Although you sometimes can forgo a topic sentence, do not be too quick to do so. Readers like topic sentences because they make a paragraph's theme unambiguous. Err on the side of including topic sentences.

2. Write Cohesive Paragraphs

Although writing a good topic sentence will go a long way toward making your theme stand out, you also must make certain that the discussion part of your paragraph supports and develops the topic sentence. When the topic sentence and the discussion work together, your paragraph will have unity and direction.

a. Write Focused Discussion Sections

In different paragraphs, the discussion sections serve different purposes. For example, the discussion section may offer an example to illustrate the point of the topic sentence, elaborate on the topic sentence, furnish a logical argument supporting the point of the topic sentence, or provide a narrative that the topic sentence introduces. In each case, the discussion section discusses the idea in the topic sentence and focuses the reader's attention on it.

In the next paragraph, the discussion section offers an example. The topic sentence tells us that a court has declined to apply strict liability when the plaintiff is an expert in dealing with a potentially dangerous product. The discussion section discusses one case in which the court refused to find strict liability for this reason.

The Washington Supreme Court has refused to extend strict liability to cases in which expert handlers suffer injury while working with a potentially dangerous product. For example, in *Spellmeyer v. Weyerhauser*, 544 P.2d 107 (1975), a longshoreman was injured when a bale of wood pulp fell on him. According to the court, strict liability was inappropriate because only expert loaders and carriers were required to deal with the bale. The court found that because of the plaintiff's status as such an expert, the policy considerations favoring strict liability were too diluted to be persuasive. *Id.* at 110.

Here is a paragraph in which the discussion section elaborates on the topic sentence:

In *Seay v. Chrysler Corp.*, 609 P.2d 1382 (Wash. 1980), the Washington Supreme Court refined the *Spellmeyer* holding to permit some expert handlers to successfully invoke strict liability. In *Seay*, a worker, an expert handler, was injured while loading a truck chassis onto a convoy trailer. He was operating a temporary device that was placed on the chassis specifically for the purpose of moving and unloading. The court imposed strict liability on the manufacturer of the temporary device, but only because the expert handler was the device's intended ultimate user. *Id.* at 1385. Although the court extended strict liability to an expert handler, it still limited the doctrine to situations in which a finished product is not safe for its intended use.

In this paragraph, the topic sentence tells us that a court used a case to refine its holding in an earlier case. The rest of the paragraph tells us about the new case and how the court used it to clarify its position on strict liability.

In the next paragraph, the discussion section presents a logical argument in support of the proposition in the topic sentence.

When the user of a product is an expert in the care and handling of such products, the product is not unreasonably dangerous if the manufacturer fails to furnish instructions on its care and handling. By definition, an expert handler knows how to handle and move a wide variety of products. The handler possesses the experience, knowledge, and judgment necessary to protect himself or herself. Although, presumably, a significant percentage of products do not come to the docks equipped with loading instructions, it would be absurd to term all these products unreasonably dangerous to their handlers.

Note that the sentences in the discussion section appear in a carefully arranged sequence. The writer thought out the argument and made it one step at a time. If we were to rearrange the sentences in the discussion group, we would upset the logical order and seriously weaken the argument.

In the next paragraph, the discussion section provides a narrative that the topic sentence introduces.

The injury occurred when the longshoremen attempted to load two steel drafts onto a barge. After both drafts arrived at the dock, the loaders safely loaded them onto the barge by using a sling of chain steel suspended from a shoreside crane. The loaders then determined that the drafts would fit better if loaded in the opposite direction. Therefore, they directed the crane operator to rehoist the drafts above the barge. Despite the availability of a nearby forklift and the obvious danger posed by the weight of the drafts, the loaders swung the drafts around in midair. The drafts collided with the forklift, slipped free from the sling, and crushed Mr. Smyth under their combined weight.

In this paragraph, the topic sentence tells you that the rest of the paragraph is going to describe the circumstances of the accident. When you read the paragraph, you may have thought that the topic sentence provided you with some help, but that it was not essential to your understanding. As discussed in Section 8.04[1], in narratives, topic sentences are not always necessary. The reader usually knows the idea of the paragraph—to tell the story. The theme of the paragraph is implicit.

b. Avoid Extraneous Sentences

In writing the discussion section, make sure that all the material in the discussion relates to the topic sentence.

Consider this paragraph:

Because the plaintiff failed to employ a sheriff to serve the garnishment writ on the defendant, the service was ineffective. Rule 402(a) permits a plaintiff to make service without a sheriff only when the plaintiff makes service within the Commonwealth. Because the plaintiff chose to make service at the defendant's Illinois office, Rule 402(a) cannot be successfully invoked. The plaintiff requests the court to overlook any error in service because plaintiff could have served the writ at the defendant's office in the Commonwealth.

In this paragraph, the first sentence is the topic sentence. It states that the plaintiff's service of process was ineffective because the plaintiff failed to employ a sheriff. The discussion section provides the supporting argument. It gives us the rule for when a plaintiff can make service without a sheriff and explains why that rule does not apply here. However, the last sentence of the paragraph is not part of that discussion. Instead of supporting the argument in the topic sentence, it puts forth the plaintiff's argument why the court should accept the service as valid. Although this sentence is about service of process, it does not directly relate to the topic sentence and is not part of the argument in the discussion section. As a result, it detracts from the unity and direction of the paragraph. It belongs in another paragraph.

Consider this paragraph:

> The discovery rule would not excuse the Johnsons from failing to satisfy the two-year statute of limitations. Under the rule, the statute would have begun running when the Johnsons should have known all the relevant facts. Although they had this knowledge shortly after their child's birth, they did not bring their action for another four years. However, the Johnsons could prevail under another exception to the two-year statute of limitations: the concealment exception. This exception tolls the statute of limitations when the defendant's fraud or concealment causes the plaintiff to relax his or her vigilance or fail to inquire further. In the present case, fraud and concealment were present and lulled the Johnsons into a false sense of security. Therefore the exception should apply.

The point of the topic sentence is that the discovery rule will not assist the Johnsons. We would expect the discussion section to explain why the discovery rule does not apply here. The first part of the discussion section satisfies our expectations. However, in the middle of the paragraph, the discussion shifts to the concealment rule. The rest of the paragraph fails to support the point of the topic sentence. Therefore, it belongs in a separate paragraph. In fact, the last four sentences of the paragraph should stand by themselves as a separate paragraph.

As the last two examples demonstrate, each paragraph can present only one central idea. Every sentence in the paragraph should deal directly with that idea. The focus on a single idea is what gives the paragraph unity and direction. Sentences that focus on some other idea are extraneous and must be omitted or placed in a different paragraph.

3. When Necessary, Use Transitions and Repeat Words

If the reader does not find a connection between the ideas within paragraphs and among paragraphs, he or she will not follow your analysis or argument. You create continuity by arranging your ideas in a logical or chronological order and by using transitional words— "for example," "however," "therefore," "in addition," "consequently," "in contrast," and "moreover"—and repeating words and ideas that you have used in earlier sentences and paragraphs. Here, we focus on transitions and repetition.

This paragraph illustrates how to use transitions and repetition:

> *The Supreme Court of Puerto Rico* has adopted the principle that rights and liabilities in tort must be determined according to the law of the jurisdiction having dominant contacts with the parties and the occurrence. *By adopting this approach, the court* has accepted the approach of the Restatement (Second) of Torts, which calls for applying the law of the state with the most significant relationship to the parties and the event. *The court thus* appears to conform to the Restatement's assertion that, in a personal injury case, a court should choose the law of the state where the injury occurred, unless another state's relationship to the injury is more significant.

The italicized words provide continuity between the sentences. The first sentence introduces the court. The remaining sentences make repeated references to the court and force the reader to remember that the paragraph is focusing on the Puerto Rico Supreme Court's resolution of a legal issue. The first four words of the second sentence refer back to the idea in the first sentence and let the reader know that the second sentence builds on the first. The third sentence contains the transitional word "thus" and tells the reader that the third sentence reaches a conclusion based on the preceding sentences. Repetition and transitions thus give this paragraph cohesiveness.

The sample paragraph contains only one transitional word, "thus." As you work on your writing, you will discover that when you place your sentences in the proper sequence and repeat words and ideas that you introduced earlier, you will not need to clutter up your sentences with a large number of transitional words.

You also may have been concerned that the subject of every sentence in the paragraph is the same. You may have been taught that if you begin sentences with the same subject, you will bore the reader. Yet, you probably did not realize the repetition the first time you read the paragraph, and you probably did not become bored. Concern over excessive repetition is greatly exaggerated. Using the same subject for a series of sentences usually gives legal writing great continuity.

We will use the next paragraph to learn about transitions between paragraphs.

Ms. Joseph should be able to make out a prima facie case for disparate treatment. To make out her case, she must persuade the court that there is sufficient evidence to prove four elements: (1) that she belongs to a protected class; (2) that she applied for an available position for which she was qualified; (3) that she was rejected; and (4) that after the rejection, the employer continued to seek applicants. She should be able to provide sufficient evidence to establish these elements. First, as a woman, she is a member of a protected class. Second, she applied for a position as a firefighter for which she was fully qualified. Third, she was rejected under circumstances that give rise to an inference of discrimination. Fourth, after she was rejected, the city continued to seek applicants.

Suppose the writer believes that it is necessary to elaborate on Ms. Joseph's evidentiary proof for each of the elements. The writer then might follow this paragraph with four paragraphs, one for each element. The first of these paragraphs might begin: "As for the first element. . . ." The second might begin: "As for the second element. . . ." In each case, the new paragraph begins with a repetition of relevant words from the first paragraph.

Suppose the writer does not believe that these four paragraphs are needed and wishes to move directly to the defendant's response. The writer might begin the second paragraph with this sentence: "If Ms. Joseph establishes her prima facie case, the defendant has the opportunity to rebut the presumption of discrimination." The first clause in the sentence repeats the idea in the preceding paragraph. It thus connects the paragraphs. Alternatively, the writer might begin the second paragraph with this sentence: "However, the defendant should not necessarily admit defeat." By using "however," a transitional word, the writer connects the paragraphs. As you can see, repetition and transitional words also are tools for connecting paragraphs.

Exercise

Here is a sequence of three paragraphs. Please rearrange the sentences to make the paragraphs more effective. You may move sentences from one paragraph to another and, if necessary, revise the sentences slightly.

Since two years have passed since the last permissible filing date, the statute of limitations, strictly read, would bar the action. Although this state's law normally imposes a two-year statute of limitations for personal injuries, the Johnsons still may be able to bring an action for wrongful birth. In medical malpractice cases, the courts have recognized an exception called the "discovery rule." The rule does not require the plaintiff to know that the physician was negligent. This exception may apply to the Johnsons' action.

In applying the rule, the courts use a three-pronged test. The discovery rule applies to plaintiffs in medical malpractice actions. Under the rule, when the plaintiff cannot reasonably ascertain the existence of an injury, the statute of limitations does not begin to run until the injury's existence is known or discovered or becomes knowable or discoverable through the exercise of due diligence.

The statute begins to run when the plaintiff knows or, through reasonable diligence, should know of: (1) his or her injury (2) the operative cause of the injury; and (3) the causal relationship between the injury and the operative.

CHAPTER 9

Help the Reader to Understand You

§ 9.01. INTRODUCTION

In this book you will learn to write documents such as legal memoranda for internal use in a law office, briefs for the courts' use in deciding your cases, and opinion letters for distribution to your clients.

Each form of legal writing has only one goal: to inform the reader in a clear and concise way. Help the reader out in every way you can. You should not try to impress your reader with your lawyering skills and language, but tell your reader your interpretation of the law in clear language.

Always assume that

1. the senior attorney who reads your internal legal memorandum may know little or nothing about the law as applied to the current case;
2. the judge who reads your brief may know little or nothing about the law as applied to the current case; and
3. the client who reads your opinion letter probably knows little or nothing about the law as applied to the current case.

Chapter 8 explained how to make your theme stand out. It thus explained one method of helping your reader to understand your writing. In this chapter you will learn other, often more subtle, methods for expressing your points clearly in writing.

Writing clearly, briefly, and precisely requires attention to detail. Many law students and young lawyers learn this lesson the hard way. A poor choice of words or a badly constructed sentence here and there really makes a difference.

We have organized this chapter into three topics: general advice, sentence structure, and sentence content. We also have included exercises to help you apply what you have learned.

§ 9.02. GENERAL ADVICE

1. Get to the Point

If you do not get to the point immediately, you will lose your reader at the outset. The reader is most often a very busy person who does not have the time or patience to ferret out what you are trying to say.

In Chapter 8 you learned one of the best ways of getting to the point: State your conclusions first. Suppose a senior attorney asks you to write a memo to address how the courts in your state would resolve a particular dispute. In the course of your research, you may learn a historical lesson on how the relevant law developed. In the relevant cases, you also may come across dozens of pithy quotations. You also may summarize dozens of cases. You may be tempted to begin your memo with a historical essay, fill the remainder with quotations, and include a series of paragraphs each furnishing a mini-brief of each case you read. However, before you fall into these traps, remember your assignment. The senior attorney asked you to answer a specific question. Instead of loading your memo with irrelevant information, include only information that answers the question.

First, state your conclusion. Then, state the controlling rule or holding in your jurisdiction and explain how the courts have applied the rule to cases with facts similar to yours. Distinguish adverse cases with different facts. Include your historical information, your quotations, and your cases only to the extent that they help you answer the question that you were asked. In other words, get to the point. Use information only to help you explain your point.

2. Use Concrete Language

Your writing should paint a picture in the reader's mind. You will not paint this picture unless you use concrete language and avoid abstractions. Do not try to achieve a lofty tone in legal writing. Your goal should be just the opposite. Follow these rules:

(1) Use the simplest language possible, as if you are telling a story orally.
(2) Use language the reader is least likely to have to look up in a dictionary.
(3) Use words that describe things in concrete terms.

Test your writing for concrete language and simplicity by reading it aloud. Does it sound interesting? Better still, read your writing to a nonlawyer, or a nonlaw student. Does that person understand it completely?

These examples illustrate how to change abstract to concrete language:

Bad: On the day the defendant's automobile collided with the minor, the precipitation level was very high, and the automobile hydroplaned.

Better: On the day Ms. Smith's car hit Sally Jones, it was raining hard and the car skidded off the road.

———————

Bad: The landlord had an obligation to secure the premises by preventing the entry of the criminal element into the domicile.

Better: The landlord should have provided adequate locks and windows on the doors to the apartment.

———————

Bad: Mr. Jones committed his signature to writing on the document conveying the real estate to the new record title holder.

Better: Mr. Jones signed the deed to the land, transferring it to Ms. Smith.

———————

Bad: The assailant brandished the weapon in the air at the victim, inflicting severe emotional distress and injuries to his person.

Better: The robber waved a gun at Mr. Jones, frightening him and severely gashing his forehead.

———————

In each of the examples, abstract language became concrete language, and complex concepts became clear pictures.

Look at each sentence you write and check to see whether you have used the simplest, most direct language possible. This instruction may appear contrary to what you think you should be learning at the professional school level. The poor writing you often see in case opinions reinforces the assumption that you should use complicated words and phrases and write abstractly. But this sort of writing is the opposite of what you should strive for. Only by writing simply and clearly can you communicate your ideas effectively.

3. Use the Active Voice

This rule is one of the hardest for writers to follow. Read the following examples:

Passive Voice: Mary was hit by Sarah.

Active Voice: Sarah hit Mary.

Passive Voice: The ball was thrown by Jeff.

Active Voice: Jeff threw the ball.

In the passive voice examples, the sentences focus on the objects of the action (Mary and the ball). The subject or actor in each sentence (Sarah and Jeff) that does something to the object takes a secondary role. In the active voice, the subject appears before the verb. It may be helpful to diagram the first example:

	(object)	(verb)	(preposition)	(subject)
(Passive)	Mary	was hit	by	Sarah
(Active)	(object) Sarah	(verb) hit		(subject) Mary

The more powerful, compelling way to express ideas in English is to use the active voice. There will be times when the passive voice is necessary, and there is no better way to express what you have said. But most of the time you can eliminate it with a little time and effort.

A few examples from legal writing may illustrate the effectiveness of the active voice. Suppose you are a district attorney prosecuting a criminal case. Which of the following would sound more persuasive in your brief for the case?

Passive Voice: The victim was hit by the defendant. Then she was raped by the defendant and shoved into the trunk of his car.

Active Voice: The defendant hit the victim, raped her, and shoved her into the trunk of his car.

The sentence in the active voice is more forceful. It makes a declarative statement, emphasizes the defendant's actions, and implies knowledge and purpose on the defendant's part.

Suppose you represent Mr. Smith in a case in which he claims a parcel of land. Which of the following would sound more persuasive in your brief for the case?

Passive Voice: Mr. Smith's intentions were evidenced by the facts that the land was occupied by him, the land was used by his sheep for grazing, and the land was used by him for planting crops.

Active Voice: Mr. Smith showed his intentions by occupying the land, using it for sheep grazing, and farming it.

Use of the active voice connotes concrete actions by Mr. Smith. The active voice also helps eliminate some unnecessary words to streamline the sentence.

Passive Voice: It was found by the court that the defendant was guilty, and he was sentenced to three years in prison.

Active Voice: The court found the defendant guilty and sentenced him to three years in prison.

Passive Voice: Title was quieted in Mr. Smith by the court, and Mr. Jones was found to no longer own the land.

Active Voice: The court quieted title in Mr. Smith and found that Mr. Jones no longer owned the land.

Passive Voice: The defendant was frisked by the detective, and this frisk turned up a loaded semi-automatic pistol, which was forcibly taken from his person.

Active Voice: The detective frisked the defendant, and this frisk turned up a loaded semi-automatic pistol, which the detective forcibly took from the defendant.

It is often difficult to eliminate the passive voice from writing. The best method is to go over your last draft, sentence by sentence, and read each sentence again for only one purpose—to eliminate the use of passive voice. As you find each use of passive voice, ask yourself, "Would converting this to active voice improve this sentence, and if so, how can I do that?"

———————

Once you have learned how to eliminate passive voice, then you will begin to learn when you can use it effectively in certain situations. For example, the following passage by the famous lawyer Clarence Darrow depends on the passive voice (italicized) for dramatic effect:

> I don't believe in man's tinkering with the work of God. I don't believe that you and I can say in the light of heaven that, if we *had been born* as he *was born*, if our brains *had been molded* as his *was molded*, if we *had been surrounded* as he *has been surrounded*, we might not have been like him.[1]

In this example, Darrow is using the passive voice to put emphasis on the verbs. One way to emphasize a word or phrase is to place it at the end of a sentence or clause. Here, Darrow places the verbs in these positions. If he used the active voice, he would have been unable to place the verbs in these positions. The desire to emphasize the verbs prevailed over any disadvantages of using the passive voice.

4. Avoid Legalese

Lawyers and judges too often use the jargon of the law, "legalese," in their writing. The frequent use of legalese is unnecessary and can result in unclear writing. You should avoid legalese not only because it results in ambiguity, but also because you may not yet fully understand the meanings of legal terms. Legal dictionaries do not always explain the full meanings of those terms. You will have opportunities to use the new language you are learning, but try to suppress the urge to overuse it in your writing.

A true story might be helpful here. Many first-year students love to use the word "dicta." They use "dicta" proudly and profusely in writing assignments. One student had been using the word in writing assignments throughout his first year of law school. At the end of the year, he told his professor that it was only then that he realized the full meaning of the word.

This student had used a dictionary definition of the term but, because of his limited experience, he did not understand precisely what that word meant. The word "dicta" refers to language in a court opinion that is unnecessary to the holding of a case. However, the student had been using the term to refer to actual holdings on issues other than those he had researched for his own research projects. He had not understood the term and had applied it too broadly.

Aside from this practical reason for not using legalese, the most important reason to avoid it is that you must write clearly, and use of legalese defeats this purpose. Legalese has developed over many centuries and stems from several languages—notably, Latin, French,

———————

1. Clarence Darrow, in defense of William D. Haywood for the murder of ex-governor Frank Steunenberg of Idaho, on the night of December 30, 1905. From G. J. Clark, *Great Sayings by Great Lawyers* (Vernon Law Book Co., 1926).

and Old and Middle English. Very little legalese is plain, simple, modern English that everyone can understand.

However, do not avoid using necessary terms of art, which you cannot replace with everyday words. The term "assault," for example, is a term of art; and you cannot use another term such as "hit" to replace it. "Proximate cause" is a term you will learn, and you should not attempt to find a substitute for it. "Exigent circumstances" is a term in criminal procedure that has its own special meaning, and you should not attempt to simplify it. Aside from certain terms of art such as these, you can eliminate most legalese from your writing.

Do not strive to impress your reader with your newly learned legalese. Strive to impress your reader with your ability to communicate effectively.

Examples

Legalese: The parties agree only to the terms and conditions set forth *herein.*

Plain Language: The parties agree only to the terms and conditions *in this agreement.*

Legalese: The plaintiff *instituted legal proceedings* against the defendant.

Plain Language: The plaintiff *sued* the defendant.

Legalese: In the event that the defendant defaults on her obligation, she will *forfeit* her rights.

Plain Language: If the defendant defaults on her obligation, she will *lose* her rights.

Legalese: Subsequent to his decision, the judge changed his mind.

Plain Language: After his decision, the judge changed his mind.

Legalese: She is to pay him $10,000 *per annum.*

Plain Language: She is to pay him $10,000 *a year.*

The examples show that you can substitute simple words and phrases for most of the terms and phrases that are peculiar to the law. Always read over your final draft of a legal document to purge it of all legalese.

5. Define Technical Terms

In the last subsection, you learned that you should avoid legalese. However, at times you cannot escape the use of technical terms. If you must use a technical term, define it immediately so you are sure the reader understands it. Of course, always consider your audience. Use your judgment when you decide whether the reader will understand the terms you use. A lawyer or judge may understand certain terms that a client would not understand. If you decide that it is necessary to define a term for your readers, either you can follow the term with a parenthesized definition, or you can define the term with a phrase or a sentence.

The following are examples of how to define technical terms in your writing:

- Mr. Barnes filed suit against Mr. Ewing to quiet title in the land. To "quiet title" means to ask the court to decide who owns the land.
- Mr. Barnes filed a suit against Mr. Ewing claiming adverse possession of the land. By invoking adverse possession, Mr. Barnes claimed he had gained ownership of Mr. Ewing's land by conducting certain acts with regard to the land for a certain time period.
- The defendant argued that a parent-child testimonial privilege should apply in this case. She argued that the court should not allow her son to testify against her in court because of the family relationship.
- Mr. Kramden argued that the insurance company's employee had apparent authority to bind the company. "Apparent authority" means that the insurance company represented to the public that the employee could make promises that the company must keep.
- The court ruled that the child should adhere to an adult standard of care (that is, that the child should have acted as a reasonable adult under the circumstances).

Never assume that your reader, whether another attorney or a judge, knows the meaning of every technical term you use. You do not want to insult your reader's intelligence, but you do not want to confuse your reader either.

6. Write in the Appropriate Tone

Much of what you have learned thus far may appear to work against using any formality in legal writing. Nevertheless, legal writing is formal writing. Although you must strive for simplicity, clarity, and brevity, you still must achieve the appropriate tone.

Setting the appropriate tone in your writing is where you can be "lawyerly" and sound "like a lawyer." Later in this chapter, you will learn the mechanics of tone at the word and phrase level—you will learn to avoid colloquialisms and contractions and not to personalize your writing with first ("I," "we") and second ("you") person pronouns. Learning those mechanics will help you write in the appropriate tone.

The tone in legal writing is similar to that in good business writing. Some helpful hints:

1. Do not use colloquialisms or slang.
2. Do not use contractions.
3. Do not personalize your writing.
4. Do not sound "preachy" or take the "soapbox" approach.
5. Do be serious. Legal documents are serious matters, and your clients have serious concerns. Legal documents are generally not the place for humor or lightness.

Although the cases you read in your casebooks may not always be the best examples of good legal writing, they usually illustrate the tone you should set in your writing. They are usually good examples for you to study.

Exercises

The following exercises give you an opportunity to put into practice some of the rules that we have just covered. Identify the errors and, to the extent possible, rewrite the sentences to eliminate those errors. You may have some difficulty rewriting some of the sentences as the original author would have because they are taken out of context. Do the best you can. For these exercises, you may assume facts not given if they are necessary.

(1) Although Pennsylvania does not provide for depositions in these circumstances, other state and the federal courts call for depositions. In *United States v. Linton*, 502 F. Supp. 878 (D. Nev. 1980), the court stressed that where testimony can be adequately secured by deposition, an incarcerated witness should not be further detained. In *Linton* the witness had been in jail for two months. At that time the trial was postponed. The court held that this was an "exceptional circumstance," and that it was "in the interest of justice that his testimony be taken by deposition." *Id.* at 879. The court delineated a comprehensive method of deposition-taking that includes videotaped examinations and cross-examinations.

Therefore, considering that Pennsylvania statute and case law strongly indicate material witnesses may not be held indefinitely, that the brothers were not afforded counsel to challenge their incarceration, and that deposition is a viable alternative to incarceration, the Fernandez brothers should be released from jail.

(2) The said canine caught the minor child's (Sally's) hand in his mouth, inflicting an injury that required ten sutures.

(3) The patient listed his unhealthy habits as the consumption of tobacco and alcoholic beverages and a lack of physical activity.

(4) The Texaco signs were put up by Bi-Rite Oil Company, which is Butterbaugh's distributor out of Monroeville and is independent of Texaco; the signs were provided by Bi-Rite free of charge.

(5) A criminal complaint was filed against defendant by the district attorney on November 5, 2013, charging the defendant with indecent assault. A preliminary hearing was scheduled by the district magistrate on November 14, 2013, but the hearing was not held because the defendant was not ready. Another hearing was scheduled for November 21, 2013, but was continued by the magistrate because a government witness was unavailable. The preliminary hearing was rescheduled for November 26, 2013, but was continued by the magistrate because defendant's attorney was unavailable. Finally, on December 10, 2013, a preliminary hearing was held by a district magistrate, and a prima facie case was established by the district attorney at that time. On December 12, 2013, the magisterial transcript was sent to the court by the clerk and was received by the district attorney on December 19, 2013. The information was filed on January 14, 2014, and the date for arraignment was set for January 22, 2014, on which date arraignment occurred.

(6) FINDINGS OF FACT

(1) The aforesaid respondent, [], Esq., is an attorney admitted to practice law in the Commonwealth of Pennsylvania, and his last place of business was located at [].

(2) Subsequent to February 2012, respondent's wife died suddenly, leaving him with two minors to care for.

(3) The sudden demise of respondent's spouse resulted in extreme mental trauma and shock to respondent thereafter.

(4) Respondent entered a period of severe depression and began heavy consumption of alcohol at or about the time of his wife's demise.

(5) Subsequent to March 2013, respondent attempted suicide and was in a state of severe psychotic depression.

(6) The suicide attempt closely paralleled the first anniversary of his wife's demise.

(7) During the period following his wife's death, and at all times material herein, respondent suffered an impairment of judgment and a diminished mental capacity.

(8) During the period of impaired judgment and diminished mental capacity, respondent committed the wrongful acts hereinafter set forth.

(9) All conditions precedent and contained in the aforesaid Agreement of Sale have been met, have been waived by defendant's aforesaid conduct or have been prevented by the defendant's aforesaid conduct.

(10) The court requested further investigation as to whether decedent was ever married or had issue. Mr. Lochner questioned, *inter alia*, whether decedent's father, Robert F. Atkinson, was in fact the uncle of Franklin A. Allen, and mentioned other possible discrepancies in the family tree. Mr. Lochner's correspondence was referred to the trustee ad litem. Franklin A. Allen died testate on March 19, 2014.

(11) In that case, where plaintiff sued a bank for conversion of checks payable to plaintiff which were paid over alleged forged endorsements to plaintiff's bookkeeper, the bank's joinder of plaintiff's accounting firm alleging negligence in permitting the embezzlement may be properly dismissed since the theory of such joinder was distinct and unrelated to the theory of plaintiff's original complaint. Moreover, the defendant and additional defendant are not joint tortfeasors.

(12) This court should not allow the lower court's decision to stand. You have a duty to protect kids from dangerous people like the defendant. You also have a duty to support the cops, who work hard to catch people like the defendant. If you don't overturn the lower court's decision in this case, you'll negate everything we prosecutors work for. The defendant didn't even provide an excuse for her actions. Our case against her should be the winner here.

§ 9.03. STRUCTURE

When you put sentences together, the most important guideline is to limit each sentence to one thought. Plan your sentences before you commit them to paper. After several weeks of intensive research and thought about a problem, you may find yourself trying to say too much too quickly. The result can be long, rambling, almost "stream of consciousness" strings of words that obscure the central idea. Here are some ways to avoid this result.

1. Write Short Sentences

The easiest way to keep your writing clear and readable is to write short sentences. The basic sentence includes a subject, a verb, and usually an object. In most cases those elements are all you need to express a single idea. Choose your words with care and work to communicate rather than impress. You then should have no trouble writing short, precise sentences, and your reader will understand you quickly and easily.

Bad: In this case, there was no public controversy involving the concert because the concert affected only its small number of participants, and even if there was plaintiff did not thrust himself to the forefront of the controversy—he was involuntarily drawn into it either by virtue of his position as promoter of the concert or by the defendant's cablecast.

Better: In this case no public controversy involving the concert existed. The concert affected only its small number of participants. If a public controversy existed, plaintiff did not thrust himself into it. He was involuntarily drawn into it, either because of his position as the concert's promoter or because of the defendant's cablecast.

––––––––––

Bad: The court in its opinion, however, found that the record indicated that hospital security was "more lax than it could have been," sufficiently so that the court decided to hold the hospital liable based solely on the issues of law presented in the pleadings, and on the facts as revealed in the deposed testimony of the hospital's own employees.

Better: However, the court found that, according to the record, hospital security was "more lax than it could have been." Therefore, it held the hospital liable solely on the pleadings and on the facts revealed in the depositions of the hospital's employees.

––––––––––

Bad: Appellant's failure to respond to the motion, however, goes to the heart of the suit, and, if he is allowed to ignore proper procedure, the judicial process will be threatened with paralysis as the court will be unable to determine when it is appropriate to assume no response will be forthcoming from appellant.

Better: Appellant did not respond to the motion. This failure goes to the heart of the suit, because it paralyzes the judicial process. When a court does not know whether a litigant plans to respond to a pleading, it is unable to proceed.

The repairs to these sentences took several forms: dividing the long sentence into several smaller sentences, removing unnecessary phrases, and rewording sentences to make them more direct. Correcting one long sentence occasionally results in a longer discussion. It is an acceptable result to have more words and sentences if the final product is clearer.

Not all the revised sentences are short one-clause sentences. Legal writing does not look like the text of a book for grade school children. If you need to use a complex sentence, use it. First, however, try to reduce your ideas to short sentences that flow.

2. Put the Parts of Your Sentence in a Logical Order

One of the most common errors writers make is failing to put sentences together in a logical sequence.

Bad: First, this court properly dismissed plaintiff's claim for fraud since plaintiff's injury, the job loss, was due to the use of information by the employer supplied by the defendant and not due to the defendant's alleged misrepresentation.

Better: First, this court properly dismissed plaintiff's claim for fraud since plaintiff's job loss was not due to the defendant's alleged misrepresentation, but rather to the employer's use of information that the defendant supplied.

Comment: Rewriting this sentence as at least two shorter sentences would be an even greater improvement.

The problem stems from "stream of consciousness" writing. Sometimes thoughts make perfect sense in a certain order in your mind but become confusing when you write them. The problem generally results from not planning sentences and trying to put too many ideas into too few words.

Avoid confusing sentences by taking the time to read what you have just written. Put yourself in the reader's shoes. Will the reader understand the sentence easily? Will the reader understand it more easily if you place the ideas in a different sequence, perhaps a sequence more chronological or logical?

The best way to catch logical errors is to put the writing aside for a while and read it later when you have greater objectivity. Then, be willing to revise it. One of the writer's hardest tasks is to proofread with a willingness to make substantial changes. It also is one of the most profitable.

Here is another example.

Bad: Any disposition of property to a third person who had notice of the pendency of the matrimonial action or who paid wholly inadequate consideration for such property may be deemed fraudulent and declared void.

Better: A court can declare fraudulent and void any disposition of property to a third person when the third person knew that a matrimonial action was pending or when that person paid wholly inadequate consideration for the property.

3. Avoid Intrusive Phrases and Clauses

Writers sometimes burden their sentences with clauses and phrases that are not needed to convey the main idea. These inserts break the sentence flow and create difficulty for the reader. Intrusive phrases appear when writers rush onto paper the many thoughts cluttering their minds.

Bad: While the Third Circuit test is on its face similar, it can lead to results such as the issue at bar, that are inconsistent with the limited public figure status determination by this Court in *Gertz.*

Better: While the Third Circuit test is facially similar to this Court's, it can lead to results that are inconsistent with this Court's definition of limited purpose public figure in *Gertz.*

Comment: The rewrite eliminates the intrusive phrase "such as the issue at bar." Awkward phrases "on its face" and "status determination" become the simpler words "facially" and "definition." To clarify the comparison between the tests of the two courts, the writer inserted "this Court's" in two appropriate locations.

———————

Bad: The Third Circuit erred in determining plaintiff was a limited purpose public figure, because in reality, under the approach taken by the United States Supreme Court, plaintiff at best would be classified as an involuntary public figure at the extreme.

Better: The Third Circuit erred in determining that plaintiff was a limited purpose public figure. Under the Supreme Court's approach, plaintiff is an involuntary public figure at best.

Comment: The rewrite eliminated the intrusive phrase "in reality." The passive "could be classified as" became "is." For further clarification, the long sentence became two shorter sentences.

Bad: With keeping the above in mind, the court of appeals notes that Plaintiff thrust himself into the public eye by actively seeking publicity for the event.

Better: As the court of appeals noted, plaintiff thrust himself into the public eye by actively seeking publicity for the event.

Comment: The phrase eliminated, "with keeping the above in mind," could almost be described as "throat clearing" before getting to the point.

Writers occasionally use intrusive phrases as a substitute for more detailed analysis. Avoid phrases like "such as the issue at bar" in the first example. Instead, make the comparison in a clear and concrete way. Other phrases, such as those removed from the second and third examples, serve no useful purpose and may create confusion.

4. Use Full Sentences

The occasional result of convoluted phrasing and writing too fast is a sentence that is not a sentence at all. Here are some examples:

- The estate failed to meet its evidentiary burden because sufficient evidence from which the trial court could have reasonably concluded that the decedent's death was the result of preexisting animosity between the assailant and the decedent.
- A position that this Court soundly rejected in *Gertz.*
- The way in which the average person viewing the statement in its intended circumstances is of critical import.

5. Use Parallel Structure

Maintain a consistent structure when joining phrases or clauses. Writers sometimes change verb tenses or use different introductory words for clauses that require the same word.

Bad: The hospital owes its invitees reasonable protection or to warn its invitees to the potential acts of third parties.

Better: The hospital owes its invitees reasonable protection or a warning about the potential acts of third parties.

Comment: The writer shifted from the noun "protection" to the verb "to warn" when discussing what the hospital owed its invitees. Using two nouns makes the sentence correct and comprehensible.

––––––––––

Bad: The plaintiff did not allege that the defendant acted specifically for the plaintiff to lose his job, but rather acted to induce the plaintiff's cooperation.

Better: The plaintiff did not allege that the defendant acted with the specific intent to have the plaintiff lose his job. He alleged only that the defendant acted to induce plaintiff's cooperation.

Comment: The failure to include some form of the verb "allege" in both parts of the sentence made the original sentence difficult to understand. Dividing the sentence into two shorter sentences clarifies it further. However, the final version still takes some effort for the reader to understand. Although revising complicated sentences makes them easier to understand, it does not remove the inherent complexity of the underlying idea. We can improve comprehensibility, but the reader still may have to do some work.

––––––––––

Bad: The security guard had no recollection of checking the laundry room doors before the murder and he also did not check the doors to the medical records office to see if they were locked.

Better: The security guard did not recollect checking the laundry room doors or the doors to the medical records office before the murder to see if they were locked.

Comment: In the first version, the combination of "had no recollection of checking" and "he also did not check" makes the sentence more complicated than it needs to be.

––––––––––

Bad: The definition established three criteria: there must exist a public controversy, into which an individual has become voluntarily or involuntarily involved for the purpose of assuming special prominence in the resolution of that issue within the controversy.

Better: The definition established three criteria: (1) a public controversy must exist; (2) the individual must become involved in that controversy voluntarily or involuntarily; and (3) the individual must intend to assume special prominence in the resolution of the controversy.

Comment: When providing a list, make sure the elements of the list are immediately apparent to the reader.

As you can see, mistakes involving parallel structure often center around verbs. Writers either use too many verbs in different forms or do not repeat the necessary verbs when they should.

§ 9.04. CONTENT

This section focuses on choosing the right words. Make sure that you choose the words that express your idea most precisely. Your words also must be appropriate for your medium of communication and your audience. They should be more formal and technical for briefs and memoranda and less formal for letters to clients. Writers sometimes choose words that obscure meaning, that are inappropriate for their intended audience, and, occasionally, that do not mean what the writers intended. Careful attention to your own writing will help you avoid these problems.

1. Use Positives Rather Than Negatives

If you emphasize the positive and avoid qualifiers, the reader probably will understand you better. Your writing also will set a tone that encourages the reader to agree with you. If you sound as if you believe what you are saying, the reader will be more likely to believe you.

Sometimes a negative word or phrase is necessary to express an idea precisely or to emphasize a point. However, use care to prevent a negative from making your message unclear or incorrect. Some writers use negatives when they are unnecessary or inappropriate. Occasionally, a writer will commit that unpardonable sin that our first grammar teachers warned us against—the double negative.

Here is an example of an awkward use of negatives:

The district court exercised its discretion in allowing seventeen days to pass before treating our opponent's nonresponse as not contesting the motion.

The sentence conveys the same idea but is easier to understand if phrased as follows:

When our opponent failed to respond, the district court exercised its discretion in allowing seventeen days to pass before treating the motion as uncontested.

Another aspect of using positive rather than negative language is the avoidance of qualifying words. Students and lawyers are sometimes less than totally confident in their positions. They reflect their insecurity in their choice of words. Avoid phrases like "it would seem," "it would appear," and "we would argue." These phrases are rarely necessary. They may even highlight areas of your argument that are particularly vulnerable.

2. Avoid Ambiguous Words and Phrases

Students and young lawyers have a natural desire to "sound like lawyers." They sometimes use ambiguous words or phrases that obscure the intended meaning but sound more "professional." Sometimes you will want to obscure the exact meaning of your message, such as when you make an argument that is less than airtight, but normally you should strive for clarity and ease of understanding. In the following examples, the writers failed to convey their meaning clearly. It is therefore not possible to rewrite the sentences in "better" form.

Bad: In such cases as *Hutchinson* and *Wolston*, this Court stressed that it is not the quantity of the relationship of the individual to the media but also the quality to which the individual subjects himself to the public.

Comment: Although there are several problems with this sentence, one of the most glaring is that the words "quantity" and "quality" are virtually meaningless. Although, in this context, these words may have a particular meaning for the writer, they do not have the same meaning for the reader. In trying to set up a stylistic contrast, the writer leaves the reader at a loss in trying to determine what the writer means.

Bad: However, as stated earlier in reference to access to the media, this would be inconsistent with this Court in the position taken in *Time* for much of the same rationale.

Comment: The writer is trying to reinforce a point made earlier without actually making the point again. The result is an almost indecipherable sentence that requires the reader to do far too much work. If you need to repeat yourself or to refer to an earlier point and explain it briefly, do so.

Bad: Plaintiff, for the most part, pleaded only conclusions that, while they may indicate that the end result of defendant's actions was outrageous conduct, do not indicate facts that show that his actions were outrageous conduct in themselves.

Comment: The writer repeats the phrase "outrageous conduct" but gives the reader no clue to what it means. The writer must provide more information.

Bad: Defendant's interview with plaintiff did not constitute the severity of an ultimatum found in *Richette*.

Bad: The defendant did not constitute an employee.

Comment: The misuse of the word "constitute" in the examples above represents the affinity some writers have for words they do not quite understand. When in doubt, use a dictionary or use simpler words that express the same idea. For example, the writer could reword the second sentence above to say "[T]he defendant was not an employee."

3. Avoid Colloquialism

Although we often hear that we should write the way we speak, certain words and phrases should rarely find their way onto paper. You can rely on common sense to identify language that is inappropriate for a written document. For example, you should not say that a court has "come up with" a particular definition. You also should avoid contractions such as "can't," "don't," and "won't." They are too conversational for the vast majority of written documents you will prepare. Here is an example from a student brief that demonstrates language you should avoid:

While these matters might be interesting to some people, the events of a small loosely run beauty pageant would hardly make a dent in the priority list of the public at large. Most people don't know when the pageant is held and a great number don't really care.

4. Do Not Personalize

Some writers cannot resist the temptation to refer either to themselves or to their readers with pronouns such as "I," "we," "our," or "you." These words may be appropriate for this book, but they are not appropriate in formal legal writing. Phrases such as "we submit," "I believe," or "our position is" only weaken your argument by reminding the reader that you are making arguments. When writing a brief or memorandum, make your arguments sound like statements of law rather than statements of personal opinion. A judge or a senior attorney may not care about your personal opinion. That judge or attorney wants to know what the law is and how it applies to your case.

When referring to the court to which a brief is addressed, use "this court." In a memorandum, you may refer to a senior attorney as "you," but many attorneys consider the pronoun too informal even for interoffice memoranda. It is safer to avoid its use. You also should avoid the more formal and often awkward "one."

5. Avoid Excessive Variation

Many students learn to use a different word every time they refer to the same person or thing. Using different words and phrases to refer to the same thing serves the laudable goal of preventing the reader from getting bored by repetition. Excessive variation, however, backfires. It is unaesthetic and sometimes comical. It also creates confusion when the writer uses inaccurate words rather than repeating accurate ones.

Legal terms of art offer an example. In torts, "standard of care" has a precise meaning that many court decisions have developed. If you use the phrase "standard of negligence" rather than repeat the term of art, the educated legal reader will not understand what you are saying. Excessive variation creates ambiguity.

In the following example, confusion results because the writer uses different words to refer to the same litigants.

> According to the record, Sam Spade had never before met the plaintiff. Although the plaintiff alleges that Mr. Spade already possessed some information about the plaintiff, there is no indication of any reason why this information might lead our client to maliciously intend to injure the appellant or to inflict losses upon him.

You might think that this excerpt mentions four people. It actually mentions two. "Sam Spade" and "our client" are the same person, as are "plaintiff" and "appellant."

In summary, the lessons are twofold. First, avoid boring the reader with repetition. Be creative, but do not overdo it. Second, be repetitive rather than imprecise or confusing.

Exercises

The following exercises are sentences taken from student briefs and memos. They give you an opportunity to put into practice some of the principles discussed above. Identify the errors and, to the extent possible, rewrite the sentences to eliminate those errors. You may have some difficulty rewriting some of the sentences as the author would have since they are taken out of context. Do the best you can.

(1) However, since the issue has been raised it has become necessary to demonstrate that even though a second motion to dismiss was not required, by submitting a letter of request to the judge and providing opposing counsel with a copy of the letter, the judge correctly found that the letter was sufficient to comply with all applicable rules of procedure regarding motions.

(2) The fundamental principle of the Fourth Amendment is ensuring "one's privacy against arbitrary intrusions by the police," *Wolf v. Colorado*, 338 U.S. 25, 27 (1949), and "intended as a restraint upon the activities of sovereign authority, and was not intended to be a limitation upon other than governmental agencies. . . ." *Burdeau v. McDowell*, 256 U.S. 465, 475 (1921).

(3) Taking into consideration the Pennsylvania Rules of Civil Procedure, which limit the amount of time in which an affirmative request for a jury trial must be made and the rulings of the courts in these cases concerning the implications of failing to file for a jury trial at all, it would be difficult, after not requesting a jury trial within the past 30 days and the trial date approaching so soon, to convince the court to allow Olive Holmes's case to be heard by a jury.

(4) The question thus is whether our client's promise that she would return to talk to the police signified voluntary willingness to be confined, or whether the Dean's refusal to allow her to leave is a detaining force sufficient from which she has no legal obligation to resist in order to prove lack of consent.

(5) In *Medico*, the court held that a press defendant could relieve itself of liability without establishing the truth of the substance of the statement reported by claiming the fair report privilege when its publication contains matters of public concern and is based on acts of the executive or administrative officials or governmental reports.

(6) Ms. Holmes can establish the tort of false imprisonment against the Law School due to the fact that Ms. Holmes's nonconsensual confinement by the school dean can be predicated as false imprisonment since Ms. Holmes was exonerated of the charge establishing the basis for the school dean's confinement of Ms. Holmes.

(7) The security guard deposed that the assailant entered the hospital through the emergency room when he confronted him about an hour before the murder and that there was no other security guard on duty who was monitoring the emergency entrance.

(8) Insofar as the court moved for a summary judgment in the Estate's favor based on the evidence in the depositions, it decided that a negligent breach of duty was shown as a matter of law and that the only reasonable inference was that its negligence, and not the criminal act of the assailant, was the proximate, legal cause of plaintiff's death.

(9) The state's patient-physician privilege imputes such information as being highly confidential and personal.

(10) The key issue to be determined is whether the Law School's answer to the complaint for false imprisonment is the last pleading directed to such issue or whether the dean's answer to the Law School's third party complaint for indemnification is not the last pleading directed to that issue, but only to the issue of indemnity.

(11) Nor is there liability if the plaintiff fails to show that the private matter of the alleged publicity is not of legitimate public concern.

CHAPTER 10

Meeting the Client

§ 10.01. INTRODUCTION

You may wonder why we talk about client interviewing and counseling in a text about legal research and writing. We do this because we want you to always remember why you research and write. Almost all lawyering work is done in the service of clients (except for government lawyers such as prosecutors, although in some sense "the people" are their clients). Keep this in mind, even when you are not working for real clients.

Most first-year legal writing programs introduce the idea that the information lawyers work with comes from clients. Some programs stage interviews for students to observe, while others allow the students to actually do the interviewing. Others do not require you to actually interview someone to get the information you need to write your memorandum or other legal writing assignments. Even if you get the facts that form the basis of your assignments from a piece of paper, you should remember that in the real world, legal research and writing are based on the information provided by clients, which may be incomplete, self-serving, or confusing.

We offer this introduction to the process of gathering information from clients to better prepare you to get the information you need to research and write documents that will provide the best possible assistance to your clients.

§ 10.02. PURPOSE OF THE INITIAL INTERVIEW

As you plan for the initial interview with a client, ask yourself what you need to accomplish in that interview. Remember that the client is not a walking, talking legal problem, but a living, breathing human being with feelings, goals, and priorities, who happens to have a current problem that may have some legal dimensions. Of course you do need to ascertain the scope of the problem that brings the client to you, but you need to find out more than the legally relevant facts. You need to understand the client. What kind of person is the client? What does he or she hope to accomplish by coming to see a lawyer?

You also need to lay the groundwork for a working relationship. Clients need to feel comfortable with you. They need to be able to trust that you will handle the problem appropriately and with sensitivity. Since the only way you will be able to make a living as a lawyer is if clients retain you, you must sell yourself. In most cases, you do not sell yourself best by overselling yourself. You sell yourself best by creating trust, by opening the channels of communication in both directions, and by conveying confidence and competence.

Remember that this is also a business relationship. It is sometimes difficult to bring up the subject of money when a client is presenting you with what may be the most pressing and difficult situation in his or her life at that moment. If you do not address the business aspects of the relationship early on, however, you open yourself up to the very real possibility of misunderstandings and unnecessary problems later. Although this may sound obvious, you need to get a clear commitment from the client to hire you before you begin working on the client's behalf.

The client will also likely want an initial assessment of the legal situation. Clients frequently ask questions such as "What are my rights?" "Can he do that?" "How can I get my money back?" "Will I have to go to jail?" Because you are a lawyer, clients expect you to have the answers to those questions. As you go through law school, you learn that there are far more questions than answers, and that you have to do research before you can answer most questions. One of the most delicate tasks to accomplish with a new client is to let the client know that you need more information, both factual and legal, before you can give an accurate answer to the problem. At the same time, you should try to give the client some idea of what might happen. What are some available dispute resolution options? How does the legal system treat these kinds of problems? Can you provide a preliminary assessment of the client's problem based on your existing legal knowledge?

§ 10.03. PLANNING THE INITIAL INTERVIEW

Here are some goals for an initial interview with a client:

- Get the facts.
- Get to know the client.
- Understand the client's feelings, goals, and priorities.
- Begin building trust.
- Explain your fees.
- Get hired.
- Offer a preliminary assessment of the problem.

You cannot accomplish these tasks without a plan. This is not the type of conversation where you can just sit back and see where it goes. As you gain more experience, you will develop a pattern for approaching interviews that allows you to accomplish your goals, but at first you must consciously structure your approach to the conversation. Plan a strategy for building trust, getting information, getting the client to retain you, and beginning to address the client's problem. It is probably a good idea to have a written form of some kind in front of you that reminds you of the various components of the initial interview. The rest of this chapter offers advice on how to structure the initial interview so you do not forget any critical steps.

§ 10.04. GREETING THE CLIENT

It may sound artificial to suggest that you plan your greeting to the client. However, as we all know, first impressions are frequently lasting impressions, and you should consider whether you want the client's first impression of you to be that you are cold, calculating, and money-hungry, or that you are a considerate, caring human being. You will be easier to confide in if you spend a bit of time in casual conversation about neutral topics such as the weather or traffic or similar "elevator" conversation. It may seem awkward and forced, particularly at first, but it does allow the client to settle down, assess the surroundings, and prepare to discuss more difficult topics. If you seem comfortable and genuinely interested in a relaxed approach to the conversation, usually the client will follow your lead. You will find it easier to get information if the tension level in your office is low.

Be careful about accomplishing your atmospheric goal by commenting on any aspect of the client's appearance. Besides being a bit personal, you never know what might be a sensitive subject. For example, if the client is coming to you about a divorce, you may start the interview off on exactly the wrong note by commenting on what a beautiful diamond ring she is wearing.

§ 10.05. PREPARATORY EXPLANATION

It is generally a good idea to offer a roadmap of the interview before you start questioning the client. You might ask whether the client has ever seen a lawyer before, as a means of gauging what the client's expectations are likely to be. If the client has never seen a lawyer before, it is a good idea to outline the procedure you intend to follow during the interview. For example, explain how long the interview is likely to last, what your goals are, that you will be asking questions and taking notes, that the client will have a chance to ask questions, that you will try to begin developing options for resolving the client's problem, and that you will discuss the likely cost of handling the problem. You may also want to remind the client of your ethical obligations relating to confidentiality.

If the client has seen a lawyer before, it is a good idea to get a feel for whether that was a positive or negative experience. If the client comes in skeptical or suspicious about lawyers because of a previous bad experience, it is helpful for you to know that sooner rather than later. If the client has had prior negative experience with attorneys, your goal is to persuade the client that you are a valuable ally, not a necessary evil. You can best do this by taking the time to show the client that you care about him or her as a whole person, not just as a legal problem or a source of money.

§ 10.06. GETTING THE CLIENT'S PERSPECTIVE

As lawyers, we frequently are in a hurry to find out what the legal problem is. We are trained in law school to spot issues, to sift through the facts presented until we find the ones that matter, and then offer an analysis of how the law applies to those facts. That is only a small part of what you must accomplish with a client. Avoid the temptation to become impatient when the client seems to ramble or starts talking about feelings. You cannot adequately represent a client without knowing how the client feels about the problem, what the client hopes to accomplish in coming to see you, and what the client's priorities are.

You will be tempted to substitute your own value system for the client's, causing you to think about how you would handle the problem if it were yours. It is not your problem, and you must never lose sight of that fact, even if the client tries to hand you the problem.

Clients frequently come to you and ask "What should I do?" The only good answer to that question is the one the client arrives at after being given a full understanding of the likely consequences of different approaches. Your job is to inform the client so that he or she can make a decision based on his or her own value system. You will do this more effectively if you understand the client's perspective on the problem.

1. Getting Started

The easiest way to begin the interview is to ask a simple, open question such as, "What brings you here today?" Or "How can I help you?" Let the client know that you want to hear the story in his or her own words and then let the client tell it. Resist the temptation to break in with constant questions. If you are afraid you will forget to ask about a needed detail, jot it down. If you derail the client's story with questions, you may end up missing key facts or elements in the story. Do not try to put legal labels on the client's problem too soon: "Oh, this is a contracts problem." If you do that you will start focusing on questions you were trained to ask about contracts, and you may never find out that the client has also brought you a tax problem and a criminal problem, or you may find out at a time and in a manner that is awkward and difficult.

If the client has difficulty knowing where to start, you might suggest a time frame. "Start at the beginning." "What event made you decide to come see a lawyer?" If the client offers unhelpful generalizations such as "I have a problem with my partner," then you want to try a few direct questions to get the story going. "Do you mean a business partner?" "What kind of business do you have?" "Does the problem relate to the business?" Once the client gets into the story, stop the questions and let the client talk.

2. Keeping Track

It is difficult to balance your need to keep track of information the client is giving you with the client's need to feel that you are listening. You will probably want to take some notes, but try not to spend the entire session staring at your legal pad as you write. Eye contact is a very important part of the conversation, not only for the client but for you. You may gain valuable clues to the client's personality and sensitive aspects of the problem by watching the nonverbal channels of communication. If you can, listen for a while and then write down only the most important aspects of the story. Jot down details such as names and dates, but don't try to record every word the client says. If you do not think that you will be able to accurately remember the client's message if you wait too long, ask the client if you may record the conversation. Having a tape recording will free you to really concentrate on the client's message and the way it is being communicated.

3. Getting the Details

You do need some details. You need detailed information about the client, including addresses and phone numbers so that you will be able to contact him or her throughout your handling of the matter. You may also need names, addresses, and phone numbers of other individuals who are involved in the matter or who may be potential witnesses. You need dates, times, places, and relevant documents. Thus you will need to ask focused, closed questions at some point in the interview. Try not to interrogate the client. If the client becomes defensive, you will likely not get information you need. It is a good idea to explain to the client why you need so much information. You may also want to have a written questionnaire for the client to take home, at least for cases such as divorce or bankruptcy, where you need a great deal of detail about personal and financial matters.

Try to get a chronological version of events. Ask for the sequence of events, and ask for dates. Find out who else is involved, and who else knows what is going on. Find out if there are any documents you need to look at and if the client can get them for you. It is a good idea to recap the client's story, perhaps several times, depending on the complexity of the story and the organization (or lack of organization) of the information provided. Telling the client what you have understood lets the client know that you were listening, and often provides an opportunity to get additional information. You may discover that you got some aspect of the story wrong, or your recap may prompt the client to fill in gaps in the story.

You will also need information the client may not think to give you because the client does not know it is important. Clients do not know the law or may have incorrect ideas about what the law says. Therefore they may have a different idea of what information is relevant than you do. They may also have personal reactions or priorities that give them a different sense of what is relevant or important. For example, it may be very important to the client that you understand that he was treated disrespectfully, while that fact may have no legal significance. Do not dismiss facts that the client thinks are important, but stay focused enough to get the facts you need.

The client may be embarrassed about certain facts; the client wants you to think that he or she is a good person and has a good case, so there may be a temptation not to tell you about things that reflect negatively on the client's character or the case. Remind the client that what is said to you will be kept in confidence (subject to certain exceptions such as information relating to imminent harm to another, which you may disclose), and that you can provide the best possible representation only if you have the full story. It is frequently a good idea to ask the client what the other party is likely to say about the situation. This allows the client to give you necessary and possibly damaging information without having to acknowledge its accuracy or validity.

4. Goals and Priorities

We have emphasized the need to get the client's perspective on the problem and potential solutions. How do you accomplish this? The simplest way is to ask: "What would you like to see happen?" or, "If you had to choose between X and Y, which would you choose?" The client may not have thought about the answers to these questions, assuming that you would tell him or her what to do or what would happen next. Do not succumb to the temptation to do that; explain the importance of understanding the client's wants and needs to your representation. If you do not accomplish this important step, you may very well present the client with what you think is a very good settlement offer, only to have the client reject it because it does not meet some fundamental need you were unaware of. For example, in a defamation case, if you think the client wants as much money as possible but it turns out the primary concern is the client's reputation, you may get a good monetary settlement but not push for an apology or retraction or some other measure that might rehabilitate the client's damaged reputation. These are the kinds of misunderstandings that lead to malpractice actions.

§ 10.07. PRELIMINARY ASSESSMENT OF THE CLIENT'S PROBLEM

You should try to offer a preliminary assessment of the client's problem, at least to the extent of determining whether it is an appropriate situation for legal intervention. Some problems simply do not lend themselves to legal solutions (some neighborhood or family disputes come to mind), or you may find that the client presents a problem you are not qualified or do not wish to handle. If so, you should tell the client that. If you think the client presents a problem with potential, you need to be honest about your expertise in the area. There is no shame in needing to do research or further investigation before deciding how to proceed with a matter, and you need to develop the confidence to present this need for further inquiry as part of your competence rather than something you need to apologize for. You should, however, share with the client any judgments you are able to make about likely actions or events that might resolve the client's problem, and you should offer some assessment of the likelihood that the client's goals can be met. You should also be very clear that these assessments are preliminary and may very well change as additional facts and law are discovered.

§ 10.08. DEVELOPING OPTIONS

Once you have preliminarily assessed the client's problem, you may begin a discussion of options to be pursued. For example, you can try to get a sense of whether the client is interested in litigating the matter or prefers a more amicable and informal resolution such as negotiation or mediation. You should take any nonlegal concerns of the client (such as a desire for an apology or to redeem his reputation) into account in developing the options, and you should encourage the client to participate in this process with you. Has the client thought about desirable outcomes, and possibly even ways to accomplish them? As you begin to develop options, explore the likely consequences of pursuing each option. What are the advantages and disadvantages? How likely is it that the option will actually work out? For example, if the dispute involves a lot of anger or other negative emotions on both sides, a quick and amicable negotiated resolution is unlikely.

§ 10.09. FEES

As we said previously, you must deal with the subject of money. There are several ways to structure fee agreements. You may bill your time at an hourly rate or charge a flat fee. In an appropriate case, where you are hoping to recover a sum of money for the client, you may take your fee out of the recovery. This is called a contingent fee because you will not get paid if the client does not recover. Many jurisdictions require that you present the client with a written statement of your fees at the outset of the relationship, at least in matters where you intend to charge a contingent fee.

You should put in writing your entire agreement with the client about the scope of your representation, including fees. This is called a retainer agreement. Even if it is not required, it demonstrates good business sense to agree in writing with the client what you will and will not do. In addition, signing the agreement will bring home to the client the necessity of paying the fee.

Most clients understand that this is a business relationship, and they will be relieved to get that part of the transaction out of the way. All you have to sell is your time and expertise, and you should not be embarrassed about that fact. If a client genuinely cannot pay or wants to work out a contingency arrangement, you will have to decide whether this is an appropriate case to handle on a reduced-fee or pro bono basis, or whether any possible recovery justifies the contingency fee. Regardless of the fee arrangement you work out, you should present it to the client in writing and get it signed, so that it is clear from the outset what you will be charging and what the client has agreed to pay.

When do you bring up the subject of money? It is not advisable to start the interview by talking about fees. This is partly because you will only reinforce negative stereotypes of "moneygrubbing" lawyers by doing so, and partly because you cannot possibly assess the most appropriate fee structure or the likely ultimate cost to the client without having some sense of what the problem is. We advise you to get the client's story and begin the assessment process before you get to the subject of fees. The beginning of the discussion regarding your client's legal and nonlegal options is a very logical point at which to bring up the subject of cost.

Remember that the client's ultimate cost concern will be the total amount of money needed to resolve the problem, so do not simply quote your hourly rate, if that is how you propose to charge the client. Try to estimate the likely total cost of the case, always remembering (and telling the client) that the final cost will depend on many factors that you may not be able to anticipate right now, such as the stubbornness of the other side, whether the other party hires a lawyer who likes to generate lots of paper and drag things out, the difficulty of finding necessary witnesses and evidence, and the like. At a minimum provide an estimate of the cost of handling the initial stage(s) of the matter. For example, tell the client how long it will take you to conduct preliminary research and generate a letter explaining the situation to the client or to other involved parties.

§ 10.10. CLOSING THE INTERVIEW

At the end of the interview, it can be very easy to simply end the conversation and say good-bye. This may be the most important point in the interview for the client's long-term confidence in you, if you handle it correctly. Clients' most frequent complaint about their lawyers is that lawyers do not keep them informed about the process. Clients who are insecure about the status of their case and who do not understand the steps in the process may make frequent phone calls to get answers. Nervous clients may make phone calls anyway, but well-informed clients should be less likely to contact their attorneys when there is nothing happening in the case that justifies contact.

Do not let the client leave without carefully explaining what happens next, when it will happen, and whose responsibility it is. If you are going to contact the attorney for the other side, tell the client when you will do so, and when you will let the client know about any response you receive. Give the client some "homework." This may sound odd, but if there is a way the client can help with the case, perhaps by retrieving documents or phone numbers, you give the client some measure of control over a difficult problem, which is usually reassuring. Handling the end of the interview in a concrete way gives the client confidence in you and gives you specific and immediate goals to achieve on behalf of the client.

Remember that you must also formalize the attorney-client relationship and confirm that the client wants you to handle the matter. If the client has not decided to hire you, do not agree to do any work for the client, unless the terms and conditions under which you will do some work are clearly specified, preferably in writing. Set a time frame within which the client must decide to hire you or you will close the file. This should help to reduce the possibility of misunderstandings about whether you were hired, the scope of your representation, and any deadlines involved. The best possible scenario is that you give the client a written retainer agreement that includes fees, and it is signed on the spot, or the client agrees to return it to you within a few days.

Exercise

Here is a draft intake form for an interview with a client who is coming to see you about a personal injury case. The only thing you know before the interview is that the injury is the result of an automobile accident. What would you add to this form? Is there another approach to structuring the interview that makes more sense to you? How will you begin the interview? What kinds of questions will you start with? What kinds of details will you need? What do you need to know about the law of your jurisdiction (e.g., is yours a comparative or contributory negligence jurisdiction)? What sorts of documents might be available that will help you prepare the case? What sorts of fee agreements might be appropriate? Write out your answers to these questions and redraft the form so you could actually use it effectively during the interview.

Client Intake Form

Name:
Address:
Phone number(s):
Email address:
Client's description of events:

Date of accident:

Other parties:

Potential witnesses:

Client's stated goal(s):

Fee structure discussed and agreed to:

§ 10.11. CLIENT INTERVIEW CHECKLIST

— Planning the initial interview: How will you get necessary information? What topics do you need to cover? Do you have fee agreements ready to be executed?

— Greeting the client: How might you best put the client at ease? Does the client seem nervous or eager to get down to business?

— Preparatory explanation: Roadmap the interview; talk about process and confidentiality.

— Getting the client's perspective: Ask about the client's goals and priorities. Let the client tell the story his or her own way! Ask what the client would like to see happen.

— Preliminary assessment: Is this problem appropriate for legal action? Is it a problem you are qualified or prepared to handle? How much additional legal or factual research do you need to do?

— Developing options: Is this matter headed for litigation, or can it be resolved amicably? What ideas does the client have for resolving the problem? What are the advantages and disadvantages of pursuing various options?

— Fees: What fee structure is appropriate for handling this case? Did you get a written fee agreement signed? Did you give the client an estimate of the likely total cost of the matter?

— Closing the interview: Was it clear what will happen next, when it will happen, and whose responsibility it is? Did you ask the client to provide you with any information or documents? Does the client understand the immediate plan of action?

CHAPTER 11

Introduction to the Memo

§ 11.01. WHAT IS A MEMO?

The memorandum of law, or memo, is a traditional internal office document. It is a research tool that analyzes the law as it applies to the facts of a client's case and offers an unbiased evaluation.[1] A memo includes both helpful and damaging information. It suggests solutions to a legal problem or predicts the outcome of a dispute. It is the precursor to informed decision making about a case.

The memo once was the most basic of legal documents and was essential to the practice of law. In the modern practice of law, formal memos of the type we teach are not as common as they once were. Supervising attorneys may ask for the results of your research in a variety of formats. Your responses to those requests will vary in length and in approach, depending on how such communications are handled in your office.

Even though you may never write a formal memo that looks exactly like the ones we teach here, the analytical approach is important for you to learn. The steps you go through in preparing these memos are the same steps you should go through even if your written product is in a different format. The memos you write in your legal research and writing class will help your instructors determine whether you are learning the fundamentals of good legal analysis; they will serve as a gauge of your ability to analyze and present a legal problem. Once you master this type of writing, you will draft other kinds of legal documents with greater skill and ease.

This chapter introduces you to the memo. It describes the purposes of a memo, the parts of a memo, and the hallmarks of a well-written memo. Chapters 12, 13, 14, and 15 focus on the parts of a memo in more detail and demonstrate how to draft each section effectively.

§ 11.02. THE PURPOSES OF A MEMO

The purpose of a memo is to provide a realistic analysis of the law as it applies to the facts of the client's case. That analysis will be the basis for giving advice or making decisions about the case.

---

1. This chapter concerns interoffice memos only. There also are memoranda of law that are submitted to the court. They are more akin to briefs and should not be confused with the office memo.

A memo can serve many purposes. Its purpose determines how extensive the research should be, what the nature of the analysis should be, and how it should be written. The memo should be written to serve the specific purpose for which it was requested. By way of example, an attorney may use a memo to

- evaluate the merits of a case;
- decide whether to settle or try a case;
- decide whether to accept a case;
- inform the reader of the status of the law;
- present recommendations as to how to proceed with a case;
- conclude that more information is needed to properly evaluate the case;
- identify the legal theories applicable to the case;
- decide whether to file any motions;
- prepare for trial;
- form the legal foundation of motions, pleadings, and briefs;
- prepare a contract, will, settlement agreement, or corporate papers;
- prepare for negotiations; or
- prepare for an appeal.

The memos you prepare during the course of a case will provide a convenient summary of the facts, issues, legal theories, and arguments involved in the case. You and any other attorneys on the case will refer to them to refresh your memories as the case progresses.[2]

§ 11.03. THE PARTS OF A MEMO

The memo is a structured document that is divided into distinct but related sections. Each section is labeled and performs a particular function. Memos do not use a universal format or a mandatory order in which their parts appear. Many law firms, corporate legal departments, and government offices prescribe a standard form. You should find out whether your office uses a standard format or, if not, whether the attorney for whom you are preparing the memo prefers a certain format. Although there are many variations in the structure of a memo, the following format is widely used:

1. Heading
2. Brief statement of the issue to be discussed
3. Conclusion
4. Brief statement of the facts
5. Discussion of the pertinent authorities

Appendix I contains sample memoranda. Please review those memoranda in conjunction with this chapter.

---

2. Many law firms index and file the memoranda of law prepared by their attorneys. These memos are a valuable asset. A question may arise in a pending case that a previous memo already addresses. The attorney need only update the research in the memo. This procedure saves the attorney time and the client money.

1. The Heading

The heading indicates the type of document, the person to whom the memorandum is addressed, the person who wrote it, its date, and its subject matter, in the following form:

MEMORANDUM

TO:
FROM:
DATE:
SUBJECT: (or RE:)

2. The Issue

The issue, sometimes called the question presented, frames the legal question to be resolved by the memo. If there is more than one issue or several subparts to an issue, number each issue and subpart separately. The issue section of the memo informs the reader of the scope of the memo. A memo should not go beyond the scope of the issue.

3. The Conclusion

The conclusion, sometimes called the short answer, provides a complete, but brief, answer to the issue. At times an attorney will refer only to the conclusion, at least initially. The conclusion includes a concise statement of the reasons for your conclusion. It also orients the reader to the general thrust of the discussion. The conclusion does not contain a detailed discussion of how you reached the conclusion. Citations to authority and cross-references to the body of the memo are inappropriate. In a memo that discusses more than one issue, number the conclusions to reflect the issues to which they refer.

4. The Facts

This section requires a clear and concise statement of the facts relevant to the legal analysis presented by the memo. The facts let the reader know what happened. The purpose of the memo is to evaluate the soundness of a particular legal position given certain facts. Therefore, present the facts objectively and include both favorable and unfavorable information. Include all the facts that you will raise in the discussion section.

5. The Discussion

The discussion section is the heart of the memo. In it you analyze the pertinent legal authorities and apply them to the facts of the problem. If there is more than one issue, address each issue separately. The discussion, like the facts, should be objective, not argumentative. Evaluate both helpful and damaging authorities. At the end of the discussion, summarize the findings presented by the memo.

§ 11.04. THE HALLMARKS OF A WELL-WRITTEN MEMO

The purpose of a memo is to inform and explain. If your memo bears the hallmarks enumerated below, it will achieve this dual purpose.

1. Thorough Research

Thoroughly research the question you are assigned. Evaluate the law you find within the context of the facts of your case. Find and analyze all of the pertinent legal authorities, those that are helpful to your case and those that are damaging, to it. Do not cite or rely on any authority without critically reading it yourself. Treatises and encyclopedias state the law only in general terms. Look up the cases on which they rely. Never rely on headnotes to cases. Remember that major decisions about the case will be made based on your memorandum, and that incomplete or inaccurate research will have far-reaching implications.

2. Good Judgment

Be certain that the memorandum you prepare is what the assigning attorney wants. When you are given the assignment, be sure you understand what purpose the memo is to serve, when it is to be submitted, and how detailed it should be. Also be certain that you understand the question that you are to research. Even if the initial instructions are clear, problems may arise later. As your research progresses, the issue may take on a different focus, unanticipated questions may arise, or additional facts may become important. Return to the assigning attorney and resolve these problems. But use good judgment. Do not trouble the attorney with questions you should be able to resolve yourself or with the help of one of your peers.

3. Objective Analysis

A memo must be objective. This is as crucial as it is simple. Your analysis of the legal authorities must be realistic and comprehensive. Examine your own arguments. Evaluate those you anticipate from opposing counsel. Consider the issues from every perspective. Honestly and thoroughly assess the strengths and weaknesses of your position. A memo is not the forum for persuasion, or for advocacy. Major choices and decisions will be made on the basis of the memo you write. Those choices and decisions can be made intelligently only on the basis of an objective memo. Indeed, the client's interests would not be served if the appraisal of his position were anything less than scrupulously realistic and objective.

4. Clear Writing Style

A memo is a complete and independent document. Another attorney who reads it should be able to fully understand the matter and make a decision. The memo memorializes, for all future readers of the file, the reasons those handling the case chose a particular course of action. By now you have read enough cases in your classes to appreciate the importance of writing style. Any poorly written legal document leads to confusion and uncertainty. A memo should be precise, accurate, and well-organized to explain a legal question effectively.

a. Good Organization

The foundation of a good memo is careful, detailed organization. The memo must be organized and written so that your thoughts are clearly presented and precisely stated. Skillful writing, thoughtful analysis, and clear presentation will be wasted unless your work is organized intelligently. The reader should not have to work at comprehending your discussion. No one reads memos for entertainment. Your legal analysis and your approach to the problem should be apparent from your organization. Make the reader's task as easy as possible.

As with other types of legal writing, memo writing requires a particular organizational framework. State your conclusions first. Follow them with your reasoning. Use mechanical aids such as headings and subheadings to help you organize the memo.

As we discussed in Chapter 7, outlining is a necessary organizational technique and one that will save you time. Outlining forces you to develop your analysis one step at a time and will expose the gaps in your discussion. Chapters 12, 13, 14, and 15 will instruct you in the principles of organization as they apply to each section of the memo.

b. Write for the Reader

Analyze and consider the problem and your memo in detail. Remember that your primary audience is the attorney who requested it. You are not writing for yourself.

Include all of the facts that you were given when you were assigned the problem. Do not assume that because the assigning attorney is familiar with the matter, he or she will remember exactly what you were told. You must include every fact you rely on in your analysis.

Explain the significance of the legal authorities in the context of the facts of the problem. Be certain that your conclusions do not appear without the benefit of the analysis that preceded them. Your discussion must progress logically. Carefully and clearly guide the reader through the memo. One way to do this, as you learned in Chapter 8, is to provide the reader with a "roadmap," a guide to the discussion contained in the memo.

The memo is the end product of your exploration of the problem and its implications. Put yourself in the position of the person for whom you are writing the memo. Ask yourself whether your memo provides that person with a thoughtful analysis of the problem. Only when you are satisfied that the memo is complete, that it fully answers the question put to you, and that it is your best work, should you submit it.

c. Precision and Clarity

To communicate your thoughts effectively, you must be precise and clear. You have been asked to resolve a concrete problem. Make certain that you provide a concrete answer and specific reasons for it. Be precise about the facts and the law, but do not miss the forest for the trees. Make it clear why the authorities you rely on are relevant. Do not just tell the reader that they are pertinent. Show how those authorities apply to your case. Draw the conclusions yourself. When reading your memo, the reader should fully understand it and should be satisfied with your resolution of the problem.

5. Creativity

Your memo should present a comprehensive and organized analysis of the law in the context of the facts of your client's problem. On occasion, it might also display some legal creativity in regard to your recommendation for further action. When you are researching and writing the memo, be alert for alternative theories or creative approaches to the problem. Because you are the one who is most immersed in the issue and who is most aware of its permutations, you are the ideal person to provide a fresh perspective. Manifesting such creativity will demonstrate your initiative, even where your theory may ultimately not be workable.

6. Correct Citation Format

Your memo must include citations to the authorities on which you rely. Moreover, the cites must be complete, accurate, and in proper citation form. Correct citation form is important for at least two reasons. First, sloppy and incomplete citations give the reader cause to suspect that the substance of your analysis is equally weak. Second, if you include an inaccurate citation in the memo, you probably will copy that citation in subsequent documents that rely on the memo's research. Simply put, bad citations can haunt you and create an extremely negative impression of your work.

CHAPTER 12

The Memo: Heading, Issue, and Conclusion

As you learned in Chapter 11, the memo is a structured document that is divided into distinct sections. Each section has a label and performs a particular function. In Chapters 12, 13, 14, and 15, you will learn how to write each of these sections.

§ 12.01. THE HEADING

The heading uses the following format to set out the most basic information about the memo.

MEMORANDUM

To:	Leslie O'Brien-Wallace
FROM:	Michael R. North
DATE:	August 7, 2013
RE:	*Smith v. Lapp*; file no. 56432-007; Recovery for negligent infliction of emotional distress under Pennsylvania law.

The centered heading indicates that the document is a memorandum. "TO" indicates the person to whom the memorandum is addressed. "FROM" indicates who wrote the memorandum. Although practices vary from one office to the next, the recipient and the sender of the memo are usually referred to by their full names. Occasionally the tone is more formal and titles are used, for example, Ms./Miss/Mrs. O'Brien-Wallace and Mr. North. Do not include job titles such as senior partner or associate after the name of the recipient or sender.

"DATE" indicates the date you submitted the memo. Including the date is important. Any reader of the memo must be able to assume that the research and analysis contained in the memo are accurate and complete as of the date of the memo. The law, however, may have changed by the time you or another attorney next refer to the memo. The date will advise the reader whether the research requires updating.

"RE" indicates the subject matter of the memo. You may also see "SUBJECT" used instead of "RE." Include the case name, or the client name if no case is pending, and the office file number. Describe briefly and broadly the legal question the memo addresses. Because most case files contain a large number of documents, including numerous memoranda, this information will make it easy to locate a particular memorandum in the future. In addition, the explanation of the subject matter facilitates indexing and filing of the memorandum for general research purposes so that it may be used for future reference in other cases.

Suppose for purposes of illustration that you have just been called into the office of a more senior attorney and given the following facts.

> Wilbur Smith has retained the firm to file suit for injuries he sustained in an automobile accident. Mr. Smith also would like the firm to file suit on behalf of his fourteen-year-old daughter, Edna. Edna witnessed the automobile accident. The accident occurred on June 10, 2012. Mr. Smith had volunteered to take Edna to school. At 8:00 a.m. Mr. Smith dropped Edna off at school and drove away, intending to go to the grocery store. Edna waved good-bye to her father and turned to talk to some friends. As she was walking through the schoolyard with her friends, Edna heard a loud crash, followed by an explosion. When she turned to see what had happened, Edna saw that a car had collided with her father's car at an intersection one block away from the school. Her father's car was on fire. Edna ran to the scene of the accident. By the time she arrived, her father had been pulled from his car. Edna saw that her father had been severely burned and that he had a large gash on his forehead. Ever since the accident, Edna has suffered from recurring nightmares, a debilitating fear of automobiles, and chronic stomach problems. These conditions did not exist prior to the accident. An investigation of the accident disclosed that Mrs. Donna Lapp, the driver of the other car, had run a red light while intoxicated.

You have been asked to research whether, under these facts, Edna can make out a cause of action for negligent infliction of emotional distress under Pennsylvania law. The sample heading at the beginning of this section incorporates the information that would be required in the heading of the memo concerning this case.

Before writing the heading for your memo, review a few recent memos prepared by other attorneys in your office to determine the preferred style. You may find that there are minor variations from the format we describe.

§ 12.02. THE ISSUE

The memo begins with the issue section, also called the question presented. The issue section of the memo states the legal question presented in your case. Here is an example of an issue concerning the *Smith* case:

> Whether, under Pennsylvania law, a daughter who witnesses the aftermath of an automobile accident involving her father from a block away can recover for negligent infliction of emotional distress when she arrives at the scene and observes his severe injuries.

Here is another equally acceptable way to frame the issue:

> Under Pennsylvania law, can a daughter recover for negligent infliction of emotional distress if she is one block away when an automobile accident involving her father occurs

and, immediately after the accident, arrives at the scene and observes her father's severe injuries?

The issue section informs the reader of the scope of the memo. The scope of the memo should never exceed the scope of the issue. Frame the question precisely. Failure to do so will mislead the reader about the limits of your discussion and analysis.

Identifying the issue is the foundation of effective analysis. On some occasions, the attorney who requests the memo will identify the issue clearly for you. More often, you will be able to identify the precise issue only after you have thoroughly researched and thoughtfully analyzed the problem. For this reason, finalize your draft of the issue only after you have written the discussion section of the memo.

To frame an issue, you must do two things. First, identify the precise rule of law. Second, identify the key facts. Key facts are legally significant facts. Key facts are those facts that determine whether and how a particular rule of law applies to your situation. These facts are of crucial importance to the outcome of the case. Once you have fully researched the law within the context of your facts, you can determine which facts are key. Finally, after identifying the precise rule of law and the key facts, draft the issue to ask whether the rule of law applies under the particular facts of your case.

Consider the following examples of poorly phrased issues, and ask yourself what the writers have done incorrectly:

> Whether a bystander to an accident can recover for negligent infliction of emotional distress under Pennsylvania law.
> Whether a bystander at an automobile accident will be able to bring a tort action to recover for negligent infliction of emotional distress.
> Whether, under current Pennsylvania law, a bystander at an automobile accident can successfully bring a tort action for negligent infliction of emotional distress.

Comment: Although the writers properly identified the ultimate legal question, they failed to include the key facts. The reader is left to wonder about the circumstances that prompted the question. The reader should understand the question without having to refer to the facts section. If you fail to include key facts, you will draft an abstract question, a question without context. The writers of two of the issues include a reference to Pennsylvania law. When possible, state the jurisdiction since the law may vary dramatically from one state to the next.

––––––––––

> Whether a daughter who witnesses the aftermath of an accident involving her father will be able to state a cause of action for negligent infliction of emotional distress.

Comment: The writer of this issue omitted one very significant fact: the daughter's distance from the accident. The writer should also have included a reference to Pennsylvania law as the controlling jurisdiction.

––––––––––

Whether Edna can recover damages for negligent infliction of emotional distress as a result of witnessing an accident involving Mr. Smith.

Comment: When including the key facts in your issue, avoid identifying any of the people, places, or things in your case by proper name. Names may have no meaning to your reader because the facts section of your memo does not come until later. Even if you, the author of the memo, return to the file after the case has been dormant, you may not recall who all the players are. Instead of using proper names, use general categories to describe the people, places, or things in the issue.

––––––––––––

The issue should consist of a concise, one-sentence question. The issue usually starts with "whether" and should call for a yes or no in response. The issue also may begin with an interrogative such as "is" or "can." Be certain that your issue is precise and complete. Do not, however, draft a question that is so complex, lengthy, and awkward that your reader cannot follow it. Ask yourself whether the rule of law is stated clearly and succinctly. Examine your facts and critically evaluate which are essential to the issue. Do not generalize because you will risk distorting the issue.

A memo can address several questions. The questions might be distinct or related and can consist of several individual questions or a question with subparts. Writing and rewriting the questions and their subparts often promotes a more thorough understanding of the problem. Generally, the more specifically the question is phrased, the more precisely it will be understood. Do not, however, divide the issue into so many questions and subquestions that the reader will become confused. Do not use a single subquestion. If the question is divided into subparts, there must be at least two subparts.

Do not forget that the memo is an informative document that realistically evaluates your client's position. Adopt an objective, nonpartisan tone. Even if a key fact is unfavorable to your client's position, you must include it. Do not draft a question to suggest a certain answer. Avoid advocacy in issue writing.

Here are two good examples of issue statements. They come from different cases:

Under the Pennsylvania Workers' Compensation Act, can an employee recover for injuries that he sustained in a personal fight with a coworker during working hours when, six months earlier, he had a work-related dispute with the same coworker?

Under New Jersey law, can the parents of a child born with Down's syndrome rely on the "discovery rule" or the "concealment exception" to bring an action for wrongful birth two years after the statute of limitations has run when:

    A. before the birth, their physician stated that amniocentesis would detect any genetic defects in the fetus;

    B. the mother underwent amniocentesis; and

    C. after the birth, the physician stated that the amniocentesis had not detected Down's syndrome, even though he knew that the technician had made errors in performing the test and had arrived at an incorrect result?

These issues are well written. Both include the legal question and the facts that are key, according to the case law. The questions are precise and objective. They advise the reader of the scope and focus of the memo. As the samples demonstrate, there is no one correct way to draft an issue. Simply be certain that your issue contains all of the necessary elements, that you have framed it succinctly and accurately, and that you have made it comprehensible.

§ 12.03. THE CONCLUSION

The conclusion, sometimes called the brief answer or short answer, provides a short answer to each question that the issue section poses. In addition to answering the question, this section includes a concise statement of the reasoning that supports the conclusion. The conclusion section provides immediate answers to the questions that the memo raises.

The conclusion section immediately follows the issue section. For that reason, some attorneys begin with a direct response to each of the questions, such as "yes," "no," "probably," "probably not," and "maybe." Because few things in the law are ever absolutely clear, and because a noncommittal answer adds little to a well-written conclusion, we prefer memoranda without this type of response. Nevertheless, opinions and practices vary; therefore, be alert to the preferences of those for whom you are working.

In writing the conclusion section, accommodate the reader. In a memo discussing more than one issue, identify each conclusion with a number corresponding to the issue to which it refers. Be certain that each answer is self-contained. While each answer should contain a succinct explanation of the reasoning that supports your conclusion, do not discuss the details of your analysis. Do not include citations to cases, statutes, regulations, or other types of authority on which you rely. Only on the rare occasion when an authority is dispositive of the question, should you note it in the conclusion. Relegate all suppositions and hypotheses to the discussion section.

You may find it helpful to draft the conclusion after you have drafted the issue and written the discussion. Drafting these sections will force you to understand fully the reasons for your conclusion. Writing the conclusion is a two-step process. First, begin the conclusion by restating your issue as a declarative sentence. Second, add a brief explanation of the reasoning supporting your conclusion. The conclusion should be ten to fifteen lines.

Consider again the facts of the Smith matter, the illustrative case for this chapter. Then, please review the following sample conclusions from student memoranda.

Under Pennsylvania law, a daughter will be able to recover damages for negligent infliction of emotional distress if the emotional distress was foreseeable to the defendant. The factors determining foreseeability include: (1) whether the plaintiff was near the scene of the accident, (2) whether the shock resulted from the direct emotional impact upon the plaintiff from the sensory and contemporaneous observance of the accident, and (3) whether the plaintiff and the victim were closely related.

Comment: The writer has done only part of the job. This conclusion sets out the elements of the test that a plaintiff must meet to recover. The recitation of the law is correct. The conclusion, however, fails to answer the question.

———————

A Pennsylvania court would hold that the bystander at the automobile accident could recover for negligent infliction of emotional distress because such emotional distress was reasonably foreseeable.

Comment: Strictly speaking, the writer has answered the question and provided a succinct explanation of the reason for the answer. The conclusion, however, lacks key facts. When the issue is devoid of key facts, the conclusion is often similarly defective. Key facts are as critical to a conclusion as they are to an issue. While you need not reiterate every key fact in your conclusion, include enough facts to give the conclusion context and meaning. Legal conclusions are based on interpretations of facts in the context of the applicable law.

Edna will be allowed to recover for her emotional distress because of her close proximity to the accident, her shock as a result of the perception of the accident, and her relationship with Mr. Smith.

Comment: The writer has answered the question and summarized the reasons for it. The writer's use of proper names, however, deprives the reader of the ability to identify the players and their roles.

A daughter bystander can recover for negligent infliction of emotional distress because the emotional distress was reasonably foreseeable to the defendant. Pennsylvania, in *Sinn v. Burd*, 486 Pa. 146, 404 A.2d 672 (1979), adopted a three-step test to evaluate whether the emotional distress was foreseeable: (1) whether the plaintiff stood near the scene of the accident, (2) whether the emotional impact and distress followed sensory observance of the accident, and (3) whether the plaintiff and the victim were closely related. The daughter stood only one block from the accident. The daughter saw her father immediately before the event, heard the event, and saw the scene and her father immediately after the event. The father/daughter relationship is a close relationship. All elements of the test are therefore satisfied and a claim for negligent infliction of emotional distress is made out.

Comment: In the conclusion, do not set out the governing standard, or the applicable law, in such detail. Do not apply the law to your facts. Application in the conclusion section is usually ineffective because it is too general. It can be misleading because it is usually incomplete. If the attorney reading the conclusion develops a misimpression, you are responsible. Do not condense your analysis. The discussion section should be the sole source of analysis. Provide only the answer and a brief statement of your reasoning. This conclusion is too long given the nature of the question. Moreover, citations to authority are improper in the conclusion.

Here are two good conclusions:

(1) A Pennsylvania court would allow a daughter who witnessed an automobile accident involving her father from one block away to recover for negligent infliction of emotional distress because: (1) she was near the location of the accident, (2) her shock was a result of her direct sensory perception of the accident, and (3) she is closely related to the victim.

(2) A Pennsylvania court would permit a daughter who heard a car accident involving her father from a block away and who then immediately witnessed his severe injuries to recover for negligent infliction of emotional distress.

As with the issue, there is no one correct way to write a conclusion. Be certain that you answer the question and that you provide a brief statement of the reasoning that supports that answer, as the writers of the above two samples have done.

Writing good conclusions and issues is difficult. If you follow the principles that have been discussed, review the sample memoranda in Appendix I, and practice by writing and rewriting your conclusions and issues, you will soon master the task.

CHAPTER 13

Practice with Drafting Memos: Headings, Issues, and Conclusions

In this chapter, we offer you four exercises to help you learn how to draft the initial parts of an interoffice memo. The exercises should help you develop attention to formalities and precision in writing and thinking.

§ 13.01. EXERCISE I

Suppose a more senior attorney, Dewey D. Delaney, has called you into his office and told you the following:

The Firm has recently been retained by Jack Montagne to file suit against Asten Lift Company, Ltd. ("Asten"), a manufacturer of double and triple chair ski lifts based in Colorado. The file number is 98876-001. The basis of the suit he seeks to bring is an accident that occurred on Devil's Mountain, located in Pennsylvania. The accident involved his stepsister, Monica Gordon, who was thrown out of a triple chair lift and killed when a cable broke. Due to the circumstances of the accident, I think we might be able to state a cause of action for negligent infliction of emotional distress.

The facts of the case as I understand them are as follows. Jack, who is apparently an avid skier, took a ski vacation last winter with his stepsister, Monica. The two went to Devil's Mountain, as I said, where they rented a chalet for two weeks. Every morning they would have a quick breakfast, step outside, snap on their skis and ski the one hundred yards to the base of the mountain and the Diamond Triple Chair Lift, which would take them to the midpoint of the mountain. From there they would ride the Devil Triple Chair Lift (the "Devil Chair") to the peak. Once at the peak, they would separate, Jack to ski the wide open "bowls" on the back of the mountain and Monica to ski the trails on the face of the mountain. However, they had a standing agreement to meet for lunch at one o'clock at Tipler's, the restaurant at the top of the Devil Chair. They had consistently followed this schedule for seven days, and would not have deviated from it on the eighth day but for the accident.

On the day of the accident, Jack was standing near the top of the Devil Chair waiting for Monica and enjoying the sunshine. It was 12:50 p.m. Waiting for her there had become his habit. Ever since their first day on the mountain she had timed her skiing so that her last run before lunch was down Go Devil, the trail which wound back and forth under the Devil Chair, and ended at the midpoint. A run down Go Devil would take approximately half an hour. Then she would take the Devil Chair back to the top and Tipler's, a ride that took approximately twenty-five minutes. Jack had met her at the top of the chairlift every day, and she had consistently arrived within five minutes of the appointed time. Jack had been scanning the skiers as they came into view for about five minutes when he heard a loud noise that sounded like a large branch breaking off of a tree. The lift slowed to a stop and the chairs rolled back approximately 25 feet. Then, as Jack and those around him watched in horror, a wave raced up the cable, abruptly pulling the chairs ten or twelve feet up into the air and dropping them again just as suddenly. The chairs had no safety bar and Jack, who could see approximately ten percent of the chairs from his vantage point, saw people hurled out of their chairs and to the ground, which he knew was at times a 35 foot drop. Some skiers were miraculously able to hold on and remain in the chairs.

Jack could think only of Monica, who he knew had been riding the lift but who might now be lying injured or dead on the mountain. Jack started down the mountain, frantically seeking Monica in her polka-dotted ski jacket. Other skiers and the ski patrol were rushing to help those who had been thrown to the ground. Screams and moans filled the air and while some skiers writhed in pain, others seemed not to move at all. Dark blotches of blood stained the snow.

When he had gone approximately one hundred yards down the mountain, Jack still had not seen his stepsister and the trail wound away from the lift. He was almost frantic with fear and worry. Abandoning the trail to continue his search, Jack skied down directly under the chair. As he made his way through the crunchy snow and around the rocks, Jack reassured the skiers lying on the ground and those clinging to the chairs that help was en route, but he did not stop. Then he saw her. She lay on the ground, perfectly still, near a large rock. Jack took off his skis and made his way to her side. She made no sound. As he held her, he saw the gash and the blood caked to the back of her head. Her pulse was weak and irregular. Jack covered her with his jacket. Within ten minutes help arrived, and Monica was taken down to the base of the mountain in a stretcher. Jack never left her side. Within minutes of reaching the makeshift emergency center she died of head injuries sustained in the fall. She had never regained consciousness. Less than four minutes had passed from the moment Jack witnessed the skiers being thrown from their chairs and the moment he reached Monica.

Since the accident, Jack has had recurring nightmares, has suffered severe depression, and has experienced significant weight loss. He has been under continuing medical supervision for these conditions, none of which afflicted him prior to the accident.

Jack and Monica had been close since his mother and her father were married when he was 16 and she was 15. Both were only children who had longed for a sibling. At the time of the accident, both were in graduate school in Philadelphia. They talked often and met regularly for meals. Ever since Monica's father had died three years ago, and Jack's mother six months later, the two had taken a skiing vacation around Christmas and New Years so that they could spend the holidays together.

Suppose you are to prepare a memo on whether Jack Montagne could successfully state a cause of action for negligent infliction of emotional distress.

1. Write the heading of the memo.
2. Review the material in Chapter 12 on the Smith case, the illustrative case in this chapter, and:
   a. identify the key facts in the Montagne case;
   b. write the issue as it would appear in the memo;
   c. write the conclusion as it would appear in the memo.

§ 13.02. EXERCISE II

Patricia Brennan, your supervising attorney, has written you this note, which tells you about one of her cases (file no. 1945-9) and asks you to draft some sections of a memo:

We are representing the Jefferson City Transit Authority, which is the defendant in a false imprisonment case. I need your help in drafting an interoffice memo on a particular issue in the case. I will use the memo in discussing the case with other lawyers in our firm. I also will use it in preparing my arguments.

Here are the facts. June 20 of this year was the last day of school for the term at Hamilton Junior High. At the end of the day, a large group of students from that school boarded a bus owned by our client and driven by its employee, William Duer. One of the student-passengers was 15-year-old Jack Jay. On that day, the students were exuberant and ultimately unruly. A number of students broke windows, ceiling panels, advertising poster frames, and dome lights. At this point, we do not know if Jack Jay was one of the vandals.

After several unsuccessful attempts to establish order on the bus, Duer stopped the bus, inspected the damage, and announced that he was taking the students to the local police station. He then resumed driving and bypassed several normal stops on the way to his announced destination. As he turned one corner, several students jumped out of a side window at the rear of the bus. As he turned the next corner (New York Road and Federalist Avenue), Jay positioned himself to jump out the window. However, as the bus turned, the right rear wheels hit the curb, and Jay either jumped or fell to the street. The right rear wheels then rolled over Jay's midsection and caused him serious injuries.

Jay and his father John have begun a legal action in the state of Madison to recover damages for false imprisonment. As you know, in our jurisdiction, to succeed in a claim for false imprisonment, the plaintiff must prove that (1) the defendant intended to confine the plaintiff, (2) the plaintiff was conscious of the confinement, (3) the plaintiff did not consent to the confinement, and (4) the confinement was not otherwise privileged. I plan on a defense of justification: a restraint or detention is not unlawful if it is reasonable under the circumstances and in time and manner, and is imposed for the purpose of preventing another from inflicting personal injuries or interfering with property in one's lawful possession or custody or damaging that property.

Jack Jay is seeking damages for mental anguish and bodily injuries. His father is seeking damages for loss of services and medical expenses.

Even if the court or jury rejects the defense of justification and finds that there was false imprisonment, we still may have a defense against damage awards. Even if a person is falsely imprisoned, that person still has a duty to use reasonable care in trying to extricate himself or herself from the unlawful detention. Here, we will argue that Jack Jay placed himself in an unreasonably perilous position when he tried to leave a moving vehicle by placing himself in the bus window.

I would like your help in getting started on one of the memos for this case, the memo concluding that even if there is false imprisonment, no damages should be awarded. Please limit your work on this memo to the issue of defense against damages in the case of false imprisonment. Other memos will deal with other issues.

I would like you to draft the three initial parts of the memo: the heading, the issue, and the conclusion.

§ 13.03. EXERCISE III

Patricia Brennan, your supervising attorney, is pleased with your work on the memo concerning Jack Jackson's ability to recover damages for false imprisonment. She is so pleased that she gives you another assignment. Here is her note to you:

Thanks so much for your work on the Jay case. Now I need more help. I asked another associate to draft the beginning of a memo on another aspect of the case: whether justification would be a successful defense to false imprisonment under the facts of this case. At this point, I am assuming that the memo will conclude that justification would be a successful defense here. I was not pleased with what I received. Here is a copy of the heading, issue and conclusion. I would be appreciative if you would revise them. I do not want to create a conflict between you and the associate, so please leave his name on it as author and do not include your name. I will make sure you get credit for the work. Here is the draft:

FROM: Mike Smith

TO: Patti

DATE: (Supply the date you completed revising this memo.)

RE: *Jay v. Jefferson City Transit Authority*; file no. 1945-9; Justification Defense to False Imprisonment

ISSUE:

Under the law of the State of Madison, can Jack sue for false imprisonment when he jumped out of the school bus window after the bus driver started driving the school bus to the police station when the students started acting up?

CONCLUSION:

When students on the school bus are acting up and breaking things, the bus driver has the right to turn them over to the police. This defense is called justification, and it is a good defense against false imprisonment.

§ 13.04. EXERCISE IV

Laura Johann, the mid-level associate who supervises you, has emailed you the following memo:

Hi. I hope you can give me a hand on a difficult case. Let me start by asking you to read this memo from our client, Attorney Kathy Clare:

In early December, William Silton telephoned me at my office and told me that he was suffering from cancer and wanted to write a will that would pass his estate to his brother Jack. He said that he was estranged from his other brother Jim and wanted to make sure that none of his estate would go to Jim. At no time did Mr. Silton tell me that he was in immediate danger of dying or that he wanted to execute the will by a certain date.

On January 15, I mailed the will and related documents to Mr. Silton. A few days later, I learned that Mr. Silton had been injured in a car accident and was now in a nursing home. The documents reached him on January 23. On January 25, I was informed that Mr. Silton was in a rapidly deteriorating condition and was anxious to sign the will. I brought the will to Mr. Silton on February 1. Mr. Silton reiterated his testamentary intent. However, he wanted to change the contingent beneficiary. In other words, in case his brother Jack predeceased him, he wanted his estate to go to a charity as the contingent beneficiary. He had changed his mind on which charity to designate. I told Mr. Silton that I would revise the will and get back to him.

On February 4, I returned to the nursing home with the revised will. When I spoke with Mr. Silton, I determined that he lacked the competence to sign the will and returned to my office. On February 16, Mr. Silton died. Because he died without a will, his estate passed to his heirs according to this state's intestacy statute. Thus, his two brothers (including Jim) and a nephew each gained a share of his estate.

Now, Jack Silton is suing Kathy for malpractice. He claims she was negligent in failing to have Mr. Silton sign the will promptly and to advise him on February 1 of the risk of dying without a will if he did not sign the document as drafted at that meeting. Thus, he argues that Kathy had a duty to insure that the will was executed promptly under the circumstances, that the duty extended to him as the intended beneficiary, and that the breach of that duty injured him financially.

The estate involved here is quite large, and, therefore, this is a big case. My partner asked me to draft an in-house memo on the primary legal issue. I am having trouble drafting the issue. I wonder if you could give me a hand by suggesting a well-phrased issue. I really appreciate your help.

How would you draft the issue?

CHAPTER 14

The Memo: Facts and Discussion

§ 14.01. FACTS

When you receive an assignment to write a memo, either the attorney tells you the facts of the case or you go through the case file to get the facts. Once you know the facts, you must determine which of those facts belong in the memo's facts section. Include only those facts that affect the outcome of your analysis, and enough background facts to allow the reader to understand the analytically significant facts.

To determine which facts are analytically significant, research the relevant legal authority. As you read the cases, identify the facts upon which the courts rely in reaching their holdings. After you complete your research, determine which facts in your case are analogous to the important facts in the decided cases. Also determine which of your facts are distinguishable from important facts in adverse holdings. Include those facts in the facts section. Include the facts even if you think the reader knows them.

The facts section must be objective. Include facts that are both favorable and unfavorable to your case. Just as you analyze adverse case law in the discussion section, you must include unfavorable facts in the facts section.

Organize the facts section logically so that the reader understands what happened. The most logical organization is a chronological organization. A chronological organization is also an objective organization because it emphasizes no one fact or set of facts.

Make the facts section clear, concise, and complete. After you write the facts section, read it again and streamline it by eliminating all unnecessary facts. Do not make your reader hunt through the facts section to find the relevant facts. At the same time, make certain you have included all relevant facts. If you discuss a fact in the discussion section of your memo, it should also appear in the facts section.

Here is an example of how to write a facts section. In order to write a facts section, you must get the facts from the client and analyze those facts in light of the relevant legal authority.

Here are all of the facts provided by the client:

On June 10, 2013, Edna Smith witnessed an automobile accident in which her father, Wilbur Smith, was injured. Edna suffered and has continued to suffer emotional distress as a result of witnessing that accident.

On the day of the accident, Mr. Smith drove Edna to school. Edna's mother usually drove her to school, but her mother was sick. Edna attended Central High School and was a ninth grader.

Mr. Smith drove a 2001 Honda Civic. He was a good driver and had never received any speeding tickets.

Mr. Smith dropped Edna off at school at 8:00 a.m. and drove away to get some groceries for Edna's mother. Edna waved good-bye and turned, to talk to her friends, Gertrude Jones and Florence Kramer.

Shortly thereafter, Edna heard a loud crash. She turned around and saw that a car had crashed into her father's car in an intersection located one block from the school. Her father's car was on fire.

By the time she arrived at the accident, her father had been pulled from the burning car. She saw that he was severely burned and had a large gash on his forehead.

Mrs. Donna Lapp was the driver of the car that hit Mr. Smith. She was intoxicated at the time of the accident and ran a red light.

Edna now suffers from recurring nightmares, a debilitating fear of automobiles and chronic stomach problems. None of these conditions existed prior to the accident.

Here is a synopsis of the governing case law:

1. *Sinn v. Burd*, 486 Pa. 146, 404 A.2d 672 (1979).

In *Sinn*, the court held that a bystander at an automobile accident has a valid cause of action for negligent infliction of emotional distress if the injury to the bystander is reasonably foreseeable to the defendant. The court formulated a three-part foreseeability test to determine whether the bystander's injury was reasonably foreseeable:

a. whether the bystander was located near the scene of the accident,
b. whether the shock resulted from a direct emotional impact upon the bystander from sensory and contemporaneous observance of the accident, as contrasted with learning of the accident from others after its occurrence, and
c. whether the bystander and the victim were closely related.

2. *Anfuso v. Smith*, 15 Pa. D. & C.3d 389 (Northampton Co. 1980).

In *Anfuso*, the court held that a mother, who was inside her home when she heard a car accident occur outside and rushed out to see her daughter injured in the accident, could recover for negligent infliction of emotional distress. The court applied the *Sinn v. Burd* three-part test to determine whether the mother's injury was foreseeable. The court found that the first part of the test was satisfied because the mother was sufficiently near the scene of the accident even though she was inside her house and the accident occurred on the street. The court further found that the second part of the test was satisfied because the mother heard the accident happen and then ran out and witnessed her daughter's injuries. The mother, therefore, had a sensory and contemporaneous observance of the event rather than learning about it from others. Finally, the court found that the third part of the test was satisfied because a mother-daughter relationship is a sufficiently close relationship.

3. *Brooks v. Decker*, 512 Pa. 365, 516 A.2d 1380 (1986).

In *Brooks*, the court held that a father did not have a valid cause of action for negligent infliction of emotional distress because he did not witness the car accident in which his son was injured, nor did he hear the accident. Instead, he merely saw his injured son lying on the ground after the accident occurred.

4. *Bliss v. Allentown Public Library*, 497 F. Supp. 487 (E.D. Pa. 1980).

In *Bliss*, the court held that a mother who heard a metal sculpture fall on her child but did not see it fall had a sensory and contemporaneous observance of the event. The mother thus satisfied the second part of the *Sinn v. Burd* test to recover for negligent infliction of emotional distress.

5. *Blanyar v. Pagnotti Enters., Inc.*, 512 Pa. 266, 516 A.2d 672 (1986).

In *Blanyar*, the court held that a cousin could not recover for negligent infliction of emotional distress after watching his cousin drown since the cousin was not a member of the victim's immediate family.

6. *Mazzagatti v. Everingham*, 512 Pa. 266, 516 A.2d 672 (1986).

In *Mazzagatti*, the court held that a mother could not recover for negligent infliction of emotional distress after learning about the accident from another person through a telephone call. The court recognized that the prior knowledge serves as a buffer against the mother observing the full impact of the accident.

Model Facts Section

On June 10, 2013, Edna Smith's father, Wilbur Smith, drove her to school. He dropped her off at the school at 8:00 a.m. and then drove away. Edna turned to talk to some friends.

At an intersection located one block from the school, Donna Lapp, the defendant, ran a red light and crashed into Mr. Smith's car. Edna did not see the accident occur, but she heard it. Edna turned around and saw the accident scene. She could see that her father's car was on fire.

By the time she arrived at the accident, her father had been pulled from the burning car. She saw that he was severely burned and had a large gash on his forehead.

Edna now suffers from recurring nightmares, a debilitating fear of automobiles, and chronic stomach problems. None of these conditions existed prior to the accident.

In the above example, the writer included only the facts that are relevant under the applicable case law and enough background facts so that the reader can understand what happened to Edna. For example, since distance from the accident is an important factor under *Sinn v. Burd*, the writer described Edna's distance from the accident. The writer eliminated extraneous facts, such as the year of the car Mr. Smith was driving and the names of Edna's friends. The writer included all of the unfavorable facts, such as the fact that Edna did not see the accident. Finally, the writer organized the facts clearly and logically by stating them in chronological order.

Here is an example of a bad facts section. Compare it with the model facts section.

Edna Smith suffers from severe emotional distress as a result of witnessing an automobile accident. The accident was the fault of Donna Lapp. In the accident, Edna's father, Wilbur Smith, was horribly injured and he almost died.

The accident occurred on June 10, 2013. Edna's father drove her to school. He dropped her off at school at 8:00 a.m. and drove away.

Donna Lapp, the defendant, ran a red light and slammed into Mr. Smith's car. His car exploded, and Edna heard the explosion. Edna saw his car enveloped in flames. Edna also saw his severely burned body and the large gash on his forehead that was spurting blood.

Edna now suffers from horrible, recurring nightmares, she is terrified of cars, and she has excruciating stomach pain. Donna Lapp negligently caused Edna's injuries.

The above example of a facts section is poorly written because it is not objective. The writer left out adverse facts, such as Edna's distance from the accident. In addition, the writer used value-laden words, such as "horrible" and "excruciating" to describe Edna's and her father's injuries.

The writer also made legal conclusions, instead of just stating facts. For example, the writer stated that the defendant negligently caused Edna's injuries. Moreover, the writer did not organize the facts clearly and logically.

§ 14.02. DISCUSSION

The discussion section is composed of legal arguments resolving the issues and sub-issues. Use the methods for writing legal arguments you learned in Chapter 6:

1. Use deductive reasoning.
2. Apply the law to the facts.
3. Make analogies.
4. Make policy and equity arguments.

Ideally, you want to use all of these types of arguments in the discussion section. Circumstances may limit the types of arguments available to you or may dictate that you emphasize one form of argument over another.

Divide the discussion into sections that correspond to the issues and sub-issues. In each section, discuss the law applicable to the issue or sub-issue, and apply it to the facts that are relevant to the issue or sub-issue. Remember that all the facts to which you refer in the discussion should be in the facts section of your memo.

Write the discussion clearly and logically. As we suggested in Chapter 8, give your reader a roadmap paragraph at the beginning of the discussion, including a statement of your ultimate conclusion. As noted previously, readers of legal prose are not looking for suspense, they are looking for explanations. Explain the organization of the discussion so the reader can follow it easily.

The discussion section must be objective. Include both favorable and unfavorable facts and legal authority. Discuss arguments in favor of your client first, and then potential counterarguments. If you can, distinguish cases that are unfavorable to your client's position.

Be objective, but think strategically. If any argument supports your client's position, discuss that argument. The senior attorney who assigned the memo wants you to find a way for your client to win. Do not, however, misrepresent the strength of your client's position. The reader relies on your research and analysis. If your client is going to lose, do not assert that the client will win. You do not want a senior attorney to take the wrong action for a client. It will come back to haunt you.

Remember to come to conclusions and make recommendations. Do not simply present the information and force the reader to reproduce your analysis. At the end of the discussion section, summarize all the conclusions you reached and recommend actions the reader can take. The conclusion at the end of the discussion should be brief but may offer more detail than the conclusion section of your memo.

Here is an example of how to write a discussion. The example is drawn from the case discussed in Chapter 12 and in the first section of this chapter.

Edna Smith has a valid cause of action for negligent infliction of emotional distress. In *Sinn v. Burd*, the court held that a bystander at an automobile accident has a valid cause of action for negligent infliction of emotional distress if the injury to the bystander is reasonably foreseeable to the defendant. 486 Pa. 146, 173, 404 A.2d 672, 686 (1979). The court formulated a three-part test to determine whether the bystander's injury was reasonably foreseeable:

1. whether the bystander was located near the scene of the accident;
2. whether the injury resulted from a direct emotional impact upon the bystander from sensory and contemporaneous observance of the accident, as contrasted with learning of the accident from others after its occurrence; and
3. whether the bystander and the victim were closely related.

Id. at 170-171, 404 A.2d at 685. The present case meets all three parts of the *Sinn v. Burd* test. Each part of the test is discussed separately below.

a. Distance from the Scene of the Accident

The issue in Edna's case is whether someone standing one block from the scene of the accident is located near the scene of the accident. The decided cases suggest that one block is close enough to meet the test.

In *Sinn*, the court held that a mother who witnessed an accident on the street from the front door of her house was located near the scene of the accident. *Id.* at 173, 404 A.2d at 686. Similarly, in *Anfuso v. Smith*, the court held that a mother who was inside her home when she heard an accident occur on the street was located near the scene of the accident. 15 Pa. D. & C.3d 389, 393 (Northampton Co. 1980). In *Bliss v. Allentown Public Library*, the court held that a mother who was twenty-five feet away from her child when she heard a metal sculpture fall on him was located near the scene of the accident. 497 F. Supp. 487, 489 (E.D. Pa. 1980).

In *Sinn*, *Anfuso*, and *Bliss*, the bystanders were close enough to the accident to see it happen or to see its aftermath. None of the cases required the bystander to be standing at the accident site in order to be located near the scene of the accident. In the present case, Edna was close enough to the scene of the accident that she could see its aftermath. Accordingly, Edna was located near the scene of the accident, and the first part of the test has been met.

b. Direct Emotional Impact

The issue here is whether someone who heard an accident rather than saw it had a sensory and contemporaneous observance of the accident. Edna's emotional distress was a direct result of hearing the accident as it occurred and, therefore, the relevant case law supports the conclusion that the second part of the *Sinn v. Burd* test has been met.

In *Bliss*, the court held that a mother who heard a metal sculpture fall on her child but did not see it fall had a sensory and contemporaneous observance of the event. *Id.* at 489. The court stated that it would not deny a suit simply because of the position of the plaintiff's eyes at the split second the accident occurred. *Id.* The court found that the entire incident produced the emotional distress the plaintiff suffered. *Id.* Similarly, the *Anfuso* court held that a mother who heard a car accident while inside her home and rushed out to see her daughter injured in the accident had a sensory and contemporaneous observance of the event. 15 Pa. D. & C.3d at 393.

The facts of the present case are similar to the facts of *Bliss* and *Anfuso*. Edna heard the accident and then turned and saw its aftermath. Her emotional distress resulted from a direct emotional impact on her from both hearing the accident and seeing its aftermath. Her observance of the accident was both sensory (hearing and sight) and contemporaneous (she heard it as it happened and then turned and saw its aftermath). Therefore, the second part of the *Sinn* test has been met.

The present case is distinguishable from *Brooks v. Decker*, 512 Pa. 365, 516 A.2d 1380 (1986). There, the court held that a father did not have a valid cause of action for negligent infliction of emotional distress. *Id.* at 365, 516 A.2d at 1383. In *Brooks*, the father did not hear or see the car accident in which his son was injured. *Id.* at 367, 516 A.2d at 1381. Instead, he followed an ambulance, which passed him. *Id.* On arriving at the scene, the father saw his injured son lying on the ground. *Id.* The court found that he did not have a valid cause of action because he did not hear or see the accident as it occurred. *Id.* at 365, 516 A.2d at 1383. Moreover, the present case is distinguishable from *Mazzagatti v. Everingham* because there the court held that a mother who learned of an accident from a telephone call was not directly impacted by the accident and could not recover damages. 512 Pa. 266, 269, 516 A.2d 672, 674.

In the present case, however, Edna heard the accident occur. She did not learn that an accident had occurred by seeing an ambulance nor did she learn about the accident from another person. Therefore, the holdings in both *Brooks and Mazzagatti* are inapplicable to the present case.

c. Close Relationship

The final issue is whether a father-daughter relationship is a sufficiently close relationship to satisfy the third part of the test. Relevant decisions suggest that Edna and her father are closely enough related to meet the third part of the *Sinn v. Burd* test, although none of the cases involved a directly analogous relationship.

In *Sinn*, the court held that mother-child relationship was a sufficiently close relationship to satisfy the third part of the test. 486 Pa. at 173, 404 A.2d at 686. In *Anfuso*, the court held that a mother-child relationship and a sibling relationship were sufficiently close relationships to satisfy the third part of the test. 15 Pa. D. & C.3d at 391.

In *Sinn* and *Anfuso*, the courts held that the two types of blood relatives satisfied the third part of the test. Edna and her father are blood relatives. Parents, children, and siblings are immediate family members. However, since none of these courts suggest that immediate family members cannot satisfy the third part of the test, we should argue that a father-daughter relationship is sufficiently close.

The present case is consistent with *Blanyar v. Pagnotti Enters., Inc.*, 512 Pa. 266, 516 A.2d 672 (1986). There the court recognized that only immediate family members can recover for negligent infliction of emotional distress.

In the present case, Edna is Mr. Smith's daughter. Therefore, the holding in *Blanyar* supports Edna's claim.

D. Conclusion

Edna Smith has a valid cause of action for negligent infliction of emotional distress. Edna was located near the scene of the accident, her injury was a result of a direct emotional impact from sensory and contemporaneous observance of her father's accident, and Edna and her father are closely related. Since all three parts of the *Sinn* test have been met, the firm should file suit on Edna's behalf.

In the above example, the writer divided the discussion into sub-issues that correspond to the three parts of the *Sinn* test. In each section, the writer discussed the law applicable to the specific part of the test and applied that law to the facts relevant to that part of the test. All of the facts referred to in the discussion came from the facts section example in the first part of this chapter.

At the beginning of the discussion, the writer provided a roadmap for the sections discussing the individual parts of the test. The writer gave conclusions at the beginning of each section and summarized those conclusions at the end of the discussions. The writer also recommended an action for the reader to take—to file suit.

Finally, the writer discussed unfavorable facts and cases. In addition, the writer distinguished an unfavorable case, *Brooks v. Decker*.

Now that you have seen an example of a well-constructed discussion section, the next segment of this chapter offers some tips on how to avoid mistakes that students and young lawyers commonly make when writing legal memoranda.

§ 14.03. MAKE YOUR REASONING READILY APPARENT

"Ambiguous" is a word that writing instructors often write on first-year law students' papers. The student will often respond by pointing out the intended meaning, perhaps not even seeing the alternate meaning that made the expression ambiguous to the reader.

Always put yourself in your reader's shoes. Assume your reader knows nothing about the subject, and strive for a self-contained document that treats your subject thoroughly. Your reader should have no trouble understanding your reasoning in applying the law to the case at hand.

1. Avoid the "Digest" Approach

A writer who uses the digest approach recites a series of mini-briefs of cases and fails to integrate the law and the facts.

In the following example of the "digest" approach, the writer "recites" the law but does not apply it.

Article 2, § 8, of New York State's Bill of Rights (McKinney 2006) reiterates the "right of the people . . . against unreasonable searches and seizures" provided by the Fourth Amendment to the United States Constitution. "Searches conducted outside the judicial process, without prior approval by judge or magistrate, are per se unreasonable under the fourth amendment . . . subject only to a few specifically established and well-delineated exceptions." *Katz v. United States*, 389 U.S. 347 (1967).

The application of the "plain view doctrine" is contingent upon a showing by the state that the officer's vantage point is a place in which it is lawful for that officer to be. *Ker v. California*, 374 U.S. 23 (1963).

The court sets forth the guidelines that govern the application of the "emergency" exception to the warrant requirement in *People v. Mitchell*, 39 N.Y.2d 173, 347 N.E.2d 607, *cert. denied*, 426 U.S. 953 (1976), as follows:

(1) The police must have reasonable grounds to believe that there is an emergency at hand and an immediate need for their assistance for the protection of life or property.

(2) The search must not be motivated primarily by intent to arrest and seize evidence.

(3) There must be some reasonable basis approximating probable cause to associate the emergency with the area or place to be searched.

Id. at 176, 347 N.E.2d 177–78.

In *People v. Gallmon*, 19 N.Y.2d 389, 280 N.Y.S.2d 356 (1967), the police officer's entry without obtaining a warrant was justified by his obligation to assist people in distress.

Under the "fruit of the poisonous tree doctrine" the government cannot use information obtained during an illegal search. *Wong Sun v. United States*, 371 U.S. 471 (1963); *Silverthorne Lumber Co. v. United States*, 251 U.S. 385 (1920).

In this example, the writer has included several paragraphs about the law, but the reader still knows nothing about the case at hand. Each time a rule is articulated, the rule should be applied to the facts of the case being discussed, using the previously decided cases to explain the application.

2. Avoid the "Historical Development of the Law" Approach

The "historical development of the law" approach, as it implies, goes through the history of the law, often needlessly. Sometimes it is necessary to give some history of the development of a rule—but not often. This approach is often appropriate in a law review article but has limited usefulness in a legal memorandum or brief. The reader—whether a lawyer, a judge, or a client—usually will care little about where the law came from or what led to its development, but will want to see what the law is and how it applies to the current situation.

Here is an example of the "historical development of the law" approach:

At common law, an action for wrongful death did not exist. Nevertheless, the Ohio General Assembly recognized such an action in title 21, section 25.01, of the Ohio Rev. Code Ann. § 2125.01. *Werling v. Sancy*, 17 Ohio St. 3d 45, 46, 476 N.E.2d 1053, 1054 (1985).

Section 2125.01 provides as follows:

When the death of a person is caused by wrongful act, neglect, or default which would have entitled the party injured to maintain an action and recover damages if death had not ensued, the person who would have been liable if death had not ensued . . . shall be liable to an action for damages, notwithstanding the death of the person injured. . . .

Ohio Rev. Code Ann. § 2125.01.

Since § 2125.01 refers only to a "person," a key question is whether a viable, unborn child is a "person" within the meaning of § 2125.01. *Werling*, 17 Ohio St. 3d at 46, 476 N.E.2d at 1054.

The most recent case involving an action for wrongful death under § 2125.01 where the decedent is a stillborn fetus is *Werling v. Sancy*, 17 Ohio St. 3d 45, 476 N.E.2d 1053 (1985). In *Werling*, the Supreme Court of Ohio reaffirmed the position of the Court of Appeals for Madison County in *Stidam v. Ashmore*, 109 Ohio App. 431, 167 N.E.2d 106 (1959). The Supreme Court held in *Werling* that a viable fetus that is negligently injured in its mother's womb and subsequently stillborn may be the basis for a wrongful death action pursuant to § 2125.01. *Werling*, 17 Ohio St. 3d at 49, 476 N.E.2d at 1054.

Notice that you have read several paragraphs and still know nothing about the case the writer is discussing. You cannot even be sure of the specific issue being discussed. Unless it is actually relevant to your discussion to explain how the rule got to its present form, simply state the rule and begin your discussion at that point.

3. Avoid the Use of Too Many Quotations from Legal Authorities

Many court opinions contain numerous quotations from other cases, legal periodicals, and treatises. It is easier and faster to quote from authorities than to paraphrase them, so some writers tend to use many quotations.

Too many quotations distract the reader, and often the quotations themselves are not clear. A frequent flaw in legal writing is overuse of the "block quote," the indented, single-spaced quote. Many judges, attorneys, and students tend to skip over them. Avoid overuse of block quotes in particular, and avoid overuse of all quotations. Here is an example from a student memo:

Mr. Walker has a valid cause of action for false imprisonment. In *Roth v. Golden Nugget Case/ Hotel, Inc.*, 576 F. Supp. 262, 265 (D.N.J. 1983), the court found that "in order to support a claim for false arrest, the plaintiffs must allege two elements: First, that there was an arrest, and second, that the arrest was without proper legal authority, which has been interpreted to mean without legal justification." In New Jersey, false imprisonment and false arrest are merely separate names for the same tort. *Roth v. Golden Nugget Case/Hotel, Inc.*, 576 F. Supp. 262, 265 (D.N.J. 1983),

The court held in *Barletta v. Golden Nugget Hotel Casino*, 580 F. Supp. at 617-618, that:

A taking into custody need not be done violently to constitute an arrest. . . . The inquiry goes to whether there was any unlawful restraint upon a person's freedom of movement. . . . Further, the assertion of legal authority to take a person into custody, even where such authority does not in fact exist, may be sufficient to create a reasonable apprehension that a person is under restraint.

Therefore, applying the law to the facts of the present case, we can conclude that an arrest was made.

The student should have used his own words instead of quoting the court. When you read the excerpt, you probably read the first quote hastily and wondered if you could avoid reading the block quote. Most people tend to skip over long quotes. The student also used quotations in place of analysis. He wanted to argue that Mr. Walker has a valid cause of action for false imprisonment. The student should have applied the rule of law to the facts in his case and compared his client's circumstances with those of the plaintiff in *Barletta*. Instead, he quoted generalities from the *Barletta* opinion.

4. Avoid the "Abstract Writing" Approach

The "abstract writing" approach reads like an essay. This form of writing is easy for students who have written essays in undergraduate school that earned "A's" in English or social sciences. Writers who use this form often discuss their viewpoints on what the law should be, but never get to what the law actually is. The following is an example of the "abstract writing" approach:

> The Court should uphold defendant's conviction for selling cocaine as a matter of public policy. This society is permeated by drugs, and courts should not allow drug dealers to go free.
>
> The President has recently declared a war on drugs. The use of drugs is so prevalent that recently many celebrities in the entertainment and sports worlds have either died or admitted drug abuse, setting a bad example for young people.
>
> Defendant's conviction should stand because she is a mother who is a bad example for her children. The evidence against her was overwhelming, and her guilt is indisputable. To let her go free to protect her constitutional rights would be an injustice not only to her drug customers but also to her family.
>
> That defendant's having to go to prison may split up her family should not be the court's major consideration. Her children will be better off in a drug-free environment. The defense argues that the police deprived defendant of her constitutional rights but ignores the fact that she is taking others' lives by selling dangerous drugs.
>
> For all these reasons, defendant's conviction must stand.

The memorandum above could also be called the "soapbox" approach to legal writing. The student quite rightly addresses public policy issues, but fails to back up any ideas with constitutional provisions, statutes, or judicial rulings. There is no legal analysis.

5. Avoid the "Law Discussion Only" Approach

The next rule concerns the opposite of the "abstract" or "soapbox" approach—the "law discussion only" approach with no factual, policy, or equity considerations. This approach often gives a very accurate recitation of the law but fails to discuss policies and equities underlying the law or the case on which the writer is working. Here is an example:

> Ohio Rule of Evidence 501 allows Ohio courts to use their discretion in deciding what privileges they will allow. The rule states that "[t]he privilege of a witness, person, state or political subdivision thereof shall be governed by statute enacted by the General Assembly or by principles of common law as interpreted by the courts of this state in the light of reason and experience." Ohio R. Evid. 501.

The Ohio courts have been consistent in their refusal to extend the privileges beyond those that are specifically listed in the statute. Section 2317.02 recognizes as privileged, communications between attorney and client, physician and patient, clergyman and parishioner, husband and wife, and professional counselor and client.

In *Whipple v. Render*, C.A. No. 2480, 1989 Ohio Ct. App. LEXIS 3493, at *3 (Sept. 13, 1989), the court refused to extend the privilege of physician-patient to include dentists or dental surgeons.

The student tells us about an evidentiary rule that gives Ohio courts discretion in making certain decisions. The student tells us that the courts have not exercised that discretion liberally. We also learn about the holding in one case. The student, however, omits vital information. We need to know what policy considerations guide the court in deciding how to exercise its discretion. We also need to know why the court decided the *Whipple* case as it did. The "law discussion only" approach fails to give us the information we need to engage in legal analysis.

6. A Good Example

The following is an edited excerpt from a good discussion of the law, accompanied by appropriate discussion of policies and equities, but avoiding abstraction or "soapboxing":

Ohio Rule of Evidence 501 allows Ohio courts to use their discretion in deciding what privileges they will allow. The rule states that "[t]he privilege of a witness, person, state or political subdivision thereof shall be governed by statute enacted by the General Assembly or by principles of common law as interpreted by the courts of this state in the light of reason and experience." Ohio R. Evid. 501.

Because the statutory privileges of § 2317.02 controvert the general policy that disclosure of all information in the possession of witnesses in trials is necessary to insure the disclosure of the truth, the Ohio courts have been consistent in their refusal to extend the privileges beyond those which are specifically listed in the statute. Section 2317.02 recognizes as privileged, communications between attorney and client, physician and patient, clergyman and parishioner, husband and wife, and professional counselor and client.

In *Whipple v. Render*, C.A. No. 2480, 1989 Ohio Ct. App. LEXIS 3493, at *3 (Sept. 13, 1989), the court followed Ohio precedent and refused to extend the privilege of physician-patient to include dentists or dental surgeons. The court noted that the Ohio statute "is a derogation of the common law and must be strictly construed. Consequently, the aforementioned section affords protection only to those relationships which are specifically named therein." *Id.* That court thus aligned itself with the earlier case of *Belichick v. Belichick*, 37 Ohio App. 2d 95, 307 N.E.2d 270 (1973). That court stressed the importance of the disclosure of all information necessary to discover the truth. "The granting of privileges against disclosure constitutes an exception to the general rule, and the tendency of the courts is to construe such privileges strictly and to narrow their scope since they obstruct the discovery of the truth." *Id.* at 96-97, 307 N.E.2d at 271. Further, the court said, "R.C. 2317.02 is in derogation of the common law and must be strictly construed and consequently, the aforementioned section affords protection only to those relationships which are specifically mentioned therein." *Id.* at 97, 307 N.E.2d at 271.

Several other Ohio decisions have refused to extend the privileges of § 2317.02. *See Weis v. Weis*, 147 Ohio St. 416, 423, 72 N.E.2d 245, 252 (1947) (no physician-nurse privilege); *State v. Hallech*, 24 Ohio App. 2d 74, 81, 963 N.E.2d 917, 922 (1970) (no parole officer-parolee privilege);

Arnovitz v. Wozar, 9 Ohio App. 2d 16, 21, 222 N.E.2d 660, 665 (1964) (no attorney-witness privilege when witness was not client).

The Ohio courts' refusal to recognize privileges outside those authorized by statute is based on the policy that justice cannot be served if vital information is kept out of the record. The court so firmly believes this that it will refuse to recognize even those privileges authorized by statute where such recognition would protect criminal conduct. In *State v. Tu*, 17 Ohio App. 3d 159, 478 N.E.2d 830 (1984), a defendant who was being criminally prosecuted for vehicular homicide claimed the physician-patient privilege to prevent the introduction of a blood-alcohol test result into evidence at his trial. The court held that the privilege was not absolute and that "statutory privileges, unless they expressly provided otherwise, were simply not designed or intended to shield criminal conduct." *Id.* at 163, 478 N.E.2d at 833.

It follows that even if Ohio did recognize a parent-child privilege, it would never uphold the privilege in a case such as this one, where a defendant seeks to use the privilege to exclude vital evidence in a criminal prosecution for possession and sale of cocaine.

If you apply the lessons of this chapter, and the approach to legal analysis discussed in Chapter 6, to all legal memoranda you write, you should find that your writing will be well received by those who use it to guide their decisions in practice. You will write clear, concrete, and concise yet thorough documents that will earn you a reputation as a knowledgeable and thoughtful lawyer.

Exercise

Below is a poorly written example of part of the discussion of Edna Smith's case. Identify what is wrong with it.

In *Sinn*, the court held that a mother who witnessed an accident on the street from the front door of her house was located near the scene of the accident. *Id.* at 173, 404 A.2d at 686. Similarly, in *Anfuso v. Smith*, the court held that a mother who heard a car accident while inside her home and rushed out to see that her daughter had been injured in the accident was located near the scene of the accident. 15 Pa. D. & C.3d 389, 393 (Northampton Co. 1980). The *Anfuso* court further held that the mother had a sensory and contemporaneous observance of the event. *Id.* In *Bliss v. Allentown Public Library*, the court held that a mother who was twenty-five feet away from her son when she heard a metal sculpture fall on him was located near the scene of the accident. 497 F. Supp. 487, 489 (E.D. Pa. 1980). The *Bliss* court also held that the mother had a sensory and contemporaneous observance of the event. *Id.*

In *Brooks v. Decker*, the court held that a father did not have a valid cause of action for negligent infliction of emotional distress. 512 Pa. 365, 516 A.2d 1380, 1383 (1986). In *Brooks*, the father did not hear or see the car accident in which his son was injured. Instead he saw an ambulance race past him with its lights flashing and its sirens on. When he arrived at home, he saw his injured son lying on the ground. *Id.* The court found that the father did not have a valid cause of action because he did not hear or see the accident as it occurred. *Id.*

Edna was located near the scene of the accident, and the first part of the *Sinn* test has been met. Edna had a sensory and contemporaneous observance of the accident, and the second part of the *Sinn* test has been met. Therefore, Edna will win her case.

CHAPTER 15

Practice with Memos: Facts and Discussion

§ 15.01. INTRODUCTION

This chapter will give you the opportunity to practice developing a facts section and a discussion section of a memo. The legal issues to be developed here are similar to those covered in the previous chapter, but with a new set of facts and case law.

§ 15.02. DRAFTING THE FACTS SECTION

After meeting with the client, you dictated the following notes of the interview:

Lisa Ellington has come to see us because she was devastated by the recent death of her son Josh. A couple of weeks ago, her husband John Ellington, a ten-year veteran of the City of Chapman police department, shot and killed seven-year-old Josh and himself. He also wounded Lisa and their three-year-old daughter Katie. There was a long history of trouble in the nine-year marriage. John beat Lisa frequently, usually when he was drunk.

Lisa called the police whenever John got out of control, including at least seven or eight times over the last two or three years. All calls were responded to, and John was taken into custody twice. She doesn't know whether he was ever actually arrested, and he was never formally prosecuted because he always promised to change and get help with his drinking and she wanted to work things out, so she didn't press charges. Lisa was hospitalized once last year with broken ribs and other injuries and contusions. John took her to the hospital that time, and they both lied and said she had fallen down the stairs. John had seemed really upset that he had hurt her so badly, and she really thought that might be a turning point in the relationship. John had never before threatened Lisa or the children with a weapon.

On the night of the shootings, Lisa called 911, asking for immediate assistance because John was drunk and threatening her with a gun. John was yelling that she was no damn good and needed to be "taught a lesson." She doesn't know exactly what set him off, but he came home drunk and missed dinner. The children were crying, and she wanted to send them to their rooms, but John said no. After she called 911, John punched her in the face three or four times and threw her against a wall, right in front of the children.

Two officers responded to her 911 call. They knocked on the door, and John answered. He was holding his service revolver. The officers, Randy Miller and Jake Holmes, asked

John to step outside. He complied, and they asked him what was going on. He started yelling again about how Lisa was no good and needed to be "taught a lesson." Randy and Jake took John's gun.

At this point, Lisa went to the door, bleeding from the nose and with a split lip, and told Randy and Jake that she had had enough, and she wanted John arrested. She said that she would follow through with the prosecution this time, and that she was going to take the children and go to her mother's. She also said she was finally going to divorce John. This seemed to enrage John even further, and he reached for his gun while screaming and cursing at her, calling her an "ungrateful *****" among other things. Randy and Jake took John away.

Lisa went back into the house to calm the children and clean up her face. She called her mother and told her they were coming. Lisa's mother was very relieved because she had been worried about the situation with John for some time. Lisa began to pack up some things for herself and the children. After about two hours, John returned home, came into the bedroom and found her packing, drew his gun, and fired at her, hitting her in the stomach. He then left the bedroom to find the children. Lisa heard the gunshots that killed her son and wounded her daughter, but did not actually see the shootings. John then took his own life.

Josh was shot in the head and died immediately. Katie was shot in the leg and will be physically okay, but she is showing signs of serious emotional trauma. She has nightmares every night and is always looking over her shoulder in fear. She jumps and screams at any sudden noise, like the phone ringing or a door slamming. She was always an outgoing child, but now Lisa can hardly get her to say three words. She hangs onto Lisa all the time. The doctors had to remove part of Lisa's spleen, but she should be okay physically as well. She has also been having nightmares and is having a lot of trouble coping. She feels as though she could have saved Josh if only she had left sooner, but it never occurred to her that the officers would keep John for only two hours. The last time they took him into custody, they kept him at the station overnight and then let him call her to see if she wanted him to come home.

Lisa believes that the officers did not take the situation as seriously as they should have, and that they gave John a break because he was a fellow officer. She told them about wanting to divorce John and taking the kids to her mother's because she wanted them to understand that she was really serious this time, and that she wanted them to treat him like they would any other criminal.

Lisa wants the police department and maybe the city to pay—it won't bring Josh back or give Katie back her smile, but she is really hurt and angry, and she is going to have a lot of bills to pay, including counseling for Katie and maybe herself. She can work as a secretary, but hasn't since Josh was born because John wanted her at home with the children. He always said he was man enough to provide for his family. Lisa doesn't know how much life insurance or pension John had, and she doesn't know whether the department will continue to pay for the health insurance she had before.

You can draft a facts section for your memo now, but it would probably be better to wait until you have read the applicable law because you won't know for sure which facts are relevant until you understand the law. When you do draft the facts section, be sure to include all facts that are legally relevant or otherwise necessary to tell a coherent story. Omit facts that do not meet those criteria. Remember to keep the tone of the facts section objective and to tell the story in a logical order.

Here is a synopsis of the governing case law:

1. *Elden v. Sheldon*, 46 Cal. 3d 267, 758 P.2d 582, 250 Cal. Rptr. 254 (1988)

In *Elden*, the court held that damages may be recovered for reasonably foreseeable emotional distress and physical injury resulting from plaintiff's witnessing of an accident in which a closely related person is injured or killed by the negligent act of the defendant. In determining whether defendant should reasonably foresee the injury to the plaintiff, the court took into account the following three factors:

(1) whether plaintiff was located near the scene of the accident as contrasted with one who was a distance away from it;
(2) whether the shock resulted from a direct emotional impact upon the plaintiff from the sensory and contemporaneous observance of the accident, as contrasted with learning of the accident from others after its occurrence; and
(3) whether plaintiff and the victim were closely related, as contrasted with an absence of any relationship or the presence of only a distant relationship.

2. *Hoyem v. Manhattan Beach City School District*, 22 Cal. 3d 508, 585 P.2d 851, 150 Cal. Rptr. 1 (1978).

In *Hoyem*, the court held that a mother, who was not present at the scene of an accident where her ten-year-old son was struck by a motorcycle, could not recover for the emotional distress that she suffered upon observing such injuries in the hospital a few hours after the accident. The plaintiff urged the court to apply the *Dillon* rule that "courts should allow recovery to a mother who suffers emotional trauma and physical injury to her child for which the tortfeasor is liable in negligence." *Dillon v. Legg*, 68 Cal. 2d 728, 730, 441 P.2d 912, 914; 69 Cal. Rptr. 72, 74 (1968). The court declined to extend the *Dillon* rule, holding that "*Dillon* requires more than a mere physical presence: . . . the shock must also result from a 'direct emotional impact' on the plaintiff caused by a 'sensory and contemporaneous observance of the accident.'" *Justus v. Atchison*, 19 Cal. 3d 564, 584, 565 P.2d 122, 135; 139 Cal. Rptr. 97, 110 (1977). Therefore, the plaintiff mother's cause of action for NEID was properly dismissed.

3. *Molien v. Kaiser Foundation Hospitals*, 27 Cal. 3d 916, 616 P.2d 813, 167 Cal. Rptr. 831 (1980).

In *Molien*, a doctor misdiagnosed a patient as having syphilis and advised her to tell her husband so he could be tested and treated if necessary. Since the doctor's negligence was expressly directed at the husband as well as the wife, the husband was permitted to pursue a claim for negligent infliction of emotional distress. The risk of harm to the husband was reasonably foreseeable, therefore the defendant owed the plaintiff husband a duty to exercise due care in diagnosing the physical condition of his wife.

The *Molien* court also found that the plaintiff was not barred from recovery by the fact that he did not suffer a physical injury. The court held that "the underlying purpose of such an action [loss of consortium arising out of infliction of emotional distress] is to compensate for the loss of companionship, affection and sexual enjoyment of one's spouse, and it is clear that these can be lost as a result of psychological or emotional injury as well as from actual physical harm." *Agis v. Howard Johnson Co.*, 371 Mass. 140, 355 N.E.2d 315, 320 (1976).

4. *Thing v. La Chusa*, 48 Cal. 3d 644, 771 P.2d 814, 257 Cal. Rptr. 865 (1989).

In *Thing*, a mother who did not witness an accident in which a car struck and injured her child could not recover damages from the driver of the car for emotional distress she suffered when she arrived at the accident scene. The court held that in the absence of physical injury or impact to plaintiff himself, damages for emotional distress should be recoverable only if

(1) plaintiff is closely related to the injury victim,

(2) plaintiff is present at the scene of the injury-producing event at the time it occurs and is then aware that it is causing injury to the victim, and

(3) as a result, plaintiff suffers emotional distress beyond that which would be anticipated in a disinterested witness.

The court applied this three-part test to determine whether the mother's injury was foreseeable. The undisputed facts established that the plaintiff was not present at the scene of the accident in which her son was injured, did not observe defendant's conduct, and was not aware that her son was being injured. Therefore, the plaintiff mother could not establish a right to recover for the emotional distress that she suffered when she learned of the accident and its consequences.

5. *Ess v. Eskaton Properties, Inc.*, 97 Cal. App. 4th 120, 118 Cal. Rptr. 2d 240 (2002).

In *Ess*, the plaintiff, sister of a nursing facility patient, brought an action for negligent infliction of emotional distress against the nursing facility, alleging that she suffered severe emotional distress as a result of the injuries her patient sister received when sexually assaulted by an unknown intruder.

The court held that damages for negligent infliction of emotional distress (NIED) may be permitted in a "bystander" case where the plaintiff is closely related to the victim of a physical injury, is present at the scene of the injury-causing event and is then aware that it is causing injury, and suffers emotional distress beyond that which would be anticipated in a disinterested witness. In *Ess*, the plaintiff could not pursue a bystander cause of action because she was not present at the event that caused the injury to her sister.

The court also stated that recovery for NIED may be permitted if the plaintiff is a "direct victim." Direct victim cases involve the breach of a duty owed the plaintiff that was assumed by the defendant, imposed on the defendant as a matter of law, or arose out of a preexisting relationship between the two. In this case, the plaintiff alleged that she had a close familial relationship with her sister and had undertaken care for her since her sister's diagnosis with Alzheimer's disease. However, the court held that when the sister became a resident of the nursing facility, the defendants undertook to provide care to the sister. Therefore, the plaintiff incidentally benefited from defendants' duty of care to her sister, but this was not sufficient to support a direct victim cause of action for emotional distress.

6. *Powers v. Sissoev*, 39 Cal. App. 3d 865, 114 Cal. Rptr. 868 (1974).

In *Powers*, the plaintiff sought damages for emotional distress resulting from seeing her daughter thirty to sixty minutes after the daughter was struck by a truck. The court found that the mother could not recover because the circumstances were not materially different from those undergone by every parent whose child has been injured in a non-observed and antecedent accident.

7. *Ochoa v. Superior Court of Santa Clara*, 39 Cal. 3d 159, 703 P.2d 1, 216 Cal. Rptr. 661 (1985).

In *Ochoa*, the plaintiffs sought damages for emotional distress arising out of the death of their thirteen-year-old son. The parents were present when the medical needs of their son were allegedly ignored by personnel of the county juvenile hall. The court found that the parents could bring an action for emotional distress under the "percipient witness" theory pursuant to the court's holding in *Dillon v. Legg*, (1968) 68 Cal. 2d 728, 441 P.2d 912, 69 Cal. Rptr. 72. Mrs. Ochoa [the mother] was a foreseeable plaintiff, looking on "as a helpless bystander as the tragedy of her son's demise unfolded before her." *Ochoa*, at 173.

8. *Fife v. Astenius*, 232 Cal. App. 3d 1090, 284 Cal. Rptr. 16 (1991).

In *Fife*, the parents and brothers of an automobile accident victim sought damages for emotional distress. From their family home, the plaintiffs heard the automobile crash and saw debris fly. The court held that the plaintiffs could not recover because they did not know that the victim was involved in the accident at the time they heard the crash.

9. *Campanano v. California Medical Center*, 38 Cal. App. 4th 1322, 45 Cal. Rptr. 2d 606 (1995).

In *Campanano*, a patient's family brought a cause of action for NIED under the "bystander" theory pursuant to the court's holding in *Dillon v. Legg*. The family sought damages alleging that the hospital had improperly placed an intravenous line in the patient's arm, and that this negligence resulted in the swelling, blistering, and eventual amputation of that arm. The court held that "the only recoverable damages are those which arose from plaintiffs' observation of the injury-producing event, the infusion. Any distress which arose from observations of subsequent injuries . . . is simply not compensable." *Campanano*, at 1329.

10. *Moon v. Guardian Postacute Services*, Inc., 95 Cal. App. 4th 1005, 116 Cal. Rptr. 2d 218 (2002).

In *Moon*, the plaintiff sought damages for NIED after he observed abuse to his elderly mother-in-law in a skilled nursing facility. While at the nursing facility, the plaintiff observed that his mother-in-law had become "malnourished and dehydrated, had lost significant weight, had become immobile and bedridden, had contracted infection, and had become incontinent." The court held that the plaintiff was not "closely related" to his mother-in-law, such as was necessary for him to establish a claim to recover for negligent infliction of emotional distress under the "bystander" theory. *Id*. at 1008.

§ 15.03. EDITING THE FACTS AND DISCUSSION SECTIONS OF A MEMO

Assume that an associate drafted the following facts and discussion sections of a memo on the Ellington case. What feedback would you give the associate?

Facts:

Mrs. Lisa Ellington (hereinafter "Lisa") is interested in filing a claim against the police department and possibly the City of Chapman for negligent infliction of emotional distress ("NIED"). Lisa desires to bring said claim as the result of a tragic incident which occurred at her home two weeks ago whereupon her husband John, a ten-year veteran of the police department, went gun-crazy and killed their seven-year-old son, Josh, and injured Lisa, as well as their three-year-old daughter Katie before he shot and killed himself. John was a wife-beater whose violent tendencies flared when he became intoxicated. There is a recorded history of domestic violence that occurred throughout John and Lisa's troubled nine-year marriage, resultant in numerous injuries, including Lisa's hospitalization one year ago for broken ribs. Lisa reportedly called the police when John was "uncontrollable," which occurred at least seven or eight times over the last two-three years. However, in typical victim fashion, Lisa never pressed charges against John, idealistically believing his promises that he would change. Prior to this event, John had reportedly never injured the children or threatened Lisa with a weapon.

On the night of the incident, Lisa telephoned 911 for emergency assistance and reported that John was drunk and had threatened her with a gun. The children were present and John refused to allow them to go to their rooms. The crying children were therefore present to witness Lisa being punched in the face several times and thrown against the wall by John. When the police arrived John answered the door holding his gun. The officers, Randy Miller and Jake Holmes, took John outside and took his gun away.

Lisa was visibly injured, with blood streaming down her face when she came to the door. She informed the police that she wanted John arrested and prosecuted. Lisa conveyed to the police that she was going to file for divorce and that she could no longer handle John's violent beatings. Lisa told the police that she was going to take the children and go to her mother's, and John was taken to the police station. About two hours after the incident had ended, while Lisa was preparing to leave for her mother's house, John entered the bedroom and shot Lisa in the stomach; he then went to find the children. Lisa heard the gunshots that killed her son and wounded her daughter, but did not actually see the shootings. John then took his own life.

Lisa believes that the police were negligent in failing to hold John at the police station given their knowledge of the danger that John presented to Lisa and the children. Lisa believes that the police violated standard protocol by allowing John, a fellow cop, to leave only two hours after he was taken into custody, when in times past, he was not released until the following day contingent to Lisa's permission. While both Lisa and Katie are predicted to have a successful physical recovery, there are still many medical bills to pay and the emotional scars are likely to plague them forever. Lisa and young Katie suffer regular nightmares and are having difficulty coping, and Katie is easily frightened and unusually withdrawn as a result of the incident.

Discussion:

Recovery under an NIED claim is an unquestionable challenge given its elemental requisites, but not an impossible one under our factual situation. Case history reveals some mixed results regarding recovery for plaintiffs who are mothers under a theory of NIED, and an often essential element is whether the plaintiff actually witnessed the trauma-inducing event, a fact which Lisa does not have in her favor, but Katie might. California's liberal courts seem to reserve a certain amount of sympathy for mother/child scenarios such as ours.

In *Elden v. Sheldon*, 46 Cal. 3d 267, 758 P.2d 582, 250 Cal. Rptr. 254 (1988), the plaintiff boyfriend sued a negligent driver who unlawfully drove his vehicle into the plaintiff's vehicle, which resulted in the injury and subsequent death of plaintiff's cohabitant girl-friend who was the automobile's driver. The plaintiff boyfriend claimed that as a result of their close relationship, and the fact that he witnessed the accident, he suffered foreseeable harm. Although the court recognized "[i]t is manifest . . . that a mother will suffer severe emotional trauma from the death or serious injury of her child in an accident whether or not she is present at the scene," not every relationship is close enough to warrant recovery. *Elden v. Sheldon*, (1988) 46 Cal. 3d at 274. While the relationship between plaintiff and victim is undoubtedly one of the primary factors for allowing recovery under negligent infliction of emotional distress (NIED), the additional elements of proximity and whether the plaintiff actually witnessed the event are becoming more of a concern for the courts.

For example, in *Hoyem v. Manhattan Beach City School District*, 22 Cal. 3d 508, 585 P.2d 851, 150 Cal. Rptr. 1 (1978), the California Supreme Court affirmed the trial court's dismissal of plaintiff mother's claims of emotional distress at having seen her son, injured in his hospital bed, hours after the event occurred. In this case, plaintiff's son was severely injured by a motorcycle while crossing the street. The trial court dismissed all causes of action, and on appeal, although the Supreme Court allowed the plaintiff to collect damages for medical expenses, recovery for emotional distress was not allowed because of the sheer fact that time and distance separated the plaintiff from the actual event and the defendant was therefore not proximately liable for plaintiff's emotional state as she was not a reasonably foreseeable victim. In the instant case, our facts are distinctly more favorable than in *Hoyem*, considering that time and distance are not mitigating factors. The son was shot in the same house as Lisa, separated only by a thin wall. Lisa was present, without being actually in the room; she heard the fatal gunshot and was able to witness the horrific results of John's brutal act within moments of him committing it. A case similar to *Hoyem* is *Powers v. Sissoev*, 39 Cal. App. 3d 865, 114 Cal. Rptr. 868 (1974), where the court refused to allow the plaintiff mother to recover for emotional distress after she saw her child almost an hour after she was hit by a truck. The court held, "we do not think that this court should extend the rule to a case such as this where the shock, as claimed, resulted from seeing the daughter 30 to 60 minutes after the accident and thereafter under circumstances not materially different from those undergone by every parent whose child has been injured in a non-observed and antecedent accident." Our facts can be distinguished from both cases on the basis of location. There was little to no time separating Lisa from the inevitable shock that she would suffer as a result of seeing her seven-year-old son dead. And her presence in the home, hearing the sequence of events unfold but unable to do anything about it, made the experience that much more visceral.

Another favorable case is *Molien v. Kaiser Foundation Hospitals*, 27 Cal. 2d 916, 616 P.2d 813, 167 Cal. Rptr. 831 (1980). In this case, a physician misdiagnosed a patient with syphilis and encouraged the patient to warn her husband so that he could be tested and treated if necessary. After the trial court dismissed the complaint pursuant to the defendant's demurrer, the California Supreme Court, with Justice Mosk writing, determined that the plaintiff husband had stated an appropriate cause of action based on the doctor's misdiagnosis and the husband's resultant emotion distress and loss of consortium. Thus, even though the plaintiff was not present when the doctor informed his wife of her misdiagnosis, and therefore was not in the "zone of danger," he was still entitled to recover under NIED. "In order to limit the otherwise potentially infinite liability which would follow every negligent act, the law of torts holds defendant amenable only for injuries to others which to defendant at the time were reasonably foreseeable." *Thing v. La Chusa*, 48 Cal. 3d 644, 685, 771 P.2d 814, 842 257 Cal. Rptr. 865, 893 (1989) (citation omitted). And the foreseeable risk may entail not only actual physical impact, but emotional injury as well. (*Id.* at 666, 771 P.2d at 828, 257 Cal. Rptr. at 879). In our situation, it was reasonably foreseeable to the police that John was clearly a dangerous man who was likely to cause severe emotional and physical injury to Lisa and her children if he was to be released on that night. The police were aware of the danger that John posed to his family. Nevertheless, they negligently released him despite his lengthy and brutal record of domestic violence coupled with Lisa's pleadings that he be arrested and prosecuted.

Thing v. La Chusa, 48 Cal. 3d 644, 771 P.2d 814, 257 Cal. Rptr. 865 (1989), is another leading case on NIED. This case also involves a mother plaintiff, who did not witness the accident wherein an automobile struck and injured her infant child. The Supreme Court held that damages for emotional distress, absent physical injury, are available only if (1) plaintiff is closely related to the victim, (2) plaintiff is present at the scene of the injury-producing event at the time it occurs and is aware that it is causing injury to the victim, and (3) as a result, the plaintiff suffers emotional distress beyond that which would be anticipated in a disinterested witness. Due to the mother's absence from the scene of the accident and the fact that she was unaware that it was occurring, she was unable to recover under NIED. Our plaintiff is mother and/or sister to the victim; both were present, in the home, at the time the injury producing event occurred and aware of what was happening; and lastly both suffer extreme emotional distress, including regular nightmares, difficult coping, and other depressive symptoms.

The final case for analysis of Lisa's position is *Ess v. Eskaton Properties, Inc.*, 97 Cal. App. 4th 120, 118 Cal. Rptr. 2d 240 (2002), wherein the plaintiff was the sister of a nursing facility patient who brought an action for NIED against the nursing facility after her sister was sexually assaulted by an unknown intruder while under the facility's care. The court acknowledged that bystanders are able to bring claims for NIED and referenced the three-factor test for recovery in *Thing v. La Chusa*. However, in this case, because the plaintiff was not a bystander when the incident occurred and was not aware of what was happening to her sister, her claim was not recognized. As has been established, Lisa was in the home with her children when John returned to the house; he had already shot Lisa and charged off to find the other children. Lisa was a bystander in this situation in every possible way; she was present and aware of what was happening in her home. While the defendant police department may offer the argument that its officers were informed, by Lisa, that she was going to be taking her children to her mother's house that evening, it is nonetheless extremely reckless and professionally negligent behavior for them to release a drunk wife-beater to undoubtedly seek out his family and finish the job only two hours after he was brought into custody. The police took a risk in allowing John to leave early that night, and it was reasonably foreseeable that a mere two hours after the incident, an understandably shaken and upset Lisa would still be at the house. She would have had to calm down two small children and herself, as well as pack for all three of them.

Pursuant to the three-factor test in *Thing v. La Chusa*, Lisa's claim for NIED will survive any demurrers filed by the defendant, and she will successfully recover damages for all medical bills resultant of the incident, and any additional claims for emotional damage. The police department made a grave mistake in allowing John to go early that night, and it was likely because he was a police officer too. John was reportedly visibly drunk, obviously dangerous, and threatening to continue to harm his family; the police department would not have allowed another person in this state to be released prematurely. The law favors

Lisa, and NIED is definitely a viable theory for recovery based on an analysis of precedent, but also because of the particularly egregious conduct by the police.

§ 15.04. DRAFTING THE DISCUSSION

Now write your own discussion section (and facts section if you have not already done so). After you have analyzed all of the case law, predict the most likely outcome for your client's claim of NIED. Your discussion should begin with a statement of your conclusion and a roadmap paragraph that describes how the analysis is organized. Your analysis must be objective—acknowledge and address weaknesses in your claim as well as strengths. Where important questions are not directly addressed by the case law, you should explain them as well.

CHAPTER 16

Writing the Client Opinion Letter

§ 16.01. INTRODUCTION

Writing and speaking to your client is perhaps the most important communicating you will do in your career as a lawyer. Attorneys sometimes become so involved in their cases that they forget the human element. Learn to communicate well with clients and you will have more work than you know what to do with. Clients like to be told what is happening in a case, why it is happening, and what is going to happen next.

One important way to keep the client informed is the opinion letter. An opinion letter advises a client how the law applies to a particular case and suggests action to be taken based on that law. The letter serves as a record of the progress of a case for the attorney and the client. This chapter gives you some simple guidelines to follow in preparing these important documents.

§ 16.02. WRITE IN AN APPROPRIATE STYLE

1. Focus on Your Audience

Remember to write for your reader. In the case of an opinion letter, your reader will usually be either an individual who does not have a great deal of legal knowledge or another lawyer, perhaps your client's general counsel, who is legally sophisticated. Such sophisticated clients often request "formal" opinion letters that involve analysis of, and citation to, relevant legal authority, much like the office memorandum. Each client is different. Your goal must be to write a letter that will help the individual client in a particular case. The better you know your client, the more likely it is that you will be able to achieve that goal.

2. Be Concrete

Your clients want to know what is likely to happen in their cases. A lengthy, abstract discussion of the law without applying it to the client's case will have very little meaning for the client. Explain the applicable rules to the client, but do it in the context of the case at issue.

In this chapter we use examples from student assignments. All of the examples in this chapter are taken from student opinion letters discussing a single case. The case involved a criminal attack on two guests at a hotel. The issue is whether the guests can sue the hotel for negligence. Under tort law, to find negligence in such a case, four elements are required:

1. The hotel must have a duty to protect its guests from criminal attacks.
2. It must unreasonably fail to perform that duty.
3. The failure must have caused the attack at least in part.
4. Damage must result.

Read this passage as if you were the clients to whom it is addressed. In this case, the clients are the hotel guests who were attacked.

Although Florida law has no statutes for a tort action for the criminal acts of third parties committed on a hotel's premises and no security standards have been adopted by the hotel industry, we think that you can bring a successful negligence action against Palm Court Hotel. Our opinion is based on past cases tried in Florida that are similar to your case and that set precedent for the courts to follow. In these past cases both motels/hotels and landlords were held liable for assaults committed by third parties on their premises when plaintiffs could prove that the hotel/motel or landlord had acted negligently in protecting its guests. These rulings are supported by Florida statutes for landlords and innkeepers.

As the clients, what have you learned? Do you understand how previous cases will help the court decide your case? Do you understand the significance of the presence or absence of statutes or industry standards? These are the kinds of questions to which clients should be able to answer "yes" after reading a letter from you. The clients who read this letter would answer "no."

Compare the next two examples and decide which you would prefer to receive if you were the same clients.

FIRST EXAMPLE

A hotel has a duty to protect its guests from harm based on the nature of the business and the social policies involved. In general, a hotel's duty is to exercise reasonable care in protecting its guests. The test for "reasonableness" is whether a reasonable person knew or should have known that there was potential danger based on the circumstances (for example, area crime rate, occurrence of similar crimes on the premises, design of the hotel, etc.) and whether appropriate precautions were taken to prevent or deter such danger. This determination is made on a case-by-case basis.

SECOND EXAMPLE

Generally, in cases like yours two things are required to find the hotel liable. First, the hotel must have had cause to believe that such an attack might occur. Second, a court must find that the hotel did not take reasonable steps to prevent such an attack.

The second example is much more concrete. The sentences are shorter and the language is simpler. Obviously, the analysis must be fleshed out and the law applied to the case, but at least you have a better understanding of the legal test. The concrete examples provided in parentheses in the first example would fit nicely in this paragraph. What else would you add?

3. Avoid Sounding Colloquial

Even when you are writing for lay clients and want to use language they can understand, maintain a formal tone. The rules for opinion letters are the same as for other legal documents. Avoid contractions, slang, and other colloquialisms. You do not want to sound stuffy or cold, but you do want to sound professional. Avoid sentences like these:

> I don't see any problem with this.
> We have several things going in our favor.
> I believe we can nail down a favorable settlement.
> FYI, the courthouse closes at 2:00 p.m. on Fridays.

4. Avoid Jargon and Stilted Language

You should avoid using unnecessary legal jargon and stilted construction. Again, remember your audience. If you are writing to a layperson, avoid legal terminology altogether if possible. But if you are writing to another attorney, he or she will expect you to use appropriate legal terminology. For example, you might include this passage in a letter to the general counsel for the Palm Court Hotel:

> Palm Court Hotel had a legal duty to exercise reasonable care for the safety of its guests. The hotel was obligated to use whatever security devices the average reasonable person would have used in the same circumstances. In view of the hotel design and location, and the criminal activity in the area, there should have been some control over access to the building.
>
> By failing to control or even monitor access to the guest building, Palm Court negligently breached its duty of reasonable care for the Smiths' safety.

Conversely, if you were writing to the Smiths, you would use simpler language, and explain legal concepts rather than using terms of art.

> Palm Court failed to provide chain locks on the guest room doors. While no hotel industry standard requires a chain lock, providing a lock in your case would have enabled Mr. Smith to keep the door locked when checking to see who was at the door.
>
> The extent of a hotel's liability depends in large part on the crime rate in the area surrounding the hotel and the occurrence of similar crimes on or near the premises. If Palm Court was not aware of the sharp increase in the crime rate in the area surrounding the hotel, it should have been. Palm Court was also aware of several similar crimes that had taken place at the Seaside Inn, a sister resort located directly across the street.
>
> A hotel's response to foreseeable danger and its attempts to exercise reasonable care can be measured most easily by the security measures and personnel it provides. Palm Court provided only one guard to patrol the entire resort, including the main buildings, four outlying guest buildings, and the grounds. The hotel also kept the access doors to the guest buildings unlocked at all times. Our security expert will testify that such security measures are clearly inadequate to protect a facility as large as Palm Court.

5. Use Correct Spelling and Grammar

It is just as important to spell correctly when you write to a client as it is when you write to the courts or to other lawyers. Avoid the grammatical errors we discuss in this book. Failure to write proper English will destroy your credibility as a professional. A client quite rightly will wonder about the impression you will make on judges and other attorneys if it appears that you cannot write grammatically or spell accurately. A few extra minutes will help you avoid this problem.

§ 16.03. ANSWER THE QUESTION

Usually a client's specific question prompts you to write the letter. Make certain that your letter gives the client all of the information necessary to make an educated decision. Here are five guidelines that will help you provide this information effectively.

1. Include Important Facts Provided by the Client

Before you analyze the problem presented by your client, you should restate the important facts the client previously provided. The client knows what happened, but your job is to connect those events to the law and give your professional opinion on the probable outcome of the case. It is important to be certain that you and the client have the same understanding of the facts. Recording the known facts in a letter to the client may jog the client's memory about something else important that happened. If other, less helpful, facts surface later, you will be able to remind your client that your more optimistic assessment of the case was based on the facts that came from the client, as outlined in the letter. Your presentation of the facts in our case might look something like this:

> I understand the facts of your case to be as follows: Palm Court is a Florida resort complex with 200 rooms and extensive grounds. It is illuminated mainly by pathway lights, and none of the five buildings have exterior lights. The access doors of the building in which you were staying were never locked. Although the steel door of your suite was spring-locked and had a doorknob with an anti-picking device, there was no safety chain on the door. The door's observation port did not permit you to see to the sides of the door. No trained security guard was on duty at the time of the attack, though there had recently been a dramatic increase in the crime rate in the area, including several thefts at Palm Court and several assaults on persons at the Seaside Inn across the street. On the evening of the attack, you heard a knock on your door. You did not see anyone when you looked out the port, so you opened the door. The attack then took place.

2. Be Accurate

You should have legal authority to support any argument you make. Although you do not cite that authority in a letter to a lay client, you should be prepared to cite appropriate authority in a formal opinion letter. In either case, you must be confident that the relevant authority supports the conclusions you state. The client will make decisions about future actions based on your advice. Provide the best guidance you can.

In our sample case, one writer declared:

> One of the areas of law that pertains to your case involves the responsibility of Palm Court for the acts of your assailants. Palm Court is responsible for the crimes you suffered while you were its guests. A hotel is in the business not only of providing lodging but also of providing its guests with reasonable care for their safety.

The last sentence in the paragraph states the law fairly accurately, but the middle sentence creates a misleading impression. It is up to a court, not the lawyer, to decide whether the hotel is legally responsible for an attack on its guests.

3. Explain Your Answer

It is not enough to tell a client that you advise a certain course of action. Explain the reasons for your recommendation. The reasons may be legal or practical. In either case, make sure you explain the reasons clearly in the letter. In explaining the legal basis for an opinion, be sure you apply the law to your client's case. You learned to integrate your discussion of the law and the facts in Chapter 6. Apply the same rules here.

FIRST EXAMPLE

> We must prove that the hotel failed to exercise reasonable care. Though the hotel exercised some degree of care in the safety measures and procedures adopted, we believe this security was inadequate. We believe that there was a need for not one, but two, patrolling security guards whose shifts would start at 7:00 p.m., not 10:00 p.m. This proposed level of security would have been sufficient to deter the type of crimes which occurred. In addition, Palm Court was or should have been aware of the increasing crime rate in the area and the recent assaults in the vicinity that make this type of crime foreseeable. Palm Court will probably say that the security provided was adequate under the circumstances and, therefore, that it exercised the reasonable care required.

SECOND EXAMPLE

> The security provisions of the hotel, both guards and physical security devices, were found to be inadequate. The number of guards was insufficient for a hotel of that size, and the hours patrolled were too few. The physical security devices were also insufficient, since Mr. Smith had to open the door to see who was there when he heard the knock.

As far as the clients could tell from either of these examples, all the writers have presented are their personal opinions. In the first example, the writer even said "we believe" in two separate places. In the second example, the writer says the security measures "were found to be inadequate." By whom? In both cases, the writer should have given the client some legal basis for the conclusions reached. The idea is not necessarily to cite cases or other authority, but to explain the legal standards by which a court will judge the actions of the parties. Here is a revision of the second example.

> A hotel has a legal obligation to take reasonable steps to ensure the safety of its guests. What is reasonable depends on the circumstances. In this case, the increase in crime in the area and the attacks at the Seaside Inn made the attack on you more likely and therefore legally foreseeable.

Our security expert will testify that these facts made the security provisions of the hotel inadequate. The number of guards was insufficient for a hotel of that size, and the hours patrolled were too few. The physical security devices were also insufficient, since Mr. Smith had to open the door to see who was there when he heard the knock.

4. Do Not Promise What You Cannot Deliver

In addition to making sure that your conclusions are accurate, be certain that your advice is honest. One student wrote:

> In regard to your claim against Palm Court Hotel for the attack that occurred on May 31, 2014, I have concluded that if you decide to proceed, you will probably recover a large sum of money in damages because the hotel was negligent in failing to prevent the crime.

This is a dangerous approach. You may create expectations that you will not be able to fulfill. Even though the law may appear to be in your favor, there are many other factors that can affect the outcome of a legal proceeding. You do not have control over some of these factors, such as the judge or jury who ultimately decides the case, so you should not make promises you may not be able to keep.

Do not interpret this rule to mean that you should take a negative approach when you advise your client. As explained by one writer:

> Not only should advice be affirmative, but the giving of it, as of all things, should be cheerful. Even as with the physicians, while clients come to us for advice, it is usually more for comfort and assurance that they seek us and this is so whether the client be a poor widow or the president of a wealthy corporation. While we must not close our eyes to the bad or disadvantageous or dangerous aspects of the client's problem or situation, we should endeavor to find its most favorable aspect and, from that vantage point, advise him cheerfully and affirmatively what to do. One who has a problem which seems dark and hopeless is not helped by a lawyer who sheds only new darkness upon it. We should remember that the leaders of lost causes were never men of dismal minds. No opinion letter should import fear into the client's mind, unless the writer of it at once eradicates that fear by strong affirmative advice.[1]

As with most legal tasks, you must strive to find the proper balance when you give honest advice to your client.

5. Address Your Client's Concerns

If you are aware of any special concerns of your client, address them in your letter. If your client is a cost-conscious businessperson, you might want to stress the cost-effectiveness of a particular course of action. If your client has never had any contact with the legal system and is somewhat afraid of it, be especially reassuring. Tell the client that you are available to answer questions and that you will be there every step of the way.

Clients like to feel that their lawyers think of them as human beings and not just as files or cases. It does not take much effort to add the little touch that lets a client know you have

---

1. Arthur Littleton, *Writing an Opinion Letter to a Client* (unpublished, 1959).

paid attention to what the client has told you. Listen carefully, be considerate, and communicate effectively.

§ 16.04. TELL THE CLIENT WHERE YOU ARE GOING

As you conclude the letter to your client, continue to think concretely. What is the next step? Who should take that step, and when will it happen? Use the final paragraph of your letter to give the client a clear idea of what happens next, so he or she feels more confident. It is not necessary to summarize what you have said previously in the letter. The document is not that long. Do not offer general predictions about what might or might not happen in the case. Avoid writing something like this:

> For all of these reasons our case against the hotel is strong. Because of previous attacks at the Seaside Inn and the size and expanse of Palm Court we should be able to prove the hotel should have realized the possibility of an attack on its patrons. Whether the judge or jury believes our security expert will be crucial to our case; however, established law does support our expert. The lack of TV monitoring equipment and security access doors also supports our case. Although I cannot assure a decision in our favor, I feel confident that the hotel will be found liable if we bring this action.

The writer could have concluded more effectively by offering to begin legal action upon instructions from the client. In some situations you might suggest a meeting with the client. Sometimes the next step is to wait for action from the court or the opposing party. If so, tell the client that you advise doing nothing and why. Tell the client what will happen next as precisely as possible. The client then will feel more comfortable with the progress of the case and with your representation.

Exercise

Rewrite the following letter using the rules you have just studied. The letter discusses the same case you have read about throughout this chapter.

> Dear Mr. and Mrs. Smith:
>
> This letter pertains to the suit we are bringing against the Palm Court Hotel where you both were assaulted in May of 2014. We are asserting that the hotel was negligent of its required duties to the two of you as guests. To establish negligence we must first prove that the hotel was negligent of its required duties to the two of you as guests. To establish negligence we must first prove that the crime committed against you was foreseeable. Secondly, we must show that the hotel responded inadequately to that foreseeable crime. In establishing foreseeability of the crime, we will try to show that criminal activity within the community and within the immediate vicinity should have alerted the management that a similar crime may occur on its premises. After establishing that the crime was indeed foreseeable, we must then assert that the Palm Court Hotel took insufficient security measures to deter or prevent the occurrence of the crime. An analysis of the security precautions taken by the hotel and testimony from an expert witness will be instrumental in deciding whether the hotel instituted the necessary security system to deter or prevent the foreseeable crime.

We expect the outcome of the suit to be in your favor. There is ample evidence of similar crime within the immediate area of the Palm Court Hotel. We feel that the court will find that the hotel neglected its duties to secure the grounds in light of the foreseeability of the crime. We have evidence that the security staff was insufficient and that the premises were vulnerable to crime. With a judgment in your favor, we can request compensatory and punitive damages. Compensatory damages are damages to compensate you for some of the injuries you sustained and some of the grief you have suffered, however inadequate this may be in reality. Punitive damages are a form of punishment levied upon the hotel for negligence.

Sincerely,

_____

CHAPTER 17

Practice with Client Letters

§ 17.01. INTRODUCTION

This chapter will give you the opportunity to practice drafting and editing a client letter, using the principles you learned in the previous chapter. Assume that you received a memo outlining the facts and law you need to know before drafting a letter to your client, Sandy Harmon. Sandy came to you looking for advice on what to do about a coworker who has been making her life difficult. The facts and legal analysis from the memo are reproduced below.

MEMORANDUM

Facts

Sandy Harmon and Kris Martin both work for a software company, Playtime, Inc. Martin asked Mrs. Harmon out several times, and she refused each time. His behavior progressed into repeated telephone calls to her home and hanging up on her husband. He told Mrs. Harmon he would convince her husband there was something going on between her and Martin so that her husband would divorce her. Shortly after, she started receiving phone calls from strange men making "seriously lewd propositions." She found out from a coworker that Martin had put her phone number and later her address on his webpage. She asked Martin to stop, and he just laughed. More recently, guys have actually come to her house wanting to engage in sex. Her husband has had to chase them off their property. Some of the men even asked if the husband would join. At one point they had to call the police for assistance. Finally, Mrs. Harmon went into work one day and threatened Martin with a lawsuit, and he responded by laughing. She began to cry and yell, trying to convince him to stop. She then had to speak to her boss and explain her situation, and she took the rest of the day off. Mrs. Harmon has suffered emotionally, from lack of sleep and from not knowing what these strange men will do to her or when they will next show up at her doorstep. She is quite frightened and wants this to stop. She wants to know if she has a viable claim against Martin for stalking, either criminally or as a tort, or even both.

Discussion

In California, one can be liable for stalking either criminally or as a tort. Stalking as a crime is defined by California Penal Code §646.9, which defines stalking as willfully, maliciously, and repeatedly following or harassing another person and making a credible threat with the intent to place the victim in reasonable fear for her safety, or the safety of her immediate family. *Id.* The three elements of the crime are (1) repeatedly following or harassing another person (2) making a credible threat (3) with the intent to place that person in reasonable fear of death or great bodily injury. *People v. Ewing*, 76 Cal. App. 4th 199 (1999).

Stalking as a tort is defined under California Civil Code § 1708.7. Although there are no cases dealing specifically with the tort of stalking, it would be appropriate to use the current cases dealing with the crime of stalking since the elements of the two are essentially the same. Under California Civil Code § 1708.7 the elements are:

(1) The defendant engaged in a pattern of conduct the intent of which was to follow, alarm, or harass the plaintiff. . . .

(2) As a result of that pattern of conduct, the plaintiff reasonably feared for his or her safety, or the safety of an immediate family member. . . .

(3) [That the defendant did] one of the following: (A) The defendant, as part of the pattern of conduct specified in paragraph (1), made a credible threat with the intention to place the plaintiff in reasonable fear for his or her safety, or the safety of an immediate family member and, on at least one occasion, the plaintiff clearly and definitively demanded that the defendant cease and abate his or her pattern of conduct and the defendant persisted in his or her pattern of conduct. (B) The defendant violated a restraining order. . . .

The main distinguishing factor is that the tort of stalking requires that the victim demand the defendant to stop his conduct.

Finally, in proving the stalking charges there are two ways the facts of the case can be interpreted. One approach would be that Martin is guilty of stalking based on his conduct of making repeated calls to Mrs. Harmon's home, hanging up on her husband, telling her that he will convince her husband there is something going on so that her husband will leave her, and publishing her phone number and address on his webpage. The second approach that can be taken is that of a co-conspirator. Although Martin did not actually make the lewd comments or appear at her doorstep soliciting sex, he knew that by placing her information on his webpage such actions would result. He actually intended those results, and as a result would be criminally liable for stalking as a co-conspirator.

The first way the facts of the case can be interpreted to determine whether Martin can be found guilty of stalking, either as a tort or criminally, is based solely on Martin's conduct. This approach is further developed throughout this memorandum and is most practically the stronger of the two. However, the second approach of viewing Martin as a co-conspirator has a viable standing in this case as well.

When Martin placed Sandy Harmon's phone number and address on his webpage he arguably met all three requirements of the crime and tort of stalking. He "harassed" Mrs. Harmon by taking her private information and making it available to millions of people. Second, the credible threat element is met through the conduct of the men who actually called her and appeared at her doorstep. They had the apparent ability to follow through on their credible threats and had to be chased away by her husband in order to stop them from committing the act. Finally, we would need to prove that both the strange men and Martin intended to place Mrs. Harmon in reasonable fear of death or great bodily injury. If we can demonstrate that Martin intended to inflict such injury, circumstantial evidence can also show that these men could have had the same intent, since they had to be chased away or the police had to be called. Martin knew that by invading Mrs. Harmon's privacy and publishing her private phone number and address she would be vulnerable to a variety of dangerous situations, which would not only put fear in a reasonable person, but actually caused Mrs. Harmon to fear for her safety.

The first element of stalking requires "repeatedly following or harassing another person, which causes that person to suffer substantial emotional distress." *Ewing*, 76 Cal. App. 4th at 199. In that case, the defendant initially was storing his belongings in the victim's garage, but became more intrusive and began to ask for food and money. *Id.* at 203. He then started to make explicit comments to the victim. Shortly after, the victim noticed that the defendant had set up residence in her garage without her permission. *Id.* He continued to stalk her by videotaping her home, calling her repeatedly, and vandalizing her yard and garage. He was finally arrested when he stole her television set and VCR. *Id.* at 204. The court began its discussion by defining the term "harass" as outlined in § 646.9(e) ". . . a knowing and willful conduct directed at a specific person that seriously alarms, annoys, torments, or terrorizes the person, and that serves no legitimate purpose." The court continued to elaborate that this course of conduct ". . . must be such as would cause a reasonable person to suffer substantial emotional distress, and must actually cause substantial emotional distress to the person." *Id.* at 206.

The court's holding in *Ewing* was that the victim did not demonstrate substantial emotional distress and therefore the defendant could not be found guilty of stalking. This holding should concern our victim, Mrs. Harmon, and we will need to get more detail from her about the nature and extent of her emotional distress. The court in the *Ewing* case went to great lengths to define every term in the statute. *Id.* at 207.

The rationale for the court's decision appeared to be based on its in-depth analysis and definition of each term in the statute, in order to demonstrate whether both the defendant and the victim met the requirements of stalking. The court went as far as analyzing what adverb precedes and qualifies the terms in the statute. The court defined "alarm" as "to strike with fear: fill with anxiety." *Id.* at 207. By placing Mrs. Harmon's private information on his webpage, Martin clearly has placed Mrs. Harmon in a position to be alarmed and anxious, not knowing who will show up at her doorstep. "Annoy" is defined as "to irritate with a nettling or exasperating effect." *Id.* Once again, Martin's conduct can easily be labeled as annoying and has had an exasperating effect on Mrs. Harmon, to the point where she had to take time off from work. The court continued to define other terms such as "torment," which is to "cause (someone) severe suffering of body or mind: inflict pain or anguish on," "terrorize," which is to "fill with terror or anxiety," and "terror," which is "a state of intense fright or apprehension." *Id.*

The court continued its analysis of these terms by pointing out that they are preceded and qualified with the adverb "seriously." So each term should be read with "seriously" preceding it. *Id.* at 208. The court then applies the reasonable person standard and rephrases the definition of "harass" as "a knowing and willful course of conduct directed at a specific person that [a reasonable person would consider as] seriously alarm[ing], [seriously] annoy[ing], [seriously] torment[ing], or [seriously] terror[ing] the person." *Id.*

Additionally, the court clarified that the reasonable person standard also applied to the victim when dealing with the course of conduct that would cause a reasonable person to suffer. *Id.* at 208. This would thus reduce the possibility that a victim's subjective reaction to a certain defendant would factor into play. *Id.* The court concluded that the "definition of 'harass' in section 646.9(e) establishes a standard of conduct which is ascertainable by persons of ordinary intelligence," so that a person could determine whether they are breaking the law by their conduct. *Id.* at 209. With that in mind, it is clear that we need to demonstrate that any ordinary person would suffer substantial emotional distress from Martin's acts of harassing phone calls and taking private information like a phone number and address and publishing them on the webpage for millions of people to access. In addition, we must demonstrate that this conduct did actually cause Mrs. Harmon to suffer substantial emotional distress.

The court in *Ewing* established guidelines to determine whether someone actually did suffer substantial emotional distress. "At the very least, we can safely assume that the phrase means something more than everyday mental distress or upset . . . the phrase . . . entails a serious invasion of the victim's mental tranquility." *Id.* at 210. The court continues its analysis of substantial emotional distress since it is not defined in the statute. By looking to the tort of intentional infliction of emotional distress as a guideline, the court concludes that substantial emotional distress means emotional distress of such substantial quantity or enduring quality that no reasonable man in a civilized society should be expected to endure. *Id.* The court wanted more than "sleepless nights" and "joining a support group." *Id.* at 211. The court concluded that ". . . there was insufficient evidence that Ewing's conduct, however offensive and annoying, actually caused Ferguson to suffer substantial emotional distress, within the meaning of §646.9." *Id.* at 212. Mrs. Harmon has mentioned that she is "furious," "frightened," and "short of sleep." There needs to be more than a mere inconvenience in her life. Therefore, more facts are needed to determine the extent of her emotional distress in order to prove that she suffered substantial emotional distress.

The second element of stalking is the making of a credible threat. Under §646.9(g), a credible threat is any verbal or written threat as well as a threat implied by a pattern of conduct. In *People v. Halgren*, the defendant stalked the plaintiff by repeatedly calling her at home and work, and saying such things like "[b]itch, you don't know who you are f *** ing with. I am going to call you whenever the f *** I want to, and I am going to do to you whatever the f *** I want to." *People v. Halgren*, 52 Cal. App. 4th 1223, 1227 (1996). He also went to her place of work, watched her, called her, and made statements like "God, I've missed you. You look great in black today." *Halgren*, 52 Cal. App. 4th at 1224. The court in that case found the defendant guilty of stalking and stated, "[t]o meet the statutory definition the threat must be made with the specific intent to cause the victim to reasonably fear for her personal safety or the safety of immediate family." *Id.* at 1231. The issue in that case was whether his conduct constituted a credible threat. The court held that the facts of the case do indeed present a credible threat.

The court's rationale was that the mere making of a credible threat was not enough and that simply expressing one's feelings or emotions does not trigger the statute. The statute clearly specifies "(1) The credible threat was made with the intent and apparent ability to carry it out so as to cause the target to reasonably fear for personal safety or the safety of immediate family; and (2) the threat was made in combination with willful, malicious and repeated following or harassing of the target." *Id.* at 1231. This definition of credible threat gives the prosecution a broad range of activities without having to prove that the stalker actually intended to execute what he threatened he would do. Therefore, we will not have to prove that Martin actually intended for Mrs. Harmon to be hurt by the strange men or that he actually intended to convince her husband to leave her. All that is needed is that he intended to make the threat, to cause her reasonable fear, and that he did so by his willful and repeated phone calls and harassing.

The court in *People v. Falck* also followed this rationale. In this case, defendant met the plaintiff when she was nineteen years old, while she was working at a restaurant.

People v. Falck, 52 Cal. App. 4th 287 (1997). The stalking behavior began when he started to repeatedly visit the victim at the restaurant. The stalking progressed to him sending her twelve black roses, and then letters being sent to the restaurant, professing his love for her and how he and the victim were meant to be together for eternity. *Falck*, 52 Cal. App. 4th at 291. He was finally arrested when he ignored the manager's request to not come to the restaurant. The defendant was given six months court probation and a court order to stay away from the defendant. *Id.* at 292.

Twelve years later the stalking commenced and by then the victim was married. *Id.* The defendant began studying astrology, and the movements of the planets convinced him that the time was right to try again. *Id.* After an exhaustive search the defendant was able to locate the victim and called her, identifying himself as George Frederick. *Id.* He said, "I found you. I can tell by your voice." *Id.* After her husband got involved the telephone calls stopped, but he started to write her letters professing his great anticipation of their impending wedding, sending pornographic pictures and astrological references. *Id.*

The defendant was finally arrested, and the search of his apartment found numerous photographs of the victim throughout his apartment. *Id.* The defendant argued that he did not have the specific intent to make a credible threat; he was just expressing his love for her and his need to marry her. The court outlined the two-prong test detailed in *Halgren* and concluded in its holding that "[b]y these requirements § 646.9 limited its application to only such threats as pose a danger to society and thus are unprotected by the First Amendment," and found the defendant guilty of stalking. *Falck* at 297.

The court explained that it is not imperative that a threat be made with the intent of actually carrying out the act that is threatened in order for it to be a credible threat. *Falck*, 52 Cal. App. 4th at 291. The court's rationale was that a ". . . true threat includes a threat which on its face and in the circumstances in which it is made is so unequivocally, unconditionally immediate and specific as to the person threatened, as to convey a gravity of purpose and imminent prospect of execution." *Id.* at 295.

The court in *Falck* continued to explain the premise of its decision by noting that § 646.9 has ". . . withstood constitutional challenge for its inclusion of the term repeatedly." *Id.* at 294. The court continued to highlight that the terms "harass," "credible threat," "willful," and "malicious" are all sufficiently defined and definite. *Id.* The defendant, however, challenged the word "safety" and claimed that the term is not defined by the statute and has no clear definition. *Id.* However, the court dismissed this reasoning and stated that the term has a commonly accepted usage and ". . . whether related to a defendant himself or to others, . . . has a commonly understood meaning which gives adequate notice of the conduct proscribed." *Id* at 295.

Although Martin's conduct was not as extreme as the defendant in the *Falck* case, there is still sufficient evidence to show that a credible threat was made and that the requirements of the two-prong test were also met. It is true that no one act of Martin's would be sufficient to trigger the statute. However, when we look at his combined efforts and his intent to convince Mrs. Harmon's husband to leave her and to scare her by placing her private information on his webpage, she not only feared him, but actually had reason to fear him, especially since he reacted by laughing at her whenever she pleaded with him to stop his stalking.

As noted earlier, there is no significant difference between the tort and the crime of stalking. However, in the tort of stalking the third element requires that ". . . on at least one occasion, the plaintiff clearly and definitely, but unsuccessfully, demanded that the defendant stop his pattern of conduct." § 1708.7. This element differs slightly from the crime of stalking by adding the additional prong whereby the victim must clearly communicate her desire for him to stop the pattern of conduct. The court in the *Falck* case concluded that the defendant intended to cause fear in the victim when he insisted on making contact with her even though she clearly asked him to stop. Additionally, the defendant was warned by her husband, the police and the court to stop his behavior, yet he ignored all requests. *Id.* at 291. Similarly to our case, Mrs. Harmon has made it clear that she wants the harassment to stop, her husband has made it clear, and Martin still continued to harass her and cause her to fear for her life by not only ignoring her repeated requests to stop but also continuing to make her vulnerable to the strange men by not removing her phone number and address from his webpage.

The third element for both the crime and tort of stalking requires that the stalker have the intent to place that person in reasonable fear of death or great bodily injury. The prosecution must prove that the stalker intended to cause the victim to be afraid and that he had the ability to carry out his threat. There is no specific intent requirement that the stalker intend to execute the threat; the prosecution must only show the ability to execute the threat if he wanted or had the opportunity to do so. Because Martin placed her phone number and address on his webpage, Mrs. Harmon was swarmed with strange men soliciting sex from her. This would clearly put any woman and her family members in fear of bodily injury or death.

Martin may try to defend his actions and say that even if he had the intent to scare her into leaving her husband, he did not have the apparent ability to carry out the threats he made. Unfortunately for him, this line of reasoning will fail. In *People v. McClelland*, the defendant and victim married while the defendant was in state prison for attempting to murder his former wife by burning down her house. *People v. McClelland*, 49 Cal. Rptr. 2d 587 (1996). Soon after he was released, he became abusive with the victim and the victim's daughter. When the daughter went away to college he became obsessed with her and wrote love letters to her, but those letters then turned abusive. In one letter, the defendant stated that if he had seen someone "'blow [Linda's] head off,' he would 'spit on [her] carcass.'" *McClelland*, 49 Cal. Rptr. 2d at 590. The victim got a restraining order, but the defendant still continued to stalk her by making repeated telephone calls, ramming into her front gate with his car, and even throwing explosive objects at her house. The defendant was finally arrested after he parked his car in front of her house. *Id.*

The defendant argued that there was not sufficient evidence that he made a credible threat with the intent to place the victim in reasonable fear; in other words, he did not have the apparent ability to carry out the threat. *Id.* at 593. The court responded and held that "[t]he circumstances leading to defendant's attempted murder conviction, his threatening display of matches to Erdman, his throwing of a bottle at the house, and his overall behavior during the period in question, constituted substantial evidence of his apparent ability to carry out the threat, a fire bomb at 6:00 o'clock." *Id.* The court's rationale was that since the defendant was convicted of attempted murder and other violent and harassing acts, he had shown he would have the apparent ability to execute his threat on this current victim. The court explained, ". . . a reasonable person, aware that the defendant had been convicted of attempted murder in burning his former wife's house, would reasonably fear for her safety. . . ." *Id.* at 154. It would be very helpful to Mrs. Harmon's case if we can determine if he had done this to any other women and, even more important, if she was aware that he is capable of this type of conduct. This is not a required element, that he stalked before or that she was aware that he was capable of violent acts against women, but it would certainly strengthen Mrs. Harmon's case if this information was known.

Our case is distinguishable from all the cases cited so far, in that the stalker in our case has not demonstrated the level of violent, neurotic, or obsessive behavior of the defendants who have been found guilty. However, the medium Martin has chosen makes his actions even more dangerous. He used his webpage, and by doing so, he has made Mrs. Harmon vulnerable to several stalkers, all at the same time. The victims in the other cases had only one deranged man after them; our plaintiff has had to deal with several men each night. What Martin has done has brought stalking to a new level by introducing a new level of fear in a victim, from several men at once. The potential for danger is far greater from several deranged men than it would be from one, who can possibly be traced because the victim knows who the stalker is. Mrs. Harmon does not have the advantage of knowing who her stalkers are or how dangerous they are.

The second approach we can take brings the analysis to another level and makes the stalking case even stronger. One can be found guilty of conspiracy to commit a crime when there is a meeting of the minds of two or more persons with the intent of performing a crime. The meeting of the minds element of conspiracy can be tacit, depending on the jurisdiction. We would need to further investigate exactly what Martin's webpage said and how he presented her private information. If her private information was portrayed in such a way that we could prove that whoever saw his webpage had an understanding that they were agreeing to some type of behavior that could be classified as stalking, then Martin would be guilty of conspiracy to stalk, as well as stalking. All co-conspirators are responsible for actions of their peers performed within the scope and in furtherance of the conspiracy. As stated earlier, more facts are needed, but we do not have to prove that Martin knew exactly what these men would do as long as their acts constituted "furtherance of the conspiracy," which in this case is stalking.

Mrs. Harmon has several avenues of retribution/justice available to her. If Martin is found guilty of the crime of stalking, the California Penal Code § 646.9 mandates ". . . imprisonment in a county jail for not more than one year or by a fine of not more than one thousand dollars ($1,000), or both that fine and imprisonment, or by imprisonment in state prison." § 646.9(a). If there is a restraining order, injunction, or any other court order, any person who violates § 646.9(a) will be "punished by imprisonment in the state prison for two, three, or four years." § 646.9(b). If a defendant is found guilty of stalking after having been convicted of a felony under § 273.5, 273.6, or 422, he ". . . shall be punished by imprisonment in a county jail for not more than one year, or by a fine of not more than one thousand dollars ($1,000), or by both that fine and imprisonment, or by imprisonment in the state prison for two, three, or five years." § 646.9(c)(1). Finally, Martin may also have ". . . to register as a sex offender pursuant to subparagraph (E) of paragraph (2) of subdivision (a) of section 290." § 646.9(d).

§ 17.02. EDITING A LETTER

Assume that an associate drafted the following letter to Mrs. Harmon based on the above analysis. What feedback would you give the associate on the draft letter?

Mrs. Sandy Harmon
32441 Mediterranean
Monarch Beach, CA 92677

RE: Stalking charges against Kris Martin

Dear Mrs. Harmon:

Thank you for contacting our offices and giving us the opportunity to represent you. The purpose of this letter is to explain your rights and remedies and tell you what we can do for you. Please remember that we are here for you and if you should need any assistance or have any questions, please do not hesitate to contact our offices.

Although we know you are aware of the facts of your case, we would like to reiterate them, just to ensure that we have the facts correct. Also, if there is anything missing or something you forgot to tell us, please be certain to notify our offices immediately. According to our last meeting you explained to us that you and Kris both work for a software company. Kris asked you out several times, but you refused each time. He then started making repeated telephone calls to your home and hanging up on your husband. He told you he would convince your husband there is something going on between the two of you so your husband would divorce you.

A couple of weeks ago, you started receiving phone calls from strange men making "seriously lewd propositions." You eventually found out from a co-worker that Kris had put your phone number on his webpage. So you confronted Kris and asked him to "knock it off," and he just laughed it off. He not only ignored your request, but Kris exacerbated the situation by placing your address on his webpage. You explained that within the past week men have actually appeared at your home wanting sexual favors from you. So, you went on his webpage and found out that he put your address on his webpage. Kris went so far as to say on his webpage that you would welcome all "comers" and that you would play hard to get, but that was part of the game, and that you really meant yes. It has become so bad that your husband has had to chase them off your property and at one point you had to even call the police for assistance.

Finally, while at work one day you once again asked Kris to stop and even threatened him with a lawsuit, and he again responded to your pleas to stop by laughing. You began to cry and yell, trying to convince him to stop. But when that failed, you were forced to speak to your boss about the situation and took the rest of the day off.

Mrs. Harmon, you have explained to us that you have suffered emotionally due to lack of sleep and not knowing what these strange men will do or when they will next show up. You have expressed how frightened you are and that you want this to stop. In our last meeting, you asked us if you had a viable claim against Kris for stalking, either criminally or as a tort, or even both. We believe you do; however we will need more facts from you to make our case stronger. The law does support your claim for stalking, but there are some weak points that we will discuss further with you. We will also discuss your remedies and the options you may pursue.

In California, one can be charged with stalking as a crime or as a tort. The requirements for the two are essentially the same, so you do have both options available to you. The basic definition that could cover both would be: willfully, maliciously, and repeatedly following or harassing another person and making a credible threat with the intent to place that victim in reasonable fear for her safety or the safety of her immediate family. The courts define "harass" as a knowing and willful course of conduct directed at a specific person that seriously alarms, annoys, torments, or terrorizes the person, and that serves no legitimate purpose. Additionally, "course of conduct" is defined as a pattern of conduct composed of a series of acts over a period of time, evidencing a continuity of purpose. Finally, the courts define "credible threat" as a verbal or written threat, including that performed through the use of an electronic communication device, or a threat implied by a pattern of conduct. The inclusion of the term "electronic communication" is important for your case because the term includes the use of computer to make a credible threat.

Kris willfully and it can be interpreted as maliciously called your house repeatedly, hanging up on you and your husband. He also harassed you by taking your private phone number and home address and placed it on his webpage. Furthermore, he made a credible threat that he will convince your husband that there is something going on between the two of you, with the intent to place you in fear. Also, by placing your private information on his webpage he has clearly placed you and your husband in reasonable fear of physical injury or death. We will argue that any reasonable person would be placed in fear if strange men showed up at her doorstep soliciting sex. However, please be aware Kris can defend his actions by saying that he did not intend to scare you or your husband and that he was just expressing his love for you. Fortunately, the law has made it clear that there is no longer free speech protection when you make a credible threat with the intent and apparent ability to carry it out and the credible threat was made in combination with willful, malicious, and repeated following or harassing of the target.

Although we went into great lengths regarding the facts of your case, we do need you to provide more specific information about the emotional stress you have suffered. This is one of the weakest areas in your case. The law is clear that you need more than sleepless nights and a few sessions of therapy. It needs to be more substantial than that. In our last meeting you explained to us that you have experienced sleepless nights and are frightened, but we need more specifics from you about how you have coped with this trauma in your life. Once we have all the details, we will be better prepared to move forward with your case.

We can also look at your case from a different perspective. Kris can still be charged with stalking, either as a tort or crime, or both; in addition, he can be charged with conspiracy to stalk. This is not the strongest perspective on your case, but it is a viable avenue. We can argue that by placing your information on his webpage Kris intended that these strange men come to your house or call you over the telephone and solicit sex from you. We can further argue that he knew this would place you in reasonable fear of physical injury or death and he intended for these men to place you in such fear for your life. Depending on what else he said or conveyed on his webpage, we can possibly prove that there was a tacit agreement between Kris and every guy who decided to telephone you or come to your doorstep harassing and soliciting sex from you.

Now we would recommend that our first step should be to send Kris a letter, asking him to stop his acts, remove your information off his webpage and to stay away from you and your husband. Although this decision is entirely up to you we think it is in your best interest that we make every attempt to convince him to stop his behavior, in order to avoid the court system. This will not only save you money, but also time and frustration. However, if he does not cooperate and insists on harassing you and continues his stalking behavior, or if you want us to altogether bypass writing a letter, we can press forward with a lawsuit against him. During this time we do ask that you document any new instances from here on out, just in case he does not cooperate and we do have to go to court. We need to have everything he has done to you well documented with dates and descriptions of the conduct. This will help make your case stronger and give us more ammunition if we have to go to court.

Finally, there are several remedies available to you. If Kris is found guilty of the crime of stalking, we can ask the court to issue a court order for him to stop his behavior and remove your private information off his webpage, in addition to facing imprisonment in county jail for no more than one year or a fine of no more than one thousand dollars ($1,000), or both. If you get a restraining order before we go to court and he continues to stalk you, then the court may punish him in state prison for no more than two, three, or four years. Also, if he has committed a felony prior to this and is found guilty of stalking, he can face county jail for up to one year, a fine of no more than one thousand dollars ($1,000) or both, or state prison of two, three, or five years. Additionally, he may have to register as a sex offender. Now, if Kris is liable for stalking as a tort, he may be liable to compensate you in damages, in addition to serving jail time.

Please advise whether you would prefer for our offices to first send him a letter, which we would provide to you for approval before we send it to him, or if you would rather we bypass that option and file suit immediately. Either way, please let us know of your decision within a week from the date of this letter. Please contact our offices if you have any further questions or information you need to provide to us. We will keep you apprised of any new findings or developments in your case.

Sincerely,

_____

§ 17.03. DRAFTING A LETTER

Now write your own letter to Sandy Harmon. Remember to include a brief synopsis of the facts to confirm that you understood them correctly and to make clear that any legal analysis in the letter relies on those facts. You should outline the legal analysis without jargon or excess detail. You should give Sandy some options to consider, along with the advantages and disadvantages of those options. You should clarify what the next steps are, and what response you seek from the letter.

CHAPTER 18

Advising the Client

§ 18.01. PURPOSE OF THE CONSULTATION

Once you have researched the client's problem and given the client some preliminary feedback in the form of a letter, you are ready to meet with the client again. This is the time to decide how to proceed with the client's matter. The process of decision making in a client-centered approach to counseling requires patience and thoroughness. Remember that the decision is not yours to make, but the client's (Model R. Prof. Conduct 1.2). Your purpose at this point in the process is to help the client arrive at a decision that will meet as many of the client's articulated goals as possible. Your purpose is not to tell the client what you would do or to substitute your judgment or priorities for those of the client. Your job is to provide the client with all relevant information so that he or she can make as informed a decision as possible. This includes discussing the most likely consequences of pursuing various options and the advantages and disadvantages of those options. Your plan for a follow-up meeting with the client should take all these considerations into account.

§ 18.02. THE SCENARIO

As we work through the planning process for a follow-up consultation, assume that you have already interviewed a client and gathered this information:

Susan Starkey is a member of a video dating service. On about December 20, she chose John Partlow from the video dating service. After speaking for hours on the telephone, the two agreed to meet at a dating service party on December 28. At the party, Partlow told Susan she was gorgeous, and she reported that she felt sparks, too. They exchanged email addresses and sent more than a dozen messages back and forth.

After five days, Susan told Partlow to "get lost," feeling that he was trying to get too close too fast. He was already starting to talk about marriage and kids. On January 6, Partlow left a message on Susan's answering machine telling her he had secretly watched her leave work. She became worried and filed a police report on January 7. Police told Partlow to have no more communication with Susan, computer or otherwise, but no official restraining order was issued.

On January 15, Partlow sent Susan another email message. "I've been trying to court you, not stalk you. If you let me, I would be the best man, friend, lover you could ever have. I just want to show you how well we go together. You've turned my innocent and somewhat foolish love for you into something bad in your own mind."

When Susan received the message, she replied via email. She sent Partlow a message stating that if he did not leave her alone, he would be sorry.

On January 24, Partlow sent Susan another email, threatening to email the story to all her computer friends, and mail it to her family and old boyfriends. He informed her that "this is the least of the many things I could do to annoy you." He said he knew she must be seeing someone else, and that he had figured out her password and was monitoring her email messages to find out who the other guy was.

This last message frightened Susan, but she is afraid that police action might not deter Partlow, or that it might make things even worse. Since the incident, she canceled her membership with the video dating service. She is afraid to use her computer for any online services and gave a friend her password, asking that the friend delete any messages from Partlow before she logs on. She also changed the hard drive on her computer and completely rebuilt her system. She is having trouble sleeping and is considering contacting a counselor to help her deal with the situation.

Susan wants to know whether there is any way she can sue Partlow, to make him pay for all the disruption he has caused in her life. She would like compensation for her distress. She feels that Partlow has diminished the quality of her life with his threats. She told you that she wants her life back.

Susan also expressed interest in finding out if she has any claim against the dating service, since it certainly seems to her that it could screen its clients better. When she called the service to complain about Partlow, the person she talked to said, "Oh yeah, him. You know, this is the second or third complaint we've had about him. We may just have to cut him off." The person she talked to was the receptionist, Sandy Adams. Ms. Adams said she would relay Susan's complaint to Tony Benton, the head of the dating service, but she never heard anything from him. Susan made the original call three or four weeks before she came to see you. Assume that the last email from Partlow arrived about two weeks before Susan came to see you.

§ 18.03. PLANNING THE CONSULTATION

As you plan the consultation, start with your understanding of the client's goals and priorities as they have been articulated to you thus far. Susan has told you that she wants compensation, both from Partlow and from the dating service, and that she wants her life back. Compare these goals and priorities with the results of your research as you have set them out in your memo and letter. Assume that your research and analysis have led you to the conclusion that you might be able to bring successful civil suits, against Partlow for intentional infliction of emotional distress (IIED) and against the dating service for negligence in screening customers.[1] It is also possible to contact the police and pursue criminal charges.

Try to estimate the likelihood of various events with some degree of precision, and think through the consequences, positive and negative, of making each decision. Then, outline the topics you and the client need to discuss. Assume that you believe the suit against

---

1. Depending on your jurisdiction, you might identify other possible causes of action as well. For example, in California it is possible to bring a civil action for stalking.

Partlow has about an even chance of succeeding, and that the odds of a successful suit against the dating service are slightly better. One distinct disadvantage of either suing Partlow or trying to have criminal charges brought is that Susan will likely have to face him in court at some point. You should also evaluate the likelihood that Partlow will be able to pay a substantial judgment. What other likely consequences can you think of? Advantages and disadvantages?

It is a good idea to find some way to keep track of all this complexity. You may want to make a chart before you begin the consultation. The chart should list the options you have considered in your planning process, and perhaps leave room for other options that might be developed during the consultation. You should identify any advantages and disadvantages that occur to you before the consultation, and leave space for others that might be identified by the client. You might want to include the client's goals and concerns in the chart, so that you will have a ready reference to check as the option development process proceeds. Here is one way you might prepare such a chart:

Options	adv.	disav.	goals/concerns
civ. suit–IIED			
civ. suit–negligence			
crim. charges			

§ 18.04. BEGINNING THE CONSULTATION

You should begin this meeting, as with the initial interview, with a friendly greeting and a little casual conversation. Again, you want the client to relax and feel comfortable. You should also offer a brief preparatory explanation, so the client knows what to expect of this meeting. Share your outline of the meeting with the client, and ask if the client has any topics in mind that you have not included. For example, your consultation with Susan might begin like this:

You: Hi, Susan. How are you today?
Susan: OK, I guess.
You: Are you feeling any better?
Susan: I'm hoping you can give me some good news today, and then maybe I will.
You: I hope so too. Can I get you something to drink?
Susan: No thanks.
You: Did you get the letter I sent?
Susan: Yes.
You: Do you have any questions about the letter?
Susan: I don't think so; not right now anyway.
You: What I am hoping we can do today is discuss the options I mentioned in the letter, and any other options or concerns that may have occurred to you. I would like us to review the advantages and disadvantages of all the options, and then try to make a decision about how you wish to proceed. I prepared a little chart that we can use to keep track of our discussion. Do you have any questions, or is there anything you want to add before we get started?

§ 18.05. REAFFIRMING THE CLIENT'S GOALS AND PRIORITIES

Early in the consultation, you should check to make sure that your understanding of the client's goals and priorities is correct, and that they have not changed since you and the client last discussed the matter. If any material facts have changed, or if the client has reassessed the desirable outcomes, you want to know that before you get too deeply into the discussion you have already prepared based on your earlier understanding. Ask if the client has had a chance to review the letter you sent, and if she has any questions about the letter.

To determine Susan's priorities, you may want to ask some questions about choices she would make. For example, ask her whether it is more important that she never have to face Partlow again or that he be forced to compensate her. Can you think of other questions that might help you prioritize her goals?

§ 18.06. DEVELOPING OPTIONS

We have identified three preliminary courses of action:

1. A civil suit against Partlow for IIED
2. A civil suit against the dating service for negligence
3. Contacting the police in the hope of criminal charges being filed

1. Likely Consequences

In order to help Susan make a decision, you need to share with her your estimation of the likely outcome of these options. You should identify the most likely and least likely outcomes, and perhaps the "best case" and "worst case" scenarios. Clients would obviously like you to predict the likelihood of a particular outcome as precisely as possible, perhaps using percentages—e.g., "we have a 50/50 chance of prevailing in the intentional infliction of emotional distress suit, and a 70 percent chance of prevailing in the negligence suit against the dating service." Many lawyers are uncomfortable with the idea of attaching numbers to their estimates, fearing that there are simply too many variables to allow such precision. The law is fundamentally a human process, and trying to predict what parties, witnesses, judges, and juries are likely to do is often little more than an educated guessing game.

If you are uncomfortable with the idea of assigning numbers to your estimated chances of success, you must come up with some other way of communicating your perceptions to the client in a way that will be understood. Remember that the client will interpret whatever you say in a way that makes it meaningful for the client. Thus, if you say "we have a pretty good chance of succeeding on this claim," what is that likely to mean to the client? You may mean 50/50 or 60/40, but the client may hear 70/30 or 80/20. You may try to offer a range of numbers, or you may try to be very conservative and guess low. Remember, however, that the client is entitled to your honest assessment of the likelihood of success of the options you discuss.

If you have previous experience in the area, or if you have researched jury verdicts in similar cases, you can share that information with the client. You can discuss the variables that make perfect prediction impossible. If the client understands the complexity of the process, the client may also understand why you can't offer guarantees, or even odds, with any degree of certainty. We do not have the perfect solution to the dilemma; you will have to experiment to find a way of communicating the likelihood of success that you are comfortable with and that gives the client a reasonable opportunity to understand the situation.

2. Advantages and Disadvantages

You also need to discuss the advantages and disadvantages of each option, and of the various ways of approaching each option. For example, as you discuss the possibility of civil suits, you should always advise the client about the time and costs involved, and of the various alternative dispute resolution mechanisms available. You should discuss the advantages and disadvantages of filing a complaint before attempting to negotiate, and vice versa. You should explain the process of mediation, along with its advantages and disadvantages. Can you think of other consequences, advantages or disadvantages that should be discussed in this case?

You should also explore nonlegal considerations that create advantages and disadvantages, and ask the client to help you think these through. For example, in this case, Susan has obviously suffered a great deal of emotional distress, to the point where she has taken the extreme and possibly irrational action of rebuilding her computer. She needs to think about how it would feel to have this matter occupy another several months, if not years, of her life. Can you think of other questions you might want to ask Susan that would help you understand the implications of the nonlegal concerns that would affect the decision-making process in this case?

It should be clear by now that this option development process can get quite complicated. It gets even more so as you actually discuss the details of each option. You will find that the discussion of one option leads you into a discussion of another, as you compare and contrast likely consequences. You will move back and forth between the options and the client's goals to check whether proposed options are meeting the client's needs. You will shift back and forth between options, and you may discover that discussing consequences leads you to other options you had not considered.

§ 18.07.   CHOOSING A COURSE OF ACTION

Once you have gone through this process of option development, it is time to make a decision. You and the client must sift through all the information you have produced as you discussed the options and choose a course of action. If your option development process has produced a clear choice in the form of a single option that has many more advantages and fewer disadvantages than other options, the choice will be easy. Unfortunately, this is frequently not the case. All of the options are likely to have advantages and disadvantages. You may find yourself with too many good choices, too many bad choices, or something in between. You should go back to the client's goals and priorities and try to make a choice that way. Is there one option that meets more goals, or does less damage to the client's goals, than other options? If not, ultimately the client will simply have to make a decision, and make the best of it. Here is one way part of your decision-making dialogue with Susan might go:

You: OK, Susan, we have discussed the advantages and disadvantages of our three options. What do you think?

Susan: I don't know. It all seems so complicated.

You: I can certainly understand that. Let's try going back to what brought you to see me in the first place. You wanted compensation, and you wanted your normal life back. Do I have that about right?

Susan: Yeah, that's about it.

You: Now, we have discussed the likelihood that you will have to face Partlow at some point if you sue him or if you contact the police about criminal charges. We have also discussed the possibility that Partlow may not be able to afford a lot of money and that it may be difficult to collect any judgment we do get. You also know how long a lawsuit might take to get resolved. Can you help me balance those concerns against what you were hoping to accomplish?

Susan: Well, that all makes suing Partlow seem like it might be more trouble than it's worth. And I don't know if I want him to go to jail. I just want him to leave me alone. What about suing the dating service?

You: I'm glad you asked that; I was going to mention that next. You would probably not have to deal with Partlow in that suit, but it could still take a lot of time to resolve. Like I said, I am hopeful that the dating service might be willing to negotiate a settlement, but you never know. Would you like me to contact them, and see how they respond?

Susan: Sure, let's see what they say. I would hope they would understand they made a mistake on this one.

You: So would I. Now, let's get back to the question of how we get Partlow to leave you alone.

If the client seems stymied, remind her that no decision is also a decision. In other words, discuss the advantages and disadvantages of doing nothing, and compare them to the other choices on the table. If the client asks you what you would do, there are two ways to present your choice. You can articulate the client's values as you understand them and tell her what choice you would make based on those values, or you can tell her what your values are and tell her what choice you would make based on those values. Either way, you should not tell her what you would do without articulating the values that guide you to that choice. For example, how risk averse are you, and how much are you guided by emotional as opposed to rational factors in making choices? You may also refuse to tell the client what you would do and insist that she make the choice.

What if you disagree with her choice? If you are satisfied that she has made an informed choice, and her decision does not pose any ethical or moral dilemmas for you, you should do whatever is necessary and appropriate to implement her decision. If you think she has made a mistake, perhaps because she does not understand some aspect of the likely consequences of her decision, you can try again to educate her by running through the advantages and disadvantages. Always remember, however, that the decision is hers and not yours, and that you owe the client an obligation of competent and diligent representation. Therefore, if you deeply disagree with what the client wants done, to the point that your representation is likely to be compromised, you should say so and offer the client the option of seeking other counsel. If the disagreement is extreme, you may seek to withdraw from the case.

§ 18.08. GETTING SETTLEMENT AUTHORITY

Once the decision is made, you should get explicit instructions from the client about the limits within which you must operate. For example, if you have decided to negotiate with the dating service on the negligence claim, you should discuss with Susan the elements of a settlement agreement that would satisfy her. How much money should you ask for, and what is she willing to settle for? If the dating service wants confidentiality of any settlement terms, does she have a problem with that? Can you think of other elements that might come up in these negotiations? If you do not have this conversation at this point, you may find yourself in a negotiation with no authority to settle. This may frustrate you, your client, and the other party. You will have to come back to her with simple questions that could easily have been answered at this stage if only you had thought to address them.

It should be obvious that we have touched only on the issues that go into helping the client to reach an informed decision. The process is much more complex, and the possibilities more numerous, than we can convey in a few pages. However, if you keep the basic principles in mind that we have discussed here, and come up with organizing strategies that help you and the client keep track of important factors, you should be able to help your clients reach informed decisions that offer as much satisfaction in the long run as is possible given the difficult circumstances that brought the clients to you in the first place.

Exercise

Make up a chart for your consultation with Susan Starkey that incorporates the issues we have already touched on, and any others that occurred to you as you were reading and answering the questions posed throughout this chapter. There is no particular format that is appropriate for such a chart; play with it until you come up with one that you think will work for you.

§ 18.09. CONSULTATION CHECKLIST

— Plan for the consultation by identifying options based on your understanding of the client's goals and priorities and the applicable law you have found. Think about likely consequences, advantages, and disadvantages of those options.

— Prepare a chart outlining those options, consequences, advantages, and disadvantages. Leave room on the chart for contributions in all these areas that may come up during the consultation.

— Remember to greet your client warmly and have a bit of casual conversation if the client seems to need an opportunity to settle down and relax.

— Check with the client to see if anything has changed, if your understanding of the facts is correct, and if you understand the client's goals and priorities. Give the client a chance to react to your letter and to ask any questions.

— Go through the options you have developed, including likely consequences, advantages and disadvantages, and give the client ample opportunity to react and contribute. Give the client the best assessment of the likelihood of success that you can.

— Get a decision from the client and discuss how you will act on it. If you are going to negotiate, make sure you understand the limits of your settlement authority.

CHAPTER 19

Negotiating

§ 19.01. INTRODUCTION

Negotiating skills are important in many aspects of life. We begin negotiating with our parents at a very young age. We negotiate with employers, with friends and colleagues. We negotiate major purchases such as cars and houses. Lawyers negotiate constantly—plea bargains, settlements, contracts, and many other types of transactions. Along with client counseling, negotiation is the most frequently performed and critical lawyering function. Nevertheless, most of us have never had any formal training or organized learning on the subject. We frequently do not even give much thought to the process. We don't plan our negotiating strategy or analyze how and why the process works the way it does. Nor do we reflect on our negotiations after the fact to figure out how we might have done better.

This chapter gives you an introduction to concepts that will allow you to plan for and learn from your negotiations in an organized way. We help you to begin to understand the inner workings of the negotiations process so that you can control both the process and results to a greater extent, and serve your clients better along the way.

As you study the material about negotiating, think about how the fact that negotiations are so common might influence your approach to research and writing. When you begin research for a memo, for example, think about the fact that the lawyer on the other side of the case is doing the same thing you are doing—looking for legal support for his or her client's position. Then imagine that after you have completed your research, you will be trying to negotiate a resolution to the problem. You will want to have thoroughly researched the law that supports both sides of the case, so you can respond to any arguments that might be put forth by opposing counsel. You will want your memo to reflect that research, so you can make cogent arguments in support of your client, and anticipate arguments from the other side. When you put your legal research and writing in the context of what lawyers actually do with the information, you will research and write more effectively.

One form of writing that is closely associated with negotiation is the settlement agreement. We explore principles that are important to drafting effective settlement agreements in Chapter 21.

§ 19.02. PURPOSES OF NEGOTIATION

The purpose of any negotiation is to reach an agreement. If that is not your purpose, you might as well save your energy and go to court. The essence of negotiation is compromise and problem solving. Whether you are trying to decide custody and visitation or how much money an injured victim is entitled to, you must assess the needs and interests of the parties and try to reach a resolution that meets as many of those needs as possible. Obviously some needs and interests will be in conflict, and there must be some balancing and decision making. The likelihood that you will be able to meet everyone's needs is very small, as is the likelihood that one party will walk away with all the marbles. Therefore, you must plan on giving as well as getting.

§ 19.03. THEORIES OF NEGOTIATION

There are many approaches to negotiating, but we will focus on two approaches here: the adversarial and problem-solving modes of negotiating.[1] Most lawyers, and probably most individuals, at least begin with an adversarial approach to negotiating—that is, the idea that someone must win while the other will lose. The problem-solving approach, which requires a great deal of trust, is less common, particularly among negotiators who have no history with each other. As you gain experience, you will develop a flexible approach to negotiating. You will adapt various methods of negotiating to suit your own personality and the many contextual variables that determine which negotiating approach is most appropriate in any particular situation.

1. Adversarial Models

We will briefly discuss three models for adversarial negotiating: game theory, economic, and social-psychological. We present the outlines of the theories so that you can gain a preliminary understanding of how theorists look at the negotiating process, and perhaps identify some frameworks that will help you in your negotiation planning. Understanding how and why the other party may be approaching the negotiation may help you plan your own strategy. Our belief is that models have some utility for conceptualizing the process, but that ultimately the process is sufficiently human and therefore unpredictable that you cannot rely too heavily on artificial constructions.

a. Game Theory

The game theory approach to negotiation views the negotiation as being composed of the usual components of a game: players and rules. If you know the rules, you can predict what the players will do. You can plot out the possible avenues of progress for the negotiation in advance because the players have limited options based on the rules. The chief

---

1. For a more in-depth discussion of the theories touched on here, see Robert M. Bastress & Joseph D. Harbaugh, *Interviewing, Counseling, and Negotiating* (Little, Brown 1990).

problem with this approach to negotiation is that it can only really work in a world of perfect information, where you know exactly what everyone else knows and how that information will affect the decisions of all the players. Fortunately or unfortunately, negotiation players do not all play by the same rules, they tend not to share all their information, and they don't behave predictably. Nevertheless, constructing a model for negotiating that uses some of the elements of game theory can be a useful organizing tool.

There are some "rules" of negotiation: for example, most negotiators don't start negotiating at the bottom line—they leave themselves some room to bargain. Also, it is frequently the case that concessions get smaller as bargainers approach their bottom lines. It is at least a convention of negotiating that it is poor form to revoke a concession once firmly made. You may learn or discover some other "rules" that offer some predictability for the process. Let us see how the first two "rules" might help you to predict the "moves" in a negotiation:

Assume that Party A, the plaintiff in a personal injury suit, demands $5 million to start. Because Party B, the defendant, knows that most negotiators set their opening demands to leave bargaining room, B knows that the next "move" is to make a counteroffer rather than simply offer to write a check. If subsequent concessions by A follow this pattern: $4 million, $3.5 million, $3.25 million, $3.125 million, then B can apply the "rule" of diminishing concessions to infer that A's bottom line is somewhere around $3 million. Of course, A can make strategic use of this assumption to suggest a false bottom line. Negotiation is nothing if not a complex strategy game!

You will rarely if ever negotiate in an environment of perfect information. Negotiations frequently take place before discovery is completed, perhaps even before it is begun. Even if discovery has been completed, the likelihood that you know everything there is to know is very small. People simply don't provide complete information in response to discovery requests—the requests may not seek the right information, the respondents may not remember everything, or there may be reasons, such as privilege, for not providing full information.

Finally, negotiators are human beings. They make decisions and choose courses of action for all sorts of reasons. Individuals have different priorities, different levels of risk aversion, and different personal styles. All of these can make it difficult to predict what a negotiator will do. This difficulty becomes compounded by the fact that a negotiator is representing a client, who also has idiosyncratic goals and preferences that may influence the negotiation.

b. Economic

The economic model of negotiation envisions a continuum along which the negotiation progresses. Each party begins at one end of the continuum, and the parties move together toward the middle until they reach their stopping point, or bottom line. If there is overlap between the stopping points, there is a "zone of settlement" within which the negotiation should settle:

(Assume that Party A starts negotiating at W and sets her bottom line at X)

W>>>>>>>>>>>>>>>>>>>>>>>>>>>>>>>>>>>>>X

($500,000)   ($250,000)

(Assume that Party B starts negotiating at Y and sets his bottom line at Z)

Z<<<<<<<<<<<<<<<<<<<<<<<<<<<<<<<<<<<<<<Y

($350,000)   ($100,000)

Here the zone of settlement is between Z and X, or between $250,000 and $350,000.

(Party A) W>>>>>>>>>>>ZoooooX<<<<<<<<<<<Y (Party B)

If the stopping points fall short of each other, there can be no settlement:

(Party A) W>>>>>>>>>>XoooooZ<<<<<<<<<<<Y (Party B)

This model of negotiation works reasonably well if the subject of the negotiation is an easily measured or relatively fungible item such as money, and the parties can take successive positions along the continuum. It does not work as well where the negotiation involves multiple items, at least some of which cannot be quantified or broken into pieces that can be given up. For example, if the negotiation involves custody of a child, there is no continuum to move along—one parent or the other will get custody, or they will share joint custody. There are no other options.

c. Social-Psychological Bargaining

We refer to this approach to bargaining somewhat cynically as the "head-game" theory of negotiation because it involves negotiation by manipulation of perceptions. "Head-game" bargainers don't bargain on the merits of the facts or law; they try to make you uncomfortable in one way or another or to affect your perceptions in a way that causes you to want to give in. They may try to make you feel intimidated ("I went to an Ivy League law school and have been practicing for twenty years"), or guilty ("How can you represent a client who did such reprehensible things?"), or physically uncomfortable or off-balance (turning up the heat or providing uncomfortable furniture), with the idea that you may give up just to get away.

There is virtually no limit to the aspects of negotiation process that can be manipulated by a bargainer determined to approach negotiation from this extremely adversarial position. The best defense against a "head-game" bargainer is to recognize the game and ignore it. If you insist on bargaining on the merits, you may be able to neutralize the tactics of your negotiating opponent.

2. Problem-Solving Negotiation

The problem-solving approach to negotiating requires a paradigm shift. The problem-solving negotiator does not think in terms of concessions, compromise, and positions, but rather analyzes needs and interests, and looks for solutions to the mutual problem facing the negotiators. That mutual problem is the dispute between the parties. If you can reframe your thinking to look at the dispute as the "enemy," rather than the party on the other side of the negotiation, you will be much more open to a problem-solving orientation.

The problem-solving negotiator looks for ways to make the pie bigger, rather than simply carving it up. A problem-solving negotiation involves more free-flowing information and brainstorming of possible solutions. The problem-solving negotiation is not constrained by the game board or the economic continuum, but moves outside the lines to address as many needs and interests as possible. Real brainstorming involves putting all possible solutions on the table, without immediate judgment, and then discussing them to see how they work with the various needs and interests at issue.

Since this mode of negotiating focuses on the parties' needs and interests rather than bargaining positions, using it should enhance the probability of success. The challenge is to determine whether both the personalities and the subject matter involved in the negotiation lend themselves to this approach. If you determine that the subject matter is appropriate, which is particularly likely in a multiple item, nonmonetary negotiation, and that you are comfortable with your negotiating counterpart, you might ask about the needs and interests of the other party. Of course, you must be prepared to honestly share your client's goals as well. Then the negotiators can work together to devise options that take into account as many of the needs and interests on the table as possible.

§ 19.04. STYLES OF NEGOTIATION

The basic personal approaches to negotiation are competitive and cooperative.[2] This is not to say that these are polar opposites; most of us could place ourselves somewhere on a continuum from highly competitive to highly cooperative. Most of us also tend to believe that other people essentially behave the same way we do. Therefore, cooperative bargainers may be vulnerable to exploitation when faced with competitive opponents because the cooperative bargainer will tend to make concessions in an effort to induce reciprocal behavior. The cooperative bargainer tends to assume that sufficient cooperative behavior must induce reciprocity from an opponent, while the competitive opponent, believing that all people are essentially competitive, will take whatever is given and push for more. This individual does not believe that cooperative bargainers exist, and therefore assumes that the concessions made by the cooperative bargainer are not real concessions—no rational person would give things away unless they did not matter!

There are more effective cooperative negotiators than there are effective competitive negotiators, at least in part because more people tend to be cooperative. In addition, competitive negotiators can sometimes be so abrasive that they cause breakdowns in the process, and so they are less effective.

Cooperative negotiators can protect themselves by making contingent concessions. In other words, do not actually give anything away until you have gotten something in return. Make it clear that all proposals on the table are contingent on the final agreement being satisfactory. For example, in a collective bargaining negotiation over compensation, management's counsel might say, "My client might be willing to contribute more to the

---

2. *See* Charles B. Craver, *Effective Legal Negotiation and Settlement* (7th ed., LexisNexis 2012). Nancy Schultz is grateful to Charlie Craver for many of the insights that guide her thinking and teaching about negotiations.

pension plan, but we would need your client to relax the demand for a large raise in salary. What is your client willing to give up?"

Negotiation models and personal styles can intersect in interesting ways. Cooperative bargainers can adopt adversarial strategies, and competitive negotiators can be problem solvers. The cooperative negotiator using an adversarial model will offer concessions and compromise, while the competitive negotiator trying to function as a problem solver will focus only on his or her own client's needs and interests, and will push solutions that meet those needs and interests.

§ 19.05. PLANNING FOR NEGOTIATION

You should plan all aspects of the negotiation: the information exchange, your opening offer or demand, and subsequent concessions. You should establish an opening offer or demand, a target point at which you would like to end up, and a bottom line below which you will not or may not go. We will discuss each of these stages in turn.

1. Evaluating the Case

The first step in your planning process is to evaluate the case as objectively as possible. In order to do this effectively, you need to have a thorough understanding of the law and the facts, and how they intersect. The beauty of negotiation is that you are not limited by what a court is likely to do with your case, but assessing the likely result in court is a good starting point for evaluating acceptable settlements. Therefore, you need to research relevant law and, if possible, find jury verdicts in similar cases. The general rule of thumb for establishing an acceptable settlement point is the likely verdict multiplied by the likelihood of prevailing. For example, if you think you could get a jury award of $800,000, but you think you only have about a 70 percent chance of winning, you should settle for $560,000.

How do you figure out the likelihood of prevailing? In addition to the strength of your legal support, look at factors such as the novelty of the claim, the credibility of likely witnesses, the availability of admissible evidence, and the track record of other players in the game, including opposing counsel, judges, and juries. You should also evaluate opportunity costs associated with litigating or not litigating. This is obviously not a science, and it is impossible to calculate the value of the case with mathematical precision, especially given that different people have widely divergent value systems, but you must start somewhere.

2. Planning to Exchange Information

Inexperienced negotiators frequently underestimate the importance of information exchange to an effective negotiation. You will feel much more confident in your negotiated result if you have sufficient information about the underlying events, needs, and interests. You will be more successful at obtaining useful information if you plan for the process beforehand. It may help to think about information as belonging to one of three categories: information you want, information you don't want to divulge, and information you want your opponents to have.

You have control over the latter two categories, and it should be relatively simple to categorize the information in your possession. You should, however, think strategically about the dissemination of information. People generally give more weight to information they have to work to get, while ascribing lesser significance to information that is easily obtained. This means that you may be able to get your opponent to devalue damaging information by simply stating it up front. This may seem counterintuitive initially, but if you think about it, it should make sense. Before fighting information requests, you should be sure that information that seems dangerous at first blush is really all that damaging. Frequently there are perfectly logical explanations for facts that seem harmful, and sometimes you may even be able to turn an apparently damaging fact into a useful tool. You will find it easier to evaluate information objectively during your preparation than you will in the heat of the negotiation.

Plan your questioning of your opponent. Identify categories of information you want, and ask questions that are precisely designed to get that information.

3. Establishing an Opening, Target, and Bottom Line

Much strategizing is done on the subject of where to begin a negotiation. Some negotiators hesitate to begin negotiating at all for fear of appearing weak. There is little evidence that either party to a negotiation gains an advantage by starting or refusing to start the process. It is possible that the party that makes the first concession will do less well in the final result. Some experienced negotiators prefer to make the first offer or demand because doing so allows them to set the stage for the negotiation and begin to limit the playing field. Other negotiators prefer to draw an opening offer or demand to respond to, on the theory that they can set the midpoint of the opening positions (where many results tend to cluster) with their response. You should probably do whatever feels most comfortable to you or whatever is appropriate in the context of a particular negotiation. For example, plaintiffs in personal injury actions frequently make the first demand.

The trick in establishing an opening offer or demand is to set the starting point at a place that is credible, but that also gives you some bargaining room. Starting too close to your bottom line in an effort to be fair or to make the negotiation more efficient may cause frustration all around. Most negotiators simply will not believe that your opening position is designed to be fair, and there will be quite a struggle to keep the final result in the range you had in mind. Conversely, an outrageous opening offer or demand may cause the other party to refuse to negotiate at all until you have come down to a reasonable point. Outrageous starting positions are difficult to defend and frequently require huge initial concessions just to get the bargaining started. Find a starting point that you can justify with a straight face and that leaves some room for bargaining, and even for the possibility that you may have miscalculated the value of the case. Remember that your opponent knows things you don't know, and this may affect the reasonable settlement point in ways you cannot anticipate.

Set a target point, a point at which you would like to settle and that you believe is reasonable based on the information you have. Head toward this target point during the negotiation and make a serious effort not to go below it unless you are persuaded that there can be no settlement in this range. Finally, set a bottom line before you go into the negotiation. This should be the point below which you absolutely do not intend to go, and you should hold firm at that point if you get there during the negotiation, unless you are satisfied that you have seriously misanalyzed the problem. Negotiators who do not preset bottom lines frequently find themselves "giving up the farm" during the negotiation.

Once you start giving, and begin to feel a commitment to settlement, it can be difficult to refuse that final concession in the interest of finalizing a deal.[3]

You should also think about a concession pattern in advance. How do you plan to get from your opening to your target, and then ultimately to your bottom line if you have to go there? Obviously the actual concession pattern will to some extent be dictated by the events of the negotiation, but you will feel more confident if you have thought about where you want to go after the opponent rejects your opening offer or demand, as is virtually inevitable. If the opening offer or demand is accepted, you have almost certainly badly underestimated the value of the case!

4. Analyzing Needs and Interests

You should make an effort to identify the needs and interests of the parties as accurately as possible before the negotiation. You may want to classify the anticipated needs as essential, important, or desirable, and then try to figure out whether those needs are likely to be shared, independent, or conflicting.[4] You should consider the importance of the needs and interests to your client: some needs will be deal-breakers, or essential, and if your client's essential needs are not met, there can be no deal. Other needs and interests will be important or desirable, and you should be able to categorize them before the negotiation, so you can prioritize the more important needs. You may find that needs and interests shift categories as the negotiation proceeds—sometimes progress toward agreement can soften earlier demands, and something that was previously essential can become "merely" important.

You should look for shared needs; for example, both parties may need to avoid litigation, or they may want to keep the agreement confidential, or both parties to a custody dispute may want the best for the children—they simply disagree about how to achieve it. Independent needs are those that can be met without creating an adverse impact on the other party. For example, if one party to a negotiation needs the terms of the settlement to be confidential, and the other party has no desire to talk about the deal, the need for confidentiality is an independent need. Independent needs are good bargaining chips— use them in exchange for things your client wants. Conflicting needs cannot be met without the other party having to give something up. Conflicting needs are obviously where the most difficult negotiating will happen.

If you can identify independent or shared needs, start the negotiation there. It is easier to get the process started if you can get an agreement on bargaining items that are not likely to create conflict. Beginning the negotiation with difficult or contentious items can lead to early breakdown. The most likely area of difficulty in the formulation we suggest is the area where essential needs of the parties are in conflict. If you arrive at this point in a negotiation, bring your creativity or prepare to go to trial!

This approach to categorizing needs is particularly appropriate for a problem-solving negotiation, but it can be useful in virtually any situation. Thinking of a negotiation in terms of needs and interests rather than positions frequently makes the bargaining more

---

3. Remember that all of this takes place in the context of your instructions from your client. You should know what your settlement authority is before you begin to negotiate, and you may not agree to anything outside of that authority. At best, you can offer to take a proposal to your client that does not satisfy the goals set by you and the client before the negotiation.

4. This formulation appears in a very useful chart in Bastress & Harbaugh, *supra* n. 1, at 483.

flexible and the conversation less strained. It may also open up possibilities for resolution that would not have occurred to you otherwise.

5. Planning for Personalities

Try to find out what you can about your negotiating partners or opponents. Negotiating style and personality can have a huge impact on the progress of a negotiation. Some people have so much trouble communicating that they simply cannot have lengthy face-to-face meetings. If you find yourself in a negotiating situation with someone who makes you so angry you cannot think straight, get out! You are likely to make mistakes if you are angry or in some other emotional state that clouds your thinking sufficiently that it becomes difficult to make rational decisions. Conversely, if you are negotiating with someone who is fair and reasonable, the process can be a pleasure. Remember that everyone's job is to represent their client, and try not to take it personally if you don't get everything you want.

§ 19.06. BEGINNING THE NEGOTIATION

If you have prepared adequately, the beginning of the negotiation should be easy. Try to establish a comfortable, constructive atmosphere for negotiating. If the negotiators don't know each other, a little small talk to allow everyone to relax may be helpful. It may be a good idea to set an agenda for the negotiation. For example, you may agree on an order of topics to be addressed; you may agree in advance that all options put on the table are contingent on an acceptable final settlement. The latter approach is a good way to avoid deadlock later on if the only item left to be discussed is a particularly difficult one, and you find yourself wishing that you had something else left to ask for or to give away. A lot of negotiators try to gain some sort of tactical advantage by playing "head games" in the early stages of a negotiation; this may be effective for some in the short run, but you will generally find that the process works better if everyone just gets down to business and concentrates on trying to deal with the joint problem to be solved that brought you to the table in the first place.

§ 19.07. INFORMATION EXCHANGE

As we mentioned earlier, this is obviously a critical phase of the negotiation. How can you reach the optimal resolution of a problem if you don't really understand what the problem is? Again, if you have prepared adequately, this phase of the negotiation should be productive. You want to find out as much as you can about the other side's needs, interests, and priorities. You want to obtain any facts that will help you understand the situation and that might be relevant if the case does go to trial. If you have filed a complaint, you may be able to get some of this information through discovery, but negotiations frequently take place before discovery is completed, and perhaps before it is even begun.

Open-ended questions, such as "What was your client doing right before the accident?", may get you more information, but they also allow more opportunities for evasion if a party is determined to evade the question. Listen very carefully to the answers you get. If the responder is hedging or seems to be choosing words very carefully, think about the precise words you used in your question and rephrase the question in a way that leaves less wiggle room or that is more precisely designed to get the information you seek. For example, if you are negotiating a settlement of the Smiths' claim against the Palm Court Hotel, and you want to establish the hotel's knowledge of criminal activity in the area, you might ask if hotel personnel were aware of any similar incidents in the area. This question allows the responder to define "similar incidents." If the negotiator chooses to interpret that phrase in a very limited way, he or she might decide that since there were no identical incidents, the answer is "no." You should ask instead whether the hotel is aware of any criminal activity within a specified radius of the hotel.

If you get questions you prefer not to answer, there are many blocking techniques available. You can answer with a question, you can "misunderstand" and answer a different question, you can hide your answer in a lot of irrelevant verbiage, you can refuse to answer, you can declare the question irrelevant or out of bounds, or you can answer part of the question. You should consider the likely effect of using too many blocking techniques on your own ability to obtain information. Why should the other party answer your questions if you refuse to answer theirs? You should also be aware of the likelihood that these techniques may be used against you and watch out for them. If you sense that information requests are being blocked, don't give up—rephrase your questions until you are satisfied that the information does not exist or will not be forthcoming. It is frequently disappointing or worse for negotiators to realize that critical information was available if only they had asked for it in the right way.

All in all, the negotiation will be much more productive if there is a constructive and thorough information exchange. If you want to obtain the best result for your client, you want to provide the information that supports the result you seek. The parties are much more likely to reach a mutually satisfactory resolution of the problem if there is genuine understanding of the issues on all sides. The exchange of information will frequently suggest possibilities for resolution that may not have occurred to anyone during preparation.

§ 19.08. TRADING

This is the point of the negotiation where the actual exchanges take place. The key here is to keep track of the concessions and to explain them in terms that are relevant and understandable. Do not make multiple unreciprocated concessions. Do not make concessions that are disproportionately large when compared to your opponent's concessions. Make sure that you explain the rationale for every concession and every refusal to make a concession. Concessions that are not justified in terms of the applicable law and facts are merely numbers or positions that come from nowhere and have little credibility or persuasive effect. There is nothing to distinguish one number from another if you cannot connect it to something concrete.

For example, if you are seeking damages for the Smiths, explain how you arrived at the number you request using factors such as lost wages and medical expenses; if you agree to accept a smaller number, explain the concession in terms if something that has happened during the negotiation—a fact of which you were unaware or a trade-off for something else that will benefit your clients. Negotiations will frequently get to a point where everyone is simply "horse-trading" to arrive at a resolution, and finally perhaps "splitting the difference" to finalize the deal. This should be the natural evolution of the negotiation—not the starting point.

§ 19.09. CLOSING THE NEGOTIATION

Once you believe you have achieved a negotiated resolution, take a few moments to find out if it is possible to adjust the agreement in some way that benefits both parties or that allows one party to benefit without damaging the other party. These few moments at the end of a negotiation can make a large difference in the parties' commitment to the agreement and willingness to carry it out. They can also go a long way toward preserving or rehabilitating the relationship between the negotiators. You will discover that the importance of reputation cannot be overemphasized in the legal community, and a reputation as a competent, fair negotiator will take you far.

You should also use this final stage of the negotiation to make sure that you have actually reached an agreement. Go back over the terms in detail and make sure that both parties have the same understanding of the agreement. Get something in writing, even if it is only an outline of the terms you plan to take to your clients for approval. You can follow up later with a more detailed writing, a formal draft, or a confirming letter. Proper handling of this crucial step will save you much grief later on. Misunderstandings can cause serious problems and may end up unraveling the whole deal if it turns out that the parties had very different feelings about the meaning of a critical term or even different understandings of what the deal actually was. If both sides are not "on the same wavelength," a thorough recap should make it clear very quickly, indicating a need for further negotiation or recognition of an impossible situation.

§ 19.10. NEGOTIATION ETHICS

There are very few written rules that govern negotiations. There will be no one there looking over your shoulder to see if you behave or not. One rule that does apply is that you may not make a false statement of material fact or law (Model R. Prof. Conduct 4.1(a)). This is obviously a simple statement of a complex range of possibilities. For example, when does an omission rise to the level of a misrepresentation? If you know that the opposing party is relying on a misconception about what the facts are, and you do nothing to correct it, are you misrepresenting the facts? Negotiators frequently try to skate this line very closely; you will have to make your own decisions about what kind of negotiator you want to be, and what kind of behavior will allow you to sleep at night. Do remember that your reputation will not only precede you, but will affect how and whether people interact with you.

It is a convention of negotiating that the client's value system is not considered a material fact. Thus you may "lie" about what your client is willing to accept and even about your bottom line. You do not have to respond honestly to direct questions about what your client wants, as you do to factual questions in other areas. You should know, however, that you may do damage to the negotiating process and to your reputation by lying about such things to the extreme. A certain amount of puffery is expected, but if people learn that you will look someone in the eye with a wounded expression and plead that you are being taken to the cleaners while you are in fact cleaning out your opponents, you will find future negotiations difficult.

Another type of behavior that causes damage to the process is lying about what kind of negotiator you are. Many competitive "sharks" can adopt the language of the cooperative problem solver while they are taking advantage of genuinely cooperative negotiators.

If discovered, however, they may find later negotiations uncomfortable. Again, however trite it may sound, you must let your conscience be your guide in negotiations.

We have obviously only skimmed the surface of the complex set of interactions that is negotiation. However, we believe that we have given you sound advice that will serve you well as you develop your own negotiating style and ideas. You will learn a lot about the process through experience, and there are plenty of books on the market if you wish to do further reading.[5]

§ 19.11. NEGOTIATION CHECKLIST

— Prepare, prepare, prepare. Research the law. Know the facts. Plan your information gathering and exchange. Analyze needs and interests. Write down your opening, target, and bottom line, and think about likely and acceptable concession patterns. Find out whatever you can about your negotiating partners and opponents.

— Exchange information until you are satisfied that real bargaining can take place in an informed environment.

— Keep track of concessions. Justify all requests and concessions with thoughtful explanations of relevant facts and law.

— Close the negotiation by checking to see if you can adjust the agreement to benefit one or more parties without damaging others. Make sure all parties have the same understanding of the agreement.

— Think about what kind of negotiator you want to be and what kind of reputation you want to have in your negotiating community.

Exercise

Here is the general information for a negotiation exercise. Your instructor will distribute confidential information for each party and give you further guidance regarding how to conduct the negotiation.

Landlord/Tenant Problem

General Information

Millie Graves is seventy-nine years old. For the past fifteen years, she has lived in a second floor apartment in Garden Grove. About a month ago, Millie was mugged outside the front door of her building. Her attacker had apparently followed her from the street, waiting until just before she entered the building, when she was in the shadow of the large bushes growing in the front yard. There is a light over the front door, but it was not on that evening. The attack took place sometime between 9:00 and 9:30 p.m. Millie was not seriously injured, but she suffered bruises and scrapes when her assailant knocked her to the ground after he grabbed her purse. She lost all her identification, credit cards, and approximately $80 in cash. There is normally a doorman stationed at the desk just inside the front door, but he was not at his desk at the time of the attack.

---

5. For example, you might want to take a look at the classic *Getting to Yes* by Roger Fisher & William Ury (Houghton Mifflin 1981), or, for some very practical advice, *Negotiating Your Salary: How to Make $1000 a Minute* by Jack Chapman (Ten Speed Press 1996).

Millie has never been a problem tenant. She doesn't complain and she pays her rent on time. For the past three months, however, she has withheld $100 per month from her monthly rent of $500 in an effort to get the landlord, Sam Simolean, to make several repairs to her apartment. There is a leak in her shower, water damage to her kitchen ceiling from a leak in the apartment above hers, and two broken windows. Her apartment has not been painted in two years, and it shows. There are also quite a number of insects running around the building, particularly in the common areas. Millie has three cats, which was perfectly fine with her previous landlord, but Simolean has instituted a "No Pets" policy for new tenants. Based on Millie's failure to pay her full rent for the past three months, he recently served her with an eviction notice, giving her sixty days to vacate the premises. The lease requires thirty days' notice of termination for failure to pay rent. Millie still has fifteen months to go on a two-year lease.

CHAPTER 20

Mediation

§ 20.01. INTRODUCTION

Mediation is an increasingly important part of being a lawyer. The odds are very high that at some point in your career you will participate in mediations as an attorney representing a client. This chapter introduces you to the process of mediation and also to the types of writing that accompany mediation.[1] We will introduce you to mediation briefs and agreements to mediate. In Chapter 21 we discuss settlement agreements.

§ 20.02. WHAT IS MEDIATION?

Mediation is facilitated negotiation. When parties can't resolve a dispute in face-to-face negotiations (with or without attorneys), they may seek the assistance of a neutral party who can help them reach agreement. A mediation is a meeting among the disputing parties and the facilitator, during which everyone works together to reach agreement. Mediations may make sense in a variety of settings—for example, a divorce dispute, a probate controversy, or a business matter. Mediations may take many forms: The parties may all sit around a table together to try to work out a resolution (conference mediation), or the mediator may engage in "shuttle diplomacy"—a series of confidential meetings (called "caucuses") between the mediator and each party during which the mediator probes for information and possible solutions and carries proposals back and forth between the disputants. Or the mediation may be some combination of the two formats.

You may hear about different approaches to mediation: facilitative, evaluative, and transformative. Facilitation is the purest form of mediation; in that form, the mediator's role is to encourage the parties to communicate with each other in order to resolve the dispute at hand. But some parties seek a mediator who will take a more evaluative role, more like a judge, and give opinions on what the case may be worth and who has the stronger legal position. Some lawyers use mediators to "talk sense" into clients who have

---

1. For additional reading on the subject, see Harold I. Abramson, *Mediation Representation: Advocating as a Problem-Solver* (3d ed., Aspen 2013); Douglas N. Frenkel & James H. Stark, *The Practice of Mediation* (2d ed., Aspen 2012); Dwight Golann & Jay Folberg, *Mediation: The Roles of Advocate and Neutral* (2d ed., Aspen 2011); James J. Alfini et al, *Mediation Theory and Practice* (2d ed., LexisNexis 2006); and Christopher W. Moore, *The Mediation Process: Practical Strategies for Resolving Conflict* (3d ed., Jossey-Bass 2003).

been unwilling to settle. Transformative mediation focuses on relationships—it is less about resolving a dispute than it is about restoring or rebuilding fractured relationships. It is possible for a single mediation to include elements of all three forms of mediation, depending on the dispute, the parties, and the mediator.

§ 20.03. WHAT DO MEDIATORS DO?

In the model of mediation generally used in the United States, mediators cannot take sides; they must treat both parties equally at all times. Mediators are both neutral and impartial; they have no preference between the parties and no interest in the outcome. Mediators can be lawyers, but they are not required to be—they just have to be trained, and good at listening and problem-solving. Mediators should probe both sides to ensure that strengths and weaknesses of positions and arguments are exposed and understood. Mediators should encourage the parties and/or their attorneys to come up with creative solutions that address the needs and interests of the parties. Alternatively, the mediator may offer creative ideas if the parties appear to be at an impasse. If agreement is reached, the mediator should make sure that everyone's understanding of the agreement is identical.

§ 20.04. CONFIDENTIALITY

Mediations are confidential in two ways. For the most part, anything that is said during a mediation stays in the mediation; mediators and parties normally cannot be forced to repeat and should not disclose things that were said during mediation if the mediation fails and the dispute continues into litigation. This does not mean that information that would otherwise have to be disclosed during litigation can be protected from disclosure merely by talking about it or presenting it during mediation. Each jurisdiction will have its own laws and rules that govern the confidentiality of mediation.

The other important aspect of confidentiality occurs during caucuses—mediators may not reveal anything a party says during a caucus to the other party without the first party's consent.

§ 20.05. THE STAGES OF A MEDIATION

1. Preparation

Both the parties and the mediator need to prepare for mediation. Many lawyers prepare for mediation the same way they do for litigation: they try to figure out how to present their case in a winning way. That is not the best approach to prepare for mediation, though. Lawyers and parties need to be thinking about what is preventing the dispute from being resolved and what real needs and interests are at stake. When mediators ask for written submissions pre-mediation, those are generally the questions they want answered.

Mediators may take a number of approaches to preparation. They may have extensive contact with the parties or their lawyers to learn everything they can about the dispute. Or they may prefer to know very little; one excellent mediator asks only one question before mediation: Why haven't you been able to settle this matter? And mediators may take every approach in between.

One common approach to pre-mediation written submissions ("briefs") is for the mediator to ask the lawyers to explain the factual background of the case and to describe what is preventing resolution. Of course, most lawyers will make their legal arguments no matter what, but in mediation they do not really matter—there is no decision being made based on the law. Pre-mediation "briefs" should really be brief—just a few pages that help the mediator understand what is going on. Sample mediation briefs appear in Appendix V.

Lawyers need to prepare their clients for mediation as they do for any occasion where the client needs to make a good impression. Clients will have ample opportunity to speak during a mediation; they should be prepared to discuss the facts of the situation and to state their needs, interests, and goals. Expressions of emotion can be helpful during mediation, but they should not be the focus of communication. Often, the reason a case goes to mediation is that the parties have simply stopped communicating. Lawyers should prepare their clients to communicate in an effective and appropriate manner, one that articulates what is at stake without name-calling and accusations that do not move the conversation forward.

2. Mediator Introduction

The mediator's introduction at the beginning of mediation is a crucial part of the process. It allows the parties to settle in and understand what is happening. It should help to calm the parties and build confidence in the process that is to follow. The mediator will generally introduce himself or herself and explain the experience he or she has in mediating. The mediator will also introduce the process of mediation, by explaining what mediation is and the many benefits of mediation. The mediator will talk about neutrality and confidentiality. The mediator will also explain what is about to happen: opening statements, caucuses and/or conferences, and what happens if agreement is reached. The mediator should also encourage creativity, resolution, and commitment to the process. The mediator will also likely set ground rules, such as no interrupting; the parties will be encouraged to demonstrate mutual respect and listen to understand each other's needs and interests.

3. Party Opening Statements

In the opening statement, the attorneys explain their clients' case. They talk about what happened and what their client seeks from the mediation. The clients contribute as appropriate—they may fill in details, add explanations, and emphasize priorities. If there are no attorneys, the clients present their stories and goals. These opening statements generally only take a few minutes. The mediator may ask clarifying questions and may allow the parties to respond to each other. The purpose of the opening statements is to get the conversation started. If the parties have taken the mediator's instructions to heart, this may be the first time the parties have actually listened to each other in a very long time.

4. Agenda Development

This is a step that not all mediators formally use, but it can be an important step toward getting the parties working together. An agenda is a simple list of issues to be discussed.

Done properly, the list will be phrased in neutral language so it does not reflect one party's interests over the other. If the parties can agree on the agenda, they are already working toward a solution. Mediators want to get as many "yeses" as possible throughout the process.

Some mediators will write an agenda themselves after they have heard the opening statements. Others will involve the parties in developing an agenda. Others skip the step entirely and just move into negotiations. There is no one right way to do this—as with most things in mediation, being flexible is key, and having as many tools in the toolbox as possible makes all the difference.

5. Caucuses/Conferences

As noted above, there are two primary ways to organize the negotiation part of a mediation: caucus and conference. Many mediators will use both processes; others may have a strong preference for one or the other.

In a caucus, the mediator will often ask if there is any additional information not disclosed in opening statements. Caucuses can be a good way to get additional information the parties did not feel comfortable sharing in an open session. The mediator should probe each party's understanding of the strengths and weaknesses of the situation. Do the parties really understand what is likely to happen if the case proceeds to litigation? The mediator will seek concrete solutions and offers to take ideas for resolution to the other side. This process may continue until the mediator feels the parties can reach resolution together in an open session.

Some mediators believe strongly that all mediation should take place in a conference, with all parties at the table at all times. They believe that true resolution cannot happen if the parties are not hearing everything that is said. Other mediators will save the conference for a time when it seems that the parties are ready to communicate directly with each other. Facilitative mediators are happiest when they are saying nothing and the parties are doing all the talking. The most logical approach seems to be to judge each situation on its own merits and use the approach most likely to lead to resolution.

6. Brainstorming/Negotiating

As discussed in the previous chapter on Negotiation, brainstorming is a particular approach to negotiating that requires parties to put ideas on the table and explore them without instantly judging them. The possible solutions should be explored for their ability to meet needs and interests, not whether they favor one party or the other. If the parties can be coaxed into exploring solutions together, and brainstorming ideas for how to get past the dispute that is negatively affecting their lives, then resolution is much more likely. Chances are that both parties will get some things they wanted and go home without some things they wanted, but if the solution is good enough, they can move on, and that is the real goal.

7. Resolution

When people talk about whether mediation is binding, this is where the concept of a binding result is relevant. Any agreement the parties reach will be a binding contract, or part of a judgment if the dispute is already in court. The big question at this point may be who writes the agreement. If lawyers are involved, they should take the responsibility for drafting the agreement. We talk about Settlement Agreements in Chapter 21. If there are no lawyers, the mediator has to decide whether to handle the drafting. Some mediators prefer not to draft the agreement, leaving it to the parties. Others believe they will do the better job of drafting a clear, enforceable agreement, and so they take that responsibility. As with most things in mediation, there is no "right" answer.

§ 20.06. WRITING FOR MEDIATION

As noted previously, writing takes several forms in mediation—agreements to mediate, mediation briefs, and settlement agreements.

1. The Agreement to Mediate

Mediators will typically ask parties to sign an agreement to participate in the mediation. The agreement may briefly explain what mediation is, but it will almost always include an explanation of confidentiality, along with a commitment by the parties to respect that confidentiality (which is likely required by the law of whatever jurisdiction the mediation takes place in). It may also include a commitment by the parties to participate in good faith, and a provision protecting the mediator from being sued if the mediation does not work. Below is an example of an agreement to mediate.

Mediation/Confidentiality Agreement

Nancy Schultz has been asked to mediate the dispute between _____ and _____ related to _____. The parties to the mediation are _____ and _____. _____ has agreed to attend the mediation as a representative of _____ with the authority to approve a mediated agreement if one is reached. The parties agree to mediate in good faith with the intent of resolving the dispute, and also agree to the following:

Role of Mediator

The mediator is an impartial, neutral intermediary, whose role is to assist the parties to clarify the facts, to explore solutions to the dispute, and to reach a negotiated settlement. The mediator cannot impose a settlement, but will assist the parties toward achieving their own settlement. The mediator does not act as an attorney or advocate or give legal advice to any participants. No professional-client or fiduciary relationship is created between any participant and the mediator.

Mediation Is Voluntary

Any party can withdraw from or terminate his/her participation in the mediation at any time, for any reason.

Confidentiality

The mediation is conducted in accordance with Sections 1115-1128 of the California Evidence Code governing the confidentiality of mediation proceedings. The mediator may not testify in any proceedings pursuant to these statutes and the parties shall not seek to have the mediator testify. Pursuant to Section 1119 of the California Evidence Code, the mediator and the parties agree that, except as otherwise provided by law,

(a) No evidence of anything said or any admission made in the course of a mediation or a mediation consultation is admissible or subject to discovery, and disclosure shall not be compelled in any arbitration, administrative adjudication, civil action, or other noncriminal proceeding in which testimony can be given.
(b) No writing that is prepared for the purpose of a mediation or a mediation consultation is admissible or subject to discovery, and disclosure of the writing shall not be compelled in any arbitration, administrative adjudication, civil action, or other noncriminal proceeding in which testimony can be given.
(c) All communications, negotiations, or settlement discussions among participants in the course of a mediation or a mediation consultation shall remain confidential.

Waiver/Indemnification

The parties agree to release the mediator from any and all claims arising out of their failure to reach agreement or their decision to enter any aspect of the mediation process. Further, the mediator makes no representation that the parties will reach an agreement on any of the issues discussed in the mediation. Any party who brings any claim of any nature against the mediator or who seeks to have the mediator testify shall be responsible to indemnify the mediator for any expenses, loss, or damage incurred, including attorney's fees and expenses incurred in connection with such claim.

Parties

_____

Date

_____

Date

Observer

_____

Date

Mediator

_____

Nancy Schultz   **Date**

2. Mediation Briefs

As discussed above, there is no set format for mediation briefs, and there are no rules governing them. The purpose of the brief is to set the stage for the mediation and help the mediator understand what is going on. The mediator will ask the parties for what he or she wants. It may be an outline of the facts, a short summary of the legal arguments, an explanation of why the parties have not been able to settle, or some combination of all of those. It is important to give the mediator what he or she asks for. There is no point in trying to dazzle the mediator with the brilliance of your legal arguments because the mediator has no power to issue a decision in your case. The mediator's role is to get the parties talking to each other.

If the mediator asks you to share your brief with opposing counsel, there may be even more temptation to load the brief with legal argument and attempts at persuasion. But if you haven't persuaded opposing counsel by the time of the mediation, it is highly unlikely your mediation brief will suddenly do the trick. Keep the brief focused on what is important for mediation—why the parties are in dispute, and what their underlying needs and interests are. That will be the basis for discussion at the mediation. We include some sample mediation briefs in Appendix V.

Exercise

Let's go back to the dispute between Susan Starkey and the dating service discussed in Chapter 18. Plan an agenda for that mediation and brainstorm some possible solutions that would allow both parties to move forward from the dispute with as many of their interests satisfied as possible.

CHAPTER 21

Settlement Agreements

§ 21.01. INTRODUCTION

We have previously discussed the processes that result in settlement agreements: negotiation and mediation. Once the parties have resolved their differences, the agreement must be reduced to writing. Clarity and precision in drafting are critical. An agreement that is ambiguous and open to interpretation invites a return to litigation if the parties find themselves at loggerheads again.

§ 21.02. WHAT DO SETTLEMENT AGREEMENTS LOOK LIKE?

In this section we show you the various parts of a settlement agreement. We give you some good and some not-so-good examples from actual settlement agreements, which you can find online. The overarching principle to keep in mind is that the agreement needs the clarity and precision referred to above, as well as an overall professional look that requires attention to detail. And, needless to say, the terms of the settlement agreement must accurately reflect the parties' actual agreement.

A good settlement agreement is well organized and uses headings to help the reader find specific provisions. It includes white space between the paragraphs, so the agreement is not dense and hard to read. It uses short sentences and simple language. It follows the golden rule of drafting: Never change your language unless you wish to change your meaning, and always change your language if you wish to change your meaning.[1] The concept of "elegant variation" that many of us learned in the early stages of our writing instruction—the concept of changing your words to make your writing more interesting—has no place in legal drafting. Precision is paramount, so use the same word for the same meaning, no matter how often and how boring it seems.

1. Descriptive Title

The first thing a settlement agreement needs is a title. The title should describe the function of the agreement. The following are some samples from the agreements we

---

1. Scott J. Burnham, *Drafting and Analyzing Contracts*, 227 (3d ed., LexisNexis 2003).

will be using throughout the chapter. Some titles are very simple, and just label the type of agreement, or simply that it is an agreement, like these:

AGREEMENT[2]
RESOLUTION AGREEMENT[3]
SETTLEMENT AND RELEASE AGREEMENT[4]

Other titles give more information and may be more useful when trying to locate a specific agreement later in time:

SETTLEMENT AGREEMENT BETWEEN
THE UNITED STATES OF AMERICA
AND
BEGINNING MONTESSORI ACADEMY, BALDWIN PARK, CALIFORNIA[5]

SHOWING ANIMALS RESPECT & KINDNESS V. PROFESSIONAL RODEO COWBOYS ASSOCIATION
N.D. ILL. CASE NO. 1:08-CV-03314
SETTLEMENT AGREEMENT AND MUTUAL RELEASES[6]

2. Caption

The function of the caption is to identify the parties. Here are the captions of three of the five agreements referred to previously:

1. From the HHS agreement: **Parties.** The Parties to this Resolution Agreement ("Agreement") are the United States Department of Health and Human Services, Office for Civil Rights ("HHS") and Affinity Health Plan, Inc. ("the covered entity"). HHS and the Covered Entity shall together be referred to herein as the "Parties."

2. From the FDIC agreement: This Settlement and Release Agreement ("Agreement") is made as of this 15th day of July, 2013, by, between, and among the fo11owing undersigned parties: The Federal Deposit Insurance Corporation, as receiver for Rainier Pacific Bank, Tacoma, Washington ("FDIC"), and Stephen Bader, Edward Brooks, Charles Cuzetto, John Hall, Brian Knutson, Carolyn Middleton, Victor Toy, Alfred Treleven, III, Bruce Valentine, and Darrren Zemanek (collectively, the "Settling Defendants") (individually, the FDIC and the Settling Defendants may be referred to herein as a "Party" and collectively as the "Parties").

3. From the Montessori agreement: The parties to this Settlement Agreement ("Agreement") are the United States of America and Beginning Montessori Academy (Montessori Academy), located in Baldwin Park, California.

---

2. You can find the full agreement at http://contracts.onecle.com/yahoo/third-point-settlement-2013-07-22.shtml (referred to elsewhere in the chapter as the "Third Point" agreement).

3. You can find the full agreement at http://www.hhs.gov/ocr/privacy/hipaa/enforcement/examples/affinity_agreement.pdf (referred to elsewhere in the chapter as the "HHS" agreement). The agreement also appears in Appendix III.

4. You can find the full agreement at http://www.fdic.gov/about/freedom/plsa/wa_rainierpacificbank.pdf (referred to elsewhere in the agreement as the "FDIC" agreement)

5. You can find the full agreement at http://www.ada.gov/montessori_academy_settle.htm (referred to elsewhere in the chapter as the "Montessori" agreement). The agreement also appears in Appendix III.

6. You can find the full agreement at https://www.eff.org/files/filenode/SHARK_v_PRCA/SHARKPRCA-settlement.pdf (referred to elsewhere in the chapter as the "SHARK" agreement).

The caption for the agreement between the USA and the Montessori Academy is the simplest of the three, and it includes everything necessary. Phrases such as "by and between" and compound prepositions such as "herein" add nothing to the meaning of the agreement and are throwbacks to an earlier time and means of communicating. You will see other examples of this kind of language as we proceed through the parts of an agreement. You will also learn that it is not necessary, and that plain English is far preferable.

In addition to identifying the parties, the caption should provide the short-form references to the parties that will be used in the rest of the agreement. These short-form references may be specific and use some part of the party's name, or they may be generic and identify the party by a role such as "employer" or "employee." The reason for using generic identifiers is that it allows the agreement to serve as a form agreement for future use between similar parties.

3. Transition/Language of Agreement

"Transition" or "language of agreement" simply refers to language in the agreement that specifically states that the parties agree to the terms of the agreement. Here are examples of transitions from two of our settlement agreements:

1. <u>From the Third Point agreement</u>: NOW, THEREFORE, in consideration of and reliance upon the mutual covenants and agreements contained herein, and for other good and valuable consideration, the receipt and sufficiency of which is hereby acknowledged, the parties hereto agree as follows:
2. <u>From the HHS agreement</u>: In consideration of the Parties' interest in avoiding the uncertainty, burden, and expense of further investigation and formal proceedings, the Parties agree to resolve these matters according to the terms and conditions below.

The second example above uses the clearest language and indicates the agreement of both parties. The statement that starts with "now, therefore" is following an old-fashioned approach that uses "whereas" for background information and "now, therefore" to signal a transition to operative language in the agreement. You will notice other rote language and unnecessary jargon in that example as well. We recommend an approach like the one used in the second example.

4. Recitals/Background

The recitals, or background, part of a settlement agreement sets forth any information the parties believe is relevant to explain why they decided to enter into the agreement. In old-fashioned settlement agreements, the recitals look like this:

WHEREAS, each of the Company and the Third Point Group has determined that it is in its best interests to enter into this Agreement and to terminate the pending proxy contest for the election of directors at the 2012 Annual Meeting

WHEREAS, Plaintiff SHARK commenced the above-captioned litigation against the PRCA by filing a Complaint on June 9,2008 (the "Action") alleging violations of 17 U.S.C. § 512(f) and for tortious interference with contract;

In a more modern, simpler settlement agreement, the recitals are usually described as "background" (although the word "recitals" may still be used, as it is in the HHS agreement) and look like this:

> On April 15, 2010, the HHS Office for Civil Rights (OCR) received notification from AHP regarding a breach of its unsecured electronic protected health information (EPHI). On May 19, 2010, OCR notified AHP of OCR's investigation regarding AHP's compliance with the Privacy, Security, and Breach Notification Rules.
>
> **I. Background**
> 3. The complainant, Ms. Kathy Castaneda, is the mother of a five-year-old, [redacted], who has autism. In a letter dated June 11, 2008, Ms. Castaneda alleges that the Montessori Academy notified her that [redacted] would not be accepted for the following school year and that as of July 1, 2008, the Montessori Academy would no longer accept any child with autism or any specialized condition or need.

We recommend the simpler approach, using clear language to explain whatever background facts are important to setting up the agreement. Using headings and clear language will let the reader know what part of the agreement they are looking at. The "whereas . . . now, therefore" approach is simply not necessary for clarity or precision.

5. Definitions

Definitions are useful if a word or phrase is subject to multiple interpretations. If an otherwise ambiguous term is used throughout an agreement, the term may be defined in a definitions section near the beginning of the agreement. If such a term is used only once in the agreement, it may be defined where it is used. None of our sample agreements include a definitions section, presumably indicating the parties' confidence that, in general, the language of the agreement is clear to both parties. (You will find specific terms defined in context on pages 4 and 6 of the Third Point agreement if you look at it online.)

> Here are some sample definitions from another agreement:
> "Action" refers to the putative class action identified in Section I.B above which is currently pending in the Superior Court of the State of California for the County of Santa Barbara.
> "Claim form" refers to a document substantially in the form of Exhibit A hereto, or as it may hereafter be modified by subsequent agreement of the Parties or order of the Court. Eligible individuals who submit valid and timely claims in accordance with this Agreement are referred to herein as "Claimants."[7]

6. Operative Language

A settlement agreement, like any contract, is a series of promises. Promises should be stated in the active voice, starting with the party making the promise as the subject of the

---

7. The full agreement may be found at http://www.missionandstate.org/ms/wp-content/uploads/2013/05/DarioPini-Settlementagreement-SantaBarbara-Alamar-ShoresInnandSuites-ChanticoInn-VillaRosaInn.pdf.

sentence. The verb should indicate the nature of the promise, and the object should clearly identify what the party has agreed to do. Here are some sample promises from the agreements we have looked at throughout the chapter:

1. From the Third Point agreement: Each member of the Third Point Group shall, and shall cause each of the Third Point Affiliates to, immediately cease all efforts, direct or indirect, in furtherance of the Stockholder Nomination and any related solicitation in connection with the Stockholder Nomination. The Third Point Group and the Third Point Affiliates shall promptly modify or disable (and not permit to be re-enabled) any websites they directly or indirectly maintain in order to comply with this section 2(b). At the same time, the Company shall immediately cease all direct or indirect negative solicitation efforts relating to the 2012 Annual Meeting concerning Third Point Group, Third Point Affiliates and members of the slate of nominees proposed by Third Point Group.

2. From the HHS agreement: **Payment.** AHP agrees to pay HHS the amount of **$1,215,780** ("Resolution Amount"). AHP agrees to pay the Resolution Amount by electronic funds transfer pursuant to written instructions to be provided by HHS. AHP agrees to make this payment on or before the date it signs this Agreement.

3. From the FDIC agreement:
A. As an essential covenant and condition to this Agreement, the Settling Defendants, collectively, agree to pay the FDIC the sum of $375,000 (the "Settlement Funds").
B. Within 10 days of the execution of an original, or originals in counterpart, of this Agreement by all of the undersigned Parties to this Agreement, but no later than August 15, 2013, the Settlement Funds shall be delivered to the FDIC by direct wire transfer into an account designated by the FDIC or by certified or cashier's check drawn upon a depository institution acceptable to the FDIC and delivered to an address provided by the FDIC.

4. From the Montessori agreement:
10. The Montessori Academy agrees that it will not discriminate against any individual on the basis of disability, including autism.
11. The Montessori Academy agrees to provide children with disabilities, an equal opportunity to attend Settlement Agreement between the United States and Beginning Montessori Academy, Baldwin Park, California http://www.ada.gov/montessori_academy_settle.htm [9/23/2013 4:48:46 PM] the Montessori Academy and to participate in all programs, services, or activities provided by the Montessori Academy, except to the extent that they are unable to reasonably participate due to their disability or unable to participate after reasonable modifications in the policies and procedures have been made as set forth in 28 C.F.R. § 36.302. The Montessori Academy agrees to make reasonable modifications in policies, practices, or procedures when such modifications are necessary to afford its child care services and facilities to children with disabilities, unless the modifications would fundamentally alter the nature of the program, service or activity as set forth in 28 C.F.R. § 36.302.

5. From the SHARK agreement: Compensation: Within five (5) business days following the execution of this Agreement, PRCA agrees to pay SHARK the amount of Twenty-Five Thousand Dollars ($25,000) by check made payable to the Electronic Frontier Foundation, as attorneys for SHARK.

You will notice that the Third Point agreement uses the word "shall." Without getting into an ongoing debate about whether "shall" is ever a good word to use, we suggest a simpler approach. "Shall" is generally used to suggest a command and frequently connotes some imbalance in bargaining power. When a party promises to do something, it is much easier, and less directive, to use the word "will" to denote the promise, as in the Montessori agreement, where the Montessori Academy agrees that it "will not discriminate."

You can also see that parties often "agree" to do something, such as make a payment, as you see in the HHS, FDIC, and SHARK agreements above. The important thing here is to make sure the party agreeing to do something is denoted as the subject of the promise, so it is clear who promised to do what. As an example of the passive voice we counsel against, you see "the Settlement Funds shall be delivered to the FDIC by direct wire transfer" in the FDIC agreement. The sentence does not specifically say who will make the wire transfer happen. While it is generally clear from the context who is responsible for doing something stated in the passive voice, it is better practice to always state promises in the active voice, so there can be no argument later about who promised to do what.

7. Contingencies

It is important to recognize that things can go wrong after a settlement agreement is reached. While the parties are still in an agreeable frame of mind, they should provide for what will happen if something does not go according to plan. Contingencies may be spelled out specifically, or the parties may agree on a form of dispute resolution to handle any disagreements. Here are some examples from our settlement agreements:

1. From the Third Point agreement: Miscellaneous. The parties hereto shall be entitled to an injunction or injunctions to prevent breaches of this Agreement and to enforce specifically the terms and provisions of this Agreement exclusively in the Court of Chancery or other federal or state courts of the State of Delaware, in addition to any other remedy to which they are entitled at law or in equity. Furthermore, each of the parties hereto (a) consents to submit itself to the personal jurisdiction of the Court of Chancery or other federal or state courts of the State of Delaware in the event any dispute arises out of this Agreement or the transactions contemplated by this Agreement, (b) agrees that it shall not attempt to deny or defeat such personal jurisdiction by motion or other request for leave from any such court, (c) agrees that it shall not bring any action relating to this Agreement or the transactions contemplated by this Agreement in any court other than the Court of Chancery or other federal or state courts of the State of Delaware, and each of the parties irrevocably waives the right to trial by jury, (d) agrees to waive any bonding requirement under any applicable law, in the case any other party seeks to enforce the terms by way of equitable relief and (e) each of the parties irrevocably consents to service of process by a reputable overnight mail delivery service, signature requested, to the address of such parties' principal place of business or as otherwise provided by applicable law.

2. From the HHS agreement: **Corrective Action Plan**. AHP has entered into and agrees to comply with the Corrective Action Plan (CAP), attached as Appendix A, which is incorporated into this Agreement by reference. If AHP breaches the CAP, then AHP will be in breach of this Agreement and HHS will not be subject to the Release set forth in paragraph 8 of this Agreement.

3. From the FDIC agreement: In the event that the Settlement Funds are not delivered to the FDIC (or its counsel) by August 15, 2013, interest shall accrue on all unpaid amounts at the rate of 5% per annum from August 15, 2013 until the date of payment. However, if said Settlement Funds are not delivered to the FDIC by August 15, 2013 as a result of the FDIC's failure to execute this Agreement, the FDIC's failure to designate an account for payment by wire transfer, or the FDIC's failure to accept or reject the sufficiency of the depository institution upon which the Settling Defendants propose to draw a certified or cashier's

check for the Settlement Funds, no interest shall accrue until ten days after the FDIC cures such failure(s).

4. <u>From the Montessori agreement</u>: The United States may review compliance with this Agreement at any time. If the United States believes that this Agreement or any portion of it has been violated, it will raise its concerns with the Montessori Academy and the parties will attempt to resolve the concerns in good faith. The United States will give the Montessori Academy thirty (30) days from the date it notifies the Montessori Academy of any breach of this Agreement to cure that breach, before instituting any court action. If the parties are unable to reach a satisfactory resolution within that period, the United States may bring a civil action in federal district court to enforce this Agreement or Title III, and may in such action seek any relief available under law.

5. <u>From the SHARK agreement</u>:
   Future Conduct.
   a. With the goal of preventing disputes of the type underlying the Action from arising in the future, the PRCA and SHARK will employ the following procedure:
   i. SHARK will designate an Internet video contact for the PRCA, which contact may be changed from time to time upon notice in writing to the PRCA in accord with section 9 hereof.
   ii. If the PRCA forms a good faith belief that any future SHARK video violates the PRCA's rights, the PRCA will notify SHARK's Internet video contact.
   iii. Once notified, SHARK will have five (5) business days to correct the problem by taking down the video.
   iv. If SHARK believes in good faith that the video does not violate the PRCA's rights, and therefore chooses not to take the video down, the PRCA may take further action with respect to the SHARK video, including, but not limited to, going to court to enforce its rights

You can see that these contingency plans range from (1) filing in a specific court, to (2) complete abrogation of the release (which will be discussed later in the chapter), to (3) something as simple as requiring interest on payments, to (4) making a good faith effort to correct any breach, to (5) an entire process for dealing with a possible violation. Dealing with contingencies can take many forms, depending on the intent and creativity of the parties. The important thing is that they are dealt with in some form in the settlement agreement. And, as always, we prefer simpler, more direct language to the more convoluted, "jargon-y" approach.

8. Declarations

Declarations are the portions of the agreement sometimes referred to as "boilerplate." They are the provisions that appear in almost any contract: governing law, integration clauses, notice provisions, and the like. Here are some examples from our settlement agreements:

1. <u>From the Third Point Agreement</u>:
   <u>No Waiver.</u> Any waiver by any party of a breach of any provision of this Agreement shall not operate as or be construed to be a waiver of any other breach of such provision or of any breach of any other provision of this Agreement. The failure of a party to insist upon strict adherence to any term of this Agreement on one or more occasions shall not be considered a waiver or deprive that party of the right thereafter to insist upon strict adherence to that term or any other term of this Agreement.

Entire Agreement. This Agreement contains the entire understanding of the parties with respect to the subject matter hereof and may be amended only by an agreement in writing executed by the parties hereto.

2. From the HHS agreement: **Effect of Agreement**. This Agreement constitutes the complete agreement between the Parties. All material representations, understandings, and promises of the Parties are contained in this Agreement. Any modifications to this Agreement shall be set forth in writing and signed by both Parties.

3. From the FDIC agreement:

Choice of Law. This Agreement shall be interpreted, construed, and enforced according to applicable federal law, or in its absence, the law of the State of Washington.

Entire Agreement and Amendments. This Agreement constitutes the entire agreement and understanding between and among the undersigned Parties concerning the matters set forth herein. This Agreement may not be amended or modified except by another written instrument signed by the Party or Parties to be bound thereby, or by their respective authorized attorney(s) or other representative(s).

Reasonable Cooperation. The undersigned Parties agree to cooperate in good faith to effectuate all of the terms and conditions of this Agreement.

Advice of Counsel. Each Party hereby acknowledges that it has consulted with and obtained the advice of counsel prior to executing this Agreement, and that this Agreement has been explained to that Party by his or her counsel.

4. From the Montessori agreement:

Failure by the United States to enforce this entire Agreement or any of its provisions shall not be construed as a waiver of its right to enforce other provisions of the Agreement.

If any term of this Agreement is determined by any court to be unenforceable, the other terms of this Agreement shall nonetheless remain in full force and effect.

5. From the SHARK agreement:

Choice of Law and Venue. This Agreement shall be interpreted in accordance with the laws of the State of Illinois. Any dispute or controversy between the Parties arising under or in connection with this Agreement shall be submitted to the court presiding over the Action, or, if the court presiding over the Action declines jurisdiction, to a state or federal court in the State of Illinois. Each Party agrees to personal jurisdiction in the State of Illinois for such purposes.

Severability: If any provision of this Agreement is found invalid or unenforceable, the balance of the Agreement, and all provisions thereof, shall remain in full force and effect. The failure of any Party to enforce any term of this Agreement shall not be deemed a waiver of that term or any other term of this Agreement.

As you look at these examples, you see how easy it is to eliminate the "heretos" and "herebys" and just say things in plain English. The choice of what to include as declarations is, of course, up to the parties, but integration clauses, severability provisions, choice of law provisions, and notice provisions are very common.

9. Closing

Although many agreements offer convoluted language and outdated formalities in their closings, the only thing that is really required is the signatures of the parties, and perhaps an effective date. If you look at the closings from our sample agreements, you will see that the HHS agreement, the Montessori agreement, and the SHARK agreement follow the simple approach. The Third Point agreement and the FDIC agreement include this unnecessary and old-fashioned language:

IN WITNESS WHEREOF, each of the parties hereto has executed this Agreement, or caused the same to be executed by its duly authorized representative as of the date first above written. [followed by signatures]

IN WITNESS WHEREOF, the Parties hereto have caused this Agreement to be executed by each of them or their duly authorized representatives on the dates hereinafter subscribed. [followed by signatures]

This language has no magic effect. It is simply not required and adds nothing to the meaning of the signatures.

§ 21.03. WHO DOES THE DRAFTING?

There are no hard and fast rules concerning who should do the drafting of a settlement agreement. A review of the literature dealing with the subject reveals advice ranging from an absolute mandate that agreements be drafted jointly to similarly strong advice that the parties prepare drafts that can then be reconciled by the mediator, if the agreement is the result of a mediation.[8] Some mediators will come to the mediation with a draft or form agreement that can be adjusted and then signed by the parties. This may be appropriate for simpler mediations that have routine terms, where the agreement will become part of the judgment if the mediation is the result of a proceeding that is already in court.

In more complex matters, the question of who does the drafting can get complicated. If lawyers are involved, they will usually want to handle the drafting. But how? Should one party's lawyer take the lead, and then send a draft to the other lawyer for "redlining"[9]? Should the lawyers draft the agreement together? Should the mediator handle the preliminary drafting? There is no one right answer to these questions. Some mediators believe it is inappropriate for them to draft an agreement, particularly where lawyers are involved. Others believe it is part of their function as neutrals, and that they may be in the best position to get the terms of the agreement precisely correct. Some lawyers always want to control the drafting process, while others prefer to take on the role of editor.

Use of a single text process, in which negotiations toward the final agreement are based on a single document amended by the parties as agreements are reached, can expedite the process.[10] Where a neutral deals frequently with similar subject matters, he or she may have basic clauses to be included in agreements prepared in advance, for appropriate modification.[11]

---

8. Thomas Denver, *Setting the Stage to Produce Comprehensive Settlements*, 16 Alternatives to High Cost Litig. 66 (1998).

9. The process in which an agreement is exchanged back and forth with the changes marked by strikethroughs and additions in a visible way so everyone can see what has changed. For example, using Track Changes in a Microsoft Word document.

10. Id.

11. Id.

The most important thing is to have any agreement memorialized, in writing, before the parties disperse. Even a rough statement of understanding is better than no written agreement at all.[12] It is simply too easy for everyone to decide that they are tired after negotiating or mediating and that they will work on the agreement later. Then they go home and think about it, and start to have "buyer's remorse" over parts of the agreement with which they may be less than entirely happy. Then the process may have to begin all over again. But if the parties sign something that encapsulates the terms of the agreement, they will feel the commitment that allows the full agreement to be drafted later.

§ 21.04. RELEASES

The release is the part of the settlement agreement where the parties agree to end any litigation that may have started or to refrain from commencing any litigation over the issues that have been settled by the agreement. Here are releases from our settlement agreements:

1. From the Third Point agreement: The Third Point Group, for themselves and for their members, officers, directors, assigns, agents and successors, past and present, hereby agree and confirm that, effective from and after the date of this Agreement, they hereby acknowledge full and complete satisfaction of, and covenant not to sue, and forever fully release and discharge each Company Released Person of, and hold each Company Released Person harmless from, any and all rights, claims, warranties, demands, debts, obligations, liabilities, costs, attorneys' fees, expenses, suits, losses and causes of action ("**Claims**") of any nature whatsoever, whether known or unknown, suspected or unsuspected, occurring at any time or period of time on or prior to the date of the execution of this Agreement (including the future effects of such occurrences, acts or omissions) in connection with, relating to or resulting from the Proxy Contest (as defined below) or the hiring or termination of employment of Scott Thompson.

2. From the HHS agreement: In consideration and conditioned upon AHP's performance of its obligations under this Agreement, HHS releases AHP from any actions it has or may have against AHP under the Privacy and Security Rules arising out of or related to the Covered Conduct identified in paragraph 2. HHS does not release AHP from, nor waive any rights, obligations, or causes of action other than those specifically referred to in this paragraph. This release does not extend to actions that may be brought under section 1177 of the Social Security Act, 42 U.S.C. § 1320d-6.

3. From the FDIC agreement: Effective upon receipt in full of the Settlement Funds and, if applicable, any accrued interest described in SECTION I above, and without any further action by anyone, and except as provided in SECTION II.D. below, the FDIC, for itself and its employees, officers, directors, representatives, successors, administrators, agents, and assigns, shall be deemed to have, and by operation of law shall have, irrevocably, absolutely, unconditionally, fully, finally, and forever released, relinquished, waived, and discharged each of the Settling Defendants and their respective heirs, executors, administrators, agents, representatives, predecessors, successors, marital communities, and assigns, from any and all claims, demands, obligations, damages, actions, liabilities, and causes of action, direct or indirect, in law or in equity, whether based on federal law, state

---

12. Id.

law, or common law, whether foreseen or unforeseen, matured or unmatured, known or unknown, accrued or not accrued, existing now or to be created in the future, that arise from or relate to the performance, nonperformance, or manner of performance of the Settling Defendants' respective functions, duties, or other actions taken as employees, officers, and/or directors of the Bank.

4. <u>From the Montessori agreement</u>: This Agreement fully and finally resolves any and all of the allegations by the complainant and the United States in this case. It is not intended to remedy any other potential violations of the ADA by Montessori Academy.

5. <u>From the SHARK agreement</u>: Pursuant to and in consideration of the Parties' promises to comply with the terms and conditions of this Agreement, including the mutual releases contained in this paragraph, the Parties, and their respective officers, directors, agents, servants, employees, parents, subsidiaries, affiliated companies, attorneys, successors and assigns, hereby release each other from any and all claims arising out of or related to the facts alleged in the Action.

You will notice that the Third Point and FDIC agreements contain an excess of verbiage, which used to be traditional in releases and which you unfortunately will still see today. If you look at the other three releases, you see that simpler language and sentence structure can accomplish the same thing. The Montessori release in particular is short and sweet and to the point. The only function of a release is to say that the parties have agreed not to sue each other or otherwise proceed on whatever grievance caused the dispute in the first place. One party will sometimes suggest language that is broader than that and purports to release any claims the parties may ever have against each other. Competent counsel, who reads carefully, will not allow such a release. Simple language makes it much easier to detect if one party is trying to secure an overbroad release.

EXERCISE

Let's go back to our dispute between Susan Starkey and the video dating service discussed in Chapter 18. Draft a settlement agreement based on the following terms of agreement:

> The video dating service (MatchesRUs.com) agrees to pay Sandy $10,000 for her emotional distress.
> MatchesRUs.com agrees to implement better screening procedures for prospective clients, and to block clients who receive two or more complaints from other clients.
> Susan agrees not to sue MatchesRUs.com.
> Susan agrees the terms of the agreement will be confidential.

Include a background section explaining why the parties have decided to enter into this agreement. Also include a governing law section (you can pick any state), an integration clause, and a severability provision. Don't forget to think about contingencies.

CHAPTER 22

Communicating Electronically

§ 22.01. THE TREND: COMMUNICATING WITH EMAIL

Increasingly, short emails are replacing the traditional ten- to fifteen-page memo. In your professional career, you will compose far more emails than memos. Your supervisor may need a quick answer to a specific question or may want to know how the law is trending in a certain area. Your client may want an update on litigation or on a project. As you compose responsive emails, you will discover that you are doing more than typing a message that looks like a streamlined version of a memo or letter. You will realize that email in a legal context has its own unique qualities.

In this chapter, we examine when an email is the appropriate vehicle for communicating, what the audience for the email expects, and the format for an email. We also review rules of email etiquette and conclude with examples of legal emails.

§ 22.02. KNOW YOUR AUDIENCE

In your professional role, your audience is different than it is when you are writing casually to a friend. If you start with a salutation, it will read "Dear Barbara," not "Hey Barb." If you are emailing your supervisor, consider what sort of response he or she expects. Your supervisor undoubtedly wants a concise and precise answer to the inquiry. At this point, he or she wants no more information or analysis than is necessary to answer the question.

If you are emailing a client, you would expect that your client also wants a short answer that quickly gets to the point and skips detailed analysis. Depending on your message, you may want to consider whether email is the best way to communicate your message. If you need to send bad news, emotionally charged news, or sensitive information, you may decide to use email or the telephone only to set up a time when you can meet and discuss the matter in person.

§ 22.03. FORMAT YOUR EMAIL APPROPRIATELY

Although email has an informal feel to it, it still requires the professional touch. For example, you want to include certain information that you normally associate with an interoffice memo. You must fill in the subject line. If you leave it blank so that it states only "RE:", the recipient's email program may relegate the message to the "junk mail" or "spam" folder. The subject heading also will help later on if you need to retrieve the email.

As for the headings and organization of your email, different readers prefer different formats. You should consult your supervisor beforehand so that you know what he or she prefers. For example, the preferred format might be: Issue; Conclusion; and Brief Explanation of Conclusion. Or it might be Summary of Assignment, possibly including some facts of the situation; Conclusion; and Explanation of Conclusion that includes citation and significant analysis. Or it might consist of Short Answer and Citations to Authorities with accompanying parentheticals. The degree of detail also will depend on the complexity of the contents.

Likewise, depending on the desired format and the complexity of the issue, the length will vary. Most likely, the email will equal a printed page or two, at most.

You will want to construct a physical layout for a document that will be easy to read on the screen of a mobile device. Long paragraphs are hard to read on a small screen, as are paragraphs that do not have spaces between them. You will want to limit the length of each paragraph to three or four lines when possible and include a blank space between each paragraph. You will want to experiment with different fonts. Some authorities state that for emails, sans serif fonts (for example, Arial, Verdana, and Georgia) are preferred over serif fonts (for example, Times New Roman).[1]

Students sometimes wonder what information to include in a signature block. Though opinions differ, we believe that shorter is better. Certainly you can note your school and year of graduation, but including your various student activities likely will not impress anyone. If you are looking for a job, send a resume to the potential employer.

Students also sometimes ask about deleting the "sent from my iPhone" line or including a line apologizing for such shortcomings as typographical errors and failings in the grammar department. There is no real value in deleting information about your iPhone, and apologizing for sloppy work will not tempt anyone to forgive you for deficient work. Instead of having to apologize for your errors, carefully proofread every message before pressing "Send."

§ 22.04. SEND A MESSAGE THAT IS NOT TOO SIMPLE OR TOO COMPLEX

To avoid sending messages that are too simple or too complex, consider the needs of your supervisor at that moment. Your research might result in a quick "yes" or "no" answer. However, it also may result in a complex one. Your email then may begin by

---

1. For example, this book is printed in a serif font, and Wikipedia articles are in a sans serif font. To learn about using fonts in briefs, see Ruth Anne Robbins, *Painting with Print*, 2 J. ALWD 108 (2004).

stating, "There's no clear answer." Or it may state, "The research favors our side, but not definitively." In any case, you will want to be as accurate and to the point as possible.

How much of an explanation follows your opening statement depends on how detailed an explanation your supervisor wants. If your supervisor is meeting with a client or opposing counsel and has just a minute or two to read your email, he or she would appreciate a short and simple response. If you want to keep your explanation short enough for an email, but fear that such an email might be misleading or believe that a longer explanation should be available, you can draft a longer response and include it as an attachment.

§ 22.05. EMAIL WITH CAUTION

1. Anticipate the Unexpected Reader

Although you are emailing one person, you do not know who else will be reading your email. The recipient may pass it on to others or accidentally send it to an opposing party. In a sense, when you send an email, you email the world. Consequently, be careful not to email more information or opinion than is required. Moreover, you never know when a matter will go to litigation and the opposing side will employ discovery to demand a copy of relevant emails.

Such cautiousness can create a dilemma. Suppose you realize that the facts of the case point to an unfavorable outcome for your client. You must email an honest answer to your supervisor; however, you fear that it could fall into the wrong hands. As a result, you should be cautious, but honest with your wording. Perhaps you might mention to your supervisor that you are keeping a copy of your email and the supporting research, so that your supervisor should feel comfortable in deleting the sensitive email.

2. Maintain a Professional Tone

When you are starting out on your legal career, other people in your firm or office are always evaluating your performance. Your performance includes not just the analytical quality of your work. Among other things, it includes your demeanor. Your demeanor is reflected in how you write. With respect to emails, an exemplary demeanor demands a certain degree of formality. Your professional email is no place for emoticons (such as happy faces), vulgar words, or cute contractions of words (for example, "How r u" or "imho"). And again, remember that your email may show up in a discovery request or in courtroom testimony. Keep it professional.

The professional email is a formal document directed to a supervisor or client and not to a close friend. Because of the nature of emails, the writer can be tempted to drop his or her guard. Even if you think you have developed a good relationship with your supervisor, you may forget that your email may be forwarded to others who will find your tone inappropriate.

Emails with an inappropriate tone can cause problems for the writer. You may know the story of the New Zealand accountant who had to fight her termination when she was fired for sending emails in all-caps with words in red and bold, which her employer argued "caused disharmony in the workplace." You may also have heard of the unfortunate email that former Federal Emergency Management Agency director Michael Brown sent during the catastrophe that Hurricane Katrina caused in New Orleans. Brown received an email stating that "thousands are gathering in the street with no food or water." His email reply: "Thanks for the update. Anything specific I need to do or tweak?" When that reply became public, Brown seemed exceedingly heartless. In the same way, a thoughtless email could cost you a client or result in a poor evaluation, a loss of promotion, or loss of a job.

§ 22.06. EMAIL ADVICE

Here are six tips to help you communicate effectively by email.

1. Begin Your Email with a Summary of the Query

If you are responding to an email, begin with a brief summary of the question that your correspondent has posed. This introduction will remind him or her exactly what the question was. Your reader undoubtedly is receiving and replying to any number of emails and will appreciate a prompt on the subject matter of your message.

2. Be Aware of Differences in Email Systems

Although email systems are becoming more uniform, you still need to watch out for changes occurring when your recipient has a different email system than you do. In particular, watch out for changes in symbols, graphics, and the formats of attachments.

3. Watch Out for the "Reply All" Button

Sooner or later, everyone seems to hit "Reply All" when they mean to hit "Reply." As a result, a private and sometimes embarrassing message travels to a wide, unintended audience. Be careful.

4. Proofread

In the professional setting, we are expected to adhere to a high standard of spelling and grammar. Because we use email for formal and informal social purposes, we sometimes blur the line. When we are stressed or in a hurry, we may unintentionally make errors. Before sending an email, be sure to proofread it once or twice.

5. Be Cautious with Humor and Avoid Sarcasm

When we speak with someone in person, we give context for what we say with our voice, our facial expressions, and our body language. They help the reader understand our message and emotions. By contrast, emails lack this context. You type out what you intend to be a humorous line, and your reader misunderstands your message. He or she may think you are emailing a criticism or insult. Efforts at sarcasm are almost certain to backfire. Including an emoticon, like a smiling face ☺, may save the day, but not necessarily. It's best to save those wisecracks for live conversations. Even then, you need to exercise caution.

6. Avoid Emotions

When we are upset, we sometimes can't help letting everyone know it. But lashing out in an email is never a wise move. Our words live on even after we gain perspective and our emotions subside. An outburst can alienate a client, a judge, a colleague, or a supervisor. The old advice about counting to ten still holds. In fact, you may want to count a lot higher.

§ 22.07. SAMPLE EMAILS

Here are three sample emails. Each deals with the same issue; however, each includes a different level of detail. The sample you would use depends on which one your supervisor would prefer in a given situation.

To understand the issue, please turn to Appendix I and read the third sample memo: RE: Jeffrey Bing—Claim of Self-defense. The following emails are based on this case. Your supervisor emails you this question:

> Our client, Jeffrey Bing and his sometime friend John Geller got into a fistfight over an old girlfriend. At one point, they were 20 feet apart, and Geller, brandishing a knife, threatened to kill Bing, and Bing pulled a gun from his knapsack. Bing apologized to Geller and pleaded with him to calm down, but to no avail. Geller charged Bing. When Geller got within 5 or 10 feet of Bing, Bing shot once, killing Geller.
>
> My question: Assuming these facts are true, under Illinois statutes, can Bing argue self defense?

The following emails offer a range of detail. The first offers the relevant statute, a conclusory application of the statute, and a reference to the case law. The second adds a more detailed analysis of how the statute applies to the facts of the case at hand. The third offers a fairly detailed analysis of the most relevant cases. Each email offers the reader the invitation to request a more detailed analysis.

Email I

> You ask whether, under the facts given, Bing can successfully argue self defense. I think yes.
>
> > Illinois Statute 720 I. Comp. Stat. 5/7-1: "However, he is justified in the use of force which is intended or likely to cause death or great bodily harm only if he reasonably believes that such force is necessary to prevent imminent death or great bodily harm to himself or another, or the commission of a forcible felony."
>
> The facts seem to fit. There are two cases with similar facts. One case is favorable to us, and one possibly contrary case is distinguishable. Please let me know if you would like me to write up an analysis at this time.

Email II

You ask whether, under the facts given, Bing can successfully argue self defense. I think yes.

Illinois Statute 720 I. Comp. Stat. 5/7-1: "However, he is justified in the use of force which is intended or likely to cause death or great bodily harm only if he reasonably believes that such force is necessary to prevent imminent death or great bodily harm to himself or another, or the commission of a forcible felony."

Here, Bing reasonably believed deadly force was necessary to prevent imminent death or great bodily harm. He first apologized to Geller and pleaded with him to calm down, kept a distance from him, and warned him by brandishing a gun. Still, Geller came within close proximity wielding a knife. At this point, Bing could reasonably believe that force was necessary.

As for cases with similar facts, there is one case favoring us and one possibly contrary case that is distinguishable. Please let me know if you would like an analysis at this time.

Email III

You ask whether, under the facts given, Bing can successfully argue self defense. I think yes.

Illinois Statute 720 I. Comp. Stat. 5/7-1: "However, he is justified in the use of force which is intended or likely to cause death or great bodily harm only if he reasonably believes that such force is necessary to prevent imminent death or great bodily harm to himself or another, or the commission of a forcible felony."

Here, Bing reasonably believed deadly force was necessary to prevent imminent death or great bodily harm. He first apologized to Geller and pleaded with him to calm down, kept a distance from him, and warned him by brandishing a gun. Still, Geller came within close proximity wielding a knife. At this point, Bing could reasonably believe that force was necessary.

There are two cases with similar facts, one favoring us and a possibly contrary case that is distinguishable. In *People v. S.M.*, 416 N.E.2d 1212 (Ill. App. 1st Dist. 1981), a group of four boys threw tin cans and asphalt at S.M. while they chased him. Eventually they cornered him. S.M. took out a gun and he fired a warning shot; however, the boys continued to advance. S.M. proceeded to shoot all four boys.

The court found that S.M. had a reasonable belief that deadly force was necessary to prevent imminent death or great bodily harm. Accordingly, the court held "where the initial use of force was justified the claim of self-defense will not necessarily be negated by the fact that several shots were fired after the attack was over."

In People v. Moore, 357 N.E.2d 566 (1976), the individuals were 50 feet apart when the defendant stated his intent to shoot the unarmed decedent and ignored pleas from others to leave. When the decedent ran toward him, the defendant shot and killed him. Under these facts, the court upheld the jury's finding that deadly force was not justified, because the defendant's fear of death or serious bodily harm was unjustified. The defendant demonstrated a readiness to encounter the decedent, who was unarmed and who knew that the defendant had a gun. By contrast, in Bing's case, the defendant was wielding a knife in close proximity. Thus Bing's fear of death or serious bodily harm was reasonable.

Please let me know if you would like more research and a more complete analysis.

Exercises

(1) When it comes to poorly composed emails, what is your pet peeve? What violation of etiquette or good format irks you the most? Please compose a short email that exemplifies your pet peeve.

(2) In Appendix I of this book, please read the first sample memo. Assume that your firm represents John E. Walker. Your partner emails you a request to email him an answer to the issue in the sample memo—a memo similar in style to the "Example II" memo above. At most, it should be no longer than one and one-half double-spaced pages.

CHAPTER 23

Drafting Pleadings

§ 23.01. INTRODUCTION

The parties in litigation use written pleadings to present their cases to the court. This chapter shows you how to write these pleadings. The pleadings determine the issues the court must decide. Pleadings also notify the parties of the allegations that each side intends to make at trial. The two most basic pleadings are the plaintiff's complaint and the defendant's answer. The litigants also may file other pretrial pleadings. For example, the defendant may file a counterclaim against the plaintiff, which may be included in the answer. Defendants may also file cross-claims against each other or third-party complaints to join additional defendants.

§ 23.02. THE PURPOSE AND LANGUAGE OF PLEADINGS

In drafting a pleading, remember that you are speaking to different audiences. When you are drafting a complaint, one audience is the defendant. Although the defendant probably knows the facts, he or she also needs to know what causes of action you are pursuing. The other audience is the court. The court needs to know both the facts and the causes of action.

To satisfy both audiences you need to tell the factual story and identify the causes of action. You will tell the story by arranging the facts in chronological order and presenting the sequence of events from your client's perspective. You do not editorialize or use unnecessary modifiers, but the reader of a well-drafted complaint should feel that a wrong has been committed and that something should be done about it. This feeling should be created even before the specific causes of action are presented.

There are different schools of thought about the level of detail that is appropriate for a pleading. There are also differences in expectations between state and federal courts. In your civil procedure class, you may learn about something called "notice pleading," which essentially means pleading only so much information as is absolutely necessary to put the defendant on notice of the nature of the claim. Additionally, some lawyers will tell you that, as a matter of strategy, they never want to tip their hands to opposing counsel by putting too much information into a pleading. You should follow the rules of your jurisdiction and the instructions of your supervisors. Nevertheless, it is our view that a good pleading tells a complete, coherent story in a persuasive way and gives the court solid perspective on your case.

The causes of action should be identified clearly and precisely. Be sure to allege all required elements. Use separate counts for each cause of action. To ensure clarity, you should follow the principles of writing set forth in this book: use plain English to the extent possible, write short plain sentences, and use concrete words.

In practice, pleadings often include substantial legalese. Court rules and decisions may require such archaic jargon as "complaint in Assumpsit" instead of "complaint in Contract" or "complaint in Trespass" instead of "complaint in Tort." Custom and practice have embedded in pleadings awkward sentences and confusing words. When local rules and precedents require you to use obscure language, you have no choice but to comply. Even when you are required to use some jargon, however, you still have considerable latitude to write short simple sentences in comprehensible English.

§ 23.03. FOLLOWING RULES

Pleadings must conform to the rules of procedure of the jurisdiction in which the action begins. Therefore, you must look at the rules in your jurisdiction before drafting a pleading. Our goal here is to give you a general understanding of how to draft a pleading.

In most jurisdictions, the party must make allegations in a pleading in consecutively numbered paragraphs so that the opposing party can answer each allegation using the same numbers. Each paragraph of the pleading must contain only a single allegation so that the opposing party can specifically deny or admit it.

You can find examples of how to draft pleadings in form books. Most jurisdictions have form books containing examples of pleadings. Law offices also develop forms over a period of time for use in many different situations.

§ 23.04. CAPTIONS

All pleadings begin with a caption that identifies the court, the number the court has assigned to the case, the parties, and the type of pleading. The caption may also include the month and year in which the action is filed. Here is an example of a caption for a complaint:

IN THE SUPERIOR COURT FOR THE STATE OF CALIFORNIA

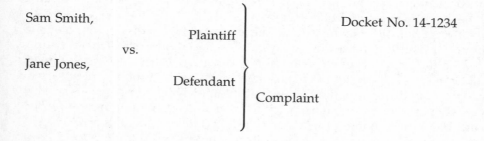

Sam Smith,
                    Plaintiff
        vs.
Jane Jones,
                    Defendant
                              Complaint

Docket No. 14-1234

Exercise

Using the following information, draft a caption for a pleading.

Bob Dob has sued Joe Doe for assault and battery. You are drafting pleadings for this case in the District Court for Lincoln County. The court has assigned the case number as 14-502, and Bob filed the case in the April Term of 2014. Joe lives at 92 High Street, Hometown. Bob lives at 110 High Street, Hometown. Write a caption to use over a complaint, an answer, or any other pleading.

§ 23.05. THE COMPLAINT

Following the caption is the body of the pleading, which contains the material allegations and request for relief.

Suppose, for example, that your client, Marilyn Smith, wants you to file suit on her behalf so that she can recover damages for injuries she received from a dog bite. Before you draft the complaint, you might write out a summary of the facts provided by the client in paragraph, narrative form. The facts alleged in a complaint must show that the plaintiff has a cause of action. The complaint also must give the defendant notice of the plaintiff's claims and an opportunity to defend against them. To show that the plaintiff has a cause of action, the complaint must allege sufficient facts to demonstrate that the plaintiff has a right to relief under the applicable law. Therefore, you must research the law before you write the complaint to determine what facts to allege in it. Suppose that the law in your jurisdiction states that the victim of a dog bite can recover under either negligence or strict liability under the following circumstances:

An individual is liable in negligence to another party if

(1) that individual owns or harbors a dog;
(2) that individual knew that the dog had previously attacked at least one other person;
(3) that individual knew that the dog was likely to harm other persons unless properly confined or otherwise controlled;
(4) that individual fails to exercise reasonable care to confine or otherwise control the dog; and
(5) the dog attacks and injures the other party.

An individual is strictly liable in tort to another party if

(1) the individual knowingly owns or harbors a dog that is of a vicious nature that is accustomed to attacking and biting other persons;
(2) the individual had personal knowledge of the vicious nature of the dog and knew that the dog was accustomed to attacking and biting other persons; and
(3) the dog attacks and injures the other party.

The complaint that you would file on behalf of your client might look like this:

Complaint

1. Plaintiff, Marilyn Smith, is an individual and citizen of the Commonwealth of Pennsylvania, residing at 12 Main Street, Anywhere, Pennsylvania 19009.[1]

2. Defendant, Samantha Jones, is an individual and citizen of the Commonwealth of Pennsylvania, residing at 14 Main Street, Anywhere, Pennsylvania 19009.

3. On June 4, 2014, at about 8:00 a.m., the defendant was the owner of or harbored a dog.

4. On June 4, 2014, at about 8:00 a.m., Plaintiff was walking in a common driveway at her residence when the defendant's dog attacked and bit her without provocation.

5. The dog had attacked at least one other person before attacking the plaintiff.

COUNT I

STRICT LIABILITY IN TORT

6. Plaintiff incorporates by reference paragraphs 1 through 5 of this Complaint.

7. On June 4, 2014, at about 8:00 a.m., Defendant knowingly owned or harbored a dog that was of a vicious nature and that was accustomed to attacking and biting other persons.

8. Defendant had personal knowledge of the vicious nature of the dog and knew that the dog was used and accustomed to attacking and biting other persons.

9. The dog attacked and bit Plaintiff, causing her to suffer various physical and mental injuries, including but not limited to lacerations of her left hand and wrist, contusions of her left thumb, and a puncture wound in her left foot. The injuries led to scarring, infection, lameness, and present and future pain, suffering, and mental anguish.

WHEREFORE, Plaintiff demands that this court enter judgment in her favor and against Defendant in an amount in excess of $10,000, exclusive of interest and costs.

COUNT II

NEGLIGENCE

10. Plaintiff incorporates by reference paragraphs 1 through 5 of this Complaint.

11. Defendant knew that the dog had previously attacked at least one other person.

12. Defendant knew that the dog was likely to harm individuals unless properly confined or otherwise controlled.

13. Defendant failed to exercise reasonable care to confine or otherwise control the dog.

14. The dog attacked and bit Plaintiff, causing her to suffer various physical and mental injuries, including but not limited to lacerations of her left hand and wrist, contusions of her left thumb, and a puncture wound in her left foot. The injuries led to scarring, infection, lameness, and present and future pain, suffering, and mental anguish.

WHEREFORE, Plaintiff demands that this Court enter judgment in her favor and against Defendant in an amount in excess of $10,000, exclusive of interest and costs.

_____

Attorney for Plaintiff

As you can see from this example, the introductory paragraphs of a complaint identify the names and addresses of the parties. Here the plaintiff is suing on two separate counts,

---

1. Some jurisdictions, including the federal courts, require a jurisdictional allegation at the beginning of the complaint. Thus, you might begin the complaint with a sentence that says something like "This Court has jurisdiction over this matter under 28 U.S.C. §1331."

or causes of action: strict liability in tort and negligence. The next paragraphs (3-5) set out any facts that are common to more than one count of the complaint. You incorporate those facts by reference in each count of the complaint. See, for example, paragraphs 6 and 10 of the sample complaint. This may appear unnecessarily repetitious, but it relates the information in the introductory paragraphs directly to each count and lets the court know that the basic information is the same with regard to each count.

The complaint shown above is written in plain English, following the principles of clear writing. You see no "hereins" or other stilted language. The writer used everyday language throughout the complaint and no legalese. The final paragraph does use "wherefore," which is the common way to end a complaint. Otherwise, however, there is no eccentric language.

Most sentences are in simple subject-verb-object structure, such as "The dog had attacked at least one other person," "Defendant had personal knowledge," and "The dog attacked and bit plaintiff." Just as you can present more than one cause of action in a complaint, you also can present alternative causes of action. Here, the two alternative causes of action are strict liability and negligence. Some jurisdictions require a demand for relief at the end of each count. Other jurisdictions require a demand for relief at the end of the complaint instead of at the end of each count. A demand for relief appears at the end of each count of the sample complaint.

The remaining paragraphs of the complaint present a concise summary of the facts that serve as a basis for the specific causes of action. Complaints do not set out case law or evidentiary matters. In the sample complaint, the writer did not discuss the elements of the strict liability or negligence causes of action. Instead, the writer set out the facts that establish the required elements of those causes of action. You must allege the required elements, but you do so with factual statements rather than legal arguments or conclusions.

§ 23.06. THE ANSWER

In an answer, the defendant admits or denies each factual allegation that the plaintiff makes in the complaint and raises any defenses to the causes of action presented in the complaint. The defendant answers each allegation by numbered paragraphs that correspond to numbered paragraphs in the complaint. The defendant's answer to the *Smith v. Jones* complaint set out in Section 23.05 might look like this:

ANSWER

1. Admitted.
2. Admitted.
3. Denied. Defendant denies that on June 4, 2014, at about 8:00 a.m., the defendant was the owner of or harbored a dog. The dog in question was owned by Frank Thomas, who had brought the dog with him while visiting Defendant.
4. After reasonable investigation Defendant is without knowledge or information sufficient to form a belief as to the truth of Plaintiff's allegation that Plaintiff was walking in a common driveway at her residence on June 4, 2014, at about 8:00 a.m., and therefore denies that allegation and demands strict proof. Defendant denies that the dog in question attacked and bit Plaintiff without provocation.
5. Denied. Defendant denies that the dog in question ever attacked anyone, including the plaintiff.

COUNT I

STRICT LIABILITY IN TORT

6. Defendant incorporates by reference her answers to paragraphs 1 through 5 of Plaintiff's Complaint.

7. Denied. Defendant denies that she owned or harbored a dog on June 4, 2014, at around 8:00 a.m. Defendant further denies that the dog in question was of a vicious nature or was accustomed to attacking and biting other persons.

8. Denied. Defendant denies that she knew that the dog in question was vicious. Defendant further denies that she knew that the dog in question was accustomed to attacking and biting other persons.

9. Denied. Defendant denies that the dog in question attacked and bit Plaintiff. Defendant further denies that Plaintiff suffered any illness or injury as a result of any action or inaction on Defendant's part.

WHEREFORE, Defendant demands judgment in her favor and against Plaintiff.

COUNT II

NEGLIGENCE

10. Defendant incorporates by reference her answers to paragraphs 1 through 5 of Plaintiff's Complaint.

11. Denied. Defendant denies that she knew that the dog had previously attacked at least one other person.

12. Denied. Defendant denies that she knew that the dog in question was likely to harm individuals unless properly confined or otherwise controlled.

13. Denied. Defendant denies that she failed to exercise reasonable care to confine or otherwise control the dog in question. Defendant did not have a duty to confine or otherwise control the dog in question. Defendant acted with all due care required of her under the circumstances.

14. Denied. Defendant denies that the dog in question attacked and bit Plaintiff. Defendant further denies that Plaintiff suffered any illness or injury as a result of any action or inaction on Defendant's part.

WHEREFORE, Defendant demands judgment in her favor and against Plaintiff.

AFFIRMATIVE DEFENSES

15. The Plaintiff's Complaint fails to state a cause of action, and this action should be dismissed.

16. The Plaintiff failed to join as defendants parties that are indispensable and necessary to a full adjudication of this action and, therefore, this action should be dismissed.

17. Upon information and belief, any injuries, losses or damages sustained by Plaintiff were caused by her own contributory negligence.

_____

Attorney for Defendant

Compare the paragraphs of the above answer with the paragraphs of the complaint in Section 23.05.

Unless you deny a factual allegation the plaintiff made in the complaint, the court will conclude that you have admitted it. Sometimes you do not have sufficient information to know if an allegation made in a complaint is true or not. In this case, the rules of procedure of many jurisdictions permit you to state that "after reasonable investigation [your client] is without knowledge or information sufficient to form a belief as to the truth of an allegation." In those jurisdictions, this statement has the same effect as a denial. See, for example, paragraph 4 of the sample answer.

After answering the plaintiff's allegations, set out any affirmative defenses that the defendant intends to raise at trial. Typical affirmative defenses in a tort case include assumption of risk, consent, contributory negligence, fraud, and the statute of limitations. Affirmative defenses operate to negate a claim even when all of plaintiff's allegations are true. The court may conclude that affirmative defenses are waived unless the defendant raises them. In some jurisdictions, the defendant can plead inconsistent defenses. Put the affirmative defenses in a separate section of the answer. See, for example, the "Affirmative Defenses" section of the sample answer. Some jurisdictions use a different title for affirmative defenses, such as "New Matter."

In some jurisdictions you also can raise counterclaims or motions to dismiss (sometimes called demurrers) in an answer. In a counterclaim, you allege that the defendant also has a claim against the plaintiff. Counterclaims are governed by the same rules that govern a plaintiff's complaint. In a motion to dismiss, you allege that the plaintiff has failed to make out a cause of action that can properly be decided by the court. In some jurisdictions, you will file a separate motion to dismiss the complaint, rather than demurring in the answer. We discuss motions to dismiss in Section 26.03.

§ 23.07. VERIFICATIONS

Attorneys must sign all pleadings. In addition, in many jurisdictions, the party signs a verification that is attached to the pleading. In it the party states that the allegations are true. Here is an example of a verification:

I, (name of party), hereby state that I am the (plaintiff/defendant) in this action and verify that the statements made in the foregoing (type of pleading) are true and correct to the best of my knowledge, information, and belief.

_____
Date

_____
Party

CHAPTER 24

Practice with Pleadings

§ 24.01. INTRODUCTION

This chapter will give you an opportunity to practice the principles we explained in the previous chapter. You will be able to go through the process of preparing a complaint and answer based on a fictitious case. The complaint and answer will be filed in your state's trial court. You should determine the appropriate format for the caption and any local pleading rules before beginning this exercise.

§ 24.02. PLAINTIFF'S FACTS

Here are the facts for the plaintiff:

Sandy Harmon works as an executive assistant to Jack Burton, the CEO of a software company, Playtime, that makes games. The company's specialty is role-playing games. She thinks one of the guys in the company has gone completely around the bend. The guy, Kris Martin, the COO of the company, has asked her out several times, but she has refused since she is married (and, frankly, wouldn't be interested anyway). Kris does not like to take no for an answer. He has been calling Sandy at home, and hanging up when her husband answers the phone. He has told Sandy that he will convince her husband there is something going on between her and Kris so her husband will divorce her. He has also told her that he will complain about her to her boss if she doesn't "wise up." Sandy has told her husband what is going on, and he, too, would like to know how to make Kris stop. This has been going on for about three months.

About three or four weeks ago, Sandy started getting calls from other guys, who were making seriously lewd propositions. Sandy couldn't figure out why these guys all of a sudden started calling, until one of her coworkers, Mark, told her that Kris had put her phone number on his webpage, and said guys could call for a good time. Sandy told Kris to knock it off, and he just laughed.

Then, in the last week or so, guys started showing up at Sandy's door, saying they were there to give her what she wants. When she told them to go away, they said they knew she didn't really mean it. Sandy's husband had to chase most of the guys away, and once they had to call the cops. When a couple of guys found out her husband was there, they said they were happy to share. One wanted to know if he could bring another woman over, too. There have been about eight or nine guys each night.

On a hunch, Sandy went to Kris's webpage and discovered that indeed he had put her address on the webpage, and said that she would welcome any men who cared to "visit." He also said that Sandy would say no, but that was just part of the game, and that she really meant yes.

Sandy went to work a couple of days ago and told Kris she was going to get a lawyer to make him stop. He laughed at her again, telling her to "lighten up," and she got pretty upset. Sandy was crying, and started yelling, trying to make him listen. Finally she gave up and told her boss she was taking the rest of the day off. Kris is a good friend of Sandy's boss, Jack Burton; they started the company together. Because of this, Sandy has not told Jack about Kris's behavior.

Sandy is absolutely furious, not to mention short of sleep. She is also getting a little frightened since she doesn't know how crazy some of these guys might be.

§ 24.03. DRAFTING THE FACT ALLEGATIONS

Remember to check whether your state requires a jurisdictional allegation at the beginning of a complaint. You should allege that both the plaintiff and any defendants are citizens of your county and state. You can decide whether to sue anyone other than Mr. Martin, such as his employer, Playtime. Your factual allegations should be clear and to the point—include only relevant facts and keep each numbered paragraph to one idea. Don't forget to request appropriate relief!

§ 24.04. DRAFTING THE LEGAL CLAIM

Here is the applicable statute to support Sandy's claim. You might also want to include other claims, such as invasion of privacy, defamation, sexual harassment, and infliction of emotional distress. If so, you should look up the applicable law to be sure that you know the required elements. Each legal claim should be presented in a separate count.

§ 1708.7. Stalking; tort action; damages and equitable remedies

(a) A person is liable for the tort of stalking when the plaintiff proves all of the following elements of the tort:

(1) The defendant engaged in a pattern of conduct the intent of which was to follow, alarm, or harass the plaintiff. In order to establish this element, the plaintiff shall be required to support his or her allegations with independent corroborating evidence.

(2) As a result of that pattern of conduct, the plaintiff reasonably feared for his or her safety, or the safety of an immediate family member. For purposes of this paragraph, "immediate family" means a spouse, parent, child, any person related by consanguinity or affinity within the second degree, or any person who regularly resides, or, within the six months preceding any portion of the pattern of conduct, regularly resided, in the plaintiff's household.

(3) One of the following:

(A) The defendant, as a part of the pattern of conduct specified in paragraph (1), made a credible threat with the intent to place the plaintiff in reasonable fear for his or her safety, or the safety of an immediate family member and, on at least one occasion, the plaintiff clearly and definitively demanded that the defendant cease and abate his or her pattern of conduct and the defendant persisted in his or her pattern of conduct.

(B) The defendant violated a restraining order, including, but not limited to, any order issued pursuant to Section 527.6 of the Code of Civil Procedure, prohibiting any act described in subdivision (a).

(b) For the purposes of this section:

(1) "Pattern of conduct" means conduct composed of a series of acts over a period of time, however short, evidencing a continuity of purpose. Constitutionally protected activity is not included within the meaning of "pattern of conduct."

(2) "Credible threat" means a verbal or written threat, including that communicated by means of an electronic communication device, or a threat implied by a pattern of conduct or a combination of verbal, written, or electronically communicated statements and conduct, made with the intent and apparent ability to carry out the threat so as to cause the person who is the target of the threat to reasonably fear for his or her safety or the safety of his or her immediate family.

(3) "Electronic communication device" includes, but is not limited to, telephones, cellular telephones, computers, video recorders, fax machines, or pagers. "Electronic communication" has the same meaning as the term defined in Subsection 12 of Section 2510 of Title 18 of the United States Code.

(4) "Harass" means a knowing and willful course of conduct directed at a specific person which seriously alarms, annoys, torments, or terrorizes the person, and which serves no legitimate purpose. The course of conduct must be such as would cause a reasonable person to suffer substantial emotional distress, and must actually cause substantial emotional distress to the person.

(c) A person who commits the tort of stalking upon another is liable to that person for damages, including, but not limited to, general damages, special damages, and punitive damages pursuant to Section 3294.

(d) In an action pursuant to this section, the court may grant equitable relief, including, but not limited to, an injunction.

(e) The rights and remedies provided in this section are cumulative and in addition to any other rights and remedies provided by law.

(f) This section shall not be construed to impair any constitutionally protected activity, including, but not limited to, speech, protest, and assembly.

§ 24.05. CRITIQUING A COMPLAINT

Here is a draft federal complaint on the same facts. Redraft any paragraphs that you think are problematic. Explain briefly the problems you see.

IN THE UNITED STATES DISTRICT COURT
FOR THE CENTRAL DISTRICT OF CALIFORNIA

SANDY Harmon,

PLAINTIFF

V.   No. 14-1234

KRIS Martin,
JACK Burton, and
PLAYTIME, INC.,

DEFENDANTS

COMPLAINT

1. This Court has jurisdiction under 28 U.S.C. § 1331.
2. Plaintiff Sandy Harmon is an individual residing in Orange County, CA.
3. Defendant Kris Martin ("Martin") is an individual residing in Orange County, CA.
4. Defendant Jack Burton is an individual residing in Orange County, CA.
5. Defendant Playtime, Inc. is a corporation organized under the laws of California.
6. Plaintiff is employed as an executive assistant at Playtime, Inc. She has always done good work and received numerous favorable performance evaluations.
7. Plaintiff's immediate supervisor is Jack Burton.
8. In July of 2013 Martin began making sexual advances toward Plaintiff.
9. Plaintiff refused all such advances, telling Martin that she was married and had no interest in extracurricular affairs.
10. Martin called Plaintiff's home and hung up when Plaintiff's husband answered the phone.
11. Martin threatened to convince Plaintiff's husband that "something was going on" between Martin and Plaintiff.
12. Martin threatened to complain about Plaintiff to Defendant Burton if she didn't "wise up."
13. In late September or early October 2013, Martin published Plaintiff's home telephone number on his webpage.
14. Martin made the outrageous and untrue suggestion on the webpage that men could call Plaintiff for "a good time."
15. Plaintiff received telephone calls from men making lewd propositions.
16. Plaintiff asked Martin to remove her telephone number from his webpage.
17. Martin demonstrated his heartlessness by laughing at Plaintiff's request.
18. In late October 2013, Martin published Plaintiff's home address on his webpage.
19. Martin's webpage, in a further demonstration of the outrageous lengths to which he would go, said that if Plaintiff said "no" to any visitors she really meant "yes."
20. Plaintiff has never had any desire to engage in sexual relations with men other than her husband.
21. Unwelcome male visitors, up to eight or nine per night, began appearing at Plaintiff's home.
22. Some visitors refused to leave voluntarily.
23. Plaintiff's husband had to chase many of the visitors away.
24. In at least one instance, the police had to be called to remove an unwelcome visitor.

25. On October 27, 2013, Plaintiff again requested that Martin remove her personal information from his webpage.
26. Martin responded by laughing and telling her to "lighten up," demonstrating a complete lack of concern for Plaintiff's physical and mental well-being.
27. Plaintiff was unable to continue working that day.
28. Defendants Martin and Burton are good friends and founded Defendant Playtime, Inc. together.
29. Plaintiff has suffered from sleeplessness.
30. Plaintiff was frightened and unsure what the unwelcome visitors might do.
31. Plaintiff no longer feels secure in her own home.
32. Plaintiff fears loss of employment.
33. Plaintiff suffers from extreme emotional distress.

COUNT I—INVASION OF PRIVACY (FALSE LIGHT)

34. Plaintiff incorporates Paragraphs 1-33 by reference.
35. Martin published outrageous, hurtful facts that falsely cast Plaintiff in a negative light.
36. Martin's portrayal of Plaintiff would be highly offensive to a reasonable person.

COUNT II—INVASION OF PRIVACY (PUBLICATION OF PRIVATE FACTS)

37. Plaintiff incorporates Paragraphs 1-33 by reference.
38. Martin published private information about Plaintiff in a manner that would be highly offensive to a reasonable person. There was no reason to put her address and phone number together with an invitation for men to come visit her for sex, other than to intimidate and harass Plaintiff.
39. There was no legitimate public interest in Plaintiff's private information.

COUNT III—CIVIL STALKING

40. Plaintiff incorporates Paragraphs 1-33 by reference.
41. Martin engaged in a pattern of conduct intended to harass or alarm Plaintiff, and maybe to cause her actual physical harm.
42. As a result of Martin's pattern of conduct, Plaintiff reasonably feared for the safety of herself and her husband. Anyone would have been scared of all these men coming to their house!
43. Martin made a credible threat with the intent to place Plaintiff in reasonable fear for her safety. What other reason could there be?!
44. Plaintiff clearly and definitively demanded that Martin cease his pattern of conduct.
45. Martin persisted in his conduct after Plaintiff's demands that he cease.

COUNT IV—SEXUAL HARASSMENT IN VIOLATION OF TITLE VII

46. Plaintiff incorporates Paragraphs 1-33 by reference.
47. Martin's conduct created a hostile working environment.
48. Plaintiff's job was threatened.

WHEREFORE, Plaintiff requests:

1. Injunctive relief, including a "stay away" order and the removal of her personal information from Martin's webpage.
2. Compensatory and punitive damages.
3. Such other relief as the Court deems appropriate.

ATTORNEY SIGNATURE

_____

VERIFICATION

I have read the foregoing Complaint, and the allegations are true and correct to the best of my knowledge, information, and belief.

PLAINTIFF'S SIGNATURE

_____

§ 24.06. DRAFTING THE ANSWER

Here are the facts Kris Martin has provided in response to the complaint:

Kris says he has just been having a little extracurricular fun. He did ask Sandy out several times, but she refused, saying she is married. Kris does not like to take no for an answer, and besides he's not sure what being married has to do with anything. He just wanted to have a little fun (i.e., sex). He did call Sandy at home, and hung up when her husband answered the phone. He told Sandy that if she didn't "go out" with him, he would convince her husband there was something going on between the two of them, so her husband would divorce her.

Kris did put Sandy's phone number on his webpage, and said guys could call her for a good time. He wasn't getting anywhere with her, and just wanted to get her attention. He thought he would look pretty good by comparison to some of the creeps who were likely to call. He also thought he could show off his understanding side if Sandy were to confide in him about the calls. However, when Sandy found out about the webpage, she got upset and told him to knock it off. Kris just laughed; this was getting more entertaining by the minute.

Kris later put Sandy's address on the webpage, and said that she would welcome all "visitors." Kris also said that Sandy would say no, but that was just part of the game, and that she really meant yes.

One day, Sandy came into work really upset (she was crying and yelling, making quite a scene), and told Kris that she was getting a lawyer to make him stop. Kris told her to "lighten up."

Kris can't figure out what he did wrong since he didn't actually *do* anything to her, and never meant for anything bad to happen to her. He just thinks she could stand to loosen up a little bit. He admitted that he might have threatened to complain about her to Jack, but didn't figure she would take that seriously since she knows how much Jack values her work.

Kris got a couple of emails from guys complaining that Sandy wasn't very cooperative when they went to visit.

Kris took Sandy's name and address off the webpage for now, but will probably come up with something else fun to do if this lawsuit goes away. He is convinced that Sandy would really appreciate his "talents" if she would only give him a chance.

Again, keep your fact allegations simple and to the point. Admit facts that you must admit, and indicate that you don't have adequate information only where that is true. Add any affirmative defenses that seem appropriate at the end of the answer.

§ 24.07. CRITIQUING AN ANSWER

Here is a draft answer to the foregoing federal complaint. Which, if any, paragraphs need to be changed, and why?

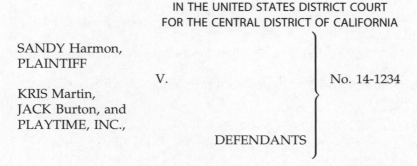

IN THE UNITED STATES DISTRICT COURT
FOR THE CENTRAL DISTRICT OF CALIFORNIA

SANDY Harmon,
PLAINTIFF

V.

KRIS Martin,
JACK Burton, and
PLAYTIME, INC.,

DEFENDANTS

No. 14-1234

ANSWER OF DEFENDANT KRIS MARTIN

1. Admitted.
2. Admitted.
3. Admitted.
4. Admitted.
5. Admitted.
6. Admitted.
7. Admitted.
8. Denied.
9. Denied.
10. Admitted.
11. Admitted.
12. Admitted, but it wasn't serious.
13. Admitted.
14. Admitted.
15. Defendant is without knowledge or information sufficient to form a belief as to the truth of this allegation.
16. Admitted.
17. Denied.
18. Denied.

19. Denied.
20. Defendant is without knowledge or information sufficient to form a belief as to the truth of this allegation.
21. Defendant is without knowledge or information sufficient to form a belief as to the truth of this allegation.
22. Defendant is without knowledge or information sufficient to form a belief as to the truth of this allegation.
23. Defendant is without knowledge or information sufficient to form a belief as to the truth of this allegation.
24. Defendant is without knowledge or information sufficient to form a belief as to the truth of this allegation.
25. Admitted.
26. Admitted.
27. Defendant is without knowledge or information sufficient to form a belief as to the truth of this allegation.
28. Admitted.
29. Defendant is without knowledge or information sufficient to form a belief as to the truth of this allegation.
30. Defendant is without knowledge or information sufficient to form a belief as to the truth of this allegation.
31. Defendant is without knowledge or information sufficient to form a belief as to the truth of this allegation.
32. Denied.
33. Denied.

COUNT I—INVASION OF PRIVACY (FALSE LIGHT)

34. Defendant incorporates Paragraphs 1-33 by reference.
35. Denied.
36. Denied.

COUNT II—INVASION OF PRIVACY (PUBLICATION OF PRIVATE FACTS)

37. Defendant incorporates Paragraphs 1-33 by reference.
38. Denied.
39. Denied.

COUNT III—CIVIL STALKING

40. Defendant incorporates Paragraphs 1-33 by reference.
41. Denied.
42. Denied.
43. Denied.
44. Denied.
45. Denied.

COUNT IV—SEXUAL HARASSMENT IN VIOLATION OF TITLE VII

46. Defendant incorporates Paragraphs 1-33 by reference.
47. Denied.
48. Denied. She can't be serious!

WHEREFORE, Defendant requests that the Court enter judgment in his favor and against Plaintiff.

ATTORNEY SIGNATURE

_____

VERIFICATION

I have read the foregoing Answer, and the allegations are true and correct to the best of my knowledge, information, and belief.

DEFENDANT'S SIGNATURE

_____

CHAPTER 25

Writing Persuasively

§ 25.01. INTRODUCTION

In discussing appellate briefs, we move from expository writing to persuasive writing. When you represent a client and argue to a court, you must do more than state the facts, explain the law, and predict how a case will be resolved. You cannot merely present information to a court and rely on it to make a decision. You also must persuade the court to find in your client's favor.

Persuasion requires constructing a clear, concrete, and tightly written argument that presents your client's case in the best light. Learning to write persuasively is not a matter of mastering a grab bag of gimmicks or tricks. It also is not a matter of using exaggerated rhetoric. Lawyers and judges have seen all the tricks and flourishes too many times. If you rely on these devices, you will impress no one.

The chapters that you have read so far teach you how to write clearly and concretely, and how to construct a legal analysis. The following chapters teach you not only the mechanics of brief writing, but also how to write persuasively. You will learn that you must construct every part of the brief in a way that advances your client's position.

This chapter summarizes the methods of persuasion that the other chapters discuss. By presenting these methods in a single chapter, we offer you an overview and reinforce the thesis that persuasive methods are not simply a number of isolated techniques, but share a common theme. To reiterate, persuasive writing consists of constructing a well-written, well-reasoned analysis that puts your client's best foot forward.

Here is a list of this chapter's lessons:

1. Make your argument clear and credible.
2. Write a well-organized argument.
3. Adopt a persuasive writing style.
4. State your facts persuasively.
5. Use equity and policy arguments.
6. Use precedent persuasively.

§ 25.02. MAKE YOUR ARGUMENT CLEAR AND CREDIBLE

1. Make Your Argument as Simple as Possible

When you write a law school exam, you expect to get credit for identifying and discussing the critical issues. You also expect extra points for discussing issues that are barely arguable or exceptionally complicated, but that would be extremely artificial if raised in a real-world legal argument. When you include complicated, artificial arguments in a brief, you cannot expect the rewards that you gained in law school. These arguments will distract the reader from the arguments with real persuasive power. They also may detract from your credibility. Stick to the arguments that have the best chance of winning.

You also can expect to hurt your case if you make your critical arguments sound unnecessarily complicated. You are more likely to persuade the reader with arguments that seem logical and simple and sound like common sense. Stick to your main arguments and write them so that they are easy to understand.

A busy judge has many cases to consider and many briefs to read. He or she does not have the time or patience to digest peripheral arguments or even major arguments that are not stated clearly. Thus, unnecessary complexity hurts your client.

Here is a simple method for rooting out complexity. State your argument to a legal associate in a very few sentences. If he or she cannot follow your train of thought, revise your words and presentation and try again.

A major part of advocacy is to place your client's arguments in clear focus: What does your client want and why? Bringing the argument into focus requires striving for simplicity.

2. Write in a Persuasive but Credible Style

Some lawyers try to be persuasive by overstating their cases and by using emotionally charged verbs, adjectives, and adverbs. This tactic inevitably marks the practitioner as an amateur. Other lawyers state their cases without adding a persuasive edge of any kind. Their style also does the client a disservice. Strive for a style that is assertive, but reasoned and even a little understated.

Consider this excerpt from a brief:

> Next we have Wilmer's ludicrous explanation of the circumstances surrounding his secret taping of various people at the dental school. Instead of coming clean and admitting that he was gathering information for his malpractice case, Wilmer asks the court to swallow his tall tale about how he was merely furthering his education.

The writer has overwritten. Words like "ludicrous" and "swallow his tall tale" do not have the effect for which the writer is striving. Judges have seen too much of this hyperbole to find it persuasive.

Compare this version:

> Wilmer admits that he secretly taped various people at the dental school, but states that he was furthering his education.

Here, the writer has underwritten and does not advance the client's position. To be persuasive, strive for a style somewhere between these extremes. For example:

Wilmer admits that he secretly taped various people at the dental school. However, he offers a curious explanation. He denies that he was gathering information for his malpractice case and instead claims that he was furthering his education.

Here is another acceptable revision:

Wilmer admits that he secretly taped various people at the dental school. However, he denies that he was gathering information for his malpractice case and instead claims that he was taping for an educational purpose. He has not been terribly specific about how he would use the tapes to further his education.

These two revisions illustrate the proper tone. In the first revision, the writer draws attention to Wilmer's unbelievable explanation by terming it "curious." "Curious" adds flair, but not too much. In the second revision, the writer adds a final sentence to subtly highlight the improbability of the proffered explanation. In both, the writer juxtaposes Wilmer's explanation with what is apparently the real reason. As a result, the writer furthers the client's cause by painting the opposing litigant as untruthful and even pathetically comical.

§ 25.03.   WRITE A WELL-ORGANIZED ARGUMENT

1. Structure Your Argument

An important key to persuasive writing is producing a document with a structure that is readily apparent. You want the reader to follow your argument as effortlessly as possible. Forgo stream-of-consciousness writing in favor of organization.

The key to organization is to write according to an outline and to put your conclusions first. Even if you are not the type of writer who is comfortable outlining first and then writing, you still can write first and then organize your results so that they fit an outline. That is, write the outline after you have finished and then, where necessary, reorganize according to the outline.

After you have written your first draft, make sure that you begin the discussion of each argument with a conclusion that applies the legal argument to the facts of your case. Briefly outline your argument in the first paragraph so that the court has a "roadmap" of where you are going. Review your paragraphs for topic sentences. In most paragraphs, you will want the topic sentence at the beginning.

2. Put Your Best Arguments First and Develop Them More Fully

When we read a document, we usually pay more attention at the beginning. After a while, our interest wanes. In addition, as readers, we expect the important arguments to come first and to be developed in proportion to their importance. The lesson is clear. Place your most persuasive arguments first and allocate more space to them.

For example, suppose you are opposing the argument that a statute requires your client to give a neighbor an easement over her property. You have three arguments. First, the statute is unconstitutional. Second, in this case, the terms of the statute do not require granting an easement. Third, the neighbor did not follow the procedure the statute prescribes. Because courts are extremely reluctant to declare statutes unconstitutional, either your second or third argument probably gives you the best chance of winning. Decide which is your best argument and develop it fully. Then set out your second argument and give it less space. Finally, set out your argument on constitutionality and allocate it the least space.

As with all rules, there are exceptions. Sometimes you will decide to put your second-best argument first because it sets a good stage for your best argument. Then you will include your best argument. Nonetheless, in the overwhelming number of cases, you will do well to put your best argument first.

§ 25.04. ADOPT A PERSUASIVE WRITING STYLE

1. Be Concrete

When you argue for a client, you are not arguing for an abstract legal principle. You are seeking a holding that has practical consequences. In the same manner, judges are not interested in debating legal abstractions; they are interested in resolving specific disputes. The lesson: write about your case in concrete terms. In doing so you drive home the fact that your case is not an academic debate, but a conflict involving real people, particularly your client.

Consider this sentence:

The unforeseeability of the event absolved the defendants of liability.

This sentence is abstract. It could be about anyone. If you include facts about the relevant events, you make the issue concrete and compelling:

Because the defendant could not foresee that a twenty-year-old trespasser would dive head first from a lifeguard chair into a shallow pool, the defendant is not liable.

Here is another example:

A reasonable adult in plaintiff's position would recognize that the attempt to execute a head-first, straight dive into the lake without prior awareness of the depth of the waters might result in severe injury from the collision of one's head on the lake bottom.

Compare this revision:

A reasonable adult like the plaintiff would know that if he dived straight down and head-first into a shallow lake without knowing its depth, he could hit his head on the lake bottom and become paralyzed.

In the revision, the changes are subtle, but telling. They make the sentence far more concrete and persuasive.

2. When You Want to Emphasize a Word or Idea, Place It at the End of the Sentence

In a sentence, the beginning and the end are the best places to put information that you want to emphasize. Use the beginning of the sentence for information already familiar to the reader, usually the subject. Also use the beginning for information that the reader expects or can understand easily. Use the end for new information that you want to emphasize.

Suppose you are arguing about which law applies to your case, Missouri law or federal law. If you are arguing in favor of applying Missouri law, you might write this sentence:

Missouri law, not federal law, governs this case.

Although this sentence states your position, it does not make the best use of the end of the sentence. You will make your point more emphatically if you end with "Missouri law." Therefore, you should rewrite the sentence this way:

This case is governed not by federal law, but by Missouri law.

Although this revision forces you to use the passive voice, the loss of the active verb is far outweighed by the power of placing "Missouri law" at the end of the sentence.

The same principle applies to sentences with more than one clause. Consider this sentence:

The court barred the plaintiff's complaint as a matter of law because the plaintiff failed to notify the bank of the forgery within the time prescribed by the statute.

Suppose you want to emphasize that the court barred the complaint as a matter of law. You would rewrite the sentence this way:

Because the plaintiff failed to notify the bank of the forgery within the time prescribed by the statute, the court barred the plaintiff's complaint as a matter of law.

By placing the main clause at the end of the sentence, you stress the idea that you want to emphasize.

3. When Appropriate, Use the Same Subject for a Series of Sentences

By using the same subject for a series of sentences, you make it clear that you are telling the story of the subject. As a result, you give your sentences unity and direction.

Consider this paragraph from the brief of a convicted criminal defendant arguing ineffectiveness of counsel:

The client and the defense counsel did not meet until one hour before the trial. As a result, there was never the personal exchange between the two parties so necessary to a strong defense. The defense counsel never had the opportunity to observe her client. Thus there was no opportunity to judge his mannerisms and overall appearance, the fact being that the defendant, being somewhat quiet and shy, would not make a strong witness at trial. When he testified at trial, he did not come across well to the jury. The tactical error of placing him on the stand could have been avoided if more time had been spent with the defendant and a personal interview had been conducted.

The argument becomes much more compelling when the defense counsel becomes the subject of every sentence and of virtually every clause:

Until one hour before the trial, the defense counsel never met with the defendant and thus never had the personal exchange so necessary to a strong defense. Because she had never had the opportunity to observe her client, she could not judge his mannerisms and overall appearance. She therefore did not know that her client was somewhat quiet and shy and, at trial, would not come across well to the jury. By placing her client on the stand, the defense counsel made a tactical error that she could have avoided by taking the time to conduct a personal interview.

The rewrite makes it clear that the writer is discussing the failings of the defense counsel and detailing what she did and failed to do. As a result, the writer is presenting a persuasive argument for ineffectiveness of counsel.

§ 25.05. STATE YOUR FACTS PERSUASIVELY

At the beginning of your brief, you will have the opportunity to present the facts from your client's perspective. Judges expect your statement of the facts to be straightforward and accurate. They dislike rhetoric here and will form a negative opinion of your credibility if you attempt to mislead them by distorting or omitting critical facts. Therefore, you must present an objective narrative.

Nonetheless, you still must write the facts as an advocate. Here is how. Stress the facts that favor your case and deemphasize those that hurt it. Instead of stating your own opinions about the facts, report that someone else offered those opinions. In this way, you are stating a fact—what someone else stated—not your opinion.

This excerpt from a brief furnishes a good example. The plaintiff dived into a pool with only three feet of water and suffered severe injuries. The writer represents the defendant, the manufacturer of the pool.

The plaintiff claimed that he perceived the water depth to be six feet and not its actual depth of three feet. At trial, several experts testified that this misperception was significant to their conclusion that the plaintiff caused the accident. As Dr. Luna, one of the experts, testified, if the plaintiff believed that the water was six feet deep, "his mental and physiological processes involving visual perception and judgment of his surroundings were impaired by his ingestion of alcohol and hallucinogens."

In this example, the writer makes the essential point without rhetoric or value-laden adjectives or adverbs. She does not call the plaintiff irresponsible or label him dissolute. She does not berate the opposing lawyer for pursuing a frivolous lawsuit. The writer simply reports the plaintiff's assertion and then reports the testimony of experts hired by the defendant.

The quotation from Dr. Luna is part of a sentence objectively reporting what happened at trial. Instead of quoting an expert, the writer might have stated the opinion as her own: "If the plaintiff believed that the water was six feet deep, his mental and physiological processes involving perception and judgment of his surroundings clearly were impaired by his ingestion of alcohol and hallucinogens." However, by placing the opinion in the mouth of another person, an expert, the writer makes it far more persuasive. (In the alternative, she might have attributed the opinion to Dr. Luna and then paraphrased his words in order to make the sentence better stylistically.) As you can see, it is possible to state facts in an objective manner and still write as an advocate.

§ 25.06.   MAKE EQUITY AND POLICY ARGUMENTS

In most cases that go to trial, and certainly in most cases on appeal, both parties have sound legal arguments. Therefore, the advocate must argue more than the law. You also need to argue the equities and social policy. To argue the equities means to argue that your client is the most sympathetic litigant and should win as a matter of justice. To argue policy means to argue that the legal holding you seek has positive ramifications for society and your opponent's does not.

Here is an example. Suppose you represent a child whose mother was seriously injured in an accident. You are suing the party that caused the accident for loss of parental consortium. In other words, you are arguing that the child should recover for losing the companionship and affection of the parent.

To argue the equities, you would enumerate the ways in which the child has suffered. You would mention activities that the child and mother used to share. You might quote the child reflecting on her loss. You thus would paint a picture of a child deserving to recover.

To argue policy, you would assert that as a general principle, the court should recognize the right of a child to sue for loss of parental consortium and should be liberal in finding that the loss has occurred in specific cases. Your policy argument might read like this:

> The importance of a child's feelings and emotions merit more than lip service. The loss of a parent is a devastating injury at least as important as a spouse's loss of consortium, which this jurisdiction recognizes. For these sorts of injuries, tort law is the appropriate avenue of redress.

Thus, while an equitable argument focuses on the particulars of a case, a policy argument generalizes. In the illustration, the policy argument states that recognizing this cause of action is desirable, is logical because it is similar to another tort that the jurisdiction already permits, and is consistent with the development of tort law.

§ 25.07.   USE PRECEDENT PERSUASIVELY

Judges prefer that their decisions be consistent with past decisions of their court. They also must be persuaded that their decisions are consistent with those of any higher court. Therefore, invoking favorable precedent is a powerful tool of persuasion.

The difficulty arises when the earlier case does not support your position or it is unclear whether the case supports it. You might argue that the earlier case was wrongly decided. However, such an argument is at cross purposes with the desire to claim consistency with existing case law. Therefore, an argument rejecting precedent should be an alternative argument of last resort. Your first argument should be that existing law supports your position or at least is consistent with it.

1. Argue that Adverse Precedent Is Consistent with Your Argument

To harmonize adverse precedent, argue that the contrary case is distinguishable from your case on its facts or that it does not address the issue in your case. If possible, go one step further and argue that the policy underlying that opinion is the one you are advancing.

Return to your argument that the court should recognize a cause of action for a child's loss of parental consortium. Suppose that in another case, the same court rejected the argument. There, the court stated that because the parent will receive compensation from the defendant, that compensation probably will give ample recovery to both parent and child. Therefore, according to the court, permitting a separate recovery for the child would be unfairly duplicative.

If, in that case, the only plaintiff was the child, and in your case, the child's claim is joined with the parent's claim, you can distinguish the cases. Argue that the previous case's holding dealt only with cases in which the actions of parent and child were not joined at trial. Argue that if the same jury is deciding the claims together, the risk of a duplicative recovery is very small. Then argue that, in both cases, the underlying goal is just compensation. Here, you are advancing this goal in a situation that will not result in overcompensation. With this argument, you distinguish the adverse precedent and also argue that you are furthering the same goal that motivated that decision.

2. Interpret Precedent Narrowly or Broadly, as Appropriate

As you have learned in law school, a holding is open to more than one interpretation. When you are dealing with precedent, select the interpretation that furthers your case. Depending on the facts of your case, this endeavor may require you to interpret the holding narrowly or broadly.

Suppose you are arguing that an adult should be able to recover for the loss of consortium of a parent. Suppose your jurisdiction has an earlier case permitting a minor child to recover for loss of parental consortium. Opposing counsel would interpret the holding narrowly to permit the cause of action only when the plaintiff is a minor child. However, you would interpret the holding broadly to permit any child to recover.

The way you deal with precedent is illustrative of the way you make a persuasive legal argument. Interpret the law and facts in a way that is both credible and in your client's best interest.

CHAPTER 26

Writing Pretrial Motions and Trial Briefs

§ 26.01. PURPOSES OF MOTIONS

Pretrial motions are filed in an effort to persuade the court to make a decision in the early stages of a case. The decision requested may be to dismiss the case entirely, to decide it without trial, or to resolve a discovery dispute between the parties. Although there are other types of motions that may be filed, we will focus on these three as representative of common motions. Motions involve advocacy; you are trying to persuade the court to do something, and so should follow all the advice about advocacy writing that is offered elsewhere in this book.

§ 26.02. FORM OF MOTIONS

There is no set format for writing motions. You should get sample motions from other lawyers in your office, or look at motions that have previously been filed in the court for which you are writing. In most courts, the motion itself is a simple statement of the basis upon which relief is requested. The motion may be supported by a memorandum that sets forth the legal arguments in support of the motion, and by other documents appropriate to the motion, such as affidavits. All memoranda, or briefs, in support of motions should include a statement of the relevant facts and an analysis of the relevant law.

§ 26.03. MOTIONS TO DISMISS

Under Rule 12(b)(6) of the Federal Rules of Civil Procedure, a defendant may move to dismiss a complaint on the grounds that it fails to state a claim upon which relief can be granted. Most, if not all, states permit a similar motion—sometimes called a demurrer—that allows a defendant to attempt to get a defective complaint dismissed. Under this standard, the defendant must demonstrate that even if the plaintiff can prove all the facts alleged in the complaint, there is no basis for legal relief. In ruling on such a motion, the court will interpret the facts in the light most favorable to the plaintiff. Motions to dismiss may also be granted when the plaintiff fails to allege some crucial element of the cause of action. In such a case, the court may dismiss the complaint with leave to amend, so the plaintiff can correct the defect.

In our case against the dating service on behalf of Susan Starkey (see Chapter 18), let us assume that you filed a complaint for negligence. Assume also that the dating service filed a motion to dismiss for failure to state a claim, alleging that it had no duty to protect persons in Susan's position, and therefore there is no basis for recovery. You should have researched the applicable law before filing the complaint, and you should have legal support for your argument in favor of such a duty. Your response to the motion should focus on establishing the duty to protect; you should not try to win your whole case on the motion because you will likely need discovery to establish the facts in support of your argument that the duty to protect was breached and that the breach was the proximate cause of Susan's damages—that is, the failure of the dating service to adequately screen its clients led to Susan's stalking and emotional distress. Proving this will require witness testimony and other evidence. The point here is that only purely legal arguments can be resolved in the context of the motion to dismiss. If the court needs to find facts in order to resolve the question presented, the case must go on. If the motion to dismiss raises factual issues, that may be reason enough to deny the motion.

Exercise

Write a paragraph or two explaining why a motion to dismiss should not be granted in the Starkey case. Focus on the facts you would like to prove and how they fit into your negligence claim, especially the issue of the dating service's duty to its customers.

Assume that you have found case law supporting the idea that the dating service may have a duty to protect customers, particularly if it makes any affirmative representations relating to safety, background checks, or similar ideas. Assume that Susan brought you an ad from the dating service that includes the language, "Looking for a safe, sane alternative to the bar scene?" Also, assume that Susan told you that she specifically asked about screening of prospective dates and was assured that the dating service took "all necessary precautions" to ensure that its clients were reputable.

Write your explanation as if it would go into your response to the motion to dismiss. In other words, your audience is the judge who will decide the motion. Remember that the judge will interpret the facts in the light most favorable to your client in deciding the motion. You do not need to cite cases; write as if you are summarizing your argument in the response to the motion.

§ 26.04. MOTIONS TO COMPEL DISCOVERY

Under Federal Rule of Civil Procedure 37(a)(3)(B), a party may move to compel discovery when the opposing party does not respond to a discovery request and the parties cannot work out the dispute themselves. For example, if

- a deponent[1] fails to answer a question asked under Rule 30 or 31,
- a corporation or other entity fails to make a designation under Rule 30(b)(6) or 31(a)(4),

---

1. The term "deponent" refers to the person being questioned in a deposition.

- a party fails to answer an interrogatory submitted under Rule 33, or
- a party fails to respond that inspection will be permitted—or fails to permit inspection—as requested under Rule 34,

then the discovering party may move for an order compelling an answer, designation, production, or inspection in accordance with the request.

The motion must include a certification that the movant has in good faith conferred or attempted to confer with the person or party failing to make the discovery in an effort to secure the information or material without court action. When taking a deposition on oral examination, the proponent of the question may complete or adjourn the examination before applying for an order.

Under Rule 37(a)(4) an evasive or incomplete answer may be treated as a failure to respond. Available sanctions under Rule 37(a)(5) include the expense of filing or opposing the motion, including attorneys' fees.

Assume that you served a request for production of documents on the dating service, and that the dating service refused to produce Partlow's file in response to your specific request, claiming confidentiality. Note that under Rule 37 you are required to confer with the dating service to attempt to obtain the material without court action. If you try to work the matter out but are unsuccessful, you may move to compel the production of the file. You would need to research the issue of confidentiality raised by the dating service and establish that under the law the service is not entitled to keep the file from you. You would make this argument in your memorandum in support of the motion.

Because the rule requires that you confer with the defendant, you should state in your motion that you have made the attempt to confer, and you should probably detail the attempts you made in your memorandum in support of the motion. It is always a good idea to put in writing all efforts you have made to comply with prerequisites to obtaining a hearing on the merits.

§ 26.05. MOTIONS FOR SUMMARY JUDGMENT

Rule 56 of the Federal Rules of Civil Procedure provides that either party may move for summary judgment. Rule 56(a) states that the motion will be granted "if the movant shows that there is no genuine dispute as to any material fact and the movant is entitled to judgment as a matter of law." This means that, as in the case of the motion to dismiss, if the question before the court is one of law, the case may be decided upon motion. The difference between a motion to dismiss and a motion for summary judgment is that the motion for summary judgment generally includes some supporting factual material, such as responses to discovery or affidavits, while the motion to dismiss focuses solely on the complaint.

Let us go back to Susan Starkey's case. If counsel for the dating service files a motion for summary judgment alleging that there was no breach of the duty to protect persons in Susan's position because the screening procedures were adequate, and attaches an affidavit from an employee of the service outlining those procedures, you would simply respond that the motion raises a genuine issue of material fact. Regardless of the existence of screening procedures employed by the dating service, you would want the opportunity to prove that those procedures either were inadequate or that they were not followed. The only way to prove these things is to cross-examine the employees of the dating service, and perhaps to hire an expert to testify that the service's procedures did not meet the standards of the industry.

The key to responding to any motion is to limit your argument to what you need to establish to overcome the motion. Many lawyers succumb to the temptation to argue the entire case at the motion stage, which only confuses the issue and may make it less likely that the motion will be decided in your favor. Thus, if in responding to the dating service's motion for summary judgment, you choose to argue the inadequacy of the screening procedures and the damages Susan suffered, you might actually suggest to the court that you think the case is ready for decision, when all you really want at this stage is the chance to prove your case in court. Understanding the standard in the applicable rule is critical. Read carefully and argue only what you need to in order to defeat the motion.

Note that the parties in some cases may actually agree upon the facts, in which case both parties may be content to submit the case for decision by summary judgment, and avoid the time and expense of a trial. This will probably be the exceptional case, but if there are no genuine issues of fact to be proved at trial, you may very well win the gratitude of the court by stipulating to the facts and submitting the case for a decision on the law.

Exercise

Write a few paragraphs explaining why Susan Starkey's case cannot be decided on summary judgment. Explain the genuine issues of material fact that must be addressed at trial. Again, assume that you are writing for the judge who will decide the motion, and do not cite cases. Focus on the basis for the motion and what you need to establish to persuade the judge to deny the motion.

§ 26.06. ETHICAL CONSIDERATIONS IN MOTION PRACTICE

As an officer of the court, you should never file a frivolous claim or make a frivolous argument. Your factual and legal support for your argument must be sufficient to justify taking up the time of the court and other parties to the matter. Rule 11 of the Federal Rules of Civil Procedure provides that pleadings and motions must be signed by the attorney of record. When you sign a pleading or motion, you represent that to the best of your

knowledge, information, and belief, formed after an inquiry reasonable under the circumstances:

(1) it is not being presented for any improper purpose, such as to harass, cause unnecessary delay, or needlessly increase the cost of litigation;

(2) the claims, defenses, and other legal contentions are warranted by existing law or by a nonfrivolous argument for extending, modifying, or reversing existing law or for establishing new law;

(3) the factual contentions have evidentiary support or, if specifically so identified, will likely have evidentiary support after a reasonable opportunity for further investigation or discovery; and

(4) the denials of factual contentions are warranted on the evidence or, if specifically so identified, are reasonably based on belief or a lack of information.

Fed. R. Civ. P. 11(b). Violators of this rule are subject to monetary and other sanctions. If you believe that another attorney has submitted papers to the court in violation of this rule, you may move for sanctions.

§ 26.07. CHECKLIST FOR MOTIONS

— Before filing or responding to any motion, make sure that you understand the standard upon which the motion will be decided. Read the rule!

— Research the applicable law.

— Find sample motions of the type you will be filing for the court in which you will be filing the motion. You may want to make copies for your files.

— Prepare your memorandum in support of the motion to carefully articulate the factual and legal basis upon which the court may grant the relief you seek. Argue no more than necessary to obtain that relief, but make sure that you have met the standard set forth in the applicable rule. Do not try your case at the motion stage!

— When responding to a motion, carefully focus your argument on what you need to establish to overcome the motion. Do not argue your entire case and confuse the issue.

§ 26.08. TRIAL BRIEFS

Much like motion briefs, trial briefs need to be focused. Trial briefs may be required by rule, or they may be requested by the judge. Sometimes counsel simply decides to file one. Trial briefs may cover all issues anticipated for trial, or they may focus on a single issue, or anything in between. There may not be any specified format for a trial brief, or there may be local rules that must be followed. You will need to adapt to the practice in your jurisdiction, and even courtroom by courtroom.

The important thing, as with any legal writing, is to not try to do too much. Your trial brief may be the first formal introduction the judge has to your case. You need to summarize the facts and to explain and apply any relevant legal authority. As with all legal documents, your brief should look professional and demonstrate attention to detail in every aspect.

Here are two local rules for jurisdictions that require trial briefs:

(1) Tennessee 26th District Local Rules of Practice § 18.04

§ 18.04. Briefs in Civil Non-Jury Cases
In all non-jury cases, except divorces and General Sessions Court appeals, trial briefs are required. Unless otherwise allowed by the Court, ten (10) days before the trial of a case, trial briefs shall be submitted to the court and furnished to opposing counsel. The trial brief format is attached to this rule as Appendix B. If an issue to be litigated at trial has been briefed in pre-trial motions and counsel believes that the motion brief adequately covered the issue, counsel may refer the court to the motion brief in lieu of briefing the issue for trial.

Appendix B

TRIAL BRIEF FORMAT NON-JURY
A. A concise statement of the facts
B. The factual issues to be decided
C. Points of Law
    1. Address all areas felt appropriate including those of an evidentiary nature, if felt controversial.
D. An argument is neither required nor desired, but may be included, if felt necessary by counsel.
E. General
    1. Briefs will not be filed with the Clerk, but sent directly to the trial Judge at his or her address.
    2. Include photostatic copies of any out-of-state or unreported cases cited and all statutes relied upon.
    3. Counsel will attach copies of their respective pleadings leading to a joining of issue, i.e. complaint and answer–amended, supplemental, etc.

(2) Local Rules for the Imperial County Superior Court, Rule 5.1.20 (California)

Rule 5.1.20. Trial Brief (Form FL-08)
(a) Each counsel and /or self-represented party shall prepare, serve, and file a Trial Brief at least ten (10) days before trial. The brief must include the following information and attachments, if applicable to the disputed issue in the case:

(1) A confirmation that the preliminary disclosure statements have been served and filed with the court;

(2) A summary of all issues resolved; if the resolution is by written agreement, a copy of the agreement; if the agreement is oral, a statement of the details;

(3) A summary of all issues in dispute, and the propounding party's proposed resolution of them;

(4) A complete and current Income and Expense Declaration (FL-150);

(5) A complete and current Schedule of Assets and Debts (FL-142);

(6) A complete and current Property Declaration (FL-160);

(7) A detailed itemization of all disputed marital assets and debt, and a proposal for an equal division of property. The proposed division shall specify any assumption or payment of debts and liabilities and any tax consequences;

(8) Proposed orders for child support, including guideline calculations;

(9) Proposed orders for spousal support, including detailed justification;

(10) Proposed orders for custody and visitation, including proposed access schedules;

(11) Proposed orders for attorney's fees, court costs, and payment of other costs of litigation;

(12) Points and authorities on any disputed issues of law applicable to the case;

(13) Values of property shall be supported by appraisals or statements, copies of which shall be attached, unless good cause is shown why no appraisal or statement has been obtained. Except for items of unusual value, personal property may be aggregated as e.g., "jewelry $1000." There shall be a rebuttable presumption that the average Kelly Blue Book value shown for a given vehicle is its fair market value;

(14) If it is claimed that an item of property is wholly or partially separate, the statement must clearly show the item or amount claimed to be separate, and the justification thereof. If any community funds have been used to purchase or maintain separate property, the amounts and the times the payments were made must be shown;

(15) A list of all witnesses to be examined, a brief synopsis of their testimony, and copies of the resumes of any expert witnesses;

(16) Any additional information which the party believes would be helpful to the Court.

(b) Failure to timely file a proper trial brief may result in the trial being vacated, the imposition of monetary sanctions including payment of costs and fees, or in trial sanctions precluding the litigation of issues or the exclusion of evidence. The Court has authority to impose these sanctions on its own motion. The sanctions may also be requested by an adverse party on noticed motion.

In these rules you can see an emphasis on efficiency. The court wants to know exactly what the status of the case is—what has been agreed upon, what is still in dispute, and what evidence you are likely to present at trial. The court wants to ensure that the case is actually ready for trial: Have all necessary documents been gathered? Do the parties have their witnesses set? Are the lawyers prepared with law to support both the elements of their claims and defenses and any evidentiary issues likely to be raised? If the court has this information beforehand, the trial can proceed much more expeditiously. You will note that the Tennessee rule even suggests that counsel refer to previous briefs submitted in connection with pretrial motions if the issue for trial has already been argued at that stage.

You may submit a trial brief for a case to be decided by either a judge or a jury. Either way, the judge is your audience. A jury will never see a trial brief, and it should be written for a legally savvy audience. Even if the judge will not be making the ultimate decision in the case, he or she will be ruling on motions and objections, and the more prepared the judge feels he or she is to make those rulings, the more likely the judge is to be happy with the performance of the lawyers.

§ 26.09. EXAMPLES

Sample motion briefs and trial briefs appear in Appendix V.

CHAPTER 27

Appellate Process and Standard of Review

§ 27.01. INTRODUCTION

Writing appellate briefs requires an understanding of the appellate process. The structure and ground rules of that process affect your ability to present an effective legal argument. In this chapter, we discuss in broad terms how cases come up on appeal, the record on appeal, and standards of review, that is, the tests an appellate court uses to evaluate the decision below. The discussion focuses primarily on the civil appellate process. If you are handling a criminal appeal, you should follow the applicable rules.

§ 27.02. HOW CASES COME UP ON APPEAL

Although each state court system and the federal system have their own rules on the proper procedure for taking an appeal, all systems share important similarities. Once a court or jury decides a case, the losing party may take an appeal to the appellate court. In a state with an intermediate appellate court, most appeals to that court are a matter of right. In most civil cases, the court of last resort, often called the state supreme court, has discretion in deciding whether to hear an appeal.

In general, the losing party can take an appeal from a final judgment, that is, a decision that disposes of the entire case. A final judgment might arise when a trial ends or when the court decides the case on a motion, for example, a motion for summary judgment. However, in certain instances, an appellant may take an appeal from an interlocutory order. An interlocutory order does not determine the final result of an action, but decides only some intervening matter, such as the grant or denial of an injunction. An appeal from an interlocutory order must follow procedural rules specifically applicable to interlocutory appeals.

§ 27.03. THE RECORD ON APPEAL

In reviewing the proceedings of the court below, the appellate court relies on the record. Rule 10(a) of the Federal Rules of Appellate Procedure sets out a typical definition of the record: "(1) the original papers and exhibits filed in the district court; (2) the transcript of the proceedings, if any; and (3) a certified copy of the docket entries prepared by the district clerk." Reliance on the record ensures that the appellate court will base its decision on only those matters presented to the district court, including both factual and legal questions.[1]

As a general rule, the court will not independently review the record for errors, but will rely on the parties to identify and brief any errors that should be reviewed. When you make your arguments on appeal, you must point to a specific reference in the record to justify each argument. In your brief, you must make constant references to the record so that the court can easily locate the parts of the record on which you are relying. If you fail to make sufficient precise references, you force the court to sift through the often voluminous stack of paper that comprises the record or you run the risk that the court will reject your argument as unsupported by the record. Such a failure will hardly endear you to the court or your client. For a further discussion of the record, see Section 29.01.

§ 27.04. THE STANDARD OF REVIEW

In deciding an appeal, a court cannot simply ignore the decision of the court below. The appellate court may decide only issues that the parties properly identified and objected to as erroneously decided at the trial level. This requirement allows the trial court to correct errors immediately, or at least gives the appellate court the benefit of the trial court's thinking on the issue. In addition, only issues or findings that are necessary to the trial court's decision may be appealed.

The test the appellate court must apply in passing on the lower court's decision is called the standard, or scope, of review. The standard of review varies depending on the jurisdiction and the type of case. You will explore the various types of review in detail in your civil procedure class. Our goal is to briefly introduce you to the most typical standards: clearly erroneous, abuse of discretion, and de novo review. These standards are part of a continuum, from extreme deference to the trial court on fact findings because of the trial court's firsthand exposure to evidence at trial, to little or no deference on purely legal questions.

1. Clearly Erroneous

The most deferential standard for review of a trial court's decision is the "clearly erroneous" standard.[2] The standard is set forth in Rule 52(a)(6) of the Federal Rules of Civil Procedure: "Findings of fact, whether based on oral or other evidence, shall not be set aside unless clearly erroneous, and the reviewing court must give due regard to the trial court's opportunity to judge the witnesses' credibility." The rationale for this standard is clear. Because findings of fact are based on in-court proceedings where the trial court can make judgments on the credibility and competence of witnesses after seeing them firsthand, these judgments are due substantial deference. Because the trial court has a greater

---

1. The appellate court may sometimes consider new legal theories or arguments on appeal, but only if those arguments can be resolved based on the facts found at trial.

2. Jury findings are accorded even more deference. The standard is the same as that employed in deciding motions for directed verdict or for judgment notwithstanding the verdict: whether a reasonable jury could have reached the verdict. Gene R. Shreve & Peter Raven-Hansen, *Understanding Civil Procedure*, 444-445 (2d ed. 1994).

familiarity with the case, the appellate court may not independently determine the weight or credibility of the evidence or assess the inferences drawn from the facts by the trial court.[3]

The Supreme Court described the standard this way: "A finding is 'clearly erroneous' when although there is evidence to support it, the reviewing court on the entire evidence is left with the definite and firm conviction that a mistake has been committed."[4] This standard obviously places quite a difficult burden on the appellant's attorney.

2. Abuse of Discretion

Slightly further along the deference continuum, and more difficult to define, is the abuse of discretion standard. This standard applies to matters that are within the discretion of the trial court because they are "largely ad hoc and situation-specific."[5] This standard is tolerant of mistakes that may be made by a trial court in the exercise of its acknowledged discretion. Trial courts have a great deal of discretion on issues relating to trial management, such as joinder, discovery, sanctions, and the grant or denial of a motion for a new trial.

The scope of the trial court's discretion in a particular instance will depend on and must be evaluated in the context of the source of its discretion. For example, Rule 35(a) of the Federal Rules of Civil Procedure gives the trial court discretion to order a mental or physical examination of a party "for good cause," when the mental or physical condition of the party is "in controversy." Such an order would normally be accorded great deference on appeal, but in *Schlagenhauf v. Holder*, 379 U.S. 104 (1964), the Supreme Court found abuse of discretion in a case where the trial court ordered that a defendant be examined in each of four medical specialties—internal medicine, ophthalmology, neurology, and psychiatry. There was nothing in the record to support any examination other than a visual examination, so the Court vacated the judgment of the district court and remanded for reconsideration and further proceedings.

The abuse of discretion standard "varies in intensity with the breadth of discretion. Accordingly, abuse of discretion really occupies a band in the middle of the spectrum of intensity of review, its precise locus in any particular case depending upon the nature of the discretionary order under review."[6] If abuse of discretion is the standard for the case you are appealing, you will need to research similar cases in order to understand and argue precisely how the standard should be applied in your case.

3. De Novo Review

The least deferential standard of review is applied to pure questions of law, or to mixed fact-law questions.[7] The appellate court is at no disadvantage in deciding these types of questions because it has the same access to relevant information that the trial court had.

---

3. Jack H. Friedenthal, Mary Kay Kane & Arthur R. Miller, *Civil Procedure* 640 (4th ed., West 2005).

4. *United States v. U.S. Gypsum Co.*, 333 U.S. 364, 395 (1948).

5. Shreve & Raven-Hansen, *supra* n. 2, at 445.

6. *Id.* at 446.

7. Friedenthal et al., *supra* n. 3, at 639, 641.

By making de novo decisions, the appellate court fulfills one of its primary functions: to provide guidance to the lower courts by ruling on questions of law.[8]

The de novo standard comes into play, for example, in reviewing pretrial motions. To illustrate, Rule 56(a) of the Federal Rules of Civil Procedure sets out the standard to apply when the federal district court grants a motion for summary judgment. According to the rule, summary judgment is proper when it appears that "there is no genuine issue as to any material fact and that the movant is entitled to judgment as a matter of law." The appellate court reads the record in the light most favorable to the party against whom the summary judgment was granted. Because the lower court heard no witnesses and weighed no evidence, the appellate court has no findings of fact to review. It therefore may decide the issue de novo. As you would expect, this standard is the one most favorable to the appellant.

4. The Importance to the Practitioner

As you can see, the appellate lawyer must know what standard of review the court should employ and should think strategically in presenting the appropriate standard to the court. If you represent the appellant, it is to your advantage to be able to characterize the issue on appeal as a question of law, or of mixed fact and law. If you succeed, the standard of review will be de novo. Conversely, if you represent the appellee, you want to characterize the issue as one of fact, or at least as one subject to the trial court's discretion. That way, the appellate court will be forced to give greater deference to the opinion of the trial court. Not surprisingly, complicated analysis and legal research may be required to distinguish the mixed fact-law question from the purely factual question.

Your understanding of the standard of review will also affect the way you argue and emphasize different aspects of the record. If you are representing the appellee and the court must find the decision below to be clearly erroneous in order to overturn it, you should stress the evidence that supports the trial court's decision and argue that the appellate court must defer to the judgment of the lower court. On the other hand, if you are representing the appellant and the court may hear the case de novo, you should point out that the decision below carries no weight and then make as few references to it as possible. Present the argument as if you are making it for the first time.

§ 27.05. AVAILABLE FORMS OF RELIEF

When the appellate court completes its review, it has the discretion to take certain specific actions. It may reverse or vacate the decision below, remand the matter to the lower court for further proceedings, or affirm. As an appellate attorney, you must tell the court precisely what action you want it to take. You may want the court to take different actions on different issues. If you fail to be precise about the relief you seek, the court can only guess at what your client wishes.

---

8. *Id.* at 639.

CHAPTER 28

Introduction to Writing Appellate Briefs

§ 28.01. WHAT IS A BRIEF?

A brief is a written argument that a lawyer submits to a court. Briefs may be written in support of motions (discussed in Chapter 26), to define issues for trial (also discussed in Chapter 26), or on appeal. As noted in Chapter 26, trial briefs do not generally follow any specific format and may not be submitted in every trial. Appellate briefs must follow very specific rules and are submitted in every appeal. In an appellate brief, the lawyer argues that the appellate court should reverse or affirm the lower court's decision, or asks for whatever other relief is appropriate. A court uses briefs to define the issues it will decide, to learn about the facts and the law, and to determine who should win.

Unlike a memorandum, which is an objective document, a brief is a persuasive document. Therefore you should write it in a way that will encourage the court to reach a decision favoring your client.

Although you should seek to convince the court that your client should win, do not overstate your case. Be sure to include a discussion of any adverse facts or cases. To win, you must not only argue that the law, policy, and equity support your client's argument, but also face up to damaging facts and contrary cases. You must downplay the significance of the facts and distinguish the cases. If you ignore adverse information, you will be embarrassed when your opponent brings it to the court's attention.

Write the brief persuasively, even the statement of facts. Argue that equity and policy, as well as the law, support your client's case. Chapter 25 describes how to make equity and policy arguments and gives an example of each. Because appellate briefs are the most complicated and involve the most precise rules, we focus on appellate briefs in the next few chapters. You should follow the rules articulated in this book for writing persuasively and for presenting the facts and analysis when writing any brief. You should try to get information from the court or from experienced lawyers who have written similar briefs if you seek guidance regarding the format or desired content of other types of briefs.

Before writing an appellate brief, read the record. The record usually consists of documents and exhibits filed in the lower court, transcripts of depositions, trial testimony and arguments before the lower court, docket entries, and the lower court's orders and opinions. The record defines the issues you may raise on appeal because you can argue only issues raised in the proceedings before the lower court. The record also limits the facts on which you can rely in your brief because you can rely only on facts that are in the record. Chapter 29 describes the record in more detail.

§ 28.02. PROCEDURAL RULES FOR APPELLATE BRIEFS

Appellate courts promulgate their own rules of appellate procedure. You must follow these rules when you write an appellate brief. These rules regulate the appearance, length, and content of appellate briefs.

Many appellate courts have rules governing paper size, paper color, size of margins, size of type, line spacing, type of binding, numbering of pages, and the format of the title page. As a general rule, each part of an appellate brief must begin on a new page. For example, even if the table of contents takes up only half of a page, you cannot put the table of authorities on the same page. You must begin the table of authorities on the next page.

Many appellate courts also limit the length of appellate briefs. Judges do not have the time to read long briefs. The shorter your brief is, the more likely it is that the judge will read all of it. Even if the appellate court's rules allow you to write a fifty-page brief, write the shortest one possible that still permits you to make a compelling argument.

All appellate courts require appellants to file their briefs first because the appellant is appealing the lower court's order. The appellee then files a brief that responds to the appellant's brief. Most appellate courts allow the appellant to file a reply brief to the appellee's brief.[1]

Most appellate courts require that appellants include the following parts in their briefs:

1. Title page
2. Table of contents
3. Table of authorities
4. Statement of jurisdiction
5. Questions presented
6. Constitutional and statutory provisions
7. Statement of facts
8. Summary of argument
9. Argument
10. Conclusion
11. Appendix (all or part of the record)

Although the appellee's brief has most of the same parts, most appellate courts do not require the appellee to include a statement of jurisdiction, questions presented, or a statement of facts. The appellee, however, is allowed to and should include its own version of the questions presented and a statement of facts.

---

1. If the parties have the right to appeal a lower court's decision, the party who initiates the appeal is called the "appellant" and the opposing party is called the "appellee." When review of a lower court's decision is discretionary, the party seeking such review is called the "petitioner" and the opposing party is called the "respondent."

§ 28.03. THE PARTS OF A BRIEF

This section briefly describes the parts of a brief that most appellate courts require. Chapters 29, 30, 31, and 32 describe the parts of the brief in greater detail.

1. The Title Page

The title page contains sufficient information to identify the case and who filed the brief. The title page usually sets out the names of the appellate and lower courts, the names of the parties, the numerical designation for the case, and the name of the attorney who is filing the brief.

2. Table of Contents

The table of contents tells the court the pages on which it will find each part of your brief. The table of contents provides a summary of your argument because it consists of the headings and subheadings of your argument in sentence form.

3. Table of Authorities

The table of authorities tells the court the pages on which it will find the cases, constitutional provisions, statutes, and secondary authorities you cite in your brief. The citation format in the table of authorities must be as accurate and complete as the citation format you use in the argument section of your brief.

4. Jurisdictional Statement

The jurisdictional statement tells the court what authority confers jurisdiction on the court to hear the appeal.

5. Questions Presented

This section frames the issues for the court. Frame the issues persuasively so that they suggest the answers you want the court to reach, but do not be argumentative.

6. Constitutional and Statutory Provisions

This section sets out the text of the constitutional and statutory provisions you cite in your brief. Do not set out the text of the jurisdictional authority you cite in the jurisdictional statement.

7. Statement of Facts

This section sets out a clear and concise statement of the facts relevant to the argument section of the brief. Write the facts in a light most favorable to your client, but do not omit adverse facts. Include references to the record but do not include arguments, conclusions of law, or citations in this section.

8. Summary of Argument

This section sets out a clear, concise, and persuasive summary of your argument. In this section, summarize your primary and most compelling arguments.

9. Argument

The argument section is the heart of the brief. In this section, analyze the pertinent legal authorities and apply them to the facts of the case. Divide the argument into as many subsections as there are issues and sub-issues. Unlike the discussion section of a memo, which is objective, the argument section of a brief is persuasive. Argue equity and policy as well as the law. You must discuss adverse facts and cases.

§ 28.04. THE HALLMARKS OF A WELL-WRITTEN BRIEF

The hallmarks of a well-written brief are the same as the hallmarks of a well-written memo, which are set out in Section 11.04:

- Clear writing style
- Good organization
- Thorough research
- Good judgment
- Writing for the reader
- Precision and clarity
- Creativity
- Correct citation format

There are certain strategic differences between memos and briefs. Your primary audience is the court, not the assigning attorney. Therefore, a brief is persuasive, not objective. The judges will not have read the case file or the applicable law before they read your brief. They usually will know less about the facts and the law than you do. For this reason, be very careful to discuss the facts and the law clearly and thoroughly.

CHAPTER 29

The Appellate Brief:
The Introductory Parts

§ 29.01. USING THE RECORD

You must have authority for every fact you state in your brief. Your authority for facts and for the history of your case is the "record." Although some courts call the record the "appendix," in this book, we use the term "record." The record consists of docket entries, trial transcripts, deposition excerpts, and pleadings filed in the court below. You will make many references to the record in your statement of facts. You will also refer to the record every time you repeat a fact in the argument section of your brief and every time you refer to any event or filing of documents in the proceedings in lower courts.

An attorney prepares the record before writing the brief. In practice, attorneys for the opposing parties on appeal usually agree to the contents of the record. In the law school situation, the instructor gives students the record from which to write the brief. The record is the "reference book" for your brief. You must not rely on any fact that is not in the record.

Rules of court usually tell you what you must include in the record. For example, the rules may require all docket entries from the lower courts and all orders and opinions from the lower courts. You also should include in the record all relevant pleadings in your case and relevant excerpts from depositions and trial transcripts.

When you prepare the record, put all items in the order the court rules specify. If the court rules specify that you arrange items in groups, arrange the items within that group in order. Put other items, such as testimony, in the order that you think is logical. The record is bound into a volume or, in many cases, several volumes. The pages of the record are then numbered sequentially as "R-1," "R-2," "R-3," and so forth. (If the record is called "appendix," the pages are numbered "A-1," "A-2," and so forth.)

When you write your brief, make references to the pages containing the facts that you include. For example:

> The defendant hit the plaintiff. (R. 35-37.) The plaintiff then skidded off the road. (R. 107-111.) The plaintiff's car was totally destroyed. (R. 103.)

If you have stated a fact that appears on several pages in the record, make references to all pages on which that information appears:

The defendant hit the plaintiff. (R. 35-37, 86-89.) The plaintiff then skidded off the road. (R. 107-111, 332, 345-346.) The plaintiff's car was totally destroyed. (R. 103, 111, 462-465, 503.)

Do not include any fact in your brief that the record does not substantiate. Do not assume any facts that are not in the record. The court that reads your brief will rely only on facts in the record. It is also very important that all your record references be accurate because the court will refer to the pages of the record you cite.

§ 29.02. THE TITLE PAGE

The title page of your brief gives the court necessary information. The title page in your brief must conform to the rules of the court with which you file your brief.

There are many ways to type title pages of briefs. The one you choose should be pleasing to the eye and easy to scan for the necessary information it contains. Some courts require typeset briefs.

A typical title page contains the following eight elements:

1. the exact name of the appellate court with which you are filing your brief;
2. the term in which the court is to consider your appeal, including the month and the year;
3. the docket number for the case;
4. the names of the parties with the appropriate appellate designation ("appellant," "appellee," "petitioner," or "respondent");
5. the exact name of the court from whose order you appeal;
6. identification of the party: "Brief for Appellant," "Brief for Appellee," "Brief for Petitioner," or "Brief for Respondent";
7. the name and address of the attorney writing the brief; and
8. the name and address of the attorney representing the opposing party (optional).

If court rules tell you how to prepare a title page, follow those rules exactly.

§ 29.03. TABLE OF CONTENTS

The table of contents is a "roadmap" for the court and the opposing counsel. This section is the first summary of your argument. It also serves as a reference tool. You must be sure that the page references are accurate and that the headings of the arguments in the table of contents are exact duplicates of the headings in your brief. For a discussion of brief headings, see Chapter 32.

§ 29.04. TABLE OF AUTHORITIES

The table of authorities is a listing of all legal authorities you have used in your brief. The first and most important part of this table is the listing of cases.

In compiling the table of authorities, follow the rules of the court for which you are writing the brief. Some rules require that you list cases alphabetically and by court—all United States Supreme Court cases in alphabetical order, all United States Court of Appeals cases in alphabetical order, and so forth. Others require a single alphabetical listing of all cases from all courts.

Follow proper citation form, including the procedural history of cases. Again, accuracy is most important. The court and opposing counsel will rely on the accuracy of the page numbers in your table to find the location of the authorities in your brief. When you prepare your brief, checking these page references is the last thing you should do because they can change at any time.

When a writer uses an authority many times throughout a brief, the Latin word "*passim*" can replace page numbers in the table of authorities; it indicates that the authority is "everywhere." Be very careful about using this term, and do not use it in the table of authorities unless you actually use the authority "everywhere." For example, you may have cited a case on virtually every page. In this situation use "*passim*." However, if you use a reference only a few times, "*passim*" is inappropriate, and you should list all the pages on which that reference appears.

In the table of authorities a listing of statutes and constitutional authorities usually follows the listing of cases. Be thorough, list every statute and constitutional provision you have used in your brief, and follow proper citation form.

After the listing of statutes and constitutional authorities, list all "secondary" sources you have cited in your brief. These include legal periodicals, treatises, restatements of the law, and other sources that are neither cases, statutes, nor constitutional provisions.

Again, list every authority you use, write accurate citations, and number the pages accurately. The court will use the page references to authorities while reading your briefs. A common question the court asks during oral argument of a case is "Where can I find that case in your brief?" Save yourself the embarrassment of referring the court to the wrong page. And remember: The court will get its first impression of the accuracy of your brief from the table of authorities section. If this section is inaccurate, the court may question the rest of your work. Attention to detail is very important.

§ 29.05. JURISDICTIONAL STATEMENT

This section of your brief tells the court what authority permits the court to consider your case. Cite the authority, but do not quote it. It is not a statement of a statute governing the substance of your case, but a statement of a statute, a rule of court, or a constitutional provision authorizing the appellate court to hear the kind of case you are appealing. This statement tells the court that your case is in the right court.

A colleague may tell you to appeal a certain kind of case to a certain court. However, you cannot rely on word of mouth. Find the provision of law specifically stating that the court in which you are bringing your appeal is the right one to consider your case.

§ 29.06. QUESTIONS PRESENTED

The questions presented section is one of the most important sections of the brief. It frames the questions you want the court to answer and frames those questions in a way that encourages the court to decide them in your favor. The number of questions presented must correspond to the number of major headings in your brief.

Courts often give you specific rules about this section of the brief; however, most rules are the same:

- State the questions clearly and concisely.
- Avoid specific names, dates, and locations unless they help clarify the issues and are persuasive.
- Let the court know precisely what your case involves.

Writing the questions presented by your case is an art in itself. You can master this art only through practice. Writing the questions presented section is not a mechanical effort, but one to which you should devote a significant amount of time.

Here are examples of issues stated in different ways to illustrate what to say and what not to say in questions presented.

Bad: Whether Mr. Barnes proved his case of adverse possession.

Better: Does an adverse user satisfy the "continuous" and "exclusive" use elements needed to establish adverse possession to severed mineral rights by mining at times that are economically feasible and allowing neighbors to mine coal for personal use at other times throughout the statutory period?

Comment: In the first example the question is too broad and could refer to any adverse possession case. The second statement of the question includes the specifics of the case in question. Note that when you begin the question with "whether," you should end with a period, and, when you begin with a word like "does" or "can," you should end with a question mark. When you phrase the question presented as a question, phrase it so that the answer is "yes" and favors your client.

Bad: Did the trial court err in admitting the evidence the officers obtained through the search?

Better: Did the trial court err in admitting evidence voluntarily given to the police by the minor child, when the child obtained it as a result of his independent search of the property and without police direction?

Comment: The first example is too general and says nothing about the particular case. The second statement of the question states the important facts concisely and clearly.

In addition to writing the questions presented with particularity and sufficient information, write your issues persuasively in your client's behalf. Here is how counsel on each side of the case might write the first example above.

Plaintiff's phrasing of the question: Can a land user satisfy the "continuous" and "exclusive" use needed to establish adverse possession to severed mineral rights by mining at times that are economically feasible and consistent with local custom, and allowing neighbors to mine coal for personal use only at other times throughout the statutory period, particularly when he acted at all times and in all other ways as a true owner would have acted?

Defendant's phrasing of the same question: Whether sporadic mining of a property only at convenient times while allowing others to use the property at their will was insufficient evidence of the continuity and exclusivity required to deprive the record owner of his superior rights to the minerals on the land.

Comment: The first statement of the adverse possession question suggests that the plaintiff has acquired rights by meeting legal requirements, and the second statement of the same question suggests that plaintiff failed to fulfill the legal requirements and should not deprive the record owner of mineral rights. Some readers may find the phrasing of the questions too argumentative. For a less argumentative version of the plaintiff's question, omit the words "only" and "particularly." For a less argumentative version of the defendant's question, omit the word "only" and substitute "sufficient" for "insufficient."

Here is how counsel on each side of the case might write the second example above.

Prosecution's phrasing of the question: Whether the trial court was correct in admitting evidence when the child who provided the evidence voluntarily conducted a search of his home, with no direction from the police, and voluntarily offered that evidence to the police.

Defendant's phrasing of the question: Whether the trial court erred in admitting evidence provided by a child, who, at the direction of the police, searched his own home and provided the evidence after further prompting by the police.

Comment: The prosecution's phrasing of the question first suggests that the trial court was correct; it then places the child's activity on the child's shoulders and not on the police. It suggests that no police search occurred and that the search was an appropriate private search resulting in admissible evidence. The defendant's phrasing suggests that the trial court erred in admitting the evidence. It suggests that the child obtained the evidence only at the direction of the police in violation of the defendant's constitutional rights.

Some lawyers phrase the question presented by using more than one sentence. This technique permits them to avoid long, complex sentences that are difficult for the reader to comprehend. For instance, in the last set of examples, the defendant's lawyer might phrase the question this way:

At the direction of the police, a child searched his own home and, after further prompting by the police, produced evidence. Did the trial court err in admitting this evidence?

§ 29.07. TEXT OF CONSTITUTIONAL, STATUTORY, AND REGULATORY PROVISIONS

This section of the brief contains the text of the constitutional, statutory, and regulatory provisions you use in your brief. Do not include the text of any of these provisions if you do not rely on them in your argument. For example, do not include the statute or rule you use in your jurisdictional statement unless that authority is at issue in your case. If you make reference to a provision that is not at issue in your case, do not include its text.

Do not include full texts of provisions when only parts of those provisions are at issue. A statute, for example, may be very lengthy and may contain much language that has nothing to do with your case. Use only relevant portions as long as those portions make sense standing alone. Follow correct citation format.

Exercises

1. Using the information provided, prepare a title page for a brief. Type it the way it would appear in final form.

(1) The appellate court is the Supreme Court for the State of Ohio.
(2) The term of court is January 2014.
(3) The docket number for your case is No. 12-43360.
(4) The appellee is the State of Ohio.
(5) The appellant is Elyse Keaton.
(6) The case is on appeal from the Court of Appeals for the State of Ohio.
(7) The brief is for the appellee.
(8) You are the attorney for the appellee. Your address is 106 Main Street, Centerville, Ohio 90207. Your phone number is (302) 777-7777.
(9) Mary Smith is the attorney for the appellant, and her address is 100 Main Street, Centerville, Ohio 90207. Her phone number is (302) 555-5555.

2. Prepare a table of contents from the following information. Omit page numbers.

(1) Conclusion
(2) Argument headings:
  I. The state did not violate the defendant's Fourth and Fourteenth Amendment rights, and the cocaine is admissible because the police found it as a result of a legal private search by defendant's child, without government involvement; and the child gave the evidence voluntarily to the police
  A. Officer Rambo did not direct Alex's search
   1. The interaction between Alex and Officer Rambo did not give rise to an agency relationship
   2. Alex conducted his search without Officer Rambo's knowledge, and he completed it before he notified Officer Rambo
  B. Alex was not acting as Officer Rambo's agent when he gave Officer Rambo the evidence
  C. Even if the search and seizure was subject to the Fourth Amendment, Alex's consent constitutes an exception to the warrant requirement
   1. Alex had authority to consent

      2. Alex voluntarily and knowingly consented to the search and seizure of the evidence

  II. Neither a husband-wife privilege nor a parent-child privilege provides a basis for defendant to exclude her child's testimony since neither would be available to defendant under Ohio law, the law of other courts and legislatures, or social policy

     A. Ohio law clearly prohibits defendant from invoking the husband-wife privilege

     B. The Ohio statute does not authorize a parent-child testimonial privilege, and the court should not recognize such a privilege where a child voluntarily testifies about a communication his mother made in his presence regarding her criminal activities

(3) Summary of the argument

(4) Table of authorities

(5) Statement of the case

(6) Constitutional and statutory provisions

(7) Statement of jurisdiction

(8) Questions presented

3. Prepare a table of authorities from the following information. Omit page numbers. Use correct citation form.

Ohio Rev. Code Ann. § 2317.02 (LexisNexis 2005)
Weis v. Weis, 147 Ohio State 416, 72 N.E.2d 245 (1947)
State v. Morris, 42 Ohio State 2d 307, 329 N.E.2d 85 (1978)
Three Juveniles v. Commonwealth, 455 N.E.2d 1203 (Mass. 1983)
Idaho Code 9-203(7) (1998)
United States v. Matlock, 415 U.S. 164 (1974)
Arnovitz v. Wozar, 9 Ohio App. 2d, 222 N.E.2d 660 (1964)
Belichick v. Belichick, 37 Ohio App. 2d 95, 307 N.E.2d 270 (1973)
Martin J. McMahon, Annotations, Presence of Child at Communication Between Husband and Wife as Destroying Confidentiality of Otherwise Privileged Communication Between Them, 39 American Law Reports Annotated 4th 481 (1985)
Fourth Amendment, United States Constitution
In re Terry, W., 130 California Reporter 913 (Ct. App. 1976)
Mapp v. Ohio, 367 U.S. 643 (1961)
Jeffrey Begens, Comment, Parent-Child Testimonial Privilege: An Absolute Right or an Absolute Privilege?, 11 University of Dayton Law Review 709, 1986
Oregon v. Scott, 729 P.2d 585 (Or. Ct. App. 1986)
Herbert v. Maryland, 269 A.2d 430 (Md. Ct. Spec. App. 1970)
Ohio Const, amend. IV. § 1

4. Rewrite the following facts into a question presented two ways: for the plaintiff/appellant and for the defendant/appellee.

    Mr. Hale is a tenant, and Ms. Petrie is his landlady. Mr. Hale's apartment is in New Jersey. A few months ago a robber attacked Mr. Hale in the parking garage of his apartment complex and robbed him at gunpoint. The robber also beat Mr. Hale, causing him injuries and a broken arm.

Mr. Hale sued Ms. Petrie for negligence for her failure to provide adequate security in the parking garage. Although a guard was usually stationed in the garage, that guard was off-duty at the time of the criminal attack. Ms. Petrie contended in the trial court that, in New Jersey, she had no duty to protect her tenants from criminal attacks and was therefore not negligent. She also argued that, even if she had a duty, she provided sufficient security and that she had fulfilled any duty she had by taking reasonable steps to provide security. Her argument won in the court below. Mr. Hale now appeals that decision and argues that, once Ms. Petrie undertook to provide security, she also undertook to provide reasonable security but failed to do so.

5. Suppose you are working on a case concerning a confidential communication to a priest. Prepare the text of the relevant statutory provision from the following statute as if you were preparing this text for a section on constitutional and statutory provisions for a brief.

Section 2317.02 of the Ohio Revised Code Annotated (LexisNexis 2005), *Privileged Communications and Acts*, provides in relevant part:
The following persons shall not testify in certain respects:

(A) An attorney, concerning a communication made to him by his client;

(B) A physician concerning a communication made to him by his patient;

(C) A clergyman, rabbi, priest, or minister, concerning a confession made, or any information confidentially communicated, to him for a religious counseling purpose;

(D) Husband or wife, concerning any communication made by one to the other, or an act done by either in the presence of the other, during coverture, unless the communication was made, or act done, in the known presence of hearing of a third person competent to be a witness; . . .

(G) A school guidance counselor . . . professional counselor, counselor assistant, social worker, social work assistant or independent social worker concerning a confidential communication made to him by his client.

CHAPTER 30

The Appellate Brief: Statement of Facts; Summary of Argument

§ 30.01. STATEMENT OF FACTS

The statement of facts, also called the statement of the case, should include all the facts that the court needs to know to decide the case. Turn to the statements of fact in the briefs in Appendix V to get an idea of what the statements look like.

For the attorney, the statement has a purpose in addition to furnishing information. Use the statement to set the stage for your argument. Tell the truth, be complete, but put your best foot forward. This part of the brief offers still another opportunity for advocacy.

Organize the facts and state them clearly so that the court can readily understand them. You are writing a statement of facts; therefore, state the facts truthfully and write without editorializing. Nonetheless, write so that the court sees your client in the most favorable light possible. The following pages show you how to perform this feat.

Here are three rules for writing the statement of facts:

1. Tell what happened.
2. Tell the truth, but put your best foot forward.
3. Hold the court's attention.

To illustrate our discussion of these rules, we will examine excerpts from the statements of the petitioners and respondents in *New Jersey v. T.L.O.*, 469 U.S. 325 (1985). In this case, a high school vice-principal searched the purse of T.L.O., a student, and found marijuana. New Jersey began a delinquency proceeding against the student.

The issue was whether the Fourth Amendment's exclusionary rule should apply when a public school teacher or official illegally seizes evidence from a student. As you may know, the Constitution's Fourth Amendment forbids unreasonable searches and seizures by government officers. Under the exclusionary rule, evidence obtained during an unconstitutional search is inadmissible in court.

In *T.L.O.*, the trial court and the intermediate appellate court ruled that the evidence was admissible. The New Jersey Supreme Court, however, ruled that the exclusionary rule applied to the search and that the evidence therefore was inadmissible. Before the United States Supreme Court, New Jersey was the petitioner and T.L.O. was the respondent.

1. Tell What Happened

In the statement of facts, you are telling a story. Tell the story so that the reader can follow along with the least amount of effort.

An important part of the story is the case's procedural history: how the case started and what decisions the courts below have issued. A court will want this information readily available. Some attorneys set it out as a short, separate section of the brief. Others include it as an introductory subsection of the statement of facts, and still others weave pieces of it into the statement of facts as the pieces naturally arise in the course of the story. You should use the method that works best for you in a particular case. If the procedural history is brief and uncomplicated, you might state it in the opening sentences of the statement of facts. If it is complicated, you might set it out as a subsection of the statement or as a completely separate section labeled "Procedural History." If you choose the latter method, you also might discuss the lower court decisions near the end of the statement.

You will help the court to follow the story if you call the parties by their names and do not refer to them as "petitioner" and "respondent." Think of the times when you have read a court opinion and the court called the litigants "appellant" and "appellee." Remember how difficult it was to recall which label went with which litigant. In the *T.L.O.* case, call the juvenile "T.L.O." as opposed to "respondent." Call the petitioner either "New Jersey" or "the State."

Most of the time, you will want to tell the story chronologically. The historical approach is easy to follow. To illustrate, here are the opening paragraphs of the statements of facts in the *T.L.O.* briefs. The first excerpt comes from the brief of the petitioner, New Jersey:

> On the morning of March 7, 1980, a teacher of mathematics at Piscataway High School entered the girls' restroom and found the juvenile-respondent T.L.O. and a girl named Johnson holding what the teacher perceived to be lit cigarettes. (MT20-1 to 25).[1] Smoking was not permitted and the girls were thus committing an infraction of the school rules. The girls were taken to the principal's office where they met with Theodore Choplick, the assistant vice-principal. (MT21-1 to 3; MT21-24 to 22-11; MT31-18 to 20; MT33-20 to 34-10).

The second excerpt comes from T.L.O.'s brief:

> On March 7, 1980, a search was made by Mr. Choplick, vice principal of Piscataway High School, of a purse belonging to T.L.O., a student at the school. Ms. Chen, a teacher, had made a routine check of the girls' restroom. She observed T.L.O. and another girl smoking tobacco cigarettes. (MT 20-7 to 25) Although smoking by students was permitted in designated areas, it was not allowed in the restrooms. (MT 33-20 to MT 34-6) Ms. Chen accompanied both girls to Mr. Choplick's office, where she advised him of the infraction. (MT 21-1 to MT 22-23)

In each paragraph, the attorneys told the story in chronological order in a way that is easy to follow. T.L.O.'s statement began with a sentence not in chronological order because the sentence offered a desirable way to begin the story. Which paragraph do you prefer?

---

1. "MT" refers to the transcript of the motion to suppress heard before the Juvenile and Domestic Relations Court on September 26, 1980. "T" refers to the transcript of trial on March 23, 1981, the transcript of the juvenile's plea of guilty to other complaints on June 2, 1981, and the transcript of sentencing on January 8, 1982, all contained in one volume.

Note that both attorneys documented their facts by making reference to the record. You are expected to furnish this documentation as a convenience to the court.

In telling the story, keep the narrative moving. Stay on point and omit irrelevant information. You should include facts that help make your client's case sympathetic, even if they are not essential to your legal argument. Here is the second paragraph from New Jersey's statement of facts:

> Mr. Choplick asked the two girls whether they were smoking. Miss Johnson acknowledged that she had been smoking, and Mr. Choplick imposed three-day attendance at a smoking clinic as punishment. (T49-24 to 50-7). T.L.O. denied smoking in the lavatory and further asserted that she did not smoke at all. (MT27-10 to 17). Mr. Choplick asked T.L.O. to come into a private office. (MT27-14 to 21; MT30-22 to 31-17).

T.L.O.'s brief does not contain a comparable paragraph. It offers a single sentence: "Upon being questioned, T.L.O. denied that she smoked." Do you understand why New Jersey's attorneys decided to include the additional information?

Here is another example. T.L.O.'s brief describes the juvenile court's disposition in the following words: "On January 8, 1982, a probationary term of one year was imposed." Here is how the New Jersey brief describes the disposition: "On January 8, 1982, T.L.O. was sentenced to probation for one year with the special condition that she observe a reasonable curfew, attend school regularly and successfully complete a counselling and drug therapy program." Arguably, the New Jersey brief includes more information than a court would need to make a decision about the applicability of the exclusionary rule. The additional information, however, helps place the state in a more favorable light. New Jersey's attorneys were correct in including it.

2. Tell the Truth, but Put Your Best Foot Forward

In writing your statement of facts, you must tell the truth and not otherwise mislead the court. If the court discovers that you have been less than truthful, you lose your credibility, severely damage your client's case, and hurt your reputation as a trustworthy attorney. Still, you should state your case in the most favorable way possible. Write in an objective, noneditorial style, but emphasize the facts that help your client's case. Here is an excerpt from the New Jersey brief:

> Once inside this office, Mr. Choplick requested the juvenile's purse, and she gave it to him. (MT27-24 to 28-7). A package of Marlboro cigarettes was visible inside the purse. (MT28-9 to 11). Mr. Choplick held up the Marlboros and said to the juvenile, "You lied to me."

This excerpt paints the picture by using facts, rather than adverbs, adjectives, or editorial statements. Instead of explicitly calling T.L.O. a liar—an editorial statement—New Jersey's attorneys furnish facts that permit the Court to reach this conclusion. The statement adds emphasis by quoting the vice-principal. Quoting another person's judgmental words is more effective than employing your own editorial words. In a statement of facts, employing your own editorial words is inappropriate.

As another illustration, consider how T.L.O.'s brief describes the items that Mr. Choplick found in the purse:

Looking further into the handbag, he found a metal pipe, and one plastic bag containing tobacco or some similar substance.[2] (MT29-10 to 16) He also found a wallet containing "a lot of singles and change," and inside a separate compartment of the purse, two letters and an index card.

Compare the description in New Jersey's brief: "There he found marijuana, drug paraphernalia, $40 in one-dollar bills and documentation of T.L.O.'s sale of marijuana to other students." Each statement tells the same story, uses objective words, offers accurate information, and yet favors the respective client.

Writing the statement of facts may require you to deal with information adverse to your client. You already have seen some examples of ways to confront the problem. For another example, compare the following accounts of T.L.O.'s encounter with the police. Here is the account in New Jersey's brief:

T.L.O.'s mother acceded to a police request to bring her daughter to police headquarters for questioning. (T18-12 to 18). Once at headquarters, T.L.O. was advised of her rights in her mother's presence and signed a *Miranda*[3] rights card so indicating. (T20-3 to 21). The officer then began to question T.L.O. in her mother's presence. (T23-4 to 6). T.L.O. admitted that the objects found in her purse belonged to her. She further admitted that she was selling marijuana in school, receiving $1 per "joint," or rolled marijuana cigarette. T.L.O. stated that she had sold between 18 and 20 joints at school that very morning, before the drug was confiscated by the assistant principal.

Compare the account in T.L.O.'s brief:

The local police transported T.L.O. and her mother to headquarters. Upon arrival, Officer O'Gurkins advised the juvenile of her *Miranda* rights. (T20-7 to T21-3). When Mrs. O. indicated that she wanted to have an attorney present during the questioning, she was permitted to telephone the office of her lawyer. (T34-10 to 24). He was not available, so the officer proceeded with the interrogation. According to Mrs. O., at no time did her daughter state that she had sold marijuana. (T35-15 to 22).

Officer O'Gurkins admitted that although it was standard practice in juvenile matters to reduce incriminating statements to writing, he did not follow this procedure with T.L.O. (T24-12 to 18). He nevertheless maintained that T.L.O. had confessed that she had been selling marijuana in school for a week. (T22-2 to 17). He conceded that T.L.O. explained to him that the $40.98, which was found in her purse, constituted the proceeds from her paper route, which she had collected the night before.

The New Jersey brief seems to deal with some adverse facts by omitting them. Controversy exists over whether T.L.O. admitted to selling marijuana. From a technical perspective, the controversy is not pertinent to the issue before the Supreme Court. Nonetheless, the possible innocence of T.L.O. on the selling charge may affect the Court's perception of the case. T.L.O.'s brief discusses the controversy. The Court might think less of

---

2. At trial it was stipulated that the bag contained 5.40 grams of marijuana. (T12-17 to 25). [Would you have advised the writer to place this information in a footnote?—Ed.]

3. *Miranda v. Arizona*, 384 U.S. 436 (1966).

New Jersey's brief for ignoring it. The New Jersey brief could have alluded to the matter without turning it into a major issue. It might have begun the critical sentence this way: "According to the officer, T.L.O. admitted that she was selling. . . ." It also might have included an additional sentence: "Her mother later denied that T.L.O. made this admission." The lesson is that you can own up to adverse facts without waving them about.

Another way to use facts to your advantage is to summarize or quote favorable opinions of the court below. These opinions are powerful support for your arguments. Use them. If a majority opinion goes against you, mention the opinion and then focus on the dissent. In either case, you have the opportunity to make your arguments while still writing objectively. You summarize the favorable words of a third party, a court. This summary is still one more presentation of your argument. In *T.L.O.*, for example, New Jersey's statement of facts summarizes the adverse holding of the state supreme court in a single sentence. T.L.O.'s statement, however, spends four paragraphs summarizing the majority opinion.

3. Hold the Court's Attention

Both New Jersey's and T.L.O.'s statements of fact hold the reader's interest. They tell the story in chronological sequence. They omit needless information. They use a concrete writing style. They refer to T.L.O.'s cigarettes as "Marlboros," as opposed to "tobacco cigarettes." New Jersey's statement quotes the vice-principal: "You lied to me." It also states that Mr. Choplick found "$40 in one-dollar bills" as opposed to "$40" or "some money." The attorneys writing these statements followed the rules of good writing style that you have learned. In these statements, the most important rules of style are using the active voice, keeping sentences and words simple and concrete, and avoiding the inflammatory rhetoric that marks the advocate as an amateur.

Exercise

Here is a paragraph from T.L.O.'s statement of facts. Rewrite it to improve it stylistically so that it more effectively holds the reader's attention.

An appeal was taken and decided on June 30, 1982. *In re T.L.O.*, 448 A.2d 493 (N.J. Super. Ct. App. Div. 1982). Two judges affirmed the denial of the motion to suppress the evidence secured by the search of the juvenile's purse, adopting the reasons set forth in the opinion of the trial court. However, they found that the record was inadequate to determine the sufficiency of the *Miranda* waiver which was allegedly made by the juvenile after her mother's unsuccessful attempt to summon counsel. *Id.* at 493. They therefore vacated the adjudication of delinquency and ordered a remand for further proceedings in light of the principles enunciated in *Edwards v. Arizona*, 451 U.S. 477 (1981) and *State v. Fussell*, 174 N.J. Super. 14 (App. Div. 1980). *Id.* One judge dissented, indicating that he would suppress the evidence found in T.L.O.'s purse because the search had been unreasonable. *Id.* at 495.

§ 30.02. SUMMARY OF ARGUMENT

In the summary of argument, you summarize your argument. According to United States Supreme Court Rule 34(h), the summary is a "succinct, but accurate and clear condensation of the argument made in the body of the brief. It should not be a mere repetition of the headings under which the argument is arranged." The summary rarely is more than one or two pages.

This part of the brief is your chance to give the court a summary of your argument. It may be all some judges read before they hear your oral argument. Because of its importance, spend the time necessary to make it readable and persuasive. When a judge turns to your summary, he or she probably knows very little about your case. Therefore write the summary for an intelligent but uninformed audience.

The task is harder than you may think. After spending weeks or months grappling with a case, you may have difficulty in accurately reducing your analysis to a page or two. Stick to your main arguments and save the subtle points for the body of the brief.

Use the table of contents as an outline for the summary. Write a topical sentence stating a point of your argument at or near the beginning of each paragraph. Then flesh out the outline a bit. If you cite any cases at all, cite only those that are essential to making your summary understandable. For example, you might cite the major case that you are distinguishing or relying on.

CHAPTER 31

Practice in Writing the Statement of Facts and Summary of Argument

§ 31.01. EXERCISE I

Please read the following excerpt from the summary of argument in T.L.O.'s brief (from *New Jersey v. T.L.O.*, 469 U.S. 325 (1985), introduced in Chapter 30). Then write an outline of the summary. Note also how the writer fleshed out the argument. What suggestions do you have for improvement?

Assuming *arguendo* that the decision of the New Jersey Supreme Court does present a federal question for adjudication, petitioner's contention that the exclusionary rule need not be applied to the fruits of the illegal search at issue in this matter is clearly erroneous. The Fourth Amendment protects against unreasonable searches conducted by any governmental agency. Because public school personnel are employed by the state, act with state authority, and are responsible for carrying out state laws and regulations, their conduct constitutes governmental, rather than private, action. Thus the search of T.L.O. by the vice-principal comes within the ambit of the Fourth Amendment.

While petitioner is correct in asserting that this Court has not found the exclusionary rule to be constitutionally required in the case of every Fourth Amendment violation, those instances where it has not been applied have involved limited, peripheral uses of the evidence so obtained. This Court has not permitted the fruits of an illegal search to be introduced into evidence on the prosecution's case-in-chief in a criminal proceeding, as the State seeks to do in the present matter. In such circumstances, application of the rule is mandatory.

Even if petitioner is correct in maintaining that a balancing test—weighing the benefits of deterrence against the societal costs resulting from implementation of the rule—is constitutionally permissible to determine if the exclusionary rule should be applied in the present circumstances, it is clear that the expected benefits would outweigh the anticipated detriments. First, educators do have an interest in the successful prosecution of juvenile delinquency proceedings and would be deterred from conducting unreasonable searches by the knowledge that the resulting evidence would be excluded. Second, if evidence illegally secured by educators was not admissible at trial, the police would be deterred from instigating teachers to conduct illegal searches in order to provide otherwise obtainable evidence on "a silver platter." With regard to societal costs, statistical studies have shown that relatively few prosecutions are dismissed because of Fourth Amendment problems. School surveys do not support the conclusion that the crime rate in schools is rising or that an increase in searches by school personnel would be a significant factor in reducing the present rate.

Petitioner has demonstrated no alternatives to the exclusionary rule which would effectively deter violations of the Fourth Amendment rights of students. In addition, the exclusionary rule serves constitutionally recognized purposes other than deterrence: it protects the imperative of judicial integrity, and teaches respect for constitutional rights.

§ 31.02. EXERCISE II

At the end of this chapter, please find the statements of the case (statements of facts) submitted by the petitioner and respondent in *McIntyre v. Ohio Elections Commission*. Please compare them. How do they differ? Why did the attorneys write them the way they did? What suggestions would you make for improvement?

§ 31.03. EXERCISE III

At the end of this chapter, please find the summaries of argument submitted by the petitioner and respondent in *McIntyre v. Ohio Elections Commission*. Please compare them. How do they differ? Why did the attorneys write them the way they did? What suggestions would you make for improvement?

§ 31.04. EXERCISE IV

In *Rosenberger v. University of Virginia*, college students sought funding for "Wide Awake," a new student publication with an expressly religious viewpoint. They were denied funding because of a university funding guideline that categorically denies funding of religious organizations and religious activities. At issue is whether this prohibition violates the First Amendment.

At the Supreme Court, the petitioner students argue that the denial violates the guarantees of freedom of speech and freedom of the press. They also argue that funding their publication would not violate the Establishment Clause, which requires separation of church and state, as long as the university extends funding to a broad range of activities and publications without regard to their differing religious and nonreligious viewpoints.

The respondent university argues that the First Amendment permits it discretion in making funding decisions. It further argues that the funding guidelines are reasonable and neutral with respect to religious viewpoints and other viewpoints and are not designed to suppress expression.

At the end of this chapter please find the summaries of argument of the petitioner and respondent and compare them. How do they differ? What suggestions for improvement would you make?

McIntyre v. Ohio Elections Commission
514 U.S. 334 (1995)

Excerpts From The Brief Of The Petitioner, Margaret Mcintyre Statement Of The Case

On March 19, 1990, Mrs. Margaret McIntyre was fined $100 by the Ohio Elections Commission for distributing leaflets opposing the passage of a local school tax levy. The Ohio Elections Commission imposed the fine because the leaflets did not contain her name and address as required by Ohio Revised Code § 3599.09, which prohibits the distribution of all anonymous campaign literature. The Ohio Supreme Court upheld the fine on September 22, 1993.

The events in this case began on the evening of April 27, 1988, outside the Blendon Middle School in Westerville, Ohio. At that time, Mrs. McIntyre; her son, a student in the Westerville schools; and his girlfriend were distributing leaflets opposing the passage of a school tax levy that was to be voted on at a nonpartisan referendum scheduled for the following week. (J.A.30). Mrs. McIntyre was distributing the leaflets at the Blendon Middle School that evening because it was the site of a previously scheduled public meeting at which the Westerville superintendent of schools planned to address the merits of the tax levy. (J.A.28). During the meeting the superintendent specifically made reference to statements contained in the leaflets. (J.A.15).

Mrs. McIntyre stood outside the school near the doorway to the meeting room and handed leaflets to persons as they entered the building. (J.A.15). Her son and his girlfriend distributed additional leaflets in the school parking lot by placing them under automobile windshield wipers. (J.A.30). The leaflets stated:

Vote No

Issue 19 School Tax Levy

Last election Westerville Schools, asked us to vote yes for new buildings and expansions programs. We gave them what they asked. We knew there was crowded conditions and new growth in the district.

Now we find out there is a 4 million dollar deficit—WHY?

We are told the 3 middle schools must be split because of over-crowding, and yet we are told 3 schools are being closed—WHY?

A magnet school is not a full operating school, but a specials school.

Residents were asked to work on a 20 member commission to help formulate the new boundaries. For 4 weeks they worked long and hard and came up with a very workable plan. Their plan was totally disregarded—WHY?

WASTE of tax payers dollars must be stopped. Our children's education and welfare must come first. **WASTE CAN NO LONGER BE TOLERATED.**

PLEASE VOTE NO

ISSUE 19

THANK YOU, CONCERNED PARENTS AND TAX PAYERS

J. Michael Hayfield, Assistant Superintendent of Elementary Education for the Westerville schools, observed Mrs. McIntyre distributing the leaflets. He examined the leaflets and told her that she was not in compliance with Ohio election laws. (J.A.28).

On the next evening, April 28, 1988, a similar school meeting was held at the Walnut Springs Middle School. . . . Again, petitioner stood outside of the school and distributed leaflets opposing the school tax levy to persons entering the building to attend the meeting. Again, Mr. Hayfield observed her distributing leaflets and noted that they did not conform to Ohio election laws. (J.A.15).

Following Mrs. McIntyre's leafletting on April 27, 1988 and April 28, 1988, the school tax levy failed. It was again defeated in a second election. In November of 1988, on the third try, it finally passed. (Pet. App. A10). On April 6, 1989, five months after the passage of the twice-defeated levy, and approximately one year after her leafletting, Mrs. McIntyre received a letter from the Ohio Elections Commission informing her that a complaint had been filed against her. (J.A.10). The complaint, filed by Assistant Superintendent Hayfield, charged her with violating Ohio Revised Code § 3599.09 and two other statutes because the leaflets she had distributed at the Blendon and Walnut Springs Middle Schools, during the two evenings in April of the previous year, did not contain her name and address.[1]

Initially, the charges were dismissed for want of prosecution. (J.A.18). A short time later, they were reinstated at the request of Assistant Superintendent Hayfield. On March 19, 1990, a hearing was held before the Ohio Elections Commission on the charges against Mrs. McIntyre. At the conclusion of its March 19th hearing, the Ohio Elections Commission found that Mrs. McIntyre had distributed unsigned leaflets and fined her $100 for violating Ohio Revised Code § 3599.09; the other charges were dismissed.[2] (J.A.41).

On September 10, 1990, the Franklin County Court of Common Pleas reversed, holding that § 3599.09 was unconstitutional as applied. (Pet. App. A33). On April 7, 1992, the Ohio Court of Appeals reversed the Court of Common Pleas and reinstated the fine. (Pet. App. A16). That decision was affirmed by the Ohio Supreme Court on September 22, 1993, which concluded that: The requirement of R.C. 3599.09 that persons responsible for the production of campaign literature pertaining to the adoption or defeat of a ballot issue identify themselves as the source thereof is not violative

---

1. In addition to being charged with violating § 3599.09, prohibiting distribution of anonymous campaign materials, Mrs. McIntyre was charged with violations of Ohio Revised Code § 3571.10(D) (failure to file a designation of treasurer) and § 3517.13(E) (failure to file a PAC report).

2. Mrs. McIntyre was unrepresented throughout the administrative proceedings and the administrative record is, therefore, a sparse one. Prior to the March 19th hearing, Mrs. McIntyre wrote a letter to counsel for the Ohio Elections Commission acknowledging that some of the leaflets she had distributed were unsigned. (J.A.12). At the hearing, she both denied any intent to violate the law and objected to the law as "an infringement of her First Amendment rights." (J.A.36, 38-39). She also testified that she had talked to many other people who were concerned about the levy and felt she was representing their views as well as her own. (J.A.38). Assistant Superintendent Hayfield repeated the statement made in his prior affidavit, that he had seen Mrs. McIntyre distribute leaflets without her name and address.

The Commission's decision upholding the complaint was issued the same day. It was not accompanied by any written opinion and contained no factual findings other than the implicit finding that Mrs. McIntyre had distributed anonymous leaflets and thereby violated the law. Thus, the only issue raised or considered on appeal by the Ohio state courts was whether the ban on anonymous campaign literature set forth in § 3599.09 is constitutional.

of the right to free speech guaranteed by the First Amendment to the United States Constitution and Section 11, Article I of the Ohio Constitution.

(Pet. App. A1).[3]

Summary of Argument

Petitioner Margaret McIntyre has been fined under § 3599.09 of the Ohio Election Code for preparing and distributing leaflets urging a vote against a school tax levy because the leaflets did not contain her name and address. The Ohio Supreme Court held that § 3599.09 does not violate the First Amendment even though it indiscriminately bans the distribution of all anonymous political campaign literature. The Ohio Supreme Court erred in upholding the statute because its decision is inconsistent with *Talley v. California*, 362 U.S. 60 (1960), which holds that a flat ban on anonymous leafletting is unconstitutional because it deters the speech of those who fear retaliation and thereby restricts freedom of expression.

This Court's protection of anonymous speech in *Talley* rests on a firm historical foundation. The drafters of the Constitution were well aware of efforts by the government of England to punish political and religious dissenters for their anonymous publications. The drafters were also aware of the frequent use of anonymous political publications to criticize the English governance of the American colonies. The use of anonymous political publications as part of public discourse continues today. Consistent with this history and practice, the Court has repeatedly held that the First Amendment protects anonymous speech. *E.g., Thomas v. Collins*, 323 U.S. 516 (1945); *Bates v. Little Rock*, 361 U.S. 516 (1960); *Shelton v. Tucker*, 364 U.S. 479 (1960); *Lamont v. Postmaster General*, 381 U.S. 301 (1965).

The constitutionality of § 3599.09 is to be measured by the compelling state interest test because it is a regulation of the fundamental right to speech and press. Most recently, this Court applied the compelling state interest test in reviewing the regulation of election related speech in *Burson v. Freeman*, 504 U.S. 191, 112 S. Ct. 1846 (1992). The Ohio Supreme Court erred in concluding that the more relaxed standard of review applicable to ballot access and voting regulations was applicable to this case. This is because § 3599.09 is a regulation of political speech in public places intended to persuade voters and is not a ballot access or voting regulation. Applying a strict scrutiny standard, § 3599.09 is unconstitutional because Ohio has not demonstrated a compelling state interest and has not narrowly tailored its law. The failure of § 3599.09 to serve a compelling state interest is demonstrated by the fact that it covers all anonymous election related leaflets and pamphlets. It is not confined to intentionally false and fraudulent statements. In addition, it extends to communications about referendum issues that cannot be smeared or libeled. *Illinois v. White*, 506 N.E.2d 1284 (Ill. 1987). Section 3599.09 is not narrowly tailored because it extends to election related publications at any time in any place. As a consequence, it is a prophylactic rule requiring disclosure, even when no legitimate interest is actually served.

Finally, § 3599.09 is unconstitutional as applied to the facts of this case. Petitioner is a street corner leafletter who has engaged in core political speech about a public issue. As a result, no law, including § 3599.09, can be applied to her speech without violating the First Amendment. *Lovell v. Griffin*, 303 U.S. 444 (1938).

---

3. According to Rule 1(b) of the Ohio Supreme Court Rules for the Reporting of Opinions, this statement, which is the syllabus of the case, "states the controlling point or points of law decided. . . ."

Excerpts from the Brief of the Respondent, Ohio Elections Commission Statement of the Case

In 1988, Petitioner Margaret McIntyre opposed passage of a property tax levy for the Westerville, Ohio school district. She prepared, or had prepared, flyers expressing this opposition.

Instead of placing her name and address on these flyers as required by Ohio Rev. Code 3599.09(A) (the "Disclosure Statute"), Petitioner identified those responsible for the flyers as "Concerned Parents and Tax Payers," Joint Appendix ("J.A.") 6-7, a fictitious organization. (J.A. 38-39). She distributed these flyers at two separate meetings that were scheduled as open forums for the public to discuss the tax levy. (J.A. 14-15).

On each occasion, an assistant school superintendent observed Petitioner distributing the flyers. *Id.* On the first occasion, he cautioned that her failure to include her name and address on them violated Ohio elections law. (J.A. 28). Petitioner, however, ignored his caution. At no time did anyone attempt to prevent her from circulating any literature, nor did anyone seek to prevent her from attending either meeting. Petitioner also was never threatened with any reprisals because of her opposition to the tax levy.

The assistant superintendent eventually filed a complaint with Respondent, the Ohio Elections Commission ("Commission"), alleging that Petitioner had violated the Disclosure Statute, among other provisions of Ohio elections law. (J.A. 3, 14-16). At a full hearing conducted by the Commission in a civil enforcement action, evidence was presented that some of Petitioner's flyers did contain the disclosure statement required by Ohio Rev. Code 3599.09(A), and Petitioner testified that she had intended to disclose this same information on all the flyers, though she had failed to do so. (J.A. 36-39). It was also revealed that no such organization as "Concerned Parents and Tax Payers" had ever existed. (J.A. 38-39). After considering all the evidence, the Commission found that Petitioner had violated the Disclosure Statute and fined her $100. (J.A. 42).

At the hearing and in the Commission's order, the viewpoint contained in the flyers, which expressed Petitioner's anti-levy message, was never considered with respect to any of the issues that were raised and determined. Instead, the sole focus was on whether the flyers included an attribution statement and whether any such statement was false or fraudulent as provided in Ohio Rev. Code 3599.09. (See J.A. 26-42.)

On appeal from this administrative order, an Ohio trial court ruled that Ohio Rev. Code 3599.09(A) was unconstitutional. (J.A. 45.) A state appeals court upheld the law and reversed. (J.A. 49).

Petitioner then took an appeal to the Supreme Court of Ohio, which analyzed her challenge to the Disclosure Statute under the established test for evaluating the constitutionality of election laws crafted in *Anderson v. Celebrezze*, 460 U.S. 780 (1983). *See McIntyre v. Ohio Elections Comm'n*, 67 Ohio St. 3d 391 (1993), Appendix to Petition for Writ of Certiorari, A1-A15. That test requires a reviewing court to weigh any burden that the challenged legislation places on First Amendment rights against the legitimate interests of the State in regulating the subject matter involved. The Ohio Supreme Court conducted this balancing test and concluded that the Disclosure Statute places only a modest burden on First Amendment rights, which is outweighed by Ohio's proper interests in the deterrence of fraud, misleading advertising, and libel, and in requiring disclosure to the public of specific information that is pertinent to the electoral process. Consequently, the Ohio Supreme Court affirmed the appeals court's holding that the Disclosure Statute is constitutional. Petitioner then sought a writ of certiorari from this Court, which granted review on February 22, 1994.

Summary of Argument

1. The court below properly applied the test established in *Anderson v. Celebrezze*, 460 U.S. 780 (1983), to analyze the constitutionality of an elections measure such as the Disclosure Statute. Under that test, a reviewing court must weigh any burden the challenged legislation places on First Amendment rights against the legitimate interests of the State in regulating the subject matter involved. Here the Disclosure Statute imposes only a modest burden, if any, on First Amendment rights. This modest burden is substantially outweighed by the State's legitimate interests in the deterrence of fraud, misleading advertising, and libel, and in requiring the disclosure to the public of specific information that is pertinent to the electoral process.

2. *Talley v. California*, 362 U.S. 60 (1960), is inapplicable to this case. *Talley* specifically left for another day whether a measure such as the Disclosure Statute, which is designed to deter fraud, misleading advertising, and libel, is constitutional. In addition, *Talley* did not involve an election law requiring the Court to weigh two competing interests of equal constitutional magnitude—protecting the right to vote by preserving the integrity of the electoral process and assuring freedom of speech. The States are authorized to act to protect the integrity of the electoral process, even when First Amendment rights are implicated, as long as any such action does not discriminate against the viewpoint expressed in any political message.

3. Even if strict scrutiny were to be applied here, however, the Disclosure Statute would withstand such scrutiny because it advances the State's compelling interest in combatting fraud in the electoral process. The Disclosure Statute, moreover, is narrowly drawn to serve that compelling state interest. *Burson v. Freeman*, 504 U.S. 191, 112 S. Ct. 1846 (1992).

4. Disclosure statutes have long been upheld by this Court in many different fields, even where they impose some burden on First Amendment activities. In the field of elections law in particular, the Court's precedents confirm the constitutionality of disclosure statutes in elections both for candidates and for ballot issues. *See Buckley v. Valeo*, 424 U.S. 1 (1976); *First Nat'l Bank of Boston v. Bellotti*, 435 U.S. 765 (1978). The same result also holds for disclosure statutes that affect such First Amendment activities as lobbying, *United States v. Harriss*, 347 U.S. 612 (1954), and charitable solicitations, *Riley v. National Federation of the Blind of North Carolina, Inc.*, 487 U.S 781 (1988). Any countervailing interest in maintaining secrecy or anonymity is less powerful than Petitioner alleges, and must yield to the State's compelling interests in requiring the disclosure of a limited amount of pertinent information to the public. In this case, for example, any burden allegedly imposed on Petitioner's First Amendment rights by the Disclosure Statute was either minimal or nonexistent, and the State has a compelling interest in requiring the limited disclosures specified in Ohio Rev. Code 3599.09(A).

Rosenberger v. University of Virginia
515 U.S. 819 (1995)

Excerpt from the Brief of the Petitioner, Ronald Rosenberger

Summary of Argument

This case involves the discriminatory exclusion of an otherwise qualified student publication from eligibility for student activity funding at the University of Virginia, solely on the basis of the content, indeed the viewpoint, of the publication.

The University of Virginia uses its Student Activity Fund to support a wide variety of student speech from different perspectives, including some 15 newspapers and magazines. Petitioners have started a sixteenth: Wide Awake, a student magazine that addresses national and campus issues of a political, personal, cultural, and educational nature from the point of view of its editors and members. They have satisfied all the necessary requirements for funding eligibility. The problem is their editorial point of view, which is rooted in their Christian religious faith. That (and that alone), according to the University, makes the magazine ineligible for funding. This raises the question: is the religious perspective of a student publication a lawful ground for excluding it from benefits otherwise available to organizations of its type?

We contend that the University's action violates the First and Fourteenth Amendments of the United States Constitution. Our argument is based on two important principles of constitutional law. First, discrimination on the basis of the content of speech, and especially its viewpoint, is presumptively unconstitutional and can be justified only on the basis of a compelling governmental purpose for the discrimination. *R.A.V. v. City of St. Paul*, 112 S. Ct. 2538, 2542-43, 2547-48, 2549-50 (1992). This principle applies to decisions involving benefits as well as regulation (*FCC v. League of Women Voters*, 468 U.S. 364 (1984); *Arkansas Writers' Project, Inc. v. Ragland*, 481 U.S. 221, 230 (1987)), and to religious as well as secular points of view (*Lamb's Chapel v. Center Moriches School Dist.*, 113 S. Ct. 2141 (1993); *Widmar v. Vincent*, 454 U.S. 263, 269-70 (1981)). Second, the nondiscriminatory funding of a broad range of publications and activities, without regard to their religious, anti-religious, or nonreligious point of view, does not violate the Establishment Clause. *Texas Monthly, Inc. v. Bullock*, 489 U.S. 1, 14-15 (1989); *Witters v. Washington Dep't of Services*, 474 U.S. 481 (1986).

Excerpt from the Brief of the Respondent, the Rectors and Visitors of the University of Virginia

Summary of Argument

Respondents' argument consists of three points:

First, in the expenditure of public funds, decisions based on the content of speech are familiar, necessary, and entirely legitimate. Routine academic decisions, such as the hiring and promotion of professors and the choice of courses for the curriculum, involve content-based evaluations of speech. To require that such decisions be made without regard to content would be to disable public universities from adopting or implementing educational policies. This the First Amendment does not require.

Second, the University of Virginia Student Activity Fee Funding Guidelines are reasonable. They exclude from funding religious, political, philanthropic, and social activities. They do not reflect, as petitioners allege, an ideologically driven attempt to suppress a particular point of view.

Third, the public forum doctrine confirms the constitutionality of the funding Guidelines. Under that doctrine, student activity fee funds constitute a non-public forum. In the non-public forum, content-based rules are allowed, "as long as the regulation on speech is reasonable and not an effort to suppress expression merely because public officials oppose the speaker's view." *Perry Educ. Ass'n v. Perry Local Educators' Ass'n*, 460 U.S. 37, 46 (1983). The University Guidelines fully meet that standard.

CHAPTER 32

The Appellate Brief: Argument and Conclusion

§ 32.01. THE ARGUMENT

The argument is the heart of the brief. Its purpose is to persuade the court that your arguments rest on the applicable law and mandate a decision favorable to your client. While the other portions of the brief are important, you generally will win or lose your case on the substance of the argument. The argument section must be written persuasively and forcefully. It must be interesting enough to hold the attention of the court, and convincing enough to warrant a decision in your client's favor. This chapter instructs you how to structure and prepare the substance of an effective argument.

1. Structuring the Argument

a. Use Headings

A heading is a concise, persuasive statement of a conclusion that you want the court to accept with respect to a segment of your argument. Headings appear both in the table of contents and in the body of the argument at the beginning of different sections and subsections; they should be identical in both places. Here is an example:

I. NALLY'S TAPE-RECORDED STATEMENTS ARE ADMISSIBLE IN EVIDENCE.
   A. Because Nally Contradicted His Taped Statements, the Taped Statements Are Admissible Under the Hearsay Exception for Prior Inconsistent Statements.
   B. Because Nally Testified About These Statements at the First Trial, They Are Admissible Under the Hearsay Exception for Judicial Admissions.

As you can see, the headings divide the argument into major sections, and subheadings further divide those sections. Together, the headings and subheadings create an outline of your argument. You can feel confident about your headings when you list them in the table of contents and they present a logical, compelling summary of your argument.

Headings, then, are an essential tool in writing an organized, logical, and therefore persuasive argument. They give the court guidance in understanding your arguments and their logic. If you write persuasive headings, they should help persuade the court to rule in your client's favor.

b. How to Write the Headings

The questions presented provide the foundation for the headings. To draft the headings, prepare a list of the specific conclusions the court must adopt to decide the case in your client's favor and identify the reasons that support those conclusions. These conclusions will become the arguments made in the headings and should serve as an excellent outline for drafting the brief. Make a separate list for each question presented. Then outline the necessary conclusions.

The order in which you present your conclusions or arguments is important. First, present your arguments in the same order as your questions presented so that the court will find it easy to follow you. Second, arrange your arguments for each question presented in a logical order, keeping related parts of the argument together. Third, begin with your strongest argument, unless doing so would strain the logic of the discussion. Your strongest argument is the one with which the court is the most likely to agree, based on your knowledge of its prior decisions and its members' predilections. It is not necessarily the one about which you feel the most strongly.

Once you have decided on the necessary conclusions and their order, you are ready to write the headings. Headings should be an integral part of the argument. They are more than section titles. A heading is a statement of the argument to follow. It should be a complete sentence and be affirmative, persuasive, and specific. It should not, however, be so partisan that it sounds unreasonable. Do not make arguments you cannot support.

Each question presented usually warrants only one major heading. If a question has several subparts, write one general major heading. Then use the subparts to write minor headings. Place a Roman numeral before each major heading and a capital letter before each minor heading. Capitalize the first word and the first letter of all words except articles, conjunctions, and prepositions, and underline each such minor heading. State the elements of the argument supporting a minor heading in subheadings preceded by numerals indicating their positions under the minor heading. Capitalize only the first word of subheadings and do not underline them. Always use a period after a heading, whether it is a major heading, a minor heading, or a subheading. However, when you list a heading in your table of contents, you need not place a period at the end. Single-space your headings. Do not use minor headings or subheadings unless you use two or more of them. The headings should look like this:

I. FIRST MAJOR HEADING.
   A. <u>First Minor Heading.</u>
   B. <u>Second Minor Heading.</u>
      1. First subheading.
      2. Second subheading.
      3. Third subheading.
II. SECOND MAJOR HEADING.

Each heading is the thesis sentence for the part of the argument it introduces. As such, a well-written heading identifies the legal issue or rule of law involved, indicates your position on the issue, and sets out the reasoning supporting that position by relating the rule to your specific factual situation. It thus includes both the law and the facts of your case. Parties are often identified by name in headings. When minor headings and subheadings are used, the major headings need include only your conclusion regarding the application of a rule of law to your particular facts, since the minor headings and subheadings will set out the reasons for that conclusion. The more specifically you state the question, the rule, your reasoning, and the facts, the more persuasive the headings will be. Framing a heading, however, remains a balancing process requiring good judgment and common sense. While the heading must contain sufficient information to effectively summarize the argument, it must also be easily comprehensible.

Here are a few examples of the types of headings that result when the writer does not adhere to the principles of effective heading drafting:

The elements of the foreseeability test.

Comment: Avoid general topical phrases that could be applicable to any number of cases.

Only blood relatives are permitted to recover for negligent infliction of emotional distress.

Comment: Avoid stating an abstract legal proposition by failing to show its relevance to your case. A better heading would be:

Because the appellant is not a blood relative of the injured person, she may not recover for negligent infliction of emotional distress.

Appellant fails to state a cause of action for negligent infliction of emotional distress since her claim does not fall within the parameters of the *Sinn v. Burd* foreseeability test.

Comment: Avoid using case and statutory citations as shorthand references to the applicable legal principle unless the reader would be familiar with them (e.g., *Miranda*). A better heading would be:

The appellant fails to state a cause of action for negligent infliction of emotional distress because she was not near the scene of the accident and was not closely related to the injured person.

c. Using Headings as an Advocate

Seek to advocate your position, to make your basic arguments, through the headings. When you write a heading, use persuasive sentence structure and language. How you phrase a heading will depend on which side you represent.

Consider the following headings as they appeared in the tables of contents of two student briefs.

As drafted by counsel for the appellant:

I. PAULA DIGIACOMO'S CLAIM FOR NEGLIGENT INFLICTION OF EMOTIONAL DISTRESS SATISFIES THE FORESEEABILITY TEST ADOPTED BY THIS COURT.
   A. Ms. DiGiacomo's Presence at the Scene Within Seconds After Farmer's Bat Struck Henry's Head Satisfies the Requirement of Physical Proximity.
   B. Ms. DiGiacomo, Hearing the Crowd's Screams After Seeing Farmer Lose His Bat, Sensed a Contemporaneous Threat of Danger to Henry.

C. Ms. DiGiacomo's Long-Term Commitment to Henry Qualifies Her as Having a Close Relationship with Him Deserving of Legal Protection.

D. Ms. DiGiacomo's Loss of Sleep, Need for Medication, and Frequent Visits to Her Psychiatrist Present Physical Manifestations of Emotional Distress.

As drafted by counsel for the appellee:

II. THE COURT BELOW CORRECTLY AFFIRMED THE SUMMARY JUDGMENT ORDER FOR THE APPELLEE BECAUSE APPELLANT DIGIACOMO CANNOT SATISFY THE REQUISITE FACTORS OF THE FORESEEABILITY TEST AND THEREFORE FAILS TO STATE A VALID CAUSE OF ACTION FOR NEGLIGENT INFLICTION OF EMOTIONAL DISTRESS.

A. The Appellant's Relationship as an Unmarried Cohabitant with the Victim Does Not Satisfy the Requirement that the Appellant Be Closely Related to the Injured Party.

B. The Emotional Distress Alleged by the Appellant Could Only Have Resulted from Her Observation of Her Cohabitant's Condition upon Arriving at the Scene of the Accident as the Appellant Neither Witnessed Nor Sensorially and Contemporaneously Observed the Accident as It Occurred.

C. The Appellant Has Not Alleged or Suffered Any Bodily Harm or Severe Physical Manifestation of Emotional Distress as a Result of the Accident.

Note how each version uses identical facts but offers a different perspective on the same arguments, yet both are persuasive.

d. How Many Headings?

Headings should reflect your organization and simplify it by providing logical breaks in your argument. A well-written brief containing carefully drafted and logically placed headings will lead the reader easily from one point to the next. Too few headings will result in an argument that is difficult to follow and often poorly organized. Too many headings will interrupt the flow of the argument and may draw attention to insignificant or weak arguments. With these considerations in mind, use your judgment.

e. Final Considerations

When you have formulated your point headings, write them out in outline form as they will appear in the table of contents. Then ask yourself whether they conform to the principles discussed in this section. Are they complete? Does each point follow logically from the ones preceding it? Is the phrasing persuasive but reasonable? Is each heading readable? Only if you can answer each question affirmatively should you be satisfied with this crucial part of the argument section.

2. Preparing the Substance of the Argument

To be an effective advocate, you must be coherent and credible. The presentation of your argument may be as important as the substance of your argument. Your research must be complete, your organization clear, your argument logical, and your writing precise.

a. General Considerations

i. Understanding the Appellate Process

Remember that the judges are the ones who must be persuaded. In every appellate case, the judges seek to render a decision that is both fair and consistent with precedent. Write your brief with these dual concerns in mind. To achieve a favorable result, write a brief that is clear, interesting, complete, and reliable. Be honest about the law. Persuade with the strength of your arguments. Avoid excessive partisanship and statements without support. Never omit or distort the applicable law. If you do so, you will sacrifice your credibility, an essential element of a successful appeal.

ii. Familiarity with the Record

The record is your sole source of information about the case. To prepare an effective argument, you must have a clear and thorough understanding of the record. Read it carefully several times. Be certain that you understand the arguments and facts presented to the lower court, as well as the legal issues raised on appeal.

iii. Research: Do It Right but Know When to Stop

A carefully crafted and persuasive argument begins with thorough research. For an approach to doing research, review Chapter 4. The following are some tips:

- Think through the legal question, approaching it from a number of perspectives.
- Be creative in using the indexes to the digests. Look under a variety of topical headings. You and the index's publisher may list a topic under very different headings.
- Keep track of what you have researched and how you arrived at each source.
- Do not rely on headnotes. Read a case critically before relying on it.
- Shepardize each case you intend to cite.
- Make certain your research is current—check the pocket parts.

How do you know when to stop? Stop researching when you begin to find the same cases again and again. You should know when you have reached the point of diminishing returns.

Students sometimes engage in excessive research for two reasons. First, they keep searching for the one case that will give them a definitive answer to the legal issue. However, if you fail to find such a case early on in your research, there probably is no such case. In law school assignments, most problems have no definitive answer and no dispositive case.

Second, students keep researching because they are avoiding the next step, organizing the material and starting to write. Avoiding this pitfall requires being honest with yourself and recognizing that doing excessive research will deprive you of the time you need to finish your brief before the deadline. Drafting an effective argument is not an easy task. Be certain that you leave yourself enough time to do it well and expect that it will take longer than you anticipate.

iv. Compliance with the Rules of Court

To be an effective advocate, you must be credible. One of the simplest ways to establish your credibility is to comply with the rules of court concerning briefs.[1] Failure to comply

---

1. All appellate courts have rules about brief format, content, and length. Your legal writing program most likely has rules that govern the briefs you write for it. Frequently these rules are online. For example, you can find the rules for briefs and other documents before the United States Supreme Court at www.supremecourtus.gov/ctrules.html.

will not reflect well on you and may have a major adverse effect, such as dismissal of your client's case.

v. Simplicity in Substance and Style

Perhaps the single most important attribute of an effective argument is simplicity in substance and style. Limit the arguments presented to the court and make them as uncomplicated as possible. If your outline is too long and complicated, rethink it. Adhere to the plain English writing style discussed in Chapters 8 and 9. Most courts have a heavy volume of cases and therefore have limited time to spend on any particular case. You are more likely to capture and hold the court's attention with a brief that is straightforward in both substance and style.

b. Formulating the Arguments

Formulating the arguments you will make is a dynamic process involving analysis and evaluation of legal authority. You should consider not only the arguments suggested by your research, but also those that you develop based on your own insight into and understanding of a particular issue. Think carefully about the kinds of arguments that would be most effective for your client.

There are six distinct types of arguments you can make:

1. Arguments based on legal precedent
2. Arguments by analogy to similar situations
3. Arguments based on public policy
4. Arguments based on a "parade of horribles," i.e., the potential consequences of a precedent-setting decision against you
5. Arguments based on commonsense notions of justice and fair play
6. Arguments that stress certain sympathetic facts and rely on the emotional appeal of your case

Consider all six types of arguments when formulating your position. Use the ones that seem most persuasive in your particular case.

c. The Organization and Substance of the Arguments

When your appeal raises several independent issues, begin the argument section of your brief with the strongest issue. Similarly, where you have formulated several arguments in support of your position on an issue, start with the most compelling argument, unless logic dictates otherwise. Your brief will be more persuasive if the strongest issues and arguments are presented first. The court's attention and time are limited. Beginning a brief with a strong argument will ensure that at least that argument will be read. Starting with a compelling argument will impress the court with the soundness of your legal position and enhance your credibility. In addition, the less persuasive issues and arguments are more compelling when they seem to support the stronger issues and arguments. Some advocates put the weakest arguments last, while others bury them in the middle.

An effective argument generally has five components. These components suggest an organization for discussion of each argument.

First, open the discussion of the argument with a fact-specific conclusion, even though you may, to a certain extent, be repeating what is contained in the heading. Do not begin with a broad statement of black letter law. If you do so, you risk losing the court's attention.

Opening with an affirmative, specific statement is more persuasive and more likely to hold the court's interest.

Second, state the specific legal question raised by the argument under discussion and provide an answer, indicating how the applicable rule of law will apply to your facts. By doing so you are, in effect, giving the court a roadmap of your argument. With the aid of a roadmap, the court will know where the discussion is leading. Knowing where the discussion is leading is invaluable to understanding it and a prerequisite to being persuaded by it. If the court does not grasp your argument on the first reading, that argument is most likely lost as the court will not take the time to grapple with it. If the discussion requires more than one reading, the fault lies with the writer.

Third, give a full discussion of the authorities on which you rely. Unless you are citing a case only for a general legal proposition, be certain that you provide the reader with the relevant facts, the court's holding, and its rationale. Failure to sufficiently develop a case you cite will rob it of its persuasive value and frustrate the court. Remember that your role here is that of an advocate. Sometimes your discussion of a case will require a paragraph; other times it will require only a sentence or a parenthetical. Present relevant authority in the light most favorable to your position, but never mislead the court. Stress those portions of the opinion that are helpful to your argument, but do not take statements out of context.

Fourth, apply, explain, or relate that analysis to the facts of your client's case. Effective argument requires that you take your facts and work them into the authorities you have cited. Develop them in the context of the facts, the rationale, the policies, or the rules those authorities set out. In this section of the brief, you must argue—you must comment, compare, distinguish, find controlling, highlight, explain away. Demonstrate to the court why it should decide the case in favor of your client and how it can do so in a manner consistent with existing precedent. Remember to cite the record each time you refer to the facts of your case.

Fifth, when appropriate, restate your specific conclusion in regard to the argument under discussion.

This sample argument illustrates the suggested organization:

The appellant, Ms. DiGiacomo, cannot state a claim for negligent infliction of emotional distress because she fails to meet the first and second prongs of the foreseeability test in *Sinn v. Burd*, 486 Pa. 146, 173, 404 A.2d 672, 686 (1979). The first and second prongs require, respectively, that the plaintiff be near the scene of the accident and that the shock result from a direct emotional impact upon the plaintiff from the sensory and contemporaneous observance of the accident. Here, the appellant was neither near the scene of the accident nor was her shock the result of a sensory and contemporaneous observation of the accident.

When invoking the *Sinn* foreseeability test, this state's highest court considers both prongs simultaneously and then strictly construes both. *See Brooks v. Decker*, 512 Pa. 365, 516 A.2d 1380 (1986); *Mazzagati v. Everingham*, 512 Pa. 265, 516 A.2d 672 (1986). Consequently, the court has refused to recognize a cause of action when, as here, the plaintiff comes upon the accident scene immediately after the accident has occurred. As recently as October 1986, the Pennsylvania Supreme Court held against the plaintiff in two such cases. *Brooks*, 512 Pa. at 368, 516 A.2d at 1382; *Mazzagati*, 512 Pa. at 268, 516 A.2d at 679.

Two Pennsylvania cases particularly illustrate why Mrs. DiGiacomo was not a contemporary observer. In the first case, *Brooks*, a father, returned to his home in the afternoon and was passed by an ambulance. After the ambulance turned up the street to his house, it stopped at a crowd of people. As the father approached, he noticed his son's bicycle lying on the ground and discovered that his son had been in an accident with an automobile. The father accompanied his son to the hospital where the boy lay comatose for ten days and then died. 512 Pa. at 366, 516 A.2d at 1381. This Court dismissed the claim for negligent infliction of emotional distress because the parent did not witness the injury causing the accident. *Id.* at 367, 516 A.2d at 1382.

As in *Brooks*, Ms. DiGiacomo did not actually witness the defendant's negligent act. The act was completed when the bat struck its victim. Witnessing the bat leave the defendant's hands and hearing the crowd's uproar was analogous to Mr. Brooks seeing the ambulance turn down his street and then seeing his son's bicycle on the ground.

In the second case, *Bliss v. Allentown Public Library*, 497 F. Supp. 487 (E.D. Pa. 1980), a federal court applying Pennsylvania law permitted a mother to recover, even though she was not looking at her child at the exact moment a statue fell on him. The court held that the mother was a percipient witness because she observed her child immediately before the accident and heard the statue fall. She absorbed the full impact of the accident as if she had personally witnessed it. *Id.* at 489. There were no intermediary forces lessening her shock in witnessing her child's condition. *Id.*

The facts in that case differ from the facts here. In *Bliss*, the mother knew where her child was located and heard the accident happen. In contrast, Ms. DiGiacomo was unaware of her friend's location before the accident. She was unaware that he had been struck by a bat. She heard the crowd roar, but she did not know that it was because of an injury to her friend. As was true of the father in *Brooks*, Ms. DiGiacomo had no sensory and contemporaneous perception of the accident.

This Court's test is not unique to Pennsylvania. The facts of the instant case most closely resemble those of *Scherr v. Las Vegas Hilton*, 214 Cal. Rptr. 343 (Ct. App. 1985). In *Scherr*, the plaintiff watched live news coverage of a hotel fire and knew that her husband was in the hotel at the time of the fire. Because she did not witness her husband's injuries and did not know with certainty that he was being injured at that time, she could not recover for negligent infliction of emotional distress. *Id.* at 910-11, 214 Cal. Rptr. at 394-395. The court held that the "decisive question . . . is whether plaintiff, through whatever medium, received a sudden and severe shock by *actually* and *contemporaneously witnessing* not just the fire but the *infliction of injuries* upon her husband." *Id.* (emphasis in original).

By simply witnessing the throwing of the bat, Appellant DiGiacomo did not know with any certainty that her friend was in danger, let alone injured. The cry of the crowd provided no greater certainty. Therefore, like the wife in *Scherr*, the appellant was neither physically proximate to the scene of the accident nor was her shock the result of sensory and contemporaneous observation of the accident.

As these cases demonstrate, the appellant cannot state a claim for negligent infliction of emotional distress. She fails to meet well-established elements of the foreseeability test set forth by the Pennsylvania Supreme Court.

d. What to Avoid

Year after year, legal writing instructors see students make the same errors in organizing and presenting their arguments. In the world after law school, judges see the same errors. These errors are both well known and easy to avoid. You can find a discussion of them in Section 14.03. Take the time to review that discussion. To refresh your memory, you are on the way to writing a well-crafted brief if you

- avoid the "digest" approach,
- avoid the "historical development of the law" approach,
- avoid the use of too many quotations from legal authorities,
- avoid the "abstract writing" approach, and
- avoid the "law discussion only" approach.

e. Using Precedent

In writing the argument portion of the brief, you must select the authorities on which you will base your argument.

i. Hierarchy of Precedent

When choosing authorities, select those that have the greatest precedential value. Binding precedent is case law from the jurisdiction whose law is controlling, particularly from the highest court in that jurisdiction or sometimes from the court that is hearing your case. Therefore, these cases have the greatest relevance. Although decisions from lower courts are not binding, they still will be persuasive. Recent cases are generally more desirable than old cases. If you are in state court, federal court decisions interpreting the law of the controlling jurisdiction are not binding, but generally provide very persuasive authority.

You often will find that there is no binding authority directly on point, that the courts in your jurisdiction have not decided the issue, or that the case is one of first impression. In such a situation, you must rely on the decisions of other courts, decisions that are not controlling. Seek to persuade the court that those decisions are based on sound policy considerations and are compatible with your jurisdiction's existing body of law.

The law of some states will be more persuasive than that of other states. Generally those states that are geographically closer to your state will have case law that is similar to that of your jurisdiction. This case law will provide you with strong arguments urging the adoption of your client's position. Certain states tend to be in the forefront of developing areas of the law and may provide you with authority for your argument. You may also make an argument based on a trend in the developing law. Suggest to the court that the conclusion reached by a number of other jurisdictions is proper and warrants adoption.

ii. Handling Adverse Precedent

In researching your argument, you will encounter decisions adverse to your position. Both ethical and practical reasons dictate that you discuss adverse decisions in your argument. The ethical reason stems from your obligation as a lawyer. The A.B.A. Model Code of Professional Responsibility requires that "legal authority in the controlling jurisdiction directly adverse to the position of [your] client" be disclosed,[2] while the A.B.A. Model Rules of Professional Conduct state that "[a] lawyer shall not knowingly . . . fail to disclose to the tribunal legal authority in the controlling jurisdiction known to the lawyer to be directly adverse to the position of the client and not disclosed by opposing counsel. . . ."[3] The practical reason should be apparent. If you have found adverse authority, it is likely that your opponent has found it as well. It is far more desirable to address and minimize the adverse authority in the context of your argument than to allow your

---

2. Model Code of Prof. Resp. EC 7-23 and DR 7-106 (ABA, 1980).
3. Model R. of Prof. Conduct 3.3 (ABA, 2009).

opponent to argue it from the opposite side. Your position will be far more credible if your argument is complete and includes adverse decisions. Seize any opportunity to explain why the authority should not be followed.

There are several ways to effectively harmonize adverse precedent. You might distinguish it on the facts of the case. You might argue that the policy goals stressed in the adverse case mandate a different result in your case. Suggest that a decision in favor of your opponent would set an unfortunate precedent with negative consequences. If the case is the most recent pronouncement of a well-established legal rule, you might want to argue that your case requires an exception to that rule. You might be forced to argue that the case is an aberration and was wrongly decided. Use this tactic only as a last resort. It is an admission that you cannot harmonize the precedent. This argument may be ineffective when there are other decisions espousing the same position.

When you are the appellant, consider as adverse authority the decision from which you are appealing. Seek to harmonize it by pointing out its errors or omissions. Counsel for appellee will stress the decision as favorable and argue that it is sound.

iii. Rebuttal of Opposing Arguments

Seek to defuse the impact of the opposing arguments by criticizing them in one or several of the ways outlined in this chapter. Do not make conclusory statements that characterize your opponent's position as wrong. A broad dismissal suggests to the court that you cannot counter the position adequately and will adversely affect your credibility.

Resist the temptation to devote too much attention to your opponent's cases and arguments. The tone of your argument must remain affirmative and not convey a defensive posture. Use paragraph structure to your advantage. Never start an argument with a rebuttal of your opponent's position or the adverse cases. Do not devote a lot of time to your opponent's position or elaborate on the adverse cases. Doing either will focus undue attention on the opposing arguments and detract from the importance of your own arguments. Your argument should recognize that there is another position, address and dispose of it briefly, and move on.

iv. Parentheticals, String Cites, Signals, Quotations, and Footnotes

Use the authorities on which you rely to persuade the court that your client's position is correct. After you have fully discussed the cases that are critical to your argument, you may want to cite additional cases that have arrived at similar conclusions based on analogous facts. Those cases may not warrant full discussion, but you may want to include them to bolster your position. In this situation include a parenthetical after your citation of the case. Your parenthetical abstractions of the case should not be more than one sentence but should contain a brief summary of the relevant aspects of the case.

> See *Pearsall v. Emhart Indus.*, 499 F. Supp. 207 (E.D. Pa. 1984) (woman who arrived home to find firefighters attempting to control the blaze engulfing her house and who saw the unconscious bodies of her husband and children was a contemporaneous observer); *Corso v. Merrill*, 119 N.H. 647, 406 A.2d 300 (1979) (mother who heard and immediately witnessed a car accident involving her daughter contemporaneously observed the accident).

Signals such as *see, accord,* and *contra* can be used effectively in the argument. You might use a signal and a parenthetical to cite an adverse case, depending on how much discussion the case requires. Such a brief reference will demonstrate to the court that you have considered the case but will reduce its impact.

Avoid string citations, except perhaps where you are seeking to demonstrate the long-standing acceptance of a rule or an emerging trend in the law. String citations add nothing to your analysis. The court does not read them. Moreover, they are a distraction and break the flow of your argument. String cites suggest to the court that you think it is responsible for locating and reading the cited cases.

Exercise restraint when using quotations. Occasionally a judge will have phrased a certain point very effectively, and you will want to use a quotation. Most often your argument will be better if you paraphrase the opinion. Avoid long block quotes. Readers will often skip them entirely. If you must use them, use them very sparingly and delete all of the language that is not relevant by using ellipses indicated by three periods.

Use footnotes sparingly. Generally, if the thought is worthy of a footnote, you can fit it into your argument. Footnotes are undesirable because they interrupt the flow of the argument.

Use underlining or other methods of emphasis only very rarely. They are distracting. Rely on language and structure to emphasize a particular word or phrase.

f. Writing Persuasively

When drafting your argument, keep in mind the general principles of clear and effective legal writing. Take the time to review Chapter 25. In addition, take note of the following points.

i. Control Tone

Carefully control the tone of your brief because it affects the court's reaction to the substance of your arguments. Seek to establish an assertive tone. Make strong arguments, but do not overstate your position. Be scrupulously accurate. Do not use colloquialisms. Avoid informality and the use of abbreviations. Do not sound stuffy or pompous. Beware of humor, as an attempt at humor may annoy the judges. Sarcasm is always inappropriate, as is insulting or attacking the integrity of opposing counsel or the parties to the lawsuit. Do not adopt an arrogant tone—it will annoy and alienate a judge who may be favorably inclined to your opponent's arguments. Refer to the judges as "the court," opposing counsel as "counsel for appellant (or appellee)." Personalize your clients by referring to them by name, while referring to opposing counsel's client as "the appellant" or "the appellee." Never refer to the court as "you" or yourself as "I."

ii. The Final Touches

Rewrite, edit, and polish your argument. Make sure your language is clear, strong, and concise. Eliminate unnecessary words. Ask yourself whether your arguments are tightly reasoned. As you examine your brief, try to read it through the eyes of the judges who will decide the case. Will they find it easy to understand and persuasive?

Proofread your argument. Typographical errors may cause the court to question how careful you were in constructing the substance of the argument.

§ 32.02. THE CONCLUSION

The conclusion is a separate section of the brief and states precisely what action the party wants the appellate court to take. Here are two typical conclusions:

> For the above reasons, appellees respectfully submit that the judgment of the court below should be affirmed.

> For the reasons discussed above, we respectfully request that the judgment of the court below be reversed and the case remanded with instructions to dismiss the complaint against the appellant.

Because a wide variety of relief is available, you must specify the relief you seek. Do not assume the court will know what relief is sought. You will annoy the court by forcing it to guess, and you risk not having the desired relief ordered. The conclusion is not a summary of the arguments presented in the brief. Such a summary should be included at the end of the argument section. The conclusion should never consist of more than a short paragraph and may be only one sentence. Close the brief with "Respectfully submitted," and your signature as counsel.

§ 32.03. A CHECKLIST

In writing and revising a brief, some lawyers and law students find it helpful to use a checklist. A good checklist lists the important mechanical and stylistic rules that the writer should follow. You may find this checklist useful.

   I. Title Page: Does the title page conform to the rules of the court?
  II. Table of Contents
    A. When you read the headings, do they present a good summary of the argument?
    B. Are the headings exactly the same as they appear in the argument?
    C. Are the page numbers accurate? Is the brief within the page limitation that the court rules prescribe?
  III. Table of Authorities
    A. Does the table include all the authorities you cite in the argument? Have you excluded the citations in the jurisdictional statement, unless jurisdiction is an issue in the argument?
    B. Have you listed the authorities in the order that the court rules require? If court rules do not prescribe an order, have you listed them in a conventional way: for example, cases alphabetically, then constitutional provisions and statutes, then other authorities?
    C. Are the page numbers accurate?
    D. Is your citation form accurate? When required, have you included a case's prior or subsequent history?
  IV. Jurisdictional Statement: Have you cited the authority that gives jurisdiction to the court?
   V. Questions Presented
    A. Does the number of questions presented correspond to the number of major headings in your brief?

    B. When you read each question, do you find it comprehensible?

    C. Is each question framed in a way that, while not argumentative, encourages the court to answer it affirmatively and in your favor?

    D. Does each question include sufficient specifics of your case without including too much detail?

VI. Constitutional, Statutory, and Regulatory Provisions

    A. Have you included the relevant text of all provisions at issue in the argument? Have you excluded the statute or rule in the jurisdictional statement unless it is at issue in your argument?

    B. Have you included only the pertinent parts of provisions, as opposed to the full texts?

    C. Are the citations in proper form?

VII. Statement of Facts

    A. Have you documented the facts with references to the record?

    B. Have you stated the facts truthfully?

    C. Have you avoided editorializing and using value-laden modifiers?

    D. Have you put your best foot forward and told the story from your client's perspective?

    E. If a court below or a dissenter supported your position, have you emphasized that fact?

    F. Have you organized the facts and stated them so that the court can readily understand the story you are telling?

    G. When appropriate, have you used a chronological sequence?

    H. Have you employed a concrete writing style?

VIII. Summary of Argument

    A. Is the summary succinct, but accurate?

    B. Does the table of contents serve as an outline of the summary?

    C. Have you avoided citing cases unless they are essential to making the summary accurate?

    D. Have you stuck to your main arguments and saved the subtle points for the argument?

    E. Will the summary be comprehensible and persuasive to an intelligent, but uninformed audience?

IX. Argument

    A. Are your headings effective?

        1. Have you structured the argument with sufficient headings and subheadings, but not too many?

        2. Do the headings correspond exactly to the headings in the table of contents?

        3. Is each heading a complete sentence?

        4. When appropriate, does each heading make specific reference to the facts in your case?

        5. Have you written the headings to be persuasive and advance your argument as opposed to just stating the law?

    B. Have you adhered to a plain English writing style?

    C. Have you chosen your arguments with care?

        1. Have you used your strongest arguments?

        2. Have you placed your strongest arguments first when it is logical to do so?

        3. Have you given your stronger arguments proportionately greater space?

        4. Have you made your arguments as uncomplicated as possible?

   D. Have you presented each argument clearly and persuasively?

        1. Have you begun the discussion of each argument with a fact-specific conclusion and an answer to the specific legal question that you are addressing so that the court knows where your argument is going? Have you briefly outlined your argument in the first paragraph so that the court has a roadmap?

        2. Have you given a sufficiently full discussion of the authorities on which you rely, including the facts of decided cases when appropriate?

        3. Have you applied, explained, or related your analysis to the facts of your case?

        4. At the end of your discussion, have you restated that your argument leads to the specific conclusion you advocate?

        5. Have you made your argument as persuasive as possible?

   E. Have you dealt with adverse arguments?

   F. Have you made the best use of authority?

        1. Have you used proper citation form?

        2. Have you relied primarily on authorities with the greatest precedential value?

        3. Have you dealt with adverse precedent?

        4. When cases have not needed extended discussion, have you briefly summarized them in parentheticals?

        5. Have you used proper citation signals?

        6. Have you avoided string citations?

        7. Have you exercised restraint in using quotations and footnotes?

   G. Have you written in an assertive tone that does not overstate your position?

X. Conclusion

   A. Have you specified the precise relief you seek?

   B. Have you closed the brief with "Respectfully submitted" and your signature as counsel?

CHAPTER 33

Basic Principles of Oral Communication

§ 33.01. INTRODUCTION

Oral presentations have several aspects that you should carefully think out or practice in advance of the presentation itself. This chapter asks you to think about the appellate argument the same way you would think about any other spoken presentation. We teach you some basic principles that will guide your preparation every time you are asked to speak, whether to a court, clients, other attorneys, or community groups. In Chapter 34, we will discuss in detail the steps that are unique to preparing for and presenting an appellate oral argument.

Knowing how to talk is not the same thing as knowing how to speak effectively; our goal is to help you do the latter. Inadequate preparation and poor presentation can so distract from a message, even a very important one, that the impact of the message can be virtually destroyed. Undoubtedly you have sat through your share of less-than-gripping speeches and presentations that have proved this rule. Make your goal to have your audiences hanging on your every word or, if not, at least processing *most* of the information you are trying to convey.

§ 33.02. CONSIDER THE AUDIENCE

If the purpose of speaking is the communication of ideas, audience evaluation is critical. How can you best communicate your thoughts to a particular audience if you have not considered who your audience is and what preconceptions they might bring to the topic and your position on that topic?

1. Do Your Homework

In the appellate context, you will seldom be faced with individuals on the bench who are unknown quantities. Your judges will likely have written opinions that you can read before you go into court. If they have written opinions on related issues, it would almost be negligence not to read them. Even if they have not written opinions in similar cases, you might gain some insight into the judges' styles of reasoning by reading unrelated opinions. You do not need to spend several days in this process, but it will be well worth your time to spend a few hours at it.

You should also try to find someone who has previously argued in front of these judges. Ask about the judges' styles of questioning, the types of arguments they seem to find persuasive, and the types of issues they like to focus on in reaching their decisions. Find out whether the judges concentrate on the facts of the cases in front of them or on policy implications for the future. When you have this kind of information, you can structure your argument accordingly.

If time and circumstances permit, consider going to court and listening to someone else argue in front of the same judges. Get a feel for the judges' reactions to various arguments and approaches, and think about what you might do to obtain the reaction you are seeking to your argument.

2. Adapt to Your Audience

Once you have developed a sense of what might persuade your audience, you need to think about how to accomplish that goal. The first thing you should consider is the image you want to present. If you have previously appeared before this court, you may already have established a certain ethos or credibility that will help you convey your message. If not, you need to determine how to suggest to the court a level of competence that will make the judges receptive to your arguments. Adequate preparation and a professional demeanor, which we will discuss in greater detail later, are good ways to accomplish this.

In order to persuade an audience, you must give them a reason and the means to identify with your position. You can do this most effectively if you establish common ground between you and the audience. Convince the audience that you are all on the same side, or at least that you have in some way attempted to adapt to your audience's perspective on the issues being discussed. If you have made some effort to ascertain your audience's attitude toward the topic before making your presentation, you will find this a lot easier to do.

If you sense, or have learned, that your audience's attitude toward the topic is different from yours, try to figure out the source of their attitude. If you understand where it comes from, your chances of changing it may improve if you can address the root cause. You should recognize, however, that extreme attitudes cannot usually be changed greatly or quickly, and that an attitude that has been expressed publicly (for example, in an opinion, article, or speech) will be more resistant to change than an attitude that has not been committed to in that manner.

There are strategies that can be employed to change audience attitudes. You can persuade the audience that circumstances have changed sufficiently that the original attitude is no longer appropriate. If there has been no change in circumstances, you may be able to persuade the audience that they were previously misinformed or that they had not been made aware of all the available facts. Or, you can point out that the situation you are discussing is sufficiently distinct from previous situations that it calls for a different result. If you are trying to "scare" your audience into changing their attitude, you should know that attitudes are generally changed more easily by moderate than by strong anxiety appeals.

§ 33.03. CONSIDER THE SETTING

The term "setting" in this context refers to both the physical surroundings in which the presentation will be made and the occasion, or reason, for convening the speaker and the audience. Spending a little time understanding the expectations created by these contextual factors will help you prepare a more effective presentation.

1. Study the Physical Surroundings in Advance

You should, if at all possible, take the time to visit the courtroom or other location in which you will be "performing." If you have a sense of the size of the space, its acoustical properties, and the location of any furniture or other objects that will be present when you speak, you can prepare in advance to deal with any problems that might be caused by any of these factors. For example, if the podium is too high or too low, find out whether it can be adjusted, as many of them can, by the simple push of a button. If you can manipulate the physical environment to make yourself more comfortable, do so. Greater comfort will mean greater confidence and, in all likelihood, a stronger presentation.

Another factor to consider is the time of day at which you will be speaking—are people likely to be tired because your turn comes at the end of a long day, or might they forget your message because it appeared in the middle of a long parade of other speakers? If you sense that these types of factors might create a problem for you, you can try to come up with ways of making your presentation stand out, such as an especially strong opening or closing statement. If you arrive early, you may even be able to make last-minute adjustments in your prepared material to account for the mood of the audience at that particular day and time.

If you need some sort of visual aid to make your presentation, you must plan for it in advance. Check to find out whether the courtroom has an easel, a projector, computers, or whatever else you might need. If not, find out whether the equipment you need can be brought in or whether you should supply it yourself.

2. Understand the Occasion

The reasons an audience convenes will largely determine the audience's expectations of what the speakers will say and of how they will conduct themselves. Make sure that your understanding of the occasion and the audience's understanding are the same. Ask questions about any traditions and conventions that must be followed to avoid surprising the audience in a way that will detract from your message.

In an appellate courtroom, for example, the expectation is that you will behave with proper formality and deference. If you go in expecting to dazzle the judges with the type of drama and emotional appeals that might be more appropriate for a jury, you are not likely to make a favorable impression or to be taken as seriously as you need to be.

§ 33.04. STRUCTURE FOR MAXIMUM EFFECT

Plan the structure of your presentation to reinforce your intended message. Remember that, from your audience's perspective, your meaning will come across sequentially and cumulatively. Thus, you want to be sure that the sequence of your ideas is logical and that the cumulative effect of your presentation is persuasive. Your ideas should progress in a manner that the audience can follow and be tied together appropriately, even explicitly where that will enhance understanding.

1. Structural Strategy

It is useful to have some basic understanding of human psychology and memory when deciding how to structure an argument for maximum persuasive effect. The concepts of "primacy" and "recency" refer to the likelihood that audiences will remember best the ideas they hear first and last, when their attention is most focused on the presenter. Bear this in mind when structuring your oral argument.

You should also consider whether to present your arguments in ascending order of impact, saving the best for last, or descending order, starting with your strongest point. Because both primacy and recency will work in most contexts, you should try to start *and* end on a strong note, and bury your weaker points in the middle, where they will be the least detrimental.

Virtually all appellate advocates will tell you to start with your strongest argument, for the simple reason that you may never get beyond your first argument if the judges have many questions. Because an appellate argument is not a "set piece," where you have total control over the presentation, but rather a dialogue between you and the court, you must plan your strategy accordingly.

2. Methods of Proof

There are two primary approaches to proving a proposition: the direct approach, from proposition to proof, and the indirect approach, which gradually builds up the building blocks of proof until the proposition being proved becomes the inevitable conclusion. The latter method is somewhat more difficult, but often more effective, particularly when dealing with a skeptical or hostile audience. The reason this method works better for such audiences is that they may decide not to listen to the proof after they hear a proposition stated with which they disagree. If they do not know what the proposition is until they have heard the proof, you may be able to keep their minds open longer.

Even so, most legal arguments will work from proposition to proof because that is the expected approach. Judges may get frustrated if they do not understand immediately where an argument is going and what an attorney is trying to prove. Because the judges have the right to interrupt at any point, the attorney trying to prove a point by indirection would probably have to be doing so in an especially fascinating manner to avoid an irritated, "Counsel, where is this going?"

Part of your proof should consist of anticipating and defusing adverse arguments. You do not need to deal with every possible argument that might be made against your position, but if you know that an opposing argument will be made, or that those who disagree with you do so for a particular reason, it is foolish not to address that point. Pretending something does not exist is not the best way to make it disappear, and it does nothing for your credibility or persuasiveness. Why should your audience believe your arguments if you ignore theirs?

Raising and then explaining away the negative arguments is known as the "straw man" approach to proof. It is called that because you are setting up the straw man arguments just to knock them down, demonstrating all the while how insubstantial they were in the first place. Just make sure that in the course of dealing with the "straw men," you do not inadvertently make them seem more substantial than your opposition would have been able to or that you do not create new arguments against your position that might not have come up at all.

3. Organizational Patterns

You must figure out which of the many ways to structure an argument makes the most sense for each project you undertake. The most important aspect of the choice, however, is that you make one. Structure does not take care of itself; you must make conscious decisions about what structure is most likely to enhance the message you are trying to convey. Here are several possibilities to consider.

a. Chronological

This approach to structure makes the most sense when you are relating a story and the exact sequence of events is important to the audience's understanding of the story. In the context of the appellate argument, a chronological organization will probably be useful in your presentation of the facts of the case you are arguing.

b. Cause to Effect

If you are trying to establish a causal relationship between two events, as you might be in a negligence case where proximate cause is an issue, you should be sure to structure the argument so that the causal link will be apparent to the audience. This will usually require you to begin with the statement of the cause and then to move on to the result, demonstrating the unbroken nature of the chain of events you are describing.

c. Problem to Solution

If you are arguing for a change in an existing rule, this structure will probably be useful. It is one of the most common approaches to persuasion. Begin by developing the need for change; discuss the harmful consequences of the current rule, being sure to connect those harms directly to the rule you seek to change. Once you have thoroughly proved that a change is necessary, move on to the solution you propose.

In order to make this structure really effective, you must establish a strong link between the benefits of your proposal and the harms you previously identified. In other words, now that you have made the case for change, you must convince your audience that your change is the right one and that it will solve all the problems previously identified. Many speakers simply present their proposal and assume the audience will immediately see that it is the perfect answer. This is very rarely persuasive—you run the risk that the audience will not find your solution as obvious as you do and will begin to think about other alternatives.

If you do a good job of convincing the audience that change is necessary, you will have created the perfect atmosphere for receptivity to your proposal. Do not waste that opportunity by failing to make explicit connections between your solution and the need for change; you may not get another chance!

d. Pro Versus Con

You may occasionally be in the position of offering an evaluation of which of two proposals is more likely to effect a desired result or of defending a proposal that you know has encountered strong opposition. If so, this might be the structure to choose. Where the positions on both sides are clearly defined, it will make sense to the audience that you choose to address those positions sequentially.

Your only remaining decision is whether to address the "pro" or the "con" first. This will depend on the context of the argument, and probably on which side you think is stronger—for example, if you think the audience is hostile to the proposition you support, you may want to deal with the "con" arguments first. If you can effectively negate those, the audience may be more receptive to hearing why you support the other side.

e. Topical

When you have several issues to address, you will generally take a topical approach to structure, presenting the various topics in any order that seems appropriate. It is here that issues of primacy and recency, and ascending versus descending order, arise. If there is a sequence that is naturally logical—for example, if one argument must be developed first to provide context for another, you should present the arguments in that order. Similarly, if you are making arguments in the alternative, or if one argument is conditional upon the acceptance of another, you should take that into consideration when structuring the overall presentation.

4. Introductions, Conclusions, and Transitions

These are important parts of the structure of any spoken presentation. We have included them last in this discussion because that is probably when you should think seriously about them. The conclusion obviously belongs at the end of the speech, but you should also construct your introduction *after* you have completed your substantive analysis. It is at that point that you will have the best idea of the tone you are attempting to create and of the central theme of your argument. Both of these should be reflected in the introduction.

The introduction and the conclusion should be short, pithy, and as powerful as you can make them, consistent with the subject of your argument. These are the first and last impressions you will leave with the audience, and you want them to be strong ones. Identify the one idea you would like the audience to take away from your presentation (assuming that that is all you can realistically expect them to take away) and then emphasize that idea in the introduction and conclusion. Ideally, the conclusion will echo the introduction in some interesting way so that the central idea is reinforced.

Consciously consider transitions after you have constructed the argument. The reason you move from one argument to another, or the relationships between arguments, will often seem obvious to you, and thus you may not state them directly as you develop the argument. After you have created the body of the argument, look at it as objectively as you can, and ask yourself whether the audience will see the flow of the argument as well as you do. Even if you think they will, consider adding brief transitions between major points. Remember that the audience has to process your message aurally; any help you can offer to make that message clearer will almost certainly be appreciated.

§ 33.05. WRITE FOR SOUND APPEAL

Remember, as you draft the language you intend to speak, that writing words to be spoken requires a different style from writing words that will be read in silence. You have additional tools at your disposal to enhance the impact your words will have on the audience. Try to hear the words as you write them and to picture how the delivery will go. What facial expressions will accompany your words? How will you use your hands to support your message? What will your volume and vocal inflection reveal about the importance of what you are saying? What tone will most enhance your message? Language shapes perceptions; use your knowledge of this fact to encourage or discourage particular responses.

1. Useful Tools

There are several ways you can maintain audience interest in your spoken message. Some of them are relatively simple but quite effective if used in appropriate contexts. Others may require more conscious effort on your part to use them effectively. Here are some of the ways you can keep an audience listening and wanting to hear more.

a. Humor

Humor can be a very good way to involve your audience in your message from the start. This is probably why so many speakers begin their presentations with a joke. Be sure that what you say really is funny and that it is appropriate to the audience. Also remember that subtle humor is often more effective than obvious humor; surprise is an important element of good humor.

b. Novelty

Novelty may also be a way to catch your audience's attention early on. If you have a different approach to an old topic or are discussing something with which the audience is not familiar, you can use the interest that most of us have in new things to your advantage. Choose an interesting way to present new information to your audience, and you may very well keep their attention longer.

As with anything else, though, do not get carried away; novelty for its own sake will wear thin very quickly. Be sure that your approach is actually novel, present it in a way that is appropriate to the audience and the topic, and avoid "cuteness" that may succeed only in turning the audience off.

c. Conflict

You may be able to use the element of surprise in another way. If your topic lends itself to the creation of conflict, for example, between light and serious tones, a sudden shift can catch the audience off guard and make them sit up and take notice. Thus if you can begin with a humorous approach and then move unexpectedly into an aspect of the topic that is decidedly not funny, you may shock the audience into listening more carefully than they might otherwise. This is a manipulative approach to getting your message across, but if handled adroitly, it can be quite effective.

d. Suspense

This is a difficult technique to use effectively, particularly in a legal setting, but if done well it can really add to the impact of a message. You can use suspense in the introduction to your presentation by finding an interesting but somewhat ambiguous way of leading into your topic. In order not to lose or frustrate the audience, make certain that your mysterious introduction is genuinely fascinating and does not go on for too long.

You may find it more effective to at least signal your topic early on, but leave the audience wondering exactly what your approach or perspective is. It can be a very effective means of persuading a hostile or skeptical audience to begin by articulating the arguments for your opponents and suggesting that you understand them, and then suddenly revealing your true position on the issue. Once again, the element of surprise keeps the audience involved in the presentation.

Be very sure that you understand the expectations of your audience before you try this technique in a legal setting. In the appellate context, where presentations tend to assume nearly identical guise and where the judges can interrupt you if they get frustrated, too much suspense could be detrimental to the persuasiveness of your argument. With a jury, however, appropriate use of this technique could be quite powerful.

e. Emphasis

A spoken presentation gives you many opportunities to suggest appropriate emphasis. You can use your voice, hands, and face to guide the audience to the conclusion that what you are saying at any given moment is particularly important. Recognize too that the audience will generally expect that important information appears at the end of sentences rather than at the beginning. They expect the beginning of a sentence to contain contextual information that will help them orient themselves in the message and prepare for what follows. Here is a powerful example of the effect an understanding of this simple expectation can have on the impact of a message. Read this excerpt and think about how you would react to it as a listener.

> I have refrained directly from criticizing the President for three years. Because I believe that Americans must stand united in the face of the Soviet Union, our foremost adversary and before the world, I have been reticent. A fair time to pursue his goals and test his policies is also the President's right, I believe. The water's edge is the limit to politics, in this sense. But this cannot mean that, if the President is wrong and the world situation has become critical, all criticism should be muted indefinitely.
>
> A fair chance has been extended the President, and policies that make our relationship with the Soviet Union more dangerous than at any time in the past generation no longer deserve American support and support cannot be expected.
>
> Reagan administrative diplomacy has had this grim result: We could face not the risk of nuclear war but its reality if we allow present developments in nuclear arms and United States–Soviet relations to continue.

This is an excerpt from a campaign speech by Walter Mondale. It seems very flat and leaves the reader wondering what exactly the speaker is trying to accomplish. If we simply restructure the sentences, leaving the meaning and vocabulary virtually intact, here is the result:[1]

> For three years, I have refrained from directly criticizing the President of the United States. I have been reticent because I believe that Americans must stand united before the world, particularly in the face of our foremost adversary, the Soviet Union. I also believe a President should be given fair time to pursue his goals and test his policies. In this sense, politics should

---

1. This example is taken from George Gopen, *Expectations: Teaching Writing from the Reader's Perspective* (A.B. Longman Publishers, Pearson Education Division, 2004, pages 145-148); he, in turn, got the example from Joseph M. Williams, and asked us to acknowledge that fact.

stop at the water's edge. But this cannot mean that all criticism should be muted indefinitely, no matter how wrong a President may be or how critical the world situation may become.

President Reagan has had his fair chance, and he can no longer expect Americans to support policies that make our relationship with the Soviet Union more dangerous than at any time in the past generation.

This is the grim result of Reagan administrative diplomacy: If present developments in nuclear arms and United States–Soviet relations are permitted to continue, we could face not the risk of nuclear war but its reality.

By simply restructuring the sentences to place emphasis on the appropriate information, we end up with something that actually sounds as though it might belong in a campaign speech.

f. Theme

One of the most important tools for effective speaking is the creation and emphasis of a central theme for any presentation. Find a way to tie your ideas together, to relate them to a single overarching principle, and be sure to clearly identify that theme for your audience and to refer to it wherever appropriate to emphasize its importance. Choose a tone for your presentation that reinforces this central theme (i.e., solemn, ironic, indignant, etc.) You should never assume that any audience will remember every subpoint of an argument, but if they walk away understanding the main goal you were trying to accomplish and why that goal is important, you will have achieved something to be proud of.

g. Language

Remembering always that your audience cannot go back for another look at something that was not immediately clear, keep your language concrete, precise, active, colorful, and simple. Most people will process information more efficiently if they can conjure up a visual representation of it. You can help your audience do this by using concrete analogies and examples to clarify points that might otherwise seem abstract. Here are some specific examples of stylistic devices that speakers have used to good effect in many contexts.

i. Rhetorical Questions

Asking questions to which you do not expect an answer can, if used sparingly, be a very effective means of keeping your audience involved in your presentation. Your goal is to frame the question in a way that suggests the desired answer but leaves enough room for thought that the audience will feel that they have arrived at the answer on their own, and thus feel a sense of commitment to it. You should be a little extra careful about using this technique with an appellate bench of course—you do not want the judges to feel that you are usurping their role!

ii. Repetition

Strategic use of repetition, whether of sentence structure (e.g., antithesis), words, or sounds (e.g., alliteration), can be an effective signal of emphasis or simply a means of increasing the memorability of what you say. Part of the reason so many people remember and quote speeches by John F. Kennedy and Martin Luther King is because they used repetition so powerfully. You should be careful to avoid monotony, however, which will almost certainly result if you overuse this technique.

iii. Imagery

As mentioned above, giving your listeners the ability to "see" what you are saying will help them process and retain the message. There are several ways to do this, all involving comparisons, sometimes literal, sometimes of very dissimilar things.

The literal analogy is the most direct comparison; it identifies similarities between things or ideas that will help clarify a point. The more figurative similes and metaphors make comparisons between very different things in order to create a picture in the listener's mind that will suggest meaning quickly and powerfully. A simile is a comparison that actually uses the words "like" or "as," while a metaphor implies the comparison.

Martin Luther King's "I Have a Dream" speech is one of the strongest and most effective uses of metaphors you are likely to see; it creates an entire landscape in your mind through the simple use of words. Most of us cannot use metaphors nearly so well. They should be used sparingly and carefully; if you create a metaphor that is too startling or confusing, you run the risk of distracting your listeners as they struggle to deal with the visual image you have created.

Personification is another type of comparison that can be used effectively to create a lasting image in the mind of the listener. This is the giving of human traits to inanimate or intangible objects, as by suggesting that an institution is "ill" or that an idea "limps." Again, you should be careful not to create images that are so strange the audience will spend substantial time puzzling over them, or laughing where you did not intend humor.

2. Not So Useful Tools

As you can see, there are many ways you can enhance your message by making it more fun for the audience to listen to you. Similarly, there are some ways you can detract from the message and alienate the audience so that they stop listening or become less receptive to your message. For example, using slang, foreign phrases, vulgarity, euphemisms, or triteness might have this kind of effect, ranging from distraction to active annoyance.

Another tactic speakers sometimes resort to, particularly in the political arena, is name-calling. By this, we do not mean only the obvious mud-slinging type of name-calling, but also the more insidious, intellectually dishonest use of labels in place of analysis. When a speaker knows that a particular word will generate an emotional reaction, such as the word "quota" in a discussion of affirmative action, it may be tempting to simply use the word and thereby short-circuit a genuine examination of the topic under discussion. This technique may get results—it is always easier, both for the speaker and the listeners, to oversimplify an issue and thus discourage reason and evaluation—but it does so inappropriately.

Particularly in a courtroom setting, where your listeners are intelligent and at least somewhat informed, you should respect them enough to offer a straightforward and thoughtful analysis of the topic you are discussing. Say what you mean and do not shy away from the difficult questions. If your audience is paying any attention at all, attempts to avoid the real issues are likely to be challenged and will cost you valuable credibility. There is simply no reason to take this kind of risk.

§ 33.06. APPLY THE FUNDAMENTALS OF GOOD PUBLIC SPEAKING

Delivery is the final element of any spoken presentation. When you have worked so hard to prepare your argument, it would be very unfortunate to diminish the impact of your efforts by not delivering the message effectively. Here are some suggestions about how to achieve maximum influence as a messenger.

1. Maintain Eye Contact

Maintaining eye contact with an audience is difficult for inexperienced or nervous speakers, but it is essential. In a courtroom, look the judges in the eye rather than at your notes or the ceiling. Eye contact lets the judges know you are interested in what they have to say. It also helps keep them interested in what you are saying.

2. Be Heard

Speak loudly and clearly enough that everyone in the room can hear you. Project but do not yell. Speaking at an appropriate volume suggests confidence in your position. If you speak so that everyone can hear you easily, you help ensure that your audience will understand your argument. You also increase the likelihood that your audience will find your argument persuasive.

3. Do Not Read

Reading will cause you to speak too fast and make you more difficult to understand. It suggests a lack of preparation and even a lack of interest in your argument. In addition, you will lose eye contact with the bench, and the judges' interest in your argument may decrease.

4. Use Emphasis

Sounding like you are interested in your arguments and believe them makes it more likely that your audience will find you persuasive. It is difficult to listen to someone who speaks in a monotone. We are not suggesting that you try to be flamboyant, but merely that you modulate your voice appropriately for the point you are making.

5. Use the Pause

Silence is often anathema to someone who is unused to speaking in public. As you develop experience and expertise in speaking to an audience, you will learn to use a well-timed pause to provide emphasis. A pause while you ponder a question or collect your thoughts can ensure that what follows the pause is more fluent and persuasive.

6. Use Appropriate Gestures

Not all people use their hands while speaking. If you are not comfortable using hand gestures, do not try them for the first time in the pressure-filled environment of a courtroom. If, however, it is natural for you to use your hands to add appropriate emphasis to your presentation, do so in your oral argument. Be careful not to use your hands excessively.

7. Watch Your Posture

The courtroom is a formal setting. Do not lean excessively on the podium. You may rest your hands on the podium, but not your elbows. Do not argue with your hands in your pockets or on your hips. Casual poses may suggest a lack of respect for the court and, at the very least, are likely to be distracting. Do not pace or rock back and forth. Stand in one place and maintain an upright, respectful posture.

CHAPTER 34

The Appellate Argument

§ 34.01. INTRODUCTION

This chapter teaches you specifically how to make an oral argument in appellate court. Although most attorneys do not find themselves in appellate court very often, the skills you learn in presenting an oral argument will be useful in other areas of practice. Attorneys also argue motions to the trial court and appear before various administrative agencies that may require argument.

Oral argument is the culmination of an attorney's efforts in an appeal. It complements the brief. You cannot expect, however, to present an argument every time you file a brief because the court has discretion about whether to grant oral argument. If you get a chance to argue, view it as a golden opportunity. You will have no other in-person, one-on-one contact with the judges who will decide whether you win or lose.

The oral argument provides you with an opportunity to interest the court in particular arguments presented in the brief and to convince the court that your client's position is correct. Generally, the argument is more provocative, more personal, and more lively than the brief. The oral argument affords an opportunity to answer the court's questions and address its concerns. Time is limited and therefore precious, which means that precision in presenting the argument is crucial.

Most lawyers will tell you there is very little chance you will win a case at oral argument that you otherwise would have lost. They will also tell you that you can lose a case based on your argument. On the other hand, some experts, including Justice Kennedy of the Supreme Court, will tell you that many cases are decided at oral argument.[1]

Many first-year law students view oral argument as an ordeal to be endured. Because the experience is new and the process unknown, the prospect of oral argument makes students nervous. Fortunately, despite their initial misgivings, most students find that the actual experience is worthwhile and even fun.

---

1. Justice Kennedy, in his address as part of the Enrichment Program at the George Washington University National Law Center, February 6, 1990.

§ 34.02. THE SETTING OF THE ORAL ARGUMENT

The appellate oral argument usually is conducted before a panel of three judges.[2] The court allots each side a specified amount of time in which to present its argument. The attorney addresses the bench from behind a podium. The appellant presents the first argument and may reserve time for rebuttal. The appellee argues after the appellant and does not present a rebuttal. If two teams are arguing in a first-year legal writing or moot court program, both appellants argue, followed by both appellees. The appellant delivers the rebuttal after the appellee has argued. The judges may interrupt at any time with questions.

As a matter of protocol, rise when the judges enter the room and remain standing until the judges have seated themselves. The court then calls the case and may ask whether counsel is prepared. After you indicate your readiness to proceed, step to the podium and begin your argument. Refer to any judge to whom you are speaking as "Your Honor." Refer to your opponent as "opposing counsel" or "counsel for appellant" (or appellee).

§ 34.03. PREPARING THE ORAL ARGUMENT

The key to a successful oral argument is preparation. If you are prepared, you will be confident and should be able to satisfactorily address any concerns raised by the judges. In preparing your argument, remember that time is limited, so you must state your arguments in general terms. Focus on controlling legal principles, policy, and equity rather than the details of case law, which should be presented in your written brief.

The judges' questions will probably force you to deviate from your prepared outline. You should be sufficiently prepared that you can shift back and forth from one part of your argument to another as necessary. The judges may not wish to follow your structure, and you should be prepared to accommodate them. Also, you must think through the consequences of your arguments and the relief you want the court to grant. Judges will want to know precisely what you want them to do and what effect your preferred result will have on future cases. Here are seven rules to help you achieve the required degree of preparation.

1. Know the Record

You must have all information about what happened in your case at your fingertips. This information includes not only the facts that gave rise to the cause of action, but also the entire procedural history of the case, including discovery. You may present a brief history of the case as part of your argument, but you must be able to answer the court's questions about any additional facts. The judges may doubt the accuracy of other aspects of your argument if you cannot tell them what happened previously in your own case.

---

2. This is true for intermediate appellate courts. The United States Supreme Court and other higher courts will have more judges hearing arguments—usually seven or nine. The party designations at the Supreme Court level are petitioner and respondent, or appellant and appellee.

2. Study the Authorities

Although you usually do not focus primarily on details of decided cases in presenting your argument, you must be able to answer questions about the major cases cited in your brief or in your opponent's brief and to use such cases in response to questions where appropriate. You must know the facts, holdings, and rationales of all such cases. The court will expect you to be able to apply them to the facts of your case.

3. Know the Arguments

You must be familiar with all arguments raised in your brief. For purposes of oral argument, however, select a maximum of three major arguments to present to the court. Use the organization of your brief as a guide. As explained in Chapter 33, try to begin with your strongest argument. This will help capture the judges' attention and set the tone for the rest of the argument. Also, the judges might ask so many questions that you never reach your second argument. You must, however, be prepared to answer questions about your weaker arguments because the judges may focus on those arguments. Also, remember that if your strongest argument does not logically come first, you may not be able to begin with it.

Be flexible about the order in which you present your arguments and be prepared to adapt your argument to what happens in the courtroom. For example, if you are the appellee, listen carefully to the questions the court asks the appellant. If the court focuses on a particular issue, you may want to begin by presenting your argument on that issue.

4. Outline Your Arguments

An outline is an essential part of preparing for an oral argument. Even if you do not use your outline during the argument, preparing one ahead of time will give your presentation clarity and structure. The outline should present the high points of your argument. When deciding how much detail to include in your outline, use the rule of thumb that you should have enough prepared material to occupy approximately half your allotted time. For a fifteen-minute argument, prepare an outline that should take you approximately eight minutes to present. Some people feel more prepared if they put virtually every word they intend to say on paper beforehand. Others prefer a sketchy outline that allows greater flexibility of word choice at the time of the argument. As a general rule, go to the podium with the fewest words on paper that will help you remember your key points. Regardless of which approach you choose, keep your arguments simple and straightforward, and use only minimal references to details such as case names in preparing your outline.

5. Prepare Argument Aids

After preparing your outline, think about the kind of notes and other aids you are likely to need while presenting your argument. You may choose to use the outline or you may find that some other form of prompting is more helpful to you. Many appellate advocates suggest putting your outline on the inside of a manila folder so that the entire argument is laid out in front of you. This approach makes referring to various parts of the argument in response to questions easier. If you are shuffling through loose papers to find needed information, you may distract the bench. Locating a particular part of your argument under pressure can be difficult.

When you go to the podium, take your brief, your outline, and notes or cards that summarize the relevant cases. The case notes should provide a short summary of the facts, holding, and rationale of each case about which you can reasonably expect questions during the argument.

Take your argument aids to the podium with you, but do not read from them. Use the argument aids only to remind you of the points you wish to raise with the court. Forcing yourself to speak without heavy reliance on notes will facilitate the all-important eye contact with the bench. One way to accomplish this is to follow the general rule stated above, and have only as many words in front of you as you really need to remember your key points. For example, use important words and phrases rather than full sentences.

6. Rehearse the Argument

Although some people may feel a bit foolish practicing an oral argument, it is an essential exercise. If you are not accustomed to public speaking, practice in front of a mirror. You will be able to see how effective your facial expressions and hand gestures are. You also may want to practice in front of other people—your friends, your family, or your partner if you are arguing as part of a team. The best way to gauge your effectiveness as a public speaker is to videotape your performance. Although videotaping is obviously not always a practical alternative, it definitely is an educational experience.

An important part of rehearsing the argument is anticipating questions the judges are likely to ask. Prepare for

- questions about the facts of your case;
- questions about the facts of cases cited in the briefs filed with the court;
- questions about arguments raised by your opponent;
- questions about arguments you intend to make but have not raised yet—that is, questions that require you to deviate from your prepared outline; and
- questions about the ramifications of your arguments and the rule or rules you are asking the court to adopt; understand and be able to articulate the policies behind the options available to the court and know your "bottom line"—what are the precise parameters of your arguments and the rule(s) you are advocating?

Although you cannot possibly predict every question the judges will ask during the argument, you will give a much more polished and persuasive presentation if you have anticipated and rehearsed answers to the majority of questions you receive.

7. Advise the Court and Your Opponent of New Information

Information or case law relevant to your case sometimes becomes available after you file your brief. You have an affirmative obligation to advise the court of any new case law that may be dispositive. If you decide that it is necessary to provide newly discovered case law to the court, do so before the argument and send a copy to your opponent at the same time. Not only is this practice a matter of courtesy, it also prevents the court from becoming distracted by reading a document you hand up during your argument.

§ 34.04. THE STRUCTURE OF THE ORAL ARGUMENT

1. Basic Argument Structure

The oral argument, whether presented by appellant or appellee, usually conforms to a basic framework that contains a number of elements:

a. The Introduction

The introduction usually begins with the phrase "[M]ay it please the court," briefly introduces counsel and the party represented by counsel, and reserves time for rebuttal if desired. For example, in the case of *Ace Trucking Co. v. Skinflint Insurance, Inc.*, counsel for appellant Ace Trucking Co. might begin:

> May it please the court, my name is Nancy Schultz, my co-counsel is Annemiek Young, and we represent Ace Trucking Co. We would like to reserve four minutes for rebuttal, with two minutes deducted from each of our arguments.

Then give a brief summary of what the case is about and indicate the relief requested. Your summary offers a good opportunity to explain briefly to the court why your client deserves to win and to set the tone for the rest of your argument. This is a good opportunity to create a "theme" for your argument. A theme is a one-sentence encapsulation of the core of your case that grabs the attention of the court. Themes are frequently used in trial court arguments, and some people will tell you they are more appropriate there, but they also have their place in appellate court. Any time you can help the judges understand the heart of your argument in an interesting and memorable way, you are advocating effectively. For example, in a Fourth Amendment case, you might introduce your case this way: "This case is about protecting our homes from unreasonable intrusion by law enforcement authorities."

b. The Roadmap and Key Facts of the Case

You should always provide the court with a roadmap of your argument. As noted elsewhere, you should be arguing two or three major points to the court, and you should tell the court up front what those points will be. This will allow the court to understand where your argument is going, and it may persuade the judges to wait to question you on particular parts of your argument until you get to them. It may not work that way, but at least you have announced to the court what you will be arguing.

The roadmap should be succinct and straightforward. For example, again assuming that you are arguing a Fourth Amendment case on behalf of the petitioner, whose mobile home was searched using a vision-enhancing device, you might offer this roadmap: "We ask this Court to reverse the decision of the court below for two reasons: (1) Petitioner had a reasonable expectation of privacy in his mobile home, and (2) the police required a warrant before using any kind of vision-enhancing technology."

Immediately following the roadmap, you should offer a very brief statement of key facts that will help the court understand what happened to your client. Ideally this statement will plant the idea that the court would like to find a way to rule for your client to right an injustice. Particularly in moot court competitions, some advocates will "waive a recitation of the facts," meaning they will not set the stage by talking about any facts, and sending the message that the facts do not matter. This is bad practice, as appellate advocates will tell you. Any time you appear in court, you are there on behalf of a client who has a story to tell. The fact that you are in appellate court, where legal issues predominate over factual ones, does not make the facts unimportant. The statement of the facts should be short, accurate, and persuasive. Frame it to present your point of view and the merits of your client's case. It must not be misleading, however, or you will lose credibility with the court. You should emphasize helpful facts, but you must appear fair.

c. The Argument

Providing the bench with a brief outline, or roadmap, of the arguments you intend to make indicates to the judges which arguments you believe are worthy of oral argument and advises them of the order in which you will be making those arguments. An outline enables you to at least mention all of the arguments you have selected, albeit broadly, and may encourage the court to defer its questions until the appropriate time. If you are arguing as appellee and will be presenting arguments in an order different from that used by your opponent, it may be wise to advise the court of that fact.

Present your arguments as you have outlined them. State conclusions first, then support them with facts and law. During your argument, refer to your client by name. This practice both humanizes your client and helps the court keep the parties straight. When referring to the opposing party, most advocates use an appropriate party designation such as "appellant" or "appellee." Expect that a substantial portion of your argument time will be devoted to answering questions from the bench.

d. The Conclusion

When your time has run out, finish your sentence and sit down. Before concluding, make sure you have answered any pending question to the questioner's satisfaction. If you finish your argument before your time has run out, do not keep talking just to fill the time. Present your conclusion and sit down. Conclude your oral argument by providing the court with a short, "punchy" statement of why your client deserves to win and is entitled to the requested relief. Depending upon how your argument has progressed and the time remaining, the conclusion may be a single sentence or it may be more detailed. You should prepare both. If, when time runs out, you have not had an opportunity to conclude, you must ask the court for permission to do so. If a question is pending, you should ask for permission to answer the question as well. The court may or may not grant such permission; for example, the United States Supreme Court will not give extra time.

2. Rebuttal

If, as appellant, you choose to reserve time for rebuttal, be prepared to use that time efficiently and effectively. If you are arguing as part of a team, usually one member of the team will present the entire rebuttal for the side and should be prepared to discuss any issues raised during the argument. In two to five minutes, you cannot rebut every argument made by your opponent. You also may not use this time to raise new issues. Select one or two major points made during the argument that you believe most require clarification or rehabilitation. Remember that your rebuttal is the last thing the judges will hear before they decide your case. Choose your arguments accordingly.

There are other effective ways to use rebuttal time. Listen carefully to your opponent's argument. Your opponent may make statements or mistakes that you can use to your advantage. If you do not have one or two major points that need reinforcing, you may want to use the time to give the court a brief and powerful summary of the reasons your client deserves to win. Some advocates choose to use the time to answer an important question they were unable to answer when the court asked it during the argument.

It may be worthwhile to prepare several possible rebuttals ahead of time. Canned rebuttals, however, are no substitute for listening to your opponent's argument. Tailor your rebuttal to the argument the court actually hears. It also is acceptable to waive your rebuttal if you are satisfied with the way the argument has progressed. The judges are likely to appreciate the time savings, and you send a distinct message of confidence when you waive rebuttal. If, however, you have reserved substantial time for rebuttal, perhaps five minutes or more, you may want to use the time to at least summarize your major arguments for the court. Also, some advocates will tell you that it is a mistake to give up the chance to have the last word. Always close your rebuttal with a request for the specific relief you seek from the court.

§ 34.05. QUESTIONS FROM THE JUDGES

Throughout your argument the judges are likely to interrupt with questions. Questions from the court are desirable because they signal the judges' interest and involvement in the matter. Questions from the bench reveal what the judges' concerns are and permit you to tailor your argument to respond. Oral argument is your only opportunity to directly address the concerns of individual judges. Do not be disturbed if the questions from the bench take you out of your prepared sequence. You use your allotted time most effectively by focusing on those matters about which the court is undecided. Do not consider every question as an attack on your position. Some questions are designed to support your view. If you are asked a helpful question, recognize it and use it to your advantage.

As noted previously, the types of questions the judges ask will vary. A judge might seek information about the facts or raise policy considerations. He or she could ask about the authorities upon which you or your opponent rely for support. You might be asked about the ramifications of a particular legal argument. If you have formulated answers to a variety of questions in advance, you should be able to use most questions to advance your argument.

To handle questions from the bench effectively, remember six basic rules:

1. Listen to the question very carefully. To respond to it, you must fully understand the judge's concerns. Never cut a judge off in the middle of a question.
2. Be sure you understand the question. If you did not understand the question, ask the court to repeat it. If you think you understand the question but are not certain, begin your answer by restating the question.
3. Think before you speak. If you need to think about the question before you can effectively answer it, do so. A brief pause will indicate to the court that you are considering the question and formulating a precise and thorough response.
4. Be responsive. Answer the question directly. If the question calls for a yes or no answer, the first words out of your mouth should be "Yes, Your Honor," or "No, Your Honor." Some first-time advocates have a tendency, particularly early in the argument, to give long, rambling answers that cover much more ground than the question requires. Such an answer may obscure the point you need to make and may bore or confuse your listeners. It also may suggest new questions to the judge.

   Do not hedge when answering a question, or the judge may think that you are being evasive. If the question seeks information you do not have, say so. If you cannot answer a question for other reasons, it sometimes helps to fall back on a general statement of your fundamental argument on the issue. Do not overuse this device.

Seek to explain and clarify your position to the judge's satisfaction. When you believe that you have answered the question and additional inquiries are not immediately forthcoming, move on. Do not wait for a signal from the bench giving you permission to proceed.

5. Be an advocate. Use your responses to the court's questions as a vehicle to present and advance your argument, even if you must depart from the order set out in your outline. If you are interrupted by a judge, be polite and answer the question immediately. Never ask the judge to wait until later in your argument for an answer. Once the court is satisfied with your answers and you have fully presented your arguments on a particular issue or point, make a smooth transition to the next issue or point. Try to get your argument back on track if it has been disrupted by questioning, but if you have fully discussed a point in response to questions, do not go back and present the argument again from your outline. You will waste valuable time and confuse the bench, and you may invite new questions that will force you back into issues you would rather not spend any more time on.

6. Prepare in advance for questions. At the risk of repeating ourselves, good preparation is the key to answering questions. A thorough understanding of your case will permit you to spot both your weak points and your opponents' strong ones. These areas will be the source of many questions from the bench.

Be prepared for a wide variety of personalities on the bench. Some benches take on personalities themselves, which may range from "cold" benches that ask very few questions to "hot" benches that rapidly fire questions at you. Sometimes the judges are not prepared and may not even have read your brief. Others may have read only parts of it. You may get very few questions or an unending stream of questions. You may get thoughtful, probing questions or questions that seem completely irrelevant. Your role in the argument is to address the particular concerns of the court, whatever they may be, and to answer all questions to the best of your ability.

§ 34.06. ORAL ARGUMENT CHECKLIST

— Identify and articulate the fundamental reason or reasons your client deserves to win; prepare a short explanatory statement for use during the argument.

— Select the two or three major points you intend to make during the argument and decide upon the order in which they will be presented.

— Think through the implications of your major arguments and identify the policy goals served by those arguments.

— Identify key facts and prepare a short statement of your client's perspective on those facts, if they are helpful to your case.

— Prepare your introduction, conclusion, roadmap, and outline.

— Anticipate questions and formulate answers to any questions you can be reasonably sure the judges will ask.

— Know the facts, holdings, and rationales of any important cases relied upon by you or your opponent(s).

— Prepare your argument aids, remembering to keep them as short as you can.

Memoranda

MEMORANDUM

TO: Jaded Old Partner
FROM: Eager New Associate
RE: John E. Walker, False Imprisonment Claim

ISSUE

Can a casino patron who is drunk and disruptive recover for false imprisonment under the law of New Jersey when security personnel detain him to "cool off" despite his repeated requests to leave?

CONCLUSION

A casino patron who is drunk and disruptive can recover for false imprisonment under the law of New Jersey when security personnel detain him to "cool off" despite his repeated requests to leave. The two requirements of false imprisonment are met because the patron was under a reasonable apprehension that the security personnel had the authority to detain him and because they did not, in fact, have such authority. There was no legal justification for the detention in this case because the patron was not cheating and had not committed a crime that the casino intended to report to the authorities.

FACTS

Our client, Mr. John E. Walker, recently visited the Empty Pockets Casino in Atlantic City, New Jersey. While there, he lost a great deal of money. Apparently believing that they had a "high roller" on their hands, casino officials instructed the waitresses on the casino floor to provide Mr. Walker with free drinks.

After accepting several free drinks and continuing to lose money, Mr. Walker became somewhat upset and began accusing the dealer and the casino of cheating and of stealing his money. He acknowledges that he was probably a bit loud and may have been annoying other patrons of the casino.

Mr. Walker was approached by two rather large men wearing suits who identified themselves as casino security guards and asked him to accompany them. Mr. Walker noticed that they were wearing identification badges that had the word "security" prominently displayed on them. Mr. Walker accompanied the men to a small room located near the casino floor, where they asked him to sit down and "cool off."

The guards remained with Mr. Walker for approximately two hours, denying his several requests to leave. At the end of this period, the guards told him he was free to go. Mr. Walker would like to know whether he can sue the Empty Pockets Casino for false imprisonment.

DISCUSSION

Mr. Walker has a cause of action for false imprisonment against the Empty Pockets Casino. Under New Jersey law, a cause of action for false imprisonment or false arrest is made out upon a showing that there was an arrest and that the arrest was without legal justification. *Barletta v. Golden Nugget Hotel Casino*, 580 F. Supp. 614, 617 (D.N.J. 1984). In New Jersey, false arrest and false imprisonment are merely different names for the same tort. *Roth v. Golden Nugget Casino/Hotel, Inc.*, 576 F. Supp. 262, 265 (D.N.J. 1983).

Mr. Walker can establish that there was an arrest in his case. He must show that his liberty was constrained as a result of force, or the threat of force, by the defendant. *Id.* New Jersey courts have held that "the assertion of legal authority to take a person into custody, even where such authority does not in fact exist, may be sufficient to create a reasonable apprehension that a person is under restraint." *Bartolo v. Boardwalk Regency Hotel Casino*, 449 A.2d 1339, 1341 (N.J. Super. L. Div. 1982, 185 N.J. Super. 534, 537).

The court in *Barletta* found that an arrest had taken place where the plaintiff was escorted to the casino security office by two security officers after an altercation between the plaintiff and another casino patron. The fact that the plaintiff accompanied the security officers under her own power did not affect her claim where she testified that she did not feel free to refuse. The court in *Roth* found an arrest under virtually identical circumstances.

Mr. Walker's situation closely parallels the cited cases. He, too, was asked to accompany security officers from the casino floor, and, by his own account, did not feel that he was in a position to refuse. Here, as in *Barletta* and *Roth*, a court should find that there was a reasonable apprehension of force.

Mr. Walker should also be able to establish that the restraint was without legal justification. There are two possible justifications for the restraint that the casino might raise, but neither of them is likely to be accepted by a court.

First, the casino might argue that the security officers were entitled to detain Mr. Walker under a broad interpretation of the New Jersey statute that allows casinos to detain patrons upon suspicion of various offenses, all of which involve cheating. N.J. Stat. Ann. § 5:12-121(b) (West 1977). Such a broad interpretation of the statute was rejected by the court in *Bartolo*. In that case the plaintiff was detained on suspicion of card counting, which the court held could not be equated with cheating. If card counting does not constitute cheating and therefore does not come within the ambit of § 5:12-121(b), being drunk and disorderly is certainly not a ground for detention under that section.

Alternatively, the casino might argue that it was entitled to detain Mr. Walker under the statutory provision that allows any person to detain another who commits a disorderly persons offense in the detainer's presence. N.J. Stat. Ann. § 2A:169-3 (West 1979). However, that statute has also been narrowly construed by the courts. In *Roth*, the court held that a disorderly persons offense must actually have occurred before an arrest without a warrant will be justified. There, the court denied defendant's motion for summary judgment because there was a genuine factual dispute as to whether plaintiff had committed the offense of criminal trespass.

It is not entirely clear whether Mr. Walker committed a disorderly persons offense, but the casino security personnel did not accuse him of committing one and took no steps to bring him before the proper authorities as is required by § 2A:169-3. Although the cases do not address the significance of the phrase "and take him before any magistrate," the previous narrow constructions of the statute would suggest that this phrase should also be read literally. Thus, the casino's failure to follow the procedure outlined by the statute should negate its claim of legal justification for the detention.

In Mr. Walker's case, the security guards simply told him that they wanted him to "cool off," and, when they were satisfied that he had done so, let him go. Such a detention is not authorized by the statutes or the decided cases. We should pursue a claim for false imprisonment on Mr. Walker's behalf.

MEMORANDUM

PRIVILEGED AND CONFIDENTIAL

TO: Paul Partner
FROM: Adam Associate
DATE: December 14, 2009
FILE NO.:   025499-0001
RE: Liability of individuals for discrimination under the DCHRA

I. QUESTION PRESENTED

Can individuals be liable for harassment and discrimination in violation of the District of Columbia Human Rights Act ("DCHRA")?

II. SHORT ANSWER

Yes. Both the plain language of the statute and case law allow individuals to be liable for violation of the statute. However, in each case to consider the issue, the court has found liability only with regard to individuals occupying a *managerial or supervisory* capacity. It is unclear whether the supervisor must have authority over the plaintiff in order to be subject to liability.

III. RELEVANT FACTUAL BACKGROUND

In February 2008, plaintiff Steven Smith ("Smith") amended his complaint to assert causes of action for discrimination under the DCHRA against individual employees of his former employer, Cafe Asia. Specifically, Smith alleged claims against May Stiltz, Karen Saweed, Joey Yimmer, Abu Baker, Elias Treer, and Shawn Yo in their individual capacities. Their specific job titles are as follows:

May Stiltz:	day manager
Karen Saweed:	operations manager
Joey Yimmer:	night manager
Abu Baker:	kitchen/chef supervisor
Elias Treer:	Abu's supervisor
Shawn Yo:	owner

IV. DISCUSSION

A. According to the Plain Language of the DCHRA, Any Individual Who Acts in Their Employer's Interest, or Who Aids and Abets Discrimination, Is Amenable to Suit.

Our analysis begins with the plain language of the DCHRA. Section 2-1402.11 provides that

(a) It shall be an unlawful discriminatory practice to do any of the following acts, wholly or partially for a discriminatory reason based upon the actual or perceived: race, color, religion, national origin, sex, age, marital status, personal appearance, sexual orientation, gender identity or expression, family responsibilities, genetic information, disability, matriculation, or political affiliation of any individual:

(1) By an employer.—To fail or refuse to hire, or to discharge, any individual; or otherwise to discriminate against any individual, with respect to his compensation, terms, conditions, or privileges of employment, including promotion; or to limit, segregate, or classify his employees in any way which would deprive or tend to deprive any individual of employment opportunities, or otherwise adversely affect his status as an employee[.]

D.C. Code § 2-1402.11(a)(1). The DCHRA further makes it unlawful "for any person to aid, abet, invite, compel, or coerce the doing of any of the acts forbidden" by the Act. *Id.*§ 2-1402.62. The DCHRA defines "employer" as "any person who, for compensation, employs an individual, . . . [or] any person acting in the interest of such employer, directly or indirectly." *Id.*§ 2-1401.02. As the foregoing citations make clear, the DCHRA is apparently not limited to constraining only the employing entity, but extends as well to "any person acting in the interest of such an employer," as well as "any person" who aids, abets, or otherwise assists in violating the DCHRA.

This broad definition appears to allow suit against individuals, especially when compared to Title VII's definition of employer. Title VII defines "employer" as "a person engaged in an industry affecting commerce who has fifteen or more employees . . . and *any agent of such a person*." 42 U.S.C. § 2000e(b). Generally, courts to construe the italicized language have held that "the obvious purpose of this agent provision was to incorporate respondeat superior liability into the statute," *Gary v. Long*, 313 U.S. App. D.C. 403, 411 (1995) (citation omitted), and that "individual employees cannot be held liable under Title VII." *Sheridan v. E.I. DuPont de Nemours & Co.*, 100 F.3d 1061, 1077-1078 (3d Cir. 1996). The DCHRA is not confined to cover only the acts of "agents," but by its terms applies to "*any person*" acting in the interest of an employer or who otherwise aids and abets prohibited conduct. Thus, based on its plain language, the DCHRA appears to apply to any employee—even nonmanagerial employees—who are deemed to have discriminated, or aided in discrimination, if the employee is also "acting in the interest" of an employer.

B. Cases to Construe the DCHRA Have Allowed Suit to Proceed Against Partners, Supervisors, Managers, and Executive Officers in Their Individual Capacity.

The majority of cases to consider the question of an individual's amenability to suit under the DCHRA have concluded that a case under that statute may properly be brought against individuals. *See, e.g., Purcell v. Thomas*, 928 A.2d 699, 715 (D.C. 2007) ("[W]e hold that because Mr. Purcell was a high level official of [the corporate defendant] who exercised extensive supervisory, management and administrative authority over the corporation, he was individually liable to Ms. Thomas under the DCHRA"); Wallace v. Skadden, Arps, Slate, Meagher & Flom, 715 A.2d 873, 888 (D.C. 1998) (holding that partners of law firm could be liable in individual capacity under DCHRA); *but see Hunter v. Ark Restaurants Corp.*, 3 F. Supp. 2d 9, 15-18 (D.D.C. 1998) (holding that individual employees cannot be liable under DCHRA);[1] Hodges v. Wash. Tennis Serv. Intl. 870 F. Supp. 386, 387 (D.D.C. 1994) (dismissing an individual defendant, who was "not a proper party because

---

1. *Hunter* was decided before the final *Wallace* opinion was published.

neither Title VII, 42 U.S.C. § 1981, nor the District of Columbia Human Rights law creates grounds for a cognizable claim against a co-worker").

1.   The *Purcell* Decision Constitutes the Most Recent Interpretation of the DCHRA.

The *Purcell* case provides the most recent analysis of whether a DCHRA claim can be asserted against an individual. In that case, the court squarely considered whether Purcell, an individual and supervisor of the plaintiff, could be liable under the provisions of the DCHRA. *Purcell*, 928 A.2d at 702. In that case, the plaintiff alleged that Purcell made numerous sexual advances toward her, continually made inappropriate comments, and eventually terminated her for refusing to give in to his demands. *Id.* at 703-706. Purcell was the president, COO, controlling shareholder, and director of Fedora, the company for which the plaintiff worked. *Id.* at 715. Purcell was also the plaintiff's supervisor. *Id.* The court held that Purcell "was individually liable to Ms. Thomas under the DCHRA" because he was "acting, directly or indirectly, in the interest of Fedora and hence fell within DCHRA's definition of employer." *Id.*

In so holding, the court referred to its decision in *Wallace*, in which law partners were found to be "employers" under the DCHRA. *Id.* at 714 (citing *Wallace*, 715 A.2d at 888-889). Next, the court observed that the District Court for the District of Columbia "has found that supervisors are subject to individual liability." *Id.* at 715 (citing *Mitchell v. Natl. R.R. Passenger Corp.*, 407 F. Supp. 2d 213 (D.D.C. 2005); *MacIntosh v. Bldg. Owners & Managers Assn.*, 335 F. Supp. 2d 223 (D.D.C. 2005); and *Lance v. United Mine Workers of Am. 1974 Pension Trust*, 400 F. Supp. 2d 29 (D.D.C. 2005)). The court also noted that "[o]ther jurisdictions have imposed individual liability upon management and supervisory employees under state law in employment discrimination cases." *Id.* at 716 (citing cases).

2.   The *Wallace* Decision Was the First Decision to Allow Individual Liability Under the DCHRA, and Is the Starting Point for Nearly All Subsequent Cases.

As with the *Purcell* decision, many cases to find individual liability under the DCHRA have cited to *Wallace* as important, if not dispositive, of their analysis. *See, e.g., Mitchell*, 407 F. Supp. 2d at 241 (discussing *Wallace*); *MacIntosh*, 335 F. Supp. 2d at 227-228 (discussing *Wallace*); *Lance*, 400 F. Supp. 2d at 31 (discussing *Wallace*). As such, a discussion of the *Wallace* decision is appropriate.

In *Wallace*, a former Skadden Arps attorney filed suit against the law firm and some of its individual partners for various causes of action, including defamation and violation of the DCHRA. *Wallace*, 715 A.2d at 875-876. After a series of procedural machinations that are not germane to the present discussion, the trial judge dismissed Wallace's DCHRA claim against the three Skadden Arps partners, holding that the individuals were "not amenable to suit in their individual capacities." *Id.* at 887. The plaintiff appealed, and the appellate court reversed.

In deciding that the individual partners could be liable under the DCHRA, the court focused on the language of the statute prohibiting "any person acting in the interest of such employer, directly or indirectly," from violating the provisions of the DCHRA. *Id.* at 888. The court attributed the "normal everyday meaning" to this language and concluded "that the partners fall within the ambit of the statute." *Id.* The court further noted that if the quoted language "does not extend to a partner in a law firm, it is difficult to conceive of any person to whom it would apply." *Id.*

The court then bolstered its conclusion by referencing the "aiding and abetting" language of the DCHRA. *Id.* ("Moreover, if Skadden, Arps unlawfully discriminated . . . then the partners who carried out the allegedly discriminatory acts aided and abetted the employer's discrimination. . . ."). The court further stated that the individual partners could be liable for violating the DCHRA under the "aiding and abetting" section "[e]ven if [the court] were to assume that the individual partners are not employers." *Id.*

The *Wallace* court then rejected the defendants' argument that the DCHRA is patterned on, and should be construed like, Title VII. *Id.* at 888-889. The *Wallace* court conceded that, in interpreting the DCHRA, courts have generally looked to, and in appropriate cases adopted, Title VII decisions. *Id.* at 889 n. 31. The court observed that the majority of relevant Title VII decisions "have held that individual employees cannot be held liable under Title VII." *Id.* at 888-889. However, the *Wallace* court declined to follow Title VII precedent because that legislation "does not contain the phrase 'any person acting in the interest of such employer,'" and because "there is no provision in Title VII proscribing 'aiding and abetting.'" *Id.* at 889. The court observed that although Title VII does define "employer" to include "any agent" of an employer, "'the obvious purpose of this agent provision was to incorporate *respondeat superior* liability into the statute.'" *Id.* at 889 n. 32 (citing cases). In contrast, the court reasoned, the plain language of the DCHRA includes "within the term 'employer' any person who acts on the employer's behalf." *Id.* As such, the DCHRA has a broader applicability than its federal counterpart.

3.   All Cases to Allow Individual Liability Under the DCHRA Have Involved Managerial or Supervisory Employees.

Notably, in both the *Purcell* and *Wallace* decisions, the courts did not rely on the individual defendants' supervisory or managerial authority in deciding that the individuals were amenable to suit under the DCHRA. Indeed, as was discussed earlier, the plain language of the statute appears to allow *any individual*—regardless of status as a supervisor—to be liable under the DCHRA. Notwithstanding the plain language of the statute, however, there does not appear to be a case in which an individual, nonsupervisory employee was found to be liable under the DCHRA.

In the cases considering whether individuals can be sued under the DCHRA, the individual is almost always a high-level manager or company executive. For example:

- *Wallace*, 715 A.2d at 889: "[W]e therefore hold that the Skadden Arps *partners* were properly joined as defendants." (emphasis added)
- *Martini v. Fed. Natl. Mortgage Assn.*, 977 F. Supp. 464, 479 (D.D.C. 1997): "[T]he Court concludes that individual *supervisors* can be held liable for their acts of discrimination." (emphasis added)
- *Russ v. Van Scoyoc Assocs., Inc.*, 59 F. Supp. 2d 20, 24-26 (D.D.C. 1999): following *Martini*, and allowing suit under the DCHRA to be brought against Stuart Van Scoyoc, the *president of the corporation* that employed the plaintiff and plaintiff's supervisor.
- *MacIntosh*, 355 F. Supp. 2d at 227-28: relying on *Wallace* and finding that the *Executive Director* and *Vice President of Advocacy and Research* for plaintiff's employer could be sued in their individual capacities under the DCHRA.
- *Lance*, 400 F. Supp. 2d at 32: citing *MacIntosh* as stating that "a plaintiff [may] maintain suit against individual *supervisors* in a DCHRA action"; and finding *MacIntosh* consistent with *Russ*, "in which this court held that under the DCHRA a *supervisor* could be sued in his individual capacity." (emphasis added)

- *Mitchell*, 407 F. Supp. 2d at 241: reasoning that "[t]he text and purpose of the DCHRA, and *Wallace*, do not suggest that it would be appropriate to follow Title VII here and preclude a claim against individual *management* and *supervisory* employees involved in committing the allegedly discriminatory conduct"; holding that "Green [the former *director of the Workforce Development* unit in the HR Department] and Porter [the *Vice President of the HR Department*] . . . are proper defendants in plaintiff's DCHRA claim." (emphasis added)

Indeed, even the magistrate judge's decision in our case suggested that only management or supervisory employees could be defendants in Smith's DCHRA claim. *See Smith v. Cafe Asia*, 598 F. Supp. 2d 45, 48-49 (D.D.C. 2009). ("[T]he amended complaint alleges that the additional individual defendants were *managers* . . . the facts alleged regarding these *supervisory management employees* reflect that they acted in the interest of their employer . . . [whether] the individual employees fit that definition is not to be resolved at this stage.") (emphasis added).

Just as no case has ever held that a nonsupervisory employee is liable under the DCHRA, no case has stated that such employees are exempt from liability. Furthermore, no case has commented on whether an individual defendant must be the *plaintiff's* supervisor or whether *any* supervisor is a proper defendant under the DCHRA.

V. CONCLUSION

Although the plain language of the DCHRA allows for any individual to be liable for discrimination, all cases to construe the DCHRA in the context of individual's amenability to suit have involved a managerial employee. There is no authority addressing whether the individual sued under the DCHRA must be one of the plaintiff's supervisors.

For questions regarding the foregoing, please contact Adam Associate.

MEMORANDUM

TO: Jayne Taylor Kacer
FROM: Regan Dean
RE: Jeffrey Bing—Claim of Self-defense

Question Presented

Will Mr. Bing's act of shooting Mr. Geller be protected by the Illinois Self-defense Statute, which specifies that an individual is justified in the use of force that is intended or likely to cause death or great bodily harm if the individual (1) reasonably believes that he or she is in imminent danger of death or great bodily harm and (2) reasonably believes that such force is necessary to prevent imminent death or great bodily harm to himself (or herself) or another, or the commission of a forcible felony? 720 Ill. Comp. Stat. 5/7-1, 1961.

1. Did Bing reasonably believe that he was in imminent danger of great bodily harm or death if his assailant was armed with a deadly weapon, had already cut another, was undeterred by attempts to avoid a confrontation, and had a known history of violent and explosive behavior?
2. Did Bing have a reasonable belief that deadly force was necessary if he made numerous attempts to avoid the use of such force either by apologizing, retreating, or warning that he would retaliate if necessary prior to shooting?

Short Answer

Yes, our client has a strong claim that he acted in self-defense in accordance with the elements of the Self-defense Statute.

1. First, Bing had a reasonable belief that he was in imminent danger of death or great bodily harm because his assailant was armed with a deadly weapon. The assailant continued to advance on our client despite knowledge that Bing was armed, threats against Bing's life were made by his assailant, and his assailant was well known as a violent individual.
2. Second, our client had a reasonable belief that deadly force was necessary to prevent imminent danger of death or great bodily harm because all of the efforts he employed to avoid the use of such force proved futile, including defendant's attempts to apologize, retreat, and warn the assailant.

Statement of Facts

Our client, Jeffrey Bing, has been charged with the murder of his close friend of six years, John Geller. Bing claims he acted in self-defense. Bing and Geller had a friendship that was occasionally marred by violence. They attended college together (four years ago), where Geller ran cross-country. During college Bing sustained injuries (swollen knuckles, bloody noses, black eye) resulting from fights with Geller (6', 190 pounds), who was slightly larger than Bing (5'11", 175 pounds). However, more serious injuries were always averted when Bing, who is not particularly athletic, pleaded with Geller to stop. They have not had any fights since college, but one year ago Bing and another friend, Newton, had to pull Geller off his roommate after a violent fight wherein the roommate suffered a broken rib, black eye, and multiple bruises.

On the day of the incident, Bing and Geller were on a camping trip with their friend, Mr. Newton. They stopped five minutes from their lodge because Bing was winded. Newton then began joking with Bing about Jill Jacoby. Jacoby was Geller's former girlfriend with whom Bing had recently spent a weekend in New York. Bing previously concealed this information from Geller, and in fact had lied to Geller about the identity of his New York companion. Upon learning the truth, Geller became enraged. Newton later told the police that Geller "went beserk."

Mr. Geller pounced on Bing, threw him on the ground, and began beating Bing's face with his fists. Bing apologized for his actions, but Geller continued to beat Bing. Newton attempted to stop Geller by shouting at him to "calm down," but Geller replied: "Stay out of this. My fight is with Jeff." Newton attempted to physically separate the men and, in doing so, was cut on the arm by Geller, who brandished a hunting knife he retrieved from his knapsack. Newton then decided to run for assistance to the lodge nearby and stated that he had "never seen [Geller] like this before." While Newton left the scene for help, Geller, who continued to brandish his knife, and Bing, at this point unarmed, began circling each other. Geller attempted to charge at Bing, and when the men were separated by about twenty feet, Bing produced a gun from his knapsack that he had carried with him for safety while hiking. Bing attempted to keep Geller at bay by waving his gun around as the men continued to circle each other for about five minutes. During this time, Bing pleaded with Geller to "calm down," but Geller told Bing that he would "kill [Bing] for this." Bing warned that he would use his gun if necessary to which Geller replied, "Only one of us is getting out of here alive." At that moment, Geller charged at Bing, and when Geller was between five and ten feet away from Bing, Mr. Bing shot Geller, pulling the trigger once.

Discussion

Mr. Bing acted in self-defense under the Illinois statute for "use of force in defense of person" (hereinafter Self-defense Statute). Pursuant to the Self-defense Statute, Bing is "justified in the use of force which is intended or likely to cause death or great bodily harm only if he reasonably believes that such force is necessary to prevent imminent death or great bodily harm to himself or another, or the commission of a forcible felony." 720 Ill. Comp. Stat. 5/7-1. In order to successfully claim self-defense, two elements must be met, namely that Bing maintained a reasonable belief that he was in imminent danger of death or great bodily harm and also that Bing reasonably believed the degree of force used was necessary to prevent such harm to himself. If belief is merely subjective, Bing cannot claim self-defense. That Mr. Bing subjectively believed that he was in imminent danger of death or great bodily harm is presumed to be true given the facts and is not addressed in this memorandum. This memorandum will discuss whether Mr. Bing had a reasonable belief that he was in danger of death or great bodily harm and that Bing reasonably believed the degree of force used was necessary to prevent such harm.

Mr. Bing Had a Reasonable Belief that He Was in Imminent Danger of Death or Great Bodily Harm.

Mr. Bing had a reasonable belief that he was in imminent danger of either death or great bodily harm. In determining whether a reasonable belief exists, the courts evaluate various factors including whether the assailant had a weapon, whether the assailant was deterred by attempts made to de-escalate the situation, the known history of violence of one or both parties, the comparative physical size of the attacker and the defendant, the mental state of the assailant, and whether the defendant was cornered. Geller not only brandished a weapon, but used it to harm a third party. Geller was undeterred by the efforts made by Bing to curtail the situation. There is a known history of violence by Geller directed toward Bing and others. Geller was said to be acting in an irrational manner, and Geller was a bigger and more athletic man than Bing.

A person reasonably believes that s/he is in imminent danger of death or great bodily harm when s/he is outnumbered by drunken, armed assailants who are undeterred by attempts to avoid a confrontation. In *People v. S.M.*, 416 N.E.2d 1212 (Ill. App. 1st Dist. 1981), the defendant's belief that he was in imminent danger of death or great bodily harm was found to be reasonable because he was outnumbered four to one and cornered by his assailants; his attackers had been drinking and were all bigger than he; the assailants had weapons, which they threw at the defendant; and his attackers were not discouraged by the defendant's gun nor by his warning that he would use it. In *S.M.*, the defendant made an offensive comment to a group of four older, more athletic boys after he was nearly hit by their car. The defendant immediately apologized for his comment upon realizing that the boys were upset. However, the boys advanced on the defendant, who then fled. The assailants continued to chase the defendant, throwing asphalt and tin cans at him. The defendant yelled out for help, but was eventually cornered and unable to escape. The defendant had a gun because he was initially intending to hunt for raccoons, and he brandished it to scare off his attackers. However, the assailants were unfazed by the gun and continued to advance, which prompted the defendant to fire a warning shot and verbally warn the attackers that he would shoot if necessary. Upon realizing that the attackers remained undeterred in their pursuit, the defendant shot and killed two of the assailants and wounded two others. The jury found the defendant guilty of the commission of two counts of aggravated battery. The court of appeal reversed, holding that the defendant's fear of imminent great bodily harm or death was reasonable under the circumstances. 93 Ill. App. 3d 105.

A person has a reasonable belief that s/he is in imminent danger of death or great bodily harm when there is a known history of the assailant's propensity for violent behavior. In *People v. Shipp*, 367 N.E.2d 966 (Ill. App. 2d Dist. 1977), the defendant knew the assailant was capable of causing her great bodily harm or death with or without a weapon. The assailant was undeterred in his pursuit of the defendant and made threatening comments to the life of both the defendant and her male friend. The facts of *Shipp* describe a long history of violence between the assailant and the defendant. The defendant sustained numerous severe injuries resulting from beatings and gunshots fired at her by the assailant, whom she knew had killed his first wife. Eventually, the defendant obtained a restraining order against the assailant, which was meant to prevent the assailant from harassing, annoying, or talking to the defendant. However, this did not prevent the assailant from continuing to harm the defendant both verbally and physically. The assailant made numerous threats against the defendant's life, including holding a knife to her throat and telling her that he would cut her throat and go to the penitentiary. The assailant further warned her that he would kill her if he ever caught her with another man. On the night in question, after leaving a bar, the assailant went to the home of a man with whom the defendant was spending the evening. When the assailant entered the bedroom, the defendant became frightened and picked up a gun; she backed away from the assailant who continued to walk toward her with his hands in his pockets, not revealing whether he was armed. The assailant continued to approach her despite verbal warnings not to come any closer or the defendant would shoot, and then cornered the defendant saying that he was going to "take care" of both the defendant and her male companion who was hiding under the bed. When the assailant was six feet away from the defendant she shot and killed him. The jury acquitted the defendant of murder and unlawful use of weapons, but convicted her of voluntary manslaughter. The Appellate Court reversed, and the court believed the defendant's fear of imminent danger of great bodily harm to be reasonable. The court stated, "It is the defendant's perception of danger, and not the actual peril, which was dispositive."

Application of the factors recognized in the aforementioned cases to the Bing situation leaves little doubt that the court will find that Bing's fear that he was in imminent danger of death or great bodily harm was reasonable. Geller had a deadly weapon, which he was clearly not afraid to use, as evidenced when he cut Newton's arm. In *People v. S.M.*, the weapons used by the assailants, asphalt and tin cans, do not merit the same potential to cause death or great bodily harm as a knife. And in *People v. Shipp*, it was unclear if there even was a weapon, yet the court found the defendant's fear to be reasonable. Thus, the fear of a defendant whose attacker is armed with a deadly weapon that he has used on a third party will most likely be considered reasonable by the court.

Like the attackers in *S.M.* and *Shipp*, Geller was undeterred despite both Newton's and Bing's attempts to calm him down, the fact that Bing had a gun, and that Bing gave several warnings that he would shoot Geller if necessary. Based on prior altercations involving Geller and Bing, Bing's efforts to plead with Geller to calm down would have been sufficient, yet his employment of those efforts immediately prior to the shooting proved futile. In fact, Geller continued to make threats against Bing's life and charge at Bing while brandishing his weapon following Bing's warnings.

Like the defendant in *Shipp*, Bing had knowledge of Geller's propensity for violent behavior and knew firsthand that he was capable of inflicting harm upon another person when angry. The court in *People v. Shipp* believed such knowledge justifies the reasonableness of one's fear of great bodily harm.

Although Geller had not been drinking, as had the assailants in *S.M.* and *Shipp*, Geller was enraged and consumed by an unpredictable state of mind. The notion that Geller was acting out of character was reinforced by Newton's comment, "I've never seen him like this before." Additionally, while each court makes reference to the stature of the parties, it does not appear to be a primary factor in their determination of whether there was a reasonable belief of imminent danger of death or great bodily harm. There was only a slight disparity in the physical size of Bing and Geller; therefore this will not be a compelling argument for our case.

In determining whether the defendant had a reasonable belief that he was in imminent danger of death or great bodily harm, the court in *People v. Moore*, 357 N.E.2d 566 (Ill. App. 1st Dist. 1976), considered many of the same factors as the courts in *S.M.* and *Shipp*, namely whether the assailant had a weapon, whether the assailant was undeterred, the comparative physical size, and a history of violent behavior. Between the parties the defendant had previously engaged in a physical altercation with the decedent in which the defendant was the aggressor. On the night in question, the defendant said something that caused the decedent to get upset with him. The defendant then informed all present that he had a gun. He left the scene and went home to retrieve his gun. Upon returning, the decedent threatened to beat up the defendant. The onlookers held the decedent away from the defendant to avoid a fight. The defendant had an opportunity at this moment to leave and put the gun away, which he was encouraged to do by the onlookers. However, the defendant remained outside and stated that he would shoot the decedent if he came near him. The defendant eventually shot the decedent while he was fifty feet away. The court held that there was no reasonable belief that the defendant was in imminent danger of great bodily harm or death and upheld the jury's finding of voluntary manslaughter. The decedent was unarmed, there was substantial distance between the men at the time of the shooting, the defendant did not attempt to flee, and the defendant stated his intention to harm the decedent. The court acknowledged the disparity in stature of the parties, but said that despite the fact that the decedent was advantaged in physical size, this factor was irrelevant because only the defendant was armed.

The *Moore* case is distinguishable from the Bing situation as the defendant in *Moore* was the aggressor, while Bing acted in self-defense. Additionally, unlike *Moore*, Geller was between five and ten feet away and charging at Bing with a deadly weapon at the moment Bing pulled the trigger. In *Moore*, the threat to the defendant was less imminent because there was fifty feet between parties, the decedent was unarmed, and there was an opportunity for the defendant to avoid the situation altogether.

Mr. Bing Reasonably Believed Force Was Necessary to Prevent Imminent Death or Great Bodily Harm to Himself.

Bing reasonably believed that his use of force was necessary to prevent imminent death or great bodily harm to himself under the circumstances of his situation. The court determines whether the necessity to prevent imminent death or great bodily harm has been fulfilled by examining the efforts made by the defendant, such as apologizing, retreating, giving verbal warnings, brandishing, or firing a warning shot to avoid a physical confrontation. Bing made several such attempts. Bing apologized to Geller, he pleaded with Geller to calm down, and he attempted to keep distance between them. Additionally Bing brandished a weapon to scare Geller off and warned that he would shoot if necessary. Each attempt Bing made was ignored by Geller, who persisted in his advancement.

A person reasonably believes that deadly force is necessary to prevent imminent death or great bodily harm to himself or another when the defendant makes repeated efforts to avoid an altercation, such as apologizing, retreating, yelling for help, pleading with attackers to stop, brandishing a weapon, giving verbal warnings as well as firing a warning shot. In *S.M.*, the defendant was clearly desperate and did not want to resort to such action, but under the circumstances, felt that it was necessary. The defendant in *S.M.* employed each of the described efforts to avoid an altercation; additionally, he did not advance toward the attackers and he unsuccessfully sought help from the onlookers before he resorted to shooting his assailants. The court acknowledged each effort made by the defendant to resolve the situation and held that the defendant maintained a reasonable belief that the force employed was necessary.

To determine whether a person reasonably believes that deadly force is necessary to prevent imminent death or great bodily harm, the court in *People v. Shipp* examined the avoidance attempts made by the defendant. Upon the assailant's entrance, the defendant in *Shipp* brandished a weapon, presupposing a threat. The defendant then verbally warned her attacker, telling him that he was violating a restraining order. She pleaded for him to stay away and to the extent that it was possible, the defendant attempted to keep distance between her and the assailant by moving backwards, and it was not until she was cornered that she shot him. There were fewer efforts to avoid the use of a firearm by the defendant in this case than in *S.M.*, but the ruling was the same. The court ruled that the defendant was justified in her actions, stating that her fear was "highly reasonable under the circumstances" and that her actions were necessary.

Bing engaged in many of the same efforts employed by the defendants in the cited cases with no success. For example, like the defendants in *S.M.* and *Shipp*, Bing apologized to his assailant and pleaded with him to calm down. Similarly, Bing retreated to the best of his ability, brandished a gun, and gave verbal warning that he would shoot prior to doing so.

In determining whether a person reasonably believes that deadly force is necessary to prevent imminent death or great bodily harm to himself (or herself) or another, the court in *People v. Moore* examined avoidance techniques. The defendant in *Moore* had ample opportunity to avoid the situation and did not. There was no pleading, apologizing, warning, or retreat, and Moore was recognized as the aggressor in this situation. The court emphasized these facts: Moore could have avoided the altercation, he expressed intent to shoot the decedent, and he shot him from fifty feet away. Moore's use of force was not found to be reasonable under the circumstances because he demonstrated intent to cause harm instead of making efforts to avoid using force.

The court should recognize the significant variances in the two situations and find that, while no reasonable belief of the necessity to use deadly force existed for Moore, it did exist for Bing. Unlike the defendant in *Moore*, Bing made repeated attempts to avoid the use of force, while in *Moore*, the defendant demonstrated intent to rely on an unjustifiable amount of force. The disparity in the distance between the parties at the moment the force was used and Bing's attempts to reconcile the conflict without force will differentiate the cases and demonstrate that Bing should be acquitted of voluntary manslaughter because a reasonable belief to justify his use of force existed.

Conclusion

Bing can successfully claim self-defense. He reasonably believed that he was in imminent danger of death or great bodily harm because his assailant was armed with a deadly weapon, his assailant was undeterred despite knowledge that Bing was armed, he had a history of violent behavior, and he demonstrated an unpredictable state of mind. He also reasonably believed that deadly force was necessary to prevent imminent death or great bodily harm to himself because all of the efforts he employed to avoid the use of such force proved futile.

MEMORANDUM

TO: Jayne Taylor Kacer
FROM: Regan Dean
DATE: November 25, 2002
RE: Andrea Johnston—Defense to Claim of Negligence

Question(s) Presented

Is Andrea Johnston liable for negligence?

1. Was it foreseeable that her car would be stolen when she parked her highly visible Porsche sportscar on a public street with the keys in the sun visor and the doors unlocked in an area she was unfamiliar with as to its reputation and crime rate, while she entered a store with the intention of being away from her car for a few minutes?
2. Was it foreseeable that an unauthorized person would cause injury while driving Ms. Johnston's Porsche, which is not an inherently dangerous vehicle and requires no special knowledge to operate other than that required to drive an automobile?

Short Answer

No, Ms. Johnston will most likely not be found liable for negligence.

1. It was not foreseeable that her car would be stolen because Ms. Johnston was unaware of the crime rate in the neighborhood, she intended to leave her car unattended on a public street for only a few minutes, and the car is one that a reasonable person would not expect to be stolen because it is so readily identifiable.
2. It was not foreseeable that an unauthorized person would cause injury while driving Ms. Johnston's car because the car requires no special skill to operate, nor is it an inherently dangerous vehicle.

Statement of Facts

Our client, Andrea Johnston, is alleged to be negligent resulting in injuries sustained by the plaintiff, Bonnie Smythe, from a car accident in which an unauthorized person operating Ms. Johnston's car collided with plaintiff's parked car. Ms. Johnston is a well-known professional racecar driver who resides in Florida. The vehicle involved in the accident is Ms. Johnston's lipstick red Porsche, which she purchased two years ago. The Porsche has been modified to include wing-like appendages attached to the doors and a manual transmission engine traditionally found in racecars. The body of the car has been reinforced with roll bars added to better withstand an impact from a collision. Additionally, the car is able to accelerate to speeds over 185 mph. The car has had celebrity exposure and is widely recognized because Ms. Johnston has raced it in various celebrity pro-am races, and the car has also been featured on the David Letterman show in a skit involving Ms. Johnston.

On the day in question, Ms. Johnston was in Missouri to attend a race and stopped at a store, Party City, on her way to the race to pick up some refreshments. Party City is located on Delmont Street, in the Central East End, which has undergone a recent transformation from a seedy, dilapidated area to a trendy neighborhood with many popular restaurants and shops. Despite its renovated appeal, the area is three blocks from the highest-crime community in St. Louis, an area called Crimtown. This area has received much publicity because of the propensity for nearby high-schoolers to steal cars. Ms. Johnston, being from Florida, was unaware of the former reputation of Delmont Street and that of its adjoining community, Crimtown. She intended to be inside Party City for only a couple of minutes to pick out a specific item. Ms. Johnston parked her car on a public street in front of the store, rolled up her windows, but placed her keys in the sun visor above the driver's seat and left the doors unlocked. While inside, Ms. Johnston checked on her car one time and it was empty. Ms. Johnston was slightly delayed while in the store, but left the car alone outside for no more than eight to ten minutes total.

When Ms. Johnston drove up to Party City, a woman standing at the bus stop across the street watched Ms. Johnston put her keys on the visor and enter the store. The thirty-five-year-old woman, Barbara Mandible, was late for a paid singing engagement and decided to take Ms. Johnston's car in order to arrive on time. Ms. Mandible drove the car over the 55 mph speed limit and was spotted by a police officer who followed her. Mandible then began to increase her speed to over 100 mph and spun out of control, colliding with the plaintiff's parked car occupied by the plaintiff. The plaintiff sustained numerous injuries when she was thrown from her Volkswagen, which was flattened by the Porsche. Upon recovery, the plaintiff will forever walk with a limp.

Discussion

Ms. Johnston will most likely not be found liable for negligence. A Missouri statute formerly addressed the issue of liability for car owners who left their vehicles unlocked, unattended with the keys readily available in Mo. Rev. Stat. § 304.150 (repealed by L.1996). The statute made it a misdemeanor for motor vehicle operators to leave the car keys in the ignition while unattended on a highway of any city with a population over 75,000, but stated that evidence of the statute and/or its violation was barred in a civil action. The statute was repealed in 1997 and will therefore not factor into the analysis contained in this memorandum. The fact that this statute was repealed, however, does seem favorable for our client, as it suggests that there is no longer any criminal liability for leaving a car unattended with the keys in the ignition. Prior case law in this area reveals that individuals who leave their vehicle unattended with the keys in the ignition are not found to be negligent when unauthorized third persons steal the car and operate it negligently. The determinative issues that will be discussed in this memorandum are the defendant's (1) foreseeability of theft and (2) foreseeability of injury resulting from unauthorized negligent operation.

Issue I. It Was Not Foreseeable that Ms. Johnston's Car Would be Stolen.

It was not foreseeable to Ms. Johnston that theft would result from leaving her keys in the sun visor while she left her car unattended for what she anticipated would be a few minutes in an area that appeared safe. In determining whether it was foreseeable that theft would result the courts evaluate various factors including the type of neighborhood, the defendant's knowledge of the neighborhood's reputation, the location in which the car was parked (i.e., a public road or a private street), the length of time the vehicle was left unattended, and the type of vehicle. Here, Johnston was new to the area and unfamiliar with the neighborhood's reputation. All Johnston could know about the area was from what she saw, and the neighborhood appeared safe. Further, she parked her car on a public street, which would seem to deter potential thieves knowing that there were many potential witnesses. Ms. Johnston left the car for only a few minutes while she entered a store nearby and did not intend for it to be unattended long. And lastly, Johnston's car is one that stands out; it is highly recognizable and would therefore seem to be a poor choice of prey for thieves as they would likely be readily caught.

It was not foreseeable that theft will result from parking a truck in an unlocked garage stall next to a business on private property with the key in the ignition despite knowledge by the defendant that the establishment had been burglarized multiple times and the truck stolen twice in the past. In *Kaelin v. Nuelle*, 537 S.W.2d 226 (Mo. App. St. Louis Dist. 1976), the defendant, who owned and operated a service station for forty-three years, customarily parked his truck in this manner in an unlocked garage. He had begun to experience thefts five years prior to the incident, but continued to park his vehicle in the same manner. On the night in question, the defendant parked his car, and it was stolen several hours later by a thief who proceeded to collide with another automobile driven by the plaintiff's husband, who was killed. The thief escaped the scene of the accident, and the plaintiff filed suit against the defendant for negligence in failing to foresee that his car was likely to be stolen because of the history of burglaries that had occurred on his property. The trial court entered a directed verdict for the defendant and the Missouri Court of Appeals affirmed, holding that the plaintiff "as a matter of law, failed to adduce sufficient evidence of negligence or proximate causation to make a submissible case even though there was some evidence that defendant's place of business had been burglarized and the truck stolen in the past." *Kaelin*, 537 S.W.2d at 231.

It was not foreseeable that theft would result from parking an unattended, unusually dangerous vehicle in a public place unlocked and ready to operate when the owner had knowledge that for a period of over one month individuals had climbed onto and operated the vehicles without permission. In *Zuber v. Clarkson Construction Co.*, 315 S.W.2d 727 (Mo. 1958), the defendant parked tractor-trailers in a public area over nights and weekends while constructing a levee. The trailers were large "earth moving" machines that required special skill to operate, yet were left unlocked and ready to operate. The defendant company had knowledge that curious passersby would climb on the trailers and operate them, yet they continued to park their trailers in this fashion. On the day in question, the plaintiff's son and his cousin engaged in this behavior, and the plaintiff's son died as a result of his lack of knowledge in operating such a dangerous vehicle and subsequent inability to curtail its movement. The plaintiff brought suit against the defendant company for negligence in his son's death because the defendant left the vehicles unlocked in an accessible place, ready to operate with knowledge of prior attempts by unauthorized individuals to operate such vehicles. The trial court overruled the defendant's motion for a directed verdict, and the Supreme Court reversed, holding that at the time of the decedent's death, he "was engaged in committing a criminal act, to wit: Driving, operating, using or tampering with a motor vehicle and trailer without the permission of the owner and, as a matter of law, no duty was owed by defendant to plaintiff's decedent to avoid negligently injuring him or causing his death." *Id.* at 732. Therefore, because the defendant owed no duty to the plaintiff's decedent, it cannot be found liable for negligence.

Theft was not foreseeable when an owner parks his Cadillac in an exposed and readily accessible parking garage with the keys in the ignition and the doors unlocked for an unstated period of time knowing there had been other vehicles stolen from the garage in the recent past. In *Dix v. Motor Market, Inc.*, 540 S.W.2d 927 (Mo. App. St. Louis Dist. 1976), the defendant parked his car in a parking garage with the keys in the ignition and the doors unlocked, behavior that was mandated by the garage owners whom the driver paid to park in that garage. The car was stolen by a thief who, while attempting to flee from the police, got into an automobile accident and killed the plaintiff's husband. Both the car owner and the garage owner were sued for negligence in failure to safeguard against theft of cars by leaving keys in the ignition and the car doors unlocked in an accessible garage where the garage owner knew and the car owner "should have known" about a history of stolen cars from the vicinity. The trial court granted the defendant's demurrer, and the Court of Appeals affirmed, stating "the defendant was under no duty to discover the presence of a thief in the vicinity where he parked his car." *Dix*, 540 S.W.2d at 930. The Court of Appeals further reasoned, "as a matter of law the duty of one who leaves keys in an unattended auto does not extend to a plaintiff injured in an accident with the thief driving the stolen auto." *Id.* at 931.

Prior case law reveals a potentially favorable outcome for our client. One fact that distinguishes our case from the other cases in a favorable manner is that Ms. Johnston did not leave her keys in the ignition of her vehicle; she attempted to conceal them by placing them in the sun visor above her seat. Although the car was unlocked and unattended with the keys inside, there was a seemingly greater effort to avoid car theft by removing them from the blatant view of potential thieves. In both *Kaelin* and *Dix*, there was no foreseeability of theft when the defendants left their keys in the ignition with the doors unlocked. While in *Zuber* there is no mention of keys, it is believed that vehicles of this type use starters not keys, which were connected and ready to operate at the time the vehicle was used. Considering there was no foreseeability of theft when keys are left in the ignition, our client's act of placing the keys in the sun visor should result in less foreseeability of theft.

In both *Kaelin* and *Dix*, cars were stolen from an area with a history of previous car thefts or burglaries, and the defendant in each case either knew this or had reason to know of it. In the *Zuber* case, the court found that the defendant was not guilty of negligence despite the fact that the defendant had knowledge that curious individuals had been tampering with the vehicles and operating them without permission and that the defendant had failed to attempt to abort this behavior. The area in our client's case had a history of car thefts by teenagers and has a notorious crime rate; however, our client was not privy to this information, as she is not from the area and had no reason to know the reputation of the neighborhood.

In both *Kaelin* and *Dix*, the vehicle was stolen from private property, while in *Zuber*, the vehicle rested on public property at the time of the theft. Yet in each case, the court found for the defendant. While location of the vehicle is a factor considered by the courts in determining whether there was foreseeability of theft, it does not appear to be outcome-determinative. Ms. Johnston parked her car on public property, which is an open and obvious location with both more accessibility and more witnesses. This factor does not appear to be especially critical particularly in light of the lack of foreseeability of theft decision rendered in *Zuber* where the vehicles were parked in a public location. This fact, coupled with the defendant's express knowledge that people were tampering with the vehicles, is decidedly a more serious situation than ours.

Ms. Johnston had no intention of being in the store for more than a few minutes. While she was delayed and therefore away from the car for slightly longer, she tried to keep an eye on the car while inside the store, and the car was actually unattended for only eight to ten minutes including the delay. In both *Kaelin* and *Zuber*, it is clear that the owner intended to leave the vehicles unattended for at least an entire night if not longer; in *Zuber*, the vehicles were unattended during entire weekends. While it is not made entirely clear what length of time the defendant in *Dix* intended for his car to be left unattended, it can be inferred from the fact that he paid for parking in a garage that it was meant to be unattended for a period of time exceeding a few minutes.

One last factor examined in determining the foreseeability of theft is the type of car driven by the defendant. Ms. Johnston drives a unique automobile that is highly recognizable not only because of its altered appearance, but also because of the media attention that Ms. Johnston has received, which has included her car. Although inviting curiosity, Ms. Johnston's car would seem to be an impractical choice for a thief because of the identity factor. The cars driven in both *Kaelin* and *Dix*, a pickup truck and Cadillac respectively, are more realistic prey because they are generic models and are found on the roads in abundance. The vehicle in *Zuber* may be more analogous to our client's car because of its unusual make and features, which would again seem to deter potential thieves based on the high level of attention one would receive simply by being seen in the vehicle. It is less foreseeable that thieves would target such easily recognizable vehicles.

Issue II: It Was Not Foreseeable that Injury Would Result When an Unauthorized Person Drove the Vehicle.

It was not foreseeable that an unauthorized driver would cause injury while driving the vehicle because Ms. Johnston's car is not an unusually dangerous car and requires no special skill to operate. Factors examined by the court to determine whether it was foreseeable to the defendant that injury could result include whether or not the vehicle was an inherently dangerous machine and whether it required special skill to operate. While Ms. Johnston's car has been equipped with an engine found in racing cars, which allows her vehicle to operate at over 185 mph, it is not inherently dangerous because of this feature. The car is able to function as a normal car, traveling at the speed limit. Additionally, the car does not require special skill to operate.

Pursuant to the decision rendered in *Zuber*, there is no foreseeability of injury when an unauthorized person operates an inherently dangerous "earth moving" vehicle, which rests on public property and requires familiarity with the technique of its operation. The vehicles in *Zuber* were large tractor-trailers known as "Euclids" (hereinafter "Eucs"), which intrigued the decedent and his cousin on the day in question to more closely examine and attempt to operate them. While the cousin of the decedent claimed to have driven one before, there is no evidence that either of the individuals who operated them on the day of the accident had ever operated a Euc before and therefore lacked the requisite skill; nor was there evidence that the users had permission from the defendant owner to operate any of the Eucs. Although the Eucs sat on public ground, the individuals' acts of climbing onto and operating them was found to be a trespass. In finding that the defendant was not liable for negligence because of lack of foreseeability of injury, the Missouri Supreme Court further stated that "no duty was owed by defendants to either (decedent or cousin) to protect them against their own criminal acts." *Zuber*, 315 S.W.2d at 735. The court reasons that the unauthorized acts of the plaintiff's son and his cousin do not demonstrate that the defendant was negligent with respect to the acts that caused the decedent's death.

There is foreseeability that injury will occur when an intoxicated, unauthorized driver operates an inherently dangerous commercial shuttle bus, which he has special skill to operate, belonging to the defendant company. In *Kuhn v. Budget Rent-a-Car*, 876 S.W.2d 668 (Mo. App. Western Dist. 1994), an employee for defendant allowed an intoxicated off-duty employee onto the company premises. The company manager learned that the individual was on the property in an inebriated state and did not request that he leave. The off-duty employee knew how to operate the shuttle bus and further, knew that the company left the keys in the vehicle's ignition; he drove the bus without permission off the company property and killed the plaintiff's decedent in a car accident. The trial court granted the defendant's motion for summary judgment, and the appellate court reversed and remanded, acknowledging that a genuine issue of triable fact does exist. The appellate court found that the trial court must determine whether the defendant company acted negligently in failing to prevent the intoxicated off-duty employee from entering the premises and operating a potentially dangerous vehicle that caused the death of the decedent. The court stated that by either failing to secure the vehicles or by allowing the off-duty employee on the premises, it was foreseeable that injury might occur.

Ms. Johnston's car does not qualify as an inherently dangerous vehicle when contrasted with the vehicles in these cases. While Johnston's car admittedly operates at high speeds, it is not a large vehicle capable of causing injury and damage to many people such as the vehicles described above. In both *Zuber* and *Kuhn*, the vehicles were both unusually large and used for purposes other than that of an automobile, namely carrying many passengers or digging up earth. While an argument may be made that if not for the racing engine in Ms. Johnston's car, the unauthorized driver would not have been able to slam into plaintiff's car at such a high speed, this argument should fail because at the time of the accident, the car was operating at just over 100 miles per hour, a speed that many cars are capable of reaching.

Similarly, Ms. Johnston's car does not require additional skill to operate other than that required to drive a car. The skill required to operate the vehicles in both *Zuber* and *Kuhn* was unique to each vehicle and therefore different than that required to drive a car. Therefore the court should not find that there is foreseeability of injury based on requisite skill to operate.

The varying outcomes in *Zuber* and *Kuhn* can perhaps be reconciled by acknowledging that while the vehicles were both inherently dangerous, the defendants in each case maintained a different responsibility because of where the accident occurred. The defendants in *Zuber* were entitled to park their vehicles on public property and therefore were not responsible for the intervening trespass. In *Kuhn*, the vehicles were parked on private property, and as such there was a higher duty to be responsible for the acts of individuals whom the defendants allowed onto their property. Thus, there was no duty attached to Ms. Johnston's behavior similar to the finding in *Zuber*. Ms. Johnston was entitled to park her car on a public road, and subsequent acts of injury to a third person based on a person's unauthorized use of the car would be the sole responsibility of the unauthorized person because of his or her criminal act in taking the car.

Conclusion

Based on precedential case law and, to a lesser extent, the state's reluctance to make it a criminal offense to leave one's keys in the ignition of an unlocked and unattended vehicle, Ms. Johnston will most likely not be found liable for negligence for the injuries sustained by the plaintiff. The negligence claim will fail because our client did not owe a duty to the plaintiff. Specifically, it was not foreseeable that Ms. Johnston's Porsche sports car would be stolen when she left her car unlocked with the keys in the sun visor while she entered a store for up to ten minutes in a seemingly safe neighborhood. Additionally the claim will fail because it was not foreseeable that once the car was stolen it would cause injury to a third person because it is not an inherently dangerous vehicle and does not require any kind of special skill to operate other than that required to drive a car.

Client Letters

The first two letters in this appendix are written for business clients. The first letter is written directly to a prospective client, offering advice on how to proceed in resolving a dispute. The second letter is written on behalf of a client to opposing counsel. Because that letter is written to another lawyer, you will notice that it includes case citations and in many ways reads like a memo or brief. The third and fourth letters were written by law students.

Thomas A. Vogele
tvogele@enterprisecounsel.com

April 27, 2009

CONFIDENTIAL AND STRICTLY PRIVILEGED; ATTORNEY-CLIENT COMMUNICATION

Mr. Lance McCann
Chairman & CEO
Bright Art Skylights
18312 S. Ritchey Street
Santa Ana, California 92705

Mr. Kevin Norton
President
Bright Art Skylights
18312 S. Ritchey Street
Santa Ana, California 92705

Re: *Bright Art Skylights adv. Jackson Chemical, et al.*

Gentlemen:

It was a pleasure to meet both of you last Thursday and discuss your interest in retaining ECG to assist you in resolving a potential product/material warranty claim your firm has against Jackson Chemical Company ("Jackson") and Startek Corporation ("Startek").

As we discussed, and after speaking with Mr. Flannigan, here is an overview of how we view the dispute and how we recommend Bright Art proceed to resolve the dispute in the most effective and expeditious manner.

First, neither I nor Mr. Flannigan believes this problem necessarily must result in protracted and costly litigation. While large corporations such as Jackson and Startek often take a "hard-line" stance at the outset, based on your description of Jackson's active involvement in specifying and supplying the defective material for your specialized requirements, Jackson's and/or Startek's liability seems clear. In the face of clear liability, even a large company can be persuaded that a fair and reasonable settlement is better than protracted litigation resulting in a potentially *"unreasonable"* damage award from a jury against an *"unreasonable"* defendant.

The key to persuading Jackson and Startek to accept your settlement demand is to have a complete and utter mastery of the facts and legal arguments on both sides of the dispute, to articulate a fair and defined statement of damages suffered as a result of their breach of warranty, and to present a highly professional, defined and commercially reasonable solution to the problem.

Faced with clear and potentially significant liability, and presented with a commercially reasonable solution, many companies will assess what is best for their own business interests and work out a settlement. This is particularly true when that company faces potentially greater risks in litigation, both to its sales and market value.

Jackson's and Startek's liability appears clear. By way of explanation, in a commercial transaction such as your purchase of specialty polymer/acrylic sheets, there are a number of warranties that can serve as the basis for recovering damages. Article II of the Uniform Commercial Code ("UCC") governs contracts involving goods with a value greater than $500.

UCC § 2-313 creates an express warranty any time a seller affirms a fact relating to the product's qualities or performance characteristics or where the seller provides a sample, performance specifications, or a description of the material such that a buyer, in this case Bright Art, relied on that specification or description. Nothing is required to create such an express warranty—it is created as a matter of law.

Similarly, UCC § 2-315 creates an implied warranty if the seller knows how a buyer will be using the product and knows that the buyer is relying on the seller's expertise to help select or specify the material. Since you indicated that Jackson worked closely with you to specify and select this material for your particular and specialized use, this implied warranty would apply and provide Bright Art with the basis for recovering damages caused by Jackson's breach of warranty. These warranties are in addition to any warranties extended by Jackson or Startek.

With that as a preface, here is how we would recommend Bright Art proceed and how we propose to assist your firm in solving this problem.

Phase I—Investigation and Testing

The first step in formulating a plan to resolve the dispute is to define the scope and exact cause of the problem. While you mentioned that Bright Art (and Tri-Star before it) has used this same material for twelve years, you did not mention any failures involving domes manufactured more than five years ago. I believe the Arizona failures were in skylights sold eighteen months ago while the Los Angeles failures were in three- to four-year-old products.

This prompts the question of whether Jackson and/or Startek have changed the composition of the material itself or the extruding process in a manner that compromised the material's formerly excellent physical properties. We need to determine, through testing, whether the problem exists in skylights shipped five to ten years ago. If not, it would seem to indicate a more recent iteration in the resin or extruding process might be the source of the induced stress and failures.

To accomplish this task, we would recommend that Bright Art retain a testing laboratory, preferably the acknowledged leader in this industry (to avoid having the results dismissed or refuted by Jackson's own testing). You mentioned a few names as possible choices in our meeting, and we would work with Bright Art to identify the premier facility for chemical, mechanical, and accelerated UV testing and to retain that firm immediately.

Concurrent with testing of Bright Art products in service for various lengths of time, we would recommend that you create a database of all installations by year of sale to enable Bright Art and ECG to quantify the scope of the problem, once testing determines if the defect afflicts all Jackson/Startek material or only that used in a circumscribed time frame. We would need to know the number and location of all skylights sold by year to then determine how best to remediate the problem with the least amount of adverse "marketing blowback."

Phase II—Remediation

To avoid allowing Jackson's and/or Startek's breach of warranty to damage Bright Art's standing in the industry and future sales, we believe a remediation plan needs to be developed and implemented as soon as the testing phase determines the scope and extent of the problem. This plan should include a short-term plan along the lines we discussed today, to minimize further UV degradation to the acrylic material. Since this is what Jackson has already recommended, it would be appropriate and commercially reasonable to follow the manufacturer's suggestions.

Next, Bright Art needs to determine whether it wishes to continue using the material in the future. If the current material is inappropriate for this application, you need to identify an alternate and make sure the alternate material will perform as intended. If testing determines the problem with the current material is limited to a quantifiable time frame, continued use will require Jackson and/or Startek to rectify their formulation or manufacturing problem and back their product with an extended warranty.

At the same time, Bright Art needs to develop a "fix" for existing installations along with an implementation cost analysis so that the "cost of cure" can be incorporated into your settlement demand. Until testing is done, it will be difficult to fully quantify the cost of remediation.

Phase III—Dispute Resolution

After we have a firm grasp on the scope and exact cause of the defect and failures, and have worked with Bright Art to develop and define a remedial action plan, ECG and Bright Art would meet with Jackson and Startek to present Bright Art's proposed solution. This "initial settlement meeting" should take place in a neutral location and involve decision makers from all parties to increase the likelihood of success.

ECG would draft and prepare Bright Art's presentation and assist and participate in presenting it to Jackson and Startek. The goal of this meeting would be to demonstrate to Jackson and Startek that they are liable for Bright Art's damages, that Bright Art's overriding goal is to solve the problem Jackson and Startek caused with the least amount of disruption to all parties, but that Bright Art is ready and willing to hold both companies responsible for their breach.

There is always the possibility that Jackson and Startek will respond to this proposal by turning it over to their attorneys; however, Bright Art will be far better prepared and equipped to deal with that potential by preparing for this meeting like it were a presentation to a jury. Compared to ECG, Jackson's and/or Startek's attorneys would be playing catch-up, and with ECG's help Bright Art could "control the high ground" throughout any litigation that ensued.

Other Considerations

Bright Art must bring a claim for breach of warranty/breach of contract within four years of any breach. Generally speaking, a breach occurs when a party has any reason to know or suspect that it has occurred. In your case, this could be the date you first learned of the failures in Arizona. However, there is also case law that holds a breach occurs, and your right to sue accrues, when the defective material is delivered, whether you knew of the defect or not. In either event, Bright Art may be limited to claims for material delivered in the four years prior to commencement of litigation.

ECG would need to review all of the correspondence between Bright Art and Jackson and/or Startek, all of the documentation you have regarding the initial decision to use Jackson's material, as well as the purchase and sale documentation for this material.

No company is fully prepared for a problem such as this, but with ECG's help Bright Art will be able to take a proactive stance and deal with the problem from a position of strength. We look forward to our next discussion and stand ready to assist you and your firm in whatever manner you feel is appropriate.

Enclosed is a proposed retainer agreement for your review and execution should you desire to retain ECG to represent Bright Art. Again, it was a pleasure to meet you, and I look forward to the opportunity to work with you to turn this problem into an opportunity.

Kindest regards,

ENTERPRISE COUNSEL GROUP
A Law Corporation

Thomas A. Vogele

Thomas A. Vogele
tvogele@enterprisecounsel.com

September 17, 2009

VIA U.S. MAIL

Ms. Heidi Hanson
Sanderson & Kimball, LLP
23226 Madero, Suite 175
Mission Viejo, CA 92691

Re: *Employment Claims of Trisha Strand v. ABCA Corporation*

Dear Ms. Hanson:

Please be advised that we represent ABCA Corporation in this matter. I received your August 30, 2007, letter to Gregory Weiss and have reviewed it with our client. ABCA does not acknowledge any liability in this matter, and we disagree with your conclusion that Ms. Strand's release is voidable.

The reasons for Ms. Strand's termination were communicated to her during a meeting she had with ABCA management on July 24, 2007. To claim she was terminated for any reason other than poor performance is to misstate the truth. While your analysis of the statutory requirements for a "knowing and voluntary" waiver under the Age Discrimination in Employment Act (ADEA) may be correct, that does not address the fact that any claim would be completely without merit.

Your sweeping conclusion that because the release may be voidable as to ADEA, it is voidable as to all claims is incorrect. Such a leap of logic is not supported by case law. In fact, the very case you cite for this proposition (*Oubre v. Entergy Operations, Inc.*, 522 U.S. 422, 428 (1998)) undercuts your assertion. Justice Kennedy wrote that, "[a]s a statutory matter, the release cannot bar her ADEA suit, *irrespective of the validity of the contract (release) as to other claims.*" *Id.* at 428 (*emphasis added*). *Oubre* narrowly holds that a terminated employee covered by the ADEA is not required to return any consideration received pursuant to a release, and a release that does not comply with the statutory requirements is voidable as to an ADEA claim. It does *not* hold that a release voidable for want of ADEA-mandated language is voidable as to non-ADEA claims.

California sought to outlaw age-related discrimination through the Fair Employment and Housing Act, Government Code sections 12940(a) and 12941, and *Guz v. Bechtel National, Inc.*, 24 Cal. 4th 317 (2000), sets out the elements of a prima facie case. That said, your conclusory statement that Ms. Strand was discriminated against *because of* age is wholly unsupported by the facts. Ms. Strand was arguably a member of a protected class by virtue of her age at termination and she did suffer an adverse employment action; however, she was not performing competently in her position as you allege.

Your claim that "there are numerous circumstances suggesting a discriminatory motive, such as the fact that she was the only person over the age of forty at the management level of the company" is belied by the fact that the manager who replaced her in the position is older than your client. The *McDonnell Douglas* three-stage burden-shifting test discussed in *Guz* requires far more than a naked allegation of discrimination to satisfy element (4) of the test.

ABCA terminated Ms. Strand for cause, as required by her executive employment agreement. She was given the reasons for her termination, and it is entirely within the purview of ABCA to make that determination. To avoid privacy concerns, ABCA will not provide the specific reasons communicated to Ms. Strand without her express authorization; however, let me assure you that every reason for her termination was related to a lack of performance, not her age.

Your claim that "the impression Ms. Strand was given was that it was a cost-cutting measure" is perhaps a form of rationalization by Ms. Strand. In the July 24th meeting, ABCA management did not discuss anything that would reasonably lead to this false impression.

The sweeping conclusion that Ms. Strand would be entitled to the balance of her contract payments cannot be based on the holding of *Martin v. U-Haul Co. of Fresno*, 204 Cal. App. 3d 396 (5th Dist. 1988). I read *Martin* to mean that contract damages cannot exceed the notice period required in the contract. The court cited *Pecarovich v. Becker*, 113 Cal. App. 2d 309 (1st Dist. 1952), for the proposition that "contract damages are limited to the notice period." *Id.* at 318. The court went on to quote *Cline v. Smith*, 96 Cal. App. 697 (3rd Dist. 1929), and the seminal case of *Jewell v. Colonial Theater Co.*, 12 Cal. App. 681 (1st Dist. 1910), as being in concert with this rule.

Ms. Strand's employment agreement did not require advance notice of termination, and thus no damages could be awarded for ABCA exercising its contract right to terminate her employment for cause. In any event, the release, although possibly voidable as to any ADEA claim, is a valid and enforceable release of all other claims. A release is a contract, *Solis v. Kirkwood Resort Co.*, 94 Cal. App. 4th 354 (3d Dist. 2001); *Matthews v. Atchison, T. & S.F. Ry. Co.*, 54 Cal. App. 2d 549 (2d Dist. 1942); and release agreements are governed by the generally applicable principles of contracts. *Vahle v. Barwick*, 93 Cal. App. 4th 1323 (1st Dist. 2001).

There is no evidence to suggest that Ms. Strand lacked capacity at the time to execute the contract. Consideration was recited and paid. There is no allegation of fraud in the inducement or false representations by ABCA regarding the release. In fact, the release specifically mentions Ms. Strand's right to consult with an attorney before entering into the contract and afforded her a five-day right of rescission. Finally, the release was not executed under duress or coercion. As such, it is binding on Ms. Strand as to all contract and tort claims.

There is no basis to suggest that ABCA and its employees acted in a manner that would constitute any form of tortuous conduct. The inclusion of *Agarwal v. Johnson*, 25 Cal. 3d 932 (1979), and *Ewing v. Gill Industries, Inc.*, 3 Cal. App. 4th 601 (6th Dist. 1992), in your letter is quite inapposite. In *Agarwal*, the conduct of the plaintiff's supervisor was so beyond the bounds of human decency and civility that a contrary decision would shock the conscience. Likewise, the facts of *Ewing* are without any relation to the facts of this matter and should not serve as a guidepost for your client.

As with your discussion of contract and tort damages, the inclusion of compensatory and punitive damages presupposes actionable conduct by ABCA and is putting the proverbial cart before the horse. Ms. Strand's termination was based on her failure to competently fulfill her contractual duties. ABCA terminated her employment in strict conformance with the terms of her employment agreement and negotiated a settlement of all her claims, as evidenced by her execution of the settlement agreement.

We hope Ms. Strand will recognize that her termination, while understandably distressing for her, was a business decision made to resolve the problems her lack of performance caused. While the release she executed may be voidable as to any ADEA claim, please keep in mind that is merely a threshold matter. There is no merit to such a claim, and the right to sue is far different from having a meritorious claim.

The settlement agreement ABCA executed with Ms. Strand is fair and final. The company regrets that Ms. Strand feels otherwise, but is confident that the company handled the matter properly and with the respect Ms. Strand deserved as a member of the ABCA organization.

Sincerely yours,

ENTERPRISE COUNSEL GROUP
A Law Corporation

Thomas A. Vogele

ADAMS & ASSOCIATES, STUDENTS OF LAW

12510 Inglenook Lane * Cerritos, CA 90703 * (888) 41 ADAMS * Fax (562) 809-2653

Ms. Mary Louise Solomon
1240 South State College Blvd.
Anaheim, CA 92806

Re: Surrogate Contract between Mary Louise Solomon and James Kelk

Dear Ms. Solomon:

Thank you for choosing Adams & Associates to represent you. We are mindful of the importance of this matter, and we will do our best to justify the confidence you have placed in us. The purpose of this letter is to acquaint you with how we see your case, what you may expect to happen and, what you need to do to assist us as we move forward. We work for you, so if you have questions, or you think there are things we should know, please do not hesitate to contact our office. If we are not available when you call, please leave a message, and we will get back to you as soon as we can. We will be providing you with a monthly itemized statement of your account with us and any amounts we are subtracting from your retainer.

Before proceeding further, there are a couple of items that require your immediate attention. First, please sign the enclosed Substitution of Attorney letter, return it to us in the envelope provided, and keep the second copy for your files. We cannot act on your behalf if you have not released your prior attorney from any obligations to you. Second, it is imperative that you keep an accurate record of all of your expenses associated with the pregnancy. Please use the enclosed expense form to keep track of your mileage to and from the doctor, and any other expenses you incur as a result of your pregnancy, such as maternity clothes.

According to information you provided during our initial consultation, you entered into a contract with James Kelk, in which you agreed to be artificially inseminated, and to conceive and deliver a child. Mr. Kelk promised, among other things, to pay all medical and collateral expenses, and to give you $15,000 upon surrender of custody of the child to him. You have abided by all the terms and conditions of the contract up to this point and are in your twentieth week of pregnancy.

Recently, your husband contacted the Kelks and informed them that your father was an alcoholic and that your mother was addicted to pain killers, facts that you confirmed were true. Now the Kelks have decided that they do not want the baby and wish to terminate the contract, despite the fact that you have no history of drug or alcohol abuse, and that tests conducted on your fetus offer no evidence of any problems with the baby. In seeking legal counsel, your goal is to have the Kelks perform the contract, i.e., do what they promised to do, including taking custody of the baby after it is born. Based on what you have told us and on our preliminary research, and with the understanding that we cannot guarantee the outcome of your case, we believe we have a reasonably good chance to either force the Kelks to pay the monies promised under the contract, or to pay any expenses and losses you might incur involving the pregnancy. We do not believe that we would be successful in forcing the Kelks to take custody of the baby.

In contract law, breach of a contract is the same as breaking one's promise. The law offers various remedies to the injured party (the party who is willing to perform on her promise). The basic goal of the courts in contract disputes is to put the parties in the same positions they were in before they entered into the contract. Usually, this involves the court either ordering the breaching party to perform as agreed in the contract, or the awarding of monetary compensation to the injured party for any expenses incurred or losses sustained as a result of the contract not being fulfilled.

Ordinarily, the law requires that a breach of the contract must occur before a legal remedy may be sought. At this point, the Kelks have not legally breached the contract because they have performed the promises that are already due under the terms of the contract, i.e., paid expenses to the fertility clinic and the costs of the medical evaluations, etc. Normally, we would have to wait until the Kelks actually broke one of their contract promises before we could take any action. However, by verbally telling you that they did not want the baby, the Kelks may have committed an "anticipatory repudiation of the contract." This is like reneging on a promise before the time when you are required to carry out that promise. We would need to prove, either through the Kelks' own admission or through other acts on their part, that they do not plan to make good on their contract promises to you.

Assuming that we can prove that the Kelks committed an "anticipatory repudiation of the contract," there are three possible responses we would advise. First, we can urge the Kelks to perform on the contract—to cancel or undo their repudiation. Second, if they still insist they do not want custody of the baby, we can try to negotiate a settlement that would be agreeable to both you and the Kelks. Third, we can immediately file an action to try and force performance of the contract or recover any damages that may be appropriate.

We recommend first sending a letter to Mr. and Mrs. Kelk urging them to honor the contract. They may have been overreacting to the information provided by your husband and may have reconsidered their position. This is the preferred approach because it accomplishes your goal and avoids the more costly alternatives. We have enclosed a copy of the letter we will send as soon as you give us your approval. Please call us and let us know what you decide.

If the Kelks refuse to reconsider and remain steadfast in their position that they do not want the baby, then we can still attempt to negotiate with them for a mutually agreeable alternative to the enforcement of the entire contract. Of course you would have to approve any final agreement we negotiated. The advantage to you of solving this disagreement through negotiation is that the outcome may be the same as through litigating the matter, but it would be resolved more quickly and at considerably less cost to you.

Should the initial negotiations fail to generate an acceptable outcome, we recommend filing an action in Superior Court for anticipatory repudiation of the contract. Based on the information you provided us and our preliminary research, we believe that filing an action would be a prudent approach and that there is a reasonable chance of prevailing. With that said, we must caution that there are no guarantees that we would win the action.

Although we would file the action in Superior Court, if you so directed us, we recommend that we enter into nonbinding arbitration, rather than court litigation. There are three reasons for this strategy. First, we can arrange an arbitration hearing more quickly than we can obtain a hearing date in our crowded court system. This means that if we are successful at arbitration, we can receive a judgment that would cover your expenses including attorneys' fees, thereby minimizing any financial burden to you. Second, it is far less costly to you than a protracted court battle. Third, we may have a better opportunity for a ruling in our favor. There has never been a case in California quite like yours, and, in general, the law surrounding surrogate contracts is very unsettled. For a number of legal reasons too complex to discuss here, how the courts would treat our case is unpredictable. In addition, an outcome in our favor in court would almost certainly result in an appeal, which would increase the costs and the length of time to a final outcome. Because the arbitration proposed is nonbinding, neither side has to abide by the decision of the arbitrator. However, having heard the other side's arguments, we will have a better idea of our chances of winning at trial if we are forced to litigate.

Thus far we have focused only on the monetary issues of your agreement with the Kelks. We realize that you want the Kelks to also honor their commitment to take custody of the baby upon its birth. However, as we mentioned before, it is our opinion that the courts would be unwilling to force Mr. and Mrs. Kelk to take custody of the child. Should you wish to put the baby up for adoption, that will be a separate issue with which our family law specialist can help. Should you decide to keep the baby, it is very likely that Mr. Kelk, as the child's natural father, would be responsible for part of the child's financial support, until he or she attains the age of eighteen. Again, that is a separate action and would be handled by our family law specialist.

To recap, upon your approval, we will send a letter to Mr. and Mrs. Kelk asking them to reconsider their position and honor the contract. If that proves unsuccessful, we will negotiate to arrive at a mutually agreed upon settlement, and, failing that, we will file an action and seek to enter into arbitration. Should arbitration fail to produce the desired results, then we will go forward with a litigated action in Superior Court.

Please contact our office no later than Friday, February 14, 2010, to inform us of your decision regarding the letter to the Kelks. Also, please mail the Substitution of Attorney letter immediately. We will keep you informed of further developments in your case.

Sincerely,

Richard G. Adams
Sr. Student

encl: Substitution of Attorney Letter (2)
        Letter to Mr. & Mrs. Kelk
        Expense Sheet

ADAMS & ASSOCIATES, Students of Law

*12510 Inglenook Lane * Cerritos, CA 90703 * (888) 41 ADAMS * Fax (562) 809-2653*

Mr. Yves Bordeaux, Esq.
Law Offices of Yves Bordeaux
2323 Main St., Suite 200
Orange, CA 92666

Reference: Surrogacy Contract between James Kelk and Mary Louise Solomon

Dear Attorney Bordeaux:

Please be advised that effective immediately I have retained the legal services of Adams & Associates to pursue my claims related to the above referenced contract.

Accordingly, please forward my file to my law student, Richard G. Adams, as soon as possible. Your cooperation is appreciated.

Sincerely,

Mary Louise Solomon

ADAMS & ASSOCIATES, STUDENTS OF LAW

*12510 Inglenook Lane * Cerritos, CA 90703 * (888) 41 ADAMS * Fax (562) 809-2653*

Mr. & Mrs. James Kelk
12345 Orange Avenue
Orange, CA 95555

Re: Surrogacy Contract between James Kelk and Mary Louise Solomon

Dear Mr. & Mrs. Kelk:

Please be advised that our firm has been retained by Ms. Mary Louise Solomon relative to the surrogacy contract entered into by Mr. James Kelk. Ms. Solomon has informed this firm that you no longer wish to take post-natal custody of the child that is the subject of the aforementioned contract, and of which Mr. Kelk is the legal father.

We believe Ms. Solomon would prevail in legal enforcement of the financial terms of her contract with Mr. Kelk. However Ms. Solomon does not wish to engage in protracted litigation to resolve this matter unless absolutely necessary. To avoid litigation, which could ultimately prove very costly to you, we respectfully request that you reconsider your position. Please indicate in writing via a letter to this office, your intention to honor all of the promises you made in the aforementioned contract.

If you have any questions, please contact me. If you have employed an attorney, then please have that person contact my office. Communicating directly with you is inappropriate if you are represented by counsel.

Sincerely,

Richard G. Adams
Student at Law

EXPENSES RELATED TO BABY

Date	Miles to Doctor	Miles from Doctor	Total Miles	Medical Expenses	Personal Expenses

RACHEL GOLDSTEIN
ATTORNEY AT LAW
426-1/2 BEGONIA AVENUE
CORONA DEL MAR, CALIFORNIA 92625
TELEPHONE: (714) 675-3242; FACSIMILE: (714) 675-3243

Mr. Dana Clark
Dana's Restaurant
101 S. Imperial Highway
Anaheim, CA 92807

Re: Ms. Julia Kidd's Right of Publicity Claims Against You

Dear Mr. Clark:

Thank you for meeting with me in my office yesterday. This letter is a follow-up to our meeting. It restates my understanding of the facts, addresses your concerns regarding whether famous chef and TV personality Julia Kidd can take legal action against you for airing a TV commercial that features an actress resembling her, and proposes a course of action for your review and consideration.

First of all, I want to be sure I have the facts of your case straight. Based on our discussion, I understand the facts to be as follows: you are the owner and chef of Dana's, a two-year-old restaurant in Anaheim, California. In January of this year you paid an ad agency to create a TV commercial (ad) that would promote your restaurant. The ad, which began airing in Los Angeles in March, appears on Channels 5, 13, and 50.

The ad you approved features an actress resembling famous cooking show chef and TV personality Julia Kidd. The actress stands in a kitchen and says, "You know me." The actress never says she is Julia Kidd in the ad, and there is no disclaimer on the ad. The ad agency titled the ad copy "Julia Kidding" for its own internal reference. You estimate the ad has increased business by 50 percent.

On October 1, you received a letter from Ms. Kidd's attorney warning you that Ms. Kidd will pursue legal action against you if you do not pull the ad by November 30th. The letter also demanded that you destroy all related ad material and give all your restaurant profits from the ad to Ms. Kidd.

Your primary concern is whether Ms. Kidd can bring any causes of action against you for continuing to run your ad. You want to continue running your ad because you have already paid for the ad and the ad time and the ad has increased your business. You are willing to put a disclaimer on the ad if it will protect you from liability. You have also expressed concern about whether you are required to give Ms. Kidd your profits resulting from the ad. Finally, you want to know what your options are at this time.

My research indicates that if you continue to run the ad, Ms. Kidd can pursue legal action against you under both state and federal laws. The California courts are especially protective of famous personalities' rights because there are so many celebrities living in the state. Therefore, the courts tend to look with disfavor upon individuals who even unintentionally use a celebrity look-alike without permission to promote their goods and/or services. In addition, a jury and not a judge will decide whether the facts support Ms. Kidd's claims against you. A jury is likely to be sympathetic to Ms. Kidd because she is trying to protect her name and reputation.

Ms. Kidd can bring two state claims against you. In order for you to prevail against the first claim, you must show the actress in the commercial does not bear an exact resemblance to Ms. Kidd, you did not knowingly intend to use Ms. Kidd's likeness, or there was no direct connection between the use of the actress resembling Ms. Kidd and the promotion of your restaurant. To prevail against the second state claim, you must show the actress does not bear a close resemblance to Ms. Kidd, you did not use the actress's physical resemblance to Ms. Kidd for commercial advantage, Ms. Kidd's consent was not required, and Ms. Kidd suffered no losses resulting from the airing of the TV ad.

With respect to the first state claim and the issue of resemblance, the court applies a strict "likeness" standard. California courts, in particular, tend to look for an exact likeness of the person being copied rather than a close resemblance. In other words, Ms. Kidd will have to prove the actress is an exact likeness of her to prevail on this issue. You may prevail by establishing that the actress merely resembles Ms. Kidd. On the other hand, Ms. Kidd may argue the resemblance is strong enough to meet the "likeness" standard. A jury will ultimately decide if the actress's resemblance to Ms. Kidd meets the "likeness" standard by viewing the ad.

Regarding whether you "knowingly" used Ms. Kidd's likeness, you could assert that the ad agency came up with the idea and you only knowingly intended to promote your restaurant. However, Ms. Kidd can argue you were aware of the actress's resemblance to Ms. Kidd when you approved the ad and that you knew the agency labeled the ad "Julia Kidding." Ms. Kidd can also say the warning letter has formally put you on notice regarding the unauthorized use of Ms. Kidd's likeness. Again, the jury will decide if the facts support the "knowing" requirement.

Regarding the existence of a "direct connection," you could argue that no direct connection exists between the use of an actress who happens to resemble Ms. Kidd and the promotion of a restaurant because the actress does not identify herself as being a chef. However, if Ms. Kidd establishes you used her "likeness," she can establish the "direct connection" between the use of an actress who is portraying a famous chef and the promotion of your restaurant. Once again, the jury will determine if the "direct connection" requirement has been met.

Ms. Kidd is even more likely to prevail against you on the second state claim because the resemblance standard is not as strict. Under this claim, the court only requires that Ms. Kidd show you used her "identity." This broader standard considers not just physical resemblance, but the ad's total impression on the viewer. Therefore, even though you could still argue the resemblance is not close, the combination of physical resemblance, a kitchen setting, and the line "You know me" is likely to be enough under this claim to show you used Ms. Kidd's identity. Ms. Kidd can show you used the actress's resemblance to Ms. Kidd for commercial advantage because the purpose of the ad was to promote your restaurant. Ms. Kidd can use the warning letter to show you did not have her consent. She can also show that she suffered lost profits because she was not paid for the ad. Finally, Ms. Kidd can show the ad damages her reputation and image because her identity has been used without her permission to endorse an unknown and, arguably, unproven restaurant that she has never visited and that is owned by a man she has never met.

Ms. Kidd can also bring a federal claim against you. To prevail against a federal claim, you must show that viewers of the ad are not likely to confuse the actress with Ms. Kidd. You may argue that viewers who know Ms. Kidd will know the actress is not Ms. Kidd. However, you have already said that people have asked you if the actress is Ms. Kidd and this evidence can be used against you. Ms. Kidd is a famous chef who has a cooking show on TV. She will try to argue that your ad features a Ms. Kidd "look-alike" who is standing in a kitchen and telling the audience "You know me" to indicate she is Ms. Kidd. She may also try to show that the absence of a disclaimer intentionally promotes confusion among viewers. Based on the facts of your case and the research I have done, it is my opinion that Ms. Kidd has a strong chance of prevailing against you on both state and federal claims if this case goes to trial.

You may consider joining the ad agency as an additional defendant if Ms. Kidd pursues legal action against you. You may then be able to recover some or all of your costs from the ad agency, assuming no agreement exists limiting your rights against the agency. I would need to see all documentation between you and the ad agency to determine if you have a potential claim against it.

You wanted to know if you could place a disclaimer on the ad to protect you from liability. As I already indicated to you over the phone on October 9th, Ms. Kidd's attorney rejected that idea. At that time, I also consulted another attorney who is an expert in the area of intellectual property. I relayed to you that he also advised immediately pulling the ad as requested to avoid having to pay punitive damages in addition to the regular damages you may have to pay if Ms. Kidd prevails against you in court. General damages can include compensating Ms. Kidd for using her identity. In addition, the court could make you disgorge all your profits from the ad to Ms. Kidd. The court could also make you pay punitive damages for acting in bad faith by disregarding the warning letter and continuing to run the ad, even with a disclaimer.

You also wanted to know if you are required to give Ms. Kidd all your profits resulting from the ad, as demanded in Ms. Steele's warning letter to you. You are not required to give your profits to Ms. Kidd. However, failure to make an alternative offer to Ms. Kidd may cause her to take legal action against you. I therefore suggest that you consider allowing me to negotiate a settlement on your behalf so that Ms. Kidd has no reason to pursue legal action against you.

The following settlement options may enable you to continue running the ad without risking liability. You may offer to pay Ms. Kidd a licensing fee in exchange for your being permitted to continue running the ad. Another option is to allow Ms. Kidd to modify the ad to her liking and agree to destroy the unmodified ad and all related material.

In the event Ms. Kidd is not receptive to either of these options, I suggest that you consider proposing a third settlement option. This option is not as appealing, but it will allow you to cut your losses. Such an option could include your agreeing to pull the ad, destroy all ad material, and pay Ms. Kidd a licensing fee that covers the entire six-month period the ad has run. This option could be proposed in the event Ms. Kidd insists on the demands made in the warning letter.

These settlement options are merely suggestions for your review and consideration. I am also happy to explore other options with you. Settlement negotiations will take approximately twenty hours and will be billed at the same hourly fee of $150.00 I quoted during our meeting. Upon your instruction, I will immediately arrange a settlement negotiation conference with Ms. Kidd's attorney.

Of course, another option you have is to continue running the ad. If you decide not to cooperate with Ms. Kidd and continue to run the ad even with a disclaimer, it is very likely that Ms. Kidd will pursue legal action against you. If you lose, you may be faced with not only paying Ms. Kidd all your profits, but also compensating her for using her identity and paying her punitive damages. You may even be forced to pay her attorneys' fees in addition to my fees. I advise you to carefully consider the possible costs and consequences of not cooperating with Ms. Kidd at this time.

If you decide to pull the ad by November 30th as requested, you could replace it with a new ad. Understandably, you may not wish to consider replacing the ad because of the expense involved. Therefore, more economical alternatives are also worth exploring at this time. You could obtain free TV, radio, newspaper, and magazine publicity by inviting restaurant reviewers, dee jays, and food critics to dine in your restaurant. You could also participate in food drive charities and local events, like "The Taste of Newport," to further publicize your restaurant. You could also submit articles to food magazines and even teach a cooking course.

If you have doubts about the strength of Ms. Kidd's claims, you may wish to consider having a random survey conducted on the TV ad to determined whether viewers are likely to identify the actress in the ad as Ms. Kidd. A random survey could give us some insight into how likely it is that a jury will identify the actress as Ms. Kidd. If you decide to enter into settlement negotiations, survey results that favor you could be used as leverage in negotiating a better settlement for you. Unfavorable results could also help you decide what to do if we cannot reach a settlement that is agreeable to you. The cost of a survey is approximately $150.00 and takes two days. Subject to your consent, I will arrange to have a random survey conducted immediately.

Mr. Clark, I recommend that you consider doing all that you can at this point to avoid what is likely to be an expensive and lengthy trial in a case that Ms. Kidd has a good chance of winning. A trial is also likely to result in negative publicity for Dana's. I understand that you want to do what you can to increase your restaurant business. I can also appreciate your not wanting to lose the cost of the ad and the ad time. However, it makes more sense to take appropriate action now while you still can to minimize your losses than to end up fighting what I believe will be an uphill battle that may ultimately cost you far more than the cost of the ad, the ad time, and lost business.

Ultimately, the decision rests with you. We can discuss the options further when I see you next week. In the meantime, please feel free to call me if you have any questions. I am here to help you in any way I can.

Sincerely,

Rachel Goldstein, Esq.

Settlement Agreements

Here are two of the settlement agreements we used as examples in Chapter 20. These are the two best examples in terms of clarity and simplicity of language.

RESOLUTION AGREEMENT

I. Recitals

1.   **Parties.** The Parties to this Resolution Agreement ("Agreement') are the United States Department of Health and Human Services, Office for Civil Rights ("HHS") and Affinity Health Plan, Inc.("the covered entity"). HHS and the Covered Entity shall together be referred to herein as the "Parties."

A.   **Authority of HHS**

HHS enforces the Federal standards that govern the privacy of protected health information (45 C.F.R. Part 160 and Subparts A and E of Part 164, the "Privacy Rule"), the security of electronic protected health information (45 C.F.R. Part 160 and Subparts A and C of Part 164, the "Security Rule"), and the notification in case of breach of unsecured protected health information (45 C.F.R. Part 160 and Subparts A and D of Part 164, the "Breach Notification Rule". HHS has the authority to conduct the investigations of complaints alleging violations of the Privacy and Security Rules by covered entities, and a covered entity must cooperate with HHS' investigation. 45 C.F.R. §160.306(c) and §160.310(b).

Affinity Health Plan (AHP) is a covered entity, as defined at 45 C.F.R. §160.103, and therefore is required to comply with the Privacy and Security Rules.

2.   **Factual Background and Covered Conduct**

On April 15, 2010, the HHS Office for Civil Rights (OCR) received notification from AHP regarding a breach of its unsecured electronic protected health information (EPHI). On May 19, 2010, OCR notified AHP of OCR's investigation regarding AHP's compliance with the Privacy, Security, and Breach Notification Rules.

OCR's investigation indicated that the following conduct occurred ("Covered Conduct"):

a. AHP impermissibly disclosed the EPHI of up to 344,579 individuals when it failed to properly erase photocopier hard drives prior to sending the photocopiers to a leasing company.

b. AHP failed to assess and identify the potential security risks and vulnerabilities of EPHI stored in the photocopier hard drives.

c. AHP failed to implement its policies for the disposal of EPHI with respect to the aforementioned photocopier hard drives.

3.   **No Admission.** This Agreement is not an admission of liability by AHP.

4.   **No Concession**. This Agreement is not a concession by HHS that AHP is not in violation of the Privacy and Security Rules and that AHP is not liable for civil money penalties.

5.   **Intention of Parties to Effect Resolution**. This Agreement is intended to resolve the OCR Complaint No. 10-150600, and any violations of the HIPAA Privacy and Security Rules related to the Covered Conduct specified in paragraph 2 of this Agreement. In consideration of the Parties' interest in avoiding the uncertainty, burden, and expense of further investigation and formal proceedings, the Parties agree to resolve these matters according to the terms and conditions below.

II. Terms and Conditions

6.   **Payment**. AHP agrees to pay HHS the amount of $1,215,780 ("Resolution Amount"). AHP agrees to pay the Resolution Amount by electronic funds transfer pursuant to written instructions to be provided by HHS. AHP agrees to make this payment on or before the date it signs this Agreement.

7.   **Corrective Action Plan**. AHP has entered into and agrees to comply with the Corrective Action Plan (CAP), attached as Appendix A, which is incorporated into this Agreement by reference. If AHP breaches the CAP, then AHP will be in breach of this Agreement and HHS will not be subject to the Release set forth in paragraph 8 of this Agreement.

8.   **Release by HHS**. In consideration and conditioned upon AHP's performance of its obligations under this Agreement, HHS releases AHP from any actions it has or may have against AHP under the Privacy and Security Rules arising out of or related to the Covered Conduct identified in paragraph 2. HHS does not release AHP from, nor waive any rights, obligations, or causes of action other than those specifically referred to in this paragraph. This release does not extend to actions that may be brought under section 1177 of the Social Security Act, 42 U.S.C. § 1320d-6.

9.   **Agreement by Released Parties**. AHP shall not contest the validity of its obligations to pay, nor the amount of, the Resolution Amount or any other obligations agreed to under this Agreement. AHP waives all procedural rights granted under Section 1128A of the Social Security Act (42 U.S.C. § 1320a- 7a) and 45 C.F.R. Part 160 Subpart E, and HHS claims collection regulations at 45 C.F.R. Part 30, including, but not limited to, notice, hearing, and appeal with respect to the Resolution Amount.

10.   **Binding on Successors**. This Agreement is binding on AHP and its successors, transferees, and assigns.

11.   **Costs**. Each Party to this Agreement shall bear its own legal and other costs incurred in connection with this matter, including the preparation and performance of this Agreement.

12.   **No Additional Releases**. This Agreement is intended to be for the benefit of the Parties only. By this instrument the Parties do not release any claims against any other person or entity.

13.   **Effect of Agreement**. This Agreement constitutes the complete agreement between the Parties. All material representations, understandings, and promises of the Parties are contained in this Agreement. Any modifications to this Agreement shall be set forth in writing and signed by both Parties.

14.   **Execution of Agreement and Effective Date**. The Agreement shall become effective (i.e., final and binding) on the date that both Parties sign this Agreement and CAP (Effective Date).

15.   **Tolling of Statute of Limitations**. Pursuant to 42 U.S.C. § 1320a-7a(c)(1), a civil money penalty (CMP) must be imposed within six years from the date of the occurrence of the violation. To ensure that this six-year period does not expire during the term of this agreement, AHP agrees that the time between the Effective Date of this Agreement and the date this Resolution Agreement may be terminated by reason of AHP's breach, plus one-year thereafter, will not be included in calculating the six year statute of limitations applicable to the violations which are the subject of this Agreement. AHP waives and will not plead any statute of limitations, laches, or similar defenses to any administrative action relating to the Covered Conduct identified in paragraph 2 that is filed by HHS within the time period set forth above, except to the extent that such defenses would have been available had an administrative action been filed on the Effective Date of this Resolution Agreement.

16.   **Disclosure**. HHS places no restriction on the publication of the Agreement. This Agreement and information related to this Agreement may be made public by either party. In addition, HHS may be required to disclose this Agreement and related material to any person upon request consistent with the applicable provisions of the Freedom of Information Act, 5 U.S.C. § 552, and its implementing regulations, 45 C.F.R. Part 5.

17.   **Execution in Counterparts**. This Agreement may be executed in counterparts, each of which constitutes an original, and all of which shall constitute one and the same agreement.

18.   **Authorizations**. The individual(s) signing this Agreement on behalf of AHP represent and warrant that they are authorized to execute this Agreement. The individual(s) signing this Agreement on behalf of HHS represents and warrants that she is signing this Agreement in her official capacities and that she is authorized to execute this Agreement.

For Affinity Health Plan, Inc.

_____/s/_____   August 7, 2013___
Bertram L. Scott   Date
President and CEO

For the United States Department of Health and Human Services

_____/s/_____   August 7, 2013___
Linda C. Colón   Date
Regional Manager, Region II
Office for Civil Rights

Appendix A

CORRECTIVE ACTION PLAN

BETWEEN

**THE UNITED STATES DEPARTMENT OF HEALTH AND HUMAN SERVICES
AND
AFFINITY HEALTH PLAN, INC.**

I.   Preamble

Affinity Health Plan, Inc. (AHP) hereby enters into this Corrective Action Plan (CAP) with the United States Department of Health and Human Services, Office for Civil Rights (HHS). Contemporaneously with this CAP, AHP is entering into a Resolution Agreement (Agreement) with HHS, and this CAP is incorporated by reference into the Resolution Agreement as Appendix A. AHP enters into this CAP as consideration for the release set forth in paragraph 8 of the Agreement.

II.   Contact Persons and Submissions

A. Contact Persons

AHP has identified the following individual as its contact person regarding the implementation of this CAP and for receipt and submission of notifications and reports:

Ms. Caron R. Cullen
Senior Vice President and Compliance Officer
Compliance & Regulatory Affairs
Affinity Health Plan, Inc.
2500 Halsey Street
Bronx, New York 10461

HHS has identified the following individual as its authorized representative and contact person with whom AHP is to report information regarding the implementation of this CAP:

Linda C. Colón, Regional Manager, Region II
Office for Civil Rights
U.S. Department of Health and Human Services
26 Federal Plaza, Suite 3312
New York, New York 10278
Voice Phone (212) 264-4136
Fax: (212) 264-3039
Linda.Colon@HHS.gov

AHP and HHS agree to promptly notify each other of any changes in the contact persons or the other information provided above.

    B.   Proof of Submissions.

Unless otherwise specified, all notifications and reports required by this CAP may be made by any means, including certified mail, overnight mail, or hand delivery, provided that there is proof that such notification was received. For purposes of this requirement, internal facsimile confirmation sheets do not constitute proof of receipt.

III.   Effective Date and Term of CAP

    The Effective Date for this CAP shall be calculated in accordance with paragraph 14 of the Agreement (Effective Date). The period for compliance with the obligations assumed by AHP under this CAP shall begin on the Effective Date of this CAP and end in one hundred twenty (120) days from the Effective Date except that, after this period, AHP shall be obligated to comply with the document retention requirement set forth in section VI.

IV.   Time

    In computing any period of time prescribed or allowed by this CAP, the day of the act, event, or default from which the designated period of time begins to run shall not be included. The last day of the period so computed shall be included, unless it is a Saturday, a Sunday, or a legal holiday, in which event the period runs until the end of the next day which is not one of the aforementioned days.

V.   Corrective Action Obligations

AHP agrees to the following:

1. Within five (5) days of the Effective date, AHP shall use its best efforts to retrieve all photocopier hard drives that were contained in photocopiers previously leased by AHP that remain in the possession of Canon Financial Services, and safeguard all EPHI contained therein from impermissible disclosure. If AHP cannot retrieve said hard drives, AHP shall provide OCR with documentation explaining its "best efforts" and the reason it was unable to retrieve said hard drives. If AHP retrieves said hard drives, AHP shall provide OCR written certification that it has completed the requirements specified in this paragraph. AHP's compliance with this corrective action will be based on the Region's review and approval of the documentation explaining why its efforts failed to retrieve the hard drives.

2. Within thirty (30) days of the Effective Date, AHP shall conduct a comprehensive risk analysis of the EPHI security risks and vulnerabilities that incorporates all electronic equipment and systems controlled, owned or

leased by AHP. AHP shall also, within this time period develop a plan, to address and mitigate any security risks and vulnerabilities found in this analysis and, if necessary, revise its present policies and procedures. The plan and any revised policies and procedures shall be forwarded to OCR for its review consistent with paragraph 3 below.

3. OCR shall review and recommend changes to the plan and any revised policies and procedures specified in paragraph 2. Upon receiving OCR's recommended changes, AHP shall have thirty calendar days to provide a revised plan and any revised policies and procedures to OCR for review and approval. AHP shall implement the plan and distribute and train staff members on any revised policies and procedures within thirty (30) calendar days of OCR's approval.

VI.   Document Retention

AHP shall maintain for inspection and copying all documents and records relating to compliance with this CAP for six years from the Effective Date.

VII.   <u>Breach Provisions</u>

AHP is expected to fully and timely comply with all provisions of its CAP obligations.

A. Timely Written Requests for Extensions

AHP may, in advance of any due date set forth in this CAP, submit a timely written request for an extension of time to perform any act or file any notification or report required by this CAP. A "timely written request" is defined as a request in writing received by HHS at least five (5) business days prior to the date such an act is required or due to be performed.

B. Notice of Breach and Intent to Impose CMP.

The Parties agree that a breach of this CAP by AHP constitutes a breach of the Agreement. Upon a determination by HHS that AHP has breached this CAP, HHS may notify AHP of: (a) AHP's breach; and (b) HHS' intent to impose a CMP pursuant to 45 C.F.R. Part 160 for the Covered Conduct set forth in paragraph 2 of the Agreement and for any other conduct that constitutes a violation of the HIPAA Privacy and Security Rules (Notice of Breach and Intent to Impose CMP).

C. AHP's Response.

AHP shall have 30 days from the date of receipt of the Notice of Breach and Intent to Impose CMP to demonstrate to HHS' satisfaction that:

1.   AHP is in compliance with the obligations of the CAP cited by HHS as being the basis for the breach;

2.   The alleged breach has been cured; or

3.   The alleged breach cannot be cured within the 30-day period, but that:

(i) AHP has begun to take action to cure the breach;
(ii) AHP is pursuing such action with due diligence; and
(iii) AHP has provided to HHS a reasonable timetable for curing the breach.

D. Imposition of CMP.

If at the conclusion of the 30-day period, AHP fails to meet the requirements of section VII.C to HHS' satisfaction, HHS may proceed with the imposition of a CMP against AHP pursuant to 45 C.F.R. Part 160 for the Covered Conduct set forth in paragraph 2 of the Agreement and for any other conduct that constitutes a violation of the HIPAA Privacy and Security Rules. HHS shall notify AHP in writing of its determination to proceed with the imposition of a CMP.

For Affinity Health Plan, Inc.

_____/s/_____   August 7, 2013___
Bertram L. Scott   Date
President and CEO

For the United States Department of Health and Human Services

_____/s/_____   August 7, 2013____
Linda C. Colón   Date
Regional Manager, Region II
Office for Civil Rights

SETTLEMENT AGREEMENT BETWEEN
THE UNITED STATES OF AMERICA
AND
BEGINNING MONTESSORI ACADEMY, BALDWIN PARK, CALIFORNIA

1. The parties to this Settlement Agreement ("Agreement") are the United States of America and Beginning Montessori Academy (Montessori Academy), located in Baldwin Park, California.

2. This matter was initiated by a complaint, D.J. No. 202-12C-367, filed with the United States Department of Justice (the "United States") against Montessori Academy alleging violations of Title III of the Americans with Disabilities Act of 1990 ("ADA"), 42 U.S.C. §§ 12181-12189, and its implementing regulation, 28 C.F.R. Part 36.

I. Background

3. The complainant, Ms. Kathy Castaneda, is the mother of a five-year-old, [redacted], who has autism. In a letter dated June 11, 2008, Ms. Castaneda alleges that the Montessori Academy notified her that [redacted] would not be accepted for the following school year and that as of July 1, 2008, the Montessori Academy would no longer accept any child with autism or any specialized condition or need.

4. The Montessori Academy is a 100% State Funded private preschool program that provides preschool educational services and is, therefore, a place of public accommodation covered by Title III of the ADA. 42 U.S.C. § 12181(7)(K) and Title V, of the California Department of Education, Code of Regulations.

5. The United States is authorized to investigate alleged violations of Title III of the ADA, and to bring a civil action in federal court if the United States is unable to secure voluntary compliance in any case that involves a pattern or practice of discrimination or that raises issues of general public importance. 42 U.S.C. § 12188(b). Preventing discrimination on the basis of disability, including

autism, is an issue of general public importance.

6. The ADA prohibits public accommodations from discriminating against an individual on the basis of disability in the full and equal enjoyment of its goods and services. 42 U.S.C. § 12182(a).

The ADA also prohibits a place of public accommodation from subjecting an individual on the basis of disability to a denial of the opportunity to participate in or benefit from the goods, services, facilities, privileges, advantages, or accommodations of an entity. 42 U.S.C. § 12182(b)(1)(A)(i). Failure to make reasonable modifications in policies, practices, or procedures, when such modifications are necessary to afford such goods, services, facilities, privileges, advantages, or accommodations to individuals with disabilities is also discriminatory unless the modifications would constitute a fundamental alteration. 42 U.S.C. § 12182(b)(2)(A)(ii).

7. The Montessori Academy denies that it violated Title III of the ADA and claims that at all times it acted consistently with the ADA.

8. Nevertheless, to demonstrate that it is committed to full compliance with the ADA, including the amendments to the ADA codified by the ADA Amendments Act of 2008, Pub. L. No. 110-325, 122 Stat. 3553 (2008) ("ADAAA"), the Montessori Academy has established and implemented policies and procedures, that are designed to afford children with disabilities a benefit equal to that provided to others, and to make reasonable modifications in policies, practices, and procedures when necessary to provide appropriate supervision or assistance to children with disabilities in order to ensure safe participation in all day care activities.

9. In consideration of the terms of this Settlement Agreement, and in particular the provisions in paragraphs 11, 12, 13, 14, 15, 16 and 17, the United States agrees to refrain from taking further action in this case, except as provided in paragraphs 18-21.

II. Terms of Agreement

10. The Montessori Academy agrees that it will not discriminate against any individual on the basis of disability, including autism.

11. The Montessori Academy agrees to provide children with disabilities, an equal opportunity to attend

the Montessori Academy and to participate in all programs, services, or activities provided by the Montessori Academy, except to the extent that they are unable to reasonably participate due to their disability or unable to participate after reasonable modifications in the policies and procedures have been made as set forth in in 28 C.F.R. § 36.302. The Montessori Academy agrees to make reasonable modifications in policies, practices, or procedures when such modifications are necessary to afford its child care services and facilities to children with disabilities, unless the modifications would fundamentally alter the nature of the program, service or activity as set forth in 28 C.F.R. § 36.302.

12. Within thirty (30) days of the effective date of this Agreement, the Montessori Academy shall designate a staff member ("ADA Compliance Officer") who shall have the responsibility for ensuring that the policies and procedures set forth in paragraphs 13-16, below, are fully complied with and implemented. The ADA Compliance Officer will review any decision to exclude from enrollment any child with a disability.

13. Within sixty (60) days of the effective date of this Agreement, the Montessori Academy shall submit to the United States, for review and approval, written policies and procedures on the Montessori Academy's obligations under Title III of the ADA. Those policies and procedures shall, at a minimum, include the following:

   (a) Adoption of the nondiscrimination policy attached as Appendix A, and inclusion of the policy in the Montessori Academy's employee and parent handbooks.

   (b) Upon receiving a request in writing for a reasonable accommodation or modification in policies, practices, or procedures from the parent or legal guardian of the child, the Montessori Academy will initiate a discussion with the parent to determine whether the child has a disability for which he or she needs a reasonable modification of any Montessori Academy policy, practice, or procedure and to explore what accommodations or modification(s) may be available.

   (c) If a request for reasonable accommodation or modification is denied, the Montessori Academy will document each reason for the denial of the request and shall submit that documentation to the ADA Compliance Officer for review.

(d) The Montessori Academy will make good faith efforts to provide a response to a written request for a reasonable modification of any Montessori Academy policy, practice, or procedure, in writing, no later than twenty (20) days from the date the request is received. If the request is denied, the Montessori Academy shall notify the child's parent(s) or guardian(s), in writing, of the reason(s) for the denial.

14. Within ninety (90) days from the date that the Montessori Academy implements the policies and procedures set forth in paragraph [13], above, the Montessori Academy shall provide appropriate training to all individuals with responsibility for interviewing applicants, reviewing applicants granting or denying enrollment, and/or considering requests for reasonable modifications of any Montessori Academy policy, practice or procedure. New employees with comparable responsibilities hired during the term of this Agreement shall be provided comparable training.

15. The Montessori Academy will provide training to the teacher(s) who is directly responsible for any child enrolled at the Montessori Academy who has been identified by his or her parent as being diagnosed with autism. That training will include a general overview of autism and typical assistance needs of the individual with autism. This training may be given by the parent or guardian of the child, or by a qualified person agreed upon by the parents or guardians.

16. Within thirty (30) days of the effective date of this Agreement, the Montessori Academy will send to Ms. Castaneda by certified mail, return receipt requested, or by overnight mail, a copy of the Agreement and the release form attached as Appendix B. Within thirty (30) days of receiving the signed release form, the Montessori Academy shall send to Ms. Castaneda a check payable to Kathy Castaneda, as parent and guardian of the minor [redacted], in the amount of $5,000.00 (five thousand dollars). The check should be sent by certified or overnight mail to the address provided by the United States. A copy of the check and the accompanying letter shall be sent to counsel for the United States.

III. ENFORCEMENT AND IMPLEMENTATION

17. This Agreement fully and finally resolves any and all of the allegations by the complainant and the United States in this case. It is not intended to remedy any other potential violations of the ADA by Montessori Academy.

18. The United States may review compliance with this Agreement at any time. If the United States believes that this Agreement or any portion of it has been violated, it will raise its concerns with the Montessori Academy and the parties will attempt to resolve the concerns in good faith. The United States will give the Montessori Academy thirty (30) days from the date it notifies the Montessori Academy of any breach of this Agreement to cure that breach, before instituting any court action. If the parties are unable to reach a satisfactory resolution within that period, the United States may bring a civil action in federal district court to enforce this Agreement or Title III, and may in such action seek any relief available under law.

19. Notices: All notices reports, or other such documents required by this Agreement shall be sent by fax and by delivery via overnight express mail to the following address:

    Eugenia Esch

    Disability Rights Section

    Civil Rights Division

    U.S. Department of Justice

    1425 New York Avenue, NW

    Washington, D.C. 20005

    (202) 515-3816 (telephone)

    (202) 305-9775 (facsimile)

20. During the term of this Agreement, the Montessori Academy will notify the United States of any written complaint, lawsuit, charge, or grievance alleging discrimination by the Montessori Academy on the basis of disability. Such notification must be provided in writing within fifteen (15) days of when the ADA Compliance Officer of Montessori Academy has received written notice of the allegation and will include at a minimum, the nature of the allegation, the name of the individual bringing the allegation, and any documentation possessed by the Montessori Academy relevant to the allegation.

21. In consideration for the terms set forth above, the United States will not institute a civil action alleging violations of the ADA based on the Department of Justice Complaint DJ No. 202-12C-367, except as provided in paragraph 18, above.

22. Failure by the United States to enforce this entire Agreement or any of its provisions shall not be construed as a waiver of its right to enforce other provisions of the Agreement.

23. If any term of this Agreement is determined by any court to be unenforceable, the other terms of this Agreement shall nonetheless remain in full force and effect.

24. This Agreement is not intended to remedy any other potential violations of the ADA or any other law that is not specifically addressed in this Agreement and does not affect the Montessori Academy's continuing responsibility to comply with all aspects of the ADA.

25. This Agreement shall be binding on the Montessori Academy, its agents and employees. In the event the Montessori Academy seeks to transfer or assign all or part of its interest in any facility covered by this Agreement, and the successor or assign intends on carrying on the same or similar use of the facility, as a condition of sale the Montessori Academy shall obtain the written accession of the successor or assign to any obligations remaining under this Agreement for the remaining term of this Agreement.

26. This Agreement constitutes the entire agreement between the United States and the Montessori Academy on the matters raised in the Agreement and no other statement, promise or agreement, either written or oral, made by any party or agents of any party, that is not contained in this written agreement, including its attachments, shall be enforceable.

27. A signatory to this document in a representative capacity for either party represents that he or she is authorized to bind that party to this Agreement.

28. The effective date of this Agreement is the date of the last signature below.

29. The Montessori Academy will not retaliate against, or coerce in any way any person trying to exercise the rights of any person under this Agreement.

30. The duration of this Agreement will be five (5) years from the effective date.

For Beginning Montessori Academy   For the United States of America:

_____
SHIV MEDIWAKE, Administrator

Beginning Montessori Academy 1969 Paseo Gabriela
San Dimas, Ca 91773

SAMUEL BAGENSTOS
Principal Deputy Assistant Attorney General

Dated: _____

RENEE M. WOHLENHAUS, Acting Chief
Disability Rights Section
Civil Rights Division

_____
Eugenia Esch
Trial Attorney
Disability Rights Section
Civil Rights Division
U.S. Department of Justice
Washington, DC 20530
Telephone: (202) 514-3816

Dated: _____

Attachment

APPENDIX A

NONDISCRIMINATION POLICY UNDER THE AMERICANS WITH DISABILITIES ACT

In accordance with the requirements of Title III of the Americans with Disabilities Act of 1990, as amended the Beginning Montessori Academy, California will not discriminate against any individual on the basis of disability. The Beginning Montessori Academy will make reasonable modifications in policies, practices, or procedures when such modifications are necessary to afford its services and facilities to individuals with disabilities, unless the modifications would fundamentally alter the nature of its services. The Beginning Montessori Academy will not exclude any individual with a disability from the full and equal enjoyment of its services and facilities, unless the individual poses a direct threat to the health or safety of others, or him/herself, that cannot be eliminated by a modification of policies, practices, or procedures or by the provision of auxiliary aids or services. The Beginning Montessori Academy will not exclude any individual from the full and equal enjoyment of its services and facilities because of the individual's association with a person with a disability.

Pleadings

ATTORNEY OF RECORD
IDENTIFICATION NO.
Mr. Noel Lerner
11240 Stillwell Dr.
Riverside, CA 92505
1-909-689-9728
Attorney for Plaintiff

SUPERIOR COURT OF CALIFORNIA
COUNTY OF ORANGE

REVEREND TOMMY SMITH
1240 S. STATE COLLEGE BLVD.
ANAHEIM, CA
  Plaintiff
 	
v.
 	
BOARD OF TRUSTEES
SALVATION BAPTIST CHURCH
1240 S. STATE COLLEGE BLVD.
ANAHEIM, CA
  Defendant
	NO. XX-00000
	
	NOVEMBER TERM, XXXX
	
	COMPLAINT FOR PUBLIC
	DISCLOSURE OF PRIVATE FACTS

STATEMENT OF FACTS FOR ALL CAUSES OF ACTION

Plaintiff argues:

1. Plaintiff is Reverend Tommy Smith, an adult individual who resides at 1240 S. State College Blvd., Anaheim, CA.

2. Defendant is the Board of Trustees of the Salvation Baptist Church, with offices located at 1240 S. State College Blvd., Anaheim, CA.

3. On or about 6/19/XX, Plaintiff entered into an employment contract with the Salvation Baptist Church, 1240 S. State College Blvd., Anaheim, CA.

4. Under the employment contract, Plaintiff's duties were to function as minister and run the day-to-day operations of the church.

5. On or about 4/17/XX, Defendant held a meeting of part of the congregation of the church. At this meeting, a vote of 101-7 was taken to terminate the employment of Plaintiff.

6. The Board told the congregation that Plaintiff was having extramarital affairs and was guilty of adultery.

7. Before this disclosure the information regarding Plaintiff's extramarital affairs was private, that is, not known to the public.

8. Fifty members of the congregation have sworn affidavits about the public statements made by the Board about Plaintiff. The members include statements that they did not know about Plaintiff's extramarital affairs before the Board's statements. The members also state that the outcome of the vote was influenced by the public statements made by the Board about Plaintiff to the congregation. These original sworn affidavits are attached to this Complaint and marked as Exhibits 1-50.

9. On or about July 10, XXXX, a second meeting was held. As a result of this meeting the congregation reinstated Plaintiff by a vote of 259-196.

10. Plaintiff has suffered damage to his reputation both personally and professionally.

11. Plaintiff has also suffered damage to his ability to be employed as a minister because of the highly personal and intimate nature of the disclosure of the extramarital affairs.

CAUSE OF ACTION

Right of Privacy—Public Disclosure of Private Facts

12. Plaintiff incorporates by reference paragraphs 1 through 11 of this Complaint.

13. On or about 4/17/XX, Defendant made a public disclosure of a private fact about Plaintiff to members of the congregation. The private fact was the extramarital affairs of Plaintiff.

14. Prior to this date, the congregation had not known of this fact.

15. The Defendant disclosed the fact either with knowledge that it was highly offensive or with reckless disregard of whether it was highly offensive or not. The fact made known was an intrusion into Plaintiff's most intimate and private sexual affairs.

16. The public disclosure of this fact caused Plaintiff to sustain injury to his reputation, damage to his emotions, and harm to his employability as a minister.

Wherefore, Plaintiff demands that this Court enter judgment in his favor and against Defendant in an amount in excess of $10,000, exclusive of interest and costs.

_____

Attorney for Plaintiff

VERIFICATION

I, Reverend Tommy Smith, state that I am the Plaintiff in this action and verify that the statements made in the foregoing Complaint are true and correct to the best of my knowledge, information, and belief.

_____

Date

_____

Reverend Tommy Smith

CERTIFICATION OF MAILING

I, Noel Lerner, certify that I personally placed a copy of this Complaint in the student mailbox of Kimchi Huynh, on November 22, XXXX.

I certify this under penalty of perjury.

_____

Date

_____

Noel Lerner

ATTORNEY OF RECORD:
IDENTIFICATION NO.

ALAN and LINDA SHERMAN
123 BIRCH STREET
PHILADELPHIA, PA,
     Plaintiffs
       v.
KATHRYN JONES
UNIT 14
130 ELM STREET
PHILADELPHIA, PA,
     Defendant

ATTORNEY FOR PLAINTIFFS
COURT OF COMMON PLEAS,
PHILADELPHIA COUNTY,
PENNSYLVANIA CIVIL ACTION—
LAW DIVISION
APRIL TERM, XXXX NO. 0000

Complaint in Assumpsit

1. Plaintiffs are Alan and Linda Sherman, adult individuals who reside at 123 Birch Street, Philadelphia, PA.

2. Defendant is Kathryn Jones, an adult individual who resides at Unit 14, 130 Elm Street, Philadelphia, PA.

3. On or about December 3, XXXX, Plaintiffs entered into an agreement with Defendant Jones to purchase real estate ("the property") owned by her at Unit 14, 130 Elm Street, Philadelphia, PA. A true and correct copy of this agreement is attached to this Complaint and marked as Exhibit "A."

4. Under the agreement, Plaintiffs paid the sum of ten thousand dollars ($10,000) to Creampuff Real Estate, Inc. ("Creampuff"), as a down payment on the property for Creampuff to deposit in an interest-bearing escrow account.

5. At all pertinent times, Creampuff acted as Defendant Jones's agent, the Defendant having agreed that Creampuff was to receive a 6 percent commission for procuring Plaintiffs to buy the property.

6. Under paragraph 19 of the agreement, Plaintiffs' duty to proceed to settlement was expressly subject to their ability to obtain a mortgage commitment within sixty days at a cost of no more than 3 percent of the principal ("three points"). Failing to obtain such a commitment, at Plaintiffs' option, Plaintiffs were to receive all deposit monies and the agreement was to become null and void.

7. At Creampuff's insistence, Plaintiffs proceeded with due diligence to apply to Security Mortgage Service Co. for a mortgage that would meet the terms of the agreement.

8. As of February 1, XXXX, however, sixty days elapsed with no commitment. On February 17, XXXX, Plaintiffs received a written commitment, dated February 12, XXXX. A copy of the commitment is attached and marked as Exhibit "B."

9. The commitment offered Plaintiffs a mortgage which would cost them four points rather than the maximum of three points set forth in that paragraph 19 of the agreement.

10. The commitment further required Plaintiffs to meet special conditions that paragraph 19 of the agreement did not contemplate, namely (a) evidence of sale or lease of their present residence, and (b) proof of XXXX income of $110,997.

11. Upon receipt of the commitment, Plaintiffs asked the mortgage company to remove the special conditions, but Security refused to.

12. In view of the circumstances in paragraphs 9-11 above, Plaintiffs on February 25, XXXX, sent a letter to Defendant Jones notifying her that they could not meet the terms of the commitment and that they desired the return of their deposit with interest. A copy of the letter is attached and marked Exhibit "C."

13. Despite the request, by letter dated February 25, XXXX, Defendant Jones refused to return Plaintiffs' deposit, and despite many subsequent requests, persists in her refusal. She additionally has directed Creampuff not to release the funds.

14. Further, by letter dated March 3, XXXX, Creampuff notified Plaintiffs they would not return the deposit unless the parties agreed or the court so directed.

COUNT I

15. Paragraphs 1-14 above are incorporated as though set forth at length.

16. Defendant Jones is liable to Plaintiffs in the amount of ten thousand dollars ($10,000), together with interest from December 3, XXXX.

WHEREFORE, Plaintiffs demand judgment in their favor and against Defendant Jones in the amount of ten thousand dollars ($10,000), together with interest from December 3, XXXX, and costs of suit.

COUNT II

17. Paragraphs 1-14 above are incorporated as though set forth at length.

18. Defendant Jones's refusal to return Plaintiffs' money has at all times been willful, malicious, and utterly without foundation in law.

19. Defendant Jones is liable to Plaintiffs for punitive damages.

WHEREFORE, Plaintiffs demand punitive damages against Defendant Jones in an amount not in excess of twenty thousand dollars ($20,000).

COUNT III

20. Paragraphs 1-14 above are incorporated as though set forth at length.

21. On April 13, XXXX, Plaintiffs notified Defendant by hand-delivered letter that unless Defendant returned the deposit by April 15, they could not pay their income taxes on time and expected to be liable for penalties and interest.

22. Defendant is now liable to Plaintiffs for consequential damages since Plaintiffs could not pay taxes on time.

WHEREFORE, Plaintiffs demand judgment in their favor and against Defendant for consequential damages calculated from April 15, XXXX, until time of judgment.

_____

Attorney for Plaintiff

ATTORNEY OF RECORD:
IDENTIFICATION NO.

_____

ALAN and LINDA SHERMAN,
Plaintiffs
v.
KATHRYN JONES,
Defendant

_____

ATTORNEY FOR DEFENDANT
COURT OF COMMON PLEAS,
PHILADELPHIA COUNTY,
PENNSYLVANIA CIVIL ACTION—
LAW DIVISION
APRIL TERM, XXXX No. 231

Answer, New Matter, and Counterclaim of Defendant Kathryn Jones to Plaintiffs' Complaint

ANSWER

Defendant Kathryn Jones, by her counsel, answers Plaintiffs' Complaint as follows:

1. Admitted.

2. Admitted.

3. Admitted.

4. Admitted.

5. Admitted in part and denied in part. Defendant admits that Creampuff was to receive a 6 percent commission for procuring a satisfactory purchaser (not necessarily Plaintiffs) for the property. Counsel advises Defendant that she need not respond to the remaining allegations in this paragraph because those allegations constitute conclusions of law which operation of law deems denied.

6. Counsel advised Defendant that she need not respond to the allegations in this paragraph because those allegations constitute conclusions of law which operation of law deems denied. Furthermore, the document speaks for itself. In any event, Defendant specifically denies that Plaintiffs' duty to proceed to settlement was subject to their ability to obtain a mortgage commitment "at a cost of no more than 3 percent of the principal ('three points')." On the contrary, paragraph 19 of the agreement provides that the commitment "shall not require the Buyer to pay more than 3 percent of the principal amount as 'points' or a 'commitment fee.'"

7. Defendant is without knowledge or information sufficient to form a belief as to the truth of the averments of paragraph 7 of the Complaint because the means of proof are within the exclusive control of adverse parties or hostile persons, and Defendant demands proof of them.

8. Admitted in part and denied in part. Defendant admits that Plaintiffs received a commitment dated February 12, XXXX, and that a copy of that commitment is attached to the Complaint and marked as Exhibit "B." As to the remaining allegations of paragraph 8 of the Complaint, Defendant is without knowledge or information sufficient to form a belief as to the truth of these averments because the means of proof are within the exclusive control of adverse parties or hostile persons, and demands proof of them.

9. Defendant specifically denies that the commitment offered Plaintiffs a mortgage which would cost them four points rather than the maximum of three points set forth in paragraph 19 of the agreement. On the contrary, the commitment expressly provided that the Buyer pay 3 percent of the principal amount as "points" or as a "commitment fee."

10. Counsel advises Defendant that she need not respond to the allegations in this paragraph because those allegations constitute conclusions of law which operation of law deems denied. Furthermore, the document speaks for itself. In any event, the commitment does not require proof of XXXX income of $110,997. On the contrary, the commitment merely requires that Plaintiffs substantiate the income that Plaintiffs claim on their application for the commitment by providing a "XXXX IRS return substantially supportive of income claimed on application of $110,997 OR complete **AUDITED** profit and loss for XXXX on both businesses supporting same income figure." Also, Defendant specifically denies that any requirement as to "evidence of sale or lease of [Plaintiffs'] present residence" is a "special condition not at all contemplated" by the agreement. On the contrary, such an occurrence is a normal, expected, and understood condition in such circumstances.

11. After reasonable investigation, Defendant is without knowledge or information sufficient to form a belief as to the truth of the averments of paragraph 11 of the Complaint, and demands proof of them.

12. Admitted in part and denied in part. Defendant admits that Plaintiffs sent the letter described, and that the letter indicated that Plaintiffs could not or would not accept the commitment and desired the return of the deposit, with interest. Defendant also admits that a copy of the letter is attached to the Complaint as Exhibit "C." Defendant is without knowledge or information sufficient to form a belief as to the truth of the remaining averments of this paragraph because the means of proof are within the exclusive control of adverse parties or hostile persons, and Defendant demands proof of them.

13. Denied as stated. Defendant admits that her counsel, by letter dated February 26, XXXX, indicated that Plaintiffs would be held liable under the agreement between the parties, based on previous indications Defendant received that Plaintiffs had obtained an acceptable commitment and Defendant's detrimental reliance on those indications. Defendant further admits that her husband informed Creampuff that any release of the deposit would be in violation of the agreement between the parties.

14. Admitted.

COUNT I

15. Paragraphs 1 through 14 of this Answer are incorporated by reference.

16. Counsel advises Defendant that she need not respond to the allegations in this paragraph because those allegations constitute conclusions of law which operation of law deems denied. In any event, Defendant specifically denies that Defendant is liable to Plaintiffs in the amount of $10,000, together with interest, from December 3, XXXX. On the contrary, Defendant is not liable to Plaintiffs.

COUNT II

17. Paragraphs 1 through 14 of this Answer are incorporated by reference.

18. Defendant specifically denies that her refusal to return Plaintiffs' money has at all times been willful, malicious, and utterly without foundation in law. On the contrary,

Defendant has at all times acted properly and within her legal rights and has acted in conformance with a good faith belief as to her legal rights.

19. Counsel advises Defendant that she need not respond to the allegations in this paragraph because those allegations constitute conclusions of law which operation of law deems denied. In any event, Defendant specifically denies that she is liable to Plaintiffs for punitive damages. On the contrary, Defendant is not liable to Plaintiffs.

COUNT III

20. Paragraphs 1 through 14 of this answer are incorporated by reference.

21. Admitted in part and denied in part. Defendant admits that her counsel received the letter described indicating that Plaintiffs sought the return of the deposit by April 15, XXXX, in order to have the money to pay their income taxes. Defendant is without knowledge or information sufficient to form a belief as to the truth of the averment that Plaintiffs were unable to pay their income taxes on time and expected to be liable for penalties and interest because the means of proof are within the exclusive control of adverse parties or hostile persons, and Defendant demands proof of them.

22. Counsel advises Defendant that she need not respond to the allegations in this paragraph because those allegations constitute conclusions of law which operation of law deems denied. In any event, Defendant specifically denies that she is now liable to Plaintiffs for consequential damages since Plaintiffs were unable to pay their taxes on time. On the contrary, Defendant is not responsible for any alleged inability of Plaintiffs to pay their income taxes on time and is not liable to Plaintiffs.

NEW MATTER

23. Creampuff, through its employee Sharon Sellit, acted for Plaintiffs as their agent.

24. Throughout the month of February, Plaintiffs or their representatives visited the property for the purpose of taking measurements and also performed other actions consistent with an intent to make settlement under the agreement.

25. On or about February 22, XXXX, Sharon Sellit indicated to Defendant that Plaintiff Linda Sherman had instructed that carpet tacking remaining on the floor after carpeting was removed pursuant to the agreement between the parties should be left there.

26. In reliance on the above, and in reliance on other indications from Plaintiffs and their agents that Plaintiffs had accepted or intended to accept the commitment, that the agreement was still in force, and that Plaintiffs intended to make settlement under the agreement, Defendant continued to act, at her own expense, pursuant to her agreement with Plaintiffs.

27. Based on the above, Plaintiffs are estopped from asserting: (1) that the commitment was not in conformity with the agreement; and (2) that the agreement became null and void.

28. Based on the above, Plaintiffs have waived the requirements and conditions of paragraph 19 of the agreement as a basis for failing to fulfill their obligations under that agreement.

WHEREFORE, Defendant Kathryn Jones requests an order dismissing Plaintiffs' Complaint.

COUNTERCLAIM

COUNT I

29. Paragraphs 1 through 28 above are incorporated by reference.

30. Plaintiffs have breached the agreement by failing to make settlement as the agreement requires.

31. As a result of Plaintiffs' breach, Defendant is entitled to the $10,000 deposit as liquidated damages under paragraph 10 of the agreement.

WHEREFORE, Defendant Kathryn Jones requests an order awarding her the sum of $10,000, plus interest and costs.

COUNT II

32. Paragraphs 1 through 31 above are incorporated by reference.

33. Based on the above, Plaintiffs have made misrepresentations of material facts for the purpose of inducing Defendant to act or to refrain from acting in reliance on those misrepresentations.

34. Alternatively, Plaintiffs' misrepresentations were negligent or fraudulent.

35. Defendant acted and refrained from acting in reliance on Plaintiffs' misrepresentations.

36. As a result, Defendant has sustained damages totaling $19,099.72.

WHEREFORE, Defendant Kathryn Jones requests an order awarding her $19,099.72, plus interest and costs.

_____

Attorney for Defendant
Kathryn Jones

Affidavit

Commonwealth of Pennsylvania
County of Philadelphia
} ss

KATHRYN JONES, being duly sworn according to law, deposes and says that she is Defendant in this action and that the facts set forth in the foregoing Answer, New Matter, and Counterclaim are true and correct to the best of her knowledge, information, and belief.

_____

Kathryn Jones

Sworn to and subscribed
before me this 27th day
of September, XXXX.

_____

Notary Public

My Commission Expires:

ATTORNEY OF RECORD
IDENTIFICATION NO. 0000

_____

ALAN and LINDA SHERMAN,
                    Plaintiffs,
                         v.
KATHRYN JONES,
                    Defendant
CREAMPUFF REAL ESTATE,
  INC.,
          Additional Defendant

ATTORNEY FOR DEFENDANT
COURT OF COMMON PLEAS
PHILADELPHIA COUNTY,
PENNSYLVANIA CIVIL ACTION—
LAW DIVISION
APRIL TERM, XXXX No. 231

Defendant's Complaint Against Additional Defendant

1. Plaintiffs have sued Defendant contending that Defendant wrongfully has refused to return $10,000 Plaintiffs deposited as a down payment toward the purchase of real estate located at Unit 14, 130 Elm Street, Philadelphia, PA. A copy of Plaintiffs' Complaint is attached as Exhibit "A."

2. Defendant has filed an Answer to Plaintiffs' Complaint in which Defendant (a) denies any liability to Plaintiffs and (b) asserts counterclaims against Plaintiffs. Copies of Defendant's Answer, New Matter, and Counterclaim are attached.

3. Additional Defendant, Creampuff Real Estate, Inc. ("Creampuff"), is a corporation organized and existing under the laws of Pennsylvania with an office at 456 Maple Street, Philadelphia, PA.

4. Creampuff is holding as escrow agent the $10,000 deposit that is the subject of Plaintiffs' Complaint under the Agreement of Sale between Plaintiffs and Defendant.

5. Creampuff, through its employee Joan Buyit, acted as Defendant's agent for purposes of the sales transaction.

6. Creampuff, through its employee Sharon Sellit, also acted as Plaintiffs' agent in this transaction.

7. Plaintiffs' obligation to make settlement under the Agreement of Sale was contingent on the receipt by Plaintiffs of a mortgage commitment that was to meet certain conditions specified in the Agreement of Sale.

8. Creampuff represented to Defendant that Plaintiffs had obtained a mortgage commitment that met the conditions specified in the Agreement of Sale.

9. Creampuff also represented to Defendant that Plaintiffs had accepted the mortgage commitment and intended to make settlement under the Agreement of Sale.

10. Prior to February 25, XXXX, and in reliance on Creampuff's representation, Defendant removed carpeting from the premises and took other action and incurred expenses in preparation for settlement under the Agreement of Sale.

11. Creampuff advised Plaintiff prior to February 25, XXXX, not to inform Defendant that Plaintiffs refused the mortgage commitment.

12. On February 25, XXXX, Joan Buyit indicated to Defendant for the first time that there was "a problem" with the Plaintiffs' commitment.

13. Plaintiffs refused to make settlement under the Agreement, allegedly because the mortgage commitment they received did not meet the conditions specified in the Agreement of Sale. Complaint, paragraphs 9-10.

14. Plaintiffs have also alleged that they never accepted the mortgage commitment. Complaint, paragraphs 11-12, and Exhibit "C" to Complaint.

COUNT I

15. Paragraphs 1-14 of this Complaint against Additional Defendant are incorporated by reference.

16. Based on the above, Creampuff is alone liable to Plaintiffs or, in the alternative, is liable over to Defendant in indemnity or contribution for any amounts which may be adjudged against Defendant.

WHEREFORE, Defendant Kathryn Jones demands judgment against additional Defendant Creampuff for any amounts that may be adjudged against Defendant and in favor of Plaintiffs.

COUNT II

17. Paragraphs 1-14 of this Complaint against Additional Defendant are incorporated by reference.

18. In the event the mortgage commitment did not meet the conditions set out in the Agreement of Sale, which Defendant specifically denies, then Creampuff misrepresented that fact to Defendant.

19. Creampuff additionally misrepresented Plaintiffs' intention to accept the mortgage commitment.

20. Creampuff further misrepresented Plaintiffs' intention to make settlement under the Agreement of Sale.

21. Creampuffs' actions violated the Real Estate Licensing Act, 63 Pa. Consol. Stat. § 455.604 (1976).

22. Based on the above, Creampuff has made misrepresentations of material facts for the purpose of inducing Defendant to act or to refrain from acting in reliance on those misrepresentations.

23. Alternatively, Creampuff's misrepresentations were negligent or fraudulent.

24. Defendant acted and refrained from acting in reliance on Creampuff's misrepresentations.

25. By reason of its misrepresentations to Defendant, Creampuff is liable directly to Defendant for any damages that Defendant does not recover from Plaintiffs under Defendant's Counterclaim against Plaintiffs.

26. As a result of Creampuff's misrepresentations, Defendant has sustained damages totaling $19,099.72, plus interest, costs, and Defendant's reasonable attorneys' fees.

COUNT III

27. Paragraphs 1-26 of this Complaint against Additional Defendant are incorporated by reference.

28. Based on the above, Creampuff has breached its duty as an agent of Defendant to act with standard care and with the skill that is standard in the locality for the kind of work which Creampuff was employed to perform.

WHEREFORE, Defendant Kathryn Jones demands judgment against Additional Defendant Creampuff for $19,099.72, plus interest, costs, and Defendant's reasonable attorneys' fees.

COUNT IV

29. Paragraphs 1-26 of this Complaint against Additional Defendant are incorporated by reference.

30. Based on the above, Creampuff has breached its duty to Defendant not to act on behalf of an adverse party in a transaction connected with its agency without Defendant's knowledge.

31. Alternatively, Creampuff has breached its duty to act with fairness to each of its principals and to disclose to each all facts which it knew or should have known would affect reasonably the judgment of each in permitting the dual agency.

WHEREFORE, Defendant Kathryn Jones demands judgment against Additional Defendant Creampuff for $19,099.72, plus interest, costs, and Defendant's reasonable attorneys' fees.

Attorney for Defendant
Kathryn Jones

THE STATE OF TEXAS COUNTY OF HARRIS   KNOW ALL MEN BY THESE PRESENTS:

BEFORE ME, the undersigned authority, personally appeared KATHRYN S. JONES, known to me to be a credible person, and after being duly sworn, upon oath deposed and stated the following:

"That the allegations in the Complaint against the Additional Defendant are true and correct to the best of my knowledge, information, and belief."

Further deponent sayeth not.

_____

Kathryn S. Jones

SWORN TO AND SUBSCRIBED BEFORE ME by KATHRYN S. JONES on this _____ day of November, XXXX, to certify which witness my hand and seal of office.

_____

Notary Public in and for
The State of TEXAS

My Commission Expires:

_____

In the United States District Court for the Eastern District
of Pennsylvania

QUALITY PRODUCTS
CORPORATION,
Plaintiff

v.

MIDDLEMAN STEEL COMPANY,
Defendant and Third-Party Plaintiff   Civil Action No. 75–4113

v.

HEAVY METALS COMPANY, Third-
Party Defendant

Plaintiff's Complaint Against Third-Party Defendant,
Heavy Metals Company

---

1. Plaintiff, Quality Products Corporation ("Quality") is a Delaware corporation having its principal place of business in New York, New York.

2. Third-Party Defendant, Heavy Metals Company ("Heavy Metals"), is a Pennsylvania corporation having its principal office and place of business in Philadelphia, Pennsylvania.

3. Jurisdiction of this claim is based upon the diversity of citizenship of the Plaintiff and Third-Party Defendant, under Title 28, United States Code, Section 1332.

4. The amount in controversy in this claim exceeds $10,000 exclusive of interest and costs.

5. Plaintiff incorporates by reference, as if set forth separately and in full, the allegations in paragraphs 5-11 of its Complaint in this action, which Plaintiff filed with the Court on October 20, XXXX, and a copy of which was served upon Middleman Steel Company on or about December 18, XXXX.

COUNT I

6. In or about November and December, XXXX, Defendant, Middleman Steel Company ("Middleman"), made a contract with Heavy Metals to purchase certain quantities of steel, which Middleman afterward sold to Quality as abrasion-resistant steel. The terms of their contract required that the quantities of steel Middleman purchased from Heavy Metals were to be abrasion-resistant steel.

7. At the time of the contract for the sale of the quantities of steel to Middleman, Heavy Metals knew that Middleman was a steel warehouse, engaged in the business of reselling steel to others, and that the steel Heavy Metals sold would come to rest in the hands of an ultimate consumer, who would be some person or company other than Middleman.

8. Quality was the ultimate consumer of the steel Heavy Metals sold to Middleman and is a third-party beneficiary of the contract between Middleman and Heavy Metals, and of all warranties, express and implied, on the part of Heavy Metals in that contract.

9. The steel that Heavy Metals sold to Middleman for resale to Quality under the contract was not abrasion-resistant steel, but was steel of different and inferior physical and chemical properties.

10. By failing to deliver to Middleman abrasion-resistant steel as Middleman had ordered, Heavy Metals breached the contract, and the express and implied warranties in that contract, causing loss and damage to Quality as alleged in its Complaint.

WHEREFORE, Plaintiff demands judgment in its favor against Third-Party Defendant Heavy Metals Company for all sums which Quality had to expend as a result of the Third-Party Defendant's breaches, plus interest and costs.

COUNT II

11. The allegations in paragraphs 1-10 are incorporated by reference.

12. Heavy Metals is engaged in the business of selling the steel it sold to Middleman and afterwards that Middleman sold to Quality.

13. Heavy Metals expected that the steel that it sold to Middleman could reach the user or consumer without substantial change in the condition in which it was sold, and the steel did reach Quality in that condition.

14. The steel Heavy Metals sold to Middleman was in a defective condition because it was not abrasion-resistant steel as Heavy Metals represented it to be, and was unreasonably dangerous to Plaintiff's property.

15. As a result of the defective condition of the steel, Plaintiff suffered damage to its property in that the machinery Plaintiff manufactured from the steel became inoperative and required the expenditure of large sums for repairs.

WHEREFORE, Plaintiff demands judgment in its favor against Third-Party Defendant Heavy Metals Company for all sums which Quality had to expend as a result of the Third-Party Defendant's sale of the steel, plus interest and costs.

COUNT III

16. The allegations in paragraphs 1-15 are incorporated by reference.

17. Heavy Metals failed to exercise reasonable care in supplying steel to Middleman under the contract in Count I by delivering steel that was labeled erroneously and described as abrasion-resistant steel when it was not abrasion-resistant steel.

18. As a result of Heavy Metals' negligence in delivering steel to Middleman knowing that Middleman was to resell the steel to another, Quality suffered damages by having to expend large sums of money to repair machinery components manufactured of the steel Heavy Metals delivered.

WHEREFORE, Plaintiff demands judgment in its favor against Third-Party Defendant Heavy Metals Company for all sums which it had to expend as a result of the Third-Party Defendant's negligence, plus interest and costs.

COUNT IV

19. The allegations in paragraphs 1-18 are incorporated by reference.

20. Heavy Metals knowingly and willfully supplied non-abrasion-resistant steel to Middleman, which had ordered the steel as abrasion-resistant, and misrepresented the character of the steel it shipped as abrasion-resistant, when it knew full well that the steel did not have the physical and chemical properties of abrasion-resistant steel.

WHEREFORE, Plaintiff demands judgment in its favor against Third-Party Defendant Heavy Metals Company for all sums that it had to expend as a result of the Third-Party Defendant's willful delivery of nonconforming steel, plus interest and costs, plus punitive damages.

_____

Attorney for Plaintiff

In the United States District Court for the Southern District of Florida

UNITED STATES OF AMERICA,
    Plaintiff,
       v.
THE GOOD CORPORATION,
    Defendant

CIVIL NO. 78-6789

Answer

Defendant, the Good Corporation, answers the Complaint as follows:

FIRST DEFENSE

1. Defendant admits that Plaintiff seeks to bring this action under the statutory sections alleged but denies that it has violated any provision of the Federal Trade Commission Act or any rule issued by the Commission and denies that the Plaintiff is entitled to recover civil penalties or obtain any other relief.

2. Defendant denies the allegations in paragraph 2.

3. Defendant denies that venue in the Southern District of Florida is proper.

4. Defendant denies the allegations in paragraph 4 and further states that they constitute conclusions of law that require no answer.

5. Defendant denies the allegations in paragraph 5 and further states that it does not know what the term "purchase money loan" means as used in the Complaint and that these allegations constitute conclusions of law which require no answer.

6. Defendant admits the allegations in paragraph 6.

7. Defendant admits that the Federal Trade Commission purported to issue a Trade Regulation Rule concerning Preservation of Consumers' Claims and Defenses on November 18, XXXX, and that

NINTH DEFENSE

73. The Rule concerning Preservation of Consumers' Claims and Defenses is vague, unspecific, confusing, and misleading, and is therefore void and unenforceable.

TENTH DEFENSE

74. The Rule concerning Preservation of Consumers' Claims and Defenses is vague, unspecific, confusing, and misleading; and Defendant and all Credit Unions identified in the Complaint attempted in good faith, to comply with it.

ELEVENTH DEFENSE

75. The Rule concerning Preservation of Consumers' Claims and Defenses attempts to regulate Defendant based upon acts of others who are not within the control of Defendant, in violation of the United States Constitution.

TWELFTH DEFENSE

76. Substantial evidence in the rule-making proceeding did not support the Rule concerning Preservation of Consumers' Claims and Defenses.

THIRTEENTH DEFENSE

77. Defendant has not engaged in an "unfair or deceptive act or practice" within the meaning of Section 5 of the Federal Trade Commission Act.

FOURTEENTH DEFENSE

78. Defendant did not accept the proceeds of purchase money loans with actual knowledge or knowledge fairly implied on the basis of objective circumstances that such acceptance was unfair or deceptive and prohibited by the Rule concerning Preservation of Consumers' Claims and Defenses.

FIFTEENTH DEFENSE

79. At the time that Defendant made any alleged sale of a used car, Defendant had no knowledge, and no reason to know, that the Purchaser had executed a consumer credit contract that did not contain the notice in the Rule concerning Preservation of Consumers' Claims and Defenses.

SIXTEENTH DEFENSE

80. No person has sustained any injury because of the matters alleged in the Complaint.

SEVENTEENTH DEFENSE

81. Defendant at all times exercised reasonable care and diligence to ensure that any consumer credit contract executed in connection with the purchase of a used car as alleged in the Complaint contained the notice in the Rule concerning Preservation of Consumers' Claims and Defenses.

EIGHTEENTH DEFENSE

82. Upon information and belief, Defendant alleges that this action is frivolous and without merit and that Plaintiff brought it under pressure from special interest groups that compete with Defendant in the sale of used cars.

WHEREFORE, Defendant, The Good Corporation, demands judgment in its favor and requests that the Court dismiss the Complaint and grant to Defendant the costs of this action and reasonable attorneys' fees, together with such other and further relief as may be just and proper.

Attorney for Defendant

By_____

Briefs and Oral Arguments

In this appendix, you will find four sample briefs that were filed in the California Superior Court. The first brief was filed in support of a motion for summary judgment. (The names of the parties have been changed.) As is true in some other courts, in the California Superior Court, the motion brief is called a "memorandum," not to be confused with an "interoffice memorandum." The second brief is a trial brief, filed in preparation for trial. The last two briefs were filed in preparation for mediation.

As for finding good examples of appellate briefs and oral arguments, the Internet is a great source. Certainly, not all the samples that you find are good ones; not even all briefs and arguments presented to the United States Supreme Court are desirable models. However, with selective searches, you can locate any number of well-constructed examples.

The Office of the Solicitor General produces very good briefs. That office conducts all litigation on behalf of the United States in the Supreme Court and supervises the handling of litigation in the federal appellate courts. To access its briefs, go to its website, http://www.justice.gov/osg. Then click on "Briefs."

You may want to examine the Solicitor General's helpful brief in *Florida v. Powell* (2009 term), which deals with the Miranda warning. You would click on "Type of Filing by Term," and then click on "2009," the term in which the Court chose to hear the case. Then, under "Merits Stage," click on "Amicus Briefs." Although the brief is an amicus brief, it is drafted as if it were the main brief on the merits. Once you access the brief, you should click on "View PDF Version" to see the brief as it was actually formatted. In order to read the Solicitor General's main brief in *Johnson v. United States* (2009 term), which deals with the definition of "violent felony" under the Armed Career Criminal Act of 1984, you would follow the same procedure, except that you would click on "Briefs" instead of on "Amicus Briefs."

The Mayer Brown law firms offers an online collection of well-constructed briefs drafted by its attorneys at http://www.appellate.net/briefs/defaultNew.asp. To find the brief in *Day v. McDonough*, a case dealing with the statute of limitations in habeas corpus proceedings, you would survey the list until you found the name of the case. If a lawyer from the firm had presented the oral argument, you could click on "Oral Argument" and find both a transcript and a recording of the argument. In this instance, another lawyer gave the oral argument. Therefore, for a recording of the argument, you would access http://www.oyez.org, find "Recently Updated Cases," and click on "More." Locate opinions filed in 2006, click on the case, find "Media Items," and click on "Oral Argument."

Another source is the United States Supreme Court's website, http://www.supreme courtus.gov. It offers transcripts of oral arguments beginning with the Court's October 2000 term. It also provides a link to briefs in recent cases on the American Bar Association's website, "Preview of United States Supreme Court Cases," www.americanbar.org/publications/preview_home.html.

A note of caution: Different courts have differing rules for formatting briefs and making oral arguments, and different lawyers have differing ways of constructing briefs and making oral arguments within the prescribed formats. Thus any briefs that you consult may not conform exactly to the rules that your law school has for formatting briefs. The value in consulting other briefs and oral arguments lies not in finding a document to imitate, but in getting a general idea of what style and level of analysis you should seek to attain.

This is a pretrial motion brief. It follows California citation rules. Your jurisdiction may also have its own citation rules that you should follow when you file documents in court. The important thing is that you use one citation form consistently throughout the document.

RUTAN & TUCKER, LLP
Brandon Sylvia (State Bar No. 261027)
611 Anton Boulevard, Fourteenth Floor
Costa Mesa, California 92626-1931
Telephone: 714-641-5100
Facsimile: 714-546-9035

Attorneys for Defendant
ABC CORPORATION, INC.

SUPERIOR COURT OF THE STATE OF CALIFORNIA
FOR THE COUNTY OF SANTA CLARA

DAVID SALAZAR,
 	
                          Plaintiff,
 	
           vs.
 	
ABC CORPORATION, INC., and
DOES 1 through 10, inclusive,[1]
 	
                          Defendants.
	Case No. 1-08-CV-126729
	
	ASSIGNED FOR ALL PURPOSES TO:
	THE HONORABLE JAMES KLEINBERG
	DEPARTMENT 1
	
	MEMORANDUM OF POINTS AND AUTHORITIES IN SUPPORT DEFENDANT ABC CORPORATION, INC.'S MOTION FOR SUMMARY ADJUDICATION OF PLAINTIFF'S THIRD AND FOURTH CAUSES OF ACTION
	
	[Notice of Motion and Motion; Separate Statement of Undisputed Material Facts; and Declarations filed concurrently herewith]
	
	Hearing on Motion for Summary Adjudication:
	
	Date: April 28, 2009
	Time: 9:00 a.m.
	Dept.: 1
	
	Date Action Filed: October 31, 2008
	Trial Date: Not Yet Set

---

1. In California, it is common for plaintiffs to leave open the possibility that additional defendants may be added when they are identified. This is typically done by naming the potential additional defendants "Does."

TABLE OF CONTENTS

                                                                            Page

I.   INTRODUCTION   398

II.   STATEMENT OF FACTS   398

      A.   *Salazar I*   398

      B.   *Salazar II*   399

III. ARGUMENT   400

      A.   In California, the Doctrine of Res Judicata Is Informed By the "Primary
           Right" Theory   400

           1.   The Doctrine of Res Judicata Bars Subsequent Proceedings That
                Present Issues That Were or Should Have Been Raised in a Prior
                Action Between the Same Parties and in Which There Was a Final
                Judgment   400

           2.   California Follows the "Primary Right Theory" in Determining
                Whether Issues Raised in an Earlier Proceeding Are "Identical" to
                Those Raised in a Later Case   401

      B.   Salazar's Third and Fourth Causes of Action Are Barred By Res
           Judicata   401

           1.   The Identical Parties Are Involved in Both Salazar Cases   401

           2.   The Prior Case Ended in a Final Judgment on the Merits   401

           3.   Because the Wage Claims Asserted in *Salazar II* Involve the Same
                Primary Right as the Wage Claims Asserted in *Salazar I*, Salazar's
                Third and Fourth Causes of Action Are Barred By the Doctrine of
                Res Judicata   402

           4.   Application of Res Judicata to This Situation Serves the Interests of
                Justice, Fairness, and Judicial Economy   403

IV.   CONCLUSION   404

TABLE OF AUTHORITIES

<u>Page(s)</u>

STATE CASES

Branson v. Sun-Diamond Growers (1994)
  24 Cal.App.4th 327 .... 402, 403
Citizens for Open Access to Sand and Tide, Inc. v. Seadrift Assoc. (1998)
  60 Cal.App.4th 1053, *review denied*, 1998 Cal. LEXIS 1960 400
Consumer Advocacy Group, Inc. v. Exxon-Mobil Corp. (2008)
  2008 Cal. App. LEXIS 2279 400
Federation of Hillside and Canyon Assoc. v. City of Los Angeles (2004)
  126 Cal.App.4th 1180 402
Gates v. Superior Court (Bonpane) (1986)
  178 Cal.App.3d 301 400
Grisham v. Phillip Morris U.S.A., Inc. (2007)
  40 Cal.4th 623 400
Murphy v. Kenneth Cole Prods. (2007)
  40 Cal.4th 1094 403
Mycogen Corp. v. Monsanto Co. (2002)
  28 Cal.4th 888 400
Sutphin v. Speik (1940) 15 Cal.2d 195 400
Tensor Group v. City of Glendale (1993)
  14 Cal.App.4th 154 402
Wick v. Wick Tool Co. (1959) 176 Cal.App.2d 677 400

CALIFORNIA STATUTES

California Code of Civil Procedure Section 998 398
Labor Code Section 226(a) 398

OTHER AUTHORITIES

8 Cal. Code Reg.
  Section 11040 .... Passim
  Section 11040(3)(A) 403
  Section 11040(11)(B) 403

I. INTRODUCTION.

Prior to filing this action, Plaintiff David Salazar ("Salazar") sued his employer, alleging failur‿ to pay overtime premium wages. Salazar eventually accepted Defendant's California Code of Civil Procedure Section 998 ("Section 998") offer and a final judgment was entered in his favor. Salazar has now filed this second wage and hour lawsuit against the same employer based on additional violations of the identical wage orders that were the subject of the first action. In his initial lawsuit Plaintiff sought and received a monetary judgment for wages, penalties, and attorneys' fees arising out of violations of Industrial Welfare Commission ("IWC") Wage Order No. 4-2001 ("IWC Wage Order No. 4") (8 Cal. Code Reg. § 11040.) In this lawsuit Plaintiff again seeks a monetary judgment for wages, penalties, and additional attorneys' fees arising out of violations of IWC Order Wage Order No. 4.

Plaintiff freely admits he was aware of the additional violations while litigating the first action, yet chose not to pursue them. By piecemealing a single lawsuit into at least two separate lawsuits, Plaintiff has succeeded in creating two opportunities to drag his ex-employer into court, and more importantly two opportunities to recover attorneys' fees for alleged wage and hour violations that absolutely could have and should have been addressed in the first wage and hour lawsuit. The two lawsuits focus on the identical plaintiff performing the identical job for the identical employer over the identical time period.

To permit Plaintiff to bring one lawsuit for overtime, another for meal breaks, theoretically another for rest breaks, and yet another for pay stub violations, violates the most basic concepts of res judicata. Since wage and hour claims typically take the form of class actions, permitting such claim splitting would transform one wage and hour lawsuit into four or five suits, encouraging multiple lawsuits, multiple claims for attorneys' fees, and create a feeding frenzy for wage and hour attorneys. For these reasons, as well as those detailed below, Defendant respectfully requests that this Court enter judgment for Defendant and against Plaintiff on Plaintiff's Third and Fourth Causes of Action for meal period premiums and penalties.

II. STATEMENT OF FACTS.

A. *Salazar I.*

On December 31, 2007, Salazar filed a complaint against ABC Worldwide, LLP ("Worldwide") in limited civil court ("*Salazar I*"). In *Salazar I* Plaintiff alleged that his employer, Worldwide, failed to pay overtime as required by the applicable IWC Wage Order, and that Worldwide had failed to provide itemized wage statements as required by Labor Code section 226(a). Salazar subsequently filed a First Amended Complaint to make minor technical corrections to his pleadings; the substance of his claims remained unchanged. (Ex. 1.)[2]

Discovery commenced, and pursuant to a Request for Production of Documents ("RFP"), Worldwide provided Salazar with his employee file, copies of Salazar's time cards, and other documents on April 21, 2008. (Decl. ¶3.) Because the photocopies of

---

2. A true and correct copy of the First Amended Complaint in *Salazar I* is attached as Exhibit 1 to the Declaration, filed concurrently herewith. All further citations to exhibits refer to exhibits attached to the Declaration.

Salazar's time cards were difficult to read, on May 28, 2008, Worldwide subsequently provided Salazar with color copies of each time card. (*Id.;* Ex. 2.) On July 8, 2008, Salazar's attorney informed Worldwide that he had lost the time cards so Worldwide *again* provided Salazar with documents responsive to the RFP, including the color copies of Salazar's time cards, on July 14, 2008. (Decl. ¶3.)

On September 9, 2008, Plaintiff was terminated. At the time of his termination Plaintiff received his final paycheck as well as an additional check for $835.81, along with a document stating, "Although we do not believe any overtime wages are due and owing you, the attached payment for $835.81 is based on the following. . . :" (See Defendant's overtime computation provided to Plaintiff, attached hereto as Exhibit 3.) The letter detailed the times, dates, and amounts of overtime that Plaintiff was allegedly owed. (Ex. 3.)

On September 22, 2008, Defendant made a Section 998 Offer to Compromise of $7,500, "for all damages, actual or statutory, reasonable attorneys' fees and costs incurred" in *Salazar I.* (Ex. 4.) On October 8, 2008, Plaintiff accepted the $7,500 offer to compromise and on December 1, 2008, judgment was entered for Plaintiff and against Worldwide for $7,500. (Decl. ¶6; Ex. 5.) Pursuant to the terms of the judgment, Plaintiff's counsel received a check for $7,500. (See check for $7,500 made out to Polaris Law Group, attached here as Exhibit 6.)

B. *Salazar II.*

On October 31, 2008, Salazar filed this lawsuit arising out of his employment with Worldwide ("*Salazar II*") in unlimited civil court. Salazar named and served ABC Corporation, Inc.[3] as the defendant, and has alleged violation of the Fair Employment and Housing Act ("FEHA") based on discrimination, as well as claims for wages and penalties for failure to provide meal periods. Plaintiff concedes that he was well aware of these violations while litigating *Salazar I.* In response to a special interrogatory seeking the factual support for Plaintiff's meal period claim, Plaintiff responded under oath as follows:

I determined these dates by reviewing the subject time cards provided to me by defendant in a previous lawsuit. The time cards confirm that I missed meal periods on the subject date because there is no clocking out for lunch on those days. (Exs. 7 and 8.)

Thus, Plaintiff concedes that despite having knowledge of these specific meal break claims, he opted not to pursue them. Instead, after prevailing in *Salazar I* on claims of wage and hour violations, and receiving payment of attorneys' fees as part of that award, Plaintiff immediately filed *Salazar II* alleging the additional wage and hour claims and seeking an additional attorneys' fees award out of the same conduct that occurred during the same time period while working for the same employer.

ABC filed an answer on November 17, 2008, consisting of a general denial of the claims alleged, and a number of affirmative defenses, including res judicata.

---

3. ABC Corporation, Inc., is a majority-owned subsidiary of ABC Worldwide, LLP, the operating partnership of ABC Conglomerate, Inc. (Decl. ¶3.)

III.   ARGUMENT.

A.   In California, The Doctrine of Res Judicata Is Informed By the "Primary Right" Theory.

1.   The Doctrine of Res Judicata Bars Subsequent Proceedings That Present Issues That Were or Should Have Been Raised in a Prior Action Between the Same Parties and in Which There Was a Final Judgment.

"Res judicata" describes the preclusive effect of a final judgment on the merits. Under the doctrine of res judicata, "if a plaintiff prevails in an action, the cause is merged into the judgment and may not be asserted in a subsequent lawsuit." *Mycogen Corp. v. Monsanto Co.* (2002) 28 Cal.4th 888, 896-97. The practical effect of the doctrine is that res judicata "bar[s] not only the reopening of the original controversy, but also subsequent litigation of *all issues* which were or *could have been raised in the original suit.*" *Gates v. Superior Court (Bonpane)* (1986) 178 Cal.App.3d 301, 311 (emphasis added).

A crucial aspect of res judicata is the *scope* of the preclusion. As the authorities quoted above imply, the doctrine does not only preclude those issues actually raised in a prior action. Instead, "[i]f the matter was within the scope of the action, related to the subject-matter and relevant to the issues, so that it *could* have been raised, the judgment is conclusive on it despite the fact that it was not in fact expressly pleaded or otherwise urged." *Sutphin v. Speik* (1940) 15 Cal.2d 195, 202 (underline added, italics in original). Thus, res judicata is properly invoked to bar a subsequent lawsuit "when that suit alleged a different theory of recovery for the same injury, or a different remedy for the same injury, or a somewhat greater factual elaboration of the same injury" already sued upon in a prior suit. *Grisham v. Phillip Morris U.S.A., Inc.* (2007) 40 Cal.4th 623, 642 (citations omitted); *see also Wick v. Wick Tool Co.* (1959) 176 Cal.App.2d 677, 687 ("The rule has the effect of coercing the plaintiff to present all of his grounds for recovery in the first proceeding, . . . ").

The doctrine of res judicata promotes judicial economy by "preclud[ing] piecemeal litigation by splitting a single cause of action or relitigation of the same cause of action on a different legal theory or for different relief." *Id.* Judicious recognition of the doctrine "benefits both the parties and the courts because it seeks to curtail multiple litigation causing vexation and expense to the parties and wasted effort and expense in judicial administration." *Gates*, 178 Cal.App.3d at 311 (internal quotation and citation omitted).

In the present case Plaintiff concedes that that he was aware of these specific wage and hour issues while litigating *Salazar I.* (Ex. 8.) Given the above-quoted authorities, this fact alone compels a finding that these issues "could have been raised in the original suit." *Gates*, 178 Cal.App.3d at 311. As detailed below, Plaintiff cannot bring a claim based on his employer's violation of IWC Wage Order No. 4 and simultaneously knowingly withhold a similar claim against the identical employer for additional violations of the same wage order.

A prior judgment bars a subsequent action if (1) the parties in the first and subsequent proceedings are the same, or are in privity; (2) there was a final judgment on the merits in the prior action; and (3) the issues decided in the prior adjudication are identical with those presented in the later action. *See Consumer Advocacy Group, Inc. v. Exxon-Mobil Corp.* (2008) 2008 Cal. App. LEXIS 2279, *15 (*Consumer Advocacy Group*) (citing *Citizens for Open Access to Sand and Tide, Inc. v. Seadrift Assoc.* (1998) 60 Cal.App.4th 1053, 1065, *review denied*, 1998 Cal. LEXIS 1960, *1 (*Citizens for Open Access*)). Additionally, even if these elements are met, res judicata will not be applied "if injustice would result or if the public interest requires that relitigation not be foreclosed." *Id.* at *16.

2. California Follows the "Primary Right Theory" in Determining Whether Issues Raised in an Earlier Proceeding Are "Identical" to Those Raised in a Later Case.

As noted above, a second suit is barred by an earlier action only if "the *issue or cause of action* in the two actions is *identical.*" *Citizens for Open Access*, 60 Cal.App.4th at 1067 (emphasis added). "To define a cause of action, California follows the primary right theory." *Id.* According to the primary right theory, "a cause of action is comprised of a primary right of the plaintiff, a corresponding primary duty of the defendant, and a wrongful act by the defendant constituting a breach of that duty." *Consumer Advocacy Group*, 2008 Cal. App. LEXIS 2279 at *16 (citing *Mycogen Corp.*, 28 Cal.4th at 904). The purpose of this doctrine is to ensure that "[a] party cannot by negligence or design withhold issues and litigate them in consecutive actions . . . on matters which were raised or could have been raised" in a prior action. *Sutphin*, 15 Cal.2d at 202.

The "most salient characteristic" of a primary right is that it is *indivisible. Mycogen Corp.*, 28 Cal.4th at 904. Thus, "[e]ven where there are multiple legal theories upon which recovery might be predicated, one injury gives rise to only one claim for relief." *Id.* (emphasis added). This is so even though the violation of one primary right "may entitle the injured party to many forms of relief," as the relief and the cause of action are "not determinative of the other." *Id.* As will be discussed below, Salazar's claims for overtime premiums (in the first case) and meal period premiums (in this case) are separate forms of relief arising from a single primary right.

B. Salazar's Third and Fourth Causes of Action Are Barred By Res Judicata.

Salazar's latest claims regarding meal period payments, and his attempts to recover penalties thereon, are barred by res judicata due to the earlier judgment between the parties. First, the parties to both cases are clearly in privity, as both are between Salazar and his employer. His transparent attempt to sue different entities does not hide the fact that he was employed by one employer during this time period. It is also indisputable that the first Salazar claim ended in a final judgment. Finally, as the following analysis will make clear, Salazar has attempted to impermissibly split his single right for unpaid wages into two separate lawsuits.

1. The Identical Parties Are Involved in Both Salazar Cases.

Worldwide and ABC are clearly in privity with one another. As noted in an earlier footnote, the defendant in *this* case is a majority-owned subsidiary of ABC Worldwide, LLP. ("Worldwide"). (Decl. ¶3.) Worldwide, in turn, is the operating partnership of ABC Conglomerate, Inc., the defendant in *Salazar I*. As such, the interests of ABC and Worldwide are identical. Furthermore, that Salazar alleged wage claims against both entities—based on the same period of employment, same shifts worked, and the same *paychecks*—essentially admits that the two are in privity with one another.

2. The Prior Case Ended in a Final Judgment on the Merits.

Salazar's first lawsuit ended in a final judgment. On December 1, 2008, judgment was entered pursuant to a Section 998 offer in Salazar's favor in the first case on all the claims alleged in Salazar's complaint—including the wage claims. (Ex. 5.) It is therefore undeniable that the first case resulted in a final judgment.

3. **Because the Wage Claims Asserted in *Salazar II* Involve the Same Primary Right as the Wage Claims Asserted in *Salazar I*, Salazar's Third and Fourth Causes of Action Are Barred By the Doctrine of Res Judicata.**

Salazar's claim for unpaid overtime (in the first case) and for failure to provide meal periods (in this case) constitute two attempts to recover for injury alleged to the same primary right. The scope of a "primary right" will necessarily depend on how the "primary injury" is defined, and "[a]n injury is defined in part by reference to the set of facts, or transaction, from which the injury arose." *Federation of Hillside and Canyon Assoc. v. City of Los Angeles* (2004) 126 Cal.App.4th 1180, 1202-03. Courts have also analyzed the *source* of the primary right to determine whether separate claims may be alleged. *See, e.g., Branson v. Sun-Diamond Growers* (1994) 24 Cal.App.4th 327, 343 (holding that a *statutory* right to seek authorization for indemnity and *contractual* action for indemnity involve different primary rights).

Because the facts and transactions forming the basis of Salazar's present wage claims are identical to the facts upon which he already recovered, his wage claims in this case should be barred. First, both of Salazar's claims arise from an alleged breach by World-wide of the statutory obligation to pay Salazar proper wages pursuant to IWC Wage Order No. 4. Furthermore, the facts underlying both claims are identical, and constitute attempts to recover wages allegedly owed to Salazar that accrued during the time he was employed by Defendant. As such, Salazar's meal break claims arise from the alleged violation of the primary right for which he already sued, and should therefore be barred.

a. **Because Salazar's Claims Both Arise From the Same Factual Scenario, a Single Primary Right Is Involved.**

Salazar's claims for overtime and meal period premium payments invoke a single primary right because the facts underlying each claim are identical. *See Tensor Group v. City of Glendale* (1993) 14 Cal.App.4th 154, 160 ("The cause of action . . . will therefore always be the *facts* from which the plaintiff's primary right and the defendant's corresponding primary duty have arisen.") (emphasis in original). Both claims allege, in different words, that Salazar's wages were not properly paid according to applicable statutes. Thus, although Salazar's claims differ superficially, they both seek recovery for the same primary injury: unpaid wages.

Additionally, the existence of all of the alleged wage and hour violations were apparent from Salazar's time cards and pay statements—documents that were *twice* provided to Salazar during *Salazar I.* (Decl. ¶3.) Plaintiff himself concedes he was aware of these wage and hour violations while litigating *Salazar I.* (Ex. 8.) Thus, Plaintiff made a conscious and knowing decision to not litigate a portion of wage and hour claims and to bring them in a separate action. Such a decision to intentionally transform one lawsuit into two violates the most basic precepts of California law. As stated earlier, "[a] party cannot by negligence or design withhold issues and litigate them in consecutive actions . . . on matters which were raised or could have been raised" in a prior action. *Sutphin,* 15 Cal.2d at 202. Salazar's meal period claims should have been brought in his first lawsuit, and because they were not, he cannot now assert them. *See Tensor Group,* 14 Cal.App.4th at 160 (explaining that res judicata bars a matter "within the scope of the [first] action, related to the subject matter and relevant to the issues, so that it *could* have been raised . . . ").

b.   Because Salazar's Right to Overtime and Meal Period Payments Both Arise From Statute, Both Claims Invoke a Single Primary Right.

Not only are the obligations to pay overtime and meal periods similar in *structure*, they share a common *source*. Both the first and second Salazar complaints refer to IWC Wage Order No. 4 as the wage order governing Salazar's employment with Worldwide. That wage order sets forth the various *statutory* obligations of an employer, including the obligation to pay overtime wages and to provide meal breaks or a premium payment for foregone breaks. *See* 8 Cal. Code Regs. §§ 11040(3)(A) (governing payment of overtime premium), 11040(11)(B) (providing for premium payment for missed meal breaks). These obligations exist independently from any employment contract an employee may have entered into. *Compare, e.g., Branson v. Sun-Diamond Growers* (1994) 24 Cal.App.4th 327, 343 (finding that *contractual* and *statutory* rights to indemnity involve *separate* primary rights). Thus, an employee's "primary right" to payment of either overtime or meal period premiums springs from a single source—the statutory obligation of the employer found in Wage Order No. 4.

c.   Because Overtime and Meal Period Premium Payments Have an Identical Function and Purpose, They Serve to Protect a Single Primary Right.

That overtime and meal period payments arise from a single primary right is further manifested by the identical purposes of the statutes under which such claims are brought. According to a recent California Supreme Court decision, "[t]he IWC intended that, like overtime pay provisions, payment for missed meal and rest periods be enacted as a premium wage to compensate employees, while also acting as an incentive for employers to comply with labor standards." *See generally Murphy* v. *Kenneth Cole Prods.* (2007) 40 Cal.4th 1094, 1109-14 (concluding that meal period payments—like overtime premium payments—are "wages"). Thus, because the purpose of overtime and meal period premium payments is identical, both forms of recovery protect the same primary right.

d.   Salazar's Fourth Cause of Action—For Penalties Due to Unpaid Meal Break Premium Payments—Is Similarly Precluded, as it Is Based on Alleged Violation of the Same Primary Right.

As already discussed, Salazar's claim for unpaid wages for foregone meal periods is precluded by res judicata. As such, Salazar's attempt to recover penalties *based on his meal period wages* must also fail. Like his meal period claim, this claim must have been brought— if at all—in the first case, where Salazar alleged that Worldwide breached its duty to pay proper wages. Thus, Salazar's Third and Fourth Cause of Action are barred by res judicata, and should be dismissed by this Court.

4.   Application of Res Judicata to This Situation Serves the Interests of Justice, Fairness, and Judicial Economy.

Although a court may decline to apply res judicata when application of the doctrine would result in injustice, such is not the case here. Instead, the interests of justice, fairness, and judicial economy all dictate that res judicata be applied to the wage claims asserted in Salazar's second lawsuit.

Allowing Salazar to bring separate lawsuits for overtime premiums and meal break premiums would open the door for the endless splitting of wage and hour claims. Within the specific realm of wage-and-hour law, a plaintiff's attorney interested in generating fees could bring separate lawsuits for minimum wage payments, overtime payments, meal break payments, rest break payments, and pay stub inaccuracies, as well as penalties for nonpayment of each form of wages. One court appearance then becomes five court appearances, one deposition of one plaintiff becomes five depositions of the same plaintiff, and one trial becomes five trials. This explosion of litigation is further incentivized because wage and hour attorneys will be permitted to collect fees for all five court appearances, all five depositions, and all five trials. To allow *separate lawsuits* for each claim would have the same effect as *encouraging* plaintiffs' counsel to bring five suits instead of one because their counsel could recover five times the attorneys' fees.

Given the frequency of wage and hour *class actions* and sheer tonnage of concomitant documents and billing, permitting such claim splitting in this area of the law will exponentially increase these inefficiencies. Permitting plaintiffs' counsel to transform one action, let alone one class action, into five separate actions, undercuts the most basic concepts of fairness and judicial economy. The entire purpose of the doctrine of res judicata is to promote judicial economy by precluding piecemeal litigation, and limiting the wasted effort and expense of multiple lawsuits. *Gates*, 178 Cal.App.3d at 311.

This unfortunate outcome is compounded by the knowledge that all the facts, evidence, and proof necessary to proceed on all five actions is typically available in the initial wage and hour action where the time records, job descriptions, and relevant information is produced and analyzed. In the case at bar, Plaintiff admittedly had all of this information while litigating *Salazar I*. As of May 28, 2008, he knew the date, time and duration of every meal break he had ever taken. (Ex. 2.) He took this information and did nothing, opting instead only to pursue a relatively small overtime claim. Now he seeks to be rewarded by garnering a second attorneys' fees award for refusing to combine these actions. As stated above, a party cannot negligently or intentionally withhold claims and then litigate them in successive actions. *Sutphin*, 15 Cal.2d at 202. This Court should prudently refuse to allow Salazar to split his wage claim into separate lawsuits, and should find that the wage claims asserted in Salazar's second case are barred by res judicata.

IV.   <u>CONCLUSION.</u>

For the foregoing reasons, ABC respectfully requests that this Court find that Salazar's Third and Fourth Causes of Action are barred by res judicata, and that the Court enter judgment in favor of Defendant and against Plaintiff on the Third and Fourth Causes of Action in Plaintiff's First Amended Complaint.

Dated: December 14, 2009

          RUTAN & TUCKER, LLP
          BRANDON SYLVIA

          By: _____
             Brandon Sylvia
             Attorneys for Defendant
             ABC CORPORATION, INC.

Here is the trial brief:

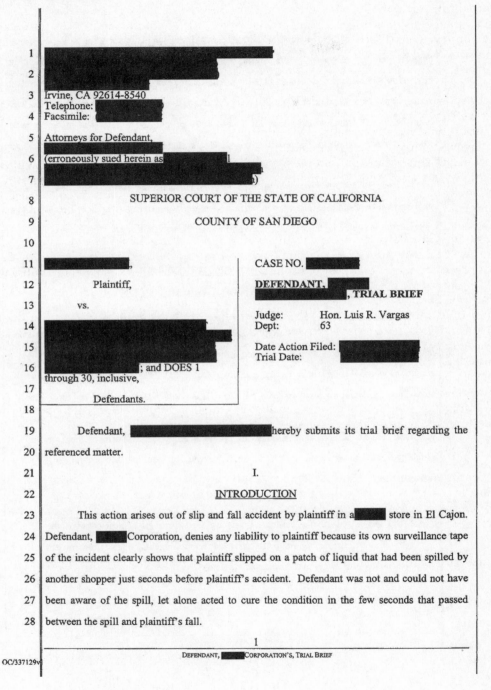

1 ▮▮▮▮▮▮▮▮▮▮▮▮▮

2 ▮▮▮▮▮▮▮▮

3 Irvine, CA 92614-8540
   Telephone: ▮▮▮▮▮

4 Facsimile: ▮▮▮▮▮

5 Attorneys for Defendant, ▮▮▮▮

6 (erroneously sued herein as ▮▮▮▮▮▮

7 ▮▮▮▮▮▮▮▮)

8   SUPERIOR COURT OF THE STATE OF CALIFORNIA

9   COUNTY OF SAN DIEGO

10

11 ▮▮▮▮▮▮▮,   CASE NO. ▮▮▮▮▮

12   Plaintiff,   **DEFENDANT,** ▮▮▮▮

13   vs.   ▮▮▮▮▮, **TRIAL BRIEF**

                                       Judge: Hon. Luis R. Vargas
14 ▮▮▮▮▮▮▮▮▮   Dept: 63

15 ▮▮▮▮▮▮▮▮▮   Date Action Filed: ▮▮▮▮▮
                                       Trial Date: ▮▮▮▮▮
16 ▮▮▮▮; and DOES 1
   through 30, inclusive,

17   Defendants.

18

19   Defendant, ▮▮▮▮▮▮▮▮▮ hereby submits its trial brief regarding the

20 referenced matter.

21   I.

22   INTRODUCTION

23   This action arises out of slip and fall accident by plaintiff in a ▮▮▮ store in El Cajon.

24 Defendant, ▮▮▮ Corporation, denies any liability to plaintiff because its own surveillance tape

25 of the incident clearly shows that plaintiff slipped on a patch of liquid that had been spilled by

26 another shopper just seconds before plaintiff's accident. Defendant was not and could not have

27 been aware of the spill, let alone acted to cure the condition in the few seconds that passed

28 between the spill and plaintiff's fall.

                                     1

1   On the night of September 13, 2003, plaintiff and her daughter went to the El Cajon

2   ███████to do some shopping. While plaintiff was making her purchase, a young man was helping

3   himself to the self-service Icee drink station located in front of the cash registers. After he

4   walked away from the machine, and just prior to exiting, the young man spilled some of his Icee

5   onto the floor. Moments later, plaintiff checked out through the register and made her way

6   toward the exit. As plaintiff approached the exit doors, she slipped and fell on the Icee that had

7   just been spilled.

8   Immediately after her fall plaintiff got up and left the store. She did not alert

9   management to her fall, or about the spot of Icee on the floor, until about an hour later when she

10   returned to the store with her daughter and son-in-law. This suit followed.

11   II.

12   THE MODE OF OPERATION RULE

13   IS NOT THE LAW OF THIS JURISDICTION

14   AND CANNOT BE A BASIS FOR LIABILITY

15   Under the Mode of Operation Rule a plaintiff is not required to prove that defendant had

16   notice of a dangerous condition if defendant could reasonably anticipate that hazardous

17   conditions would regularly arise. Jackson v. Kmart Corp., 251 Kan. 700 (Kan. 1992). California

18   courts, however, have expressly rejected this line of reasoning. Moore v. Wal-Mart Stores, Inc.

19   (2003) 111 Cal. App. 4th 472, 478. In *Moore*, plaintiff attempted to argue that Wal-Mart's mode

20   of operation and business practice of allowing patrons to enjoy food and drink in the store while

21   shopping created an unreasonable risk of harm. The court, rejecting plaintiff's argument,

22   reasoned that:

23

24   [A] store owner's choice of a particular 'mode of operation' does not eliminate a
         slip-and-fall plaintiff's burden of proving the owner had knowledge of the
         dangerous condition that caused the accident. Moreover, it would not be prudent

25   to hold otherwise. Without this knowledge requirement, certain store owners
         would essentially incur strict liability for slip-and-fall injuries, i.e., they would be

26   insurers of the safety of their patrons. Id. at 479.

27

28

                                    2

1   Accordingly, a defendant's mode of operation is irrelevant and inadmissible.

2   The facts of the present case are remarkably similar to those in *Moore*. Kmart allows its

3   patrons to enjoy food and drink in the store while shopping. In fact, and not unlike nearly every

4   fast-food restaurant in the state, and many similarly styled department stores, it provides a self-

5   service drink machine for its patrons. This method is cost efficient and convenient for both

6   ████ and its customers. Still, the fact that ████ provides this service is not relevant to the

7   issues presented in this case. Here, plaintiff's slip and fall occurred away from the self-service

8   machine, and immediately after another customer spilled Icee on the floor in front of her. In

9   order to prevail, plaintiff must prove that ████ had actual or constructive notice of the

10 dangerous condition that caused plaintiff's injuries, i.e., the spill itself, without utilizing a "mode

11 of operation" argument.

12   III.

13   ████ DID NOT HAVE ACTUAL OR CONSTRUCTIVE NOTICE

14   OF THE SPILL CAUSING PLAINTIFF'S FALL.

15   In an action for damages arising from a slip and fall accident, the plaintiff must prove that

16 a defendant knew or should have known of the existence of a dangerous condition and a potential

17 for injuries arising therefrom. Megeff v. Doland (1981) 123 Cal.App. 3d 251, 256 Tucker v.

18 Lombardo (1956) 47 Cal.2d 457, 463 ; BAJI No. 8.01. A landowner only has the obligation to

19 cure or warn of dangerous conditions for which the landowner has actual or constructive

20 knowledge. Peterson v. Superior Court (1995) 10 Cal.4th 1185, 1197. See also, Bridgman v.

21 Safeway Stores, Inc. (1960) 53 Cal.2d 443, 447. For liability to attach, the allegedly dangerous

22 condition which caused injury on a premise must have existed for a sufficient period of time to

23 notify the property owner of the potential danger. Oldenburge v. Sears, Roebuck & Co. (1957)

24 152 Cal.App. 2d 733, 741.

25   For example, in Perez v. Ow (1962) 200 Cal.App.2d 559, the plaintiff was injured after

26 slipping and falling on chocolate ice cream in the parking lot of defendant's store. The plaintiff

27 alleged that the defendant had constructive notice of the condition because the spill existed for

28 sufficient time to have been discovered and remedied. The Court held that there was absolutely

3

OC/337129v

1   no evidence from which any conclusion at all could be drawn as to the length of time the ice

2   cream had been there, and that plaintiff had the burden of producing evidence of the existence of

3   the condition complained of for at least a sufficient time to support a finding that defendants had

4   constructive knowledge. Id. at pp. 560-561.

5   In Brown v. Poway Unif. Sch. Dist. (1993) 4 Cal.4th 820, 826, the plaintiff slipped on a

6   piece of lunch meat while delivering computers to a local high school. The defendant moved for

7   summary judgment on the ground that there was no evidence that the defendant either created the

8   condition or had notice of its existence. The trial court granted summary judgment, a decision

9   affirmed by the Supreme Court. The Court held that "slips and falls are not so likely to be the

10 result of negligence as to justify a presumption to that effect … even when the fall is associated

11 with a slippery object, because objects all too often appear on floors without sufficient

12 explanation." Id. at 826.

13   In Gold v. Arizona Realty Co. (1936) 12 Cal.App.2d 676, the plaintiff slipped and fell

14 down a flight of stairs in an apartment building after stepping on a "soapy" liquid substance. The

15 trial court entered judgment for the defendant. The Court of Appeal affirmed, noting that there

16 was "no evidence that the substance which caused plaintiff's fall had been on the stairway any

17 length of time." Id. at 677.

18   In Oldenburg v. Sears, Roebuck & Co. (1957) 152 Cal.App.2d 733, the plaintiff was

19 injured after stepping on a piece of chalk outside the store, which caused her to fall. The jury

20 returned a verdict in favor of the plaintiff, and the defendant appealed. The Court of Appeal

21 reversed, holding that an action alleging constructive notice of a dangerous or defective condition

22 must be supported by "substantial evidence" as to how long the condition existed prior to the

23 accident in question before the matter goes to a jury.

24   In Nicholson v. City of Los Angeles (1936) 5 Cal.2d 361, the plaintiff suffered injuries

25 after tripping over a one-and-one-half inch break in a sidewalk. There had been no reports of any

26 prior falls at the same premises. The trial court entered judgment in favor of the plaintiff. The

27 Supreme Court reversed. The Court held that plaintiff could not rely on constructive notice since

28 only those conditions which are conspicuous could give rise to constructive notice. Since the

1   plaintiff testified that she did not believe the sidewalk was dangerous, and since there were no

2   prior accidents, the trial court improperly charged defendant with constructive notice. Id. at 364-

3   365.

4   The case of Girvetz v. Boys' Market, Inc. (1949) 91 Cal.App.2d 827, is remarkably

5   similar to the case at bar. In *Girvetz*, the plaintiff was injured after slipping on a banana peel

6   which was thought to have been on the floor for 1-2 minutes. The defendant had several cashiers

7   stationed within a 15-foot radius of the subject location, and several other employees who

8   conducted regular inspections of the subject area. Despite uncontested inspection practices, the

9   jury found in favor of the plaintiff. The trial court then granted defendant's motion for a directed

10   verdict. The Court of Appeal affirmed, noting that "[t]he fact alone that a dangerous condition

11   existed at the time the accident occurred will not warrant an inference that the defendant was

12   negligent. There must be some evidence, direct or circumstantial, to support the conclusion that

13   the condition had existed long enough for the proprietor, in the exercise of reasonable care, to

14   have discovered and remedied it." Id. at p. 829.

15   Finally, prior incident-free experience is also relevant to prove no notice of a dangerous

16   condition. Romeo v. Jumbo Market (1967) 247 Cal.App.2d 817.

17   In this case plaintiff's fall came immediately after another customer spilled his Icee drink

18   on the floor in front of the exit doors. After his spill, the man continued on his way without

19   alerting anyone, including ▮▮▮personnel, to the event. In any case, however, plaintiff's fall

20   could not have been avoided as she proceeded over the same area only seconds after the spill.

21   Liability simply cannot exist without evidence that "support[s] the conclusion that the condition

22   had existed long enough for the proprietor in the exercise of reasonable care, to have discovered

23   and remedied it." Oldenburge v. Sears, Roebuck & Co., supra.

24   ///

25   ///

26   ///

27   ///

28   ///

OC/337129v

IV.

████ DID NOT HAVE

ACTUAL OR CONSTRUCTIVE NOTICE

THAT USE OF THE ICEE DRINK MACHINE

PRESENTED A DANGER TO OTHERS

Assuming, *arguendo*, that use of the Icee machine did, in fact, present a dangerous condition to others ████ is still not liable. A property owner is not an insurer of a visitor's personal safety. Ortega v. Kmart (2001) 26 Cal.4th 1200, 1205; 7735 Hollywood Blvd. Venture v. Superior Court (1981) 116 Cal.App.3d 901, 905; CACI 1011. Its responsibility is not absolute; it is not based on a duty to keep the premises completely safe. Brunelle v. Signore (1989) 215 Cal.App.3d 122, 130-131 ████t was only obligated to repair or warn of those dangerous conditions for which it had actual or constructive knowledge. Peterson v. Superior Court, supra.

████ had no knowledge, actual or constructive, of any danger posed by the placement of its self-service Icee machine at the front of the store. Quite the contrary, there has never before been a slip-and-fall accident at this store between the self-service Icee machine and the exit door that could be attributed to the Icee machine.

V.

THE LOCATION OF THE SELF-SERVICE ICEE MACHINE

IS NOT A DANGEROUS CONDITION

A condition is considered dangerous or defective only if it presents an unreasonable risk of harm to persons using the premises in a foreseeable manner. Akins v. County of Sonoma (1967) 67 Cal.2d 185, 193; BAJI 8.21. In other words, a dangerous condition "must be one which a person of ordinary prudence should have foreseen would appreciably enhance the risk of harm ... A latent condition that would not be perceived as dangerous in the exercise of due care by a reasonably prudent landlord does not present a substantial risk of injury." Constance B. v. State of California, (1986) 178 Cal.App.3d 200, 209.

DEFENDANT, ████ CORPORATION'S, TRIAL BRIEF

1   As a matter of law, the self-service drink station did not "appreciably enhance" any risk

2   of harm. Plaintiff claims that the location of the drink station, near the exit doors, was itself, the

3   dangerous condition of which ███ was aware because ███ had knowledge of the presence of

4   heavy foot traffic in that area. It is not enough, however, for plaintiff to allege tha███rt

5   operated the drink station in an accessible location. Nevertheless, ███ took necessary

6   precautions to prevent wet floors, i.e. a black rubber mat was placed beneath the drink station to

7   catch spills and to prevent customers from falling in the event a customer spilled a drink at the

8   drink station. Furthermore, the drink station was placed in a location where numerous███t

9   personnel could supervise and inspect the floor in case of a spill. If the drink station was located

10 in the back corner of the store, it would be more dangerous due to the reduction in work force

11 readily available to address issues of spills and the condition of the floor. Accordingly, the drink

12 station was appropriately located.

13 Finally, the subject incident did not occur due to the location of the drink station. The

14 accident did not occur in front of the drink station or even near the drink station. The incident

15 occurred after a patron spilled a drink on the floor while proceeding through the exit doors. That

16 same patron had the freedom, after obtaining his drink, to go anywhere within the store or to exit

17 the store. Accordingly, there is simply no connection between plaintiff's fall and the location of

18 the self-service drink station.

19   VI.

20   PLAINTIFF'S ACCIDENT WAS NOT REASONABLY FORESEEABLE.

21 No suggestion of negligence arises from the mere happening of an accident. Edwards v.

22 California Sports, Inc., (1988) 206 Cal.App.3d 1284, 1287. A property owner is only required to

23 take measures to protect against *reasonably foreseeable* accidents, not all possible accidents.

24 (Emphasis added.) Perrine v. Pacific Gas & Elec. Co., (1960) 186 Cal.App.2d. 442.

25 Foreseeability is essential to a finding that a duty of care to plaintiff existed, and a finding

26 that injury was not reasonably foreseeable precludes a finding that a legal duty existed, regardless

27 of what other factors may weigh in favor of imposing a duty. Ludwig v. City of San Diego

28 (1998) 65 Cal.App. 4th 1105 (summary judgment for defendant was proper based only on finding

7

1 that injury was not reasonably foreseeable.) Slips, trips and falls "are not so likely to be the

2 result of negligence as to justify a presumption to that effect." <u>Brown v. Poway Unified School</u>

3 <u>Dist.</u> (1993) 4 Cal.4th 820, 826; <u>Akins v. County of Sonoma</u> (1967) 67 Cal.2d 185, 195.

4 Sometimes, "people are hurt in accidents, and the consequent loss must remain where it falls."

5 <u>Nunez v. R'Bibo</u> (1989) 211 Cal.App.3d 559, 565. It is, therefore, incumbent upon the plaintiff

6 to prove that her accident was reasonably foreseeable, an element which she simply cannot

7 prove.

8   A dangerous condition: "must be one which a person of ordinary prudence should have

9 foreseen would appreciably enhance the risk of harm ... A latent condition that would not be

10 perceived as dangerous in the exercise of due care by a reasonably prudent landlord does not

11 present a substantial risk of injury." <u>Constance B. v. State of California</u> (1986) 178 Cal.App.3d

12 200, 209.

13   The Icee machine has been at the store for years. In that time, there is no history of any

14 slip-and-fall accident related its use, along the main thoroughfare between the machine and the

15 exit doors. In fact, plaintiff has had been frequenting thi███████t several times a week for the

16 past decade and she never perceived any danger such that she thought to take any precaution

17 when traversing the area. This incident did not occur at or directly in front of the machine, where

18 one might expect a spill might occur. Rather, it occurred away from the machine, and away from

19 the area where it would be reasonable to expec█████t to take precautionary steps, such as the

20 placement of a mat. And, there is no dispute tha███████k reasonable measures to protect its

21 customers in the immediate vicinity of the machine – it placed the machine in an area where it

22 could easily be monitored and it placed a mat where spills might occur. This is the standard of

23 practice for most commercial venues that have self-service drink machines.

24 ///

25 ///

26 ///

27 ///

28 ///

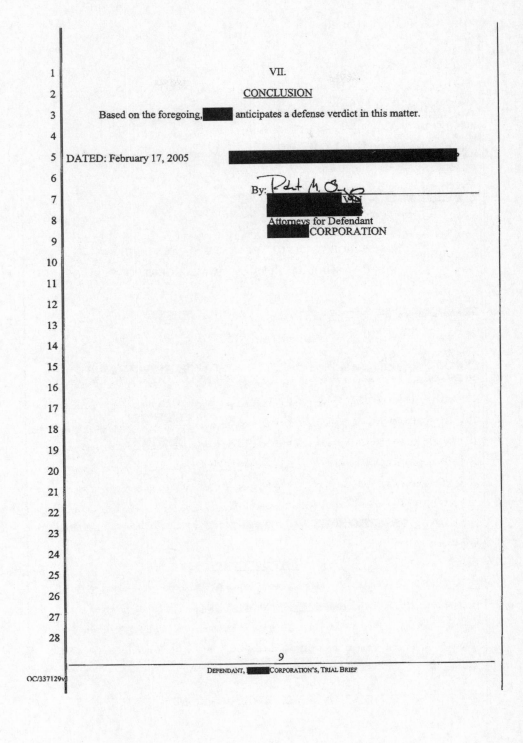

VII.

CONCLUSION

Based on the foregoing, ███ anticipates a defense verdict in this matter.

DATED: February 17, 2005   ████████████████████████

By: _Robert M. O_____

████████

Attorneys for Defendant
████ CORPORATION

9

OC/337129v

Here are the two mediation briefs:

Robert M. Beggs (SBN 232834)
THE BEGGS LAW FIRM
3151 Airway Ave, Building S-1
Costa Mesa, California 92626
P | (949) 878-3773 F | (949) 608-1741
E-Mail: robert@thebeggslawfirm.com

Attorneys for Plaintiff,
[redacted] **JR.**

SUPERIOR COURT OF THE STATE OF CALIFORNIA

COUNTY OF LOS ANGELES – NORWALK COURTHOUSE

[redacted] **JR.**, an individual Plaintiff(s), vs. **KENNETH** [redacted] an individual, and **DOES 1-10**, Defendant(s).	**CASE NO.:** [redacted] Judge: Raul A. Sahagun Department: SE "F" **PLAINTIFF** [redacted] **JR.'S CONFIDENTIAL MEDIATION BRIEF** **<u>Judicate West Mediation</u>** **JW Case No.:** [redacted] Mediator: Hon. William Sheffield, Ret. Hearing: [redacted] Time: 2:30 p.m. Case Filed: July 15, 2011 Trial: September 18, 2012

Plaintiff, [redacted] **JR.** ("Mr. [redacted] hereby submits the following **<u>confidential</u>** mediation brief.

<u>INTRODUCTION</u>

This is a very simple case. On December 27, 2010, [redacted] was riding his motorcycle to work when the defendant, **KENNETH** [redacted] ("Mr. [redacted] made an unsafe, unprotected, and illegal left-hand turn across two lanes of traffic and a center divider and into [redacted] Liability is not contested. As a result of the accident, [redacted] suffered severe, life-changing injuries, and significant damages.

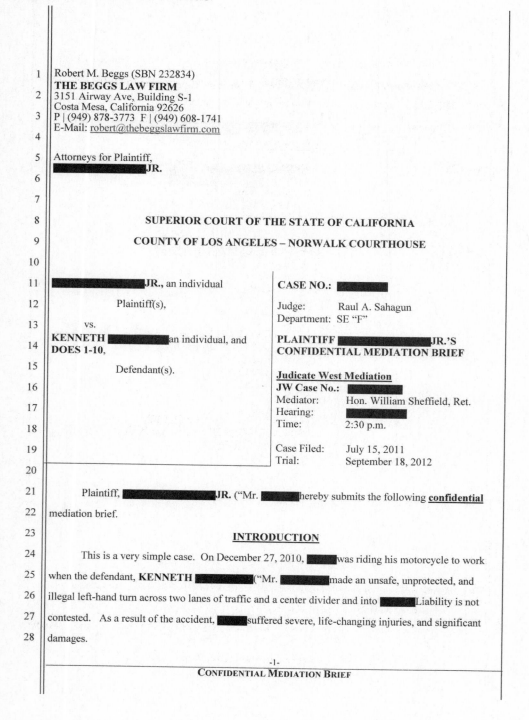

1   To date, the biggest impediments to settlement of this action have been the lack of sufficient

2   insurance coverage and the passing of Mr. ███████[1]. Following his death, Mr. ████████ widow, Mrs.

3   Jeri L. ████████ was in mourning and subsequently required a surgery –rendering her unwilling and/or

4   unavailable until now to address and resolve this action.

5   **PARTIES TO THE ACTION**

6   **Plaintiff:**   ███████████████
    Counsel: Robert M. Beggs, Esq.

7   The Beggs Law Firm
                         3151 Airway Ave., S-1

8   Costa Mesa, CA 92626

9

10   **Defendants:**   **KENNETH** ████████ (████████
    Insurance Counsel: Margaret Ann Dunne, Esq.

11   Richardson, Fair & Cohen
                         3700 Central Ave., 3rd Floor

12   Riverside, CA 92506

13

14   Cumis Counsel: Marvin Louis Wolf, Esq.
                         Law Offices of Marvin Louis Wolf

15   433 N. Camden Drive, Suite 400
                         Beverly Hills, CA 90210

16

17   **Defendants who have not appeared**[2]:

18   **DOE 1:** The Estate of Kenneth ████████
                         DOE 2: Jeri L. ████████ Personal representative of the Estate of

19   Kenneth ████████

20

21

22

23

24

25

26   [1]/ Mr. ████████ liability coverage is only $25,000. He passed on November 18, 2011. His passing was unrelated to the
accident that is the subject of this lawsuit.

27   [2]/ The Estate of Kenneth ████████ and Mrs. ████████ have both been served with the Summons and Complaint. However, we
are informed that a probate estate has not yet been opened for ████████ As discussed below, if the matter does not resolve at

28   mediation, we will immediately file a petition for probate and appointment of a personal representative on behalf of ████████
estate.

-2-
CONFIDENTIAL MEDIATION BRIEF

1   **FACTUAL AND PROCEDURAL HISTORY**

2   **A.   Factual History**

3   On December 27, 2010, Mr. ███ was riding his motorcycle eastbound on Centralia Street

4   within the city of Lakewood, at a speed not exceeding the posted speed limit. Just prior to the collision,

5   Mr. ███ was traveling westbound on Centralia Street and proceeded to make an unprotected and

6   unsafe left-hand turn across two lanes and the center divider ("U-turn") directly into Mr. ███[3].

7   As a direct result of Mr. ███ failure to yield, he collided with Mr. ███ Upon impact,

8   Mr. ███ was thrown from his motorcycle and sustained severe bodily injury. The force of the

9   collision also caused extensive damage to Mr. ███ motorcycle, which was declared a total loss.

10   Following the collision, Mr. ███ was rushed via ambulance to the Long Beach Memorial

11   Hospital Emergency Room where, after full examination and x-rays were obtained, it was confirmed

12   that he sustained multiple rib fractures, a lacerated spleen, a left lung contusion, and a severely

13   comminuted fracture of his left proximal femur (hip). Not surprisingly, Mr. ███ was also suffering

14   from intense pain.

15   Mr. ███ was immediately admitted to the intensive care unit in serious condition and

16   underwent emergency surgery on his left hip and femur. During the procedure, Mr. ███ had a

17   titanium rod implanted through the center of his left femur and an intersecting titanium screw implanted

18   through the femoral neck and head in order to repair the fracture. The surgical hardware implanted into

19   Mr. ███ body will remain permanently, or until the hip is replaced. Mr. ███ remained at Long

20   Beach Memorial Hospital for more than a week.

21   Upon discharge from the hospital, Mr. ███ was bed ridden for several weeks. Due to the

22   nature and extent of his injuries, Mr. ███ was unable to walk or place any weight on his left side for

23   nearly six months after the accident. When he was finally cleared to get out of bed, he received

24   extensive physical therapy, including range of motion therapy, endurance training, bed/transfer mobility

25   training, gait training, and therapy to help him regain his balance and coordination.

26   ///

27

28   _____
[3] At his deposition, ███ admitted to pulling to the curb on the right-hand side of the street in order to check traffic before making the U-turn. He then proceeded from the curb, across the two lanes of traffic going in his direction and the double-yellow median between the opposing lanes of traffic, and struck ███

CONFIDENTIAL MEDIATION BRIEF

1   Though he is recovering, Mr. ████continues to undergo physical therapy in order to restore full

2   function and further alleviate his pain. His leg is now ¾" shorter than it was before the accident, and he

3   walks with a cane. He also recently underwent a second surgery on his hip to grind down the pin, which

4   was causing him severe pain when walking and sitting. And, his doctors believe that he will need a hip

5   replacement surgery within the next 10-12 years, if not sooner.

6   **B.   Procedural History.**

7   This action was filed on July 15, 2011 and was originally scheduled for trial on July 9, 2012.

8   The parties have completed all fact discovery, including the depositions of Mr. ████and Mr. ████

9   Following Mr. ████passing this past November, and at the request of Mrs. ████*cumis*

10 counsel, Mr. ████agreed to give Mrs. ████time to grieve, and then to recover from surgery before

11 continuing with litigation in earnest.

12 The parties stipulated to a trial continuance in order that we could attend mediation and attempt

13 to resolve the matter without incurring further costs. Trial is now set for September 18, 2012.

14 <u>**ARGUMENT**</u>

15 **A.   Mr. ████is liable for negligence.**

16 Mr. ████failed to yield the right-of-way to Mr. ████when he attempted to complete an

17 illegal U-turn across several lanes of traffic. As a direct and proximate result of his failure to yield, Mr.

18 ████sustained serious injuries and damages.

19 **B.   Mr. ████may enforce a judgment against Mr. ████separate and community**

20 **property.**

21 Mr. ████death has delayed and, perhaps, complicated resolution of this action –but it has

22 not reduced or eliminated the assets available for satisfaction of a judgment in this case. Indeed, the

23 California *Family Code* clearly provides that the community estate is liable for debts, including

24 obligations arising from tort, incurred by either spouse during the marriage. CAL. FAM. CODE §§ 900,

25 910(a). Since a tort debt is incurred at the time the tort is committed, to the extent that Mr. ████

26 separate assets cannot satisfy his debt, all community assets still held by Mrs. ████may be targeted.

27 See, CAL. FAM. CODE § 903.

28 ///

-4-
CONFIDENTIAL MEDIATION BRIEF

1   Mr. ▓▓recognizes that in order to gain access to Mr. ▓▓▓▓assets (beyond insurance

2   proceeds) he has to make a claim against Mr. ▓▓▓estate. CAL. PROBATE CODE §§ 554, 9390. We

3   are informed and believe that a probate estate has not yet been opened. And, barring settlement at

4   mediation or written confirmation of Mrs. ▓▓▓intention to open a probate action within 30 days,

5   we will immediately file a petition for probate and appointment of a personal representative, as well as a

6   section 9390 claim against the estate.

DAMAGES

A.   Medical Expenses

9   Mr. ▓▓has incurred significant medical expenses as a result of his injuries. Following the

10   accident, he spent a week at Long Beach Memorial Hospital (four days in the Intensive Care Unit),

11   where he underwent surgeries to remove his spleen and repair his hip and leg. Since his discharge from

12   the hospital, he has had extensive physical therapy. And, he had a follow-up surgery just two weeks ago

13   to grind off a portion of the pin that is holding his hip together. Mr. ▓▓▓billed medical expenses to

14   date are $88,442.75[4].

15   We are informed and believe that the cost of Mr. ▓▓▓recent surgery to adjust the pin in his

16   hip will be approximately $30,000.

17   Our expert orthopaedic surgeon and life care planner inform us that as a result of his injury, Mr.

18   ▓▓will likely need a full hip replacement within the next 10-12 years. They estimate the total cost of

19   the hip replacement and associated care and treatment to be $100,000.

20   As such, if the matter proceeds to trial, we anticipate putting on evidence of past and future

21   medical expense damages of not less than **$218,442.75**.

22   ///

23   ///

24   ///

25

26

27

28   [4]/ The charged amount of Mr. ▓▓▓medical expenses to date is $141,863.06. The above-referenced amount is after
Howell reductions. *Howell v. Hamilton Meats* (2011) 52 Cal.4th. 241.

CONFIDENTIAL MEDIATION BRIEF

1   **B.   Lost Earnings**

2   Mr. ▮▮▮ has been working as an amateur radio technician for more than a decade. He is full-

3   time hourly employee, who enjoys significant overtime. Mr. ▮▮▮ was unable to return to work for six

4   months following the accident. During that time, he was unable to earn any income. A review and

5   analysis of Mr. ▮▮▮ earnings statement for the three years prior to his accident confirm that for the

6   six months that Mr. ▮▮▮ was out of work, he lost a total of $**36,754.35**.

7   **C.   Pain and Suffering**

8   Mr. ▮▮▮ is 60 years old and was in good health prior to the collision. The injuries he sustained

9   have caused a significant impact to his physical condition and have lowered his overall quality of life.

10   He currently lives with constant pain in his left hip, right knee, and lower back, which makes sitting,

11   standing, walking, rehabilitation, and exercise difficult. Further, his injuries have permanently affected

12   the anatomical function of his hip, including his range of motion and gait, which adds to his current

13   difficulties. Moreover, because the side effects of the prescribed pain medication affect his mental

14   awareness and acuity, Mr. ▮▮▮ is forced to suffer constant pain in exchange for remaining mentally

15   alert.

16   For the first several months following his surgery, Mr. ▮▮▮ was confined to bed and then a

17   wheelchair. During that time, he was in constant pain and discomfort. Even his mental health suffered

18   as he battled with anxiety and depression. When he was finally cleared to begin bearing weight on his

19   leg, he had to re-learn how to walk. At first, he couldn't walk without the assistance of a walker. He

20   eventually transitioned to a cane, and can now walk without the cane for short periods of time. Each

21   step of the rehabilitation process was, quite literally, excruciatingly painful. Even now, walking

22   exacerbates the severe pain in his right knee and lower back (resulting from the modified gate

23   necessitated by a shorter leg).

24   A review of settlements and verdicts in similar cases (i.e., similar factual circumstances, injuries,

25   and/or treatment) confirms that, on average, plaintiffs with Mr. ▮▮▮ injuries can expect to recover

26   between $475,000 and $600,000 in pain and suffering damages.

27   ///

28   ///

1 **SETTLEMENT POSTURE**

2 .In consideration of his chances of success, a preliminary review of the defendant's assets, and in

3 an effort to avoid unnecessary litigation costs, Mr. ███████made a pre-suit settlement demand of

4 $400,000.00. Though Mr. ████████insurance provider immediately offered the policy limits of

5 $25,000, the defendant has never offered any additional sum to resolve this matter.

6 Mr. ███████conservatively estimates that his chances of prevailing at trial are between 80% and

7 95%. The combined total of his economic and non-economic damages are between $730,000 and

8 $850,000. Therefore, we believe the appropriate settlement range to be between $584,000 and

9 $808,000.

10 Mr. ███████understands, however, that Mr. █████████estate (including the community property

11 interest in Mrs. ████████assets) is not large enough to fully compensate him for his injuries and

12 damages. Therefore, we are presently amenable to reduced settlement sum that will reasonably

13 compensate Mr. ███████without forcing Mrs. ██████████(who owns two homes) onto the street. Should

14 this matter fail to settle at mediation, however, Mr. ██████is prepared to open a probate action on behalf

15 of Mr. █████████estate and he will seek to enforce, **in full**, any judgment he recovers at trial.

16 **CONCLUSION**

17 This is a very simple case. Mr. ████████negligence in the operation of his motor vehicle caused

18 the accident and severe and life-changing injuries to Mr. ████████Liability is not disputed. The

19 reasonableness and necessity of Mr. ████████medical care and expenses is not disputed. Mr. ███████

20 potential damages exceed $800,000. Still, he is willing to consider a significant discount on that amount

21 to allow Mrs. ████████to remain in one of her homes on a going forward basis.

22

23 **DATED:** June 13, 2012   **THE BEGGS LAW FIRM**

24

25   By:_Robert M. Beggs_____

26   Robert M. Beggs, Esq.
                                     Attorneys for Plaintiff,
27   ██████████████**JR.**

28

CONFIDENTIAL MEDIATION BRIEF

1   Robert M. Beggs (SBN: 232834)
     THE BEGGS LAW FIRM
2   3151 Airway Ave., Building S-1
     Costa Mesa, California 92626
3   P | (949) 878-3773   F | (949) 608-1741
     E-Mail: robert@thebeggslawfirm.com
4

     Neil B. Fineman (SBN: 177915)
5   **FINEMAN & ASSOCIATES**
     155 N. Riverview Dr.
6   Anaheim Hills, California 92808
     P | (714) 620-1125 F | (714) 701-0155
7

8   Attorneys for Plaintiff,
9   ███████████

10

11   **SUPERIOR COURT OF THE STATE OF CALIFORNIA**

12   **COUNTY OF LOS ANGELES – STANLEY MOSK COURTHOUSE**

13

14 ███████████ on behalf of herself and all others similarly situated,	**CASE NO.:** ███████
15	Judge: Mary H. Strobel
16 Plaintiff(s),	Department: 32
17 vs.	**PLAINTIFF'S MEDIATION BRIEF**
18 ███████████**INC.**, a California corporation; and **DOES** 1 through 50, inclusive,	
19 Defendant(s).	Mediation Date: ███████████
20	Time: 9:00 a.m. Dept.: Judicate West – Santa Ana
21	
22	Complaint Filed: October 18, 2011 Trial Date: TBD

23   **TO THE HONORABLE JOHN LEO WAGNER:**

24   Plaintiff, ███████████hereby submits the following mediation brief for your review.

25   ///

26   ///

27   ///

28

-1-

PLAINTIFF'S MEDIATION BRIEF

I.

INTRODUCTION

The legal issues in this case are straightforward: Plaintiff, ███████████ (███████) alleges that defendant, ██████████████ INC. (███████ has and continues to blatantly, systematically, and unapologetically violate the *Song-Beverly Credit Card Act* of 1971 (specifically California *Civil Code* Section 1747.08) and the common law privacy rights of each of its credit card customers. Specifically, ██████ alleges that ██████ unlawfully requested and recorded each of its credit card customers' full addresses and telephone numbers, and utilized a credit card form containing preprinted spaces specifically designated for filling in its customers' personal identification information. ██████ brought the instant consumer class action in order to (1) require ██████ to pay civil penalties of up to $1,000 per violation to each class member; (2) compel ██████ to destroy the personal identification information it has already collected, and (3) enjoin ██████ from requesting and recording personal identification information from future credit card customers.

II.

STATEMENT OF FACTS

A.   ██████ **Personal Identification Information Capture Program**

██████ has been unlawfully collecting its customers' personal identification information for several decades. In fact, ██████ sales representatives are trained to request and record the customer's name, address and telephone number during each transaction. Initially, customer personal identification information is recorded in ██████ computer information system, but it is thereafter printed to hard copy and stored at ██████ corporate offices and warehouses. ██████ contends that the primary purpose of requesting personal identification information is to facilitate delivery of its products and process warranty claims. However, ██████ collects personal identification information even when the customer takes possession of the purchased products at the point of sale, and even though it does not actually use the information to validate warranty claims.

Strikingly, ██████ freely admits that it has used its customers' personal identification information in direct mail marketing campaigns.

///

-2-

1   B.   **The Personal Identification Information of Every ███████Customer is Requested**

2   **and Recorded**

3   ████████concedes that it is its policy to request and record personal identification information

4   for each and every transaction processed in its stores. It further acknowledges using a credit card

5   form containing preprinted spaces specifically designated for filling in the personal identification

6   information of its credit card customers. By so doing, ██████has violated California *Civil Code*

7   Section 1747.08 for every credit card transaction it processed from at least October 18, 2009 through

8   the present. ████████personal experience at ██████is demonstrative:

9   ████████went shopping for a box spring for her son at ██████Laguna Niguel location on July

10 3, 2011. After entering the store, she was greeted by a sales representative and shown various

11 products that might meet her needs. When she decided on a particular box spring, she inquired if it

12 was in stock and told the sales representative that she intended to take her purchase with her that day.

13 When she learned that the box spring was in stock, she informed the sales representative that she

14 would like to make the purchase and pay with her Discover Card.

15   The sales representative then invited ██████to the counter to process the transaction. At that

16 time, she handed ██████a piece of paper and requested that she write down her full name, street

17 address, and telephone number. ████████who believed that she was required to provide the

18 information, complied. Thereafter, the sales representative entered ████████personal identification

19 information into ██████computer system and generated an invoice.   The sales representative then

20 swiped ████████credit card and took an imprint of the card on a form containing a preprinted space

21 for filling in ██████customers' driver's license numbers.

22 ///

23 ///

24 ///

25

26

27

28

-3-

PLAINTIFF'S MEDIATION BRIEF

III.

LEGAL BASIS FOR LIABILITY

California *Civil Code* section 1747.08 generally states it is unlawful for any retailer which accepts credit cards to request and record personal identification information from a customer paying with a credit card. Section 1747.08 is part of the *Song-Beverly Credit Card Act* and was designed to promote consumer protection. *Florez v. Linens 'N Things, Inc.* (2003) 108 Cal.App.4th 447, 450.

Section 1747.08 was originally enacted as a response to two principal privacy concerns: first, that with increased use of computer technology, very specific and personal information about a consumer's spending habits was being made available to anyone willing to pay for it; and second, that acts of harassment and violence were being committed by store clerks who obtained customers' personal identification information. *Id.* at 452. Additionally, there is the risk that credit card customers will be subjected to identity theft, unwanted marketing and solicitations.

A.   ██████**Argument for Liability and Civil Penalties**

██████argument is simple: she contends that every time ████requested and recorded personal identification information from a credit card paying customer in California who took possession of the purchase at the point of sale, ████violated California *Civil Code* section 1747.08. And, every time ████used a credit card form containing preprinted spaces specifically designated for filling in its customers' personal identification information, it violated Section 1747.08. Any retailer that violates Section 1747.08 shall pay civil penalties of up to $1,000 per violation. CAL. CIV. CODE § 1747.08(e).

B.   ██████**Argument Against Liability and Civil Penalties**

████admits that it requests and records personal identification information from all its customers, including those paying by credit card. It argues, however, that its practice is acceptable because: (1) the majority of its customers require an in-home delivery of the purchased products; (2) it needs the personal identification information of its customers to process warranty claims; and (3) that the collection of personal identification information is voluntary and not a condition precedent for completing a transaction.

///

-4-

PLAINTIFF'S MEDIATION BRIEF

1   C.   ▆▆▆▆▆**Counter-Argument**

2   1.   <u>The fact that some transactions may necessitate the collection of personal</u>

3   <u>identification information does not exempt all transactions from the general</u>

4   <u>prohibition</u>.

5   California *Civil Code* section 1747.07 makes it unlawful for any retailer which accepts credit

6   cards to request and record personal identification information from a customer paying with a credit

7   card, except where the "personal identification information is required for a *special purpose*

8   *incidental but related to the individual transaction*, including but not limited to, information relating

9   to shipping, delivery, servicing, or installation of the purchased merchandise, or for special orders."

10   Cal. Civ. Code § 1747.08(c)(4) (emphasis added).   By definition, the delivery exemption does not

11   apply to credit card customers who took possession of their purchase at the point of sale. Therefore,

12   ▆▆▆▆▆practice of collecting personal identification information from those customers is unlawful.

13   2.   <u>Retailers cannot collect personal identification information from credit card customers</u>

14   <u>under the guise of warranty processing.</u>

15   The processing of warranty claims is not a special purpose incidental but related to the

16   individual transactions, and no court has ever ruled that a retailer may request personal identification

17   information at the time of sale for this purpose. It is not surprising that such an exception does not

18   exist because, if it did, it would obviate the carefully drafted consumer protections contained within

19   *Civil Code* section 1747.08. Moreover, it is well established that warranties are voluntarily registered

20   *after purchase and delivery* of the product by the completion of a warranty card. Regardless, the

21   extensive discovery completed in this case confirms that ▆▆▆▆does not use any personal

22   identification information to process or validate warranty claims. Instead, it process is limited to

23   identifying the customer by name and invoice number. Therefore, ▆▆▆▆cannot collect personal

24   identification information from its credit card customers under the guise of warranty processing.

25   ///

26   ///

27   ///

28

3. <u>The voluntary provision of personal identification information during a credit card</u>

   <u>transaction is not a defense.</u>

Pursuant to California *Civil Code* section 1747.08 retailers are prohibited from requesting that their credit card customers voluntarily provide their personal identification information. In this regard, *Florez v. Linens 'N Things, Inc., supra,* is instructive:

> [S]ection 1747.8 is designed to prevent a 'request' for personal information, because a customer might perceive that request as a condition of credit card payment. In effect, <u>the 1991 amendment prevents a retailer from making an end-run around the law by claiming the customer furnished personal identification data 'voluntarily.'</u> In fact, the Enrolled Bill Report of the California Department of Consumer Affairs, Assembly Bill No. 1477 (1991-1992 Reg. Sess.), specifically addressed this problem, noting '[t]his bill would prohibit requesting or requiring that information.' As we read it, the legislative intent suggests the 1991 amendment simply clarified that a 'request' for personal identification information was <u>prohibited if it immediately preceded the credit card transaction, even if the consumer's response was voluntary</u> and made only for marketing purposes. *Florez, supra,* 108 Cal.App.4th at 453 (emphasis added).

The California Supreme Court has since confirmed that there is no "voluntary" defense in section 1747.08 cases. *Pineda v. Williams-Sonoma Stores, Inc.* (2011) 51 Cal.4th 524. In *Pineda,* the Supreme Court emphasized that retailers could not avoid liability under section 1747.08 by claiming the customer furnished personal identification data "voluntarily." *Id.* at 535. The Court went on to hold that, "the legislative history of the Credit Card Act in general, and section 1747.08 in particular, demonstrates the Legislature intended to provide robust consumer protections by prohibiting retailers from soliciting and recording information about the cardholder that is unnecessary to the credit card transaction." *Id.* at 535-36.

Similarly, consumers cannot "waive" the prohibition against requesting and recording personal identification information during a credit card transaction. The *Song-Beverly Credit Card Act* contains an "anti-waiver" statute, which effectively deprives ███ of its "voluntary" defense. California *Civil Code* section 1747.04 provides that "[a]ny waiver of the provisions of [the *Song-Beverly Credit Card Act*] is contrary to public policy, and is void and unenforceable."

///

PLAINTIFF'S MEDIATION BRIEF

1   Accordingly, even if ▮▮employees followed a script and requested a credit card

2 customer's personal identification information so that the customer could receive information from

3 ▮▮the customer cannot waive the prohibition against retailers requesting and recording personal

4 identification information during a credit card transaction.

5   For each of these reasons, ▮▮believes the class will be awarded substantial civil penalties

6 if this action proceeds to trial.

7   **IV.**

8   **RELEVANT DATES AND CLASS SIZE**

9   ▮▮has failed to meaningfully respond to ▮▮discovery requests regarding class size.

10 In fact, as recently as September 4, 2013, ▮▮confirmed that it has not made any effort to calculate

11 the actual or potential number of credit card customers who made purchases from its California stores

12 from October 18, 2009 through the present. According to its discovery responses, ▮▮estimates

13 that is processes approximately 4,000 credit card transactions per month. The customer takes

14 possession of the purchase at the point of sale in approximately 5% of those transactions.

15   Accordingly, and though ▮▮concedes that business card and debit card purchases (and

16 any form of return) are not considered violations of the *Song-Beverly Credit Card Act*, she believes

17 the number of actual violations of *Civil Code* section 1747.08 and, thus, the number of class members

18 exceeds 190,000. More specifically, ▮▮violated *Civil Code* section 1747.08 by utilizing a credit

19 card form containing preprinted spaces specifically designated for filling in its customers' personal

20 identification information on at least 190,000 occasions. And, ▮▮violated *Civil Code* section

21 1747.08 by requesting and recording each of its credit card customers' full addresses and telephone

22 numbers, despite the lack of a special purpose incidental but related to the individual transaction, on

23 at least 9,600 occasions.

24 ///

25 ///

26 ///

27

28

-7-
PLAINTIFF'S MEDIATION BRIEF

V.

BASIS FOR CLASS CERTIFICATION

The California Supreme Court has long held that *Civil Code* section 1747.08 cases are proper class actions, and there is no doubt that the class will be certified in this case. *See, Linder v. Thrifty Oil Co.* (2000) 23 Cal.4th 429.

Here, █████principal argument against certification is that: (1) class members cannot be identified without unreasonable expense; and, (2) █████is not a qualified to serve as the class representative because of a conflict of interest between her and her counsel. Both arguments fail. First, █████cannot avoid class certification by claiming it is too expensive to identify and notify potential class members. See, *Hypertouch, Inc. v. Superior Court* (2005) 128 Cal.App.4th 1527, 1552-1553. Second, the court has already ruled that there is no conflict of interest between █████ and her counsel, Robert Beggs. Therefore, █████argument will be not be sufficient to defeat certification.

Moreover, █████has since retained Neil Fineman, who has successfully won certification in several other nearly identical *Civil Code* section 1747.08 cases over strong opposition by defendants. Accordingly, there is little doubt that this action will be certified with a potential class of over 190,000 consumers.

VI.

█████EXPOSURE EXCEEDS $190,000,000.00

Pursuant to *Civil Code* section 1747.08(e), violators of the statute shall be liable for a civil penalty of up to $250.00 for the first violation and up to $1,000.00 for each subsequent violation. The trial court has discretion as to the amount of penalties awarded, but the duty to impose a penalty for each violation is mandatory. *Pineda*, 51 Cal.4th at 536; *The TJX Companies, Inc. v. Superior Court* (2008) 163 Cal.App.4th 80, 85. The inclusion of a civil penalty provision in a statute presumes the statute affects important public rights. Thus, "[p]enalties are designed to deter as well as compensate." *State of California v. City and County of San Francisco* (1979) 94 Cal.App.3d 522, 531. "[C]ivil penalties may have a punitive or deterrent aspect, [but] their primary purpose is to secure obedience to statutes and regulations imposed to assure important public policy objectives."

-8-

1   *Kizer v. County of San Mateo* (1991) 53 Cal.3d 139, 147-148. "A penalty statute presupposes that its

2   violation produces damage beyond that which is compensable." *People ex rel. State Air Resources*

3   *Board v. Wilmshurst* (1999) 68 Cal.App.4th 1332, 1351; see also, *City and County of San Francisco*

4   *v. Sainez* (2000) 77 Cal.App.4th 1302, 1315.

5   Once ████ has proven that there has been a violation of a penalty statute, it becomes

6   "defendant's burden to establish . . . that the amount of penalty imposed should be less than the

7   maximum." *State of California v. City of San Francisco*, 94 Cal.App.4th 522, 546-47; *See also, Rich*

8   *v. Schwab* (1998) 63 Cal.App.4th 803, 817. Ultimately, the amount of the penalties awarded to

9   ████ and the class members for ████ violations of *Civil Code* Section 1747.08 "rests within the

10   sound discretion of the trial court". *Pineda*, 51 Cal.4th at 536. However, "achieving deterrent

11   purposes supposes that the penalty is large enough to hurt overall, not just diminish the value" of

12   ████ assets. *Starving Students, Inc. v. Department of Industrial Relations* (2005) 125 Cal.App.4th

13   1357, 1367.

14   With a class size exceeding 190,000, civil penalties could be more than $190,000,000.00.

15   ████ counsel recognizes the judge in this action may not order the full $1,000-per-violation

16   penalty against ████ However, even if each class member is awarded a mere 10% of the statutory

17   maximum (e.g., $100), ████ will be ordered to pay out $19,000,000.00 into a common fund for the

18   class. And that figure does not include defense fees and costs, ████ counsel's fees and costs,

19   class administration fees and costs, etc. Even a 10% penalty will not constitute a large expenditure

20   for ████ which grosses $45 million a year.

21   ///

22   ///

23   ///

24

25

26

27

28

-9-

PLAINTIFF'S MEDIATION BRIEF

1   **VII.**

2   **SIGNIFICANT PENALTIES ARE JUSTIFIED IN THIS ACTION**

3   As set forth above, civil penalties are meant to, among other things, deter a defendant from

4 engaging in the proscribed conduct. Here, despite full knowledge of its bad acts, ████continues to

5 do what it has for several decades: blatantly, systematically, and unapologetically violate California

6 *Civil Code* Section 1747.08 and the common law privacy rights of each of its credit card customers.

7 Moreover, ████unlawfully collected its credit card customers' personal identification information in

8 order to do exactly what the statute was designed to prevent – to compile mailing lists and conduct

9 direct mail marketing campaigns. Accordingly, ████flagrant disregard for the law will not go

10 unpunished.

11   **VIII.**

12   ████**PROPOSED TERMS FOR SETTLEMENT AT MEDIATION**

13   At this point in the litigation, ████would agree to settle the matter on the following terms:

14   1.   ████agrees to a permanent injunction requiring it to fully comply with *Civil Code*

15 section 1747.08 in all of its California stores;

16   2.   ████agrees to purge and destroy all of the personal identification information it has

17 collected from credit card customers from one year prior to the filing of the complaint to the present;

18   3.   ████stipulates to a certified settlement class and pays all fees and costs associated

19 with class administration and class notice;

20   4.   ████agrees to directly mail or email a cash payment, in an amount to be negotiated,

21 to each identifiable class member;

22   5.   ████agrees to provide a modest enhancement award to the class representative; and,

23   6.   ████agrees to pay attorneys' fees and costs consistent with the fees and costs agreed

24 upon in other 1747.08 actions.

25 ///

26 ///

27 ///

28

-10-

PLAINTIFF'S MEDIATION BRIEF

1   ████ and her counsel seek a fair result from this mediation and look forward to the

2   assistance the mediator will provide in reaching this goal.

3

4   **DATED:** September 20, 2013   **THE BEGGS LAW FIRM**

5

6   By:_____

7   Robert M. Beggs, Esq.
                                                 Attorneys for Plaintiff,

8   ██████████████ and the Class

9

10   **DATED:** September 20, 2013   **FINEMAN & ASSOCIATES**

11

12   By:_____

13   Neil B. Fineman, Esq.
                                                 Attorneys for Plaintiff,
                                                    ██████████████ and the Class

14

15

16

17

18

19

20

21

22

23

24

25

26

27

28

Grammar and Punctuation

Some people enjoy the great fortune of having learned the rules of grammar and punctuation in eighth grade, high school, or college. Others have learned a few rules here or there or by osmosis. If you fall into the latter group, it is time to make sure that you know at least the basics. If you are very deficient, you need to consult one of the many books on writing composition and grammar. If you do not already have one of these grammar books from college or high school, you should get one. You also should consult with a writing specialist at either your law school or college.

This appendix is not designed to be a comprehensive remedial handbook. Instead, it reviews the rules of grammar and punctuation most likely to create difficulties for the law student. Part A explains six rules of grammar and offers exercises to help you test your learning. Part B reviews the main rules for using commas, semicolons, colons, and dashes. It also discusses quotations.

Part A: Grammar

Part A discusses six rules:

1. Make sure each modifier unambiguously refers to the word that you want it to modify.
2. Make sure each pronoun clearly refers to the word for which it is a substitute.
3. If you are referring to a singular noun, use a singular pronoun. If you are referring to a plural noun, use a plural pronoun.
4. Make the subject agree with the verb.
5. Use "its" to denote the possessive and "it's" to abbreviate "it is."
6. Use "which" to introduce a nonrestrictive clause. Use "that" to introduce a restrictive clause.

Rule 1. Make sure each modifier unambiguously refers to the word that you want it to modify.

A modifier is a word, phrase, or clause that describes, alters, or clarifies another word in the sentence. For example:

The statute gives manufacturers a second incentive to comply with the regulations.

"Second" tells us more about "incentive." It modifies "incentive." "To comply" also is a modifier. It tells us more about "incentive." The incentive is designed to encourage manufacturers to comply with the regulations.

Watch out for misplaced modifiers. A sentence has a misplaced modifier when the reader might think that the modifier applies to a word different than the one the writer intended. The problem arises when the modifier is in the wrong location. Here is an example:

> The court discussed the need for a written contract in a brief paragraph.

"In a brief paragraph" might modify "discussed" and tell us how much space the court's opinion devotes to this topic. Alternatively, it might modify "written contract" and tell us how long the written contract should be. Because of the location of the modifying phrase, the reader may not know which message you intended to communicate. Presumably the phrase modifies "discussed." If so, the sentence has a misplaced modifier. You can clear up the ambiguity by relocating the phrase. Here are some acceptable alternatives:

> In a brief paragraph, the court discussed the need for a written contract.
> The court discussed, in a brief paragraph, the need for a written contract.
> The court, in a brief paragraph, discussed the need for a written contract.

Sometimes, a poorly written sentence contains the modifier, but not the word to which the modifier applies. Here is an example:

> Faced with a statutory deadline, it is important to proceed quickly.

Who is faced with a statutory deadline? The sentence fails to tell us. The initial phrase is a dangling modifier because the sentence does not contain the word it modifies. The problem is easy to fix:

> Faced with a statutory deadline, counsel must proceed quickly.

The next example illustrates a related problem:

> Faced with a statutory deadline, quick action by counsel becomes necessary.

As written, the initial phrase seems to modify "quick action." However, the phrase must modify the actor, "counsel." To solve the problem, place the modifier next to the word it modifies:

> Faced with a statutory deadline, counsel must act quickly.

Exercise

Please rewrite so that the modifiers unambiguously refer to the words you want to modify.

1. To prevail before an appellate court, a sound record must be developed before the trial court.

2. Once considered a major part of the civil procedure course, only modest attention is paid to the forms of action in today's law school curriculum.
3. The commission encouraged the companies immediately to go into production.
4. They only praised the decision, but not the rationale.
5. After examining the complaint, it is necessary to consider possible pretrial motions.

Rule 2. Make sure each pronoun clearly refers to the word for which it is a substitute.

The professor questioned the student about the issue that he was exploring.

Does "he" refer to the professor or the student? Was the professor exploring the issue or was the student exploring it? The sentence does not tell us in an unambiguous fashion. Here are three ways to rewrite the sentence, assuming "he" refers to the professor:

1. The professor questioned the student about the issue that the professor was exploring.
2. In exploring the issue, the professor questioned the student about it.
3. The professor explored the issue and questioned the student about it.

Be particularly careful when you use "this," "that," or "those." Make sure the pronoun clearly refers to an antecedent. For example:

The court encountered criticism for making a de novo review of the evidence. This is not the function of an appellate court.

To what does "this" refer? We can solve the problem with a simple revision:

The court encountered criticism for making a de novo review of the evidence. Making such a review is not the function of an appellate court.

Exercise

Please revise these sentences so that the pronouns clearly refer to the words for which they are a substitute.

1. A friend of the decedent testified that she had been harassed at work in the weeks before the assault.
2. The plaintiff granted a single interview to a reporter. This would be inconsistent with the court's definition of media access.
3. The evidence was quite scanty. That made the prosecutor nervous.
4. Although taking exams dominates the month of December, it rarely is as taxing as students expect it to be.
5. The distinction between public and private figures is that they have media access to refute any defamation.

Rule 3. If you are referring to a singular noun, use a singular pronoun. If you are referring to a plural noun, use a plural pronoun.

Study this sentence:

If the corporation files for bankruptcy, they must notify their creditors.

"Corporation" is singular. The proper pronouns are "it" and "its." "They" and "their" are incorrect.

> If the corporation files for bankruptcy, it must notify its creditors.

Here is another example:

> Although the insurance company's representatives accepted the premiums, they now refuse to honor the policy.

The subject of the second clause is the insurance company, not the insurance company's representatives. Therefore, the correct pronoun is "it."

> Although the insurance company's representatives accepted the premiums, it now refuses to honor the policy.

Exercise

Please revise these sentences so that single pronouns refer to single nouns and plural pronouns refer to plural nouns.

1. The Third Circuit was correct in determining that the statements were capable of defamatory meaning. Their decision should be upheld.
2. This practice creates a monopoly-like situation for the third party in which they are free to do whatever they wish.
3. The appellant's punitive damage claim should be dismissed because their fraud claim has been dismissed.
4. Every person in the neighborhood was asked to sign their name to the zoning petition.

Rule 4. Make the subject agree with the verb.

If the subject of the sentence or clause is singular, the verb must be singular. If the subject is plural, the verb must be plural. Although we know this rule, we sometimes break it by being careless.

In each of these examples, the subject and verb do not agree:

1. A variety of rhetorical devices appear in the appellate brief.
2. A lay dictionary, as well as a legal dictionary, are essential to an office library.
3. Either of the appellant's rationales require the court to accept a highly innovative argument. ("Either" means "either rationale.")

Exercise

Please revise these sentences so that subjects and verbs agree.

1. Everyone in the office say they met the deadline.
2. None of the memoranda recommend pursuing the matter.
3. The newspaper coverage in the surrounding counties were extensive.
4. Neither of the cotenants wish to partition the acreage.
5. The best part of the brief are the last five pages.

Rule 5. Use "its" to denote the possessive and "it's" to abbreviate "it is."

"It's" is the contraction of "it is." "Its" is the possessive of "it." Just as the possessive pronouns "her" and "his" have no apostrophe, the possessive pronoun "its" has no apostrophe.

Although the argument appears innovative, its roots extend well into the last century.

"Its roots" means the roots of the argument. The pronoun refers to the argument. Because "its" is a substitute for "the argument's," it is in the possessive and has no apostrophe.

Because legal writing is formal, contractions should be used only rarely. Therefore, rarely, if ever, will you use "it's." If you tend to confuse "it's" and "its," remember that in legal writing, the correct word almost always is "its."

Here are two correct examples.

1. Although both parties claimed the privilege of using the easement, neither was willing to pay for its maintenance.
2. According to the first witness, the defendant shouted, "It's time for a couple more beers."

Rule 6. Use "which" to introduce a nonrestrictive clause. Use "that" to introduce a restrictive clause.

Here is a simple way to decide when to use "which" and when to use "that." If you can or should place a comma before the clause, use "which." Otherwise use "that."

The memo that I wrote under considerable time pressure is surprisingly good.

Suppose I wrote only one memo. The clause gives the reader additional information: I wrote it under time pressure. The information in the clause is not essential to identify the memo that is discussed in the sentence. We call this clause a nonrestrictive clause because it adds information but is not essential to identifying the word or clause that it modifies. In a sense, it is parenthetical. We should place a comma before the clause and begin the clause with "which."

However, suppose I wrote several memos and wrote one of them under time pressure. In this case, the clause does more than give the reader additional information; it identifies the memo that I am discussing. We call this clause restrictive clause because it is essential to identifying the word or clause that it modifies. We do not place a comma before the clause, and we begin it with "that."

Exercise

Please rewrite the sentences that use "which" and "that" improperly.

1. Every business that qualifies can seek a tax exemption.
2. The building, which overlooked the river, attracted many tenants. (Assume several other buildings also overlooked the river.)

3. The building which overlooked the river attracted many tenants. (Assume that only this building overlooked the river.)
4. The comma that precedes the clause is unnecessary. (Assume that the sentence contains two commas.)

Part B: Punctuation

Part B explains how to use the comma, colon, semicolon, and dash correctly. It also discusses how to punctuate quotations.

1. The Comma

The rules concerning commas are in flux. The conventional rules require commas in specified situations. In many of these situations, however, the trend is to omit the comma when it does not help the reader to understand the sentence.

Here are six rules for using commas:

1. When using a conjunction to separate the independent clauses in a compound sentence, place a comma before the conjunction.
2. Use a comma after an introductory phrase or clause.
3. Use commas to set off words, phrases, and clauses in a sentence.
4. Use commas to separate words, phrases, and clauses in a series.
5. Use a comma between two adjectives that modify a verb.
6. Use commas in dates.

Rule 1. When using a conjunction to separate the independent clauses in a compound sentence, place a comma before the conjunction.

An independent clause is a clause that could stand alone as a sentence. A compound sentence has two or more independent clauses joined by a semicolon, colon, or a conjunction, such as "or," "but," or "and." Place a comma before the conjunction. Here are two correct examples:

An independent clause must have a subject and a verb, but a phrase need not have them.
    An independent clause must have a subject and verb, and it must be able to stand alone as a sentence.

When the subject of both clauses is only in the first clause, place a comma before the conjunction, unless the conjunction is "and." Here are two correct examples:

An independent clause must have a subject and verb and must be able to stand alone as a sentence.
    An independent clause must have a subject and verb, but need not include a preposition.

Pitfall: Do not separate two independent clauses with a comma. This construction is called a comma splice. Here is a bad example:

An independent clause can stand on its own as a sentence, a dependent clause cannot.

If you wish to place two independent clauses in the same sentence, separate them with a semicolon or with a comma and a conjunction. We can correct the bad example this way:

An independent clause can stand on its own as a sentence, but a dependent clause cannot.

Pitfall: Do not confuse a conjunction with a transitional word that functions like an adverb. Such transitional words include "however," "therefore," "thus," and "moreover." Do not treat these words as conjunctions. Consider this bad example:

The word "and" is a conjunction, however, the word "however" is not.

This sentence is a compound sentence consisting of two independent clauses. Because "however" is not a conjunction, no conjunction separates them. In the absence of a conjunction, you must separate them with a semicolon:

The word "and" is a conjunction; however, the word "however" is not.

Rule 2. Use a comma after an introductory phrase or clause.

The rule is self-explanatory. Here are two good examples:

1. After an introductory phrase, use a comma.
2. In the absence of a conjunction separating independent clauses, you may decide to use a semicolon.

Rule 3. Use commas to set off words, phrases, and clauses in a sentence.

Use commas when the word, phrase, or clause is really parenthetical or otherwise interrupts the sentence. Here are three good examples:

1. A comma, one type of punctuation mark, is overused more than other punctuation marks.
2. A comma, however, has many uses.
3. A grammarian would agree that, as a general rule, a writer should use commas to set off a parenthetical.

Instead of using a comma, you also can use parentheses or dashes. See the discussion of dashes later on in this appendix.

Rule 4. Use commas to separate words, phrases, and clauses in a series.

Here is an example:

Punctuation marks include the comma, the period, the colon, the apostrophe, the question mark, and the semicolon.

Sometimes writers find the last comma unnecessary—here, the comma after "question mark"—and omit it. However, sometimes the last comma is necessary to avoid ambiguity:

The curriculum includes courses in property, contracts, trusts and estates, and legal writing.

Here, the last comma makes it clear that trusts and estates is a separate course from legal writing.

Rule 5. Use a comma between two adjectives that modify a noun.

Here is an example:

An obtrusive, well-placed comma helps the reader out. If the clause does not seem necessary, you may omit it: A comma helps the reader to understand a long, complex sentence.

Rule 6. Use commas in dates.

Place a comma between the day of the month and the year:

September 22, 1945.

Under the traditional rule, you should use a comma between the month and the year when you are not specifying the day:

March, 1952.

However, most writers omit the comma.

2. The Colon

A colon indicates that the words before the colon lead the reader to expect what comes after the colon. For example:

There are three ways to punctuate the end of a sentence: a period, a question mark, and an exclamation point.

The words before the colon lead us to expect the writer to tell us what three punctuation marks can end a sentence. The words after the colon fulfill the expectation. Sometimes a comma will serve the same purpose:

In legal writing, there is one punctuation mark that we almost never use, the exclamation point.

Here we could have used a colon instead of the second comma. Because a colon is more dramatic and legal writing tends to prefer understatement, most legal writers use a comma instead of a colon when they can.

You also can use a colon to introduce a quotation:

The judge frequently quoted Justice Holmes: "The life of the law has not been logic; it has been experience."

3. The Semicolon

Use the semicolon in three situations:

a. When you want to combine two sentences into one sentence, separate them with a semicolon. The semicolon indicates that the two sentences—now independent clauses—have a close connection, but not close enough to use a conjunction. For example:

A semicolon can separate two independent clauses in a sentence; its use indicates a close connection between the clauses.

b. When the second independent clause in a sentence begins with a transition acting as an adverb—such as "however," "therefore," or "moreover," separate the clauses with a semicolon. For example:

You can join independent clauses with a conjunction; however, sometimes a semicolon seems more appropriate.

c. Use a semicolon to separate items in a series when there are commas within some of the items. For example:

Use a semicolon to show the close connection between independent clauses; to precede a transitional adverb such as "however," "therefore," or "thus"; and to separate items in a series when there are commas within some of the items.

4. The Dash

Use dashes to set off words that interrupt the continuity of a sentence. For example:

Use dashes—make one by typing two hyphens next to one another—to set off words that interrupt the continuity of a sentence.

Use dashes when the interruption is a major one. Otherwise, use commas or parentheses, whichever seems appropriate. Usually parentheses draw the least attention to the interruption. For example:

A dash (not a parenthesis) signals a major interruption in a sentence.

5. Quotations

The Bluebook, Rule 54 and the ALWD Citation Manual, Rules 47-49, prescribe the rules for punctuating quotations. Here is a summary of important rules:

a. Do not enclose block quotes with quotation marks.
b. When you omit words from the middle of a quoted sentence, insert three periods separated by spaces and put a space before the first period and after the last one (. . .). For example:

James Madison recognized a limitation on the danger of factions: "The influence of factious leaders may kindle a flame within their . . . states, but will be unable to spread a . . . conflagration through the other states."

c. When you are using the quotation as a full sentence and are omitting words at the beginning of the quoted sentence, do not use the three periods. If the first word you are quoting is not capitalized, capitalize the first letter and put it in brackets. For example:

James Madison recognized a limitation on the danger of factions: "[F]actious leaders may kindle a flame within their particular states, but will be unable to spread a . . . conflagration throughout the other states."

d. When you are using the quotation as a full sentence and are omitting words at the end of the quoted sentence, use four periods. Separate the periods with spaces and put a space before the first period. The last period is the period that ends the sentence. For example:

James Madison recognized that factions could disrupt the political process in an individual state: "The influence of factious leaders may kindle a flame within their particular states . . . ."

e. When you are quoting two consecutive sentences and omitting words at the end of the first sentence and at the beginning of the second sentence, use four periods. Separate the periods with spaces and put a space before the first period and after the fourth period. If the first word of the second sentence, as quoted, is not capitalized, capitalize the first letter and put it in brackets. For example:

For James Madison, the cure for factions lay in the great size of the republic: "In the extended republic of the United States . . . a coalition of the majority of the whole society could seldom take place on any other principles than those of justice and the general good . . . .[T]he larger the society . . . the more duly capable it will be of self-government."

f. Place a period or comma inside the quotation marks. Place a semicolon or colon outside the quotation marks. Place a question mark inside the quotation marks if it is part of the quoted material. Place a question mark outside the quotation marks if it is not part of the quoted material.

A

A.B.A. Model Code of Professional Responsibility, 303
A.B.A. Model Rules of Professional Conduct, 303
Abbreviations, 305
Abstract language, use of, 94-95,150, 252, 317
Abuse of discretion standard of review, 267
Active voice, 95-97, 214-216, 285
Adjectives and adverbs, use of, 250, 254
Adversarial models of negotiation, 190-192
Adverse information in statement of facts, 269, 271, 284-285,
Adverse precedent, 256, 303-304
Advising clients. *See* Client interviewing and counseling
Agency interpretation of statutes, 20
Agreement to mediate, 207-208
A.L.R. *(American Law Reports),* 28
ALWD Citation Manual, 5
Ambiguous words and phrases, 106-107
American Jurisprudence (West), 27
American Law Reports (A.L.R.), 28
Analogy, use of, 318
Analysis. *See* Legal analysis
Anger or emotional responses
  email, 227
  initial client interview, 111
Answers. *See also* Pleadings
  generally, 3
  drafting of, 235-237
  exercises, 244-247
  sample, 378-381, 390-392
  verifications, 237
Appeals
  generally, 265
  process of, 265
  record on, 265-266
  standard of review, 266-268
    abuse of discretion, 267
    clearly erroneous, 266-267

de novo review, 267-268
  importance to practitioner, 268
  state law issues, 14
Appellant, use of term, 270*n* , 322*n*
Appellate briefs
  generally, 269-270
  argument, 272, 295-305
    checklist, 306-308
    headings, 295-298
    sample, 393-394
    structure of, 295-298
    substance of, 298-305
    summary of, 272, 285-294
  checklist, 306-308
  conclusion, 306, 308
  editing, 305
  hallmarks of well-written brief, 272
  headings, 295-298
    advocacy with, 297-298
    checklist, 306-307
    number, 298
    outline, 298
    use of, 295
    writing, 296-297
  jurisdictional statement, 271, 275, 306
  parts of, 271-272
  persuasive writing, 249, 305. *See also* Persuasive writing
  precedent, use in, 303-305
    generally, 303
    adverse, 303-304
    footnotes, 304-305
    hierarchy, 303
    quotations, 304-305
    rebuttal, 304
    signals, 304-305
    string cites, 304-305
  procedural rules for, 270
  question presented, 271, 276-277, 279-280, 306-307
  record, 265-266, 269-270, 271, 273-274, 299
  research, 299
  statement of facts, 270, 271, 281-285, 288, 307. *See also* Record

Appellate briefs (*cont.*)
    substance of argument, 298-305
        appellate process, understanding, 299
        checklist, 307-308
        editing, 305
        formulation of arguments, 300
        organization and, 300-302
        persuasive writing, 305
        precedent, use in, 303-305
        record, familiarity with, 299
        research, 299
        rules of court, 299-300
        simplicity and, 300
        types of arguments, 300
        what to avoid, 302
    summary of argument, 270, 272, 285-286,
        287-294, 307
    table of authorities, 270, 271, 275, 279, 306,
        397
    table of contents, 270, 271, 274, 278, 306, 396
    text of constitutional, statutory, and
        regulatory provisions, 270, 271, 278,
        280, 307
    title page, 270, 271, 274, 278, 306
Appellate courts, 14, 15, 16
Appellate oral arguments, 321-328, 393
    generally, 6, 321
    argument, 326
    argument aids, 323-324
    authorities, 323
    checklist, 328
    conclusion, 326
    introduction, 325
    new information, advising court and
        opponent, 324
    outline, 323, 326
    preparation, 322-324
    questions from judges, 310, 322, 327-328,
    rebuttal, 326-327
    record, 322
    rehearsal, 324
    roadmap, 325-326
    sample, 393-394
    setting, 322
    structure, 325-327
    techniques and tools. *See* Oral argument
Appellee, use of term, 270*n* , 322*n*
Attorneys
    fees
        initial client interview, 116-117
        sanctions, 259, 261, 263
    signature, 218-219, 244, 247, 306, 308

Audience for documents. *See also* Reader
    understanding
    client opinion letter, 163
    email communication, 223
    memoranda, 125
    oral presentations, 309-310
    purpose of documents, 72

B

Binding authority. *See* Mandatory
    authority
Bluebook: A Uniform System of Citation, 5,
    275, 441
"Boilerplate" term, 217
Brief answer in memoranda, 123, 131-133,
    135-137
Briefs. *See also* Case briefs
    generally, 3
    appellate briefs. *See* Appellate briefs
    case briefs compared, 2. *See also* Case
        briefs
    format, 3
    mediation briefs, 208-209, 414-431
    memoranda as, 2, 121*n*

C

Canons of statutory construction,
    20-21
Captions in,
    pleadings, 232-233
    settlement agreements, 212-213
Case briefs, 35-46
    generally, 2
    class preparation, additional, 45-46
    defined, 35
    format, 36
    parts of brief, 36-42
        analysis, 41
        citation, 39
        facts, 39
        holding, 41
        issue, 40
        name, 39
        procedure, 39-40
    purpose, 35-36
    sample briefs, 38-39, 41-45
Case law. *See* Common law
Causal relationships, establishing, 313

Checklists
  appellate briefs, 306-308
  consultation, 187
  context and structure, 78-79
  initial client interview, 118-119
  legal analysis, 70
  motions, 261
  negotiation, 200
  oral arguments, 328
  research strategy, 33-34
Chronological order
  fact statements, 141, 282-283
  oral presentations, 313
CIRAC, 48
Circuit courts, federal, 15, 16, 17
Citations
  appellate briefs, 275, 304-305, 307, 308
  case briefs, 39
  form, 5
  memoranda, 126
  signals, 304-305
  string cites, 304-305
Citators, 31
Class preparation. *See* Case briefs
Clearly erroneous standard of review, 266-267
Client intake form, 118
Client interviewing and counseling
  communication skills, 5-6
  consultation, 181-187
    beginning, 183
    checklist, 187
    client's goals and priorities, 183, 184
    course of action, choosing, 185-186
    keeping track of information, 183
    option development, 184-185, 185-186
    planning, 182-183
    purpose of, 181
    scenario, 181-182
    settlement authority, 187, 196*n*
  initial client interview. *See* Initial client
      interview
  opinion letter. *See* Client opinion letter
  settlement authority, 187, 196*n*
Client opinion letter, 163-170
  generally, 2, 163
  answering client question, 166-169
    accuracy, 166-167
    client's concerns, 168-169
    facts, 166
    honest advice and conclusions, 168-169
    recommendations, 166-169
  authority in, 163, 166

exercises, 169-180
  instructions and future planning,
      168-169
  samples, 351-367
  style of, 163-166
    audience focus, 163
    colloquialisms, 165
    concrete discussion, 163-164
    jargon and stilted language, 165
    spelling and grammar, 166
Closing in appellate brief, 306,308
Colloquialisms, 99, 107-108, 165, 305
Colon, use of, 440, 442
Comma, use of, 438-440, 441, 442
Common law, 16-18. *See also* Precedent
  annotations, 26, 27, 28
  case analysis, 55-64
  case briefs. *See* Case briefs
  headnotes to cases, 124
  mandatory authority, 16-17, 77, 303
  persuasive authority, 17, 77, 303-304
  relationship between statutory law and
      common law, 20-21
  sources of law and hierarchy, 13, 303-304
  weight of authority, 18, 77
Communication, electronic. *See* Email
      communication
Communication skills, 5-6
Competence of witnesses, 266-267
Competitive negotiators, 193-194, 199
Complaints. *See also* Pleadings
  generally, 3
  drafting, 233-235
  exercises, 241-244
  sample, 373-377, 383-389
  verification, 237
Computer research, 29-31
  books vs. computer, 30-31
  nonlegal sources, 30
  traditional research sources, 29-30
Conclusion
  appellate brief, 306, 308
  beginning of argument or discussion with,
      81, 83-85
  at end of argument or discussion, 83
  memoranda, 123, 131-133, 135-137
  oral arguments, 314, 326
Concrete language, use of, 94-95, 252, 317
Concurring opinions, 41
Confidentiality in mediation, 204, 207-208
Conflict, use in oral argument, 315
Congress, U.S., 18

Constitutions
  appellate briefs, text in, 270, 271, 278, 280, 307
  state, 13, 14
  United States, 13, 15
Consultation with clients. *See* Client
    interviewing and counseling
Context of documents, 72, 78-79
Contingencies, 216-217
Contractions, 99, 107, 165, 225, 437
Cooperative negotiators, 193-194, 199
Corpus Juris Secundum (West), 27
Counterclaims, 3, 231, 237, 378-382
Court of appeals, U.S., 15, 16
Courts of general jurisdiction, 14
Courts of last resort, 14, 15, 265
Court system
  federal courts, 15-16
  state courts, 14-15, 17
CRAC, 48
Credibility of witnesses, 194, 266

D

Damage claims against United States, 15
Dash, use of, 441
Declarations, 217-218
Definition section of,
  settlement agreements, 214
  statutes, 18, 19, 20
Demand for relief, 235
Demurrer, 257
De novo review, 267-268
Dicta, 17, 41, 97
Digests, 28
Discovery
  mental or physical examination of party, 267
  motions to compel discovery, 258-259
Discussion
  client opinion letter, 167-168
  memoranda, 123, 144-152. *See also* Legal
    analysis
    abstract writing approach, 150, 303
    "digest" approach, 147-148, 303
    example of, 151-152
    exercises, 152, 157-161
    historical development of law, 148-149, 303
    "law discussion only" approach, 150-151, 303
    quotations, overuse of, 149-150, 303
    reasoning, make readily apparent in,
      147-152

Dissenting opinions, 41
District courts, federal, 15, 16
Double negatives, 106
Drafts and revisions, 83

E

Economic model of negotiation,
    191-192
Editorial statements, 281, 283
"Elegant variation," concept of, 211
The Elements of Style (Strunk & White), 4
Email communication, 223-229
  generally, 3, 223
  advice, 226-227
  audience, knowledge of, 223
  composition guidelines, 224-226
  emotion in, 227
  exercises, 229
  formatting of, 224
  humor in, 226-227
  proofreading, 226
  tone, 225-226
  unexpected reader, 225
  use policies, 225-226
  samples, 227-228
  systems, differences in, 226
Emphasis
  in oral argument, 316-317, 319
  word placement for, 253
Equity and policy arguments
  appellate briefs, 255
  legal analysis, 51, 63
  persuasive writing, 249, 255, 305
  structure of documents, 78
Ethical considerations
  adverse precedent, 303
  motions, 260-261
  negotiation, 199-200
Excessive variation of words and terms, 108
Expository writing, rule of, 83
Eye contact in public speaking, 319

F

Facts
  appellate briefs, 265-266, 269-270, 271,
    281-285, 288, 307. *See also* Record
  application of law to, 50-55

case briefs, 39
client opinion letter, 166
findings of fact, 266, 268
memoranda, 123, 141-144, 153-161
oral argument, 325-326
persuasive writing, 254-255
pleadings, 239-240
False statements of material fact or law,
    199-200
Federal courts, 15-16, 17
Federal Rule of Appellate Procedure
    Rule 10(a), 265-266
Federal Rules of Civil Procedure
    Rule 11, 260-261
    Rule 12(b)(6), 257-258
    Rule 35(a), 267
    Rule 37, 258-259
    Rule 52(a)(6), 266
    Rule 56, 259-260, 268
Fees, attorney, 116-117, 259,
Findings of fact, 266-268
Flag burning, statutory interpretation
    example, 22-24
Footnotes, 35, 41, 304-305, 308
Form books, 232

G

Game theory approach to negotiation,
    190-191
Gestures in public speaking, 319-320
Google Scholar, 30
Grammar. *See also* Paragraphs; Sentences
    active voice, 95-97
    adjectives and adverbs, 250, 254, 283
    client opinion letter, 166
    correct use of, 166
    double negatives, 106
    parallel structure, 104-105
    passive voice, 95-97
    rules of, 433-438

H

Headings
    appellate briefs, 295-298
        advocacy with, 297-298
        checklist, 306-308
        number, 298

outline, 298
use of, 295
writing, 296-297
    memoranda, 123, 127-128, 135-137
    settlement agreements, 211
Headnotes to cases, 30, 124, 299
Historical development of law, 148-149, 303
Holding in case briefs, 41
Hornbooks, 17, 25, 34
House of Representatives, 18, 23
Humor
    appellate briefs, 305
    email, 226-227
    oral argument, 315
    reader's understanding, 99
Imagery, use in oral argument, 318
Index to periodicals, 25n , 28
Initial client interview, 111-119
    generally, 111
    checklist for, 118-119
    client's perspective, 113-115
        detailed information, need for, 114-115
        getting started, 114
        goals and priorities, 115
        keeping track of information, 114
    closing interview, 117-118
    fees, 116-117
    goals for, 115
    greeting client, 112-113
    option development, 116
    planning for, 112
    preliminary assessment of client's problem,
        116
    preparatory explanation, 113
    purpose, 111-112

I

Interlocutory orders, 265
Intermediate appellate courts, 15
International trade cases, 16
Interoffice memoranda. *See* Memoranda
Interview with client. *See* Initial client
        interview
IRAC (Issue, Rule, Application/Analysis,
        Conclusion), 48
Issue. *See also* Question presented
    case briefs, 40
    memoranda, 123, 128-131, 135-139
Its vs. it's, 437

J

Jargon, 5, 165. *See also* Legalese
Judges
    addressing during argument, 322
    opinions, review of, 327-328
    questions in oral argument, 310, 322,
        327-328,
Jurisdiction
    defined, 13*n*
    federal courts, 15, 16
    mandatory authority, 16-17
    state courts, 14-15
    statements
        appellate brief, 271, 275, 306
        complaint, 234*n*
Jury findings on appeal, 266*n*

K

Kennedy, Anthony, 321
Kennedy, John F., 317-318
KeyCite, 31
King, Martin Luther, Jr., 317-318

L

"Law discussion only" approach, 150-151,
    303
Law review articles, 17, 25*n*, 29
Legal analysis, 47-70
    generally, 47
    case analysis, 55-64
    case briefs, 35-36, 41
    checklist for, 70
    deductive argument, 48-50
        generally, 48
        application, 49-50
        limitations, 49
        use of, 49
    facts, law applied to, 50-55
        basic approach, 51
        example, 51-55
    legal system and, 1-2
    statutory analysis, 64-70
    steps for legal argument, 47
Legal encyclopedias, 27, 124
Legalese, 4, 97-98, 232, 235
Legal periodicals, 25*n* , 28-29, 149, 275

Legal system, 13-24
    common law, 16-18
        mandatory authority, 16-17, 77, 303
        persuasive authority, 17, 77, 303-304
        sources of law and hierarchy, 13, 303-304
        weight of authority, 18, 77
    court system, 14-16
        federal courts, 15-16, 17
        state courts, 14-15, 17
    legal analysis and, 1-2
    sources of law and hierarchy, 13, 303-304
    statutes, 18-24
        canons of statutory construction, 20-21
        mandatory authority, 16-17
        relationship between statutory law and
            common law, 20-21
        role of court and legislature, illustration
            of, 22-24
        sources of law and hierarchy, 13
        supremacy of legislature, 18-20
Legislative history, 20, 21
Legislative process, 18-20
LexisNexis, 29, 31
Loislaw, 29*n*

M

Mandatory authority, 16-17, 77, 303
Mayer Brown law firms, briefs by, 393
Media and legal system, 1-2
Mediation, 203-209
    generally, 6, 203-204
    agreement to mediate, 207-208
    confidentiality, 204, 207-208
    exercise, 209
    mediation brief, 208-209, 414-431
    mediator, role of, 204, 207
    sample mediation briefs, 414-431
    stages of, 204-207
        agenda development, 205-206
        brainstorming, 206
        caucus, 206
        conference, 206
        introduction, 205
        opening statements, 205
        preparation, 204-205
        resolution, 206-207
    voluntary, 207
    waiver, 208
    writing for, 207-209

Mediation brief, 208-209, 414-431
Mediator, 204, 207
Memoranda
  generally, 2
  citation format, 126
  conclusion, 123, 131-133
    exercises, 135-139
  defined, 121
  discussion, 123, 144-152. *See also* Legal
    analysis
    exercises, 152, 157-161
    reasoning in, 149-152
  facts, 123, 141-144, 153-161
  hallmarks of well-written memo,
    124-126
    citation format, 126
    clear writing style, 124-125
    creativity, 125-126
    good judgment, 124
    objective analysis, 124
    thorough research, 124
  heading, 123, 127-128, 135-137
  issue, 123, 128-131, 135-139
  negotiation and, 189
  organization, 125
  parts of, 122-123
  precision and clarity, 125
  purposes of, 121-122
  reader understanding, 125
  sample, 329-349
Metaphor, use of, 318
Modifiers, use of, 433-435
Motions. *See also* Persuasive writing
  generally, 3
  checklist, 261
  to compel discovery, 258-259
  to dismiss, 257-258
  memorandum in support, 2
  pretrial motions. *See* Pretrial motions
  for summary judgment, 259-260, 268

N

Name-calling, 205, 318
Names in briefs, using parties', 274, 282, 393
Negative implication, rule of, 21
Negative words or phrases in writing, 106
Negotiation
  generally, 189
  beginning of, 197

  checklist, 200
  closing of, 199
  communication skills, 5-6
  ethics, 199-200
  information exchange, 194-195, 197-198
  planning for, 194-197
    analysis of needs and interests, 196
    evaluation of case, 194-197
    information exchange, 194-195
    opening offer, target, and bottom line,
      195-196
    personalities involved, 197
  purposes of, 190
  settlement authority, 187, 196*n*
  styles of, 193-194
  theories of, 190-193
    adversarial models, 190-192
    economic model, 191-192
    game theory, 190-191
    problem-solving negotiation, 192-193
    social-psychological bargaining model,
      192
  trading, 198
New information, advising court and
    opponent about, 324
Notice pleading, 231-232
Novelty, use in oral argument, 315

O

Office of the Solicitor General, briefs
    by, 393
On-point authority, 16-17, 18, 32, 33, 77, 78
On Writing Well (Zinsser), 4
Opinion letter. *See* Client opinion letter
Opposing arguments, 304, 305, 312
Oral argument, 309-320
  generally, 6, 309
  appellate oral argument, 321-328. *See also*
    Appellate oral arguments
  audience considerations, 309-310
  fundamentals of good public speaking, 6,
    319-320
    emphasis use, 319
    eye contact, 319
    gestures, 319-320
    pauses, use of, 319
    posture, 320
    reading, 319
    speaking to be heard, 319

Oral argument *(cont.)*
  language use in, 317-318
    imagery, 318
    repetition, 317-318
    rhetorical questions, 317
  organizational patterns, 313-314
    causal relationships, establishing, 313
    chronological, 313
    problem to solution, 313
    pro vs. con, 313-314
  setting, 310-311
  structure of, 311-314
    introductions, conclusions, and
      transitions, 314
    methods of proof, 312
    organizational patterns, 313-314
    strategy, 312
  style and tools for, 315-318
    conflict, 315
    emphasis, 316-317
    humor, 315
    inappropriate tools, 318
    language, 317-318
    novelty, 315
    suspense, 315-316
    theme, 317
Organization
  appellate brief arguments, 300-302
  within arguments, 77-78
  memoranda, 125
  oral argument, 313-314
  persuasive writing, 251-252
Outlines
  appellate oral arguments, 323, 326
  argument and discussions, 81, 82-83
  headings, 298
  memoranda, 125
  persuasive writing, 251
  structure in legal writing, 72-74

P

Paragraphs
  generally, 81
  cohesive paragraphs, 87-89
    extraneous sentences, 88-89
    focused discussion sections, 87-88
  roadmaps, 76-77, 84, 125, 144, 251
  structure of documents, 77-78
  thesis, 84
  topic sentences, 76-77, 85-86, 87-89, 251

  transitions and repetition words, 89-90,
    317-318
Parallel structure, 104-105
Parentheticals, 304-305
Parties
  in briefs, 270, 271, 296
  in complaints, 231, 232, 234
  in settlement agreements, 212-213
Passim, use of, 275
Passive voice, 95-97
Patent cases, 15
Penal statutes, 19, 20, 21, 23
Personalized writing, 99, 108, 305
Personal jurisdiction, 13*n*
Personification, use of, 318
Persuasive authority, 17, 77, 303-304
Persuasive writing, 249-256
  generally, 249
  appellate briefs. *See* Appellate
    briefs
  clear and credible arguments, 250-251
  equity and policy arguments, 255
  facts, 254-255
  motions. *See* Pretrial motions
  precedent, 255-256
  well-organized argument, 251-252
    best arguments first, 251-252
    structure of, 251
  writing style for, 252-254
    concrete words and terms, 252
    same subject in series of sentences,
      253-254
    word placement for emphasis, 253
Petitioner, use of term, 270*n* , 322*n*
Plain English, 1, 4, 98, 232
Plain meaning rule, 21
Pleadings, 232-247
  generally, 3, 232
  answers
    generally, 3
    drafting, 235-237
    exercises, 244-247
    verification, 237
  captions, 232-233
  complaint, 233
    generally, 3
    drafting, 233-235
    exercises, 241-244
    sample, 373-377, 383-389
    verification, 237
  numbered paragraphs in, 232,
    235, 240

purpose and language of, 231-232
rules of procedure and, 232
sample, 373-392
verifications, 237
Pocket parts, 27, 299
Policy arguments. *See* Equity and policy
arguments
Positive words or phrases in writing, 106
Posture in public speaking, 320
Preamble of statutes, 18, 20
Precedent. *See also* Common law
appellate briefs, 303-305
generally, 303
adverse, 303-304
hierarchy, 303
rebuttal, 304
footnotes, 304-305
mandatory authority, 16-17, 77, 303
other jurisdictions, 21, 78
parentheticals, 304-305
persuasive authority, 17, 77, 303-304
persuasive writing, 249, 305
quotations, 304-305
rebuttal, 304
relationship between statutory and common
law, 20-21
signals, 304-305
string cites, 304-305
weight of authority, 18, 77
Pre-law writing experience, 4
Pretrial motions, 257-261
checklist for, 261
ethical considerations, 260-261
form of, 257
motions to compel discovery, 258-259
motions to dismiss, 257-258
purposes of, 257
Problem-solving negotiation, 192-193
Procedural history of case, 39, 282
Procedural provisions of statutes, 19, 20
Procrastination. *See* Time Management
Pronouns
personalized writing, 99, 108, 305
use of, 433, 435-437
Proofreading
appellate briefs, 305
email, 226
Protocol for appellate oral arguments, 321
Puffery in negotiation, 199
Punctuation rules, 438-442
Purpose of documents, 72

Q

Qualifiers, 106
Question marks, use in quotations, 442
Question presented, 271, 276-277, 279-280,
306-307. *See also* Issue
Quotations
appellate briefs, 304-305
overuse of, 149-150, 303
punctuation rules, 441-442
statement of facts, 285

R

Reader understanding, 93-109
generally, 93
content, 106-109
ambiguous words and phrases,
106-107
colloquialisms, 99, 107-108, 165, 305
contractions, 99, 107, 165, 225, 437
excessive variation, 108
personalized writing, 99, 108, 305
positives vs. negatives, 106
general advice, 94-101
active voice, 95-97, 214-216, 285
concrete language, 94-95, 252, 317
getting to the point, 94
legalese, 4, 97-98, 232, 235
technical terms, 98-99
tone, 99
sentence structure for, 101-105
full sentences, 104
intrusive phases and clauses, 103-104
logical order, use of, 102-103
parallel structure, 104-105
short sentences, 101-102
Rebuttal of opposing arguments, 304, 325, 326-327
Recitals, 213-214
Record
appeals, use in, 265-266
appellate briefs, use in, 265-266, 269-270,
271, 273-274, 299
oral arguments, 322
Rehearsal of oral arguments, 324
Releases, 220-221
Relief
appeals, forms of, 268
in appellate briefs, 306
demand for, 235

Repetition, use of, 86-87, 317-318
Research strategy, 25-34
    A.L.R. and legal periodicals, 28-29
    appellate briefs, 299
    books vs. computer, 30-31
    checklist for, 33-34
    computer research, 29-31
    digests, 28
    keeping track of research, 33
    legal encyclopedias, 27
    memoranda, 124
    negotiation and, 189, 194
    nonlegal sources, 30
    statutes, 26
    traditional research sources, 29-30
    updating research, 31
    when to stop, 31-33
        appellate briefs, 299
        finding same citations, 32
        not following all leads, 32-33
        on-point cases first, 32
    where to start, 25-27
        legal encyclopedias, 27
        restatements, 26-27
        statutes, 26
        treatises, 26
Respondent, use of term, 270n , 322n
Restatements, 26-27
Rhetorical questions in oral argument, 317
Roadmaps
    appellate oral arguments, 301, 325-326
    conclusion first in, 81, 83-85
    memoranda, 125, 144
    persuasive writing, 251
    structure of documents, 76-77
Rules of procedure, 232, 257, 259, 260,
        265-268, 270. See also specific rules of
        procedure

S

Sanctions
    discovery, 259
    Rule 11, 260-261
Sarcasm, 226-227, 305
Secondary authority, 17, 78, 271. See also
        specific types
Semicolon, 441
Senate, U.S., 18
Sentences
    extraneous, 88-89

    full sentences, 104
    intrusive phrases and clauses, 103-104
    logical order of, 102-103
    parallel structure, 104-105
    persuasive writing style and, 252-254
    short sentences, 101-102
    structure, 101-105
    topic sentences, 76-77, 85-86, 87-89, 251
Settlement agreement, 211-221
    generally, 3, 211
    drafting, 219-220
    exercise, 222
    headings, 211
    parts of, 211-219
        caption, 212-213
        closing, 218-219
        contingencies, 216-217
        declarations, 217-218
        definitions, 214
        operative language, 214-216
        recitals, 213-214
        title, 211-212
        transition, 213
    release, 220-221
    sample settlement agreements, 212n, 214n,
        369-371
Settlement authority, 187, 196n
Shepard's Citation Service, 31, 32, 33, 299
Short answer in memoranda, 123, 131-133,
        135-139
Short sentences, use of, 4, 101-102
Signals, 304-305
Signature of attorney, 218-219, 244, 247, 306, 308
Slang, 99, 165, 318
Social-psychological bargaining model of
        negotiation, 192
Sources of law and hierarchy, 13, 303-304
Spelling, 11, 166, 266
Stages of mediation, 204-207. See also Mediation.
    agenda development, 205-206
    brainstorming, 206
    caucus, 206
    conference, 206
    introduction, 205
    opening statements, 205
    preparation, 204-205
    resolution, 206-207
Standard of review on appeal, 266-268
    abuse of discretion, 267
    clearly erroneous, 266-267
    de novo review, 267-268
    importance to practitioner, 268

Stare decisis, 16, 47, 78. *See also* Precedent

State constitutions, 13, 14

State courts, 14-15, 17

State legislatures, 18

Statement of facts in appellate briefs, 270, 271, 281-285, 288, 307. *See also* Record

Statutes, 18-24
   appellate briefs, text in, 270, 271, 278, 280, 307
   canons of statutory construction, 20-21
   legal analysis, 64-70
   mandatory authority, 16-17
   relationship between statutory law and common law, 20-21
   research strategy, 26
   role of court and legislature, illustration of, 22-24
   sources of law and hierarchy, 13, 303-304
   supremacy of legislature and legislative process, 18-20

"Straw man" approach to proof, 312

String citations, 304-305

Structure of documents, 72-79. *See also specific documents*
   checklist, 78-79
   organization within arguments, 77-78
   outlines, use of, 72-74, 81, 82-83, 125, 233, 251, 298
   placement of policy and equity arguments, 78
   roadmaps, topic sentences, and transitions, 76-77, 85-86, 87-90, 251, 317-318
   strategy and, 74-76

Style of writing. *See* Writing style; *specific documents*

Subject matter jurisdiction, 13*n*

Subject-verb agreement, 436-437

Substantive provisions of statutes, 19, 20

Summary judgment motions, 259-260, 268

Summary of argument in appellate briefs, 270, 272, 285-286, 287-294, 307

Supreme Court, U.S., 15-16, 17
   oral argument transcripts, 394
   Rule 34(h), 285-286

Surprise, use in oral argument, 315-316

Suspense, use in oral argument, 315-316

T

Table of authorities in appellate briefs, 270, 271, 275, 279, 306, 397

Table of contents in appellate briefs, 270, 271, 274, 278, 306, 396

Technical terms, defined, 98-99

Terms of art, 108

That vs. which, 437-438

Themes of argument or discussion, 81-91
   generally, 81
   conclusion first, 81, 83-85
   oral argument, 305, 313
   outline, 81, 82-83
   paragraphs, effective writing of, 81, 85-91
      cohesive paragraphs, 87-89
      topic sentences,76-77, 85-86, 87-89, 251
      transitions and repetition words, 89-90, 317-318

Thesis paragraph, 84

Thesis sentences. *See* Topic sentences

Third-party defendant, complaint against, 387-389

Time management, 7-11
   generally, 7
   assignments, 8-9
   workload, 7-8
   writer's block, 8-9
   writing methods, 8
   writing process
      planning, 10
      complications, 11
      deadlines, 10-11
      details, 11
      drafts, 10

Title page in appellate briefs, 270, 271, 274, 278, 306

Tone
   appellate briefs, 305
   email, 225-226
   reader understanding, 99

Topical organizational pattern, 314

Topic sentences, 76-77, 85-86, 87-89, 251

Torts, 26, 27, 60, 61*n*, 108

Transitions, 89-90, 213, 317-318

Treatises
   appellate briefs, 275
   persuasive authority, 17
   research strategy, 26, 124

Trial courts, 14, 15

Types of legal writing, 2-4. *See also specific documents*

U

United States Constitution, 13, 16
United States Court of Appeals for the District
    of Columbia, 16
United States Court of Appeals for the Federal
    Circuit, 16
United States Supreme Court. *See* Supreme
    Court, U.S.

V

Verbosity, 5
Verb-subject agreement, 436
Verification and pleadings, 237
Vetoes, 18
Visual aids in oral presentations, 311

W

Weight of authority, 18, 77
Westlaw, 23, 24
Which vs. that, 437-438
Wikipedia, 30
Witness credibility, 194, 266
Word choice, 106-109
  abbreviations, 305
  ambiguous words and phrases,
      106-107

colloquialisms, 99, 107-108, 165, 305
concrete language, 94-95, 252, 317
contractions, 99, 107, 165, 225, 437
excessive variation in, 108
jargon and stilted language, 5, 165
legalese, 4, 97-98, 232, 235
oral argument, 317-318
personalized writing, 99, 108, 305
positives vs. negatives, 106
qualifying words, 106
slang, 99, 165, 318
technical terms, 98-99
terms of art, 108
tone, 99
Writer's block, 8-9
Writing, process of, 10-11. *See also* Time
    management.
  planning, 10
  complications, 11
  deadlines, 10-11
  details, 11
  drafts, 10
Writing style, 4-5, 124-125. *See also specific
    documents*
  abstract writing approach, 94-95,150, 252,
      303, 317
  client opinion letter, 163-166
  "digest" approach, 147-148, 303
  memorandum, 124-125
  persuasive writing, 252-254